MITCHELL BEAZLEY

THE WINE ATLAS OF
SPAIN
AND TRAVELLER'S GUIDE
TO THE VINEYARDS

by

HUBRECHT DUIJKER

MITCHELL BEAZLEY

THE WINE ATLAS OF

SPAIN

AND TRAVELLER'S GUIDE

TO THE VINEYARDS

by

HUBRECHT DUIJKER

For Julie
... who has often had to give me up to the country
of our honeymoon.

The Wine Atlas of Spain
Edited and designed by Mitchell Beazley
Publishers, Michelin House, 81 Fulham Road,
London SW3 6RB

Copyright © Mitchell Beazley Publishers 1992
Text copyright © Hubrecht Duijker 1992
Maps and illustrations copyright © Mitchell
Beazley Publishers 1992
All rights reserved

No part of this work may be reproduced or
used in any form or by any means, electronic
or mechanical, including photocopying,
recording, or by any information, storage and
retrieval system, without the prior written
permission of the publishers.

A CIP catalogue record for this book is
available from the British Library.

The author and publishers will be grateful for
any information which will assist them in
keeping future editions up to date. Although all
reasonable care has been taken in the
preparation of this book, neither the publishers
nor the author can accept any liability for any
consequences arising from the uses thereof, or
from the information contained herein.

Editor Alexa Stace
Senior Executive Art Editor Nigel O'Gorman
Map Editor Zoë Goodwin
Index Marie Lorimer
Picture Research Brigitte Arora, Ellen Root
Production Ted Timberlake
Managing Editor Anne Ryland
Illustrations Lesli Sternberg
Cartography Lovell Johns
English translation
by Raymond Kaye

ISBN 0-85533-910-1

Typeset in Century Old Style by
Servis Filmsetting Ltd, Manchester, England
Reproduction by Mandarin Offset, Hong Kong
Printed and bound by Printer Industria
Grafica, S.A., Barcelona, Spain

ACKNOWLEDGMENTS

This book would not have been possible without the help of many people. During
my journeys through the Spanish wine regions a great many people not only
received me most hospitably, but were wonderfully forthcoming with information. I have also been most appreciative of the way that wine producers and
others have fitted themselves in with my travel schedules – enabling me to make
and keep many dozens of appointments, including at weekends. It has been the
wine producers in particular who have provided information, but I also owe a debt
of gratitude to the *Consejos Reguladores* and other wine authorities and agencies,
such as the *Instituto Español de Comercio Exterior*; the *Instituto Nacional de
Denominaciones de Origen*; various oenological stations; wine importers in a
number of countries; and the *Spaans Nationaal Verkeersbureau* (Spanish National
Tourist Office) in the Netherlands.

A number of individuals deserve special mention:
María Antonia Fernández-Daza who, when still at Icex, assisted me in word and
deed – which resulted in impeccable travel arrangements and first-class
information.
Steve Metzler and his wife Almundena de Llaguno of Classical Wines from Spain
(Seattle) who, specializing as they do in Spanish quality wines, have an
outstanding knowledge of the country and of many of the best producers. They
have given me excellent advice in every possible way.
Wim Mey is the author of *Sherry*, a standard work that has appeared in Dutch and
English editions. He has made it possible for me to benefit to the full from his
incredible knowledge of this region and of neighbouring Condado de Huelva.
Marianne Nuberg, Director of *Vinos de España* in the Netherlands, who for about a
year devoted herself wholeheartedly to assisting in every possible way, making
arrangements on my behalf with persons and authorities in Spain. Her excellent
knowledge of Spanish has been of tremendous help to me.
Jeremy Watson, Divisional Director of Wines of Spain in the United Kingdom, has
done his utmost to provide the publishers with the basic material for the maps, and
has furnished me with useful advice.
I must also make grateful mention of a number of other people who have been
exceptionally helpful:
Berta Bartolomé, *Consejo Regulador de la Denominación de Origen Rioja*, Logroño
Véronique Brink, *Vinos de España*, The Hague, Netherlands
Mercedes Chivite, *Julián Chivite*, Cintruénigo
Joaquin Delgado, Expounión, Sevilla
Rafael Delgado, Pérez Barquero, Montilla
Lourdes Fernández, *Consejo Regulador Denominación Especifica Tacoronte-
Acentejo*, Tacoronte
José Fco Garriques, Icex, Valencia
Antonio Hernandez, *Economía y Comercio*, Murcia
Pascual Herrera, *Estación Enológica*, Rueda
Manuel Julve, Reporter, Palma de Mallorca
José Antonio López, Bodega Morgadío, Albeos
Manuel Llamas, Montebello, Montilla
Annemarie Nuberg, San Sebastián
Agueda del Pilar, *Consejo Regulador de la Denominación Cigales*, Cigales
Desiderio Rodriguez, Bergidum, Almere, Netherlands
Jaime Sancho, Sancho Trading, Nieuw-Vennep, Netherlands
Pedro Scholtz, Scholtz Hermanos, Málaga
Peter Schoonbrood, Vinites, Vilafranca del Penedès
José María Silla, Icex, Murcia
Alexander Stom, Het Zuiden, Oosterhout, Netherlands
Miguel A. Torres, Miguel Torres, Vilafranca del Penedès
Félix Valencia, Larios, Málaga
José Vera, Icex, Alicante Esther Verheul, Salvador Poveda, Monóvar
Paulino Vinuesa, Codorníu, Barcelona
Monique Wassen, Vinos de España, The Hague
Finally I must record the fact that to an important extent the quality of this book is
the outcome of the energetic efforts and great expertise of the editorial team who
have supported me: Chris Foulkes – succeeded by Anne Ryland – (Managing
Editor), Alexa Stace (Editor), Nigel O'Gorman (Art Editor), and Zoë Goodwin (Map
Editor).

The introductory sections on History and Legend, Vineyards and Grape Varieties,
Laws and Labels, and Geography and Climate were written by Richard Mayson.

Contents

Foreword

It was truly great news to hear that Hubrecht Duijker was to write a book on the wines of Spain. For most Spanish wine producers, this *Wine Atlas of Spain* will be their introduction into the society of world-class wines. It is the recognition of many years of hard work in anonymity, and now, transported by Duijker's pen, they can travel the world, consolidating the image and prestige of their wines.

I first met Hubrecht at the beginning of the seventies, in his native Holland, and still remember vividly the lunch in a restaurant in Amsterdam. With his grey eyes flicking from glass to glass, he was eager to learn the intricacies of winemaking, and to understand the care involved in the cultivation of vineyards. Now, nearly 20 years later, he still retains the spirit of that student who travelled the world via its vineyards, searching in each bodega for the philosophy behind the winemaking by evaluating their vineyards and all the different vintages. With these years of experience, my friend has built up an enormous wealth of knowledge on viticulture and winemaking techniques. I had the opportunity to confirm this at first hand on a recent visit of his to Penedès, some 12 months ago. As we strolled through the vines at Milmanda, a vineyard dating back to the Middle Ages, we talked of geology and rootstocks, of clones and fertilizers, and of biology as applied to viticulture.

This is the author to whom Mitchell Beazley has chosen to entrust the *Wine Atlas of Spain*.

Given its worldwide distribution, this book will open the doors once and for all to the toughest markets for our wines. It explains why Spain, which has the largest surface area under vines in the world, produces only just over half the volume of wine that France or Italy does. This is because here, vines have traditionally been planted on the poorest and driest soils, on hillsides or the high plains, leaving the richer lands in the valleys for other crops. However, even in the most remote regions, there was always great potential for quality, which is now being realised with the arrival of modern winemaking techniques.

The Spain that made its wines in dark and dusty bodegas and kept them in pigskins, leather bags and gourds, to be drunk from pitchers and *porrones* – that Spain has gone forever. Many years of hard work have successfully constructed the umbrella of 39 *denominaciones de origen* which our wines now come under. The average quality of Spanish wines has risen rapidly in recent years. Great companies, cooperatives and even ordinary bodegas have bowed to oenological common sense, enabling them to make wines that are truly competitive in an ever tougher market-place.

Hubrecht, who has visited Spain many times, and has written the best book to date on Rioja, has put all his wealth of experience into this Atlas. Its success is assured, and I have not the least doubt that the *bodegueros* and winemakers of Spain, the *Consejo Reguladores*, together with the Ministry of Agriculture and ICEX (the Spanish Foreign Trade Institute) will all do their utmost to make sure that this work reaches as wide a public as possible.

In the faces of great works, men are sometimes moved to a childlike wonder. El Cid must have felt something very similar when, seeing the rising sun, he exclaimed, "*Ixié el sol. Dios que fermoso apuntava!*" (The sun rose. My God, how beautiful the rays!) Sometimes the same thing can happen with great wines; and wine becomes that "cosmic phenomenon" that the great

Spanish philosopher Ortega y Gasset talked about. Hubrecht Duijker's book brings a new day for the great wines of Spain. And as Mauricio Wiesenthal wrote to introduce one of his books, "Let the author decant his wines, and let the sun rise for all of us."

Miguel A Torres
Mas la Plana, June 1991

6

Above: Grapes have been grown around the monastery of Poblet, Conca de Barberà, for more than eight centuries.

Introduction

The history of wine in Spain goes back at least 2,000 years – to the time when the country was being colonized by Greek and Phoenician traders. Most regions have had a more or less continuous history of winemaking ever since, until today Spain has the largest acreage under vines in the world. Yet it is only in the last few decades that it has been worth discovering as a winegrowing country. Hitherto most producers had worked with obsolete equipment that made it impossible, for example, to produce fresh, fruity, exciting white wines in the many hot areas of Spain. Besides, the country had spent decades under Franco in political isolation, which did the quality of its wine no good, for this isolation meant that the Spanish market was closed to imported wines, so that foreign competition was lacking – and with it any strong stimulus to improve the native products. The Spanish home market was thus not a very critical one, partly because no comparison with foreign wines was possible.

Membership of the EC

The departure of the Generalissimo, however, and the restoration of democracy have resulted in great changes, which have also involved Spanish winegrowing. Spain has become a member of the EC, which means that its frontiers have been opened to other wines. At the same time, the country has benefited on a large scale from EC subsidies, enabling all kinds of investment to be made in vineyards and wine cellars. Until the end of the 1970s the sherry country, Rioja and Penedès were the only regions with a goodly number of quality-minded bodegas; over the rest of the Spanish wine map darkness prevailed, with just a few points of light here and there, where individual producers were making wine of an international standard. Today that same wine map is ablaze with light. Quality wines are now made practically all over the country, from tiny Alella to the vastness of La Mancha; from long-established Navarra to recent Costers del Segre. In less than 20 years Spanish winegrowing has advanced further than in the foregoing 20 centuries.

This fact has been recognized well enough among the winegrowers themselves. They have, after all, put a great deal of time, money and energy into improving their stocks of vines and their cellar equipment, often investing in oak casks, bottle lines, laboratories and new buildings as well. Among the public, however, Spain's spectacular leap forward has scarcely been acknowledged as yet, and the same is true of many wine merchants and restaurateurs. Just as millions of holidaymakers associate Spain almost exclusively with beaches and cheap tourist hotels, so millions of wine lovers still see the country as mainly a supplier of cheap plonk.

This is understandable really, for in many wine districts the development has been so swift that even the experts would have been hard pressed to keep up with it all. Rías Baixas in Galicia offers a striking example of this, for in an unbelievably short space of time the situation has changed completely from what it was at the end of the 1980s; practically all the information available in 1985 had to be replaced in 1990, including data concerning the producers.

Technical improvements

The regional oenological stations have played an important part

Above: Vines growing in Bierzo, Castilla y León, where wine production was first recorded in the twelfth century.

in the whole process of improving quality. The countless experiments they have carried out have been of inestimable importance for Spanish winegrowing. The process is obviously still going on, for although many producers now have modern equipment, others are still working with old-fashioned installations. In the vineyards there are still improvements to be made in places to plantings. But in most cases this will only be a temporary state of affairs, for in the face of increasing international competition both in the export field and at home, and of rising standards in Spain itself, improving quality is no longer a luxury but a necessity. Another spur to improvement comes from the EC measure that links the right of a wine to a *denominación de origen* or other such designation to the bottling of a specified proportion of the vintage – usually at least half.

Mapping of the regions

This atlas shows what wine the Spain of today has to offer. All the Spanish wine regions are mapped here in various ways, in geographical order from north to south. Completely new maps have been made for nearly all the *denominaciones de origen*, Spain's highest wine classification, showing the most important wine communities and a suggested wine route. The latter feature is of course meant for travellers who are going to visit the areas; and for them I have also given lists of recommended hotels and restaurants, compiled with the help of the best local producers. This atlas is not just a handbook for the traveller, however, for it also forms a source of documentation and information for the wine lover in his own home. In every chapter the text and photos have the same function as descriptions of paintings, musical compositions and other art forms, for the same maxim applies: the more you know, the more you enjoy. Finally, this book is also a buyer's guide, for it gives sketches of the most interesting bodegas in each region, and names their most delicious wines.

Incidentally, you will discover that the Spanish producers have their own customs for naming their wines. Thus the word *viña* –

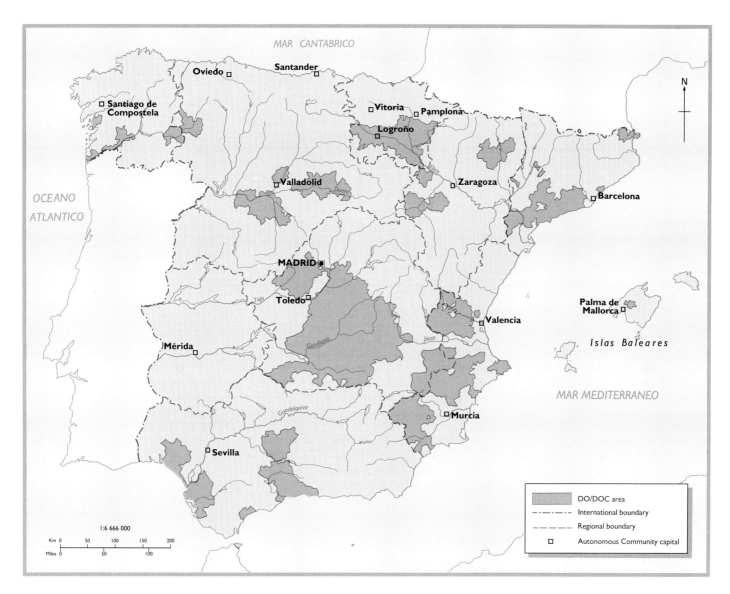

MAR CANTABRICO

OCEANO ATLANTICO

Oviedo

Santander

Santiago de Compostela

Vitoria

Pamplona

Logroño

Valladolid

Duero

Zaragoza

Barcelona

MADRID

Toledo

Tajo

Valencia

Júcar

Palma de Mallorca

Islas Baleares

Mérida

Guadiana

MAR MEDITERRANEO

Guadalquivir

Murcia

Sevilla

N

1:6 666 000

Km 0   50   100   150   200
Miles 0   50   100

DO/DOC area

International boundary

Regional boundary

Autonomous Community capital

literally vineyard – is rarely used for wines produced from grapes from one vineyard, but is usually part of a brand name. The same is true for *castillo*: the concept of a "castle" is not the same in Spain as that of "château" in France. Also interesting is the large number of marquesses who appear on Spanish wine labels.

To collect the data for this book I travelled extensively in Spain, acquiring not only copious notes, but also delightful memories: fresh large prawns and cool *manzanilla* on the front at Sanlúcar de Barrameda; Chardonnay and asparagus from the garden at Raimat; shrimps in coarse salt with white Mallorcan wine on my visit to Binissalem; roast leg of kid with a mature *reserva* in Rioja; hake croquettes in Rueda accompanied by a young Rueda Superior; lamb cutlets grilled out of doors, with a rosé from Navarra . . . I am quite sure that your own journey of discovery through the wine regions of Spain will also be rewarded with many a fragrance and savour.

Hubrecht Duijker
Abcoude, Netherlands

History and Legend

Iberia has nearly 3,000 years of wine history, dating back to a time long before the Spanish nation was established. The marauding Greeks and Phoenicians are credited with bringing wine to the Iberian Peninsula: between 1100 and 500 BC, they founded trading settlements along the Mediterranean coast as far west as Cádiz on the Atlantic. They brought their own vines from the east, and by the time the Carthaginians conquered the coastline around Cartagena and Sagunto in the third century BC, there is evidence of a flourishing trade in wine.

The wine industry developed rapidly under the Romans, who swept into Spain at the end of the third century BC. As the Roman legions marched inexorably westwards, fighting off unruly Celts along the way, they developed a healthy thirst for wine. It took them nearly two hundred years to conquer the whole of the peninsula but by the end of the first century BC the Romans had planted vineyards from Catalonia to Galicia.

The Romans revolutionised wine-making in Iberia. They fermented grape-juice in large earthernware jars called *orcae* and used smaller clay *amphorae* for storage and transportation. The *tinajas* that are still used today by some producers in Montilla, La Mancha and Valdepeñas are a Roman legacy.

After the disintegration of the Roman empire, Iberia was overrun by successive tribes of Swabians and Visigoths, wine-loving Christians from northern Europe. But, following the Battle of Guadalete in 711, the Moors advanced from the south, rapidly taking over the peninsula. Muslim domination lasted over five centuries. In deference to the Koran, they uprooted large areas of

Below: Detail from the Columbus monument, Passeig de Colom, Barcelona.

vineyard although there is evidence that Christian small-holders continued to grow grapes and make wine.

The Christians fought back, but their wars of reconquest took seven hundred years to complete. As they drove south, vineyards were quickly re-established. Monks planted vines around monasteries and made wine for the celebration of Mass. The Catalonian wine-region of Priorato is reputed to date back to this time, when the medieval priors first started to cultivate vines. Scala Dei, though no longer a monastery, continues to make wine today.

The final defeat of the Moors at Granada in 1492 saw the emergence of a Christian Spain united under a single crown. Having channelled their energy into defeating the infidels, the Spanish now set about conquering an empire overseas. Christopher Columbus discovered the West Indies in the same year, opening up the New World and a captive market for Spanish products. The expulsion of the Jews gave rise to a new merchant class, some of them foreigners with a keen interest in wine.

Jerez and Málaga, both close to major ports, were the first Spanish wine regions to attract the attention of foreign settlers. Traders from Italy, France and England helped to improve the quality of of the local wine, and sherris-sack, or sack as it was then called, became a popular drink at the English Court.

English merchants residing in the wine-producing town of Sanlúcar de Barrameda were given special tax privileges by the Duke of Medina Sidonia in 1517 and a church of St George was built to encourage more traders. But relations between the Spanish and the English soon began to deteriorate and the occasional skirmish between the two countries erupted into full-blown conflict at the end of the sixteenth century, after Sir Francis Drake seized 2,900 pipes of sherry in a raid on Cadiz in 1587. English settlers fled under threat from the Spanish Inquisition and, for a time, the wine trade dried up. Jerez obtained a new business: the manufacture of ship's biscuits for the Spanish Armada.

After the defeat of the Armada and the death of both Philip II of Spain and Elizabeth I of England, the wine trade resumed and sack once again became a popular drink at the English Court. Taxes were raised to control consumption but hostilities between the two countries resumed after the English captured Jamaica in 1660. Once again trade declined and the Spanish responded by seeking new markets both in Europe and in South America.

The conflict took its toll on the sherry industry. By 1754 there were just nine traders left in Jerez, only one of whom was English. But in the second half of the eighteenth century, the situation started to improve. In 1772 Sir James Duff, then British Consul in Cádiz, began to export sherry to England under his own name. He was quickly followed by an Irishman, William Garvey, the Scottish Gordon family and Thomas Osborne.

They heralded a new era of prosperity for Jerez which lasted until the Peninsular Wars broke out in 1808. Andalucía was a battleground, occupied for a time by French soldiers. They pillaged the sherry bodegas and forced British families to flee to the safe haven of Cadiz garrison. With the defeat of the French, merchants set about re-building their businesses. Names like Sandeman, Domecq, Burdon, Gonzalez Byass and Mackenzie initiated a sherry boom. Exports rose from 17,000 casks in 1840 to 70,000 in 1873, a quantity not exceeded again until the 1950s.

Above: Lucrezia Borgia, whose infamous family originally came from Borja, in Aragón.

Málaga also enjoyed an unprecedented increase in sales, producing an estimated 175,000 hl (3097 gal) of wine in 1829. "Mountain", as the wine was called, became popular in Britain and North America alongside sherry, port and madeira.

Elsewhere in Spain, wine-making had developed little since Roman times. In central Spain, most table wines were still being made in earthernware *tinajas* or open stone *cisternas*, while further north, wooden barrels were used for both fermentation and maturation. Nineteenth-century wine-writers like Richard Ford and Cyrus Redding commented on the unscientific and haphazard methods of production used by Spanish wine-makers. Most wines were oxidized and acetic due to the hot climate and unhygienic storage conditions. Wine was often kept in *cueros*: pig skins lined with pitch or resin which imparted peculiar flavours to the wine. As late as the 1850s, these *cueros* filled with wine and suspended from the rafters of bodegas were the same "big-bellied monsters" attacked by the legendary Don Quixote in the early seventeenth century.

The dual plagues of oidium and phylloxera forced change on the Spanish wine industry in the latter part of the nineteenth century. Oidium, or powdery mildew, was found in the vineyards of Catalonia in the 1850s, and it swept through much of Spain destroying vineyards before it was brought under control. Phylloxera, a minute but devastating aphid which feeds on the roots of vines, arrived in Málaga in 1878 where it inflicted enormous damage. Thousands of livelihoods were ruined and, with no cure in sight, many growers abandoned their land and left Spain for a new life in the colonies in South America.

But for Spain, the phylloxera cloud had at least one silver lining. The French, who had also been been suffering from oidium since the 1850s, crossed the Pyrenees in search of wine. Rioja, the closest Spanish wine region to Bordeaux, was still unaffected. At first, the French merely bought and began shipping wine. Then, after phylloxera had really taken hold, wiping out over half the country's vineyards, they began building wineries in Spain similar to those they had left behind in Bordeaux. The Bordelais introduced the 225 litre (50 gal) oak *barrique* or *barrica*, and refined wine-making practices to meet their own standards. Bodegas like those belonging to Murrieta, Riscal, López de Heredia and Cune all date back to this period, when up to half-a-million hl (11 million gal) of wine were being shipped monthly to phylloxera-ridden France.

Due to the vast distances between vineyards, it took longer for phylloxera to take hold in Spain. After initially destroying Málaga, it reached Jerez in 1894 but only arrived in Rioja in 1901 by which time the epidemic had been successfully controlled. *Vitis vinifera* vines, susceptible to attack by the phylloxera, were grafted on to resistant American rootstock. Vineyards all over Spain were re-planted and by 1910, phylloxera had ceased to be a problem.

In Cataluña, re-planting in the wake of phylloxera coincided with the development of a new wine industry. Following a visit to the Champagne region, Don José Raventós began making sparkling wine for the family firm of Codorníu in 1872. The wine, originally called *champaña*, caught on and whole swathes of vineyard around the little town of Sant Sadurní d'Anoia were planted with white Macabeo, Xarel-lo and Parellada grapes as growers jumped on the band-wagon. Today, Codorníu is one of the largest producers of sparkling wine in the world. The Raventós family were joined in 1901 by Freixenet and together they now sell over 70 million bottles of Cava a year.

Spain has suffered a turbulent history in the twentieth century. Following the abdication of King Alfonso XIII in 1931, political infighting rose to fever pitch and erupted into civil war. For four years, Spain tore itself apart. Vineyards were neglected and wineries destroyed. Recovery following Franco's Nationalist victory in 1939 was hampered by the Second World War which effectively closed European markets to Spanish wine exports. It was not until the 1950s that progress was made when, with government support, wine-making cooperatives were set up all over Spain and export markets began to revive.

Exports were dominated by sales of bulk wine sold as brands like Don Cortez, or labelled with spurious names like "Spanish Burgundy" or "Spanish Sauternes". But since the early 1970s, government authorities have exercised an ever greater degree of control over Spain's principal wine-producing regions. Alongside sherry, which continued to boom throughout the 1950s and '60s, Rioja has emerged in recent years as one of Spain's best known wines. Since the death of General Franco and the restoration of the monarchy in 1975, the growth of an urban middle class has created a new market for quality wine. A programme of investment in modern wine-making technology was initiated in the early 1980s, helped further by Spain's entry into the European Community in 1986. With the market for ordinary *vino de mesa* continuing to shrink and new regions like Ribera del Duero, Penedès and Valdepeñas coming to the fore, Spain is gaining an ever better reputation for the quality of her wines. But three millennia of tradition, albeit tempered by modern practice, continues to survive.

Vineyards and Grape Varieties

When it comes to vineyards and vines, Spain can lay a few claims to the biggest and the most. In between the Pyrenees and Portugal are around 1.5 million ha (3.6 million acres) of vines – more than any other nation in the world. But when it comes to production, Spain's annual average harvest of between 30 and 35 million hl ranks a poor fourth behind France, Italy and the Soviet Union.

By European standards, vineyard yields are low. Much of the country is dry and infertile and vines have to be widely spaced to survive the summer drought. Compared with France, where yields average 60 hl (1,319 gal) of wine per ha, and Germany, where many vineyards top 100 hl (2,199 gal), Spain produces a paltry average of 23 hl (450 gal) per ha of vines. But yields vary sharply from one region to another. In Galicia on Spain's cool, damp northwestern seaboard vines produce up to 100 hl (2,199 gal) per ha, whereas in La Mancha scrubby old vines yield tiny quantities of shrivelled grapes.

Faced with a surplus, the European Community is eager to keep Spanish production under control. Grants encourage farmers to uproot their vines and plant other crops. Vineyards in the better DOs regions are unlikely to disappear, but the ocean of vines in the poorer parts of La Mancha, Levante and the south is likely to contract over the next few years as EC policies begin to take effect.

Irrigation, which tends to promote vineyard yield, is forbidden by EC legislation drawn up with damp northern Europe in mind. But in the drier parts of Spain, there is a strong case for allowing irrigation. One or two properties, such as the Raimat estate near Lérida, have been granted "experimental" status which permits them to side-step the law. With judicious use of water, arid waste has been planted with foreign grape varieties that would otherwise struggle to survive.

Spain claims to have 600 different grape varieties, though just 20 cover 80 percent of the country's massive area of vineyards. Understandably, farmers looking to maximize their returns favour the grapes that are best adapted to Spain's extreme climate. White Airén is the most popular and takes up almost three times as much land as any other grape variety. Garnacha Tinta, a grape that flourishes in arid, windy conditions, is the second most widely planted. Since phylloxera ravaged the country a number of the troublesome varieties have been abandoned and are now close to extinction. For example, grapes such as Malvasía which were once important in Rioja and Penedès have been replaced by productive but bland varieties such as Macabeo. However, there is now an encouraging move to replace poor quality vines with grapes which produce better wines. Tempranillo is currently the most fashionable but French imports like Cabernet Sauvignon and Chardonnay are now being produced in commercial quantities.

The following list includes all of Spain's most important native grape varieties, along with the major foreign interlopers:

White grape varieties

Airén In a country which is best known for its red wines, it comes as a surprise to find that the most widely planted grape variety is white. There are over 450,000 ha (1 million acres) of Airén growing in Spain, making it the single most planted grape variety in the world. It is largely confined to one area: La Mancha. Here, in Don Quixote country at the centre of the Spanish *meseta*, it has traditionally produced vast amounts of basic, alcoholic dry white wine for swilling around parched mouths in Spanish bars and cafes. Recent improvements in wine-making technology have improved the quality of much Manchegan wine and Airén, used to its full potential, makes a simple but refreshing, appley dry white. Airén also crops up under the name of Lairén around Málaga and Montilla-Moriles.

Albariño This sweet, small, low-yielding grape has attained cult status in fashionable restaurants. It is grown in Galicia where in DO Rías Baixas it makes some particularly good, firm, aromatic dry white wines. Demand has forced up prices and Albariño wines count among the most expensive whites in Spain.

Albillo Neutral grape making dry white wines in the country around Madrid and Avilla as well as DO Ribeiro in Galicia. In the Duero valley it occasionally finds its way into red wines and plays a small part in the composition of the legendary Vega Sicilia.

Alcanón White grape of DO Somontano.

Caiño A native of Galicia, the white Caiño is mainly planted in Rías Baixas. It is not highly prized for quality.

Chardonnay Burgundy's finest white grape has travelled the world, and growers in Spain have been seduced, quite late in the day, by its global popularity. It is grown in commercial quantities by a number of leading producers in Catalonia, among them Jean León, the Raimat estate near Lérida and Torres's Milmanda vineyard in DO Conca de Barberà. Chardonnay is also creeping in to a number of the better Cavas where it adds depth and dimension to the neutral base wines made from local grapes Parellada, Xarel-lo and Macabeo.

Chenin Blanc This Loire grape crops up in some unusual places: Alella, Penedès and in the Mallorcan DO of Binissalem. It is notoriously difficult to handle.

Doña Blanca Planted inland in Galicia where it is slowly giving way to varieties with more character.

Garnacha Blanca The Grenache Blanc, as it is known in France, grows in the vineyards of Aragón and Catalonia where it makes fairly flat, neutral, alcoholic dry white wines.

Gewürztraminer Aromatic grape with a strong hint of spice and lychee fruit. It is grown successfully in Somontano, and also in Penedès, where Torres uses it for the Viña Esmeralda.

Godello This aromatic variety is planted in Galicia, especially inland in DO Valdeorras. It can make good, dry white wine.

Hondarribi Zuri Grape planted in the tiny Basque DO of Chacolí where it produces fresh, acidic dry white wines.

Lairén The local name for Airén in Andalucía (*see* Airén).

Listán Synonym for the Palomino grape (*see* Palomino).

Loureira Along with Albariño, Loureira is one of the best grapes of Galicia, making fragrant, floral dry white wines. It is often used in conjunction with Treixadura which helps to compensate for Loureira's low sugar levels.

Macabeo Grown all over the north of Spain, at best Macabeo makes fresh but fairly neutral dry white wine. Under the name of Viura it accounts for over 90 percent of all white Rioja, with 6,000 ha (14,820 acres) of vines mostly planted in the higher reaches of the region. In Cataluña, Macabeo is one of the "big three" varieties used in making Cava. Wines made from Macabeo tend to age rapidly and are therefore best drunk in the bloom of their youth

Above: Vineyard in the Valdeorras DO, Galicia.

when they can be crisp and perfumed if well made. Plantings of Macabeo amount to 35,000 ha (86,485 acres).

Malvar Variety producing bland white wines from vineyards around Madrid and Toledo.

Malvasía There is a number of different types of Malvasía and few people seem to be sure which one of them grows in Spain. In Rioja it is likely that Malvasía, formerly an important element in oak-aged white wine, is different from the grape of the same name that crops up around Zamora and on the Canaries. It now accounts for less than five percent of Rioja's white grape varieties, having been overtaken by the more productive Viura. The quality of white Rioja has suffered as a direct result.

Merseguera The mainstay of vineyards around Valencia and Alicante where the better producers make light, refreshing slightly fruity wines from it.

Moscatel The variety of Moscatel planted extensively along the Mediterranean coast of Spain and on the Canaries is the Muscat of Alexandria, which is distinct from the Muscat à Petits Grains planted in the southern Rhône for Muscat de Beaumes-de-Venise. As a consequence, Spanish muscats tend to be unctuous but clumsy, lacking in delicacy and refinement. Some good, rich dessert wines are however made around Valencia and Málaga.

Palomino By nature Palomino is a big, juicy white grape producing flabby, neutral white wine. It is planted extensively in Spain, especially in Rueda and Galicia where it is now slowly being replaced by varieties that make wines with more character. In one Spanish wine region however, Palomino excels. In the chalky *albariza* soils around the city of Jerez da la Frontera, Palomino produces the vast majority of the base wine for one of

the most distinctive of all drinks, sherry. But even here it is fortification followed by a unique maturation process that transforms the blowsy base wine into crisp, nutty dry *fino* or *amontillado*. When it comes to rich *olorosos*, the Pedro Ximénez grape (*see* Pedro Ximénez) also plays an important part.

Pansá Blanca *see* Xarel-lo.

Parellada Reputed to be the best of Catalonia's white grapes, Parellada is used in the making of both still and sparkling wines. On its own it produces wines that are light and low in alcohol with a floral aroma and crisp flavour. More often than not, Parellada is blended with Macabeo and Xarel-lo to make a crisp but often neutral base wine for Cava.

Pedro Ximénez In the warm sunshine of Andalucía, Pedro Ximénez (or PX as it is affectionately known for short) attains incredibly high sugar levels. In Montilla, without the help of fortifying brandy, PX wines have an alcohol content that is sometimes in excess of 15 degrees. Pedro Ximénez is found in vineyards all over southern Spain where it has a variety of uses. In Málaga and Jerez generous dollops of syrupy PX juice are used for sweetening, while in Montilla-Moriles, PX is the mainstay of all the region's wines. Elsewhere, Pedro Ximénez produces rather coarse, alcoholic dry white wines.

Planta Nova Authorized in the DO of Utiel-Requena where it makes undistinguished dry white wine.

Riesling Unfashionable as it is, Riesling has crept into Spain. A small amount is planted in the hills of Penedès where Miguel Torres makes a typically perfumed, fresh-tasting white wine.

Sauvignon Blanc Authorized grape in the DO Rueda where it has been grown since 1985. Also planted in Penedès. A qualified success. Spanish Sauvignons are typically fragrant and grassy.

Torrontés With careful wine-making, this Galician grape yields distinctive, balanced wines sometimes with an attractive almond and pine kernel flavour.

Treixadura Increasingly important quality grape in the vineyards of Galicia (especially DO Ribeiro) where it is often used to fill out wines made from other local varieties.

Verdejo Some authorities consider this to be one of Spain's best native white grapes. Verdejo is planted in the DO of Rueda where it is gradually superseding Palomino. With modern technology, Verdejo makes a fresh, dry white wine with the aroma of apples and pears; good and sometimes exciting.

Verdil A popular variety around Murcia and Alicante.

Viura The name for Macabeo in Rioja and some other regions (*see* Macabeo).

Xarel-lo One of the "big three" grapes planted in Catalonia (*see also* Macabeo and Parellada). Xarel-lo is an important constituent of Cava. On its own, it often produces a neutral white wine that needs the aromatic uplift of Parellada. In Alella, the same grape masquerades under the name of Pansá Blanca.

Zalema Grown around Huelva where it is an important constituent of the local sherry-like wine, Condado de Huelva. Oxidizes rapidly.

Red grape varieties

Alicante *See* Garnacha Tintorera.

Aragón Local synonym in parts of Spain for Garnacha.

Bobal An important grape in Levante where there are over 100,000 ha (2,471,000 acres). Bobal produces deep, dark wine that seems to retain its acidity in spite of the hot climate. It can also produce delicious dry rosés.

Brancellao Makes light but fruity wines in Galicia.

Cabernet Sauvignon Like Chardonnay, Cabernet Sauvignon is a world traveller that has been planted in vineyards all over Spain. Cabernet ripens well under the warm Mediterranean sun, making rich, minty wines packed with blackcurrant fruit. It was brought from France at the end of the last century, and a few vines have remained in the vineyards of Marqués de Riscal and Vega Sicilia ever since. But over the last twenty years Cabernet has really caught on and significant quantities are now planted all over Spain, particularly in the DOs of Penedès and Costers del Segre. The wines of Marqués de Griñon from a plot near Madrid show the ripe flavour of Spanish Cabernet.

Caiño Grows like its white namesake in Galicia where it produces some good, light, spicy red wines.

Cariñena Alias Carignan in France, the Cariñena originates from a town with the same name in Aragón. It produces dark wine that is often fairly alcoholic, tannic and astringent. In Rioja, where it now represents only a tiny proportion of the total vineyard area, Cariñena is called Mazuelo (and sometimes Mazuela).

Cencibel The local name for Tempranillo in La Mancha and Valdepeñas (*see* Tempranillo).

Espadeiro Found in Galicia where it makes light but fragrant red wine.

Forcayat Productive variety producing washed-out wines in the country around Valencia.

Garnacha Tinta Spain's most widely planted red grape with a total of over 170,000 ha (420,070 acres). The high yielding Garnacha is cultivated all over the north of Spain, especially in Rioja Baja, Navarra, Aragón and Catalonia. On its own it tends to make rather brutish red wines, mostly lacking in finesse, though it can make fresh, fruity rosés. In Rioja, red made from Garnacha helps to fill out lighter more delicate Tempranillo-based wines. Pure Garnacha wine tends to age rapidly.

Garnacha Tintorera Red-fleshed grape making solid, deeply coloured wines in central Spain and Levante. Also christened Alicante.

Graciano It is sad that this high quality variety has almost disappeared from Rioja's vineyards. Low yields have made it unpopular although it makes fine, powerful wine that ages well.

Hondarribi Beltz Basque grape making light, astringent red wine in DO Chacolí and the province of Viscaya.

Malbec Originating from Bordeaux, Malbec is found in tiny amounts in Vega Sicilia's vineyards.

Manto Negro Grows on the Balearic islands where it makes sound, but unexciting reds.

Maria Ardona Grape growing in DO Valdeorras.

Mazuelo *see* Cariñena.

Mencía Thought to be related to the French Cabernet Franc, Mencía makes sound wines with a slightly metallic taste in Bierzo, as well as in Valdeorras.

Merlot Usually planted as a partner to Cabernet Sauvignon by those growers looking to emulate the classic Bordeaux blend. Raimat in DO Costers del Segre make a varietal Merlot that shows off the soft, plummy flavour of the grape. Torres works with Merlot too, as do some producers in other regions, such as Navarra.

Monastrell This, the second most widely planted red grape in Spain after Garnacha, is popular with growers because of its high yield and sweet fruit. Monastrell is mostly found in Penedès and Levante where, with good wine-making, it can produce big, meaty, alcoholic but balanced red wines. Sometimes these are fortified. Monastrell also produces good rosé.

Moristel Not to be confused with Monastrell, Moristel is mainly found in the Aragón hills. It is one of the main grapes in DO Somontano.

Negramoll Canary Islands grape producing light, insubstantial wine in spite of the sub-tropical climate.

Pinot Noir Notoriously difficult to grow outside its native Burgundy, Pinot Noir has been cultivated with some success in Costers del Segre and Penedès. The wines are characteristically soft, round and perfumed, sometimes with more body than most Burgundies.

Preto Picudo Grows around Zamora and León where it makes pale wines without much distinction.

Samsó Catalan name for Cariñena (*see* Cariñena).

Souson Grape making ink-black wines in Galicia. Now increasingly scarce.

Tempranillo Undoubtedly one of Spain's best indigenous varieties, 33,000 ha (81,543 acres) of Tempranillo crop up in different guises all over Spain. It performs best in cooler parts of the country like Rioja and the Duero region, where it makes elegant wines with a whiff of cherries and strawberries when young. Wine made from Tempranillo responds well to ageing in oak. Most Rioja *reservas* and *gran reservas* are made mainly if not entirely from Tempranillo. In DO Ribera del Duero it is christened both Tinto Fino and Tinta del País, in La Mancha and Valdepeñas it becomes Cencibel, and in Catalonia Ull de Lebre. Other local synonyms include Tinto de Madrid, and Tinta de Toro.

Trepat Grows mainly in DO Conca de Barberà where it produces refreshing rosés.

Ull de Llebre Catalan name for Tempranillo (*see* Tempranillo).

Laws and Labels

Regulations controlling the production and sale of wine were drawn up as early as the thirteenth century, but it was not until the 1920s that a serious attempt was made to protect the authenticity of regional wines.

Rioja was the first region to attract the attention of the men from the ministry when, in 1926, they set up a *Consejo Regulador* (Regulating Council) to ensure fair play within the boundaries of a newly delimited wine region. Jerez and Málaga joined the ranks in the 1930s and they were followed by a rash of new regions in the period after the civil war. At a time when Madrid was keen to stamp its authority on Spain, it is surprising that it was not until the twilight years of Franco's regime that a central body was established to co-ordinate the activities of the *Consejos*. Following a comprehensive statute promulgated in 1970, the Ministry of Agriculture formed INDO (*Instituto Nacional de Denominaciones de Origen*) to administer a national system of authenticity and quality control. Since 1979, when Spain reverted to federal administration, direct responsibility for the *Consejos* has been devolved to regional government. INDO however continues to play a central role as in policy making and promotion.

Spanish wine legislation corresponds closely to the AOC (*Appellation d'Origine Contrôlée*) system devised by the French in the early part of the twentieth century. It is founded on the DO (*denominación de origen*) which, like the AOC, defines boundaries within which the grapes must be grown. The laws have been revised to meet the needs of the European Community (EC), which Spain joined in 1986. Like France, Germany and Italy, Spain currently has four different principal quality control categories as follows.

Vino de Mesa (Table wine) This, the most basic category, covers wine made from grapes grown in unclassified vineyards or wine which has been declassified by blending. If bottled, labels may not normally display a grape variety, vintage or geographical origin. Much of Spain's *Vino de Mesa* is sent for compulsory distillation in an effort to prevent Europe's wine lake from overflowing.

Vino de la Tierra A wine of which more than 60 percent is from a specific region within Spain may be categorised as *Vino de la Tierra* if it complies with governing laws. This category is the equivalent of the French *Vin de Pays* but few wines are, as yet, of exportable quality. A notable exception is the wine of Marqués de Griñon, which has recently been designated a Vino de la Tierra.

Denominación de Origen (DO) This category is the mainstay of the Spanish quality control system which, at the time of writing, had been given to thirty-nine wine-producing regions. Each region is governed by a *Consejo Regulador* made up of representatives from the Ministry of Agriculture and growers, winemakers and shippers earning their livelihoods in the region. The *Consejo*, in conjunction with the regional government and INDO in Madrid, decides on the boundaries of the region, permitted grape varieties, maximum yields, alcoholic strength and any other limitations pertaining to the district. *Consejos* run control laboratories to carry out regular chemical analyses of the wine to ensure strict control of standards, as well as helping growers and winemakers with research and development. Back labels or neck seals are granted to certify that the wine meets regional standards.

The category of *Denominación de Origen Provisional* (DOP) may be awarded to regions on their way to becoming full DOs.

Denominación de Origen Calificada (DOCa) This, the newest category to be added to Spanish wine regulations, is reserved for regions making wines of the highest quality, complying with certain stringent regulations including tasting. So far, the one and only region to benefit is Rioja, which was awarded DOCa status in 1991.

The language of the label The following explanatory terms can currently be found on the labels of Spanish wines:

Año: year. 2o, 3o, 4o año is no longer permitted, but still occasionally seen on bottles.

Bodega: wine cellar or wine-producing company.

Brut: dry sparkling wine.

Brut de Brut or *Brut Extra*: the driest of all sparking wines.

Cava: DO, applying to certain designated regions producing sparkling wine by the traditional or "champagne" method.

Crianza: a wine that is released for sale in its third year, having spent a minimum of six months in 225 litre (50 gal) oak casks. In Rioja, where the term is most commonly used, the wine must have spent at least 12 months in oak casks.

Cosecha: year of harvest or vintage.

Dulce: sweet

Elaborado por: produced by

Embotellado por: bottled by

Extra Seco: sparkling wine that is not quite as dry as *Brut*.

Gran Reserva: wine from a supposedly excellent vintage that has been subject to lengthy ageing. Red wines must spend a minimum of two years in cask followed by three years in bottle (or vice-versa). The wine may not leave the bodega until the sixth year after the vintage at the earliest.

Granvas: sparkling wine produced by inducing the secondary fermentation in tank. The equivalent of *Cuve Close*.

Lágrima: literally "tears"; it also refers to a wine made from free-run juice without any mechanical pressing.

Metodo Tradicional: Spanish term denoting sparkling wine made by the "champagne method", i.e. the secondary fermentation has taken place in the bottle in which the wine is sold.

Pasada: term used to describe a well-aged sherry.

Quinado: fortified wine aromatized with quinine.

Reserva: red wine from a good harvest with a minimum of three years in cask and bottle of which a year should be in cask. It may not leave the bodega until the fourth year after the vintage.

Roble: oak

Rosado: rosé

Seco: dry

Semi-seco: medium dry

Viejo: old

Vendimia: vintage

Viña: literally means vineyard but it is often used as part of a brand name, e.g. Viña Arana. The EC is currently tightening up on the use of the term.

Vino espumoso: general term for sparkling wine.

Vino generoso: fortified wine developed under *flor*.

Geography and Climate

The relief map of Iberia looks rather like a table with a rim around the edge. Mountains rise steeply from the coast around much of the Iberian Peninsula, reaching a height of 3,400 m (11,400 ft) in the Sierra Nevada just 50 km (120 yds) from the Mediterranean. But the most dominant feature is an immense plateau that takes up the heart of the country. The *meseta* ranges in altitude between 600 and 1,000m (1,968 to 3,279 ft). Spain is the second highest country in Europe, with an average height of 650m (2,130 ft).

Mountains divide Spain into distinct regions. The northern fringe, from Galicia to the Pyrenees, is cool and damp. Winds blowing off the Atlantic and the Bay of Biscay give a year-round rainfall of 1,300 mm (51 ins). This is the most intensively cultivated part of Spain. Vines grow in profusion on the granite soils of Galicia which produces some of Spain's most refreshing white wines.

The Cantabrian Cordillera, a westerly spur of the Pyrenees, acts as a climatic shield for the rest of Spain. The land rises to a height of 2,600m (8,600 ft) in the Picos de Europa which protects the northern *meseta* from cool, rain-bearing winds. If you travel from Bilbao to Rioja's wine capital Haro, a distance of some 100 km (62 miles), the difference is immediate. Clouds piling over the Sierra de Cantabria give way to brilliant sunshine by the time you reach the upper Ebro valley. Fertile south and west-facing slopes and long, warm summers help to ripen grapes slowly, making soft, smooth red wines.

Towards the centre of the *meseta*, the climate becomes more extreme. Winters are long and cold with temperatures often falling well below zero for days on end. In summer the heat is gruelling. Daytime temperatures regularly rise above 30°C (86°F), even 40°C (104°F), and little, if any, rain falls between May and September. It is the country south of Madrid, in particular the vast plain of La Mancha, that suffers the cruellest climate of all. The landscape, which is green in spring, quickly turns burnt ochre in July and August as rivers dry up, only to turn to a shade of grey as winter sets in. But wine is an important crop and doughty Airén vines seem to defy the drought.

Further to the south and east the climate becomes more Mediterranean. This part of Spain is protected from the climatic extremes of the *meseta* by lofty sierras. On the narrow strips of land between the mountains and the sea, the climate is especially mild with long, warm summers giving way to mild winters. These coasts are Spain's holiday playground but inland, olives, almonds and vines are important crops. Penedès perhaps has the most favourable climate for wine grapes, but the country around Valencia and Alicante is also heavily planted with vines. The long, hot summers in Málaga and Montilla are ideal for making high-strength wines from sweet Pedro Ximénez grapes.

The south-west corner of Andalucía has a climate of its own which favours a unique wine. Palomino grapes flourish on the chalky *albariza* soils, producing a delicate, dry wine which is fortified to make sherry. Cool winds blowing inland from the sea help to promote the growth of *flor* in the bodegas of Jerez de la Frontera and Sanlúcar de Barrameda.

Of all the grape-growing countries of the world, it is difficult to think of another making such a broad range of wines, from the light, crackling table wines of cool, damp Galicia to the rich, nutty fortified wines of warm, dry Andalucía.

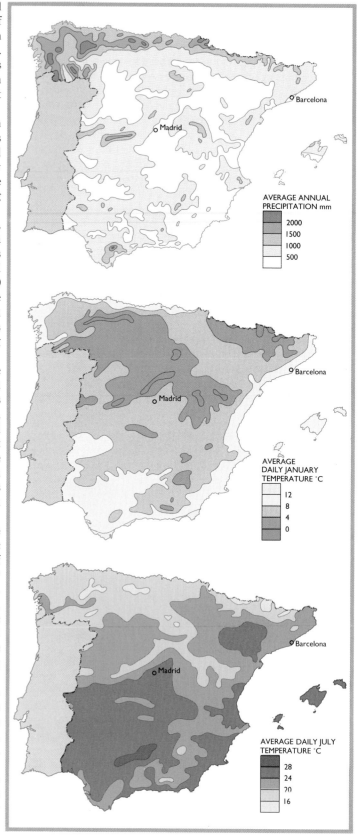

AVERAGE ANNUAL
PRECIPITATION mm

2000
1500
1000
500

AVERAGE
DAILY JANUARY
TEMPERATURE °C

12
8
4
0

AVERAGE DAILY JULY
TEMPERATURE °C

28
24
20
16

How to Use This Atlas

As a basic reference to the wines of Spain, this Atlas provides a fund of knowledge in words, maps, and pictures that can be studied or consulted at home. It is also designed to be used as a travel guide, with entirely new maps of the wine zones that suggest routes through the wine villages, and point out places of interest in the vicinity.

The Atlas takes a thorough look at the special characteristics that make Spanish wines unique. It focuses in depth on the vineyards, describing the lay of the land and the climate and soil, giving an insight into each zone's winemaking practices and describing the producers who use them most effectively. For the traveller it also suggests restaurants, hotels, and places of interest to visit along the way.

The book is designed to appeal to both the student of wine and the enthusiastic amateur. The text may be read following a north to south geographical sequence through Spain, which has been divided into four main areas for the purposes of this book – the North, the East and Centre, the South, and the Islands. It can also be used as a reference book, to find out more about a certain wine region or bodega, or to get an idea of what to expect from the bottle to be opened at dinner. The Atlas can also be used as a buyer's manual, but only in a general way, since its lasting value as a reference does not permit it to be an up to the minute guide to vintages.

Each region is introduced by an overview of wines and production trends, with notes on the landscape, history, customs, and foods that give it a special flavour. Then comes information of the vineyards and grape varieties and a survey of the geographical conditions of the DO wine zones shown on the accompanying regional map. The wines of each DO within the region are discussed in detail. (See page 15 for an explanation of the *denominación de origen* [DO] system.) The descriptions, which include both praise and critical appraisals, mix fact and opinion in a fashion designed to enlighten without being pedantic. The fine points behind the DO category convey the technical side of winemaking, but even casual readers might be curious to know how grape varieties and such factors as yields, alcohol strength, acidity, and ageing determine a wine's type and style.

The maps

The maps vary widely in scope and detail, depending on the complexity of the wine zones in each region or area. The four levels of maps used in the Atlas are as follows:

National maps

The areas shown – which roughly correspond to the geographical divisions of Spain – have been chosen to highlight the various wine regions. The Introduction maps (pages 1–19) show the nationwide distribution of DO zones, average temperatures and rainfall, and major routes: road, rail, airports and ferries.

Area maps

These correspond to the major areas of Spain followed in geographical order in the Atlas. These maps show the broad geography of the sector, with roads, railways, and physical features. They also show regional boundaries, thus acting as a key to the regional maps. Note that the Islands have no area map –

instead, each has its own regional map.

Regional maps

Each of the 10 regions has a general map, showing all the DOs within it. There are a few anomalies: the wine zones of Rioja, Navarra and Chacoli de Getaira are shown together on a map of Central North (page 76), although they are all in different geographical areas. In addition, The Islands, i.e. the Balearics and the Canary Islands, each have their own regional map, showing the DOs.

The regional map shows all DO areas and these are marked by coloured boundaries. The DO names are indicated on the map. In Cataluña, where space doesn't permit, the wine area is given a number in a box and the name is indicated by the side (underlined in a distinct colour).

Detailed maps

Thirty-one of Spain's most important DO zones are shown in varying degrees of detail, showing the various wine villages. The remaining DOs appear in outline on the regional maps. To check the precise location of an individual DO, you can refer back to the regional map which locates all DO wine zones within the region's boundaries. The suggested wine routes shown on the maps lead through wine villages and places of special interest.

As a key to reading the regional and detailed maps, names of physical or geographical points (eg towns, mountains) are in black type and wine data is in red.

All the boundaries for DO areas have been compiled from the most authoritative and up-to-date information available. Each map (except for those in the introductory pages) is enclosed by a lettered and numbered grid. Important points on the maps have a grid reference so they can be easily located. These grid references are listed in the index and gazetteer.

Wine terminology

Some of the more common terms used on Spanish wine labels are listed in the section on Laws and Labels (page 15). For a complete list of Spanish terms and expressions used in this book see the Glossary (page 230).

Travelling in Spain

The only way of making a really thorough tour of the Spanish wine regions is by car. This can be very agreeable even at the height of the season, for the millions of tourists who visit Spain every year stay mainly on the coast. The interior therefore remains peaceful and pleasant to drive around in, especially if you avoid the trunk roads (indicated by an N followed by a Roman numeral) which are used by many heavy goods vehicles. And whereas the coast has been spoiled in a lot of places by huge concrete hotels, inland the country is often undeveloped from the point of view of tourism. There are many advantages in this – but also one drawback: it means that the interior has a shortage of comfortable, congenial hotels. Practically all the good four- and five-star hotels are on the coast or in the bigger towns. What you usually find in the smaller towns are either *hostales* (a roadside combination of bar, restaurant and hotel), or simple hotels with at most three stars. Most are downright ugly, and very noisy. The noise comes in the first place from passing traffic – so always ask for a room at the back. But the hotel itself can generate a good deal of noise through stone floors, running water, and thin walls. The quietest rooms are usually on the top floor, but these are also the hottest if there is no air conditioning. Anyone who values a good night's sleep should therefore take great care in choosing accommodation. You will find the addresses given in this book a great help, for they have been selected with great care.

Paradores

Favourable exceptions to the general hotel scene are scarce, but fortunately they do occur. The most important group are the *paradores*. These state hotels are to be found not only in the towns, but also in the villages and out in the countryside, and what is pleasant about them is that each *parador* has its own character. Many of them are accommodated in large, interesting old buildings, like the one at Zamora; others are very modern, as at Segovia. A third category rather comes in between, being quite modern outside and stylish inside – Vilafranca del Bierzo is an example. Unfortunately there is only a limited number of *paradores*. In the whole of Spain, including the islands, there are some 10,000 hotels and *hostales* – of which just under 90 are *paradores*. This means there is no *parador* in or near many of the wine districts, and if there is one it may be difficult to get a room; early reservations are usually essential. If you have a choice of hotels or *hostales*, always check whether there is going to be an engagement party or other celebration during your stay. Some establishments do well out of these, especially at weekends, and the fact that their hotel guests are kept awake well into the small hours by the thump of the music is of no concern to them.

You should also allow for the fact that without maps or detailed directions hotels may be hard to find. Things are worse at night, as there are seldom any illuminated signposts or direction boards. I have always made grateful use of the town plans and directions in the *Guide Michelin España-Portugal*. The Michelin maps are also very reliable, particularly the 1:400,000 scale regional ones.

A Spanish hotel breakfast is usually a meal of no consequence, and for good, fresh coffee and a decent roll it is often better to go to a bar. Lunch and dinner on the other hand are more exuberant affairs, bringing brisk business to tens of thousands of restaurants, large and small. By general European standards, prices of

Above: Romanesque church at Ujué, Navarra.

both food and wines are reasonable, especially if you choose regional varieties – which are usually the nicest. Food in Spain is generally tasty and nourishing, without fussiness or great subtlety. It is only in and around the big cities that you find establishments where the cooking has finesse and creativity. I myself have tremendously enjoyed grilled lamb cutlets from Rioja, and much other such unadorned fare. But the absolute high point of all my Spanish travels was a meal at the Sibaris restaurant in Vigo, where dishes of the utmost refinement were served along with Rías Baixas wines.

Tempo and service

There is much to be enjoyed at various levels in Spanish restaurants. But bear in mind that waiters are often more interested in getting through the meal quickly than in the welfare of their guests; the main course often arrives on the table while the starters are still being eaten. Such surprises can only be avoided by giving the waiter strict instructions. If you want to have butter – on bread, with ham or cheese – you must always ask for it specially. For non-Spaniards, it seems strange to have cheese served as a starter and only rarely as a dessert – although the

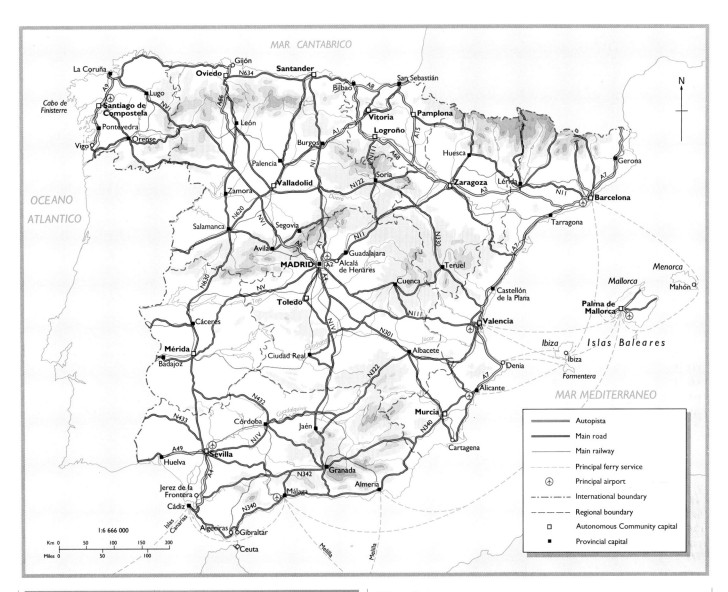

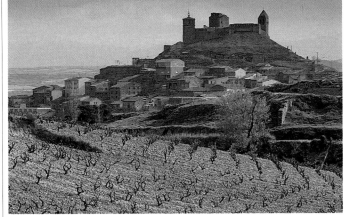

Above: Vineyard below San Vincente de la Sonsierra, Rioja Alavesa.

latter is always possible. In the simpler eating houses you must be prepared for the TV to be on, loudly – probably more for the benefit of the staff than for the customers. In a hotel in Ponferrada I once even ate dinner to the accompanying noise from two TV sets, tuned to different channels. You will look in vain for that hotel in this book!

Wine lists

Spanish wines have made tremendous advances in quality in recent decades, but in many restaurants they are obviously still regarded as unimportant. The average wine list is characterized by a slipshod approach, with vintages not stated and an absence of .descriptions. As vintages are so often not given it may be difficult, for example, to order a young, fresh white wine. Often the only answer is to ask the waiter to show you the various bottles. In some establishments part of the stock of red wine is kept standing in the dining-room. This carries the risk of dried-out corks, and spoiled wine; and the wines will mostly be too warm. If the wine is too warm, don't hesitate to ask for the bottle to be stood in a bucket of cold water with a few ice cubes.

Another problem for the wine lover is the impossibly small wine glasses that most restaurants use. Water, on the other hand, is served in a more generous-sized glass, which would be just right for wine. This fault is easily remedied: just change the glasses round. Make sure that wines you have ordered are offered for you to taste; in many simple restaurants this will just be forgotten otherwise. It will take time before wine in Spain is given the appreciation and the treatment it deserves. The customers have the power to speed up this process – for it is to them that restaurateurs will listen first.

Above: The castle of Peñafiel dominates the area of Ribera del Duero.

The North

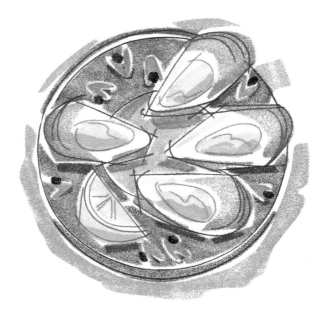

Variety is the key word for northern Spain, for it offers an unbelievable range of landscape, climate, culture and tradition, and the wines made here are very diverse. The largest part of the area's northern boundary is in fact composed of the Costa Verde, the Cantabrian coast. This has many quiet sandy beaches, but also important industrial cities such as Bilbao, San Sebastián and Santander. Immediately behind the coast lie the foothills of the Cantabrian Mountains, a chain that separates the maritime provinces from Castilla y León. In the west the coast takes on a fantastical aspect because of the many reefs and *rías* – broad inlets something like fjords. The Atlantic brings a good deal of rain to these coastal areas, which as a result are very green. In late spring in Galicia, the *autonomía* in the far north-west consisting of four provinces, the traveller may encounter grey, overcast skies, brilliant sunshine and heavy showers several times over on the same day. The result of all the rain is exuberant vegetation. Even the smallest patches of land are planted and there is also extensive woodland: Galicia accounts for about a quarter of Spanish timber production.

Between the Atlantic Ocean and the Mediterranean are the towering Pyrenees, Spain's natural frontier with France. The rivers that rise there water great areas of the *autonomías* to the south of this mountain range, namely Aragón, Cataluña and Navarra. Sometimes the river valleys act as funnels for cold mountain winds. The valley of the Río Gallego brings a biting wind to Zaragoza, capital of Aragón. There is hardly any winegrowing along the cool, damp north coast or the Pyrenees. Chacolí de Guetaria is the only *denominación de origen*; this little entity lies just west of San Sebastián and covers less than 50 ha (124 acres). The climate is sunnier and more benign in Galicia, which means that grapes can be grown there without too many problems, from the coast to further inland. Galicia has three DOs:

The North

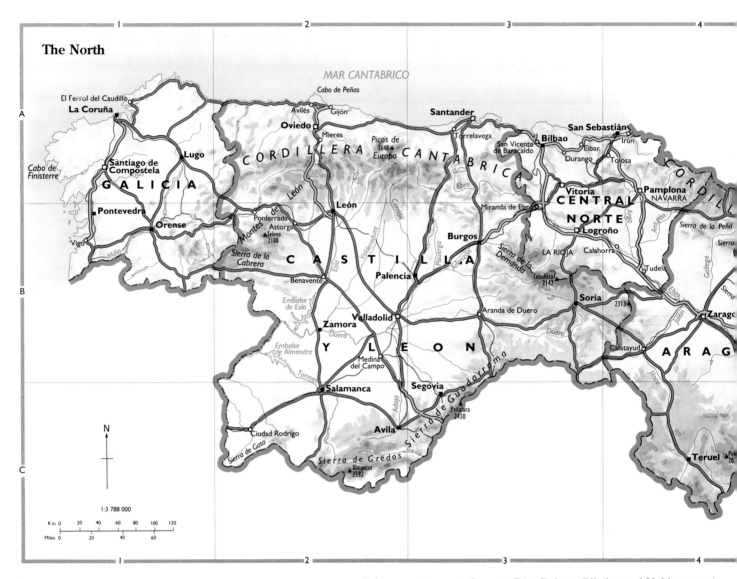

MAR CANTABRICO

1:3 788 000

from west to east they are Rías Baixas, Ribeiro and Valdeorras.

Beyond the Cantabrian range the climate becomes gentler and drier. This is particularly noticeable in Rioja, some 100 km (about 60 miles) south of Bilbao. Once you are through the last mountain pass you immediately sense that the weather is Mediterranean. This, in combination with the various soil types, limestone among them, has enabled Rioja to develop into one of Spain's leading wine regions. It also has the advantage of having had a very busy trade with Bordeaux at the end of the nineteenth century, resulting in the adoption of French winemaking techniques. Until well into the twentieth century neighbouring Navarra made its wines chiefly for its own region, with the emphasis on rosé. Since the 1970s and 1980s, however, Navarra has had a more cosmopolitan outlook, with new, high-quality grape varieties planted and a great increase in the quantity of red wine produced.

A famous pilgrim way

Although the wine regions of Navarra, Rioja and Galicia display great differences, they are clearly connected in the cultural and historical sense, for they are linked by the *Camino de Santiago*, the busiest pilgrim route in Europe. It was believed that early in the ninth century the stone coffin of the Apostle James had been washed up near Iria Flavia, the former Roman capital of Galicia. Eventually it was found by a hermit who said a star had showed

Above: The Casa Batlló in Barcelona is a remarkable example of the architecture which made Gaudí world famous. It stands in a street of Modernista houses called Manzana de la Discordía (Block of Discord)

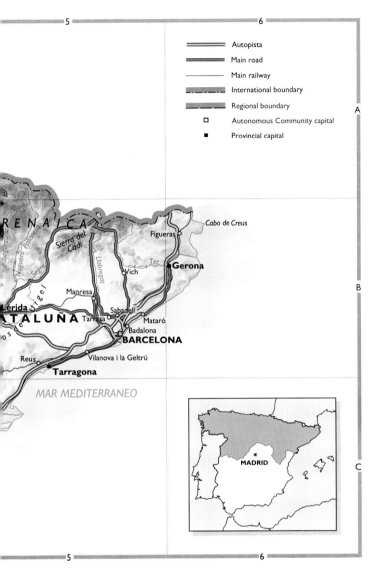

Above: New Arinzano estate of Julián Chivite, Navarra.

The Duero basin

Between Galicia and Rioja lies Castilla y León, an *autonomía* of nine provinces. At its heart is Valladolid, a great city connected through a network of roads with such other centres of population as Burgos, León, Salamanca, Segovia and Soria. The landscape consists mainly of plateaux with low hills, and with the Duero basin as its dominant feature. Only here and there are the contours more dramatic – as in the Ribera del Duero wine region, where the vines sometimes grow against a backdrop of high table mountains. The climate here begins to take on a continental character with hot, dry summers and cold winters. Besides Ribera del Duero (a rising star by dint of its red wines), Castilla y León has among its DOs Bierzo (mainly red wines), Cigales (rosé), Rueda (white) and Toro (mostly red). The region offers the tourist an amazing wealth of monuments, both in the wine districts and beyond. One fine example is the imposing Roman aqueduct at Segovia.

Aragón nestles between Castilla y León and Cataluña. It is a former kingdom that now comprises three provinces. The flat Ebro valley runs across this *autonomía*. Winegrowing is carried on some miles out from this valley, both to the north and the south of it. In the four DOs – Calatayud, Campo de Borja, Cariñena and Somontano – both the traditional local grapes and imported varieties are used and this results in very divergent kinds of wines. There is a similar situation, although on a bigger scale, in Cataluña. It was in this triangular area between the Pyrenees and the Mediterranean that Spain's first vines were probably planted. Here the landscape varies greatly according to DO, and sometimes even within a DO. The plateaux of Costers del Segre are in sharp contrast to the rugged mountain contours of Priorato, and the rolling landscape of the central Penedès looks very different to the peaceful hills of Alella. The other DOs here – Ampurdán-Costa Brava, Cava (95 percent of which lies within Cataluña), Conca de Barberà, Tarragona and Terra Alta – all have their own physical features, and their own wines. The Catalan wines alone have enough variation in type, style, quality and price to please the most pampered of wine lovers. And to these yet more can be added – all the wines from the other regions. Northern Spain deserves to become an important place of pilgrimage once more – but this time for its wine.

---

him the way, and so the place was called *campus stellae*, or "field of the star". This became corrupted to Compostela. The name Santiago – which is what St James is called in Spanish – was added. In 829 a small chapel and monastery were built at the spot where the sarcophagus was found, and the shrine began to attract many pilgrims.

In about 900 the chapel was replaced by a church, then in 1075 the building of a cathedral was begun. The town of Santiago de Compostela grew up around it. The importance of this destination increased greatly during the eleventh century, for the Turks had made the journey to Jerusalem too perilous. Every year an estimated half a million pilgrims crossed the Pyrenees to Santiago de Compostela. As a result many bridges, hospitals, monasteries, churches and inns were built along the route, which also passed through Navarra and Rioja. Cistercian and Benedictine monks, particularly those from Cluny, probably brought French vines to Spain by way of the *Camino de Santiago*. Winegrowing was encouraged so that the many pilgrims could be supplied with wine: the monastery of Roncevalles alone provided something like 40,000 litres (8,800 gal) of wine a year. Santiago de Compostela declined in importance after 1589, when the relics were hidden for fear of a raid by Sir Francis Drake, but by then this pilgrim way had for five centuries exerted great influence on the artistic, political and social development of the region.

Cataluña

Capital: Barcelona
Province: Calaluña is an *autonomía*
Area: 31,930 square kilometres
Population: 5,977,008

The coastal areas of north-eastern Spain have always attracted both the seafaring nations of the Mediterranean and peoples who migrated across the Pyrenees. Phoenicians and Greeks are the earliest known settlers, followed by the Carthaginians and the Romans, who made Tarraco (later Tarragona) the capital of their Hispania Citerior. The Moors arrived in the eighth century AD, but were driven out in 801 by Charlemagne, who established his Marca Hispánica in the north of Spain, intended as a buffer zone between the Moors and the Christians. Not long afterwards this Spanish March was divided into countships. The most easterly of these included Barcelona and Gerona, and was assigned to Wifredo the Hairy. His descendants, the Counts of Barcelona, were to rule for centuries over this region which become known as Cataluña.

After the marriage of Count Ramón Berenguer IV and Petronilla of Aragón in 1137, Cataluña and Aragón were forged into a single, mighty kingdom – in which the actual power was in the hands of the Counts of Barcelona. Cataluña enjoyed a period of great prosperity throughout the thirteenth and most of the fourteenth centuries, but then a decline set in, brought about by wars and economic problems, and in 1412 the Catalan element of the Aragón monarchy was replaced by a new Aragonese dynasty. This was to lead to the unification of the kingdoms of Aragón and Castilla later that century. Despite this political fusion, Cataluña kept its own identity and a strong sense of independence, resulting in 1640 in a 12-year war fought with French help against Philip IV. In the end Cataluña was able to demand political autonomy, but suffered great damage in the process. There was more strife at the beginning of the eighteenth century, this time in the War of the Spanish Succession. The Catalans took the side of Archduke Charles of Austria, but when he lost Philip V took away some of Cataluña's privileges. Self-government was achieved once more in 1932 but was subsequently abolished by Franco. It was eventually restored in 1977, and the present *autonomía* comprises the provinces of Barcelona, Gerona, Lérida and Tarragona.

This new independence within the Spanish political system has greatly stimulated a revival of Catalan culture. Thus Cataluña is now officially bilingual. Among themselves the people of the region speak Catalan, which developed from Latin independently of Spanish. This language is also spoken in the French region of Roussillon, which for centuries belonged to the same kingdom as Cataluña (and was ceded to France in 1659 by Philip IV). The earliest extant texts in Catalan date from the end of the twelfth century. This is a rich and vigorous language with a considerable body of original literature. The somewhat fanatical attitude the Catalans have towards their language can be very frustrating for visitors: sometimes even tourist literature is only available in Catalan.

Modernista architecture

In the late nineteenth and early twentieth century another aspect of Catalan culture manifested itself: architecture in the Moder-

Above: The fantastic cathedral of Sagrada Familia in Barcelona, designed by Gaudí.

nista style. This Spanish equivalent of art nouveau, or the German Jugendstil, found brilliant expression in the work of Antonio Gaudí (born 1852), and is characterized by richly imaginative, daring concepts and flowing lines. Followers of Gaudí designed buildings for wine firms in Cataluña, at Codorníu (Penedès), Raimat (Costers del Segre) and elsewhere, and for a number of cooperatives (Conca de Barberà, Tarragona, Terra Alta). Painterly talents have also developed in Cataluña; museums devoted to some of these artists have been established, including those to Salvador Dalí, Joan Miró and Pablo Picasso (born in Málaga).

As well as being concerned with culture the Catalans are hard-working, enterprising and business-minded. There is a saying: "A Catalan makes bread from stones." The city of Barcelona alone accounts for roughly a fifth of Spain's total industrial production, as well as having the biggest port in the country. Cataluña has had notable commercial success with its wines, both sparkling and still. In addition, the region is very much geared to tourism: there are more hotels along the coast of Cataluña than in the whole of Switzerland.

Climatic differences

Cataluña is triangular in shape and dominated by its coastal mountains and the Pyrenees, which meet here. Just how rugged the mountain landscape can be is exemplified by Terra Alta and Priorato, two wine districts to the west of Tarragona. Anyone driving around here on the twisting roads and along the deep ravines will find it hard to imagine that the coast is not all that far away. Generally speaking there are golden beaches stretching along that coast, but there are also large areas of weathered rocks

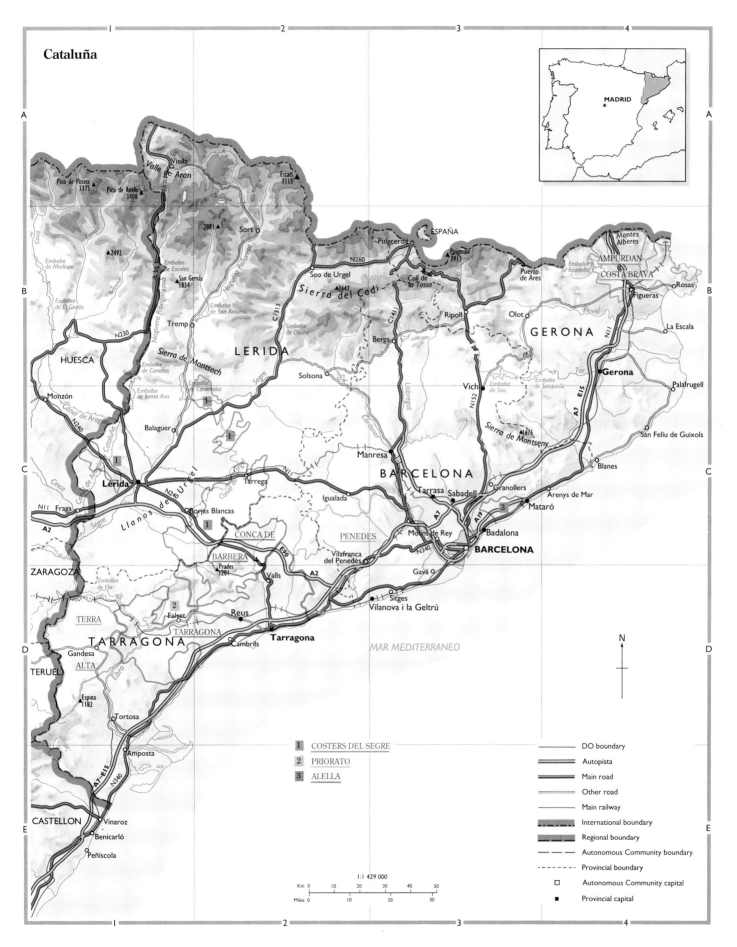

Cataluña

MADRID

Pico de Posets 3375
Pico de Anelo 3408
Valle de Aran
Viella
Estats 3115
▲2881
Sort
ESPAÑA
Puigcerdá
N260
Puigmale 2913
▲2492
Embalse de Mediano
Embalse de Escales
San Gervás 1834
Cinca
Noguera Ribagorzana
Embalse de El Grado
Seo de Urgel
Sierra del Cadi
▲2647
Coll de la Tossa
Puerto de Ares
Embalse de Boadella
AMPURDAN-
Montes Alberes
COSTA BRAVA
Figueras
Rosas
HUESCA
N230
Tremp
Noguera Pallaresa
Embalse de San Antonio
CI313
Embalse de Oliana
Ripoll
Olot
Fluvia
GERONA
La Escala
Berga
Sierra de Montsech
LERIDA
CI141
NI52
Embalse de Sau
Gerona
Monzón
Embalse de Canelles
Embalse de Camarasa
Solsona
Cardoner
Ter
Embalse de Susqueda
Palafrugell
N240
Embalse de Santa Ana
Segre
Vich
Llobregat
Sierra de Montseny
Canal de Aragón
Balaguer
1
Llanos de Urgel
1
Cinca
Manresa
▲676
San Felíu de Guixols
Canal de Urgel
Lérida
N240
Tárrega
BARCELONA
Tarrasa
Sabadell
Granollers
Blanes
NII
Arenys de Mar
NII Fraga
Segre
Borjas Blancas
Igualada
A7
3
Mataró
A2
CONCA DE
1
PENEDES
A19
Molins de Rey
Badalona
ZARAGOZA
BARBERA
Prades 1201
Vilafranca del Penedès
N340
BARCELONA
Embalse de Flix
Valls
A2
Gavá
TERRA
2
Falset
Reus
Sitges
Vilanova i la Geltrú
TARRAGONA
TARRAGONA
Tarragona
MAR MEDITERRANEO
ALTA
Gandesa
Cambrils
TERUEL
Ebro
Espina 1182
Tortosa
N
Amposta
A7 E15
N340
1 COSTERS DEL SEGRE
2 PRIORATO
3 ALELLA
CASTELLON
Vinaroz
Benicarló
Peñíscola

DO boundary
Autopista
Main road
Other road
Main railway
International boundary
Regional boundary
Autonomous Community boundary
Provincial boundary
□ Autonomous Community capital
■ Provincial capital

1:1 429 000
Km 0   10   20   30   40   50
Miles 0   10   20   30

and cliffs. This is particularly the case along the Costa Brava, north of Barcelona. In the Ampurdán-Costa Brava district there even used to be slopes planted with vines right down to the sea – and the grapes were picked from boats. Any flat land between the coast and the mountains is narrow as a rule, and intensively cultivated with all kinds of crops. Vegetables and fruit are also grown far inland.

The whole coastal zone enjoys a Mediterranean climate, but it becomes drier and more extreme further inland. In the Costers del Segre wine district, near Lérida, the annual rainfall is only 300 mm (11.8 ins), compared with 500 to 600 mm (19.7 to 23.6 ins) in windy Ampurdán-Costa Brava.

Progressive management

These differing climatic zones in themselves mean that Cataluña produces a great variety of wines. This effect is further reinforced by differences in soil, and by the human factor. In their stubbornly independent way the Catalans have not cared much for notions prevailing elsewhere in Spain; at an early stage they were already planting superior French grape varieties alongside the native ones. In addition, they did not hesitate to invest in modern cellar equipment sooner than most other regions. Pioneering work in these aspects was carried out in particular by such wine houses as Codorníu and Torres. Cataluña has reaped the rewards for this progressive approach by selling tens of millions of bottles of its wine, both in Spain and in a large number of other countries. The leading DOs in qualitative and commercial terms are Cava (sparkling wines), Penedès (mainly red and white wines), and

Below: A picturesque corner in Falset.

Above: Vineyard at Espolla in Ampurdán-Costa Brava, the most northerly wine area.

Costers del Segre (still and sparkling wines). The other DOs have not come so far but here, too, technology and quality are making steady progress: Alella (principally white), Ampurdán-Costa Brava (red, rosé, white and fortified), Conca de Barberà (white, rosé and red), Priorato (red, rosé, white and fortified), and Terra Alta (white, red, rosé and fortified). Few wines of any significance are made outside the DO districts in Cataluña. Artès would seem to have the best chance of such recognition, thanks to a very active cooperative; Cabernet Sauvignon and Chardonnay grapes are grown in addition to native varieties in this small district northwest of Barcelona. Anoia produces chiefly rosés; but the wines of Bajo Ebro-Montsía and Conca de Tremp are rarely encountered any more.

International influences

The Catalans enthusiastically drink both their still and sparkling wines with their many regional dishes. Since Cataluña has had close political and trade connections with the south of France and with Italy, there are influences from both countries in its regional cuisine. The *bullabesa* fish soup occurs in Provence as *bouillabaisse* and the *canalones* of Cataluña (traditionally eaten on 26 December) are Italy's *cannelloni*. There is also the remarkable fact that one of the world's first printed books was a Catalan cookbook, the *Llibre de Coch* by Ruperto de Nola, which came out in 1477. Five sauces are used in many Catalan recipes: *allioli* (garlic mayonnaise), *picada* (a paste of toasted almonds or hazelnuts with bread, garlic, parsley, saffron or other herbs), *romesco* (sweet red peppers, toasted almonds, garlic, bread, tomato), *samfaina* (onion, tomato, pepper and vegetables such as aubergine), and *sofrito* (tomato, onion, olive oil, and sometimes garlic and peppers). Catalan dishes usually include sausage or nuts (almonds, pinenuts or hazelnuts). Fresh or dried fruit is included in many recipes and there is chocolate in certain traditional sauces (both sweet and savoury). Rice and fish, as in the rich *zarzuela*, are also on the menu, and Catalans are extremely fond of roast dishes. Despite its many classic recipes, Catalan cuisine is by no means static, for in many restaurants in Barcelona and other towns new, elegant dishes are always being created. Cataluña does not like standing still: not in its cultural life, its trade, its industry, its wines or its cuisine.

Ampurdán-Costa Brava

It is quite possible that the first vines were planted here as early as the fifth century BC, but it was the Romans who developed winegrowing here, and gave the region its name: Ampurdán comes from the Roman town of Ampurias. Benedictine monks were the next to stimulate winegrowing, and one of them, Ramón Pedro de Novas, even wrote an essay on winemaking in 1130. This monk lived in the Monasterio de San Pedro de Roda, high up in the mountains, and the slopes are still ribbed with the remains of ancient vineyard terraces, some of which come down close to the sea; the grapes were sometimes harvested by boat.

A smaller vineyard area

The terraced vineyards were abandoned after phylloxera had arrived; and elsewhere in the region a great deal of winegrowing land was also lost for good. The present area of around 3,100 ha (7440 acres) is only a fraction of what it once was. Most of the vines in this DO, created in 1975, grow in the northern part of the region which stretches out over the broad plateaux and low foothills of the Pyrenees. The soil has a brownish tinge and often contains limestone. In the southern, lower-lying zone there are hardly any vineyards, for the soil is too fertile for quality winegrowing.

Ampurdán-Costa Brava is made up of 35 communities that roughly speaking lie in the area bounded by the French frontier, the coast, and a line from Figueras to Rosas. A Mediterranean climate prevails, with an annual rainfall of 500 to 600 mm (19.7 to 23.6 ins). A special aspect of this climate is the almost ever-present wind. Most dreaded is the *tramontana* from the north, which can reach 140 to 160 km per hour (90 to 100 mph), and often blows for days on end. As protection, farms are often surrounded by thick cypress hedges. On the estates vines have to be trained along extra wires, and extra poles put in to support them. One advantage of these winds is that they keep the grapes healthy. There are said to have been periods in the sixteenth and seventeenth centuries when the winds didn't blow, and humidity in the vineyards was so great that there were plagues of insects, and people were afflicted with epidemics. Prayers were apparently said for the wind to return. The wind also protects the region from night frosts.

New grape varieties

Grape picking normally starts around mid-September, when a three-day wine fair takes place in Figueras. The varieties harvested are mainly black Garnacha and Cariñena. More than 80 percent of all the grapes are black. The most important white grapes are Macabeo and Xarel-lo, and some new varieties are gradually making their appearance. The Cavas del Ampurdán concern has planted a good many other types in an experimental vineyard, and research is going on with each variety into the best rootstock and the best pruning methods. Among the grapes growing here are black Cabernet Sauvignon, Merlot, Syrah and

Below: Wine village of Rabós, Ampurdán.

Tempranillo, together with white Chardonnay, Chenin Blanc, Gewürztraminer and Riesling. The most successful of these so far appear to be Cabernet Sauvignon, for wines for keeping, and Merlot and Tempranillo for wines for drinking young.

The dominant cooperatives

To be able to make a living, a grower here needs to have about 20 ha (nearly 50 acres), but the average area is half this. Most winegrowers therefore need to have other sources of income, such as cattle or sheep farming, or cultivating cereals or vegetables. Traditionally, many work in the cork factories, which have been here since the eighteenth century; corks from this region are among the best in the world. As a result of the small size of the holdings, most of the growers do not process their grapes but take them in to a cooperative. Ampurdán-Costa Brava has 13 cooperatives, which are in a totally dominant position, producing about 95 percent of all the wine here. A good proportion of this wine is nurtured and bottled by Cavas del Ampurdán. This bodega, which is connected with Cavas del Castillo de Perelada, has also set up a joint venture with the Mollet de Perelada cooperative under the name of Covinosa. True to their traditions, many cooperatives sell the greater part of their production in bulk. Quite a few of them work with old-fashioned equipment and supply rustic, potent and totally uninteresting wines. However, there are others that have invested heavily in technology. With these you find stainless-steel tanks and cooling equipment alongside concrete vats.

It was these modernized cooperatives that at the beginning of the 1980s launched supple, fruity wines for drinking young. They had names like Vi Novell and Vi de l'Any. The quality of these red (and rosé) wines varies and has not yet reached the level of comparable examples from Roussillon across the frontier. In general the best kinds of Vi Novell come from the cooperatives in Espolla, Garriguella, Mollet de Perelada and Pont de Molins. A complete contrast is formed by the luxuriantly sweet and aromatic Garnatxa. As the name indicates, Garnacha is used for this wine. This strictly traditional product owes its sweetness either to residual sugar, which results from adding alcohol to stop fermentation, or to supplementary *mistela*, sweet must made from the same grape variety. Garnatxa is usually 15 percent alcohol and its colour can range from cherry red to orange brown.

Various bodegas market wood-aged red wines. The biggest number of casks, about 1,000, are in the cellars of Cavas del Ampurdán. The wines from this firm have various brand names, Castillo de Perelada among them. The *crianzas* are as rule supple, with a smooth taste with fruit (tending to cherries); the *reservas* and *gran reservas* clearly have more maturity and wood to offer. In the great range of Spanish wines they come somewhere around the middle; they seldom have a great deal of depth, refinement or personality. And the same is true of cask-aged wines from other producers. Increasingly now the region is producing fresh white wines, both with and without the DO. Some contain quite a lot of carbon dioxide. At cellars near the fourteenth-century castle at Perelada there are some tens of thousands of bottles of Gran Claustro Cava stored. This is one of the sparkling wines from Cavas del Castillo de Perelada, whose main cellars are in Villafranca del Penedès. Wines from this company are mostly sold with the Castillo de Perelada label; Gran Claustro is the prestige brand. Wines with the Ampurdán-Costa Brava DO are still by definition. Only through further investment in quality will this region be able to gain a strong position in the market both at home and abroad.

Above: The monastic church of the wine village of Perelada.

PRODUCERS OF SPECIAL INTEREST

Oliveda 11750 Capmany
This bodega owns 120 ha (297 acres) which supply 10 percent of the grapes required. The most appealing wines in its comprehensive range are the Vi Novell rosé and red, both made from Garnacha and Cariñena. The red wood-aged Don José is very decent and correct in taste, as is the *gran reserva* Cabernet Sauvignon; both are given six months in cask.

Cellers Santamaría 17750 Capmany
A small family concern with 15 ha (37 acres) that produces wood-aged red wines. The Gran Recosind *crianza* has a good deal of vanilla in scent and taste; and the latter is supple and almost fat. This is a product for those who like rustic, old-fashioned wines. A *gran reserva* has the same brand name.

Covinosa (Comercial Vinícola del Nordeste) 17752 Mollet de Perelada
This was set up in 1977 by the Mollet cooperative (50 percent), Cavas de Ampurdán (45 percent), and its affiliated Cavas del Castillo de Perelada (5 percent). Most of the wines from the 300 ha (740 acres) owned by the cooperative members are used for both the still and sparkling wines made by the two other shareholders. But Covinosa also produces wines on its own account. Among these are Conde Bravo, a decent red; the supple, readily drinkable red Vi de l'Any (mainly Garnacha); and the classic, sweet, 15 percent strength Garnatxa de l'Emporda.

Cavas del Ampurdán 17491 Perelada
The group that runs Catalonia's three casinos also owns Castillo de Perelada. Sharing the site of this splendidly preserved stronghold is the Cavas del Ampurdán bodega. This was founded in 1926 and consists of two underground cellars, a laboratory, and bottling and storage facilities. Wines are ordered from the Mollet de Perelada cooperative through the Covinosa arrangement (see left). Wines also come in from other cooperatives. In addition Cavas del Ampurdán has a 15 ha (37 acre) vineyard of its own where the activities include experimenting with new grape varieties, rootstocks and pruning methods. The wines from this firm are also exported in considerable quantities. A commercially successful example is the Castillo de Perelada Blanc Pescador, a sparkling wine without the DO, or any very pronounced characteristics. Blanc de Blancs, a pale, likeable and slightly fruity product does have the DO. In terms of life expectation the red range runs from a 1-year wine to an 8 to 10-year-old *gran reserva*, the Don Miguel Mateu. One of the firm's *crianzas* is the Tinto Cazador, a firm, attractive, but again not especially distinctive wine. The Castillo de Perelada *reserva* has a good deal of vanilla in fragrance and taste, a quite elegant structure, and comes over as mellow but not tired.

Travel Information

HOTELS AND RESTAURANTS

Mas Pau, 17741 Aviñonet de Puig Ventós, tel (72) 546154
This restaurant in a fine old building is one of the best in the province of Gerona. The cooking is imaginative, with plenty of fresh fish and shellfish, and the wine list is very comprehensive. This quietly situated establishment also has seven comfortable hotel rooms.
El Tinell, 17750 Capmany, tel (72) 549068 Typical restaurant of the region in a wine village.

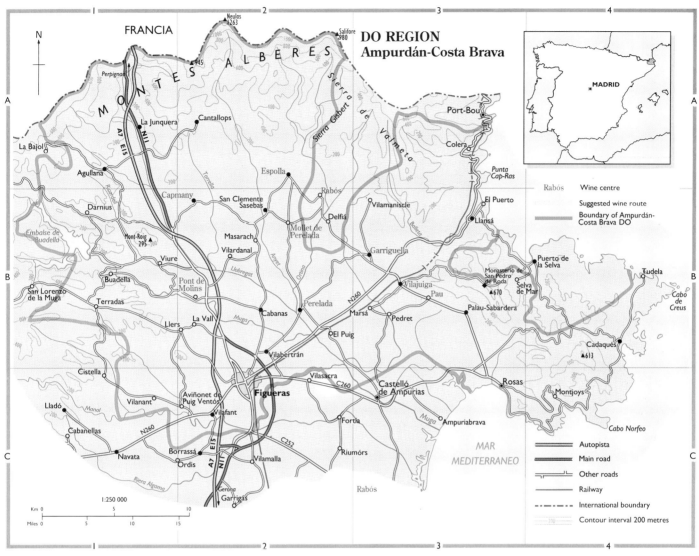

**DO REGION
Ampurdán-Costa Brava**

Rabós — Wine centre

Suggested wine route

Boundary of Ampurdán-
Costa Brava DO

Autopista

Main road

Other roads

Railway

International boundary

Contour interval 200 metres

1:250 000

Km 0   5   10

Miles 0   5   10   15

Hotel Ampurdán, N11, 17600
Figueras, tel (72) 500562
Plain, square-looking building on
the north side of town. The rooms
lack atmosphere, but have all the
necessary comforts. In the
restaurant it is sometimes cheaper
to eat à la carte. The food is
middling to very good (fish, game,
beef stews).
Hotel Durán, Lasauca 5, 17600
Figueras, tel (72) 501250
Renovated, with very neat rooms
and a well-known restaurant, where
Salvador Dalí often dined. The
cuisine is regional.
Ca la María, 17752 Mollet de
Perelada, tel (72) 563382
Meals from the grill, hotpots and
other country fare.
Cal Sagristá, 17491 Perelada, tel
(72) 538301 Pleasant restaurant,
with terrace. Regional dishes.
Mas Molí, 17491 Perelada, tel (72)
538381 This restaurant is in a
nineteenth-century mill just west of
Perelada, on the road to Vilabertrán.
The regionally based cuisine is

supervised by the casino in the
Castillo de Perelada (which has its
own restaurant).

PLACES OF INTEREST

Ampurias South of the actual wine
district, near La Escala, are
excavations of the Greek and
Roman towns. A number of the
finds can be seen in the Museo
Monográfio nearby. Some are
copies, the originals having gone to
museums in Barcelona and Gerona.
Castelló de Ampurias Fine
Gothic cathedral here with a
Romanesque tower.
Espolla Wine village with a
dolmen: follow the signs to this
prehistoric monument.
Figueras This town with its
population of more than 30,000 is
dominated by a large fifteenth-
century fortress, the Castillo de San
Fernando, whose walls are 5 km (3
miles) in length. The former town
theatre now contains the Salvador
Dalí museum, one of the most

visited in Cataluña: the painter was
born in Figueras in 1904. Also
interesting are the Museo de
Juguetes (toys) and the Museo El
Ampurdán (art from Greek and
Roman times to the present). There
is a memorial here in honour of
Narcisco Monturiol, the inventor of
the submarine, who also came from
Figueras. A three-day wine fair is
held around mid-September.
Mollet de Perelada Important
wine village with a Romanesque
church.
**Monasterio de San Pedro de
Roda** This tenth-century
Benedictine monastery stands more
than 600 m (1970 ft) above sea level,
giving a magnificent view. Many of
the slopes here are terraced with
abandoned vineyards.
Perelada This village has a rich
history, as shown by the fourteenth-
century Castillo de Perelada and the
Carmelite house beside, both
perfectly preserved. From July to
mid-September there are guided
tours, taking in the fourteenth-

century cloisters, an impressive
library with more than 70,000 works
(including 1,000 editions in 30
languages of *Don Quixote*), Spain's
biggest glass museum, with a
considerable amount of pottery as
well, wrought-iron work, a
fourteenth-century church with a
tapestry designed by Rubens, and
an underground wine museum.
Some 700 kinds of trees grow in the
garden by the castle, which is used
as a casino in the evenings.
Concerts and recitals are held here
in the summer.

WINE ROUTE

As you drive further north, and
closer to the coastline, the landscape
becomes rich in contrasts. The route
leads through some of the most
important wine villages, branching
off to the lofty Monasterio de San
Pedro de Roda, and offers some
splendid panoramas. Another
beautiful stretch of road is between
Mollet de Perelada and Espolla.

Alella

As elsewhere along the Mediterranean coast it was probably the Greeks who planted the first vines here. Certainly the Romans practised viticulture here and were shipping wines to Rome in the first century. The town of Tiana, where one of the most important producers is established, was founded by the Romans, who called it Titiana. The wine region starts just northeast of Barcelona, only a few miles separating the first of the vineyards from the advancing suburbs. Various communities in the region have grown considerably with the increasing number of commuters, and the effect of all this urbanization has been that a good few Alella vineyards have been lost. For many winegrowers the high prices paid for land have made selling their vineyards more attractive than cultivating grapes. Alella has only about 550 ha (1,360 acres) left, whereas 30 years ago the area was nearly three times as large.

The wine zone extended

The *denominación de origen* lies between the coast and the A7 *autopista*, and takes its name from Alella, 15 km (9.5 miles) from the heart of Barcelona and with a population of 4,000. The landscape is decidedly hilly, rising to more than 470 m (1,540 ft) from the sea. Two small streams traverse the area, flowing north to south to meet not far from Alella. A subtropical climate prevails, with mild winters and hot summers. The annual rainfall is about 600 mm (23.6 ins), supplemented by sea mists which

Below: Alella wines for sale next door to the cooperative.

often bring extra moisture. Until 1989 the wine zone consisted of 14 communities, but since then four more have been admitted, on the northern and eastern edge of the area. This extension was presumably decided on to secure the continued existence of the DO, for the urbanization in the southwestern sector seems unlikely to be checked. There has in fact been criticism of the admission of the four new communities: not only is the climate there somewhat cooler than elsewhere in Alella – with night frosts in spring – but the soil is different, being chalky whereas the original area is mainly on granite.

Most of the vineyards consist of small plots of land, often on south-facing hill slopes, and in some cases they are surrounded by houses. Large expanses of vineyard are rare here. One such stretches over a plateau behind the cellars of Alta Alella (the producer of Marqués de Alella) in Santa María de Martorella. The higher parts of the district are well wooded, and along the winding roads there are quite a few restaurants where Barcelona families come to eat Sunday lunch. In fine weather it is very busy along the coast, and the outskirts of Alella are full of parked cars, so the best time to visit is during the week.

Mainly white

More than 80 percent of Alella wine is white. The basis is usually Pansá Blanca (Xarel-lo). According to the local producers, this variety gives wines with more potency and character than in Penedès, thanks to differences in soil and climate. Other white grape varieties here are Macabeo, Chenin Blanc and Chardonnay. The last of these is very much on the increase and practically all new plantings reflect this. In general the vineyards on the higher ground give wines that are fresher and lighter than those from sites down near the coast. Picking usually starts about two weeks later on these higher vineyards as it does not get as hot up there. Ull de Llebre (Tempranillo) and Garnacha are the grapes principally used for the red and rosé wines, with some Pansá Rosado. Roura, however, has also planted Cabernet Sauvignon and some Merlot. Already on the market is an attractive, quite elegant *tinto* of 40 percent Cabernet Sauvignon and 60 percent other grapes. In addition to still wines a few producers make sparkling varieties and these have the Cava DO.

Changes in style

Until the beginning of the 1980s white Alella was not a particularly exciting wine. It was semi-sweet in taste, lacked freshness, and also spent an obligatory period in cask. The wood of these casks was usually old, so that the effect on the wine was negative rather than positive. All this changed when Ismael Manaut and three others, including the lawyer Juan Pelaez y Fabra, Marqués de Alella, took over the Alta Alella concern – and decided to build a 20th-century cellar. With the permission of the local *Consejo* stainless-steel tanks and other modern plant were installed, and subsequently the white must was fermented at a lower temperature. Manaut cut out the wood-ageing phase and bottled his wines young. Then, in addition to a white wine with residual sugar, he introduced a dry variant. This was exceptionally well received and has remained in the range. Called Marqués de Alella Seco, this wine is made from 50 to 60 percent Pansá Blanca, supplemented by Macabeo and Chenin Blanc. Next Ismael Manaut began to plant Chardonnay and the first vintage came in 1985, although this was not bottled. Of later harvests, too, only a part was marketed as Alella, as some of the grapes went into Cava from Parxet (which had been owned by Manaut since 1982). In terms of quality, the Marqués de Alella Chardonnay offered still more class than the other wines, which resulted in a great demand for it. Since 1989 therefore Alta Alella has been steadily increasing plantings of Chardonnay. The few other Alella producers have now acquired Chardonnay, too. This applies to Roura and to the Alella cooperative, which uses the brand name Marfil. The example of a low temperature, slow fermentation has also been followed. Roura uses stainless-steel tanks exclusively; the cooperative has been fitted with them since 1989. Until 1990 there was a fourth Alella producer, Jaime Serra, but this bodega has now withdrawn from the DO to concentrate wholly on Penedès.

PRODUCERS OF SPECIAL INTEREST

Alella Vinícola 08328 Alella
Founded in 1906, this is by far the biggest Alella producer. The members, about 100 of them, cultivate around 330 ha (740 acres). There was a complete updating and replacement of equipment in 1989, following which the quality of the wines improved spectacularly. Of the five kinds of white wines made, four are dry. The best of them is the Marfil Xarel-lo, a slightly sparkling, very refreshing wine made from 90 percent Pansá Blanca and 10 percent Chardonnay. This too has a hint of carbon dioxide, a light structure and a good measure of freshness.

Bodegas Roura 08328 Alella
Around 1980 Juan Antonio Roura started to plant 25 ha (62 acres) of vineyard in the Valle de Rials, near Alella. A few years later he built an ultra-modern cellar where, thanks to a computer, one person can do all the work. White Alella comes in both an exhilarating dry version, sold as Voramar, and in the traditional semi-sweet form. The red wine is composed of 45 percent Cabernet Sauvignon, a little less than 25 percent Tempranillo, with other varieties making up the balance. It is an elegant product that develops well in bottle. As these vines mature, so the resulting wine will gain in depth. Cavas are also produced at this bodega; the three-year-old Cava Roura Nature Reserva is the most attractive of them.

Parxet/Alta Alella 08391 Tiana
After Ismael Manaut and his three associates had bought the Alta Alella concern in 1981, he then went on to acquire Parxet a year later. The first house made still wines exclusively, the second only sparkling; then in 1987 he merged the two. The offices and storage cellars – on three floors

underground – are at Tiana, where the premises date from 1920. From the romantic garden there is a view of the sea, and bougainvillaea grows at the gate.

The wines are made high up at Santa María de Martorella. Behind the old, seventeenth-century Alta Alella building (very tastefully furnished) Manaut has put up a modern vinification and bottling plant. Here grapes from the bodega's own 40 ha (99 acres), and from 110 ha (272 acres) under contract, are processed. The growers are given strict instructions as to which grapes should be picked, and when.

The firm markets three still wines, all of them white. They bear the Marqués de Alella name. The Clásico is fermented slowly at 15°C (59°F) and contains residual sugar. Usually it is made only, or mainly, from Pansá Blanca grapes and is a juicy, pure, attractive wine. Since 1987 Manaut has also made a Seco, for which the grapes used are 50 to 60 percent Macabeo and more or less equal parts Pansá Blanca and Chenin Blanc. This wine is fresher, leaner, drier and more fragrant than the traditional Clásico, and has fruit. Its fermentation temperature is 18°C (64.4°F), which is the same as for Manaut's Chardonnay. The latter has a nutty aroma, plenty of fruit, a smooth freshness and excellent balance. At present it is the best white Alella on the market.

None of the white wines here undergoes malolactic fermentation, since the aim is to keep them as fresh as possible. The volume of sparkling wines produced by this concern is three to four times that of the still wines. They are sold under the Parxet brand name. The range comprises six wines of which the *brut nature* Chardonnay is the most interesting with its fine bubbles and fresh, exciting taste. Bottles of this Cava spend 24 to 30 months in the underground cellars.

Above: Urbanization threatens the vineyards of Alella.

Travel Information

HOTELS AND RESTAURANTS

Can Casals, 08328 Alella, tel (3) 5556415 Typical Catalan restaurant in fine premises.
Níu, 08328 Alella, tel (3) 5551700 The cooking here shows refinement and is of a high standard; Spanish, French and Italian influences are all perceptible. An Alella Chardonnay goes deliciously with the turbot.
Racó d'En Binu, 08310 Argentona, tel (3) 7970101 Restaurant with much character, where fresh regional ingredients are excellently and inventively prepared. Be sure to leave room for dessert.
Mont Bell, 08185 Vallromanas, tel (3) 5680791 Simple eating house serving tasty Catalan dishes. It lies just outside Vallromanas, a hamlet in a hilly setting.

PLACES OF INTEREST

Alella This old wine community has a fifteenth-century Gothic church, the San Felíu, with a twelfth-century Romanesque belfry. There is also a monolith dedicated to the architect Antoni Gaudí. Next to the cooperative bodega there is a small shop that carries a good selection of Alella wines. Alella usually celebrates its grape harvest on the last Sunday in September.
Argentona The Museo del Cántir Joan Rectoret i Rigola holds a collection of water pitchers from all over Spain. It has 6,500 inhabitants, a parish church, and distinguished sixteenth-century town houses. Outside Argentona are the ruins of Castillo de Burriac, from where there is a marvellous view.

WINE ROUTE

The best way to reach the zone from Barcelona is to drive east on the A19 and take the Mongat exit. Then follow the coast road in the Masnou direction and turn off left for Alella. From Alella a beautiful stretch of road leads to Vilanova de la Roca. You can then turn off right towards Argentona and Mataró, on the coast. If you go left at the Vilanova de la Roca intersection the road brings you to Martorella. From there you can drive either to Santa María de Martorelles, where Parxet/Alta Alella makes its wines and has a large vineyard, or to Tiana, the headquarters of this same firm, with underground wine cellars. For anyone who does not know the area well, stops at regular intervals to ask the way are essential.

Penedès and Cava

In one of the rooms of the wine museum in Vilafranca del Penedès stands a row of amphorae, used by the Romans for transporting wine. With some of their very large vessels they could ship 10,000 of these to their homeland and the colonies. Well-to-do Romans had their own estates in the Penedès – Marcus Porcius, for example, who built the amphitheatre at Pompeii. The amphorae furnish the evidence that wine has been made in this area throughout recorded history. Indeed, there was probably wine-growing here centuries before the Romans came in about 100 BC, albeit on a much more modest scale. A second period of prosperity came in the early Middle Ages, after the Moors had been driven out, when the clergy needed considerable quantities of wine for the daily celebration of Mass. In the eighteenth century wine was the second most important agricultural product after grain. Exports were on a big scale, too, during that century: between 1756 and 1785 more than half the total tonnage shipped to the Indies consisted of wine, spirits and liqueurs.

Mass production

In the nineteenth century Penedès went over to mass production. This happened under pressure from the French, whose vineyards were being ravaged by phylloxera and so had urgent need of cheap wine. Very productive grape varieties were planted at this time, with such nicknames as *afarta pobles* (people filler) or *quebranta-tinajas* (barrel burster). Between 1868 and 1886 Cataluña produced nearly a half of all Spanish *vin ordinaire*. Growers earned a great deal of money and many new wine houses were founded. But then in 1887 phylloxera made its appearance in Penedès and all the vines there were destroyed. Nevertheless, the overall damage remained less than in other regions, for the infestation advanced more gradually – it was to go on until 1910 – and the growers had a lot of money put by. Also, the practice of cooperation emerged. The first, at El Vendrell, dates from 1906.

Until the 1950s Penedès led an inconspicuous existence in among the other wine regions, except for one thing: it began to produce sparkling wine in increasing quantities. This was due in the first place to the pioneering work carried out by Josep Raventós, who in 1872 had used the *méthode champenoise* to make Spain's first sparkling wine. The popularity of these wines led to an increasing demand for the white grapes they are based on, namely Macabeo, Parellada and Xarel-lo, and the region largely went over to growing them. For still wines the break-through was not to come until the 1960s and 1970s.

New grape varieties

To a great extent this was due to Miguel A. Torres who, after studying oenology at university in France, planted a number of superior French grape varieties. Among them were Cabernet Sauvignon, Pinot Noir, Chardonnay, Sauvignon Blanc, Riesling and Gewürztraminer. Miguel also carried out thoroughgoing research into soil types and microclimates to ensure that the right variety would be planted in the right place. At the same time he introduced the latest wine technology. All this effort and investment resulted in a most engaging series of wines, of immaculate quality. The good example set by the house of Torres induced many others to follow it. Few Spanish wine regions are so well equipped technologically as Penedès; and many of the grape varieties imported by Torres have been officially admitted to the *denominación de origen*. At present they represent some five percent of the 25,000 ha (61,800 acres) of vineyard in Penedès – a proportion that is going to increase. Cabernet Sauvignon is by far the most important of these "foreign" varieties.

Most Penedès grapes – around 80 percent – are white. An important reason for this is the phenomenal success of the sparkling wines, which are usually made on the basis of three regional white varieties. Production of these, at about 125 million bottles a year, is several times greater than that of the still wines. Many growers deliver their grapes directly to the bodegas. During the harvest, tractors drive up and down, hauling their loads of grapes. At Codorníu the wine presses work day and night; at peak periods they are hidden behind walls of stacked-up baskets of grapes, while a long line of carts waits at the entrance for unloading. Not all white grapes, however, are used for sparkling wines and the region also produces numerous still wines. These are often made from a combination of grapes, but single-variety wines are also quite common. The commonest black grapes are Tempranillo (often called Ull de Llebre), Garnacha, Monastrell and Cariñena. When used in combination at least two varieties are generally involved, Tempranillo with Cabernet Sauvignon being one of the most successful blends.

Three zones

Three wine-growing zones are distinguished in Penedès. The Bajo Penedès comprises the generally flat coastal belt, and it is as hot here as, for example, central Spain and the warmest parts of the sherry country. Large quantities of Malvasía and Moscatel grapes used to be grown here, but with the decline in demand for fortified sweet wines, the accent has shifted to black grapes, including Monastrell, Cariñena and Garnacha. The soil here has limestone, clay and sand. The Medio Penedès is separated from the coastal strip by a mountain ridge and comprises a large valley. This looks flat when seen from above, but in reality it consists of a series of low hills broken up by various streams and ravines. Vineyards are everywhere here and some 60 percent of all Penedès grapes come from this zone. The average height above sea level is 200 metres (656 feet), the soil has limestone and clay, and the climate is warm – although cooler than on the coast. Many grape varieties, white as well as black, thrive here. Still further inland is the very hilly Penedès Superior zone, where the vineyards climb from 500 to 800 m (1,640 to 2,625 ft). A relatively cool climate prevails, comparable with that of Bordeaux. The zone is very chalky and white varieties are cultivated, with Parellada the most important. Riesling, Muscat and Gewürztraminer are also grown. It is possible that Penedès will be enlarged in the future through federation with Conca de Barberà. Many producers already obtain grapes from Conca de Barberà, and both Codorníu and Torres have their own vineyards there.

The Cava *denominación*

Because of the historical connection with Penedès the Cava industry is centred on Sant Sadurní d'Anoia in that region, in Barcelona province. It was here in 1898 that Josep Raventos began to build the impressive cellar complex of Codorníu. Wine lovers all over the world know such names as Codorníu and Freixenet, but by no means always associate them with Cava. Since 1986 Cava has been a separate *denominación* for the sparkling wines from the giants Codorníu and Freixenet, and some 200 other producers. Cava refers only to these wines made by the *méthode champenoise*, in the specified area of origin. They

come from some 155 communities, spread over eight provinces in northern Spain. Altogether Cataluña produces more than 95 percent of all Cava; besides Penedès, it also comes from the wine regions of Alella, Ampurdán-Costa Brava (Gerona province), Conca de Barberà, Costers del Segre (Lérida) and Tarragona. Non-Catalan Cava may be supplied by Cariñena (Zaragoza) and Rioja (Alava, Navarra and Rioja provinces). The total Cava area of origin covers just under 40,000 ha (98,800 acres). The producers put Cava on their labels, without any geographical data. They are free to get their grapes and basic wines from the whole area, which is why the big Penedès bodegas buy vast quantities of these in other parts of Cataluña in particular.

The bulk of the Cava made in Cataluña – and therefore in Spain – is produced from the three local grape varieties, the proportion varying according to bodega and type of wine. Xarel-lo is used most, giving colour, structure, alcohol and acids, Macabeo adds a fruity aroma, and Parellada finesse. The latter is the finest of the traditional Penedès grapes and costs more than the other two. Besides these three types Chardonnay is increasingly being included; Codorníu, for example, uses it a great deal. The quite special and distinctive aroma of this grape adds an extra dimension to the Cava, and greater nobility. Up until now practically all Cavas have been based exclusively on white grapes. However, some are beginning to appear that are made from a blend of black and white varieties – just like champagne.

Above: The imposing Montserrat monastery, founded in the 11th century. Pilgrims still come to visit the famous Black Madonna, above the high altar in the basilica.

PRODUCERS OF SPECIAL INTEREST

Can Rafols dels Caus 08739 Avinyonet del Penedès
A bodega dating from 1980, with modern equipment; it produces a number of good wines from its own 33 ha (82 acres). The nutty element of Chardonnay (50 percent) can be discerned in the juicy, wood-aged Gran Caus *blanco*; the red is made from three Bordeaux grape varieties.

Can Feixes 08785 Cabrera d'Igualada
This wine estate of about 120 ha (297 acres) has gravelly soil that is poorer than elsewhere in Penedès. The vines are planted up to 400 m (1,310 ft) above sea level and undergo great changes of temperature between day and night. These factors combine to give high-

quality grapes, much in demand by famous houses. The owners, Josep Huguet and his sons, also produce their own wine. This carries the estate name and in all its versions is of high quality. The white (60 percent Parellada, 40 percent Macabeo) is very clean and stimulating in taste; the Cava (about 60 percent Parellada, 20 percent Chardonnay, 20 percent Macabeo) has refinement, particularly the Gran Reserva; and the red (70 percent Tempranillo, 30 percent Cabernet Sauvignon) has a splendid balance between wood and fruit – it is one of the best wines of the region. The Cabernet Sauvignon, too, is excellent.

Manuel Sancho e Hijas 08732 Castellví de la Marca
The wine estate of Mont-Marçal on its hill was bought in 1975 by Manuel Sancho, who subsequently

33

modernized and enlarged the cellars. The vineyard was also extended to its present area of about 70 ha (173 acres). An ample series of wines, half of them Cavas, is produced from the firm's home-grown and bought-in grapes. Of the sparkling wines the *brut nature, gran reserva* and *rosado* are very attractive. The still white Mont-Marçal has a fruity aroma (partly from the Muscat grape); the Chardonnay, grown on 2 ha (5 acres) gets better by the year; and the red Cabernet Sauvignon (with 10 percent Merlot) seems to develop well in bottle. The red Mont-Marçal Reserva tastes somewhat more complete and full. Vi Novell, a young wine, is made in red and white. Amadeus and Opus-4 are the names used for still wines of simpler quality, largely bought in. Vincent and Palau refer to secondary brands of Cava.

Rondel 08758 Cervelló
A Codorníu subsidiary that markets decent Cava under its own name. The firm cherishes a collection of old wine objects and has almost 8 km (5 miles) of underground cellars.

Cavas y Bodegas Ferret 08758 Guardiola de Font-Rubí
After a complete renovation of this 25-year-old bodega in 1986, Ferret launched a number of good wines. The Ferret *brut* is a fresh, lively Cava. The elegant white Celler del Mingo contains 65 percent Parellada.

Julià & Navinès 08739 Guardiola de Font-Rubí
The Schaefers, a German family, produce mainly Cava from their 10 ha (25 acres) here. The best example is the exciting *brut nature*, with fruit, making a delightful aperitif. The still white wines are lightweights.

Cavas Hill 08734 Moja
In June 1990 the house of Cavas Hill, founded in 1887, opened a new cellar complex, enabling a considerable increase in production. The collection is made up of both sparkling and still wines, the grapes for which come partly from the firm's own 50 ha (124 acres). The Brutísimo Cava is full of taste and is among the best in Penedès, but the Reserva Oro also has its merits. The Cavas Hill *blanc brut* is a still wine, rounded and with charm and a hint of peach. The red Gran Toc (wood-aged and with 60 percent Tempranillo) tastes good, as does the Castell Roc rosé. The range has recently gained a Chardonnay and a Cabernet Sauvignon.

Marqués de Monistrol 08770 Monistrol d'Anoia
This bodega has 800 ha (1,980 acres) around the white-walled hamlet of Monistrol d'Anoia, 3 km (2 miles) north of San Sadurní. In the coming years 500 ha (1,235 acres) of this will supply grapes – a good part of it is already productive. About 70 percent of the volume here is made up of Cavas, of a very respectable standard. The still wines, however, offer rather more class, the Marqués de Monistrol Blanc en Noir in particular is delicious.
Its fragrance comes partly from the fact that the grapeskins are left in the must (90 percent Xarel-lo, 10 percent Parellada) for 12 to 18 hours. Then only the juice produced by the weight of the grapes themselves is used. The still Blanc de Blancs, the dry rosé and the red *gran reserva* are all attractive in their categories.

Cellers Josep María Torres 08374 Olérdola
A family estate that besides its 30 ha (74 acres) of land has up-to-date cellars. The star of a modest range of wines is the fruity Mas Rabassa Gran Blanc, full of character and composed of 85 percent Macabeo and 15 percent Xarel-lo.

Ramón Nadal Giro 08733 El Plá del Penedès
This producer has made a speciality of vintage Cavas. The Brut Salvatge is very dry and fresh in taste, with fruit and a light structure. The Brut Especial is only made in outstanding years and tastes rather firmer and more mature. Besides these a non-vintage *brut* is also produced. In all cases the name used is Nadal. The grapes come exclusively from the firm's own 100 ha (247 acre) wine estate.

Masía Bach 08781 Sant Esteve Sesrovires
After making their fortune during the First World War supplying cotton to the French army, the Bach brothers built themselves a neo-classical mansion in the middle of a 350 ha (865 acre) estate where grapes and olives were grown. Since 1975 Masía Bach has belonged to Codorníu. This giant of a firm keeps the mansion and gardens in perfect condition, and has drastically modernized and extended the bodega that stands behind them. Only still wines are made, from grapes bought from 300 growers.

Below: Torres have an ultra-modern vinification plant near Vilafranca del Penedès.

Since the take-over production has risen from an annual 12,000 cases in 1975 to around 500,000 now; the hope is that 800,000 will be reached before the turn of the century. Despite their great quantity, the quality of the wines is most reliable. The white Extrísimo Seco tastes dry, fresh and enlivening, as does the Masía Bach rosé, made from six grape varieties. The red wines age first in French casks, then in small barrels of American oak. The Viña Extrísima (45 percent Tempranillo, 35 percent Garnacha, 20 percent Cabernet Sauvignon) tastes supple and pleasing; the Cabernet Sauvignon (with 10 percent Merlot) is rather firmer in structure and has a good deal of vanilla as well as currant-like fruit. An elegant, balanced Masía Bach Reserva, with a fragrance tending to plum, is also carried.

Oriel Rossell 43720 Sant Marçal
There are 80 ha (198 acres) of vineyards around the splendid Can Cassanyes estate. The Oriel Rossell *brut* has a lively taste. The *brut nature* is somewhat finer in its fragrance and there are more subtleties to it; it is a delicious aperitif, fresh and pure. So too is the *rosado brut*; this has rather more

body than the two white wines, and is made solely from Tempranillo.

Cavas Rovellats 08731 San Martí de Sarroca
A substantial Cava producer. The grapes come from an estate of more than 210 ha (520 acres). The best wine, the Grand Extra Brut, contains some Chardonnay besides the three traditional Penedès grape varieties.

Celler Rámon Balada 08731 San Martí de Sarrocan
Ramón Balada is able to make a number of excellent single-variety wines from grapes grown in the firm's own 70 ha (173 acres). Among them are the light, stylish Parellada; the fresh Macabeo with its suggestion of exotic fruit; the quite firm, more distinctive Xarel-lo; a fleshy Chardonnay with fruit – a hint of melon; and a juicy Cabernet Sauvignon, matured in cask only. The Cava, made from three grape varieties, is clean in taste and well balanced.

Albert i Noya 08739 San Pau d'Ordal
Small, expertly run vineyard of 20 ha (49 acres) that makes good sparkling and still wines. Among

them are the Cava rosé and *brut nature*, as well as the fragrant still white wine. All three wines carry the Albert i Noya brand name.

Antonio Mestres Sagues 08770 Sant Sadurní d'Anoia
This firm dates from 1928 and enjoys a good reputation for its aromatic, dry Cavas. Particularly worthy of mention are the vintage Mestres Clos Nostre Senyor and the rather younger Mestres Coquet. The grapes come from the bodega's own 90 ha (220 acre) vineyard.

Castellblanch 08770 San Sadurní d'Anoia
A big Cava producer, part of the Freixenet group since 1984. This firm, which has no vineyard of its own, makes a relatively large quantity of semi-dry wine. However, its Brut Zero tastes best.

Castillo de Perelada 08770 San Sadurní d'Anoia
Although the Cavas from this producer are named after the castle of Perelada in Ampurdán-Costa Brava, they originate in a cellar in San Sadurní. Only the distinguished Gran Claustro wine from the top of the range is actually aged at Perelada itself. Of the other

kinds produced, the Brut Castillo has a fresh, dry taste with a hint of fruit. At a blind tasting held in 1988 by the Spanish consumers' organization this wine came first out of 28 Cavas. The *rosado brut* has something of a strawberry aroma and comes from three black grape varieties.

Cavas Domecq 08770 Sant Sadurní d'Anoia
The international sherry and brandy firm of Pedro Domecq has an establishment of its own in the Penedès. Here a delicious Cava is produced, with more personality than most. There is also a rosé version, based on Garnacha. In some markets the brand name Lembey is used for the same wines.

Codorníu 08770 Sant Sadurní d'Anoia
The history of this house goes back to the mid-sixteenth century, but it only became really prosperous after Josep Raventós had produced Spain's first sparkling wine in 1872. His descendants have built Codorníu up into one of the world's leading makers of sparkling wine. During the harvest more than 1 million kg (2.2 million lb) of grapes, from around 1,000 growers, are

pressed daily. Only juice from the first pressing is used by Codorníu itself; the second and third are sold on. The average quality of the firm's Cavas was steadily improved throughout the 1980s. This was due in part to the most up-to-date techniques and increasing use of Chardonnay in all dry white wines. In addition the range was gradually extended. Besides the exceptionally reliable Brut Clásico, and the smoothly fresh Blanc de Blancs, there is the Anna de Codorníu. In with the usual grape varieties this firm, vital Cava also has 15 percent Chardonnay and 20 percent of wines reserved from earlier years. A beautiful, smooth, almost buttery Chardonnay (with 10 percent Parellada) was also introduced, as was the Jaume de Codorníu 1551, the first Cava on the basis of just Pinot Noir and Chardonnay. This elegant, fruity, delightful wine comes very close to a good champagne. The Codorníu cellars are among the most impressive in the country. They are surrounded by a park and were built in Modernista style at the end of the nineteenth century by Puig i Cadafalch, a brilliant pupil of Gaudí. Underground there is a system of galleries that totals 30 km (19 miles) in length, divided over five levels. An average of some 120 million bottles are stored there.

Conde de Caralt 08770 Sant Sadurní d'Anoia
A medium-sized bodega belonging to the Freixenet group. The Conde de Caralt still white and red are no high-fliers, but they are competently made and good value for money. Of the Cavas the *brut nature* has the most to offer. This fresh wine with its fine bubbles is always sold with its vintage indicated.

Freixenet 08770 Sant Sadurní d'Anoia
In 1889 Pedro Ferrer and his wife Dolores Sala started a small wine business. At first they just sold wine. Then in the early years of this century they began to make sparkling wine. The descendants of Pedro (who lost his life in sad circumstances in the Spanish Civil War) have enlarged Freixenet's sphere of operation from regional to worldwide. In 1986, for example, the house first sold a million cases to the United States alone. Factories were built in various countries and the Ferrer family even acquired a champagne firm, Henri Abelé. The Freixenet success is due both to extremely efficient, highly mechanized methods of production

Above: At Codorníu some wine is still fermented and stored in oak casks.

and to strict quality standards. The firm processes both grapes and made wines, and from these produces a series of attractive Cavas. The best-selling brand is Cordon Negro Brut, a fruity, light creation with a generous touch to it. The vintage *brut nature* is drier and fuller in taste, and contains about 30 percent Chardonnay. Another splendid Cava is the Carta Nevada Brut, with a taste that in its richness hints at toast, butter and pears. The Brut Barroco in its striking bottles has great distinction.

Heredad Segura Viudas 08770 Sant Sadurní d'Anoia
Since its take-over by Freixenet in 1984 this firm has grown considerably. With its Cavas it aims at the upper end of the market, and its wines are of a very good quality. At the head of the range is the stylishly presented Aria, a wine of class with the aromas of both fruit and flowers. The Reserva Heredad and Brut Vintage are similarly delightful in taste.

Juvé y Camps 08770 Sant Sadurní d'Anoia
This firm founded by Juan Juvé and his wife Teresa Camps has been making wine from its own vineyards since 1921: it has around 400 ha (988 acres) divided among three *fincas*. Although still wines are made here it is the dry Cavas that are the most interesting: the *brut*, *brut naturel* and Grand Cru.

Raventos i Blanc 08770 Sant Sadurní d'Anoia
From the architectural point of view this is the most amazing of San

Sadurní's bodegas. Here in 1986 the architects Jaume Bach and Gabriel Mora created a contemporary set of buildings that fits beautifully into the landscape. Part of the complex is sited around a 100-year-old oak tree, and in the interior there is a splendid interplay of form and light. The wines, from the firm's own 130 ha (320 acres) of vineyard, are strikingly labelled, and lively in taste and excellent in quality: descriptions that apply to the still white Vi de Tiratge as well as the Chardonnay and the Cava.

René Barbier 08770 Sant Sadurní d'Anoia
It was a Frenchman who founded this house in 1880, but nowadays it belongs to the Freixenet group. Only still wines are made here, a proportion of them from grapes from the firm's 250 ha (620 acres) of vineyards. The bulk of the wines here are of a decent standard, examples being the fruity white Kraliner; the René Barbier rosé; and the Cabernet Sauvignon, aged for two years in cask.

Josep Ferret i Mateu 08730 Santa Margarida i Els Monjos
A family concern that has been producing wines for 4 generations. The most pleasing are the rosé and white Viña Vermella – deliciously refreshing on a summer's day. The firm's own vineyard of 20 ha (49 acres) supplies some of the grapes.

Cellers Robert 08870 Sitges
The once famous Malvasía de Sitges is an almost forgotten wine. One of its few producers is the family firm of Cellers Robert. The sweet juice of Malvasía grapes gives a rich wine

that, after being fortified, is aged in large wooden casks. The ordinary version is 5 to 7 years old, the Reserva Especial almost 15. They also produce a sweet Moscatel.

Chandon 08739 Subirats
This Spanish branch of the Moët & Chandon champagne house consists of a very modern complex with 4,000 sq m (43,000 sq ft) of underground cellars and 90 ha (220 acres) of vineyard. The quality of the two-year-old *brut* puts it among the better Cavas.

Molí Columa 08739 Subirats
After making Chandon's Cava for two years, this family firm came on to the market with its own wines around 1990. The Cava Sumarroca, the *brut nature* in particular, has class and a basis of 50 percent Parellada grapes. Also worthy of attention are the Chardonnay (clear, fresh taste, melon-like fruit); the Riesling (dry, elegant, a flowery perfume); and the Muscat (with 15 percent Gewürztraminer – fragrant, clear in taste, slightly sparkling). The name Claverol is used for wines of simpler quality.

Olivella Sadurní 08739 Subirats
Although the roots of the Olivella family go back for centuries in the Penedès, this wine business was only founded in 1986. It works exclusively with grapes from its own 100 ha (247 acres). The white Prima Juventa is a clean, pleasant product, but there is more taste and character to the Prima Lux; this is made with the skins of the Xarel-lo and Parellada grapes in the must. The red wine is a *crianza* of Cabernet Sauvignon and Merlot.

Jean León 08775 Torrelavit
After emigrating to America, Jean León ended up in Hollywood, where he succeeded in opening his own restaurant, La Scala. Then by chance, when he was on holiday on the Catalonian coast, he saw a vineyard for sale in Penedès. He bought the land, took a crash course in oenology back in California, and began to replant his property with high-quality French varieties. The first harvest came in 1969 and since then León's wines have been spectacularly successful. The Chardonnay is fermented in oak casks and has a meaty, nutty, generous taste and a long aftertaste. The Cabernet Sauvignon wine is made from that grape together with Merlot and Cabernet Franc. It is characterized by noble wood and vanilla, a firm structure, elements of blackcurrant fruit, and enough

backbone to mature in bottle. All the grapes that Jean León works with come from the firm's own estate, which at present covers about 160 ha (395 acres).

Vranken-Naverán 08775 Torrelavit
Since 1989 the champagne house of Vranken Lafitte has collaborated with the Gillièron Parellada de Naverán family on their 100 ha (247 acre) wine estate. This is at San Martín Sadevesa, a hamlet near Torrelavit. The oenologists from the two firms work together here. The Vranken Cava has a fine mousse, good fruit and a pure taste in which the Chardonnay (60 percent of the blend) can clearly be discerned. The same wine is also sold under the Louis Drescher name. Besides a Cava of its own – with less Chardonnay – the Spanish partner also makes still wines, with the brand name Naverán. The best of these is the Cabernet Sauvignon, which has a good balance between wood and fruit, but is somewhat lacking in depth.

Jané Ventura 43700 El Vendrell
After working exclusively with bought-in grapes, this family concern planted 15 ha (37 acres) of its own mainly with Cabernet Sauvignon vines. The resulting first vintage will be on the market in 1992-3. The existing collection consists of the fresh, fruity white Jané Ventura; the rosé with its fruit reminiscent of preserves; and a fragrant, elegant Cava, the *brut nature*. The firm is experimenting with a rosé Cava.

Antina Vins 08720 Vilafranca del Penedès
Producer of *pétillant* wines, usually slightly sweet, with ample fruit and the brand name Antina. The owners of this house, in operation since 1990, are Bodegas Olarra (Rioja) and Domingo Montserrat.

Cavas Masachs 08720 Vilafranca del Penedès
A dynamic house that completed the building of an entirely new bodega in 1987. All the grapes for the Masachs range of Cavas come from the firm's own 55 ha (136 acre) estate, and 30 percent of those for the younger, simpler Louis de Vernier wines. The dry Brut de Brut Josep Masachs has a slightly earthy element in its taste. This contains no Chardonnay, but the dry Caroline de Masachs does have around 10 percent of this grape in its blend.

Cellers Grimau-Gol 08720 Vilafranca del Penedès
A producer of supple, pleasurable, easy wines. Among the most attractive are the Cava Duart de Siò Brut Nature; the white Duart de Siò Vi Novell; the Cabernet Sauvignon rosé; the voluptuously labelled red Gitaneta, made from Tempranillo and Cabernet Sauvignon; and the red *reserva*. This bodega, which has been in business since 1986, has no vineyards of its own.

Mascaró 08720 Vilafranca del Penedès
A locally well-known distiller who also makes Cava and, in 1991, launched a still red Cabernet Sauvignon. This had been given three years in cask, and had been fined with fresh white of egg. Being from young vines it still rather lacked depth, but tasted good. The Mascaró family is extending its 60 ha (148 acre) wine estate, planting more Cabernet Sauvignon, Merlot and Parellada. This last grape is used in their Cavas, which are rather earthy with a tendency to sweetness.

Miguel Torres 08720 Vilafranca del Penedès
In 1856 Jaime Torres emigrated to Cuba, where he eventually did well in the oil business. In 1870 he returned to Penedès and established a bodega there. In the cellars he installed what was then the world's biggest wine vat, with a capacity of 600,000 litres (132,000 gal). Shortly before the bodega opened, a banquet for 50 guests, including King Alfonso XII, was held in this vat.

Jaime's grandson Miguel took over the firm in 1932 and, with his wife, began to travel the world to open up export markets. By this time all Torres wines were being sold in bottle. The successful development of the house was given a new stimulus at the beginning of the 1960s with the arrival of Miguel Jr, a brilliant, French-trained winemaker. He was the first to introduce French grape varieties into Penedès, and under his leadership the vinification plant was modernized. He also considerably extended the firm's own vineyard area, both in Penedès and in Conca de Barberà. The Torres family now owns around 830 ha (2,050 acres), divided between the two districts.

Usually there are some 200 trials carried out every year: with grape varieties, with all aspects of their cultivation, with the ageing of wine, and with other facets of the business. Thus in the Torres cellars there are some metal casks with

Above: Sampling from a cask in the cellars at Torres.

wooden sections let into their sides. Quality is what shines through everywhere in the extensive range of wines. The white Viña Sol is the best seller, a pure Parellada, juicy, clean and fresh. The white Gran Viña Sol is more complex, more fragrant, and firmer; it contains at least 40 percent Chardonnay and spends a modest period in wood. Sold under the same name is the Green Label, a full-tasting, wood-aged, balanced combination of Parellada and Sauvignon Blanc. Viña Esmeralda is a generous, charming wine made from Muscat (strongly present in its fragrance) and Gewürztraminer. The rarest, greatest and most expensive of the white wines is Milmanda, originating from a plot in the vineyard of that name in Conca de Barberà. Fermented in casks of new French wood, there is a splendid charm to it. Among the red wines are the generous Sangre de Toro and the Gran Sangre de Toro, rich in vanilla, both made with grapes of the region, Garnacha and Cariñena. The engaging, more elegant Coronas is based on Tempranillo. A small proportion of this grape is present in the Gran Coronas, a fine, meaty wine made mainly from Cabernet Sauvignon. The Gran Coronas Black Label is made only from Cabernet Sauvignon, from the Milmanda vineyard. It was this sublime, finely nuanced wine that defeated a number of renowned Bordeaux *Grands Crus* during the wine olympiade organized by the French periodical *Gault-Millau*. Pinot Noir and Tempranillo together result in the pleasing Viña Magdala. But Torres also makes a pure Pinot Noir, the Mas Borras. Of the other wines, the Da Casta rosé deserves a mention.

Jaume Serra 08735 Vilanova i la Geltrú
In 1975 when its founder, Jaume Serra, was 80 years old, this firm was taken over by the sherry producer Ramón Rato. Serra had started in Alella in 1943, but the cellars there were abandoned. Since 1986 the firm's headquarters have been housed in the seventeenth-century castle of El Padruell, which looks out to sea near Vilanova i la Geltrú. With its up-to-date equipment the bodega makes an annual 1.5 million bottles of Cava, and more still wines. On average the wines with the Jaume Serra brand are of good quality. The Seco Macabeo is wonderfully refreshing; the Chardonnay tastes fresh and fruity – tending to melon; and the Parellada is elegant and refined. The red *reserva* generally has a likeable taste with a slightly rustic wood element to it. The Cava tastes pleasant, with a hint of lemon in the bouquet and some sweetness to the taste and aftertaste. The wines originate in part from the firm's own 125 ha (310 acres) of vineyard. Cristalino is used as the brand name for a simpler quality of Cava.

Cavas Loxarell 08735 Vilobí del Penedès
Although housed in old premises, this bodega has modern equipment. It produces only Cavas, of a very worthwhile standard. The best is the Reserva Familiar; but the Brut Daurat, for example, is a firm, fruity product with a pleasant freshness and a generous mousse. The wines come from the bodega's own 80 ha (200 acre) estate.

Masía Vallformosa 08735 Vilobí del Penedès
The Domènech family, owners of this house, have been bottling wine since 1977. Sales have developed to such an extent that the cellars had to be considerably enlarged at the end of the 1980s. The wines – two-thirds of them Cavas, one-third still – originate in part from the firm's own 230 ha (570 acres) of vineyard. The Vallformosa Brut Nature, a very dry Cava, has won prizes in Spain itself; the Gran Reserva Brut is somewhat firmer and more mature in taste. The still rosé Viña Rosado is generally a success, as is the dry white wine. The nicest red wine is usually the *reserva*, with 20 percent Cabernet Sauvignon.

Travel Information

HOTELS AND RESTAURANTS

Licorella, 08880 Cubelles, tel (3) 8950044 Artistically furnished four-star hotel in a typical resort. The cooking in the fairly expensive restaurant is excellent and includes splendid dishes with *merluza* (hake).

L'Avi Pau, 43881 Cunit, tel (77) 674861 The best place to eat in this coastal village. The cuisine follows the seasons and offers a lot of fish. Try the crêpes with lobster and small prawns.

Sol i Vi, 08739 Lavern, tel (3) 89930204 Hotel-restaurant halfway between Vilafranca and Sant Sadurní. The rooms are not excessively luxurious, but nice. You can eat well here and the wine list is extensive. Try to avoid weekends.

Cal Recolons, 08731 Sant Martí de Sarroca, tel (3) 8991020 A small restaurant serving mainly regional dishes including a delicious prawn and tuna tortilla.

Mirador de las Cavas, 08770 Sant Sadurní d'Anoia, tel (3) 8993178 This locally renowned eating house is in Els Casots, just under 4 km (2.5 miles) out of town in the Ordal direction. Local specialities and more international dishes are prepared from ingredients fresh from the market.

Hotel Antemare, Verge de Montserrat 48, 08870 Sitges, tel (3) 8940600 A reasonably comfortable and not too expensive place to stay, in a quiet situation a short distance from the beach. Also a restaurant.

El Velero, Passeig de la Ribeira 70, 08870 Sitges, tel (3) 8944846 For imaginative fish dishes.

El Vivero, Passeig Balmins, 08870 Sitges, tel (3) 8942149 Enjoy the fresh fish and paella, with a view of the sea.

Airolo, Rambla de Nuestra Señora 10, 08720 Vilafranca del Penedès, tel (3) 8921798 Various fine local dishes based on fresh fish.

Cal Ton, Casal 8, 08720 Vilafranca del Penedès, tel (3) 8903741 Fairly large restaurant serving tasty, carefully prepared dishes.

Casa Juan, Plaça de l'Estació 8, 08720 Vilafranca del Penedès, tel (3) 8903171 Both the fish and the meat dishes are good here.

Hotel Domo, Calle F Marcía 24, 08720 Vilafranca del Penedès, tel (3) 8172426. The Domo was opened in the spring of 1991. It offers modern four-star comfort and there is also a restaurant.

La Cucanya, Racò de Santa Llucia, 08735 Vilanova i la Geltrú, tel (3) 8;151934 Specialises in fish and Italian dishes.

Peixewrot, Paseo Marítimo, 08735 Vilanova i la Geltrú, tel (3) 8150625 For fish and shellfish, with a fine view thrown in.

PLACES OF INTEREST

Castellví de la Marca Wine village with the ruins of a medieval castle.

Llorenc del Penedès There is a neo-Romanesque high altar in the parish church.

Martorell Here you can see the Puente de Diable (Devil's Bridge), a medieval gate, and a triumphal arch of the Roman period. Modern Catalonian art is displayed in the Vicente Ros museum.

Monistrol d'Anoia Small hamlet among the vineyards. The houses are plastered white and there is a small church. This hamlet is where the Marqués de Monistrol bodega is established.

Montferri Just outside the actual wine region. There are castle ruins here and a tower. To the northeast is the Sanctuario de Montserrat built in Modernista style.

Montserrat In silhouette the Montserrat summit presents what looks like a mouthful of broken teeth. A monastery, which still exists, was built up there in 1025, and about 80 Benedictine monks live there. The present building is nineteenth century. Montserrat is an important place of pilgrimage because of its "Black Madonna", a twelfth-century sculpture in a glass case above the high altar of the basilica, where one of Europe's oldest-established boys' choirs, the Escolania, sings daily.

Olérdola There are the remains here of an Iberian fortification from the third century BC.

San Martí de Sarroca A twelfth-century church with both Eastern and Italian stylistic elements.

Santa Oliva The church of Santa María has a Romanesque porch. The Santa Juliá, too, is Romanesque. There are castle ruins here with a large tower.

Sant Pere de Riudebitlles The parish church has a Romanesque façade and a Gothic interior. The house of the Marques of Llió is also Gothic. An annual festival here celebrates the must.

Sant Quinté de Mediona Here there are castle ruins and inhabited caves.

Sant Sadurní d'Anoia The most interesting sights here are the bodegas of Codorníu and Raventos i Blanc, both just outside the village. There is also an eleventh-century Romanesque chapel, the Espiells, and a Roman bridge over the Anoia.

Sitges In mid-May a carnation show is held here – this is Spain's national flower. Then in mid-September the town celebrates the grape harvest. The Museo Cau Ferrat has a collection of wrought-iron work, as well as archaeological finds and paintings, including two El Grecos. The Museo Maricel del Mar, linked with the Cau Ferrat, houses religious art. A brilliant assembly of old dolls and nineteenth-century art objects and furniture is displayed in the Museo Casa Llopis. The parish church of this famous resort is baroque.

El Vendrell The house where the famous cellist Pablo Casals (1876-1973) was born can be viewed. The

DO REGIONS
Penedès
Conca de Barberà

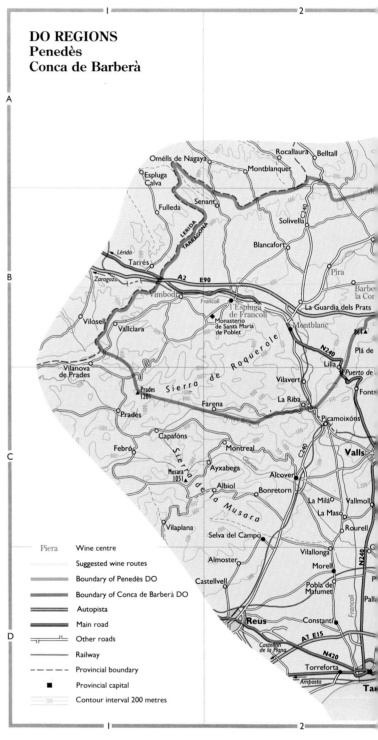

Piera — Wine centre
— Suggested wine routes
— Boundary of Penedès DO
— Boundary of Conca de Barberà DO
— Autopista
— Main road
— Other roads
— Railway
— Provincial boundary
■ Provincial capital
— Contour interval 200 metres

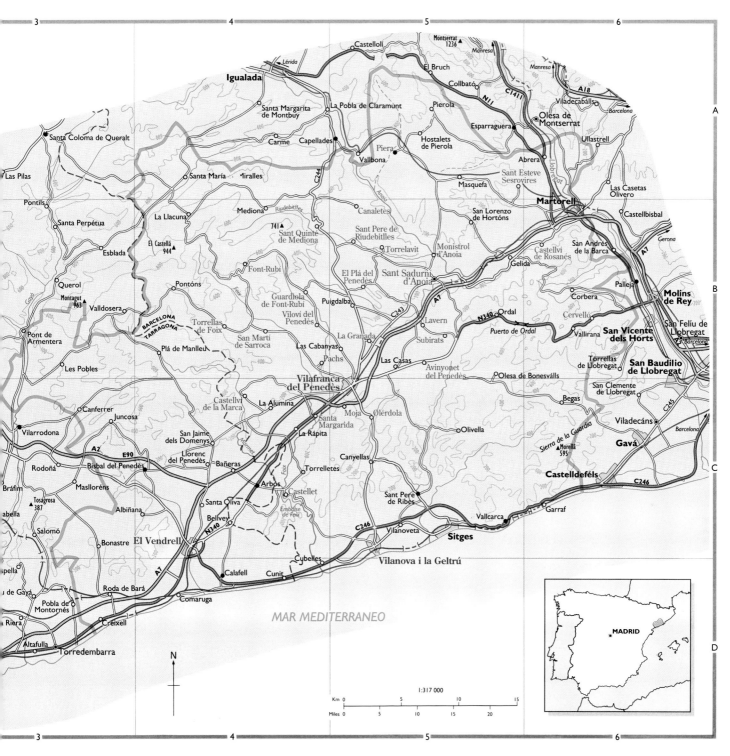

MAR MEDITERRANEO

1:317 000

Km 0   5   10   15

Miles 0   5   10   15   20

MADRID

town also has two defensive towers; a parish church with an organ dating from 1772; noblemen's houses that are centuries old; and a municipal museum with prehistoric, Roman and medieval exhibits.

Vilafranca del Penedès A busy, thriving town with some 30,000 inhabitants. Only the old centre has any atmosphere and here are to be found an excellent wine museum (in a former 14th-century palace), a municipal museum, and the 13th-century basilica of Santa María. All these buildings are around the Plaza Jaume I, where the grape harvest is celebrated. The San Francisco monastery, now a hospital, dates from the 13th century and has some fine monumental tombs.

Vilanova i la Geltrú Ceramics and other arts are displayed in the twelfth-century castle of la Geltrú. The Museo Romántico is furnished to show how a well-to-do family lived in the nineteenth century.

Sculpture, an Egyptian mummy, and paintings (including an El Greco) can be seen in the Victor Balaguer museum. To see colourful glazed tiles go to the Museo Joaquín Mir. The Santa María church has a seventeenth-century altarpiece.

WINE ROUTE

The suggested route swings back and forth from east to west, through large areas of the Penedès. On the way it passes through many of the most important wine villages in the Medio Penedès, but it also takes you through part of the Bajo Penedès, and such villages as Font-Rubí, San Martí de Sarroca and Sant Quintí de Mediona in the Penedès Superior zone. You can make special excursions to Montserrat, high up on its massif to the north, and to Sitges. Due west of the Penedès are the Conca de Barberà and Tarragona wine regions.

Conca de Barberà

Directly west of the Penedès, and some 50 km (31 miles) north of Tarragona, the valleys of the Francolí and Anguera form a natural basin surrounded on all sides by mountain ridges. The district is called Conca de Barberà: *conca* indicates a basin or hollow and Barberà is a reference to Barberà de la Conca, the first village reconquered by the Christians centuries before. Wine-growing became significant here in the twelfth century, after the Cistercians had founded the monastery of Poblet. One feature that shows its importance at the time is the monastery's large wine vault. Around Poblet the monks also built fortress-like farms, such as Castellfollit, Milmanda and Riudabella, where grapes were among the crops grown.

Fresh, fruity wines

Conca de Barberà lies at an average 500 m (1,640 ft) above sea level, rather higher than the Penedès, and with a somewhat cooler, damper climate. Average rainfall is about 500 mm (21.7 ins) a year. Winters can be very cold, with the thermometer dropping to − 10° C (14° F). The days are hot in summer, but then cool air comes in from the sea, lowering the temperature and making the nights agreeable. This change of temperature has a beneficial effect, giving the vines maximum retention of their fruit. The limestone content of the soil is another of the natural factors that together provide Conca de Barberà with such excellent potential for making elegant, fresh and fruity wines. These are produced here in plenty, along with hazelnuts and almonds. But you seldom see these wines, for most of them disappear anonymously into the Penedès Cavas.

Cava

Penedès wine houses, large and small, have discovered that the white wines of Conca de Barberà make a perfect basis for Cavas of high quality. These basic wines are made from Parellada and Macabeo grapes, which together account for nearly two-thirds of the total 7400 ha (18,285 acres) of vineyards. Chardonnay also appears to do extremely well here: Codorníu has planted many acres with this variety, in the Castillo de Riudabella estate and elsewhere. Torres, a firm producing still wines in the Penedès, makes its best Chardonnay wine from grapes grown in Conca de Barberà; it is called Milmanda, after the castle of that name. This variety was planted there by Torres at the end of the 1970s.

However, the district is able to supply not only excellent white wines, but reds too. Climate and soil are well suited to Cabernet Sauvignon, Pinot Noir, Merlot and Tempranillo. Pinot Noir is not only used for still wines (with Torres as the most important customer), but also on a modest scale for sparkling ones. The other black grapes are meant exclusively for still wines. Just what class the Cabernet Sauvignon grown in Conca de Barberà can have is shown – once again – by Torres. For this house chooses grapes from the Milmanda estate for its famous Gran Coronas, including Black Label. These superior black grape varieties are gradually supplanting Garnacha, which has been here for ages. Trepat is a strictly local grape from which delicious rosés are made hereabouts; they enjoy a considerable reputation and Catalonians are very fond of them – which is why rosé makes up a quarter to a third of the total volume of wine produced here. All wines have a relatively low minimum alcohol content, namely 9.5 percent. The producers are therefore able to make relatively light

wines – which is good for whites and rosés which must be drunk young. There is no doubt that Conca de Barberà has the potential to produce high quality wines, both still and sparkling.

Since most of Conca de Barberà's grapes are made into wines that do not carry the district name, this small DO has to contend with being relatively unknown. It is also the case that the designation is quite recent – December 1989 – and there are few private producers here. The bulk of the wine is made by cooperatives, of which only a few do their own bottling, and then only of a small part of the vintage. Efforts at marketing are therefore minimal. One of the few really energetic firms is Concavins, which produces splendid rosé and white wines under the Xipella brand name. Elaboradores y Comerciantes de Vinos, a Montblanc house that uses the name Làscaris, also makes itself known. But so long as Penedès remains by far the biggest customer for the wines from the 14 communities of Conca de Barberà, the latter will remain one of Spain's least-known districts. It is therefore quite logical that serious discussions should have taken place between Penedès and Conca de Barberà on the formation of some kind of federation. If this were to come about, Conca de Barberà would presumably become a district of the Penedès, just as the Médoc is of Bordeaux, or Chablis of Burgundy. This would be no startling change, rather the confirmation of a situation that already largely exists.

Below: The monastery at Poblet, surrounded by vineyards.

PRODUCERS OF SPECIAL INTEREST

Concavins 43422 Barberà de la Conca

This bodega, which lies a few miles west of the village, was a cooperative until 1988. It went bankrupt, however, and was subsequently bought by a group of private individuals. These have invested in modern equipment for the cellar, which has greatly benefited the quality of the wines.

All the grapes are bought from 25 to 30 growers who between them work 200 ha (494 acres). Concavins processes only the very soundest fruit: the rest goes to cooperatives. The best of the wines are sold under the Xipella name. The pale pink Clos Rosado rosé is perfect of its kind: fresh, light, and very fruity. It is made from 95 percent Trepat and 5 percent Tempranillo. The Xipello Blanco Seco is also light in taste, pure, and with an apple freshness. The grapes used for this wine are about 60 percent Parellada and 40 percent Macabeo.

In terms of quality the Xipello Tinto leaves something to be desired; at present it is made from Garnacha, Tempranillo and Trepat grapes, but the firm hopes eventually to made a better wine with Cabernet Sauvignon and, perhaps, Merlot. Simpler qualities of wine are sold as Molí Sec or Les Marinades. Concavins also markets goat's milk cheeses in olive oil, made with real craftsmanship.

Travel Information

Above: General view over the vineyards of Conca de Barberà.

HOTELS AND RESTAURANTS

Hostal del Senglar, 43440 l'Espluga de Francolí, tel (77) 870121 Anyone driving through the village on the way to Poblet will see this hotel-restaurant. Its rooms are simple, but the restaurant has more atmosphere and character, and there is a small museum. You eat well here; the most expensive white wine on the list is the Milmanda Chardonnay from Torres.
Masía del Cadet, 43448 Les Masies de Poblet, tel (77) 870869 Charming small hotel in a fifteenth-century country house. Tasty Catalonian dishes are served in the restaurant, including confit of duck.
Hostal del Centre, 43440 Monestir de Poblet, tel (77) 870058 Simple but pleasant, quietly situated country hotel. Decent food in the restaurant.
Fonda Colom, 43400 Montblanc, tel (77) 860153 Roast meats and other regional dishes.
Les Tines, Finca de Riudabella,

43430 Vimbodí This restaurant, in an old farmhouse, enjoys an excellent reputation locally – which makes reservations necessary. Ingredients are bought fresh from the market.

PLACES OF INTEREST

Barberà de la Conca This small wine village with fewer than 500 inhabitants stands on a hill, offering a view out over almost the whole of the district. There are the ruins of a large, eleventh-century castle here. The wine cooperative was built in Modernista style by César Martinell.
Castillo de Riudabella This stronghold dating from the thirteenth and fourteenth centuries used to be one of the farms belonging to the monastery at Poblet. Since 1820 it has been owned by the artistic Moreno de Mora family, who have lovingly

restored it. The vineyard, planted mainly with Chardonnay and Pinot Noir, has been leased for 30 years to Codorníu.
l'Espluga de Francolí Many tourists drive through this village on their way to the monastery at Poblet. The Romanesque and Gothic church of San Miguel is a national monument, as is the fourteenth-century former hospital with its beautiful courtyard. Also here is a Modernista wine cooperative. Near l'Espluga the river Francolí flows for 300 m (330 yds) underground.
La Guardia del Prats Very ancient village with some castle remains.
Monasterio de Santa María de Poblet Founded in 1151, for hundreds of years this was the most powerful monastery in Cataluña. In the centuries that followed, the Cistercians continued to enlarge it. The present complex has three surrounding walls and many

Right: The castle at Riudabella, not far from Poblet. Codorníu rents the vineyard here, and Chardonnay and Pinot Noir are the most important grapes.

features of interest. Among them are the Romanesque Santa Catalina church; the cloisters, also Romanesque; a huge wine vault; the cathedral-like monastery church with its sixteenth-century alabaster altarpiece; the abbot's palace; and the chamber with two gigantic sarcophagi containing the remains of seven kings of Aragón and Castile. Within the walls is a 15 ha (37 acre) vineyard that Codorníu works. With Rome's permission, Torres bought the land around the monastery. Called La Muralla, there are 130 ha (320 acres) of it that can be cultivated. For about a century the monastery was neglected, and even overgrown, but in the 1940s, the Cistercians started on a total renovation. It was discovered then that in spite of the repeated waves of pillage many works of art had survived, including the vast library which contained many works which had been given to monastery by the kings. The rarest work was the Chronicle of Jaime I, dating from

1343, written in Catalan. It is currently in the university library of Barcelona, but thousands of other works can still be admired at Poblet.

Montblanc This capital of Conca de Barberà was founded, as Vilasalva, on the north bank of the Francolí, but moved not long afterwards to the south bank, where it acquired its present name. The whole of Montblanc has been declared a national monument. A 2

km (1¼ mile) wall around the centre has four gates and 17 towers still intact. Within the wall there are old churches, such as the thirteenth-century San Miguel; the fourteenth-century Santa María, on a hilltop and never completed; a royal palace; the Casa Josa museum of pottery; and Gothic houses. Just outside these town walls stands the Hospital de Santa Magdalena, a fourteenth-century structure with beautiful cloisters.

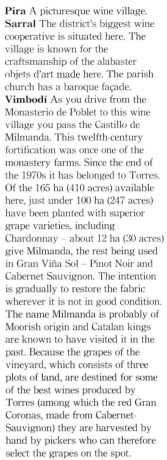

Pira A picturesque wine village.

Sarral The district's biggest wine cooperative is situated here. The village is known for the craftsmanship of the alabaster objets d'art made here. The parish church has a baroque façade.

Vimbodí As you drive from the Monasterio de Poblet to this wine village you pass the Castillo de Milmanda. This twelfth-century fortification was once one of the monastery farms. Since the end of the 1970s it has belonged to Torres. Of the 165 ha (410 acres) available here, just under 100 ha (247 acres) have been planted with superior grape varieties, including Chardonnay – about 12 ha (30 acres) give Milmanda, the rest being used in Gran Viña Sol – Pinot Noir and Cabernet Sauvignon. The intention is gradually to restore the fabric wherever it is not in good condition. The name Milmanda is probably of Moorish origin and Catalan kings are known to have visited it in the past. Because the grapes of the vineyard, which consists of three plots of land, are destined for some of the best wines produced by Torres (among which the red Gran Coronas, made from Cabernet-Sauvignon) they are harvested by hand by pickers who can therefore select the grapes on the spot.

WINE ROUTE

The village of l'Espluga, or any of the nearby hamlets such as Les Massies de Poblet or Monestir de Poblet, forms an excellent starting point for an exploration of Conca de Barberà. You could drive first to the Poblet monastery, continue in the direction of Prades and then turn off right for Vimbodí. Next you return to Poblet (with Castillo de Milmanda on your left), and on via l'Espluga to Montblanc. From there take the road to Barberà de la Conca, Sarral, Rocafort de Queralt, then return by way of, first, part of the road to Solivella, turning left for Sarral at a T-junction; then go south for Pira and La Guàrdia dels Prats. In the latter village turn north for Solivella, via the C 240, and then from Solivella drive back to l'Espluga.

Left. Although the summer days can be hot in Conca de Barberà, the area has cool nights. This is good for the scent of the grapes.

Tarragona

Consilium Vinorum Tarraconensium is the name of the Tarragona wine fraternity set up in 1989. A Latin name was chosen because of the Roman influence here in the past. The town of Tarragona was founded in 218 BC by Publius Cornelius Scipio and was later the residence of Roman emperors, including Augustus and Hadrian. Tarraco, as the town was called then, also functioned as capital of Hispania Citerior. There are many monuments to remind you of Roman times, including the remains of an amphitheatre that seated 12,000 spectators, and about a quarter of the 4 kilometre (2.5 mile) wall the Romans built around the town. Winegrowing flourished in this period and the wine was even shipped to Rome, where it was valued almost as highly as that grown in Latium, on the hills near the Eternal City. Tarraco's wine was also praised by such writers as Silvius Italicus, Martial and Pliny the Younger.

Communion wine

Until well into the 20th century Tarragona wines were mainly strong and sweet. The biggest foreign customer was Britain, where the wine was looked on as a cheap alternative to port; this particular export trade got under way in the second half of the nineteenth century and continued until the 1930s. Tarragona was also, and continues to be, a supplier of communion wines. The house of De Muller, which dates from 1851, ships various styles of communion wine all over the world. All kinds of conditions are attached to their production, including two years in cask, fining with fresh egg white, and a ban on filtering. Since the 1960s and 1970s, however, the region has increasingly produced dry, unfortified wines. In 1959 these were officially admitted to the classification then applicable; the actual Tarragona *denominación de origen* came in 1976.

Public unfamiliarity

The present wine region consists of 80 communities, or parts thereof, in Tarragona, the most southerly of the Catalan provinces. The vineyards cover some 18,200 ha (40,000 acres). The area used to be greater, but economic problems have led many growers to go over to other crops; in particular to hazelnuts, which are produced in vast quantities here. In some parts of Tarragona 70 percent of the agricultural land is covered with hazel trees, and there are even cooperatives that process these nuts as well as grapes.

The root cause of the economic problem is the greatly reduced demand for the traditional Tarragona wines, and the generally low prices paid for the other wines. Most of the wine – around 65 percent of it – is sold anonymously and in bulk, so that although Tarragona is among the 15 biggest DOs, wines bearing this name are seldom seen. Those producers who do bottle wines have to contend with public unfamiliarity and a lack of a reputation, which has direct repercussions on the price. This situation

Below: Further inland in Tarragona the landscape becomes more mountainous.

Above: The wine village of Tivissa, built on a hill.

resulted in the failure of various bodegas around 1990. The only firm that has so far been dynamic and successful enough to lift the Tarragona DO out of its anonymity is Pedro Rovira.

Wine for Cava

Like nearly all the other houses, Pedro Rovira depends on the cooperatives for most of the grapes and wines it needs. There are some 180 cooperatives in the province of Tarragona, with more than 95 percent of production in their hands. This handicaps the development of the wine region, for progressively managed cooperatives are in the minority. For example, many of these establishments concentrate their production on wine to be used for Cava. About 70 percent of all Tarragona wine is white and around a third of this is bought by Cava makers in Penedès. Some 25 communities of the Tarragona wine region also belong to the Cava DO.

El Campo de Tarragona

The subzone El Campo de Tarragona with its wine communities is the part of Tarragona that most resembles Penedès. It stretches around the town of Tarragona for 25 to 30 km (15.5 to 19 miles) in all directions. The landscape is mostly made up of flat plateaux and low hills, the contours becoming more pronounced as you go further inland. The soil is light, on a limestone base, and a Mediterranean climate prevails, with an average annual rainfall of 500 mm (19.7 ins). Most of Tarragona's vineyards – about two-thirds of them – are here, and 85 percent of the area is planted with the same grape varieties as in Penedès: Macabeo, Parellada, Xarel-lo and, increasingly, Chardonnay. Ull de Llebre (Tempranillo) and the indigenous Sumoll are the principal grapes grown for red and rosé wines.

La Comarca de Falset

A second subzone is La Comarca de Falset, which lies directly to the west of El Campo de Tarragona and in the north borders on the Priorato DO. The terrain is distinctly hilly, and often even mountainous, with a subsoil of limestone and granite. The weather is cooler and damper – at 650 mm (25.6 ins) a year – than in the coastal zone. Production is chiefly of red wines, for which Cariñena and Garnacha grapes have long been grown, though new varieties are on the increase. The cooperative in the village of Falset is working closely with Pedro Rovira and now has plots with Ull de Llebre, Cabernet Sauvignon and Pinot Noir.

La Ribera d'Ebre

The third and last of the subzones is called La Ribera d'Ebre, which is just slightly larger in area than Falset and lies to the west of it. As the name indicates, it is to be found in the valley of the Ebro, or Ebre. This is separated from the coast by a range with rugged peaks rising to more than 700 m (2,300 ft). Just past the beautifully situated upland village of Tivissa the country opens out and vineyards come into view, as well as many nut and fruit trees. Lower-lying fields here are apt to flood; locally they say this usually happens once every four years. The vines grow down in the valley, on the slopes and up on the plateaux, on limestone and gravel. On a hill near Móra la Nueva the house of Pedro Rovira has two sizeable plots planted with Cabernet Sauvignon, with a sprinkler system fitted in one of them. In Ribera d'Ebre this is no luxury, for only 385 mm (15.2 ins) of rain falls annually, significantly less than in the other two subzones. The summers are also hotter here, and the winters colder. For white wines Macabeo and Garnacha Blanca are the grapes mainly grown, with Cariñena and Garnacha for the red. Experiments are being conducted with other varieties, including Colombard (white) and Syrah and Merlot (both black).

Trends and traditions

The bulk of the unfortified bottled wines from these three subzones is of little merit. The quality is seldom inspiring, and the personality is usually indeterminate. Attempts are being made, however, to improve this situation. One example was provided by the José Lopez Betrán concern, which had an ultra-modern cellar and produced wines on the basis of a single grape variety. This bodega, however, went bankrupt. The only firm at present in a position to increase the prestige of the Tarragona DO is Pedro Rovira. What Torres once did for the Penedès still wines, Pedro Rovira hopes to do for those of Tarragona. To this end this family firm is not only working and experimenting with different, high-quality grapes, but is also investing a great deal in new technology. In his extensive cellar complex at Móra la Nueva, director Pedro Rovira Solé can ferment millions of gallons of wine at low temperatures, and for ageing his better red wines he has around 1,500 small casks at his disposal, most of them of French oak. Since the 1980s the quality of the Rovira wines has been improving steadily – a trend that seems likely to continue through the 1990s.

At De Muller, in Tarragona's harbour district, the traditional sweet, heavy wines are still held in honour along with the communion wines. The cellar here is full of large old casks. Some of them belong to a *solera* system that goes back decades, even into the last century. In this, wine drawn off is replaced by younger wine, giving rise to a system of perpetual blending. Tasting the classic De Muller wines is an experience in itself: they are unbelievably concentrated and offer a rich, lingering taste with impressions of figs, raisins and apple syrup. It is good that this kind of sumptuous curiosity is still being made, for it truly contains the whole history of Tarragona wine.

PRODUCERS OF SPECIAL INTEREST

Pedro Rovira 43770 Móra la Nueva

It was almost a century before this firm turned to making wine. Founded in 1864, Pedro Rovira at first was simply blending and selling wine, and only began to produce wine on its own account in 1962. The firm owns various bodegas in Cataluña, as well as a distillery. The establishment that makes wines with the Tarragona DO is in the village of Móra la Nueva, in the Ribera d'Ebre subzone. The grapes come from 100 ha (247 acres) of its own vineyards as well as from some 2,500 growers belonging to cooperatives. There is a particularly close relationship with the Falset cooperative, and both Pedro Rovira and this organization have planted plots with Cabernet Sauvignon. Tests are also being carried out with Pinot Noir.

Thanks to a big investment in modern equipment a large proportion of the wines can be fermented at low temperatures: white and rosé at 18°C (64.4°F), the red at 22° to 25°C (71.6° to 77°F). In addition to barrels, about 1,500 small casks are used for ageing in wood, most of them of French oak. The firm is working hard at improving quality under the director Pedro Rovira Solé, a dynamic fourth-generation member of the family.

Almost without exception the most recent vintages are the best in each type of wine. The Viña Montalt is not the fresh, fruity kind of white but an agreeable, smooth wine that is supple in taste and also has a measure of development. It is in fact matured for a year in the cellars. It is made from around 80 percent Macabeo and 20 percent Parellada. The red Viña Mater is given some 18 months in cask and is generally a mature, juicy wine with something of plums and distinct wood about it. It is made solely from Ull de Llebre, which is also true of the Pedro Rovira Gran Reserva. This, too, spends 18 months in cask, followed by five years' rest in bottle. Despite its age it is a reasonably vital, firm wine, very good with roast meat and game.

De Muller 43000 Tarragona

The house of De Muller, founded by a German, has stood near the harbour area at Real 38 since 1851. It is a bulwark of tradition – but on the other hand it was the first Spanish firm to stabilize wines cold. The range coming from this family firm is vast, with very many fortified and unfortified wines. Communion wine is its great speciality: this goes all over the world and has been supplied to various popes. Splendid sweet and dry fortified wines age in its cellars, sometimes according to a *solera* system. These are sold with such names as Aureo, Dom Berenguer, and Dom Juan Fort. Alongside these De Muller carries a considerable range of unfortified wines. The most exciting of these is its Moscatel Seco, a dry, fragrant and fresh wine with a floral aroma. A number of acceptable wines are offered under the Viña Solimar brand name, including a pleasant red and a dry rosé. De Muller owns 20 ha (49 acres) within the Tarragona DO and 5 ha (12.5 acres) in Priorato; wine from the latter is described below in the relevant section.

Travel Information

HOTELS AND RESTAURANTS

Can Bosch, Jaime I 19, 43850 Cambrils, tel (77) 360019 Cambrils on the coast belongs to the Tarragona DO, but has a reputation for its gastronomy rather than for its wines. This is the best-known restaurant in the area and people come from far and wide to eat here. It produces delicious, elegant creations based on fresh fish and shellfish. Booking is necessary.

Hotel Sport, 43202 Falset, tel (77) 830078 This simple hotel is a good starting point for trips through the western part of the Tarragona DO, Terra Alta and nearby Priorato. On the ground floor is a bar and restaurant.

Enric, 43770 Móra la Nueva, tel (77) 401166 A well-known local eating-house and pizzeria. In fine weather you can eat on a terrace at the back. Country cooking with shellfish, *jamón serrano*, *chuletas de cordero*, etc.

C'al Brut, San Pedro 14, 43004 Tarragona, tel (77) 210450 Congenial restaurant in the port area with fresh fish on the menu.

Lauria, Rambla Nova 20, 43004 Tarragona, tel (77) 236712 Friendly service and reasonable prices characterize this centrally situated hotel. It has a garage and swimming pool, and there is a restaurant on the first floor.

Sol Ric, Vía Augusta 227, 43007 Tarragona, tel (77) 232032 This famous restaurant is in the eastern part of the town, and tradition and quality are its hallmarks. It has a well-stocked cellar with many old vintages. In sunny weather you can eat on the shady terrace.

PLACES OF INTEREST

Cambrils Atmospheric seaside resort with a fishing harbour and many restaurants. The Marqués de

Above: Fresh fish from Cambrils is served in numerous local restaurants.
Left: Detail of Tarragona's medieval cathedral, which took about a century to build. Chapels and other elements were added later. A collection of more than 50 tapestries is among the treasures here. Communion wines made in Tarragona are used not only here but in churches and other religious centres all around the world. Their production is subject to strict rules.

Above: A timeless landscape in Tarragona: olive trees and vines. The wine enjoyed a considerable reputation in Roman times.

Mariano palace is in the Samá park.
Constantí Less than a mile from this village is the mausoleum at Centcelles which dates from Roman times (fourth century AD) and consists of two square buildings with fine interiors with mosaics.
Falset Important winemaking community at the foot of a ruined castle. The Santa María church is eighteenth century; the Casa Consistorial, a former palace, is in Renaissance style; and the wine cooperative owes its striking form to the architect César Martinell, a pupil of Gaudí. Regional wines are sold in the La Vinícola shop next to the cooperative.
Miravet Village with the ruins of a Moorish castle, in the Ebro valley.
Tarragona Capital of the province of the same name, and with a population of 110,000. Its oldest part is built on a rocky hill and is rich in monuments, especially from Roman times. The Paseo Arqueológico is a path that runs along the foot of a town wall of Roman origin, 1,000 m (1,100 yd) long, with gateways and towers. There are Roman statues in the park and the remains of a Roman forum and amphitheatre. Many Roman finds are displayed in the Museo Arqueológico, including sculptures and mosaics, the famous "Head of Medusa" among them. The Romano-Christian necropolis and the museum associated with it display tombs, sarcophagi, and objects from the third and fourth centuries including a fine ivory doll. Tarragona's cathedral is medieval. Beside the Romanesque and Gothic structure there are large, richly decorated cloisters, as well as a museum with paintings and dozens of Brussels tapestries. About 4 km (2.5 miles) north of the town, on the N420, is a splendidly preserved

Roman aqueduct 217 m (712 ft) long, called El Puente de Diablo (The Devil's Bridge).
Tivissa A pleasant wine village, built on a hill, which belongs to the Ribera d'Ebre subzone.

WINE ROUTE

The wine route covers the western, more interesting part of the Tarragona DO. As you travel along you will clearly see how different the landscape is in the three wine subzones. The vineyards run from close by the sea up to a height of more than 360 m (1,180 ft) at Falset, and are divided up by rugged mountains. Part of the wine route corresponds with that of Priorato, but the latter goes further into the mountains.

An alternative route leads past the cooperatives built by the architect César Martinell. This pupil of Gaudí lived from 1888 to 1973 and designed these remarkable cooperatives in the Modernista style, the Spanish version of art nouveau. There are seven of them, all within the province of Tarragona and scattered over various wine districts. From east to west they are to be found in Rocafort de Queralt, Sarral, Barberà de la Conca, and Montblanc (all in Conca de Barberà); Falset (in Tarragona); and El Pinell de Brai and Gandesa (both in Terra Alta).

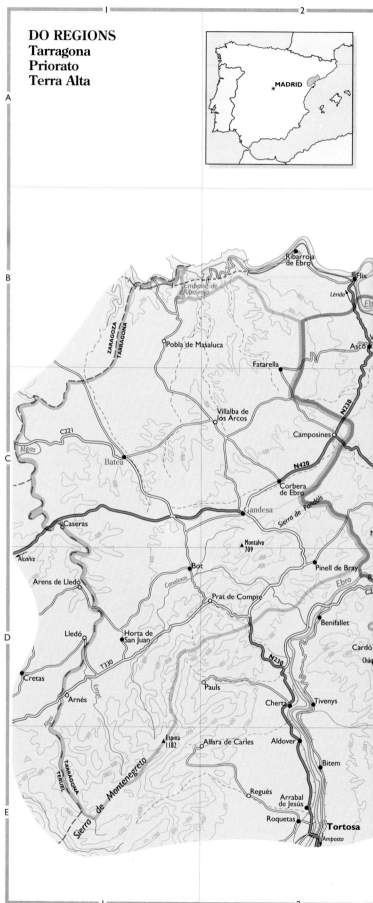

DO REGIONS
Tarragona
Priorato
Terra Alta

N

Batea   Wine centre

Suggested wine routes

Boundary of Tarragona DO

Boundary of Priorato DO

Boundary of Terra Alta DO

Autopista

Main road

Other roads

Railway

Provincial boundary

Provincial capital

Contour interval 200 metres

1:317 000

Km 0   5   10   15

Miles 0   5   10   15   20

Priorato

Above: Various kinds of wines are on offer in the Cellers Scala Dei saleroom.

The origins of Priorato go back to prehistoric times. More recently, the Romans were active here, growing grapes and mining for lead and silver. Because of its natural resources the area was once one of the most populous in Cataluña: the mountain streams provided water, the forests were full of game, and there was trout for the catching in the rivers. A long period of prosperity dawned in the twelfth century after a villager from Poboleda had a vision of angels ascending and descending a stairway to heaven. Subsequently, in 1163, Alfonso II of Aragón founded a Carthusian monastery on the spot. It was given the name Scala Dei (Stairway of God). For some centuries the monks dominated the district, which thereby acquired the name Priorato, from the Spanish word for priory. The monastery made an income from the sale of medicinal plants, herbs and mountain spring water, and also took up winegrowing. But in 1835 the monks finally left the priory, and today it is simply an overgrown ruin. The little hamlet, also called Scala Dei, still stands nearby, with some 30 inhabitants. The legend of the heavenly stairway is

commemorated on all bottles of Priorato wine: the seal of the *Consejo Regulador* shows a stairway flanked by angels and bunches of grapes.

Small plots

Winegrowing in Priorato became a lucrative occupation in the eighteenth century with large exports to Italy, Russia and other countries. Then at the end of the nineteenth century France suddenly became a big customer, because of the phylloxera raging there. The stately houses built for wealthy families in Poboleda and elsewhere are a reminder of these periods of prosperity. Today, however, Priorato is quiet and largely deserted. Most of the population in the 11 villages that make up the DO live on their pensions. Only at weekends does the district spring to life when families come visiting, not only for the traditional Sunday meal, but also to work on the land – the 1,850 ha (4,450 acres) of Priorato vineyards are mainly divided into small plots. Most of the grapes are therefore taken to cooperatives, which control about 85 percent of wine production.

Rugged beauty

The landscape of Priorato – which was once a great inland sea – is characterized by a rugged beauty, with its mountains and the deep valleys of the Siurana and its tributaries. Wild vegetation covers most of the slopes, scented in summer with wild herbs. The roads without exception are very winding. The villages seem positively mediaeval, and their narrow streets were never designed for cars. Olives, almonds and grapes are the most important produce. Not many other crops will thrive here, for the rocky subsoil is poor – mainly slaty, often with mica and iron as well. The climate is mainly dry, with less than 400 mm (15.75 ins) of rain a year. A dry wind, the *seré*, blows from the north, and in July and August the daytime temperature can rise to 40°C (104°F), yet drop to 10 to 12°C (50 to 54°F) at night. This great fluctuation is ideal for grapes, for it helps them keep their aroma. The slate is helpful too, forming an ideal medium for vines to grow in, as shown elsewhere in the world – in the German Mosel valley for example.

Very low yields

Winegrowing has always been carried on under very difficult circumstances in this region. The steep slopes make terracing necessary; and where this has not proved possible, ropes have had to be used to keep plants, animals (mules and horses) and people from plunging headlong down the hillsides. Many vineyards can still only be worked by hand. In addition Priorato has to contend with an extremely low yield; in many places this is no more than 5 to 15 hl per ha (45 to 135 gal per acre). It is only in the more logically laid-out vineyards with relatively young, vigorous vines that 40 hl per ha (360 gal per acre) is reached; but sites of this kind are the exception rather than the rule. The height at which the vineyards are situated also varies greatly. They are found on valley floors 200 m (655 ft) above sea level and on slopes more than 1,000 m (3,275 ft) up.

Tremendous potency

As with the natural factors of soil and climate, the low yield is also an advantage. It contributes quite a lot to the special character of Priorato wine, particularly the red. The latter is one of the most concentrated and potent made in Spain – if not the world. The legal minimum alcohol content is 13.5 percent, but in practice this is exceeded perfectly naturally and without difficulty, sometimes reaching 18 percent. These wines have an inky colour, an aroma of sun-drenched fruit, often with wood as well, and their taste fills the mouth in a quite massive way. Some of the reds tend towards sweetness and almost suggest a dry kind of port. Practically all the reds are made from Garnacha and Cariñena grapes; Garnacha Peluda is planted here, too, but in smaller quantities. Most of the winegrowers keep stubbornly to these varieties. There is, however, a new trend in winemaking here, with non-native grapes given a role and the alcohol content of the wines kept as close as possible to the legal minimum. This has all been set in motion by Cellers Scala Dei, in the hamlet of that name. Thus one of its red wines was made from 70 percent Garnacha and 30 percent Cabernet Sauvignon, and its alcohol was kept at exactly 13.5. New wines of this type are regarded as heresy by traditional winemakers, and by some critics. If viewed objectively, however, they are among the very best in the region, and much less

heavy and soporific to drink. Their lightness is in fact relative, for they are still among the strongest and most substantial in the country.

Styles in rosé and white

High alcohol percentages are also obligatory for the small amounts of rosé and white wine produced – 13.5 and 13.75 percent respectively. Here, too, there are contrasts between the classic kinds of wine and the new wave. The former lack fruit and freshness; often they are oxidized to a greater or lesser degree. Like certain kinds of sherry, some of the white wines develop *flor*. The Solera from the very traditional estate of Masía Barril suggests a light type of dry Amontillado. Cellers Scala Dei, on the other hand, vinifies its rosé and white wines at low temperature so that they do have fruit and freshness. Some Chenin Blanc goes into the dry white wine from this house. The usual white grape varieties are Garnacha Blanca, Macabeo and Pedro Ximénez. Finally, Priorato produces fortified wines, in sweet, semi-sweet and dry forms. Exports from this exciting, unspoiled region are as yet of little significance, but since 1988 the *Consejo Regulador* has very sensibly allowed bottled wines only to be exported, to ensure that only authentic Priorato wine goes abroad – the wine whose pleasures are looked on locally as nothing less than heavenly.

Below: The 12th-century Carthusian monastery of Scala Dei, whose monks developed winegrowing in the region. The building, overshadowed by the surrounding mountains, has stood empty since 1835.

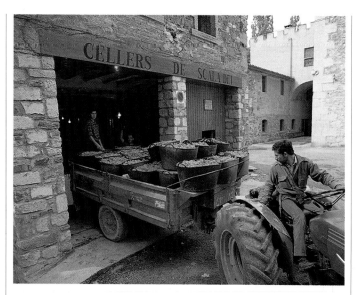

Above: Vintage time in Priorato – Garnacha Blanca grapes arriving at Cellers de Scala Dei.

PRODUCERS OF SPECIAL INTEREST

Masía Barril 43738 Bellmunt del Priorato

This wine estate lies hidden in the hills between Falset and Bellmunt del Priorat, covering 15 to 20 ha (37 to 49 acres), spread over various plots. It is energetically directed by Rafael Barril, a resident of Madrid, whose father bought it in 1931. Since 1980 he has bottled a proportion of his wines which are almost all traditional in type. One exception is the Masía Barril Virgen, which looks like a red wine, but possesses a fresh, rosé-like taste. The skins of the Garnacha (70 to 80 percent) and Cariñena grapes are left in the must for 36 to 48 hours before fermentation starts. The unfiltered En Rama is a supple, pleasant and reasonably mature wine in which the 16.5 percent alcohol is barely perceptible. Usually the latest vintage is the best; after four to five years the wine begins to show evidence of oxidation. The firm's Clasico is indeed a classic red Priorato: opaque and with a tremendously mouth-filling taste, with ripe fruit and around 16.5 percent alcohol. It consists of 75 percent Garnacha and 25 percent Cariñena. The same proportions are the basis of the firm's Extra, a strong product with a lot of taste and tannin, and "only" 14 percent alcohol.

Rafael Barril is a great believer in the future of aromatic wine, marketing a sweetish Vino Aromatizado, based on old white wine and herbs from the bodega's own botanical garden. The Solera is the most interesting of the white wines. This aperitif is made up from various vintages and develops *flor*. The Barril family strives to respect nature as far as possible on its wine estate, and to make Masía Barril a bodega that embodies many aspects of the life and culture of Priorato.

Cellers Scala Dei 43379 Scala Dei

The reception area of this progressively run firm stands next to the De Muller cellar and is much visited by day trippers at weekends. Its own cellars have stainless-steel tanks where wines from the bodega's own 100 ha (247 acres) are fermented. The company also has cellars where wines are aged in casks and bottles. The bottle cellar is vaulted and dates from 1692.

Wines from Cellers Scala Dei are generally of an exemplary quality. Its Blanc Scala Dei, made from Garnacha Blanca and 35 percent Chenin Blanc, is clean in taste, with hints of spice, and the alcohol is restricted to the legal minimum (and can even be a little lower). The Rosat Scala Dei (100 percent Garnacha) goes well with food, and is characterized by a firm, fruity, juicy taste. Besides its Garnacha the Negre Scala Dei now has 30 percent Cabernet Sauvignon. It is a firm wine with meaty fruit, suppleness and some wood (it spends six months in cask).

More classic in character is the Cartoixa de Scala Dei, a *gran reserva* made exclusively from Garnacha grapes. It has a good deal of wood and vanilla, with some spice and a firm, mouth-filling, fully rounded taste.

De Muller 43004 Tarragona

The house of De Muller, based in Tarragona, has a cellar beside the little square in Scala Dei. The grapes processed here include those from the firm's own 5 ha (12.5 acres) in Priorato. The resulting wine is the Legitimo Priorato de Muller. This has a purplish, inky colour and a well-rounded, sinewy taste with sun-drenched fruit, 15.5 percent alcohol, and a long aftertaste. It is usually made from half Garnacha and half Cariñena grapes.

Travel Information

HOTELS AND RESTAURANTS

Hotel Sport, 43202 Falset (*see* Tarragona) Part of the Falset community comes under Priorato, so this village is a suitable starting-point for a visit.

Antic Priorat, 43376 Poboleda, tel (77) 827006 Pleasant, very peaceful 15-room hotel with restaurant. The view is lovely, the swimming pool cooling.

Racó del Priorato, 43374 La Vilella Baja, tel (77) 839065 Tasty country dishes are prepared here. It attracts a lot of customers at weekends in particular: at Sunday lunchtime people sit and wait a long time for a table to be free. Park on the other side of the village, near the wine cooperative.

PLACES OF INTEREST

Bellmunt del Priorat Ancient village with an abandoned lead mine that was worked by the Romans. Turn round here, for this is where the surfaced road ends.

Gratallops Situated in the centre of the wine region. La Pastera is a cake and confectionery shop that makes pastries with local wine, and in the village square is a cooper's workshop. High on a mountain not far from Gratallops is a hermitage dedicated to the Virgen de la Consolación, patron saint of Priorato.

El Lloà A medieval atmosphere and a view over the surrounding country.

Poboleda The elegant houses and decorated doorways demonstrate this town's former prosperity.

Scala Dei Behind this hamlet, with 30 inhabitants and a couple of bodegas, stand the ruins of the abbey of the same name which served as a model for many other Carthusian abbeys in Spain. A plan is displayed on a wall by the car park.

Torroja del Priorat In the San Miguel church is an eighteenth-century organ, installed here in 1880. There are also some fine houses.

La Vilella Baja Medieval village, by an old bridge.

WINE ROUTE

On the map the total distance looks relatively short, but as the roads through Priorato are so narrow and winding, a good part of a day is needed to reconnoitre this wine district – certainly if there are stops on the way to walk round a village or to visit bodegas. The southern part of the route is shared with Tarragona. The Priorato *Consejo Regulador* has set out a wine route, which is indicated by yellow boards bearing the words *Ruta del vi*, but its course is not clear throughout.

Terra Alta

The best place from which to look out over Terra Alta is the Colle del Moro, a high hill near the village of Gandesa. Franco stood here in 1938 when he led his troops in one of the bloodiest and most important engagements of the Spanish Civil War, the Battle of the Ebro. The distant view from this hill is limited by the mountain chains that surround Terra Alta on practically all sides. The highest peaks lie to the south, from 1,000 m (3,280 ft) to about 1,400 m (4,600 ft). Between the rough, grey mountain masses the countryside, peaceful now, appears as a green oasis with many vineyards, almond and olive trees. Wheatfields provide yellow patches here and there. Terra Alta ("High Land") is in fact a whimsically shaped plateau at an average 400 m (1,300 ft) above sea level. Its terrain is made up of plateaux, gentle slopes and low ridges of hills.

The Iberians were some of the earliest inhabitants and remains of their culture have been found near Colle del Moro. Much later the area was to become the property of the Knights Templars. For centuries Terra Alta led an extremely isolated existence; it was only opened up this century, when the building of better roads and the growth in motor traffic led to increased communication with the outside world.

Wine communities

The climate in Terra Alta is less congenial than on the coast. The summers are very hot and it freezes in winter. The winds that blow here are dry, such as the warm *autan* from the east, and the cold northerly *bise*. Rainfall is an average 400 mm (15.75 ins) a year. The vines grow low to the ground so as to keep as much of the available moisture as possible. Limestone occurs nearly everywhere in the porous substrata; the amount of clay present varies greatly according to location. This wine region, which received its *denominación de origen* in 1982, consists of 12 communities and covers 10,800 ha (26,700 acres). Batea and

Below: The old wine village of Corbera de Ebro lies at the foot of a hill with the parish church perched above.

Gandesa are the most important villages, for each has a third of all the winegrowing land; the rest is distributed among the other 10 communities. Gandesa also serves as the commercial centre of the region.

White grapes

For a long time Terra Alta customarily produced *rancios*, dry or sweet fortified wines that were aged for 12 months in large casks. Some were also used as communion wine, and others were flavoured with herbs. The unfortified wines used to be heavy and soporific, with alcohol at 15 percent and more. The emphasis lay very much on white wines, which accounted for about 80 percent of the vintage. Not much of the wine was bottled locally – less than a third of the total. The equipment was old-fashioned and the vines were very old – 60 years on average – and so yielded only 11 hl per ha (98 gal per acre). Taken together, these factors offered a dispiriting prospect. On the one hand the demand for fortified or highly alcoholic white wines was waning, and on the other, the low yield per hectare made any economically sound use of resources impossible from the outset. Drastic measures were therefore needed if Terra Alta was to survive in the modern world of wine.

Drastic changes

It speaks well for the regional *Consejo Regulador* that these measures were taken. It was decided drastically to change the stock of vines, the primary aim being to reduce their average age to 20 years and at the same time to increase the yield eventually to 25 to 30 hl per ha (223 to 267 gal per acre). By 1990, 22 hl per ha (196 gal per acre) had been reached – double what it had been previously. This restructuring was not confined to the age of the vines, but also involved the varieties planted. At the beginning of the 1980s 77 percent of the vines were of the Garnacha Blanca variety, with Macabeo also cultivated. Cariñena, Garnacha and the latter's close relative, Garnacha Peluda with its smaller grapes, were grown for red and rosé wines. Barely 10 years later the situation looked quite different. The overall total of white varieties had dropped to half and many of the Garnacha Blanca vines had been replaced by Macabeo. In addition, Parellada had made an appearance. For the black grapes the proportion of Garnacha had risen and Cabernet Sauvignon had been planted on a modest scale. Efforts are being made to have the latter variety admitted to the DO. About 4,000 ha ((9,880 acres) have so far been reorganized in this way.

Lighter wines

In the area of winemaking, too, the necessary changes were made. Evidence of this is the introduction of lighter wines in the mid-1980s. Pioneering work was carried out by the house of Pedro Rovira, which is very active here in Terra Alta as well as in Tarragona. This firm laid down that grapes would have to be picked earlier than was customary in the area. Traditionally the grape harvest began around 12 October, but Pedro Rovira brought the date forward by about a month, since the fruit was fully ripe by 10 or 12 September. As a result of picking earlier, less alcoholic wines could be made. Stainless-steel tanks and cooling equipment were installed in the Pedro Rovira bodega, which made it possible to ferment the wines at lower temperatures. This firm also decided to use only the must for its white wines, without the grape skins: the custom in Terra Alta was to leave the skins in during fermentation. Pedro Rovira's example has in the meantime been followed by other producers.

Encouraging results

Results with the new-style wines were extraordinarily encouraging, both commercially and in terms of quality. The whites in particular showed improvement in quality that was impressive; an outstanding example is the smoothly fresh, very pleasing and lightly fruity Blanc de Belart from Pedro Rovira. This wine, made from 75 percent Macabeo and 25 percent Garnacha, was launched in 1989. The quantity in that year was 5,000 bottles; three years later Pedro Rovira was selling 250,000. During the 1990s the Terra Alta red wines will also be making themselves known, both those for drinking young and the wood-aged kinds. And as the Cabernet Sauvignon vines become fully grown, it will be clear how far this variety will influence the character of the red wines. All the bodegas will continue to make fortified wines, in limited quantities, if only for the Catalan market.

In 1990 only three of the eleven cooperatives and three of the thirteen private producers were bottling wine. The number of those bottling their wines is expected to have increased greatly before the turn of the century, with a decrease in the amount of bulk wine per bodega. All the signs indicate that Terra Alta is on its way to new heights.

Below: A typical old farmhouse in Terra Alta. This "High Land" had little contact with the rest of the country until the beginning of the 20th century.

PRODUCERS OF SPECIAL INTEREST

Cellers J. Pedrola 43006 Gandesa
This modest firm founded in 1850 is housed in a very old building with equally old cellars, but has invested a great deal in modern equipment. As well as the traditional fortified wines the range here includes unfortified whites, reds and rosés in the new style. The best of them are marketed under the name of the firm. For the simpler qualities the brand names Compte Rei and Viña Daurada are used.

Pedro Rovira 43006 Gandesa
The Pedro Rovira bodega stands outside Gandesa and was thoroughly modernized in the 1980s, so it now has a battery of stainless-steel fermentation tanks. In its cellars there are casks, both large and small. The director, Pedro Rovira Solé, is experimenting with fermenting white wine in new oak casks. The grapes and wines come principally from cooperatives, which are to be found in 11 of the 12 Terra Alta communities. The firm does, however, have land of its own in the neighbourhood of Gandesa. Its estate is called El Mas and covers 22 ha (14 acres). In line with the regional programme of restructuring, 14 ha (9 acres) of this has been replanted. The star of the range is the Blanc de Belart, presented in a stylish bottle. There is something of exotic fruit in its fragrance and taste, and it is supple, smoothly fresh and very agreeable. Its basis is 75 percent Macabeo and 25 percent Garnacha grapes. Another attractive white wine is the slightly sweet Alta Mar, clean and with a melon-like aroma. To date the most important red wine is the Viña d'Irto, an obviously mature *reserva*, with a firm core of alcohol and a distinct element of wood. Eventually the range will be augmented by other red wines. There are fortified sweet wines here too, seven kinds in all, among them a communion wine and the aromatized Mas dels Frares.

Travel Information

HOTELS AND RESTAURANTS

Hostal Piqué, 43006 Gandesa, tel (77) 420068 This simple hotel is the best of the scarce places to stay in Terra Alta itself. It has just under 50 rooms, and you can eat well in the restaurant with its regional bias.
Fonda Miralles, 43596 Horta de San Juan, tel (77) 435114 Offers a delicious, very affordable lunch. Lamb is often on the menu.
Parador Castillo de la Zuda, 43500 Tortosa, tel (77) 444450 Tortosa lies 40 km (25 miles) south of Gandesa and thus makes a good base for excursions in Terra Alta. You can stay in peace and comfort in this *parador*, a former Moorish castle surrounded by a fine garden.

PLACES OF INTEREST

Corbera de Ebro An old wine village built on a hillside. The church stands at the top of the hill, the wine cooperative at the bottom.
Gandesa This is the capital of Terra Alta and has some 3,000 inhabitants. It has a thirteenth-century Romanesque and Gothic church and possesses the oldest wine cooperative in the area. This was founded in 1919 and is strikingly housed in a building that was far ahead of its time when designed by the Gaudí-trained architect César Martinell. Four or five km (2.5 to 3 miles) west of Gandesa, along the N420, is the Colle del Moro hill which commands such a fine view.
Pinell de Bray Here, too, César Martinell built the wine cooperative, which has colourful ceramic tiles, the work of Xavier Nogués.
Horta de San Juan Picasso lived in this atmospheric wine village at the foot of the mountains. The church is Gothic.
Tortosa This town with its population of about 31,000 lies 24 km (15 miles) from the southernmost point on the Terra Alta wine route. Monuments here include the Gothic cathedral with its impressive interior; the Lonja or market hall (fourteenth century) with its striking design; the Bishop's Palace (fourteenth century) with a fine courtyard; and the Convento Santo Domingo, of the Renaissance period. The Museo Municipal de Arqueología is in the last building.

WINE ROUTE

Coming from the Tarragona wine district it is easy to get on to the Terra Alta wine route by crossing the Ebro at Mora la Nueva and driving in the Gandesa direction via the N420. You can also make the connection at Pinell de Bray by way of the T324/N230. This road – from Mora de Ebro – is narrower and more winding, but an advantage is that it goes through Miravet with its Moorish castle. The Terra Alta route passes through 7 of the 12 wine communities.

Above: The wine route through Terra Alta leads alongside Miravet, which has a ruined Moorish castle.
Left: The wine route also passes numerous old houses such as this one in Corbera de Ebro.

Costers del Segre

When in 1914 Manuel Raventós visited the Raimat estate, 15 km (9.5 miles) west of the town of Lérida, he found a wide expanse of land lying fallow around a seventeenth-century castle built on a bare hill. For hundreds of years vines had grown here: this was clear not only from the archives, but also from a weathered stone in a Moorish graveyard, on which was depicted a bunch of grapes and a hand; and it is from the original Arabic words for these (*raim* and *mat* respectively) that the estate derives its name. It was the agricultural crisis in the nineteenth century that had driven the growers from this land. The journey Raventós made to Raimat was part of his search for a suitable location for producing still wine: his Codorníu bodega in Penedès was making sparkling wine in plenty. He was also aware that the Canal de Aragón y Cataluña was to be cut right through the property, bringing down meltwater from the Pyrenees and so making irrigation possible – essential in a very dry area with an annual rainfall of only 300 mm (11.8 ins).

The Raimat estate

That Manuel Raventós decided to buy the whole 3,200 ha (7,900 acres), plus the castle, bears witness both to his great vision and optimism. For one thing, the salt content of the soil was so high that it had to be drastically reduced: the whole area was first sown with lucerne (the plant used for cattle fodder) then subsequently planted with pine trees. Some 20 years after the purchase the Raimat castle was surrounded by dense woods. After the trees had been felled large areas of the land were levelled out; up to 90 cm (3 ft) of earth from surrounding hills was added to raise some of the lower-lying places. The result was a gigantic plateau. Then an irrigation and drainage system was dug. For his workers Raventós created a village, complete with church, school, sports facilities, railway station and café. This still exists and accommodates some 160 families. A wine cellar was built at an early stage. Raventós wanted Gaudí to be the architect, but had to be content with one of his students – who acquitted himself splendidly in carrying out his task. The structure looks almost like a cathedral, and the stepped construction of the roof makes it possible to cool the space beneath by running cold water over it. Erected in 1918, this was Spain's first building in reinforced concrete.

American advice

Part of the land was planted with cereals and fruit trees, and of the original 3,200 ha (7,900 acres), 200 ha (494 acres) went to the church and to the army – a customary donation at that time. The first experiments with vines were unsuccessful. The traditional varieties from Penedès which had been planted did not thrive here. Research showed that there were problems with the rootstocks, and that non-native types would probably give better results. A conclusive report was written by Vincent Petrucci of Fresno University in California, who carried out a study in depth of all the natural factors at Raimat and provided a series of specific recommendations. Another American university that Raimat maintains close contact with is Davis, also in California.

The Raventós family decided to follow this American advice, and so in 1975 the first plantings were made with American rootstocks; Raimat now uses rootstocks grown on the estate. Codorníu in fact has the services of its subsidiary, Agro 2001, which carries out viticultural studies into subjects that include

Above: The 18th century Canyeret district of Lérida near the Segre.

clones and rootstocks of grape varieties. The Raimat vineyard today covers around 1,250 ha (3,090 acres), which is almost one-third of the 3,700 ha (9,140 acres) total area of the Costers del Segre DO. That this DO came into being is due to an important extent to Raimat and the Raventós family. For the first time in the history of the region it was shown that distinguished wines could be made, here at Raimat – wines that could compare with the best in Spain.

A tour of the property, which is at an average 330 m (1,083 ft) above sea level, shows broad plateaux with tall-growing vines. These level expanses are ringed by low hills. Reservoirs and pump installations enable the vines to be watered, and this happens automatically whenever the temperature rises above 35°C (95°F) or falls below 1°C (34°F). In both cases the water has a protective function, against scorching and freezing respectively. These installations regularly come into operation, for the summers are hot, while night frosts can occur from December to mid-May, and snow falls in the winter. The northern part of Raimat is rather flatter and cooler than the southern. Most of the white varieties grow in the former, and the black grapes are mainly cultivated in the warmer southern part. Black Cabernet Sauvignon and white Chardonnay are the most-grown varieties by far, and together they represent 60 percent of plantings. Next come Tempranillo (black), Parellada (white) and Macabeo (white), all with just under 100 ha (297 acres). The other varieties grown are black Merlot, Pinot Noir and Monastrell, and white Xarel-lo. Growers elsewhere in the region have

Above: The entrance to Raimat's futuristic cellar complex.

followed Raimat in planting Cabernet Sauvignon and other imported varieties.

A new winery

The first full harvest at Raimat came in 1978 – about 60 years after the purchase of the estate. To start with the wines were still made in the old bodega, but as production grew, the Raventós family decided to invest further in an entirely new winery complex. This was ready in 1988 and suggests a pyramid without its top. A hill was levelled, the building was erected, and some of the earth was replaced – so vines now grow on top. The entrance, flanked by an ornamental lake, is a rectangular, very modern construction with reflecting glass. The actual cellar space measures 120 by 90 m (394 by 295 ft) and has a height of 20 m (66 ft). Part of it serves for maturing the wine in wooden casks and large barrels, most of them of American oak. The 300 litre (66 gal) size is preferred here to the more usual 225 litre (50 gal) kind, so as not to have wine with too much wood. "It's fermented grape juice we aim to sell, not oak sap", a member of the firm once joked. A conveyor belt system devised by Codorníu enables the casks to be cleaned quickly; the process requires only five to seven minutes per vessel.

Four subzones

Costers del Segre acquired its *denominación de origen* in the year that Raimat's new bodega was opened, and the quality of the latter's wines was a very great inducement in this direction. The wisdom of the Spanish authorities is seen here in giving Raimat official recognition, thus avoiding the ridiculous situation that arises in other wine-growing countries where particular kinds of *vino da tavola* or *vin de pays* clearly have more class than many wines with a protective appellation or its equivalent. A subzone was created within the new DO especially for Raimat. The Raimat subzone is the only one west of Lérida; the three others are east of the town. From north to south they are Artesa, Valls de Ríu Corb, and Les Garrigues. The last two border on each other; Artesa consists of two parts and is separate from the others.

Few other producers of quality

While the Raimat wines have a high average quality, this does not apply to the products of the other zones, where far fewer of the non-traditional grape varieties are grown. The producers in the three eastern subzones sell the greater part of their wines in bulk: the Penedès Cava houses are faithful customers. The conscientious kind of bodega doing its own bottling is hardly to be found here. The undisputed star in this darkness is Cellers Castell del Remei in La Fuliola. Since 1992 it has owned 100 ha (247 acres), with grapes that include Cabernet Sauvignon, Merlot, Tempranillo, Chardonnay and Sauvignon Blanc. In addition it has invested a great deal in improving its cellars and in new equipment. Undoubtedly an increasing number of good wines will come from east of Lérida; but for the moment it is for the delightful wines of Raimat that this wine district on either side of the Segre will be known.

Above: The atmospheric bodega of Cellers Castell del Remei.

PRODUCERS OF SPECIAL INTEREST

Cellers Castell del Remei 25333
La Fuliola

In La Fuliola the Cusiné family lived by growing lucerne. Then in 1982 the Castell del Remei bodega was put up for sale and the Cusinés decided they should take it on. This complex, sited southwest of the town, consists of a castle, a chapel, a park, a restaurant, spacious cellars, and 400 ha (988 acres) of agricultural land.

A great deal of money had to be invested both in the bodega and the land. In 1983 the brothers Tomás and Manuel Cusiné started on an intensive replanting programme, while the cellars were completely renovated and modernized. Most of the 6,000 old casks were replaced with better ones. The first wine from the new owners was the Castell del Remei 1985. The Costers del Segre district had no DO at that time, but this first product was selected by a large Spanish wine club. It was made from 70 percent Tempranillo, 20 percent Cabernet Sauvignon and 10 percent Garnacha. The present Gotim Bru *crianza* has roughly the same composition and is given six months in cask. It is a refined sort of wine, with wood and fruit. The first Cabernet Sauvignon grapes from this estate were picked in 1988. That year's wine also contains 15 percent Tempranillo and has a beautiful taste that includes vanilla and toast. The Merlot is still to come into production. Of the 100 ha (247 acres) of vineyard, 7 are planted with white grapes such as Chardonnay and Sauvignon Blanc. White grapes are also bought in.

Raimat 25111 Raimat
A few decades ago, when Raimat was being developed, the Spanish government awarded it a diploma as a model enterprise. Raimat still sets an example, not only in its own region, but also for bodegas in other districts – and abroad. Planting is very thoroughly worked out and the vines growing here have been selected with the greatest possible care and expertise. The varieties grown on the 1,250 ha (3,090 acres) are, in order of importance, Cabernet Sauvignon, Chardonnay, Tempranillo, Parellada, Macabeo, Xarel-lo, Merlot, Pinot Noir and Monastrell. Besides the old cellar, dating from 1918 and modernized, the bodega has an ultra-modern complex that was built seven decades later. By 1995 there will be around 15,000 casks of 300 litre (66 gal) capacity here.

At Raimat an increasing number of excellent wines are being produced, both still and sparkling. Among them are the pale gold, regular still Chardonnay (firm, nutty aroma), and the Chardonnay Selección Especial (fermented and matured in new casks, complex in fragrance and taste). The biggest wine in terms of volume is the red Clos Abadia, made from 50 percent Cabernet Sauvignon, 35 percent Tempranillo, 12 percent Merlot, and 3 percent Garnacha (percentages may vary). This is a smooth, supple *crianza* with body to its almost peppery taste and distinct elements of wood and vanilla. Since 1987 Raimat has produced a pure Tempranillo. Besides wood and vanilla there is in this sound, pleasing wine a suggestion of ripe blackberries. Also deserving of favourable comment are the generous Merlot; the surprisingly successful Pinot Noir (a notoriously difficult grape); and the excellent, lingering, well-structured Cabernet Sauvignon (88 percent of the grape of that name, with 12 percent Merlot). These three wines are all matured in wood. The sparkling Chardonnay with its outstanding quality is brilliantly successful. It is a Cava that has a clean, exciting taste with exotic fruit in it. The *brut* Raimat (50 percent Chardonnay, 20 percent Parellada, 20 percent Macabeo, 10 percent Xarel-lo) is somewhat simpler, and for the present this wine is sold only in Spain itself. Wines from young vines have the brand name Parnàs.

Wines in this range that can be recommended are the white Garbi, the *rosado*, and Cava *brut nature*.

Vall de Valdomar 25737
Baldomar

A bodega, established 1990, that mainly processes grapes from its own 25 ha (62 acres). Its first wine was a dry, fruity rosé to which it has given the brand name Cristiari, made from half each Cabernet Sauvignon and Monastrell. White wines, such as a Riesling, and wood-aged reds with Cabernet Sauvignon and Merlot are on the way. The firm has modern equipment and uses cellars in the centuries-old Castell de Montsonis, 4 km (2½ miles) from Baldomar.

Travel Information

HOTELS AND RESTAURANTS

Restaurant del Remei, Castell del Remei, 25333 La Fuliola, tel (73) 718165 Simple establishment next door to the Cellers Castell del Remei bodega. It specializes in grilled meat dishes.

Fonda del Nastasi, N 240, 25001 Lérida, tel (73) 249222 This restaurant is 3 km (nearly 2 miles) northwest of Lérida, on the road that leads to Raimat. The cooking is reliable and very Catalan.

Forn del Nastasi, Salmerón 10, 25004 Lérida, tel (73) 234510 Locally famous restaurant, where both traditional and modern dishes can be enjoyed. Extensive wine list.

Sansi Park Hotel, Avenida Alcalde Porqueras, 25008 Lérida, tel (73) 244000 There are various hotels situated outside Lérida, but this is the biggest one in the centre of the town. It has modern rooms with double glazing, air conditioning, and a restaurant.

El Molí de la Nova, 25690 Villanueva de la Barca, tel (73) 190017 Excellent restaurant, established in an old mill. Dishes are served based on fresh fish, beef (*tournedos al cabernet*), game, and many kinds of fruit. Villanueva de la Barca lies 15 km (9.5 miles) northeast of Lérida.

PLACES OF INTEREST

Balaguer Partly walled town with a pleasant medieval square. The Romanesque San Salvador church contains fine paintings on stone. Santo Domingo has Gothic cloisters.
Bellpuig de las Avellanas Just south of here is the Santa María abbey which dates from the twelfth century.

Lérida This city, often fought over, is the capital of the province of the same name. Its nickname is *ciudad de los nombres* (city of names). In the past it has been called Iltírda, Ilerda and Lareda; and its Catalan name is Lleida. The Lérida skyline is dominated by the remains of a great fortress built on a hill, the Azuda. The old cathedral, the Seu Vella, stands within its walls. Between 1707 and 1948 this served as a barracks. In style it is Romanesque and Gothic; note the beautiful portals and cloisters. Lérida also has a "new" cathedral, dating from the eighteenth century, containing a collection of paintings. Two museums are housed in the former Santa María hospital: the Museo Arqueológico Provincial displays numerous prehistoric and other finds; the Museo Jaime Morera has over 500 works by Catalan painters (Jaime Morera, for example) and others.
Raimat For wine lovers a visit to this estate is obligatory, if only for the extraordinary contrast between the 1918 and 1988 cellar buildings (see page 55).

WINE ROUTE

This is set out so that the two key producers of Costers del Segre can be visited. These are Raimat in the subzone of the same name, and Cellers Castell del Remei in the Artesa subzone. Raimat lies along the N240 and is easy to find from signposts and the very noticeable vineyards. Cellers Castell del Remei is on the road from Bellpuig de las Avellanes to Castellserá, a few miles south of the junction with the C148.

Aragón

Capital: Zaragoza
Provinces: Huesca, Teruel, Zaragoza
Area: 47,669 square kilometres
Population: 1,214,729

The origin of Aragón goes back to the town of Jaca, strategically situated at the foot of the Pyrenees and on the left bank of the Aragón. This is where the countship of Aragón was established in AD 824; and after Ramiro I Sánchez had proclaimed Aragón to be a kingdom, in 1035, it was Jaca that functioned as its capital. However, the fact that the court eventually moved to Zaragoza, a much more centrally situated city that had been won back from the Moors in 1118, was a token of the coming development of Aragón. For its ruler at that time, Alfonso I, called El Batallador (the Battler), had expansionist plans that went far beyond being an insignificant little mountain kingdom. Not for nothing was a – temporary – alliance being sought with Navarra.

The Kingdom of Aragón

Alfonso El Batallador died before he had provided an heir to the throne and so his brother, a monk, was fetched from his monastery to oblige. The new king, Ramiro II, was successful in his task and a daughter, Petronilla, was the outcome. In due course she was given in marriage to Count Ramón Berenguer IV of Barcelona, in 1137. The result was that Aragón and Cataluña became a single kingdom with a sphere of influence that was eventually to include Murcia, the Balearics, Roussillon, Montpellier, Naples and Sicily. Jaime (or James) I, El Conquistador, greatly extended the kingdom in the thirteenth century by driving the Moors out of large areas of eastern Spain. Then in the course of the fifteenth century Aragón was united with Castilla. Once again this came about through a marriage, that of Ferdinand II of Aragón to Isabella of Castilla in 1469.

Contrasts of landscape

The present Aragón *autonomía* is roughly the same size as the eleventh-century kingdom. It is made up of three provinces: Huesca in the north, Teruel in the south, and Zaragoza between

Below: The flat, intensively cultivated valley of the Ebro surrounded by rugged mountain ranges.

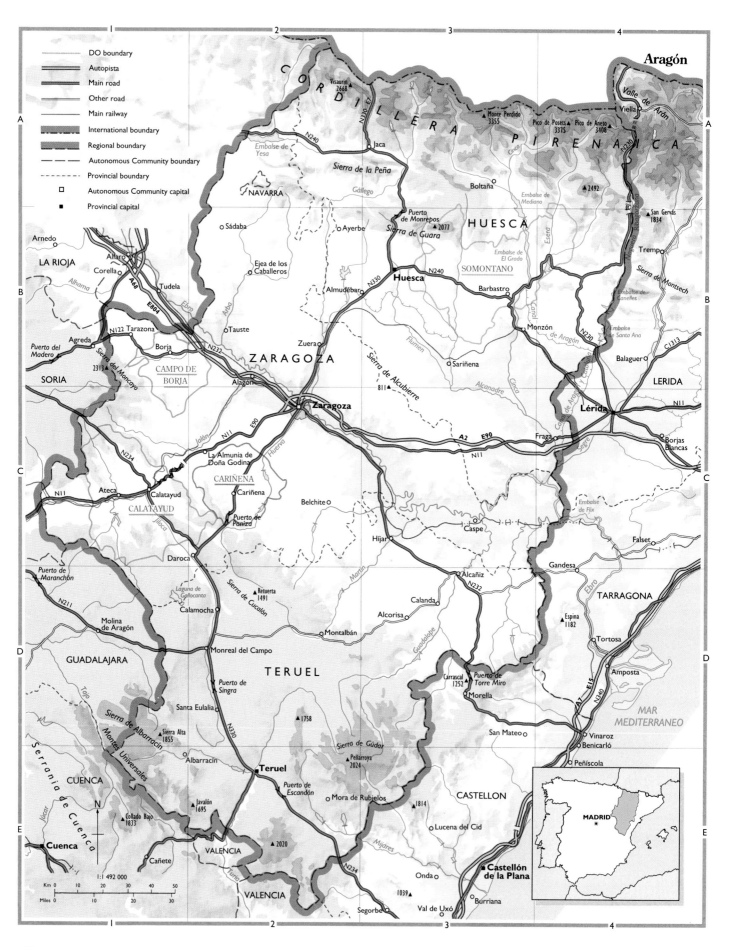

DO boundary
Autopista
Main road
Other road
Main railway
International boundary
Regional boundary
Autonomous Community boundary
Provincial boundary
□ Autonomous Community capital
■ Provincial capital

Aragón

CORDILLERA PIRENAICA

Visaurin 2668
Monte Perdido 3355
Pico de Posets 3375 ▲
Pico de Aneto 3408 ▲
Valle de Arán
Viella
N230

Jaca
N330-E7
Sierra de la Peña
N240
Embalse de Yesa
Gállego
Boltaña
Embalse de Mediano
▲ 2492
San Gervás 1834
Cinca
Esera
Noguera Ribagorzana

NAVARRA
Sádaba
Ayerbe
Puerto de Monrepos ▲ 2077
Sierra de Guara
HUESCA
Trempo
Sierra de Montsech

Arnedo
LA RIOJA
Alfaro
Corella
A68
E804
Tudela
Ejea de los Caballeros
Almudébar
N330
Huesca
N240
SOMONTANO
Barbastro
Embalse de El Grado
Monzón
Embalse de Canelles
Embalse de Santa Ana
C1313
Balaguer

N122 Tarazona
Agreda
Puerto del Madero
Sierra del Moncayo 2313 ▲
Borja
N232
Tauste
Zuera
Flumen
Sariñena
Alcanadre
Cinca
Canal de Aragón y Cataluña
LERIDA
Lérida

SORIA
CAMPO DE BORJA
ZARAGOZA
Alagón
Sierra de Alcubierre
811 ▲
N11
E90
Zaragoza
A2 E90
Fraga
N11
Segre
Borjas Blancas
N11

La Almunia de Doña Godina
N234
Jalón
Huerva
CARIÑENA
Cariñena
Belchite
Caspe
Embalse de Flix
Falset

Ateca
N11
Calatayud
CALATAYUD
Puerto de Poniza
Jiloca
Hijar
Alcañiz
N232
Gandesa
Ebro
TARRAGONA

Daroca
Puerto de Maranchón
N211
Laguna de Gallocanta
Sierra de Cucalón
Retuerta 1491
Calanda
Alcorisa
Espina 1182
Tortosa

Molina de Aragón
Calamocha
Montalbán
Guadalope
Amposta

GUADALAJARA
Monreal del Campo
TERUEL
Puerto de Singra
Carrascal 1252 ▲
Puerto de Torre Miro
Morella
E15
N340

Santa Eulalia
Sierra de Albarracín
Sierra Alta 1855
▲ 1758
Sierra de Gúdar
San Mateo
Vinaroz
Benicarló

Montes Universales
Albarracín
Peñarroya 2024
Peñíscola

Sierra de Albarracín
Teruel
Puerto de Escandón
CASTELLON
MAR MEDITERRANEO

Jávalon 1695
Mora de Rubielos
▲ 1814
CUENCA
Serranía de Cuenca
Collado Bajo 1833
N
Lucena del Cid

Cuenca
Júcar
▲ 2020
VALENCIA
Cañete
Onda
Castellón de la Plana
Burriana

1:1 492 000
Km 0   10   20   30   40   50
Miles 0   10   20   30

VALENCIA
Turia
N234
Segorbe
1039 ▲
Val de Uxó

MADRID

them. There are great contrasts of landscape here. The whole of the northern area is dominated by the Pyrenees and their weathered foothills. Streams, rivers, reservoirs and waterfalls, together with the requisite rainfall, provide green forests; but life here is hard for the small-scale growers and farmers. As you go south you find ever-larger plateaux with vines growing in places, as in the Somontano district. Further south again there stretches the steppe-like Ebro plain; the Moors discovered that only irrigation makes cultivation possible here. It is applied on a large scale and the river basin grows large amounts of fruit and vegetables. A continental climate prevails, with long, harsh winters and a scorching summer sun. The city of Zaragoza in the middle of the river valley is often plagued by a cold mountain wind. How the plain would look without irrigation is clear from the Monégros, a desert-like area between Zaragoza and Lérida; you would think yourself in North Africa here. To the south of the river valley the terrain again becomes very rugged, with low hills leading up to mountains, as in the wine regions of Cariñena and Calatayud. The river valleys in this latter area grow many other fruits beside the grapes, including pears, cherries, and splendid peaches.

Mudéjar architecture

Besides contrasts in landscape, Aragón also has contrasts in architecture. Part of the north was never conquered by the Moors; they were in fact beaten back at Jaca in 760. Also, pilgrims travelled through the north for centuries, on their way to or from Santiago de Compostela, and here the architectural style is decidedly Romanesque. However, south of the Ebro, which often formed the frontier between Christians and Moors, the architecture shows strong Arabic influences. In particular the Mudéjar style, the work of Muslims under Christian rule, is present everywhere. The brick church towers in the provinces of Teruel and Zaragoza are among Spain's most beautiful examples of Mudéjar art. You can even follow a Mudéjar trail through the area.

Country cooking

Aragonese cuisine is very rustic in character and makes use mainly of simple ingredients. *Chilindrón*, a substantial sauce of peppers, tomato, onions and garlic, is famous; on feast days chicken and lamb are prepared with it. *Esparragos montañés* is a dish that can give rise to misunderstanding, for this is no "mountain asparagus", but lamb's tail stewed with tomatoes. Garlic soup with egg and almonds is warming during the cold winters and *migas*, pieces of crusty bread, taste extremely good with it. Numbers of restaurants have *costillas*, or spare ribs, on their menus. Ham from Teruel (which has its own *denominación de origen*) is a delicacy that is served in various ways.

Winegrowing

The history of wine in Aragón goes back a very long way, certainly to Roman times, and has continued more or less without interruption ever since. But in terms of quality it is only since the 1980s that this *autonomía* has really given an account of itself. Before this the various districts mainly produced very heavy wines, particularly those from Cariñena which could often have a natural alcohol content of at least 17 to 18 percent. The wine was also distinguished by its dark, purply red colour. The red wines were therefore almost exclusively made for blending with lighter wines. At the height of the phylloxera epidemic in France, in the nineteenth century, a great deal of this wine was shipped to Bordeaux, where it was in great demand.

Top: Nesting storks are a familiar sight in northern Spain.
Bottom: Detail from the Aljafería, the 11th-century Moorish palace in Zaragoza.

Up till recently, most of the wines continued to be sold in bulk, and the majority of the bodegas (90 percent of them cooperatives) were working with the equipment of a generation ago. But now, all this has been changing at express speed. Many producers have acquired modern equipment, or intend to do so; and in their wines they are increasingly seeking for fruit, freshness and refinement. They have realised that the highly alcoholic, heavy wines are unsuitable for export markets, and the minimum alcohol content for red Cariñena has now been reduced to 12 percent.

New varieties

New grape varieties have come in to replace or complement Garnacha, whose high sugar content was in the past responsible for such potent, highly alcoholic wines. These new grapes are most strongly represented in Somontano; but in Cariñena the proportion of both Tempranillo and Mazuelo is rising. Tempranillo is also present in Campo de Borja and Calatayud, the other two DOs. All this has made the wines of Aragón a good deal more interesting than hitherto. Under the guidance of viticultural stations advice is also offered, and experiments conducted, outside the DOs as well as in them. This has brought very promising results in, for example, Valdejalón, a district between Cariñena, Campo de Borja and Calatayud. The Garnacha is totally dominant, but seems to be able to give astonishingly good wines here – provided that there is about 25 percent Tempranillo included. In Bajo Aragón, the biggest non-DO area, the light reds and rosés are beginning to claim attention. Signs of progress are as yet less obvious in Alto Jiloca-Daroca (red) and Muniesa (red).

Above: Castillo de Loarre, Aragón.
Right: Vineyard near Barbastro, below the Monasterio del Pueyo.

Somontano

In 1100 Barbastro, established where Roman roads crossed, was finally liberated from the Moors. Here 37 years later a meeting took place between the rulers of Aragón and Cataluña at which it was decided to unite the two states into a single kingdom. At the same time a marriage was arranged between Princess Petronilla of Aragón and Count Ramón Berengher IV of Barcelona. Later the town acquired a cathedral and became the seat of an archbishop. Until the nineteenth century Barbastro was greatly renowned for its cattle markets. Since then the glories of the past have gradually dimmed and for decades the town has attracted little notice. Thanks to wine, however, this may well change; for Barbastro today is the centre of Somontano, Aragón's most promising wine district.

The name Somontano ("at the foot of the mountains") perfectly conveys the character of the district, which consists of a natural amphitheatre at the foot of the Pyrenees. Most of its 2,000 ha (4,950 acres) of vineyards are on a large plateau of broken ground north of Barbastro, with loose soil which often contains a reddish-brown limestone. In places olive and almond trees grow among the vines. To the south the Monasterio de Pueyo, built on a steep hill, forms a striking point of reference. The river Vero winds through the plateau, which is bounded to east and west by two more rivers, the Cinca and the Alcanadre. Mountains from 700 to 1,100 m high (2,300 to 3,600 ft) form a barrier to the north that to some extent protects the area from the biting Pyrenean winds, so it does not usually get as cold in Somontano as in other parts of Aragón – in Zaragoza, for example. The summers are dry, but enough rain falls in winter and spring to allow winegrowing to be carried on without problems. The average annual rainfall is almost 500 mm (20 ins); and in addition the rivers bring in the necessary amount of moisture. The area does not escape the cooling influence of the Pyrenees, with an average annual temperature of 11°C (51.8°F). This is some two to three degrees Celsius lower than in Aragón's other wine districts.

Grape varieties

Grape varieties different from those usually grown in Aragón can readily be cultivated in Somontano, thanks to its cooler, more humid type of climate. Since the late 1980s the Compañia Vitivinícola del Somontano has been planting hundreds of acres with new black varieties that include Cabernet Sauvignon, Merlot, and Pinot Noir; and new white varieties such as Chardonnay and Gewürztraminer. This firm has ultra-modern equipment for winemaking. The first wines from these new vineyards came on the market at the beginning of 1990 and their high quality caused surprise. Since then this firm has gone on steadily building up its reputation – and thereby that of the whole district as well.

Cabernet Sauvignon, Merlot and Chardonnay were already there on the estate of Bodegas Lalanne, a winery founded here by Frenchmen in the nineteenth century. Yet so far results have been disappointing; the reason undoubtedly lies in vinification with out-of-date plant. Technological improvements can, however, be expected, for so powerful has been the illuminating influence of the Compañia Vitivinícola del Somontano that the other five producers simply cannot let themselves be left behind. Thus the Somontano de Sobrarbe cooperative – by far the biggest producer – has invested in a battery of stainless-steel fermentation tanks

Above: Thousands of pilgrims visit the Santuario de Torreciudad every year.

and the cooling equipment that goes with them. In addition, of the 900 ha (2,225 acres) owned by its members, more than 25 percent has now been planted with Cabernet Sauvignon.

Moristel

The advance of these new varieties in Somontano does not mean that all the native grapes will be discarded. The proportion of Garnacha vines will decrease, but that of Tempranillo – already present in large measure – will increase considerably. Moristel, too, will remain in abundance; the cooperative's members have something in the order of 400 ha (990 acres) planted with it. According to the Somontano growers Moristel is closely related to the Monastrell grape, but definitely not identical to it – as is often maintained. The wine from this strictly regional grape has a well-defined character of its own, with a distinct scent of berries, a suggestion of spice, and great suppleness. It is more apt to oxidize than Tempranillo and therefore is not suitable on its own for long maturing in wood. Surprisingly enough, until the mid-1980s Moristel was practically always mixed with other grapes. This changed when Steve Metzler, an American importer, tasted a pure Moristel from one of the cooperative's tanks. Metzler, who specialized in Spanish quality wines, became so enthusiastic that he ordered several thousand bottles of pure Moristel. The wine from this and subsequent vintages was warmly received in the United States by experts and consumers alike. Indeed, it has often been compared to a Beaujolais. With this grape and the new varieties, Somontano holds most of the aces in Aragonese winegrowing. The way these advantages are made use of in the coming years will determine the success of this wine district.

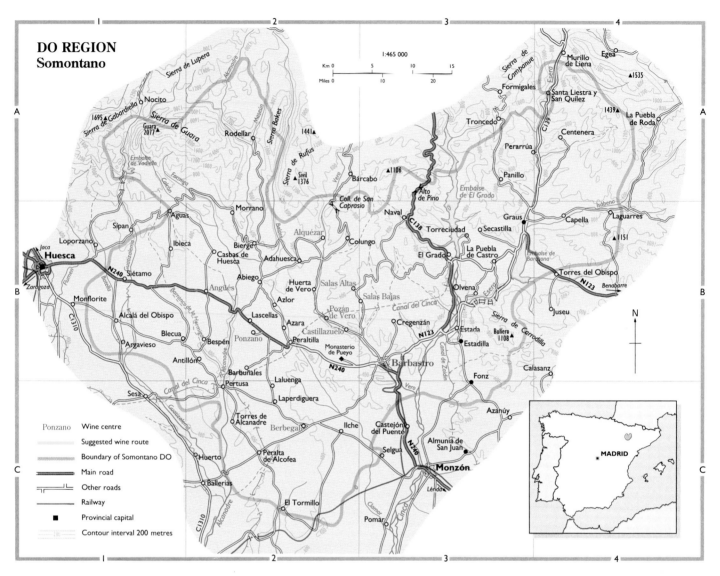

DO REGION
Somontano

1:465 000

Km 0   5   10   15
Miles 0   10   20

Ponzano — Wine centre

⎯⎯ Suggested wine route

⎯⎯ Boundary of Somontano DO

⎯⎯ Main road

⎯⎯ Other roads

⎯⎯ Railway

■ Provincial capital

⎯⎯ Contour interval 200 metres

Above: The Moorish castle which stands above the wine village of Alquezar. In the village itself the Plaza Mayor is well worth a visit.

PRODUCERS OF SPECIAL INTEREST

Bodega Cooperativa Somontano de Sobrarbe 22300 Barbastro
This cooperative, about 30 years old, has been rejuvenated since the beginning of 1990, acquiring stainless-steel fermentation tanks and other modern equipment. In addition, the concern has built itself an underground cellar. The members (about 500) work some 900 ha (2,225 acres), which makes this Somontano's biggest producer. Roughly 400 ha (990 acres) are planted with Moristel, and more than 25 ha (62 acres) with Cabernet Sauvignon. At present a third of production is bottled, but this proportion will certainly be increased. The best red wine for drinking young is the pure Moristel, with its taste of berries and touch of spice, which goes under the brand name of Montesierre. The same name is used for a wine with 50 to 60 percent Moristel, the rest being Tempranillo. A fairly recent creation combines Cabernet Sauvignon with Tempranillo.

A more traditional kind of red wine is represented by the Señorío de Lazán, a *crianza* with about 80 percent Tempranillo and 20 percent Moristel. This type may yet lose its rusticity and gain in quality if the cooperative speeds up the replacement of its 500 or so casks. Both the white Montesierra (100 percent Macabeo) and the rosé (various grapes) have gained in fruit and freshness since the arrival of steel casks.

Bodegas Lalanne 22300 Barbastro
In 1894 the Lalanne family from Barsac in Bordeaux decided to settle in Somontano. Their winery was established a few miles out of Barbastro – near where the cooperative stands now – and plantings included such Bordeaux grapes as Cabernet Sauvignon and

Merlot. The family went on to produce sparkling as well as still wines. At present Bodegas Lalanne owns 16 ha (40 acres) of vineyards; grapes are also bought in. The cellars, above and below ground, have a good deal of atmosphere, but also show that the firm now needs to modernize its equipment: the wines will then undoubtedly gain in quality.

Of the present range the reds are preferable by far: for example, the Laura Lalanne (made from four grape varieties, with Cabernet Sauvignon and Merlot accounting for half); the Lalanne *crianza* (40 percent Moristel, 30 percent Cabernet Sauvignon, 20 percent Merlot); and the Viña San Marcos about eight years old (60 percent Moristel, 30 percent Tempranillo, 10 percent Cabernet Sauvignon). The white and rosé wines, which are aged in wood, lack freshness.

Bodegas Borruel 21124 Ponzano
A small producer who makes San Lorenzo (80 percent Moristel), an engaging red wine. Most of the grapes come from the firm's own vineyard of just under 15 ha (37 acres).

Compañia Vitivinícola del Somontano 22314 Salas Bajas
This young firm has been operating since 1987 and leads Somontano in terms of quality. Its equipment is very modern and includes all stainless-steel fermentation tanks, a pneumatic grape press and apparatus that allows the skins of white grapes to remain in the must at low temperature.

This concern, which belongs to the Daysa group, has a cellar with a 2,500-cask capacity. It buys casks of French and American oak. The area under vine totals 600 ha (1,480 acres). About a quarter of this grows native varieties such as Moristel. In addition there are Cabernet Sauvignon (about 20 percent), Chardonnay (15 percent), Tempranillo (10 percent), Merlot (10 percent), Pinot Noir (10 percent), and some 10 percent of other varieties including Gewürztraminer. When the vineyards are fully productive, an annual volume of 400,000 cases can be reached.

The firm's first wines, of the Viñas del Vero brand, showed exemplary quality both in red (including a Cabernet Sauvignon *crianza*) and in white: Chenin Blanc, Gewürztraminer, Riesling and two Chardonnays, one normal and one fermented in new casks.

Travel Information

HOTELS AND RESTAURANTS

Flor, Goya 3, 22300 Barbastro, tel (74) 311056. Elegant restaurant that besides regional dishes serves more cosmopolitan fare. The best place to eat in Somontano.

Rey Sancho Ramírez, N120, 22300 Barbastro, tel (74) 310050. Hotel just west of Barbastro with friendly service. Take a room as far from the road – and the discothèque – as possible. Has a swimming pool as well as a restaurant.

Hostería El Tozal, 22390 El Grado, tel (74) 304000. Small, very quietly situated hotel and restaurant on the road to Artasona. With pleasant views of the surrounding area this is the best place to stay.

Tres Caminos, 22390 El Grado, tel (74) 304052. A simple hotel and restaurant that offers traditional cuisine (wild boar, partridge, fresh fish) which is very good value.

PLACES OF INTEREST

Alquézar Beautifully situated wine village at the foot of a castle built by the Moors and later altered. Next to the castle is a small church and cloisters with frescos. The Plaza Mayor in this village is very atmospheric.

Barbastro Close to the shaded *rambla* in the centre of this community of 15,000 inhabitants are the late Gothic cathedral and the sixteenth-century town hall. Two Flemish tapestries hang in the archbishop's palace. Since 1989 the grape harvest has been celebrated in Barbastro in the second half of October, signalling the rise of Somontano as a wine district.

Graus Photogenic village with numerous old houses whose fronts carry coats of arms or are otherwise adorned (particularly those around the Plaza de España).

Monasterio de Pueyo Worth visiting, especially for the view over the whole of Somontano. The monastery is built on a steep rock just west of Barbastro along the N240.

Torreciudad On the initiative of a priest from Barbastro a huge sanctuary was built here in honour of the Virgen de los Angeles. It draws thousands of pilgrims annually from all over the world and offers a panoramic view of the El Grado reservoir.

WINE ROUTE

The two circuits as plotted show various aspects of Somontano, including the plateau with its vineyards, the most important wine communities, some of the nicest-looking villages, and the mountain landscape around the reservoirs of El Grado and Barasona.

Below: Romanesque cloisters in the church of San Pedro El Viejo, Huesca.

Cariñena

For generations the red wines of Cariñena were almost exclusively made for blending with lighter wines. They had so much colour that someone described the bodegas of the time as "dye works", while their alcohol content was usually 17 to 18 percent, achieved in a natural way by harvesting the grapes as late as possible. Until 1990 even the minimum alcohol content for red Cariñena was 14 percent. This has since been lowered to 12 percent, but many producers still have difficulty in giving up the habits of days gone by. So it was that at a small firm in Almonacid de la Sierra I sampled attractive white, red and rosé wines for drinking young. My only point of criticism was that I thought they had rather too much alcohol. To this the owner's reaction was: "But alcohol belongs in Cariñena". Then he cajoled me into visiting his underground cellar where, besides a dining and tasting room, there were large wooden casks which proved to contain oxidized rosés. Proudly my host revealed their alcohol content: 18.4 percent and even 19.5. The latter had an almost liqueur-like taste.

Climate

That such potent wines can emerge from Cariñena is partly due to the dry Aragonese climate. Moreover, the area is surrounded by mountain ranges which have a sheltering effect. The harsh, cold *el scherzo* wind that blows from the Pyrenees towards Zaragoza – with the Galileo valley acting rather as a wind tunnel – is somewhat less fierce in Cariñena. This area and the small town of the same name in fact lie some 50 km (30 miles) southwest of Zaragoza at a height of about 300 m (980 ft). The average annual rainfall is 480 mm (18.9 ins). A large part of the vineyard area stretches over a reddish, slightly undulating plateau with hard stony soil. It is mainly planted with Garnacha, a vine that bears grapes with a very high sugar content, and thus gives potent wines. There are also vineyards on the outlying slopes of the Sierra de Algairén, a mountain ridge with peaks above 1,200 m (3,950 ft) directly to the west of Cariñena. The soil is lighter here, and is used for most of the other grape varieties grown.

Above: Local wine for sale in Cariñena.

In Cariñena, as elsewhere in Spain, the wine industry is busy breaking with the past. One step in that direction was the lowering of the minimum alcohol content, as has been mentioned. In addition, making red wines from Garnacha alone is more and more giving way to the use of this grape blended with other varieties. The proportion of Garnacha – still 52 percent at the end of the 1980s – will therefore gradually decrease. The cooperatives are playing a key role in this process of change, for they produce more than three-quarters of all the wine here. The large Cooperativa San Valero with its modern plant is encouraging its members (about 950 of them) to plant Tempranillo. By the beginning of the 1990s this had already resulted in its members having 35 to 40 percent Tempranillo vines, significantly above the 10 percent average for the area. The cooperative hopes to have reached 60 percent by 1995. Another black grape that can produce good results is Cabernet Sauvignon. This has been officially permitted in the *denominación de origen* since 1990. Bodegas Martínez Gutiérrez has planted some 4 ha (10 acres) with it, and the Cooperativa San Valero has experimented on a small scale with this grape. Other bodegas are also looking into the possibilities of Cabernet Sauvignon. At the Zaragoza oenological station I was given a most palatable, elegant and fruity Cabernet Sauvignon rosé from Cariñena to taste. However, growing this variety is a problem, for in Cariñena's hot, dry summers it has to be regularly watered. In addition, Cabernet Sauvignon is best planted on the higher ground where the soil is lighter, fresher and has lime, so any increase in this variety will be modest.

Mazuelo

Another variety, one that is characteristic of Cariñena, is Mazuelo (often called Mazuela). Locally it is also known as Cariñena, because it presumably originated in this area. It is also present to a modest extent in Rioja and elsewhere, and it is very closely related – if not identical – to the French Carignan. Mazuelo has the advantage of giving a wine with a good deal of acid and tannin; Garnacha wines gain structure and ageing potential from it. The disadvantage of this variety is its susceptibility to mildew and other diseases. At present around 18 percent of the vines are Mazuelo, and this proportion will probably increase. Pure Garnacha wines are being produced less and less, and if they are made, they are usually intended for quick consumption. This is true of both red and rosé wines. The future seems to lie with blends of Garnacha with Tempranillo or Mazuelo in which the proportion of Garnacha will continue to be reduced. There are already wines available that are only half Garnacha; and it is in the cask-aged *crianzas*, *reservas* and *gran reservas* that it will diminish quickest. The blended wines seem to have more depth than the pure Garnacha offerings and stand up better to spending time in cask.

White wines

When Cariñena celebrates the grape harvest around September 15, with a wine show included in the festivities, whites are served as well as reds and rosés. Of the total vineyard area of about 21,600 ha (51,900 acres), a fifth is planted with white grapes, with a great preponderance of Macabeo. Garnacha Blanca and Moscatel Romano are also grown, and since 1990 Parellada has been allowed. For the wineries that ferment Macabeo at a low temperature, this grape produces fresh, light, fruity and lively wines. All that they lack is an individual personality. Perhaps use of such additional techniques as skin contact and blending with Parellada may bring improvement.

PRODUCERS OF SPECIAL INTEREST

Bodega Cooperativa San José
50408 Aguarón
The white buildings of this cooperative can be seen on the way into the peaceful village of Aguarón with its surrounding wine slopes. The concern has 400 members who cultivate about 2,000 ha (4,950 acres). Until the 1989 vintage the wines were at best of middling quality, but the average standard has risen somewhat thanks to the arrival of stainless-steel fermentation tanks. The best are sold under the Monasterio de las Viñas brand name.

Manuel Moneva Muela y Hijos
50108 Almonacid de la Sierra
Most of the grapes this family firm processes come from its own 40 ha (99 acres). From the vines planted here it is clear that the changes to the varieties grown are well advanced: Tempranillo and Mazuelo altogether cover 24 ha (59 acres) of the estate, exactly twice the area growing Garnacha. This bodega has concrete tanks, cooling equipment and, since 1989, a shiny new bottling line. Prizes were won with the vintage of that year, the rosé and the white wine taking first prize at the grape harvest celebrations. Both wines are generally characterized by a good deal of fruit in scent and taste, combined with a pleasing freshness. Their alcohol content is usually around 18 percent. This is also the case with the firm, quite meaty red wine and this, too, has fruit. These wines for drinking young carry the brand name Viña Vadina. Tío Manuel is used for an old-fashioned type of Garnacha wine with 15 percent alcohol.

Bodegas Martínez Gutiérrez 50108
Almonacid de la Sierra
This winery, which dates from 1780, comprises a large hall with subsidiary buildings above the village of Almonacid de la Sierra. Here wines are made from the firm's own 15 ha (37 acres), and also from a few dozen other vineyards under contract. In addition wine is bought in from cooperatives. In his own vineyards the owner, Jesús Martínez, has 3 ha (7.5 acres) planted with Tempranillo and 4 ha (10 acres) with Cabernet Sauvignon. The vines of this latter variety grow quite high up on a hillside and there are sprinklers to water them if necessary. Martínez advocates making wines that are not too heavy. He therefore has the grapes

Above: A wine fair takes place annually in Cariñena around the middle of September. During the fiesta wine flows from this fountain, which stands in front of the 16th-century Renaissance-style ayuntamiento.

picked earlier than is customary for the area (normally Cariñena harvests from September 10 to mid-October). Viña Valerma is a very pleasant red wine for drinking young, a somewhat spicy, fruity blend of 70 percent Garnacha and 30 percent Mazuelo. At the beginning of the 1980s the Señorio de la Obra, aged in tanks and in casks, was almost pure Garnacha. It now consists of 60 percent Garnacha, 30 percent Tempranillo and 10 percent Mazuelo, which has improved the quality. For enthusiasts there is the 70-year-old *rancio*, the Gran Paulet.

Bodega Cooperativa San Valero
50400 Cariñena
Roughly half the wine that Aragón exports comes from this cooperative, founded in 1944, which is housed in a large, craggy building on the outskirts of Cariñena. There are approximately 950 growers who together own 1,300 ha (3,210 acres) of vineyards. The cooperative promotes the planting of high-quality varieties, particularly the Tempranillo. By 1995 this will represent 60 percent of production. In its own experimental vineyard it is conducting trials with Cabernet Sauvignon and other grapes.

Despite the considerable volume involved, the cooperative is able to make successful, often prize-winning wines. Among them are the Don Mendo rosé (100 percent Garnacha) and the still fresher, more vital Monte Ducay rosé (90 percent Garnacha, 10 percent Tempranillo). The Monte Ducay white (100 percent Macabeo) also has commendable quality.

Among the reds Don Mendo (Garnacha, with 30 percent Tempranillo and some Mazuelo) is characterized by a pleasing, almost jam-like aroma and a supple taste. The Monte Ducay red *crianza* (55 percent Garnacha, 35 percent Tempranillo, 10 percent Mazuelo) is given six months ageing in cask and a further six months in bottle. It is an attractive, mellow but quite firm wine with a tinge of wood and dusty fruit. There is also a *gran reserva* (40 percent Tempranillo) with the same name, which as well as greater maturity also offers more wood and vanilla. The Marqués de Tosos *reserva* forms an intermediate quality. San Valero also produces a sparkling wine, Gran Ducay, from grapes bought in from Penedés. This lacks class, however, and is characterized by a rather earthy taste.

Vinícola Cariñena (Vincar) 50400 Cariñena
A firm with up-to-date equipment, it works exclusively on the basis of bought-in grapes and wines. The white Viña Oria (100 percent Macabeo) and the rosé (100 percent Garnacha) are among the region's better wines. The slightly fruity red *crianza* (80 percent Garnacha, 20 percent Mazuelo) has a quite elegant structure and a refined taste with wood and vanilla in it.

Travel Information

HOTELS AND RESTAURANTS

Mesón El Escudo 50400 Cariñena, tel (76) 620081. This restaurant on the Zaragoza road is the best place to eat in the area. Well-prepared regional dishes are served at very acceptable prices.

Hostal Cariñena, 50400 Cariñena, tel (76) 620250. Simple hotel on the N330, almost opposite the San Valero cooperative. The restaurant serves local dishes.

El Balcón, 50480 Paniza, tel (76) 620518. Situated by the Puerto de Paniza mountain pass, so the view is splendid. Straightforward cuisine with good meat dishes.

PLACES OF INTEREST

Aguarón Can be reached from Cariñena via a beautiful route through undulating vineyard country. Part of an old castle wall still stands in this peaceful wine village. A few miles further into the mountains, to the right of the road, is the convent of Nuestra Señora de las Viñas.

Almonacid de la Sierra Situated at the foot of castle ruins it has some very old houses, a pleasant church square (with a covered market dated 1904) and many underground wine cellars, marked by their ventilation shafts.

Cariñena The origins of this little town, the centre of the wine district, go back to prehistory. In the late nineteenth century so much wine was being exported from Cariñena to France that the Bordeaux house of Violet even opened a branch here. The church of La Asunción is interesting, built of brick in the baroque style. One of the altarpieces has reliefs depicting the secrets of the rosary. The *ayuntamiento* dates from the sixteenth century; in Renaissance style, it has a gallery and round-arched doorways. During the grape harvest celebrations (September 15) the fountain in front gushes not water but wine. The Santiago chapel was formerly a mosque.

Cosuenda Atmospheric village on a hillside surmounted by the remains of a castle.

Fuendetodos Francisco de Goya was born here in 1746. The birthplace of the renowned painter is still standing, and is now a museum.

Longares Old village with a fine church where there is an Ecce Homo worth seeing. The tower is in Mudéjar style.

Muel In the fifteenth and sixteenth centuries this place was already known for its pottery. Near the park along the Río Huerva is the Ermita de Nuestra Señora de la Fuente, where the young Goya painted four frescos.

Puerto de Paniza Pass about 900 m (2,950 ft) high offering a splendid view over a landscape of vineyards, and the town of Cariñena.

Zaragoza This great city about 50 km (30 miles) from Cariñena has many monuments. The cathedral of Nuestra Señora del Pilar is the most impressive of them, standing beside the Ebro and built in various styles. Its silhouette is characterized by tall towers at the corners, a dome and numerous cupolas. Goya painted a fresco over the choir. La Aljafería was originally a Moorish palace, which might be expected in Andalucia rather than Aragón, and has an abundance of vaulting. One room is the prison cell made famous in Verdi's *Il Trovatore*. The Lonja is a fine sixteenth-century exchange near the cathedral where exhibitions are regularly held. Not far from here is the former metropolitan church of La Seo, built in various styles, where Flemish and French tapestries are among the objects on display.

WINE ROUTE

With Cariñena as its central point, the wine route leads through the most attractive parts of the area, and the nicest villages. There are three short trips to places outside the actual wine district that are also suggested: to Fuendetodos (Goya's birthplace), the monastery of Nuestra Señora de las Viñas, and the observation point at the Puerto de Paniza pass. Connection with the Calatayud route can be made via the very winding C221. The town of that name can also be reached via La Almunia de Doña Godina and the N11.

Left: The winegrowing landscape between Cariñena and Aguaron.

DO REGIONS
Cariñena
Calatayud
Campo de Borja

Miedes	Wine centre
	Suggested wine routes
	Boundary of Cariñena DO
	Boundary of Calatayud DO
	Boundary of Campo de Borja DO
	Autopista
	Main road
	Other roads
	Railway
	Provincial boundary
■	Provincial capital
	Contour interval 200 metres

1:440 000

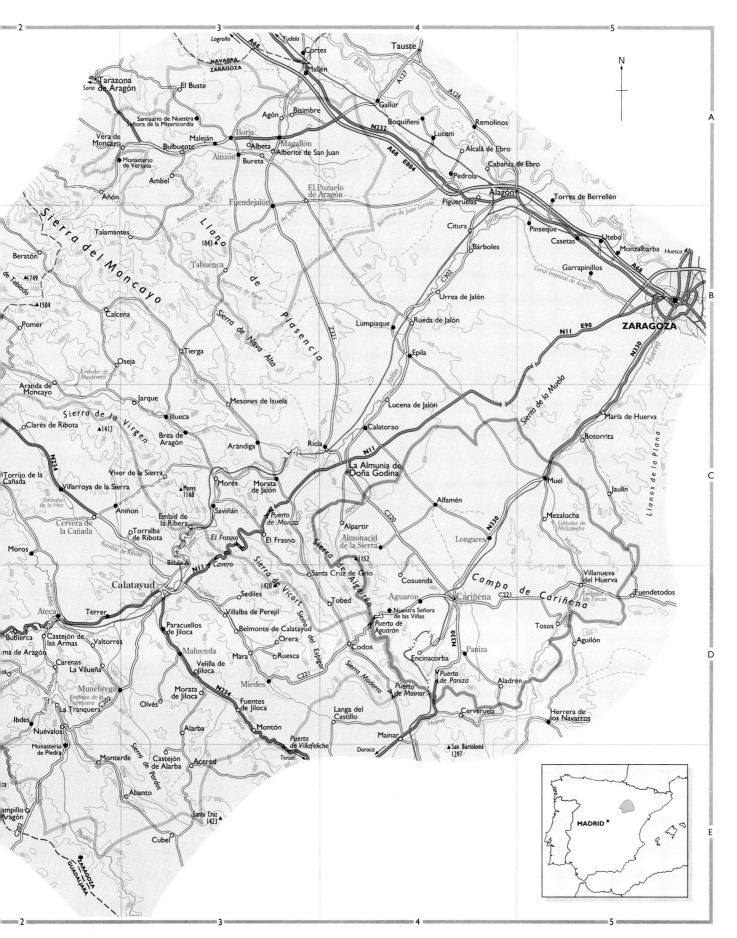

Calatayud

The Celtic settlement of Bilbilis was renamed Bilbilis Augusta by the Romans. Excavations show that they built a temple, theatre and bathhouses. Marcus Valerius Martial, who lived in the first century AD, was born here and at the age of 23 journeyed to Rome, where he not only described life among the ruling classes in satirical vein, but also praised the wines of Bilbilis – where he was to spend the last years of his life. In the eighth century the Moors built a castle, the *calat* of the ruler Ayub, on a hill not far from Bilbilis. The town that grew up around it acquired the name of Calatayud. Today it is a dusty, untidy sort of place, serving as the centre of the wine district that was made a *denominación de origen* at the beginning of 1990. So, 20 centuries after being praised by a Roman, the wines have been officially recognized in Spain.

Fertile valleys

The town of Calatayud lies in the valley of the Jalón, on the busy N11 which links Madrid and Barcelona. The distance to Zaragoza to the northeast is slightly under 90 km (56 miles). Cariñena is only 35 km (22 miles) away, but the climate in the two wine districts is different. In Calatayud it is somewhat moister, with an average annual rainfall of 510 mm (20 ins), and half a degree Celsius cooler, so the grapes are picked later. The vineyards are found at a height of 500 to 700 m (1,640 to 2,300 ft), and even at an exceptional 1,000 m (3,280 ft). They are mostly in the valleys of the small tributaries that feed the Jalón. Most of the valley land is heavily planted with fruit trees. Calatayud produces apples, pears, cherries and other fruits, and the area is known throughout Spain for its luscious peaches. The 11,000 ha (27,181 acres) of vines are usually grown around the margins of the valleys. They are also found on the uneven ground of plateaux – as along the C202, which leads from Calatayud to the Monasterio de Piedra. Sometimes almond orchards are interspersed among the vineyards. Running parallel with most of the rivers here are considerable mountain ranges, which form part of the Iberian massif. The Sierra de la Virgen (1,427 m/4,682 ft), Sierra de Vicort (1,411 m/4,629 ft) and Sierra de Algairén (1,279 m/4,196 ft) screen the area off from the Ebro valley. The Sierra del Caballero (1,147 m/3,763 ft) and Sierra de Pardos (1,423 m/4,669 ft) form a natural boundary to the south.

Varieties

Mainly black grapes are cultivated here in the loose, stony soil. In the first place comes Garnacha, with about a 60 percent share, while Tempranillo accounts for 20 percent. In contrast to many other wine areas the planting of replacement varieties is little encouraged here, if at all. One bodega, Langa, has planted some Cabernet Sauvignon, but I found the wine made from it (which also contained some Tempranillo) to be disappointing; Cabernet Sauvignon is not even accepted within this DO. The third most important grape is Macabeo, called Viura here. This leaves 4 percent made up of various other kinds.

Modernization

Although the *Consejo Regulador* is largely content with the wine varieties in their present proportions – except for wanting to increase the percentage of Tempranillo – numerous changes are being carried through in the cellars. This has brought about considerable investment, especially in the cooperatives, which produce more than 80 percent of the wine here. Stainless-steel fermentation tanks and cooling equipment have already appeared on a large scale, and this process will continue. On the other hand large halls above or below ground for lines of vats are not being built, for throughout this district the aim is fruity wines that can be drunk young.

Rosés

Because of this emphasis on young wines, the accent is being laid more and more on rosés. These now represent around a third of production, but this may still increase, especially if the home market drinks more dry *rosados* and international demand for them develops. Garnacha makes a good basic ingredient for rosés, the more so since this grape gives less heady wines in Calatayud than, for example, in Cariñena. The trick is simply to pick the Garnacha grapes in their optimal condition (this calls for full information to the growers) and then to vinify them to perfection.

At the Bodega Cooperativa San Alejandro in Miedes I sampled the difference between an ordinarily made rosé and one from stainless-steel tanks. The second wine had more fruit and tasted lighter, fresher – and significantly better than the first. With the red wines, too, modern techniques have brought about improvements. In the best kinds the fruit that is so much sought after is clearly present, and in addition they soon develop suppleness. Charm is the key word for Calatayud red. It is obvious that the whites too have benefited from low-temperature fermentation in steel tanks.

Bottling

For long the district concentrated mainly on bulk sales. However, with the arrival of the protective DO the proportion of bottled wines has kept on increasing. A great leap forward came with the opening of Embico, a collective bottling enterprise comprising six cooperatives and Bodegas Gabriel Ibarra. It is situated next door to the Miedes cooperative and became operational at the end of 1990. Since Calatayud has only 14 bodegas, this means that adequate bottling plant is available to two-thirds of all producers, while private concerns such as Langa already had such equipment. The next challenge for Calatayud is to sell its bottled wine, for it is as yet little known outside its own region.

PRODUCERS OF SPECIAL INTEREST

Bodegas Gabriel Ibarra 50300 Calatayud

A firm that is run with great zest and sells a lot of its wine in cask (it has some 10,000 of these), but more and more in bottle. The wines strongly resemble those of the San Alejandro Cooperative at Miedes, with which commercial agreements have been made. The red, white and rosé are all of good average quality and are agreeably fruity. They are meant for quick consumption and are sold under the Marqués de Sandañon brand name.

Bodegas Langa Hermanos 50300 Calatayud

A family business on the N11, which was founded in 1982. The firm's own vineyards – nearly 20 ha (50 acres) – provide 30 percent of the grapes required. The owners, José Langa Fuentes and his sister María Teresa, have planted Cabernet Sauvignon, Chardonnay and Chenin Blanc as well as the usual grape varieties. Both the white grapes are used for Cava, stylishly presented but weak in the glass (a special cellar has been constructed underground for it). The Cabernet Sauvignon blended with some Tempranillo produces a less than brilliant wine. This is indeed characteristic of all the wines here, including the ordinary kinds that carry the Portalet name. Remarkably enough Bodegas Langa Hermanos is well equipped technically; the potential here is simply not exploited to the full.

Cooperativa del Campo San Isidro 50340 Maluenda

Together the 1,000 members here own around 4,000 ha (9,880 acres) of vineyard, which makes this the biggest of Calatayud's cooperatives. The concern has invested lavishly in stainless-steel tanks for its red, white and rosé wines for drinking young; and it now has its own bottling line. The Viña Alarbra rosé is usually the best wine, and is supple and fruity in taste. The white of the same brand is rather less vivacious, but a very decent product nevertheless. Bringing up the rear is the red, for drinking young.

Cooperativa Comarcal del Campo San Alejandro 50330 Miedes

This was the first of the cooperatives in the area to install stainless-steel fermentation tanks and cooling equipment. Since the 1990 vintage all the wines here have been fermented at relatively low temperatures. They are characterized by their fruit and freshness. The *rosado* is excellent, the white pure, and the charming red wine contains about 25 percent Tempranillo. The brand name is Marqués Nombrevilla. There are about 500 members here and they cultivate a total of 1,400 ha (3,460 acres). A joint bottling plant, the Embico, has been built nearby, where wines from five other cooperatives as well as from Bodegas Gabriel Ibarra are bottled.

Cooperativa Comarcal del Campo Virgen del Mar y de la Cuesta 50219 Munébrega

The 450 members of this

Above: Valley near Miedes, with vineyards as well as fruit trees and other cultivation.

cooperative work 450 ha (1,110 acres). Garnacha is predominant, with about 75 percent; the percentage of Tempranillo, however, is steadily increasing. The stainless-steel tanks on the premises are used to vinify the better wines, which are bottled at Miedes. The white wine is very decent, the rosé rather livelier, with more fruit. The red is made principally from Garnacha grapes, with some Tempranillo. It is a supple wine, rounded out and with fruit. This cooperative uses the brand name La Olmedilla.

Above: Thanks to stainless-steel fermentation tanks and cooling apparatus, the quality of Calatayud's wines for drinking young has improved dramatically. This battery of equipment stands beside the Cooperativa Comarcal del Campo San Alejandro.
Right: The play of light and shade in the Monasterio de Piedra. This dates from 1195 and is surrounded by a splendid park with waterfalls.

Travel Information

HOTELS AND RESTAURANTS

Hotel Calatayud, N11, 50300 Calatayud, tel (76) 881323 Typical trunk road hotel, on the north side of the town on the N11. Ask for a room at the rear (even though a railway line runs at the back). The rooms are noisy and lack character. In the restaurant food and service are equally indifferent.
Lisboa, Paseo Calvo Soleto 10, 50300 Calatayud, tel (76) 882535 Traditional, unadorned dishes, some based on fresh fish. A fresh rosé from the region is appropriate with the tasty *cordero asado* (roast lamb). For dessert, ask for *melocotón con vino* (peaches with wine) in season.
Monasterio de Piedra, 50210 Nuévalos, tel (76) 849011 This is the best place to stay in the area. The 60 or so rooms are in a former monastery, other parts of which contain a museum. There is a view out over a fine park (see Places of Interest below). In the Reyes de Aragón restaurant fresh salmon trout from the lake in the park is served, with a choice of dishes.

PLACES OF INTEREST

Belmonte de Gracián The writer Baltasar Gracián was born in this pleasant wine village, situated on a hillside. A striking church tower is found here.
Calatayud This is not one of those really attractive or atmospheric towns, but in the old centre there are some buildings worth seeing. Among them is the Colegiata de Santa María la Mayor, in Mudéjar style. Its notable octagonal tower remains from the mosque that stood here. Another fine tower, also of the Mudéjar period, belongs to the San Andrés church. In the Museo Municipal the history of the town and its surroundings is enlivened by archaeological finds and other objects.

High above the town are the remains of the Moorish castle that gave Calatayud its name (the *calat Ayub*). Just a few miles from this stronghold are excavations of Bilbilis Augusta, the Roman settlement.
Cervera de la Cañada The Santa Tecla church here is built in Gothic Mudéjar style.
Maluenda On a height over the village are the ruins of a tenth-century castle. The local wine cooperative is the biggest in the Calatayud district.
Mara Here there is a church in the Mudéjar style, a little square redolent with atmosphere, and a fountain you can drink from.
Miedes Narrow streets lead to the heart of the village, where the church is surrounded by very ancient houses. A little way past the cooperative the road affords marvellous views on either side over the valleys.
Monasterio de Piedra About 30 km (19 miles) from Calatayud, this is the area's greatest tourist attraction. The monastery was founded by Cistercians in 1195 by order of Alfonso II of Aragón, and one tower still dates from that time. The building, which is now partly a hotel, retains the fine cloisters, but most visitors come mainly for the splendid park.

Two walks through the park include various waterfalls, the biggest of which is some 50 m (165 ft) high, and a trout farm. Try to avoid visiting at weekends, when you may have a long wait for a parking space, though weekdays, too, can be very busy. The road to the monastery leads past a large reservoir, the Embalse de la Tranquera.

WINE ROUTE

The wine route runs from Calatayud to the Monasterio de Piedra and back. At three points routes branching off to ancient Bilbilis, to Maluenda and to Miedes are indicated. From this last village you can connect with the Cariñena route via the Puerto de Aguarón.

Campo de Borja

The wine district of Campo de Borja ("field" or "estate" of Borja) takes its name from the little town of Borja. The ruins of an old castle bear witness to the fact that this was the seat of the Borja family until the fourteenth century. They then emigrated to Italy, where the name was changed to Borgia. In 1492 one member of the family was even elected pope – the corrupt Alexander VI.

The first vines were probably not planted in Borja but further west at the Monasterio de Veruela, which dates from the twelfth century. Today, however, the monastery no longer has vineyards and in fact lies outside the Campo de Borja *denominación de origen*. The wines come from a roughly triangular stretch of country around the valley of the Huecha, in the west of Zaragoza province. In a few places this wine district borders on that of Navarra.

Climate

The vineyards, some 10,000 ha (24,700 acres) in all, lie in the transitional zone between the Iberian massif and the Ebro valley. A large part of the landscape is made up of rolling open terrain, with olive trees here and there. The dark green of vineyards alternates with the pale yellow of wheatfields. Vegetables, such as asparagus and beans, are also grown here. The lower-lying, flatter parts of Campo de Borja have an average annual rainfall of 350 mm (13.7 ins), compared with 450 mm (17.7 ins) on the higher ground. But those lower areas do not actually suffer from summer drought, for during the winter months the humidity is increased by mists from the Ebro valley. Night frosts can occur here into the spring. On the lower ground Garnacha is the variety mainly grown, while grapes such as Tempranillo and white Macabeo are chiefly found on the slopes and the higher plateaux. There are two spells of picking as the grapes in the lower vineyards ripen earlier than those higher up. Faithful to tradition Borja holds a vintage festival, usually around September 21 and between the two harvest periods. It lasts for five days and besides the usual celebrations includes a wine parade – and *encierros*, when bulls run through the street.

Until the 1970s the loose soils of Campo de Borja with their gravels and limestone yielded mainly heavy red wines for blending. A good deal of the wine is still sold in bulk, but significantly less than before. The Borja cooperative, one of the leading, and most influential, of the area's wine firms, now bottles more than half its production. Another example is provided by the biggest regional cooperative, that at Fuendejalón which began bottling in 1983, after having sold not a drop of wine in bottles for 30 years. Campo de Borja has about 10 producers altogether, most of them cooperatives. Until the early 1980s these were still using equipment from the 1950s and 1960s when they were founded. Now after considerable investment most of them are at least partly provided with modern plant, including not only bottling lines but stainless-steel tanks and cooling equipment. Nor do the private bodegas lag behind.

New grape varieties

While these necessary technical improvements have been effected, changes out in the vineyards have also been taking place. Thus the predominance of Garnacha – at about 80 percent – is being reduced by the planting of other black grapes, primarily Tempranillo. This has already gained an important position in Campo de Borja. Thus of the 1,800 ha (4,450 acres) worked by the members of the Borja cooperative, a quarter is now planted with Tempranillo vines. And in 1989 the cooperative at Fuendejalón launched its first red wine to contain Tempranillo as well as Garnacha. On a small scale Cabernet Sauvignon and Merlot have also made their appearance. Bodegas Ruberte in Magallón is probably the first grower to have planted these varieties. Whether they have a future in this area remains to be seen, for the results from these Bordeaux grapes have not so far been remarkable.

Ageing in cask

Most of the red wines that Campo de Borja produces are meant for drinking young. The best kinds are characterized by firmness and fruit, and are pleasantly supple. Some of the grapes – usually Tempranillos – undergo *macération carbonique*. The alcohol content of wines of this kind is limited to 12 to 13 percent. However, the region also produces cask-aged wines. The casks may be of the 225-litre (50-gal) Bordeaux model, or much bigger – 2,000 litres (440 gal), for example.

The oenological station at Zaragoza has shown that even a pure Garnacha wine can usefully spend some time in wood. At this research station I was allowed to taste a wine that had been two years in small *barricas* of new American oak, followed by two years in bottle. It was a most successful wine, and without the pronounced oxidization that can occur with Garnacha. This particular Campo de Borja had been scientifically nurtured. I was not served such quality anywhere out in the region. There most of the wines aged in wood were either dull or strictly traditional: alcoholic (13.5 to 14 percent), very ripe, and with old wood predominant in the rustic manner. The cooperative at Borja is probably the only establishment that produces decent *crianzas* and *reservas*. It has built a special cellar underground for its casks and replaces them every four years.

White wines

In parallel with the emergence of the new style of Campo de Borja red – of a type for drinking young and unmixed, not for blending – rosé and white wines have also been receiving more attention. Provided they are well made, *rosados* from this district can be agreeable and refreshing, with a good dose of fruit. They represent nearly a fifth of production. White grapes were formerly used here specially to make the red wines somewhat lighter; this still happens at some bodegas.

White DO

In fact white wines were originally not even included in the DO. This was changed in 1989 when white Campo de Borja came into being officially. It is nearly always made from Macabeo grapes alone; other white varieties that might be involved are hardly worth mentioning. However, trials are being conducted with Chardonnay and Riesling, and other new grapes. When Macabeo grapes are fermented at low temperature they can give clean-tasting, juicy thirst-quenchers. The best of these wines come from grapes grown on the higher ground. Aragón's first sparkling wine was made at Bodegas Bordejé in Ainzón, an example later followed by the cooperative in the same area. Both of these taste just a little too coarse and earthy to be interesting; the future for Campo de Borja lies with still wines.

PRODUCERS OF SPECIAL INTEREST

Bodegas Bordejé 0570 Ainzón
This family firm has its cellars in a hillside facing the village of Ainzón. Its own vineyards – about 80 ha (200 acres) extend behind. In these atmospheric old cellars the grapes are made into powerful, rustic *reservas* and *gran reservas* (Don Pablo), as well as wines for drinking young. The red Abuelo Nicolas usually has some fruit and is good quality. Its alcohol content varies from 13.5 to 14 percent. The Cava, exclusively from white grapes, is an indifferent product with a rather coarse, earthy taste.

Sociedad Cooperativa Agricola Limitada de Borja 50540 Borja
That they take things seriously at the Borja cooperative is shown by the many prizes that its wines have won, both in and beyond its own area. Tempranillo planting has been encouraged among the 1,200 members with their 1,000 ha (2,470 acres), and it now represents a quarter of the total. In addition, the vineyards have some 5 percent Cabernet Sauvignon. The bodega's red Borsao is made from 50 percent Garnacha, 30 percent Tempranillo

(half of this by *macération carbonique*), and 20 percent Cabernet Sauvignon. The wine has a supple, meaty taste, with elements of both fruit and flowers in it. It tastes best when freshly poured.

With their qualities of fruit and freshness, and their clear, clean taste, the white and rosé Borsaos (made from Macabeo and Garnacha respectively) are also attractive and are among the very best of the area's products. Gran Campellas (50 percent Garnacha, 50 percent Tempranillo) is a smooth, balanced wine with a modest touch of wood. More wood and more alcohol are present in the somewhat rustic Señor Antares, a pure Garnacha wine. The cooperative has an underground cellar where it stores some 250 *barricas*. Anyone visiting this establishment to buy a few bottles should not forget that fine, fruity olive oil is also produced here (as well as grain, asparagus etc).

Cooperativa del Campo San Juan Bautista 50529 Fuendejalón
The area of land held by the 400 members of this cooperative is relatively large, for between them they cultivate 3,000 ha (7,400 acres), which makes it the biggest cooperative of the district. At the

beginning of the 1990s there were just a few stainless-steel tanks here for making rosé; the rest were concrete. The concern was established in 1952 and has been bottling since 1983. Its wines are normally sold under the name of a commercial subsidiary, Bodegas Aragonesas, which works with a number of brand names: for the ordinary reds, whites and rosés these are Viña Tito and Don Ramón Perez Juán. Of these the red reaches the best standard; since the 1989 vintage this has had 20 percent Tempranillo in it, the rest being Garnacha. However, these wines for drinking young have not as yet attained a really good level of quality.

The red Duque de Sevilla brand of wine used to come from Cariñena, but is now a Campo de Borja. It comes in a frosted bottle and possesses a pleasing, quite mellow taste and an unpretentious personality. It matures for one year in the tank, nine months in cask, then two years in bottle. A wine sold particularly in Aragón itself is Mosén Cleto, with grains of sand on the bottle.

Bodega Cooperativa Santo Cristo
51520 Magallón

Above: In Magallón are the remains of cloisters in Mudéjar style and a church built on the top of a hill.

Until this cooperative, too, has stainless-steel tanks and cooling equipment at its disposal, only its red wine (sold as Magallón or Molilla) will be of interest. This is supple in taste, reasonably firm, with a modicum of freshness and fruit. Besides its Garnacha it has a very little Tempranillo, but the proportion of the latter is going to increase markedly in the years to come. In 1990 the 760 or so members produced 50,000 kg (50 tons) of Tempranillo grapes from their 1,300 ha (3,210 acres) compared with 30,000 kg (300 tons) of Garnacha. Grain and olive oil are two other products of this cooperative.

Bodegas Ruberte Hermanos
51520 Magallón
On its 50 ha (124 acres) of vineyards the Ruberte family has planted Tempranillo (30 ha/75 acres, Merlot (8 ha/20 acres) and Cabernet Sauvignon (2 ha/5 acres), as well as Garnacha (10 ha/25 acres). In principle, therefore, it should be possible to produce an exciting range of wines here. Yet both the

making and the maturing of the wines seem to proceed rather less than flawlessly. All the wines I tasted could have been better, from the red and rosé Vino Joven to the Cabernet Sauvignon (no *denominación de origen*, and with 60 percent Cabernet, 30 percent Tempranillo, 10 percent Merlot), the *crianza* Viña Bona, and the *gran reserva*. But given more expertise, Bodegas Rubarte Hermanos has the potential to distinguish itself in a positive way from the other winemakers here. A firm making a table wine, La Magallonera, operates on the same premises. Wooden dolls and other knick-knacks are set out for sale to visitors.

Travel Information

HOTELS AND RESTAURANTS

La Bóveda, 50540 Borja, tel (76) 868251 The best restaurant in the area, with quite inventive dishes: do not expect typical Aragonese cuisine here. The ambience, too, is special, partly due to its situation on the Plaza del Mercado with its arcades.

Mesón Gabas, 50540 Borja, tel (76) 867295 There are quite a few traditional dishes on the menu here.

El Churro, 50529 Fuendejalón, tel (76) 862048 Restaurant in an old wine cellar. The *migas* (savoury, crispy pieces of bread) and *costillas* (spare ribs) are some of the specialities here.

Rodi, 50529 Fuendejalón, tel (76) 862030 A quite elegant décor in this restaurant (black chairs, pink linen), with country dishes such as cold, marinated rabbit (*conejo escabechado*), *costillas* and peaches in white wine.

La Corza, 50592 Monasterio de Veruela, tel (76) 649036 Restaurant opposite the monastery. Regional dishes can be ordered as well as the more standard items.

Hotel Brujas de Bequer, 50500 Tarazona, tel (76) 640404 Campo de Borja's only decent hotel, it lies outside the actual wine district, to the east of Tarazona. Nicely kept, fairly small – and noisy – rooms. Book a room at the back, because of the traffic. There is good cooking in the restaurant, and full-flavoured regional cheese to go with that last glass of red wine.

You could also stay in Navarra or eastern Rioja (Alfaro, for example; see the relevant chapters).

PLACES OF INTEREST

Ainzón Beautiful seventeenth-century parish church. The grape harvest is celebrated around September 14.

Borja This small town with about 4,500 inhabitants has a rich history. The Borja family (later known as the Borgias) lived here in a castle built on a hill, the ruins of which remain. Wine cellars were dug into the slope of that same hill and some of these are still in use, distinguished by their small entrances and stone air shafts. The heart of Borja consists of two small squares, one with the sixteenth-century *ayuntamiento*, the other being the Plaza del Mercado with its galleries. Have a look at the library on the latter square, which has a carved doorway and a fine hall in blue-grey tints. Borja also offers the visitor the restored Santa María church, an old gateway, the sixteenth-century Casa de las Conchas, and the Convento de la Concepción. The *fiesta de la vendimia* is celebrated here around September 21,when the best wines of the district are chosen.

Fuendejalón Around this peaceful little village there are small cellars where the growers used to make their wine. A few are still used. The sixteenth-century Gothic church of San Juan Bautista has a fine altarpiece, and on the remains of an old fort there stands the eighteenth-century Ermita de la Virgen del Castillo.

El Pozuelo de Aragón Wine village with a small free-standing tower in Mudéjar style in the square by the church.

Magallón Famed for its pottery. One of the churches stands on a hill above the village. On the eastern side the remains of a monastery in Mudéjar style can be seen.

Monasterio de Veruela This monastery was founded by Cistercians in the twelfth century and was probably where winegrowing in Campo de Borja had its birth. The vineyards at this particular spot have gone, but what does remain is the great Romanesque and Gothic abbey, and the cloisters with their carvings.

Santuario de Nuestra Señoría de la Misericordia A hill a few miles from Borja where people come on summer Sundays to keep cool. The best view is from the bar terrace. There is also a round chapel on the hill, the Ermita Calvario.

WINE ROUTE

The suggested route runs through the most important wine communities of the Campo de Borja, through the hills, plateaux and valleys of the countryside. Trips to Santuario de Nuestra Señoría de la Misericordia are also marked.

Above: Detail from the porch of the cathedral of Zaragoza, with sculptures in classical style.
Right: General view of the centre of Zaragoza, showing the old Plaza de Toros, formed by a circle of houses. The cathedral, seen in the background, stands on the bank of the Ebro. (For information on Aragón's capital city see page 66.)

Rioja

Capital: Logroño
Province: La Rioja is an *autonomía*
Area: 5,034 square kilometres
Population: 262,611

Above: Young Tempranillo vines near Baños de Ebro.

The earliest words to have come down to us in Castilian, the standard Spanish of today, are four lines of verse that end with: *un vaso de bon vino* (a glass of good wine). They date from the beginning of the thirteenth century and come from the pen of Gonzalo de Berceo, a monk who lived in the Riojan monastery of San Millán de Suso. The lines are one of the many pieces of evidence of Rioja's long history of winemaking, which goes back to before the Roman occupation. Winegrowing certainly flourished here under the Romans, as shown by the number of their pressing troughs that have been preserved: they are amazingly like those still used today by small growers following the traditional methods. After the Moors had been driven out of northern Spain winegrowing began to develop once more, this time under the stimulus of the monasteries. The first Riojan wine laws were probably in force as early as the ninth century, promulgated by Bishop Abilio.

The name Rioja first appeared in writing – as Rioxa – in 1092 in a local statute, or *fuero*, from Miranda de Ebro. It probably referred at that time to lands in the immediate basin of the Oja, a river that nowadays flows into the Tirón near Haro, shortly before the combined streams join the Ebro. Later the name came to be used for the whole region, an area that lies some 100 km (62 miles) south of Bilbao, San Sebastián and the Atlantic coast, around the Ebro valley. Despite the closeness of the ocean Rioja does not have a maritime climate, for a series of mountain ranges forms a natural barrier against the chill winds and rains from the sea. From Rioja you can often see clouds lying along the Sierra de Cantabria, the nearest of the mountain ridges. This means it is misty and cool north of the mountains while Rioja is basking in sunshine. Riojan vegetation is more southern and exuberant than in surrounding areas. Many Basques come to their holiday homes here in the summer; it is said that their children get not only a better colour, but better appetites too.

Geographically speaking there are two Riojas, the province and the wine region. They do not altogether correspond: certain parts of the province do not lend themselves to grape growing; and the wine region takes in small areas that belong to other provinces, Alava and Navarra. The wine region stretches from northwest to southeast for a distance of about 120 km (75 miles). It is not heavily populated – around 250,000, almost half in the capital Logroño. There has been no development of mass tourism here, so large parts of Rioja are peaceful and unspoiled.

Rioja Alavesa

The Riojan wine region is divided into three districts: Rioja Alavesa, Rioja Alta and Rioja Baja. The first two comprise the western zone, the third the eastern zone. The border between them runs near Logroño. The composition of the soil varies according to the area, and there are distinct microclimates. As its name indicates, Rioja Alavesa belongs to the Basque province of Alava. Its vineyards extend from the foot of the Sierra de Cantabria to the steep north bank of the Ebro. The terrain has a terrace-like structure, rising from just below 400 m (1,310 ft) above sea level to nearly 800 m (2,620 ft). In many places the soil has a whitish colour as there is a lot of limestone here, as well as clay. Because of this limestone content red wines tend to have less colour than those from the other districts; they are also more elegant in structure and fresher in taste. With some 10,000 ha (24,710 acres) Rioja Alavesa is the smallest of the three districts.

Rioja Alta

In this western zone Rioja Alavesa follows the winding north bank of the Ebro while Rioja Alta is bounded by its south bank, except for certain communities in Rioja Alta that for political and administrative reasons make up an enclave within Rioja Alavesa. The most important of these Alta communities on the north bank are Abalos and San Vicente de la Sonsierra. Considerable areas of Rioja Alta are composed of clay with limestone, but alluvial soils occur too, and others still with clay and iron. This makes it almost impossible to speak of the specific characteristics of Rioja Alta wines: soils can vary according to commune, and even according to vineyard, resulting in different wines. The landscape has much high ground, with vineyards in the south climbing to 600 to 700 m (1,970 to 2,300 ft). The microclimates of Rioja Alavesa and Rioja Alta do not differ greatly, though the further southeast you go, the warmer and drier it becomes. In the wine town of Haro in the west the average annual temperature is 12.7°C (54.9°F), with a rainfall of 500 mm (19.7 ins). For Logroño 50 km (31 miles) to the southeast the figures are 13°C (55.4°F) and 390 mm (15.4 ins). Differences in the microclimates are partly due to respective heights above sea level: Haro is 480 m (1,575 ft), Logroño nearly 100 m (328 ft) lower. The total area of vineyards in Rioja Alta is more than twice that of Rioja Alavesa.

Rioja Baja

Rioja Baja begins to the east of Logroño. Height above sea level drops further here, down to around 300 m (980 ft) at Alfaro right over in the east, where the valley widens and the landscape flattens. Alluvial clay brought down by the river is the most common kind of soil. Large areas with clay and ferruginous subsoils are also found. The Rioja Baja climate is relatively warm and dry. Alfaro records an annual average of 14.4°C (57.9°F) with a rainfall of only 280 mm (11 ins); drought can be a problem here. As well as the grapes, fruit and vegetables are grown on a big scale on the fertile valley floor, including peaches, potatoes, artichokes, asparagus, beans, peppers, sprouts, sugar beet, tomatoes, onions and carrots. Much of this produce is processed locally by the canning industry that flourishes here. The Rioja Baja wines are generally the strongest of the region. In Rioja Alavesa and Rioja Alta the red wines reach a natural alcoholic strength of 10 to 13 percent, while in Rioja Baja 13 to 15 percent is quite normal – although an increasing number of producers now prefer somewhat lighter wines. In terms of quantity Rioja Baja, with about 15,000 ha (37,000 acres) of vineyards, is the second largest of the three districts.

A golden age

The natural attributes of Rioja make it eminently suitable for winegrowing, which is why it developed here so early. Yet it was not until the nineteenth century that Riojan wine became known outside its own region when better communications arrived, first the roads and then the railway. In 1852 the Marqués de Murrieta bodega was established, the first on a commercial basis. Then in the second half of the nineteenth century came a dramatically increased demand from France, as vineyards were afflicted first with mildew, then with phylloxera, the parasite that was to destroy practically all the French vines. This brought the Bordeaux merchants to Spain in large numbers, and there was a marked increase in French orders to Rioja after the rail link

Left: During the harvest celebrations in San Vicente de la Sonsierra a feast is held in this church, which stands high above the village.

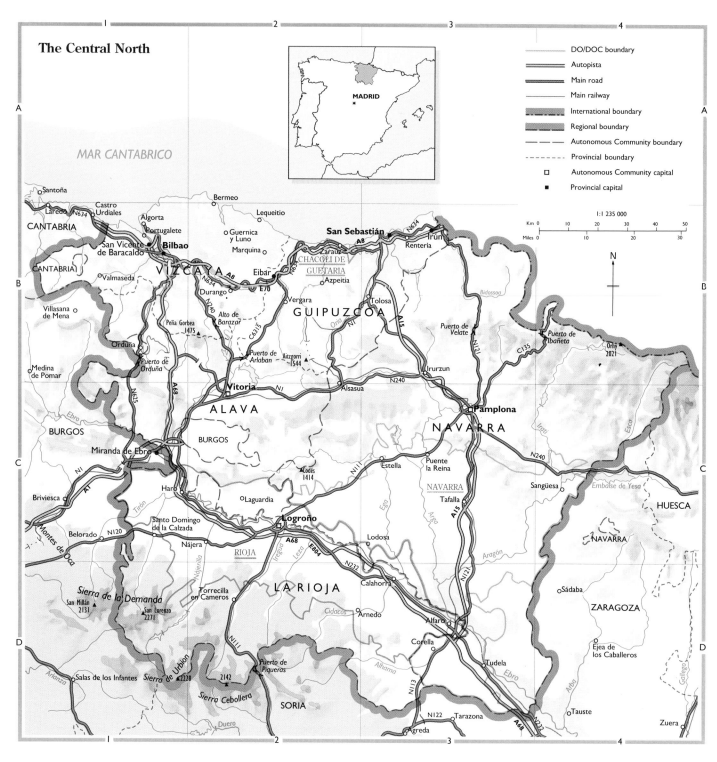

The Central North

MADRID

DO/DOC boundary
Autopista
Main road
Main railway
International boundary
Regional boundary
Autonomous Community boundary
Provincial boundary
□ Autonomous Community capital
■ Provincial capital

1:1 235 000

between Haro and Bilbao had been opened in 1880. At times Rioja was sending 50 million litres (11 million gal) a month to France. By the end of the century many new bodegas were established, often on the French model, and many Frenchmen themselves set up in the region. The total vineyard area grew to 52,000 ha (128,500 acres), its greatest extent ever.

Decline and restoration

By about 1900, however, this golden age was over. The French had at last found a means of preventing phylloxera – by grafting the vines on to American rootstocks, which still happens – and

the pest had appeared in Rioja itself. In addition, French import duties were raised and Spain lost her colonial export markets such as Cuba and the Philippines. Misery was the general outcome. After a temporary revival in the early 1930s, further development was checked first by the Spanish Civil War, then by the Second World War. It was not until the 1960s and 1970s that a marked upturn came. During the 1970s this resulted in the creation of a new group of bodegas with modern equipment, exemplified by Berona, El Coto, Domecq, Lan, Olarra and Unión Viti-Vinícola/Marqués de Cáceres. At the same time a number of existing houses was taken over by large groups, multinationals

Above: View over the Ebro and Rioja Alta, where the vineyards are interrupted by flat-topped hills.

among them. Then new, often small bodegas came into being in the late 1980s, after Spain's entry into the EC and the liberalization of Riojan wine exports that flowed from this.

Small-scale growers

Although there are 15 or so producers in Rioja who own between 100 and 500 ha (245 to 1,480 acres), around 85 percent of the grapes come from small growers. Thousands of them cultivate grapes as a sideline, and have no winemaking facilities of their own. This explains why the wine cooperatives play such an important role. There are about 30 of them and they receive some 45 percent of all the grapes. Most of the cooperatives sell by far the greater part of their production, in the form of must or wine, to the merchant bodegas. The latter also have contracts with individual growers, and in addition buy wine from growers who do their own vinification. Altogether these merchants control more than 90 percent of production. Nevertheless, a number of cooperatives are having increasing success with bottled wine.

Tempranillo

The number of grape varieties that producers are now working with is much more limited than before. There was a time when some 40 different varieties were grown in the region; today the regulations allow only seven, generally with a special dispensation for Cabernet Sauvignon. The most characteristic and widely planted grape is black Tempranillo, which represents about a half of all plantings. Tempranillo ripens excellently on the clay and chalk soils in the relatively cool Rioja Alavesa and Rioja Alta. It is also grown increasing in Rioja Baja, and the *Consejo Regulador* recommends a quota of at least 25 percent Tempranillo

when replanting is carried out in this district. It can be too hot and dry for Tempranillo in the lower-lying areas of Rioja Baja, but this grape seems to thrive in the higher, somewhat cooler vineyards. The Monte Yerga estate southwest of Alafaro covers hundreds of acres and rises to 640m (2,100ft) above sea level; here Tempranillo represents 60 percent of plantings.

Other varieties

Rioja's second grape is black Garnacha. This is found particularly in Rioja Baja, where the prevailing weather pattern and the clay soil are ideal for it. Garnacha Tinta bears fruit that is rich in sugar, giving highly alcoholic wines. However, colour is not its strong point, still less acid, and it also oxidizes rather readily. By itself, therefore, Garnacha is mainly made into rosé wines, for which this grape is perfectly suited (*see also* Navarra, page 95). For red wines it is principally blended with Tempranillo.

The same happens with two other varieties, Mazuelo and Graciano. These are planted in very limited numbers as both are very susceptible to disease. Basically Tempranillo gives a red wine with a straightforward, not markedly aromatic taste, good fruit, a relatively low degree of acidity, just enough alcohol, and a strong, stable colour. It can be delightful pure, but many producers add other grapes to endow it with yet more qualities. Garnacha provides extra strength and alcohol, Mazuelo acidity and tannin, and Graciano aroma. Often, too, some white Viura or Macabeo goes into it, which also adds acidity. When composing their wines the big bodegas attend not only to the varieties of grapes used, but also to their origin, for with each variety the differences in grapes from various sites can be considerable. Most bodegas work with grapes from all three districts.

Traditional winemaking

Besides the usual methods of production, in some parts of Rioja red wine is still made in the strictly traditional way. It is estimated that more than half the small growers in Rioja Alavesa who vinify their own grapes maintain this practice. It is a very simple system. The black grapes are neither destalked nor crushed, but go into an open concrete fermenting trough or *lago* with their skins, stalks and pips. A little juice collects in the bottom of the tank as a result of the grapes being tipped in, and from the weight of the fruit. This begins to ferment and the carbon dioxide released envelops the grapes, which are therefore deprived of oxygen. The enzymes present in the fruit begin to work and fermentation inside the skins ensues. In this way the primary aroma of the grapes remains trapped in the skin cells, giving an exceedingly fragrant, fruity wine. The *cosechero* or winegrower does not just look on in anticipation during this process. He regularly treads the grape pulp and also brings the lowest layers to the top (*remonta*) to produce the optimum fermentation. During fermentation the grapes gradually swell up and, after 9 or 10 days, finally burst. In this way the amount of fermenting must steadily increases, and therefore the wine. This method resembles *macération carbonique*, but is not identical: in Rioja the troughs remain uncovered and no extra carbon dioxide is added.

The fruity, supple and meaty red wines that are obtained in this way (nearly always from Tempranillo alone) are enthusiastically drunk in the region. You can order them in all the bars and restaurants there by asking for a *vino de cosechero*. It is served fresh and can be quite delightful. Yet remarkably enough this traditional Riojan wine is little known outside its own region, and only a trickle is exported. This has mainly to do with the image that importers, restaurateurs and consumers have of Rioja: for them a good red Rioja has to be aged in wood. So far there has been little understanding of, or interest in, a less "serious" type of wine. This is a matter for regret for lovers of *vino de cosechero*: all too often it seems impossible to obtain such a young, fruity wine.

Bordeaux-style barrels

It is hardly surprising that red Rioja should be so strongly associated with barrel ageing: there are few regions in the world where such large quantities of wine are matured in oak. The first step in this direction came from Manuelo Quintano who in 1780 aged some wine in a few large wooden casks. The experiment was successful, but the local mayor would not give Quintano permission to sell his improved, and more expensively produced, wine at higher prices. The idea was taken up again in 1850 by Luciano de Murrieta, the later Marqués de Murrieta. He had a number of small casks brought to Logroño from Bilbao and used them to ship Riojan wine to Cuba. Later this pioneer matured some wine in wood in his own cellar. Not long after this, and under Bordeaux influence, the 225 litre (50 gal) measure in use there came into vogue in Rioja. The *barrique bordelaise* became Rioja's *barrica bordelesa*. Today the barrels are still called *barricas*, and their form and capacity are laid down by law.

American and French oak

The regulations also state how long each category of wine should be aged in cask. For *crianza* and *reserva* the minimum is one year, and for *gran reserva* two years. As more than 40 percent of all

Above: Bottles of Reserva 904, a gran reserva, *being placed in a wire mesh in the cellars of La Rioja Alta.*

Rioja comes in these categories, many tens of thousands of barrels are stored with the 110 firms that make these wines. In Luciano de Murrieta's time there was not a single cooper to be found in the whole of Rioja. Now the region has cooper's workshops large and small, and some bodegas have their own *toneleros* in service. As elsewhere in Spain, American oak is used for most casks. It is denser and less porous than the French oak, and the staves are usually sawn thicker. This means there is less contact with oxygen than in French oak casks, with a slower development of the wine. However, the number of French casks is increasing steadily since the oak used gives the wine a softer, more noble aroma. In some bodegas French casks already represent half or more of the stock – at Unión Viti-Vinícola/Marqués de Cáceres and Montecillo, for example. Wood-ageing of red Rioja on such a large scale, and sometimes for long periods, has to do with the fact that Tempranillo is very resistant to oxidization.

Large stocks of bottles

The wine laws stipulate that wood-aged red Riojas must subsequently be rested in tanks or bottles, or both. For *crianzas* this extra period is one year (tank and/or bottle); for *reservas* two years (tank and/or bottle); and for *gran reservas* three years (bottle). This means that as well as barrels there have to be enormous quantities of bottles in stock – millions in quite a number of the bodegas. The idea underlying these rules for maturing and resting is to market wines that are at their best and ready for drinking. Many of the world's famous wine-growing areas expect the consumer to lay down their products for years to mature, but in principle any red Rioja on sale can be drunk right away. It doesn't have to be, of course: many Riojas have backbone enough to stay drinkable for years, if not decades, and may benefit from further bottle-ageing. Another aspect of these wines is that there are seldom any lees, even in bottles of very mature wines, which makes decanting unnecessary. Sediment is left behind in the *barricas* during ageing.

The recurring vintage

Because of the various categories of wood-aged Rioja the region has the remarkable phenomenon of the recurring vintage. What happens is that a bodega may bring out various wines of the same vintage with long intervals in between. Thus the *crianza* may be sold out first, next a *reserva* of the same vintage may appear – and then a *gran reserva* some considerable time after that. Most of the bodegas select their wines according to type. This implies that the strongest wines, with usually the highest percentage of Tempranillo, are chosen for the longest ageing. It may be, however, that all a bodega's wines are identical in their composition and only the length of time they have been matured decides the category they belong to at any given moment. Every bodega cherishes its own ideas about choice of grapes, winemaking, and the duration and manner of ageing. The result is a very varied range of red wines on offer: from purplish red to light brown, from fruity and fresh to mature, from elegant to potent, etc.

Whites and rosés

Besides the red Riojas there are also whites. For these the main grape is Viura, a variety that represents about a fifth of plantings. As has already been indicated, some Viura goes into red wines to give them more acidity, but a considerable amount is also bottled pure. Sometimes Malvasía and Garnacha Blanca may be added, but so little of these varieties is grown that most white Riojas are made exclusively from Viura. Until the 1960s these wines lacked freshness and fruit. They were flat in taste and yellowish in hue, and white grapes were vinified like the black. However, modern winemaking techniques were introduced, with progressive firms like Unión Viti-Vinícola/Marqués de Cáceres in the lead. In addition white grapes were picked earlier than had been usual and some remarkable results were achieved. From being dull and uninteresting the Viura wines evolved into vivacious, fruity products with light colour, a fine perfume and a pure taste.

Wood-aged whites

The new style of white Riojas vinified at lower temperatures were a great success commercially, and so the example of the pioneering houses was widely followed. Most of these wines made in the modern way are meant for drinking young and undergo no wood ageing. However, the region also produces a modest number of white wines that have been in contact with wood. In general these have more character, depth and complexity than the others. Firms that carry them include CVNE, Federico Paternina, López de Heredia, Marqués de Murrieta, and Palacio. Another, very small-scale development is to ferment white wine in new oak barrels. Martínez Bujanda and Bretón have been doing this for several years now. The technique of slow

Below: Red wine matured in barrels at Bodegas Muga.

Above: An art nouveau tower dating from 1892 adorns the bodega of R. López de Heredia Tondonia in Haro.

fermentation at low temperatures that is used for most white wines is now being employed for many rosés as well. These, too, have gained in freshness and fruit. Garnacha is the basic grape for the bulk of the rosés.

Quality control

Measures were taken centuries ago in Rioja to ensure the quality of its wines. A league of winegrowers came into existence in Logroño in 1560. This forbade the importing of wine, from Arnedo and elsewhere; obliged its members to declare their vintages (with the weight and type of grapes); and introduced a monogram to authenticate the wines. The amount of regulation has been greatly increased in the course of the twentieth century. Thus in 1925 Spain's first *denominación de origen* was created for this region. This was five years after it had been legally recognized as constituting a wine region. In 1928 the *Consejo Regulador*, then two years old, stipulated the precise geographical zone within which Rioja wines could be grown and made, a demarcation that was confirmed by the Spanish wine laws of 1933. But the *Consejo Regulador* was not really effective as yet, certainly not as far as its monitoring function was concerned, and for many years it was not in the picture at all. An attempt to breathe new life into it in 1945 failed. The *Consejo* did not regain its significance until 1953, which is now regarded as the year of its official foundation.

Supported by the new *Estatuto de la Viña* (replacing that of 1933) and a decree of 1976, the *Consejo Regulador* has grown into a powerful body that in an effective manner regulates, administers, monitors and promotes the Riojan wine world. Monitoring

is the most important of these functions. The *Consejo* not only has registers of all the vineyards and bodegas, and inspectors in full-time service, but it also has at its disposal a very efficient computer system. This came into operation – after it had long been urged by a group of quality-conscious winemakers – at the time of the 1981 vintage. From that moment it was no longer possible to interpret the term "vintage" with more flexibility than was desirable. If a Rioja was sold with its vintage stated then no more than 15 percent of its contents could be from any other year. The computer system works in conjunction with the so-called *cartilla del viticultor*. This is a form that in principle follows every litre of wine from the picking of the grapes through to bottling. Every year each winegrower receives a *cartilla* on which is stated how many grapes he may pick in relation to the size of his vineyard, the varieties planted there, and the expected crop. This form passes to the cooperative or bodega when they buy the grapes from the grower. After the grape harvest the *Consejo Regulador* uses the *cartillas* to calculate how many bottles of wine may be made and provides numbered back or neck labels accordingly. Since 1982 every bottle of Rioja has had to be provided with these; sales without them are not allowed. By means of these forms and the computer the *Consejo Regulador* also follows the wines through the maturing processes, and any movement of them between bodegas. The use of legally defined terms such as *crianza*, *reserva* and *gran reserva* is also monitored by this body.

Two testing stations

The *Consejo Regulador* is also concerned with quality control of the end product, and for this purpose chemical and organoleptic tests are carried out. The most stringent are those applied to wines for export. For political reasons the region has two viticultural stations. Accordingly wines from Rioja Alta and Rioja Baja are tested at Haro, where the station has been in operation since 1892, while Rioja Alavesa has its own station in Laguardia, later established in 1982. Both stations have modern equipment, and experts to call on. At Haro all wines for export are approved by a committee of five to seven members. Permission to export is granted only after a majority vote in favour.

The first DOC

All these measures to safeguard quality formed the basis for the *Consejo Regulador*'s application for a *denominación de origen califica* (DOC). This is a superior version of the *denominación de origen* – and on 3 April 1991 Rioja was the first Spanish wine region to be granted one. Acquiring this qualification came after a long period of uncertainty and manoeuvring. After the idea of creating a DOC first took shape in the 1970s, the Riojan *Consejo Regulador* sought to discover the conditions under which the new qualification would be granted. But it was not until 1988 that the formulated rules emerged from Madrid. The most important of these were a grape price higher than the national average; the sale of the entire production in bottle; and effective monitoring procedures. Rioja already fulfilled this last condition. The full *Consejo Regulador* also declared that it agreed in principle with the other conditions. The higher grape price – eventually fixed at 200 percent of the national average – was easy to accept since Riojan grapes were already among the most expensive in the country. The longest discussions centred on the problem of compulsory bottling within the region. Finally, it was agreed that from 1 January 1993 all Riojan wine would be sold in bottle, to guarantee its origin wherever it was sold.

PRODUCERS OF SPECIAL INTEREST

Bodegas de la Real Divisa 26339
Abalos

In its present form this small bodega dates from 1972, but wine has been made here for much longer than this – as the fourteenth-century cellar shows. Real Divisa specializes in wood-aged red wines, all from its own vineyard of about 40 ha (99 acres) and matured in its 900 or so casks of American oak. The best quality at present is offered by the Marqués de Legarda *reserva* with its elements of wood, fruit and spices, but the *crianza* sold under the same name certainly has its merits.

Bodegas Campo Burgo 26540
Alfaro

This concern has gone under quite a number of different names since it began in 1895. It acquired its present one in the course of the 1980s, and it was during this decade that the quality of the wine improved. Only a fraction of its annual production of five million bottles comes from its own vineyards. Some 80 percent of the grapes and wines bought in come from Rioja Alta and 20 percent from Rioja Baja. In the extensive cellar complex (a former sugar factory) there are about 7,000 casks, around 500 of them of French oak. The bodega principally uses the Campo Burgo name for its red, white and rosé wines.

Bodegas Berberana 26350
Cenicero

The modest little firm that Martínez Berberana set up in Ollauri in 1877 grew in just under a century into one of the biggest and most modern in the Rioja, sited now in Cenicero. This was where Melquíades Entrena built a completely new, spaciously laid-out bodega. After various changes of owner, almost half the shares in the company were acquired in 1989 by the Spanish subsidiary of the Italian Carlo de Benedetti. Most of the remaining shares are held by cooperatives in the region, from whom Berberana obtains 70 percent of the grapes, must and wines it requires. For wood ageing the firm has about 30,000 *barricas* at its disposal. Despite the large scale on which Berberana operates, its wines are of very good quality. The white Carta de Plata is given no cask ageing,

Right: The wine village of Elciego is easy to recognize because of its church with two different towers.

but the Carta de Oro on the other hand has five or six months ageing, and thus has rather more body, and much charm. The Carta de Plata name also refers to a pleasing rosé and an elegant, supple *crianza* that has 12 months in cask. The red Carta de Oro is also a *crianza*, but is given longer in wood – 24 months – and has a rather broader, more mature taste. The Berberana *reservas* and *gran reservas* are both highly agreeable in character, with ample wood and vanilla, and of impeccable quality. Subsidiary trade names used by the concern are Bodegas Mariscol, Viña Arisabel, Viña Canda and Viña Mara. Bodegas de Abalos is a subsidiary firm.

Bodegas Riojanas 26350 Cenicero

In 1990, with a big programme of renovation and expansion behind it, this firm celebrated its centenary. The bodega is located in the main street in Cenicero. Visitors are received in a reproduction castle tower, complete with Gothic windows and crenellations. Everything is in excellent technical order. There are around 18,000 casks in the cellars and the intention is to increase this number gradually to 24,000. Bodegas Riojanas belongs to the Artacho family and has 200 ha (494 acres) of vineyards which supply roughly one-third of the grapes needed. The rest of the requirement is bought in, either as grapes or as wine. The house has built up its good reputation principally with red *reservas* and *gran reservas*. Two names are used for both categories: Viña Albina is a fairly elegant style of wine; Monte Real is stronger, with more colour, tannin and alcohol. There is also an engaging Monte Real white *crianza*. The most important brand name for the young wines, in red, white and rosé, is Canchales. The modernization here means that since the 1990 vintage the young wines are of a more attractive quality than they used to be.

Bodegas Velázquez 26350
Cenicero

The new premises for this medium-sized family concern were completed in 1973 and are situated on the road to the railway station. Part of the firm's wine comes from its own land of about 45 ha (110

acres). The rest is bought in, either as grapes or wine. This bodega makes only red wines, not remarkable in quality, but certainly decent enough. Monte Velaz is the most important name used. For maturing its wines Velazquez has more than 2,200 *barriccas*.

Compañia Internacional de Vinos
26350 Cenicero

This is a subsidiary of Bodegas Montecillo and thus belongs to Osborne. Its policy is to make wines exclusively for export, and its products are based on bought-in wines as well as what it vinifies itself. The resulting wines are generally rather less fine than those of Montecillo. Brigadier Miranda is the most important name used.

Unión Viti-Vinícola/Bodegas Marqués de Cáceres 25350
Cenicero

At the end of the 1960s, after a successful career in Bordeaux, Enrique Forner decided to return to Spain and establish a bodega there. He opted for Rioja and sought the advice of Professor Emile Peynaud. Together they selected Cenicero as the place for the bodega – partly

because of the high quality of the black and white grapes grown there – and Peynaud also advised on the construction of the cellars, which were ready in 1970. To ensure a sufficient supply of grapes, Forner set up the Unión Viti-Vinícola with 16 winegrowers. Altogether members own 70 to 80 ha (173 to 188 acres). In 1975 the concern began to sell its first wines, under the Marqués de Cáceres name. Production in that first year was 28,000 cases; it now runs at 520,000 to 550,000. This spectacular growth is mainly due to the high quality of the wines. Enrique Forner and his experts give all the growers precise instructions concerning the time to start picking. In addition, fermentation temperatures are meticulously controlled. This bodega was the first to ferment white and rosé Rioja wines at low temperatures; both are characterized by liveliness and fruit. For maturing the better red wines the bodega has some 22,000 casks available, half of American oak and half of French. And there are also some *barricas* of Spanish oak. Forner believes that in Riojan wine wood should not be predominant, but should be balanced with fruit. He is therefore in favour of a shorter period in cask, complemented by a considerable time maturing in bottle. The Marqués de Cáceres *crianza*, *reserva* and *gran reserva* are characterized by a beautiful balance between wood and fruit, great purity, and enough backbone for further ageing. They are among the very best that Rioja has to offer. Enrique Forner is a subsidiary brand of Marqués de Cáceres, and among the names used for young wines are Rivarey and Costanilla.

Castillo de Cuzcurrita 26214
Cuzcurrita de Río Tirón
This is one of the most beautifully housed of the Riojan bodegas, established in and around the fourteenth-century castle of that name. Since 1945 it has been the property of the Count of Alacha, who has tastefully restored it. The wines – wood-aged reds only – come from the estate's own 12 ha (30 acres). Generally they are quite slender in structure and of an introvert character.

Bodegas Domecq 01340
Elciego
In 1973 the Jerez-based house of Pedro Domecq decided to build a completely new bodega in Rioja, and 500 ha (1,235 acres) of vineyards were bought in Rioja Alavesa. No other producer in this

district has so much land. Efficiency prevails in the cellars with their modern equipment. A system has been developed to give the Alavesa wines rather more colour than usual by improving the colour extraction as the wines are being made. Not all the wines originate solely from the bodega's own vineyards; grapes and wines (mainly red) are also bought in. The name Viña Eguia is used – in Spain only – for the simplest wines in the range. The better qualities go under the name of Marqués de Arienzo. These have always spent time in wood; the bodega using 15,000 casks for this purpose. In general these wines have a supple, elegant and refined taste, with wood, fruit and other nuances.

Herederos del Marqués de Riscal
01340 Elciego
In the mid-nineteenth century Camilo Hurtado de Amázaga, Marqués de Riscal, returned to Rioja after long exile in Bordeaux. He planted 200 ha (494 acres) of vineyard with French as well as native grape varieties, and built what for those days was a very modern cellar. The wines from his bodega earned a great reputation both in Spain and beyond. The heirs of the Marqués comprised four families, and these still own the estate. The vineyard area has remained the same and supplies 40 percent of the grapes. Cabernet Sauvignon and Graciano each account for about one-eighth of the total here. The French grape is

mainly used in the *reservas*. In the second half of the 1970s and the first half of the 1980s, a series of mediocre, disappointing wines was produced. Since then, however, there has been renovation and investment – including replacement of 8,000 of the 21,000 casks. The quality of the wines has subsequently improved considerably, as is shown by the Marqués de Riscal *reserva*, a vital, thoroughly sound and elegant wine with a noble aroma of wood to it. The *crianza* has also improved. Since 1988 this house has also made a fresh, exciting rosé solely from Tempranillo. Baron de Chirel is a special, classic Rioja, aged for more than 2 years in oak.

Viña Salceda 01340
Elciego
The Viña Salceda buildings stand near a bridge over the Ebro, between Elciego and Cenicero. This bodega, in existence since 1976, belongs to a large group of shareholders. Two red wines are produced here, the Viña Salceda *crianza* and the Conde de la Salceda *gran reserva*. Both are of a reliable quality, with the *gran reserva* showing distinctly more potency and class. For ageing these wines the firm has nearly 7,000 casks. As its own 30 ha (74 acres) supply only one-eighth of requirements, both grapes and wines are bought in.

Bodegas Heredad de Baroja
01309 Elvillar de Alava
In the cellars of this recently established bodega (1988) more

Above: Vines growing in Rioja Alavesa, the most northerly of the Riojan zones, near the Ermita de San Juan.

wine can be stored in the 23,000 casks available than in tanks. This means that even the Baroja red wine for drinking the same year comes into contact with wood, and is of its kind a very successful and pleasant wine. There is another such wine, the Viña Baroja, which is made by the *macération carbonique* method. This does not spend time in cask. The best wine is usually the Rincón de Baroja *crianza*, a juicy product in which wood and vanilla are markedly present. A big wholesaler and two others own this bodega, which has 40 ha (99 acres) of land, providing 10 percent of the wine. The rest is bought in as ready-made wine. The bodega's most curious building is a remarkable little reproduction castle near Fuenmayor.

AGE Bodegas Unidas 26360
Fuenmayor
For years AGE has been the biggest exporter among the Riojan bodegas. It was created in 1967 by the merger of three producers. Since then AGE has changed owners several times. In 1987 Guinness acquired a majority shareholding in the AGE concern and went on to invest some millions of pounds in what is one of Spain's most modern production facilities. About three years later Guinness withdrew from AGE, which is now owned by the Spanish Banesto group. About 60

percent of the wines sold carry the Siglo name. The best wine in this range is the *saco*, which comes wrapped in jute sacking, and is a smooth-tasting, generous Rioja that undergoes two years' ageing in wood – AGE has 30,000 *barricas* at its disposal. A higher quality is offered by the Marqués del Romeral *gran reserva*, a wine that also has more personality. The bodega's own 50 ha (124 acres) of vineyard supply only a fraction of the grapes required. AGE has quite a number of subsidiary brands, among them Bodegas Romeral, Bodegas Las Veras, Viña Tere, Agessimo and Credencial.

Bodegas Lagunilla 26360 Fuenmayor

At a distance the white buildings of Lagunilla, owned by the British group International Distillers and Vintners (IDV), look rather like a grain silo. The firm, which dates from 1885, works exclusively with bought-in wines, which are blended and put through their various stages in the cellars. Some of the wine is then matured in the 10,000 or so casks. The reds generally taste smooth, supple and easy, without much depth to them. They are not bad, but neither are they exciting.

The most interesting are usually the Viña Herminia *reserva* and the Lagunilla *gran reserva*. Of the young wines the Lagunilla rosé can taste very good.

Bodegas Lan 26360 Fuenmayor

The name Lan is formed from the initial letters of Logroño, Alava and Navarra, the three Riojan provinces (though Logroño is no longer a province). This functional-looking, technologically advanced bodega was set up in 1973 and, after various changes of ownership, is now in the hands of a Basque industrialist. The 70 ha (173 acre) vineyard yields an eighth of the required grapes. The bodega produces three main lines of wine. The youngest wines are sold under the Lan name. Next come the somewhat more mature Lander, and finally the Viña Lanciano *reservas* and *gran reservas*. Of the young wines the Lan rosé is usually tastily fruity. The more mature wines nearly always have a quite elegant and clean taste. And the successful Lander red *crianza*, besides its wood, has fruit and a gentle freshness. The wood aroma is more dominant in the *reservas* amd *gran reservas*. That all of the Lan wines are made with care is clear

from the more than satisfactory level achieved over the whole range. The bodega has around 10,000 casks at its disposal. Lancorta and Señorío de Ulla are among its subsidiary brands.

Bodegas Marqués del Puerto 26360 Fuenmayor

Nearly 20 years after its foundation in 1968 this bodega was bought by the Bodegas y Bebidas group, which also owns Campo Viejo in the Rioja. This take-over has brought an improvement and 2,000 casks have been purchased. The wines have benefited from this and are now around the middle of the quality range. The Marqués del Puerto *reserva* and *gran reserva* in particular are worth discovering. About one-sixth of production comes from the firm's own 22 ha (54 acres) of vineyards.

Bodegas Montecillo 26360 Fuenmayor

The good reputation that the Bodegas Montecillo wines enjoy in Spain was the reason for its take-over in 1973 by Osborne, the sherry and brandy maker. Two years later a whole new cellar complex had been completed. It looks rather like a chalet and is splendidly equipped

for the production of quality wines. In principle the firm buys in only grapes, and no wines, so as to be able to do its own vinification. More than three-quarters of its 14,000 or so casks are made of French oak, which is an unusually high percentage for Rioja. The better the wine, the greater the use of French oak. Thus the Viña Monty *reserva* is aged exclusively in French *barricas*. This is a balanced, beautifully matured and charming wine of a high standard; at a blind tasting it once won more points than some renowned Bordeaux *grands crus*. Another delightful wine is the Montecillo *gran reserva*, which has more wood. The young wines from this bodega also merit attention. They are sold under the Montecillo and Viña Cumbrero brand names and include reds, whites and rosés.

Bodegas Berceo 26200 Haro

The Gurpegui family has tastefully restored an old bodega, dated 1872, in the Calle de las Cuevas, in the heart of Haro. Even new wooden fermentation vats were installed in 1983, to be in keeping with the rest of the building. Some of the red wine is aged on the premises here, in cellars dug into the hillside, where 3,200 casks, 40 percent of them of French oak, are stored. Generally the best of the red wines are the Viña Berceo *reserva* and Gonzalo de Berceo *gran reserva*, which is only sporadically made. Sometimes the Viña Berceo *crianza* is also marvellous. A fifth of the grapes come from the firm's own 50 ha (124 acres). The Gurpegui family also owns Bodegas Gurpegui in San Adrián; the Bodegas y Viñedos de la Plana in Andosilla; and it produces Navarran wine.

Bodegas Bilbaínas 26200 Haro

It is said that Viña Pomal was served at the Spanish court, and that Winston Churchill and Salvador Dalí were very fond of it. This red wine is the best known of the Bodegas Bilbaínas products and is also made as a *crianza* and *gran reserva*. The former has a quite broad, decently matured taste complemented by wood; the latter is meant for those who like a really aged Rioja. It is surpassed in its quality by the Gran Zaco, a meaty wine with rather more fruit and depth, as well as excellent ageing potential. Viña Zaco is a pleasant, but not really substantial *reserva*.

Left: One of the oldest bodegas is the Marqués de Riscal. The company dates from 1860.

Above: Since 1979 La Rioja Alta has been headed by Guillermo de Aranzabel. The bodega celebrated its centenary in 1990.
Right: In 1984 Pedro López de Heredia received the Spanish Royal couple here in his dark, atmospheric cellars, with their mouldy walls and cobwebs on the ceiling.

As well as some younger wines this firm also produces a Cava and a brandy. Bodegas Bilbaínas was founded in 1901 and has remained in the possession of the Ugarte family. About a half of the total production comes from its own 250 ha (618 acres). The rest is bought in as grapes or wine. For ageing in wood the firm has 13,000 casks.

Bodegas Carlos Serres 26200 Haro

There is little of visual interest in the Carlos Serres cellars. They are situated on the southwest side of Haro and are strictly functional. Since 1987 the bodega has belonged to the Monthisa group and in terms of standard it is in the middle ranks. The wines only become interesting after wood ageing – the Carlos Serres *crianza*, for example, a fairly rounded Rioja. The best wine in an unremarkable collection is the *reserva* Onomástica. This undergoes three years' ageing in cask. Carlos Serres, a firm that dates from 1896, has 3,000 *barricas* of American oak.

Bodegas Martínez Lacuesta 26200 Haro

Although there is modern equipment in the cellars of this bodega, the place as a whole gives a traditional impression. Thus for storing the wine there are large wooden vats as well as some 7,000 *barricas*, and the bodega has its own cooper's workshop. The most celebrated Rioja from this firm, founded in 1895, is the Reserva Especial, served at the Spanish

court and often adorning the menus at state banquets. The wine is in the *gran reserva* category and despite its age – at least 10 years – it remains fully vital. Usually, too, it develops nicely in the glass. The Campeador *reserva*, produced only in good years, has a meaty, firm taste and is the wine with the highest sales from this firm. The Martínez Lacuesta *crianza*, too, has its merits. This bodega, which has no vineyards of its own, belongs to descendants of its founder.

Bodegas Muga 26200 Haro

There are few bodegas that work in so craftsmanlike a manner: thus the wines here still ferment in wooden vats and are fined with white of egg. The accent is on red wines and three kinds are produced, all of good quality and wood-aged. The firm, which belongs to the Muga family, has 7,300 casks, half of them of American oak, half of French. The Muga *crianza* has a silky, smooth taste with some fruit and a restrained aroma of wood. Besides having more wood, the Prado Enea *reserva* and *gran reserva* possess more power and distinction. Bodegas Muga also produces one white, one rosé and one sparkling wine. About one-third of its production stems from its own 35 ha (86 acres), the rest being bought-in in the form of grapes.

Bodegas Ramón Bilbao 26200 Haro

This is a medium-sized concern on the west side of Haro, founded in

1924 and owning about 10 ha (25 acres) of vineyard. This provides only a small fraction of the grapes required, and the bodega mostly buys in wines. The number of casks here has grown gradually from 2,500 in 1981 to around 4,500. The best wine nurtured in them is the Viña Turzaballa *gran reserva* – although this would benefit from rather more depth and character. The other wines here are of a decent average quality.

Bodegas Rioja Santiago 26200 Haro

Angel Santiago Munilla started a small bodega in Labastida in 1870, then in 1904 he transferred his activities to Haro. Here his Bodegas Rioja Santiago grew steadily. The Santiago family remained owners until 1970, when the business was taken over by the American Pepsico concern. The latter was not so much interested in the wines as in sangria, an extremely successful by-product. A huge factory was built for its production just outside Labastida. But at the end of the 1980s American demand for sangria dropped and Pepsico sold the enterprise to the Julián Cantarero group (*see also* Bodegas Campo Burgo). Rioja Santiago has no vineyards of its own and does no vinification. It works solely with bought-in wine. The younger red wines from this bodega lack class, but its *reserva* has a pleasant scent, a smooth taste, and possesses the right amount of wood. There are two *gran reservas*, the regular one

and the Gran Fino Enológica made only in the very best years. The same wines are brought out under various brand names, including Rioja Santiago, Gran Condal, Vizconde de Ayala, Bilibio and Castillo de Ezpeleta.

CVNE 26200 Haro

After its foundation in 1879 by Eusebio Real de Asúa, family, and friends, this bodega grew so fast that considerable extensions had to be carried out three years later. In order to obtain capital, the structure of the business had to be altered and in the process it acquired a new name: Compañía Vinícola del Norte de España, abbreviated to CVNE. Under the direction of the Real de Asúa family, who hold a majority of the shares, CVNE evolved into one of the leading, most influential Rioja producers. In Spain and beyond the name of this house is synonymous with quality. A characteristic of CVNE is its continuing investment in better facilities and in its own vineyards. The firm now has nearly 500 ha (1,236 acres), which yield about half the grapes required. There are about 25,000 casks in the cellars, one-third of French oak. One of CVNE's best-selling wines is its white Monopole, a fresh, balanced product that is given a year's ageing in cask. There is also a white Rioja that is not wood-aged, the refreshing Cune Lanceros. The red wines are exceptionally reliable, examples being the supple, charming Rioja Clarete 3er año *crianza*; the rather more mature and

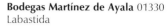

firmer Viña Real *plata*; the Cune 5o año, which is almost like a *reserva*; the generous, slightly spicy Viña Real oro *reserva* and *gran reserva*; and the velvety Imperial. This last wine represents the best selections from the best years and comes as a *reserva* and a *gran reserva*.

Federico Paternina 26200 Haro

This firm has what is probably the biggest hall in Europe for storing wine casks. Around 35,000 *barricas* are stacked here. In them Banda Azul, Federico Paternina's best-selling brand, is matured. Elsewhere in the vast complex there are a further 12,000 casks for other wines. The bodega still bears the name of the man who founded it in 1898, but it has had various owners. Since 1985 it has belonged to the Marcos Eguizábal group, which also owns Franco-Españolas and has sherry interests. The firm works only with bought-in must for its whites and rosés, and wine for its reds. The white Banda Dorada is somewhat neutral in taste. There is more personality to the Federico Paternina Reserva, a fresh wine with plenty of taste and a fine aroma of wood. The red Banda Azul *crianza* is supple, reasonably firm and decent. The standard improves with the Viña Vial *reserva*. The Federico Paternina *gran reserva* and the Conde de los Andes (made only in exceptional years) are aged in Ollauri, in underground cellars. Their aroma is dark-toned, with a lot of wood, and they remain vital even for several decades after their year of vintage.

La Rioja Alta 26200 Haro

Like a number of the other Riojan top producers – CVNE, López de Heredia, and Muga among them – La Rioja Alta is located in the area around the railway station in Haro. It has in fact been there since 1890. The present owners are descendants of the founders and industrialists. About half the production derives from the firm's own 300 ha (741 acres) of vineyards; bought-in grapes account for the rest. Some 85 percent of the output consists of *reservas* and *gran reservas*. These are matured in about 32,000 casks. The Viña Ardanza is a complete, harmonious and fragrant wine of a quite generous kind that is usually given at least three years' ageing in cask. For the Reserva 904 (a *gran reserva*) the figure is seven years, and eight years for the Reserva 809. Wood, vanilla and tannin are strongly present in the 904, which is a traditional, robust Rioja that lasts well in bottle. This last point also

applies to the 890, which can be very mature without being tired, and is made only in exceptional years. In 1990 the house produced another, special *gran reserva*, the Centenario 1890-1990. Other good wines that deserve mention are the Viña Arana *reserva* and the Viña Alberdi *crianza*. The firm also has wine interests in Ribera del Duero and Riás Baixas.

R. López de Heredia Viña Tondonia 26200 Haro

The most striking feature of this bodega's collection of buildings is a small tower in art nouveau style. It dates from 1892, when Rafael López de Heredia, a wine producer from Chile, began to build new cellars, offices and a dwelling house. People who visit López de Heredia today often have the feeling of going back in time. This bodega is a bulwark of conservatism. Wooden fermentation vats are still in use; all the wines are aged in cask – in 15,000 *barricas*; transferring wines is done by hand

in underground cellars with black mould on the walls; and all the *reservas* are fined with white of egg. The firm vinifies all its wines itself. Its own 170 ha (420 acres) supply half of the grapes required and the rest are bought in.

Style and refinement characterize the red wines. Thus the Viña Tondonia *reserva*, from the vineyard of that name, is a splendid Rioja with elegance and a good balance between wood and fruit. There is also a *gran reserva* with the same name in which there is more firmness and development to be found. The elegant *crianzas* Viña Cubillo and the rather more mature and substantial Viña Boscoñia are fine younger wines. About a quarter of production consists of white wines, among them the smoothly fresh Viña Gravonia and the complex Viña Tondonia with its pronounced bouquet. This traditionally-run bodega is still the property of the López de Heredia family.

Left: At López de Heredia they still work with wooden fermenting vats.

Bodegas Martínez de Ayala 01330 Labastida

Here you can sample the atmosphere of a small family bodega, founded in 1870, where the work is carried out in a strictly craftsmanlike way. It processes the grapes from its own 10 ha (25 acres), and also buys in wine. After ageing in the 400 or so casks and in bottle, the resulting red wines are elegant and fresh, and often remain drinkable for 30 to 40 years. Besides the Martínez de Ayala brand name, Viña Mediate, or Viña Mendiguria, are used for the oldest wine.

Granja Nuestra Señora de Remelluri 01330 Labastida

This idyllically situated bodega at the foot of the Sierra de Cantabria mountains works mainly (85 percent) with grapes from its own 60 ha (148 acres) of vineyard. The owner, Jaime Rodriguez Salis, and his family have invested a great deal of time and money in restoring this *granja* (farm), replanting the vineyard, and building the cellars – where the contents include stainless-steel fermentation tanks and 3,000 casks, a fifth of them made of French oak. Red Remelluri – *crianza* and *reserva* – possess exemplary quality, with fine nuances, noble wood, mature fruit and an elegant firmness.

Unión de Cosecheros de Labastida 01330 Labastida

For quality this is one of the best cooperatives in the Rioja, and a number of renowned houses are among its customers. But it also bottles some of its production, using names that include Montebuena (for young wine), Viña Solagüen, Castillo Labastida, and Castrijo. For ageing its better wines 1,000 *barricas* were bought. The cooperative has about 160 members who between them work 450 ha (1,110 acres) of vineyards.

Bodegas Alavesas 01300 Laguardia

It was the industrialist Miguel Angel Alonso Samaniego who in 1972 brought together a group of wine growers with the aim of setting up a bodega, Alonso putting up the capital and the growers the land. After the death of the founder all the shares passed to his family. The grapes come from the bodega's own 100 ha (247 acres) and from 200 to 300 ha ((495 to 740 acres) elsewhere. The most important brand is the Solar de Samaniego, applied both to young and to wood-aged wines. Generally the wines are typical of Rioja Alavesa in being elegant rather than rounded and seldom dark in hue. Their taste is pure and nearly always has fruit. The wood aroma is by no means excessive even in the *reservas* and *gran reservas*. The bodega holds 6,000 casks. Other brand names used, for the *crianzas* or younger wines, are Solar de Iriarte and Señorío de Berbete.

Bodegas Campillo 01300
Laguardia
The official opening of this bodega took place in September 1990. The elegantly designed T-shaped building stands in the middle of a 25 ha (62 acre) vineyard. It is a subsidiary of the Martínez Zabala group, which also owns Bodegas Faustino Martínez in Oyón – where Bodegas Campillo's first vintages were made. In fact the latter's wines come not only from its own vineyard, but also from the Faustino Martínez estate, which covers about 350 ha (865 acres). Yet the wines from the two bodegas are not identical. Those from Campillo – exclusively red so far – are made solely from Tempranillo, which makes them somewhat lighter. The quality of both the *reserva* and the *gran reserva* is high. For wood ageing the Laguardia bodega has 8,000 casks, a quarter of them of French oak. The name Campillo was formerly used for a subsidiary brand of Faustino Martínez.

Bodegas Palacio 01300 Laguardia
In 1987 this firm was taken over by the management, who had bought all the shares from Seagram, the owners. A great deal has been invested since then. French casks have replaced some of the stock of 10,000. It is hoped that eventually only *barricas* of French oak will be used.

Two new wines were launched in the year of the take-over, the red and the white Cosme Palacio y Hermanos, named after the man who founded the original bodega in 1894. Both wines are aged in cask, the white for a somewhat shorter period than the red. They are of a very good standard. The Glorioso name represents a much bigger production, covering a considerable range of wines. The young wines have improved in quality since 1987 – the white and rosé included – and this may be expected to be the case with the wood-aged types. The pre-1987 quality is quite simply good, with the Glorioso *gran reserva* out in the lead. At the beginning of 1991

the firm introduced its Mil Flores, a fruity and floral red wine in a millefiore bottle.

Cosecheros Alaveses 01300
Laguardia
In 1985 six independent producers decided to set up a bodega together to enable a proportion of their wine to be processed, bottled and sold under a new name, and so Cosecheros Alaveses came into being. The red wines are produced by the individual shareholders – from 100 ha (247 acres) – and a selection from these goes on to Cosecheros Alaveses. Under the brand name Artadi the bodega offers an excellent red wine for drinking young, with plenty of colour and fruit, and a lively taste. The Viñas de Gain is also delicious: a meaty Tempranillo wine that is matured for one year in cask. The firm has 500 casks in store, a quarter of them made of French oak. The Artadi rosé and white are somewhat less interesting although these, too, are carefully made. Valdepomares is a second brand name used for simpler wines.

Viñedos del Contino 01309
Laserna
In 1974 a splendid wine estate was created by CVNE and a group of private individuals at the foot of a broad, flat hill halfway between Logroño and Laguardia. It was given the name Viñedos del Contino and covers 52 ha (124 acres). Partly because of a very low yield per ha the wine, a red *reserva* is very concentrated, with a deep colour, delicious taste, and a creamy wood aroma. It is nurtured in casks of which half are of American and half of French oak. The estate has a total of 1,500 *barricas* in stock.

Bodegas Bretón y Cía 26000
Logroño
This enthusiastically managed firm has been in existence since 1985. It has 50 ha (124 acres) of its own land and buys in grapes from a further 50 ha. The Bretón family, who together with a group of growers are the owners of the estate, make fragrant, elegant red wines, namely the Loriñon *crianza* and *reserva*. In addition to the regular white Loriñon, one fermented in new

casks was introduced from the 1990 vintage. This experiment was not successful, however, and it remains to be seen whether it will be repeated.

Bodegas Campo Viejo 26000
Logroño
Since its establishment in 1963 Campo Viejo has grown into the biggest Rioja producer: it sells more than 5.5 million bottles per annum. About a fifth of this amount is yielded by the bodega's own 300 ha (741 acres) of vineyards, of which some 50 ha (124 acres) are planted with relatively young vines. In the early years Campo Viejo produced mainly cheap wines that were not given wood ageing. In the 1980s, however, the firm began to make wines of *crianza* or still more mature quality, and as a result the number of casks was greatly increased – to the present 45,000. Around 80 percent of them are of American oak and the rest of French. A wine that is aged only in French casks is the Marqués de Villamagna *gran reserva*, a stylish, balanced wine with a beautifully

Above: The owner of Bodegas Marqués de Murrieta, Vicente Cebrián Sagarriga, Conde de Creixell.
Left: The outstandingly beautiful landscape near Laguardia.
Below: Cleaning barrels with burning sulphur at CVNE.

mature and distinguished taste. Other wines to be recommended from the extensive range are the elegant Viña Alcorta *reserva*, a pure Tempranillo wine from the firm's own estate; the Campo Viejo *reserva*, rather more rounded in taste and a frequent prize-winner; and the Selección José Bezares, with a lot of fruit and again a pure Tempranillo. This last name also applies to a pleasant white and rosé. Like Marqués del Puerto and a

number of other concerns, Campo Viejo belongs to the Bodegas y Bebidas group. Subsidiary brands are Castillo de San Asensio, Foncalada, Almenar, Tres Ducados and Marqués de Ciria.

Bodegas Franco-Españolas 26000 Logroño
It was in 1890 that the Frenchman Frédéric Anglade arrived in Logroño, where he not only bought grapes for the Bordeaux house of

Anglade, but also purchased land where he could grow his own. In 1901 he set up his own wine business, Bodegas Franco-Españolas, with Spanish capital. However, the firm regards 1890 as its foundation year and so the centenary was celebrated in 1990 by the present owners, the Marcos Eguizábal group (to which Federico Paternina and a number of sherry houses also belong). The estate's own vineyards were sold long ago, which means that the 10 or so wines in the present range are made on the basis of bought-in grapes. The bodega produces both classic, wood-aged wines – reds and whites – and fruity kinds for drinking young. In the latter category there are the white Diamante and the agreeably aromatic Viña Soledad in its slender brown bottles. There is also a Viña Soledad Reserva Tête de Cuvée. This is aged for four years in cask and in addition to its pronounced vanilla aroma has a smoothly fresh, refined taste. The best-selling red wine is the pleasant Rioja Bordón *crianza*, which also comes in *reserva* and *gran reserva* form. The most

special of the wines is the Excelso *gran reserva*, which is made only in exceptional years and in small quantities. There are some 25,000 casks in the cellars of Bodegas Franco-Españolas. The firm carries a number of subsidiary brands, among them Casa de la Reina, Conde Bel and Conde Lar.

Bodegas Marqués de Murrieta
26000 Logroño
Just outside Logroño, beside the road to Zaragoza, is the Ygay estate. Since 1872 the cellars of Bodegas Marqués de Murrieta, a business established 20 years earlier, have stood here. The bodega bears the name of its founder, Luciano de Murrieta, who was made a Marqués on his 50th birthday. This dynamic personality not only carried out pioneering work in the viticultural sphere (this included the first export of Spanish wine in casks), but also in the social field – which is why a street in Logroño was named after him. The present owner is Vicente Cebrián Sagarriga, Conde de Creixell. All the wine today comes from the bodega's own vineyards – around 300 ha (741 acres) – and is vinified and nurtured in a cellar complex that was greatly enlarged in the 1980s. All the wines undergo wood ageing for a minimum of two years, and to this end there are 13,000 casks – some of them very old. The firm's red Etiqueta Blanca is a reliable, firm *crianza*. More nuances and charm are present in the *reserva*; and the Castillo Ygay *gran reserva* usually goes on sale only after 40 years or so – but despite this shows no tiredness. It is a beautiful, majestic Rioja of the highest possible standard. A 20-year-old white wine is sold under this same name. Its perfume and taste offer both subtle nuances and maturity, along with freshness, juice, and a restrained aroma of vanilla. The white *crianza*, *reserva* and *gran reserva* are also glorious products.

Bodegas Olarra 26000 Logroño
"The Cathedral of Rioja" is the nickname for the premises in which Olarra is established. This revolutionary piece of architecture is in the form of a letter Y, its three wings symbolizing the three districts of Rioja. Beside this structure there is an underground cellar for casks beneath 111 hexagonal, pointed roofs. Housed here are 25,000 casks, 20 percent of them of French wood. This bodega was completed in 1973 and was named after one of the shareholders, Luis Olarra, who left the company

in 1984. Since then it has been owned by the Guibert and Ucín families. Bodegas Olarra possesses no vineyards of its own and its wines are made in the modern premises here exclusively from bought-in grapes. Most of the wines are sold under the Añares name. These are very clean-tasting, whether red, white or rosé, slightly fruity and graceful – with wood and vanilla progressively more perceptible in the *crianza*, *reserva* and *gran reserva*. Somewhat firmer in character are the wines that are offered under the Cerro Añon name. The white wine called Reciente is fresh and clean in taste. The subsidiary brand name Otoñal is used for the simpler wines produced by this bodega.

Bodegas Palacios Remondo 26000 Logroño
Although this bodega's head office is in Logroño (almost opposite Bodegas Olarra) the wines are made in Alfaro and Haro. It was in fact in Alfaro that José Palacios began his own wine business in 1947; and his son Antonio created a château-like estate near Haro in 1990. The Palacios family also runs a hotel in Alfaro (*see* Travel Information).
 The firm has a total of 150 ha (370 acres) of vineyard, able to supply 60 percent of the grapes

required. In addition contracts have been drawn up with growers for the supply of grapes. Antonio Palacios and his team usually specify the precise date for picking to start. All the better wines go under the Herencia Remondo brand name. The reds are all harmonious, with a mild taste, a firm core, good fruit and a pleasant, but not exaggerated touch of wood. The whites and rosés, too, are successful. The José Palacios name is used for the simpler wines. The firm has 2,500 casks, 20 percent of them of French wood.

Barón de Ley 31587 Mendavia
The splendidly restored sixteenth-century Imaz hunting lodge stands in the middle of a 90 ha (220 acre) vineyard and is the headquarters of the Barón de Ley bodega. This was set up in the second half of the 1980s by the owners of El Coto. Both concerns now belong to the same group, Mercapital. The installations at Barón de Ley are ultramodern, but honour is done to tradition in the form of 4,000 casks, nearly 60 percent of them of French oak. The wines generally have a graceful structure, with a good balance between wood and fruit of the berry type. Cabernet Sauvignon vines grow in the vineyard as well as Tempranillo.

Bodegas Corral 26370 Navarrete
This is the only Riojan bodega that actually stands beside the old pilgrim route, or "St James's Way", to Santiago de Compostela. This is why Corral uses Don Jacobo as a brand name. The concern was founded in 1898 and has 40 ha (99 acres) of land, which is good for 20 to 25 percent of the grapes it needs; the rest are bought in. Nearly 6,500 casks are stored in the cellars, variously of American, French and Yugoslav oak. The red *crianza* and *reserva* are not too much dominated by wood and have a firm, substantial taste. The *gran reserva*, sold under the Corral name, is rather more mature and rounded.

Bodegas A. Navajas 26370 Navarrete
This small bodega has stainless-steel fermentation tanks and around 1,200 casks. Production is increasing steadily and comes mainly from bought-in grapes: the firm itself has only 5 ha (12 acres) of vineyard. The Navajas family makes good, quite meaty red wines. Both the Navajas and the Gustales *crianza* also have a measure of wood and vanilla. The white Navajas *crianza* also deserves recommendation for its lively and delicious taste with a lot of juice and a noble wood aroma.

Above: In autumn almost all Riojan wine villages have a celebration, including Laguardia.

Bodegas Beronia 26200 Ollauri
After the sherry and brandy firm of Gonzalez Byass took over this bodega in 1982, its capacity was increased fourfold. Beronia was then four years old. The 10 ha (25 acres) of vineyards around the building are all that this firm owns, and it therefore works chiefly with bought-in grapes (and sometimes wine). The younger kinds of wine are sold under the Berón name. The white is fresh in taste, with something of exotic fruit in it; and the red, after 12 months in cask, has some wood and a supple, pleasant taste. Beronia is the name on the label of the more mature wines. These are aged in the nearly 7,000 casks here and are characterized by a firm elegance, purity, suppleness and a fine aroma of wood.

Bodegas El Coto 01320 Oyón
After having belonged to the Alexis Lichine group, Bodegas El Coto was taken over in 1991 by the Spanish Mercapital organization – which bought Barón de Ley at the same time. About a quarter of the production comes from the firm's own land, which covers almost 100 ha (247 acres) in the neighbourhood

of Cenicero. In the technologically well-equipped cellar complex graceful, well-balanced wines are made; they are not particularly deep in colour, but wood and tannin are there to a pleasant degree. The *crianza* is called El Coto or Coto Mayor; the *reserva* and *gran reserva* is Coto de Imaz, as is the fresh white and rosé. About 12,000 *barricas* are stored in the cellars.

Bodegas Faustino Martínez 011320 Oyón

The best-known wines from this family concern are the red Faustino V and Faustino I. Both come in bottles of dark frosted glass. The Faustino V is a creamy *reserva* with considerable wood and a hint of freshness; the more matured, aristocratic Faustino I comes in the *gran reserva* category. These two products probably make Faustino Martínez the biggest Riojan exporter of mature wines. This does not mean that the bodega makes no other kinds – on the contrary, it follows a policy of diversification. Thus it produces splendid white and rosé wines for drinking young (under the Faustino V name) plus a range of simpler wines (Faustino VII), as well as Cavas. The best of them is the Faustino Martínez Brut Reserva, which is given 27 months' cellar rest; finely sparkling, it also has some fruit. The grapes for the Cavas and for about 40 percent of the other wines come from the firm's 350 ha (865 acres) of vineyards. The firm has a stock of about 20,000 casks. Bodegas Campillo in Laguardia is a subsidiary owned by the Martínez family, who have been making wine in Oyón since 1860. Señor Burgues is used as a subsidiary brand name.

Bodegas Maese Joan 01320 Oyón

Larios, a very important gin producer in Spain, has various wine interests including a firm in Málaga and Bodegas Maese Joan in the Rioja, established in 1989. This was formed with 15 or so wine growers who between them had 170 ha (420 acres) of land at their disposal. The grapes are processed in cellars with up-to-date equipment. Various brand names are used. For young wines in Spain itself it is mainly Viñalzada, and Armorial for the *crianzas*. For special sections of the market the names mostly used are Coro for young wines and Vega Vieja for wood-aged types. A charming red Rioja from the Coro range is the Black Label, which is given two months' wood ageing. The Vega Vieja *crianza* and *reserva* are both characterized by an attractive taste with both wood and a suggestion of fruit – especially raspberries. This young firm has just under 2,000 casks in store – to be increased to around 3,000.

Bodegas Martínez Bujanda 01320 Oyón

In 1991 the Spanish magazine *Gourmets* placed no fewer than eight Bodegas Martínez Bujanda wines among the best in the country. This is just one example of the many compliments and honours that have come the way of this perfectly equipped wine concern and the man who directs it, Jesús Martínez Bujanda. In 1984 he built a completely new complex to replace the old bodega dating from 1890, now arranged as a museum. Every possible style of wine can be made in the new cellars, and for the 11,000 casks two halls have been built where both temperature and humidity can be regulated. The grapes come exclusively from the firm's own 270 ha (667 acres) of land. The Martínez Bujanda range is characterized by a high average quality. The red wine for drinking young is dark in colour, with fruit of berry type, and is absolutely delightful. The white and rosé, too, are fruity and refreshing with plenty of taste. In 1989 some of the white wine was fermented in new vats and then aged in them for about seven months. The experiment was a success and has subsequently been continued on a bigger scale. In its various manifestations, from *crianza* to *gran reserva*, the red Conde de Valdemar is characterized by a vital, balanced taste with a smooth fruitiness, adequate tannin, an agreeable wood aroma and a good finish.

Bodegas Otañon Quel 26570

After years of supplying grapes to the big bodegas, the Perez Marco family decided in 1985 to set up their own wine business, Bodegas Otañon. The grapes come from their 70 ha (173 acres) of land. The equipment is modern and there are some 1000 casks in the cellars. The wines – such as the Artesa *crianza* and *reserva* – are of a decent quality. Other names used are Boyante, Comportilla, Señorío de Villoslada and Valliciergo.

Bodegas Virgen del Valle 01307 Samaniego

Strict selection of bought-in grapes forms the basis that this bodega has worked on since 1987. The Cincel *crianza* – given a year's ageing in some of the 850 casks here – is juicy, neither too heavy nor too light, and attractively supplied with wood and vanilla. In addition a young red wine, called Chocante, is produced by the *macération carbonique* method.

Bodegas Gurpegui 31570 San Adrián

This was the first house in the Rioja to produce rosé on a large scale. Luis Gurpegui, whose father founded the bodega in 1921, was in fact known locally as the "king of rosé". Bodegas Gurpegui owns 150 ha (370 acres) of land in San Adrián and the immediate neighbourhood which provide for about 8 percent of the wine. The rest is bought in as grapes or wine. In all the kinds of wine made – mostly sold under the Viñadrián brand name – the character of the grapes used is retained. Most of these are young wines, with no wood ageing. Wines that are aged in the 6,000 or so *barricas* in the cellars include some for a subsidiary firm, Bodegas Berceo of Haro, which does not have enough room of its own. Aplauso, Don Quintiliano and Riazán are in use as subsidiary brand names. Another subsidiary, Bodegas y Viñedos La Plana, was established in neighbouring Andosilla in 1990. The dynamic Gurpegui family also produces Navarra wine.

Bodegas Muerza 31570 San Adrián

In 1986 the white-painted Bodegas Muerza cellars with their green shutters and doors were taken over by the Cenalsa group of Navarra. The company, founded 1882, has 26 ha (64 acres) of their own land which is not sufficient to support their own production. They therefore have to buy in both grapes and wine. Their present policy is to produce more and more mature wines, hence the 1,500 barrels. The red Riojas are supple and fruity, with wood, and often have a light, earthy taste. The young wines are relatively neutral, but certainly clean and pleasant. The main label is Rioja Vega. Bodegas Ugaldes, (with Señorial) is used as a subsidiary label.

Bodegas Antigua Usanza 26338 San Vicente de la Sonsierra

In 1989 the distillery Licorera Albendense founded its own bodega in Rioja, called Antigua Usanza. This has been equipped with

Left: At Bodegas Muga the white wine is fined with fresh egg white.

89

Above: Drinking wine out of a porron.

stainless steel tanks and 500 barrels (half of them French). The company buys wines mainly from Rioja Alavesa. The young ready-to-drink wines carrying the label Viña Azai are fruity and clean. The *crianza* Antigua Usanza is usually supple and soft, with a slight taste of fruit. The company's subsidiary label is Peña Bajenza.

Bodegas Sierra Cantabria 26338 San Vicente de la Sonsierra
Originally called Bodegas Eguren, the name of this company, founded in 1979, was changed to the present one during the 1980s. The owners, who are members of the Eguren family, have 100 ha (247 acres). The (mainly red) wines are produced with great skill and have more colour and strength than the average Alavasa product. Murmurón, a young red wine made by *macération carbonique*, is fruity and meaty in taste. The rather rustic Sierra Cantabria is full of taste and comes in *crianza, reserva* and *gran reserva* variants.

Bodegas Sonsierra 26338 San Vicente de la Sonsierra
During the 1990s this cooperative specialized increasingly in selling bottled wine. It also got in about 650 *barricas*. Under the Sonsierra name red, white and rosé wines for drinking young are offered, as is an engaging *crianza*. In quality this in turn is rather surpassed by the Viña Mindiarte. The cooperative has just under 250 members who between them cultivate some 640 ha (1580 acres).

Bodegas Valgrande 26338 San Vicente de la Sonsierra
Gregorio García, who also owns Bodegas Valduero in Ribero del Duero, is the biggest shareholder in this wine business, founded in 1983.

The accent here is on the production of wood-aged red wines. About 30 to 40 percent of the volume comes from the firm's own 40 ha (99 acres), the rest from bought-in grapes. Most of the red wines have an elegant taste and at the same time substantial wood; this is true for the Rincón de la Navas and Viña Saseta. There is more depth in the fine Rincón de la Navas *reserva*. The Azkueta is a pleasant, smoothly fruity young red wine. The complement of 1,500 casks is to be steadily increased in coming years.

Bodegas Amézola de la Mora 26359 Torremontalbo
In 1986 the lawyer Iñigo Amézola de la Mora built a completely new cellar complex in the middle of his own 70 ha (173 acres) of vineyards. Subsequently good red wines have been marketed. These are all matured and have a quite firm, vital taste with some fruit, as well as wood and vanilla. About a third of the 2,500 casks are of French oak. This is a rising star among the smaller Rioja estates. Viña Amézola and Señorío Amézola are the brand names.

Bodegas Ondarre 31230 Viana
In 1985 three young people opened their own, very modern bodega. It had financial difficulties and in 1987 was taken over by the Guibert and Ucín families, of Bodegas Olarra. The red Ondarre *crianza* and *reserva* are balanced, with a pleasing aroma of both wood and fruit. This house has 1,500 casks at its disposal, a proportion of them of French oak. As well as the wood-aged kinds, wines for drinking young are produced (Ondarre and Tidon are the names) and various types of Cava. These bear the name Cava Añares. Besides the fresh *brut* and *brut nature* with their fruit, there is also a rosé.

Bodegas SMS 01307 Villabuena de Alava
This bodega was founded at the end of the 19th century and acquired its present name in 1943. It uses only grapes from its own estate, which is being increased from 35 to 50 ha (86 to 124 acres). All the wines – red without exception – are matured in wood, and the bodega has 900 casks for this purpose. The Valserrano *reserva* is somewhat dominated by (old) wood. The very pleasant *reserva* and *crianza* with the same brand name have more juice and fruit. Part of the cellars is underground, dug out of the rock, and probably dating from the seventeenth century.

Travel Information

HOTELS AND RESTAURANTS

Asador San Roque, 26540 Alfaro, tel (41) 182888 Good for regional dishes; also has a bar.
Hotel Palacios, 26540 Alfaro, tel. (41) 180100 The same owners as Bodegas Palacios Remondo (next door). Decent rooms, friendly service and a good restaurant, where the originals of some of the paintings used on the bodega's labels can be seen on the walls. There is an attractive wine museum in the cellar.
Sopitas, 226580 Arnedo, tel (41) 380266 Atmospheric eating place in a former bodega. Roast kid is one of the specialities.
Hotel Virrey, 26580 Arnedo, tel (41) 380150 The restaurant has an excellent reputation locally because it is such good value. Simple rooms.
Casa Mateo, 26500 Calahorra, tel (41) 130009 Congenial, unpretentious restaurant. Marvellous lamb cutlets and good wines.
Chef Niño, 26500 Calahorra, tel (41) 133104 Regional cuisine; has been a small hotel since 1988.
Montserrat 2, 26500 Calahorra, tel (41) 130017 The place for fish and shellfish.
Parador Marco Fabio Quintiliano, 26500 Calahorra, tel (41) 130358 Columns and other remains from Roman times have been set out in the garden, which has a splendid view out over the broad Ebro valley. Regional cooking in the restaurant.
La Taberna de la Cuarta Esquina, 26500 Calahorra, tel (41) 134355 Inventively cooked and presented dishes.
El Valenciano, 26360 Fuenmayor, tel (41) 450227 The *cabrito asado* here is delicious, and also the Valencian rice dishes.
Los Agustinos, 26200 Haro, tel (41) 311308 By far the best hotel for the western part of Rioja, located in a beautifully restored convent.
Beethoven II, 26200 Haro, tel (41) 311181 Regional fare is lovingly prepared here. Beside the restaurant is a well-patronized bar that serves good *tapas*.
La Kika, 26200 Haro, tel (41) 311447 Very small, so it is wise to book. Food comes fresh from the market and is mostly served without a menu. Lunch only on weekdays.
Mesón Tercte, 26200 Haro, tel (41) 310023 The best-known local eating place. Leg of lamb here is roasted in a wall oven.

Jatorrena, 01330 Labastida, tel (41) 331050 Riojan cooking. There are a few rooms here.
Mesón los Claveles, 01330 Labastida, tel (41) 331053 Enjoy the lamb cutlets *al sarmiento* (grilled over vine twigs) and the fruity red *vino de cosechero*.
Hostal Marixa, 1300 Laguardia, tel (41) 100165 Well-thought-of restaurant with Basque and Riojan cuisine.
Avenida 21, Avenida Portugal 21, 26000 Logroño, tel. (41) 228602 Pleasing ambience, dishes full of taste, good wine list.
Los Bracos Sol, Bretón de los Herreros, 26000 Logroño, tel (41) 226608 The most comfortable and most expensive place to stay in Logroño. Centrally situated.
El Cachetero, Laurel 3, 26000 Logroño, tel (41) 228463 This has been a famous restaurant for nearly a century. Traditional fare and a simple ambience.
Carabanchel, San Augustín 2, 26000 Logroño, tel (41) 223883 Regional dishes of high quality.
Carlton Rioja, Gran Vía del Rey Don Juan Carlos I, 26000 Logroño, tel (41) 212100 Fairly characterless but adequate hotel situated near the old centre.
Ciudad de Logroño, Menéndez Pelayo 9, 26000 Logroño, tel (41) 250244 Pleasant new hotel beside a park.
Gran Hotel, General Vara del Rey 5, 26000 Logroño, tel (41) 252100 Recently renovated; centrally situated.
Machado, Portales 49, 26000 Logroño, tel (41) 248456 Contemporary cuisine and a stylish interior. On the first floor.
Meson la Merced, Marqués de San Nicolás 109, 26000 Logroño, tel (41) 221166 Indisputably the best, and most beautiful, restaurant in the town – if not in the whole of Rioja. Three floors with brilliant décor, refined and inventive cooking, and an impressive wine list.
Murrieta, Marqués de Murrieta 1, 26000 Logroño, tel (41) 224150 Partly renovated three star hotel in the centre, with restaurant.
San Remo, Avenida de España 2, 26000 Logroño, tel (41) 230838 Famous for its "Avión" entrecôte.
Mesón la Cueva, 01320 Oyón, tel (41) 110022 In this good regional restaurant you have a view out over the terrace during lunch.
Hostal Tony, 26338 San Vicente de la Sonsierra, tel (41) 334001

Regional cuisine.

Parador, 26250 Santo Domingo de la Calzada, tel (41) 340300 Established in a former hospital, which was built on the site of a royal palace. It stands opposite the cathedral and also has a restaurant.
El Rincón de Emilio, 26250 Santo Domingo de la Calzada, tel (41) 340990 Carefully prepared Riojan dishes.
Mesón Borgia, 31230 Viana, tel. (48) 645781 Cooking of a high, creative order here, plus an excellent wine list.

PLACES OF INTEREST

Abalos The parish church has a baroque tower and there is a number of fine paintings in the palace of the Marqués de Legarda.
Aldeanueva de Ebro Also called the "Town of the Three Lies", because it is not an *aldea* (hamlet), still less is it *nueva* (new), and it is not even on the Ebro. There is a sixteenth-century altarpiece in the parish church, by Pedro de Troas.
Alfaro This is Rioja's biggest wine community. Bulls play an important part during the fiestas here – from mid-August to the beginning of September, and the Alfaro *corridas* are renowned. In the centre there are noblemen's houses and also the sixteenth-century church of San Miguel Arcángel. This has an unusual brick façade; doves and storks make their homes on and around this building.
Anguiano Village in the Sierra de la Demanda. Dancers on stilts take part in the festivities here around 22 July and on the last Sunday of September.
Arnedillo Spa where the waters are said to be therapeutic for rheumatism, bone disorders and sciatica.
Arnedo This town is dominated by a steep hill, frequented by doves and topped by the ruins of a Moorish castle. Arnedo has three churches of interest, including Santo Tomás from the first half of the sixteenth century, and a number of shoe factories; during the festivities at the end of September a Golden Shoes Trophy is presented. Near Arnedo is the monastery of Vico, where the church has a rich baroque interior, and where painted pottery is on sale.
Briñas Near this village the Ebro winds through a narrow ravine, the Conchas de Haro.
Briones This village is on a high hill and so the road in climbs steeply. For a splendid view over the Ebro valley stand beside the church, which has a high tower and is visited evey year by nesting storks. According to the local growers, the day the storks arrive indicates the quality of the coming vintage. Briones also has the ruins of a castle and what is probably the oldest dwelling-house in the region.
Calahorra This was already an important town two centuries before the beginning of the present era. The Romans, who arrived in 189 BC, changed the name from Calagorios to Calagurris. It became one of the most important towns of the empire, with its own coinage. Many Roman remains have been found around Calahorra, including the Lady of Calahorra, a marble head from the first century. The Roman orator Marcus Fabius Quintilianus, or Quintilian, was born here, as was the poet Aurelius Clemens Prudentius. On the top of the hill stands Calahorra's Gothic cathedral, the building of which went on from the twelfth to the eighteenth centuries. Carved bunches of grapes decorate the upper parts of the columns here. Other architectural interest comes from the churches of San Andrés and Santiago, and the eighteenth-century Bishop's Palace.
Cañas The building of the Santa María convent began in the twelfth century. The windows are very fine and here, too, is the tomb of Abbess Urraca López de Haro and an eighteenth-century crib. The nuns of the convent paint pottery and do embroidery.
Cenicero This wine village may owe its curious name (literally ashbin) to the fact that the Romans cremated their dead here. But it could also have arisen because cattle dealers used to keep themselves warm at nights here by burning dung – with a great deal of ash to show for it next morning. A miniature replica of the American Statue of Liberty stands in a small park here. Sometimes you can see women in the street busy plaiting *alambrados*, the metal meshes that go on bottles of Bodegas Berberana wine.
Clavijo In 844 a famous defeat was inflicted on the Moors here; according to tradition the Christians won because Santiago – the Apostle James – appeared to them on a white horse. An enormous painting depicting the battle hangs in the basilica here. Above the village the ruins of a great fortress stand proudly on an awe-inspiring rock.
El Cortijo Hamlet on a steep slope on the south bank of the Ebro, with

Below: The peaceful landscape near Briones.

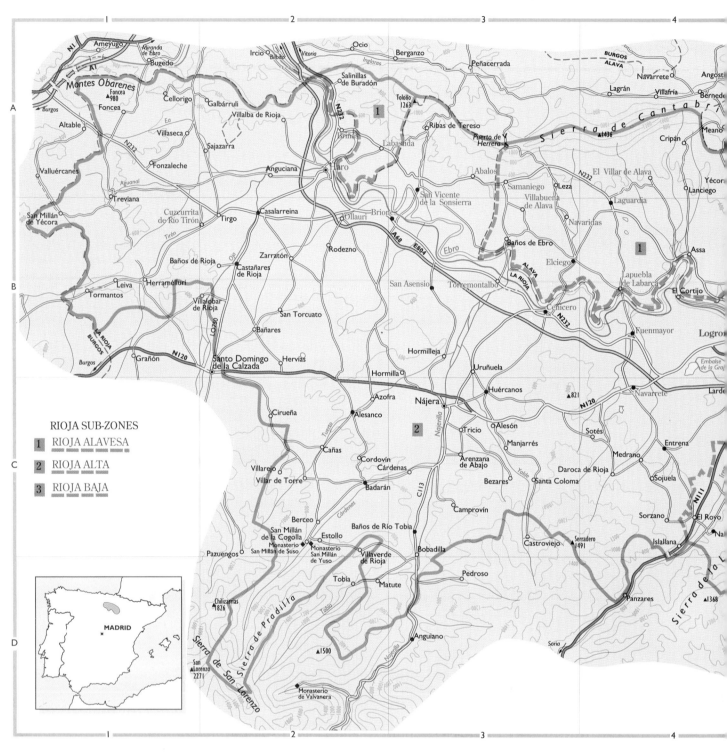

RIOJA SUB-ZONES

1 RIOJA ALAVESA

2 RIOJA ALTA

3 RIOJA BAJA

a marvellous view out over Rioja Alavesa. In the neighbourhood are the remains of the Puente Mantible, a great Roman bridge over the Ebro.

Elciego On a hill, with two churches. The larger of these has two dissimilar towers, and a striking arcade between them over the main door. There is a number of noblemen's houses with family crests adorning their frontages.

Fuenmayor It is said that the

mortar in the parish church was once mixed with wine. The retables in the church are well worth seeing.

Haro This is the wine capital of Rioja. Wine has always played an important role throughout the town's rich history. In the fourteenth century it was already the most important source of income, and acquired the byname *ciudad de jarreros* (city of jar makers). After the railway line to Bilbao was opened, many bodegas

moved from the Calle de Las Cuevas, with its cellars cut into the rock, to the station area lower down. A number of famous names are still there, including CVNE, López de Heredia, Muga, and La Rioja Alta. In the centre of Haro a number of *palacios* bear witness to the prosperity that wine brought to the town. Among them are the Palacio de Paternina, Palacio de la Cruz, and Palacio de los Condes (this is now a cultural centre). Of later date

are the impressive *fin de siècle* buildings around the Plaza de la Paz, the central square, and elsewhere. The late-eighteenth-century town hall is also here. Haro's most beautiful church is the Santo Tomás, a Gothic structure with sixteenth-century sculptures grouped around its two doors. The town celebrates in the last week of June, which is when the Batalla del Vino takes place and people splash one another with wine. Then in the

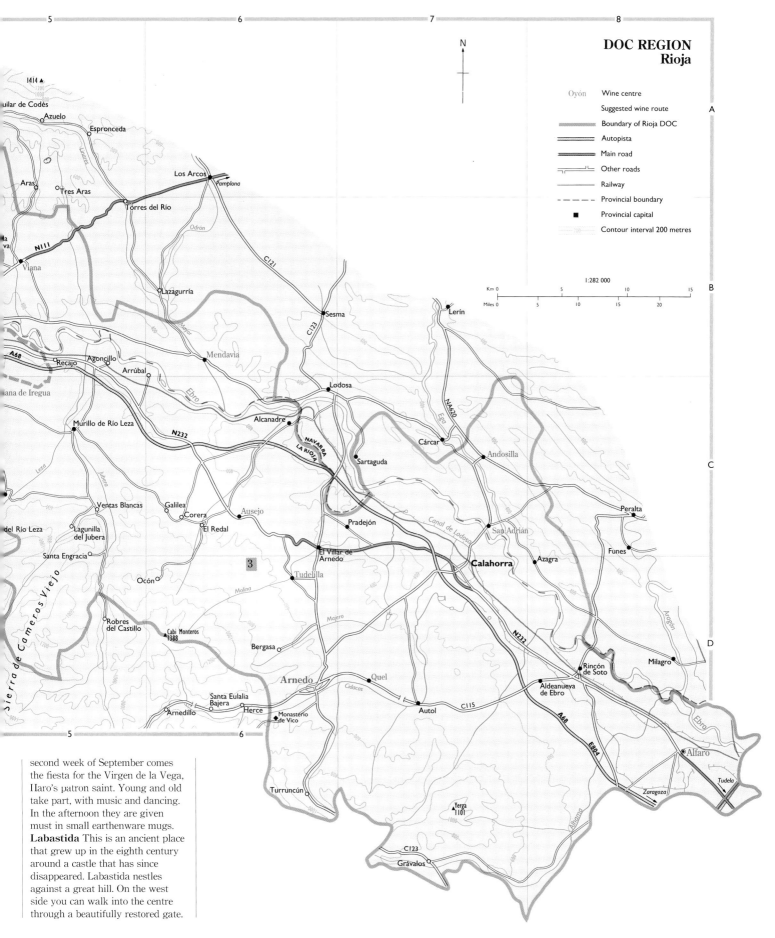

DOC REGION
Rioja

Oyón   Wine centre

Suggested wine route

Boundary of Rioja DOC

Autopista

Main road

Other roads

Railway

Provincial boundary

■   Provincial capital

Contour interval 200 metres

1:282 000

Km 0   5   10   15

Miles 0   5   10   15   20

second week of September comes
the fiesta for the Virgen de la Vega,
Haro's patron saint. Young and old
take part, with music and dancing.
In the afternoon they are given
must in small earthenware mugs.
Labastida This is an ancient place
that grew up in the eighth century
around a castle that has since
disappeared. Labastida nestles
against a great hill. On the west
side you can walk into the centre
through a beautifully restored gate.

The *ayuntamiento* here is eighteenth century and the church has one of the most prized organs in the region. Up from the church is the chapel of Nuestra Señora de la Piscina, built after Jerusalem had been captured during one of the Crusades. The authorities have placed seats near this little building so that people can enjoy the views from here. Unfortunately, to the east the scene is spoiled by a huge sangria and wine factory; and around the centre there has been some ugly new building.

Laguardia This rather ship-shaped village used to serve as a fortress defending Navarra from Moorish incursions. In fact Laguardia is still largely walled. The narrow streets here mean that cars are banned in some of them. Behind a number of the house fronts are cellars where in autumn grapes ferment in open concrete troughs with their skins, stalks and pips, and the sweet scent of must wafts through the streets. The twelfth-century church of Santa María de los Reyes has a magnificent fourteenth-century porch with lifesize sculptures of the Apostles. Félix de Samaniego, who wrote fables, lived here in Laguardia. His former house now serves as the viticultural station for Rioja Alavesa; and the authorities have placed a bust of this famous villager in an open cupola in a small park. The prehistoric village of La Hoya has been excavated just a few hundred yards from Laguardia and finds from it are displayed in the local archaeological museum. Also in the neighbourhood of Laguardia are a number of dolmens and Bronze Age burial chambers.

Logroño This sizeable provincial town with its 115,000 inhabitants has a lot of traffic and a skyline with noticeable blocks of flats. Atmosphere seems lacking – until you visit the old centre. This is made up of mainly narrow streets, between the large Paseo de Espolón square and the bank of the Ebro. Here, too, are the churches, built when Logroño was an important stopping-place for pilgrims travelling to and from Santiago de Compostela. One of these churches is the Santa María de Palacio, which dates from the twelfth and thirteenth centuries and has a spire 50 m (164 ft) high. Even more imposing is the cathedral of Santa María la Redonda, fifteenth to seventeenth century, with a Gothic nave and two baroque towers (these are called San Pablo and San Pedro – St Paul and St Peter). Art treasures are displayed in the provincial museum here, an

Above: Rioja Alavesa and Sierra de Cantabria. In the foreground is the church of San Vicente de la Sonsierra.

eighteenth-century building where General Baldomero Espartero once lived. A bronze statue of him stands in the Paseo del Espolón, surrounded by fountains. Almost opposite this museum is a fine post office, dating from the 1930s. The old centre of the town is very pleasant in the evenings. The Calle Laurel is particularly bustling then, for there are about 25 bars here and various restaurants. Logroño's bodegas have largely gone from the centre and are now out on the edge of town.

Monasterio de Valvanera This Benedictine abbey stands 1,000 m (3,280 ft) up a side valley of the Najarilla, a remote establishment with a fifteenth-century church and a twelfth-century figure of the Virgin. It also has a hotel, restaurant, cafeteria and bar.

Nájera This was once the capital of the Rioja, for the kings of Navarra held court here, and it was later a residence of Castilian monarchs. Navarra's first coinage was struck in "Nájera of the Kings" and many kings, queens, princes and princesses lie buried in the abbey of Santa María la Real, founded in 1032. The most beautiful of the tombs is that of Doña Blanca (or Blanche) of Navarra with its twelfth-century carving. The Gothic cloisters are also worth a visit. It is said that the Benedictine monks of this abbey used to grow "mysterious" plants for a liqueur they made.

Navaridas About 70 percent of all the land here is planted with vines – a higher proportion than in any other Rioja Alavesa community. After seeing the old parish church

you can make your way up to the Balcón de la Rioja, a viewing point 1,100 m (3,610 ft) above sea level.

Navarrete The fifteenth-century parish church has a sixteenth-century Flemish triptych and goldsmith's work. Potters practise their craft in the narrow streets around. Since 1875 an entrance that came from a former pilgrims' hospital of 1185 has stood by the churchyard. Joan of Arc once slept in this hospital.

Oyón Village with a growing community of Logroño commuters, various important wine firms and a beautifully ornamented church. The road from Oyón to Laguardia leads through a fine landscape of vineyards.

Salinillas de Buradón A once thriving community that derived its prosperity from a saltmine (still in existence). Note the gateway into the town and the gallery supported on wooden posts behind it.

Samaniego This was once a fortified outpost for Laguardia. Even the church was built for defence.

San Millán de la Cogolla Named after San Millán, the saint who lived here somewhere between 473 and 574. The village has two notable monasteries. That of San Millán de Suso stands high up on a wooded hillside and dates from the tenth century. Clear Moorish influence can be seen in the austere interior. A twelfth-century Romanesque tomb commemorates the saint. It was in this monastery that the earliest known written words in Castilian, the official Spanish of today, were discovered. At the foot of the same hill stands the much bigger abbey

of San Millán de Yuso. The impressive size and brilliant interior of this fifteenth to seventeenth century abbey have led to its being called "the Riojan Escorial". A visit to Yuso is both a visual and a spiritual experience, the high point of which is the abbey church with its many treasures. The remains of San Millán lie here, in a monumental tomb ornamented with ivory.

San Vicente de la Sonsierra Here a castle and a church were built on a hill that rises high above the village roofs. During the traditional September festivals a feast is held on this hill, followed by a procession back down into the village. Dancing follows, and many people end up in the fountains. At Easter the atmosphere is quite different: penitents wearing tall pointed hats walk in procession through the streets, scourging themselves.

Santo Domingo de la Calzada A small town founded in the second half of the eleventh century by the saint of this name, who built bridges and improved roads for the benefit of pilgrims. The cathedral, mainly thirteenth-century, is distinguished by a beautiful baroque tower. Inside there is a cage with a white cock and hen, commemorating a local legend. A pilgrim who had been wrongfully accused of theft was condemned by the judge and hanged. When his parents returned four weeks later their son proved to be still alive. They pleaded with the judge to let him be taken down. But the judge, seated at table, declared that after four weeks a hanged man would be as dead as the roast chicken in front of him, whereupon it immediately grew feathers and began to run about. The town also has two fine monasteries and a chapel. The local festival is held 10 to 15 May.

Villabuena de Alava Wine village with a number of noblemen's houses.

WINE ROUTE

Following the suggested route will give you an excellent impression of the three Rioja districts. The journey leads through most of the important wine communities and offers many scenic views, particularly in Rioja Alavesa. One day is definitely too short a time for seeing the whole region. For this you should set aside at least two, and preferably three days. It would then be possible to make trips to interesting places off the actual wine route, such as the monastery at Valvanera and the castle at Clavijo.

Navarra

Capital: Pamplona
Province: Navarra is an *autonomía*
Area: 10,421 square kilometres
Population: 512,676

Above: The heavy rainfall and moderate climate in the northern wine zones of Navarra is responsible for the intense green of the landscape, as at Ayeguí.

Navarra is Spain in miniature: to the north are the rugged Pyrenees with their green valleys and tumbling mountain streams, while to the south is the flat Ebro valley with its dry Mediterranean climate. North of the capital, Pamplona, the peaks rise to more than 1,400 m (4,590 ft), while Tudela on the river Ebro is much lower at 275 m (900 ft) above sea level. Produce from the mountains includes the distinctive sheep's milk cheese Roncal, while the lower, flatter areas are covered with vineyards, orchards and fields. Extensive irrigation means that the Ebro valley grows a great deal of vegetable produce, including beans, artichokes and the famous Navarrese asparagus.

The history of Navarra is a tumultuous one. It became an independent kingdom at the end of the eighth century AD, after Charlemagne had driven the Moors out of Pamplona. At its most flourishing under Sancho III the Great, it stretched from León to beyond Bordeaux, but after his death in 1035 a decline set in, and from 1234 to 1512 Navarra was ruled by French dynasties. Spanish Navarra was integrated into the kingdom of Castilla, but French monarchs went on styling themselves kings of Navarra right up to the French Revolution.

The pilgrim way

The pilgrim route to Santiago de Compostela, which passes through the region, has been of great importance in the political, social and artistic development of Navarra. Thousands went on pilgrimage along this route, particularly from the eleventh to the end of the sixteenth centuries. Every year, Navarra was visited by around half a million pilgrims from all over Europe, and inns, monasteries, churches and chapels were built to cater for their

Above: The 11th-century bridge of Puente la Reina was built for pilgrims on their way to Santiago de Compostela. The bridge emerges in the main street.

spiritual and bodily needs. The monastery at Roncesvalles alone, on the French-Spanish border, provided pilgrims with around 40,000 litres (8,800 gal) of wine annually.

Quenching the thirst of pilgrims obviously provided a strong stimulus to winegrowing, and for centuries wine was second only to grain as a source of income in Navarra. It was the Romans who brought vines to this region. At Olite a tombstone from the second century BC was found with bunches of grapes depicted on it; at Cascante an amphora from the first century BC was discovered; and at Funes the remains of a large Roman wine-cellar of the first or second century have been excavated. After declining under Moorish rule, winegrowing revived strongly during the Middle Ages. Attention was given to quality in the thirteenth century under King Teobaldo I who brought vines from his native Champagne.

The fame of Navarra's rosé

Exporting began in the fourteenth century, when casks were shipped to Normandy and elsewhere. However, this was as nothing compared to the quantities that were to go to the New World after 1492. The quality of Navarra wines was often praised by Spanish writers in the sixteenth century, and this was when references to the district's rosés first began to occur. In 1592 Philip II and his treasurer, Enrique Cock, visited the wine village of Puente la Reina, noting that it had ample stocks of rosé.

At the beginning of the seventeenth century Navarra had 18,500 ha (45,700 acres) of vineyards, 30,000 ha (74,100 acres) in the first half of the 19th century, and 49,000 (121,000) in 1891. A great deal of wine was being sold to producers in France by this time, after phylloxera had destroyed the French vines. But Navarra itself suffered in this catastrophe; the first of these

parasites being reported in 1896. Yet in spite of the total devastation of the winegrowing areas, the region recovered fairly quickly. It had regained 10,000 ha (24,700 acres) by 1906, and more than 26,000 ha (64,200 acres) by 1920. Another upswing came between 1952 and 1968 when many new cooperatives were set up in Navarra. At that time the vineyards covered 40,000 to 45,000 ha (98,000 to 112,000 acres). Increasing competition and other problems then brought about a decline that lasted until around 1980. The area of Navarra's DO has now stabilized at about 18,000 ha (44,500 acres).

The northern zones

The vineyards are spread over five zones, all of them south of Pamplona. In the wine district – which is shaped like a goblet with a rather hefty foot – the Baja Montaña zone, which has 20 percent of the vineyards, is in the northeast. This comprises 14 communities with mainly reddish or yellowish soil, often with gravel and sometimes with limestone as well. A little under 600 mm (23.6 ins) of rain falls annually here, and the average temperature is 11.7°C (53.1°F). The best *rosados* are produced here and the highest yield per ha (acre) is registered. The central northern zone is called Valdizarbe. The climate is very like that of Baja Montaña – it is at most a fraction warmer. The soil is chalky, often with a reddish-grey tint. This zone has 24 communities and 6 percent of the vineyards. In the northwest there is Tierra Estella, where climate and soil are practically identical to those of Valdizarbe. Its vineyards are distributed over 26 communities and represent 12 percent of the total.

The southern zones

The northern zones are certainly hilly, but in the two southern ones the landscape flattens out. Ribera Alta, with the larger area, forms the heart of the Navarra DO. Except in the river valleys with their sandy clays, limestone predominates here. Rainfall varies according to location, but is always lower than in the northern zones. At Olite, to the northeast, an annual 513 mm (20.2 ins) is recorded; at Lerín to the west 472 mm (18.6 ins); and 444 mm (17.5 ins) at Marcilla in the south. The average annual temperature varies around 13.5°C (56.3°F). The 24 communities here cover 30 percent of the vineyard area. Ribera Alta is the second most important zone on this reckoning – although the average volume per ha (acre) is lowest here. The more southerly zone, around Tudela, is called Ribera Baja. It is dry here, with a rainfall of 448 mm (17.5 ins), and warm at an average 14°C (57.2°F). The Ebro valley is characterized by alluvial soils, whereas further north in the zone there is reddish limestone. With 32 percent of the vineyards Ribera Baja outrivals the other zones. This percentage may decrease in the long run, however, as it is in the somewhat cooler, damper north that a great deal of new planting is going on. The Señorío de Arínzano forms a striking example, for here Bodegas Julián Chivite is creating a wine estate of 150 ha (370 acres) in Tierra Estella.

Garnacha

The whole southwest side of Navarra borders on Rioja, and six Navarrese communities actually belong to the Riojan DO. This does not mean that the pattern of grape variety plantings is the same in the two areas. Tempranillo is the most important variety in Rioja, with Garnacha in second place. But in Navarra the scene is dominated by sweet, purple Garnacha. At the start of the 1990s it accounted for more than 85 percent of the total; Tempranillo came a long way behind with 5 percent; white Viura (or Macabeo) was 3 percent; Graciano 1 percent. The remaining varieties all had a less than 1 percent share. The past tense is used deliberately because an intensive programme of replanting has been started in the district. Navarra's *Consejo Regulador* hopes to have reduced the proportion of Garnacha to a half by the turn of the century, in favour of Tempranillo and Cabernet Sauvignon in particular. Chardonnay has also made its appearance: the Señorío de Sarría has planted 30 ha (74 acres).

The oenological station

In their selection of the replacement grape varieties the *Consejo Regulador* and the producers associated with it were advised in brilliant fashion by the Estación de Viticultura y Enología de Navarra (Evena). This was established at Olite in 1981 and has been continually extended and modernized since then. It has at its disposal five experimental vineyards and a fully equipped vinification complex, where it is possible to conduct numerous small-scale experiments. Research into native yeasts here, for example, must eventually result in a yeast bank.

New varieties

Experiments with more than 35 kinds of new grape varieties are being conducted. The research station has discovered that besides Tempranillo, Cabernet Sauvignon and Chardonnay can offer excellent results, as can Merlot and Ruby Cabernet (a Cabernet Sauvignon and Carignan cross). Evena can show the producers how the new varieties taste when by themselves, and when blended with other kinds, either wood-aged or not. One of the most potent blends is Tempranillo with Cabernet Sauvignon

(and possibly with some Merlot). The wine firm Guelbenzu has had success with this blend.

There are various reasons why Navarra is going over to a different range of grapes. One is that red wines made exclusively from Garnacha are almost by definition unable to rise above a middling quality. Often, too, they are light in colour and rather apt to oxidize. In the fiercely competitive world of wine it is vitally important for the Navarrese wine growers to give their *tintos* status and an identity of their own – and with Garnacha on its own the cause would be lost before they had started.

One kind of wine to which Garnacha lends itself extremely well is rosé – something that is also demonstrated in France, with Tavel, for example. True to tradition, Navarra produces large quantities. Its rosés are dry and often quite firm; if fermented at low temperature they can also have fruit and liveliness in their taste. The problem is that while this rosé sells well in its own area and on the Spanish home market, its international prospects are poor. In order to be effective abroad, the Navarra *Consejo Regulador* wants to reduce the proportion of rosé from around 45 percent to 30 percent. This strategic decision will also influence the future position of the Garnacha grape.

The cooperatives

A number of individual producers have adopted the conversion programme with enthusiasm. One example is Navarra's biggest exporter, Julián Chivite, who pays up to 60 percent more for high quality grapes, and replanting is vigorously promoted among growers who have long-term contracts with this bodega. In the new estate of Señorío de Arínzano Tempranillo, Cabernet Sauvignon, Merlot and Chardonnay are there in abundance. If the plan is really to succeed, however, the cooperatives will have to give their support, for they supply about 90 percent of all grapes. The cooperative idea is strong in Navarra. It was here in 1911 that one of the first Spanish wine cooperatives was founded, in Olite. On the front of the building are painted the words: *Unos por otros Dios por todos* (One for others, God for all). The movement advanced particularly strongly in the 1950s and 1960s, then during the difficult period that followed the cooperatives maintained a considerable area of by now languishing vineyards. Whether these concerns, often very conservative, will accept the new challenge facing Navarra remains to be seen. However, there are hopeful signs: a key role seems to be reserved for Bodegas Cenalsa, a large modern winery that has close links with many of the cooperatives.

Technical advance

Navarra's quality policy is not confined to the varieties of grapes planted. A great deal also needs to happen in the area of winemaking. At various bodegas hundreds of millions of pesetas have been invested in modern plant and others have their plans ready. In the 1980s these investments made many Navarra wines better than they had ever been in their long history. In general they were less alcoholic, with more fruit, and better balanced and more clean-cut than before. This applied to the red, rosé and white wines – with red and rosé giving better results than the white. With its reds and rosés Navarra seems to be able to differentiate itself positively with regard to other wine districts – but hardly with the whites. Probably there are no surprises in store here, with the exception of a few Chardonnays. Navarra sees red and rosé wines as its strongest suit and its producers now give them the fullest attention, which is probably a wise decision.

PRODUCERS OF SPECIAL INTEREST

Bodegas Irache 31240 Ayeguí
In 1991, when this firm was a century old, its capacity was doubled. Among other items it acquired a battery of stainless-steel fermentation tanks. An impressive cellar for casks was also built, and the bodega now has room for 10,000 altogether. This family business has 40 ha (99 acres) of vineyards and also buys-in grapes. In the 1970s its wines were usually rather dull, but the average quality has improved steadily since then. This applies particularly to the Castillo Irache, made for drinking young, in white (100 percent Viura) and rosé (100 percent Garnacha). The red Viña Irache is made from varying percentages of Tempranillo, Garnacha and Graciano; there is usually a lot of fruit in its supple taste. With the purchase of thousands of new casks improvement may be expected in the standard of the wood-aged Gran Irache (*crianza*), Castillo Iracha (*reserva*) and Real Irache (*gran reserva*).

Bodegas Magaña 31532 Barillas
This wine estate was created by the brothers Juan, Carlos and Luis Magaña on the lines of a Bordeaux château. The grape varieties planted in their 60 ha (148 acres) are mainly French – for example, Merlot (about 40 percent), Cabernet Sauvignon, Cabernet Franc and Malbec. In addition the wines are generally aged in casks of French oak. Because the vines were quite young the early vintages rather lacked

depth, but nevertheless they were already among the better Navarrese red wines. The Viña Magaña is made nowadays from Merlot, Cabernet Sauvignon, Cabernet Franc and Malbec. The *reserva* Merlot of this same brand is a pure Merlot wine, with a smoothly generous character and a wood aroma that bring Pomerol to mind.

Vinícola Navarra 31397 Las Campanas
Its large nineteenth-century casks are a reminder of when this bodega was founded, but otherwise it makes a very contemporary impression with several dozen fermentation tanks of stainless steel. The firm, which belongs to the Bodegas y Bebidas group, is one of the biggest in Navarra. Its grapes are mostly bought in from growers, with its own 12 ha (30 acres) providing the rest. The quality of most of the wines is better than correct. The rosé Las Campanas has Garnacha as its basis and is fruity, with a suggestion of raspberries in aroma and taste. The white Las Campanas is made from Viura alone and is characterized by a cool fruitiness. A red *crianza* is also produced under this label. This tastes velvety, again with a hint of ripe raspberries, and is rounded, with a touch of spice. Its grapes are 80 percent Tempranillo, 20 percent Garnacha. The Castillo de Tiebas *reserva* was somewhat middling in quality, but this may change as new small casks have been purchased.

Bodegas Beamonte 31520 Cascante
The class of the wines made here

matches that of the Julián Chivite products – for the simple reason that Beamonte is a subsidiary. The stars in the range are the Beamonte *crianza* and *reserva*, both made from about 70 percent Tempranillo and 30 percent Garnacha. Wood and vanilla are present in both wines, though naturally the *reserva* tastes more mature. The Beamonte cellars, dating from 1938, were completely modernized in 1986. The name Viña Sempronia is used as well as Beamonte.

Bodegas Guelbenzu 31520 Cascante
In the mid-nineteenth century the Guelbenzu family was already offering its wines for sale in London, but the name temporarily disappeared from the scene when the estate joined the Cascante cooperative. In the 1980s, however, the eight Guelbenzu brothers and sisters decided to continue independently. They invested both in their own vineyards – about 40 ha (99 acres), with more than 25 ha (62 acres) planted – and in cellars. In addition a French-trained oenologist was brought in. The grapes, which are fermented in stainless-steel tanks, all come from their own vineyards and consist of 50 percent Cabernet Sauvignon, 40 percent Tempranillo and 10 percent Merlot. These grapes are present in the red Guelbenzu in the same proportions. It is matured in casks of French oak and is at the same time intense and elegant, with the potential to become one of Navarra's top wines. In addition this bodega produces a special, more expensive wine on the basis of Cabernet

Sauvignon and Merlot. This, too, has real class.

Bodega Nuestra Señora del Romero 31520 Cascante
This Cascante cooperative is one of the few that exports independently. It dates from 1951 and has 1,200 members with a total of some 1,800 ha (4,450 acres) of vineyards, which makes it the biggest cooperative in Navarra. The red Nuevo Vino (100 percent Garnacha) and the rosé Malon de Echaide (100 percent Garnacha) are pleasant wines for drinking young, but would benefit from more liveliness and depth. The Plandenas *reserva* and the Señor de Cascante *gran reserva* both taste fairly rustic and lack refinement. Yet there is good basic material here, as was shown by a pure Tempranillo I tasted from one of the tanks.

Bodegas Julián Chivite 31592 Cintruénigo
It is thanks to this firm that Navarra wine has acquired a strong image abroad, because for years Julián Chivite has accounted for half the region's total wine exports. This has benefited the region, since the firm is very quality conscious. The family has been making wine since 1779, but the establishment of the bodega came in 1860. The modern installation, totally renovated and updated in 1990, processes grapes from the Chivite 115 ha (284 acres) of vineyard, and from growers with long-term contracts. Wine is also bought in from cooperatives in the north of the DO, and vinification is carried out there under Chivite supervision (the firm usually takes at least half of the crop). Julián Chivite has 5,000 *barricas* for ageing its red wines.

The wines from this bodega are distinguished by their flawless quality. The white Gran Feudo (100 percent Viura) and rosé (100 percent Garnacha) are fermented at low temperature and have a lively taste with fruit and freshness. The rosé is among the best that Navarra produces. The red Gran Feudo is a very pleasant, balanced *crianza* made from 70 percent Tempranillo and 30 percent Garnacha. An exquisite red wine that is given no wood ageing is the Viña Marcos (50 percent Tempranillo, 50 percent Garnacha). A distinguished *reserva* is produced under the name Parador Chivite (70 percent Tempranillo, with the rest Garnacha and a little

Left: Pamplona in silhouette. The famous San Fermín fiesta is held here every year in July.

Mazuelo). Chivite's most beautiful wine, now scarcely to be found, was the *gran reserva* 125 Aniversario, a concentrated, lingering jubilee wine of 1981 vintage. Only Tempranillo grapes were used for this.

The Chivite family also owns Bodegas Beamonte in Cascante, while a new wine estate is being created in the Estellazone, near Aberín, with a total of 150 ha (370 acres) of vineyard. The Chivites are convinced that excellent wines can be made on this estate.

Bodegas Bardón 31591 Corella
After Luis Olarra had left Bodegas Olarra in Rioja, which he had founded, he started a new wine firm in Navarra with a number of partners. They called it Bodegas Bardón, but the concern also operates under the name Luis Olarra. The grapes come from 10 ha (25 acres) of Bardón land as well as from growers in the neighbourhood; wine is also bought in. Among the names on the labels are Togal, Larums and Don Luis. The supple, smooth red wines are usually of average quality, but lack depth. A better standard is offered by the Viña Arcadia, a Cabernet Sauvignon that is given a year in cask (American oak) and has in its taste a hint of wood and vanilla, dark fruit, and a touch of pepper.

Bodegas Camilo Castilla 31591 Corella
In the inner courtyard of this bodega stands the bust of the man who founded it in 1856, but since 1987 it has belonged to Arturo Beltrán, an Aragón firm. The 60 ha (148 acres) of vineyards yield about 60 percent of the grapes required, particularly Moscatels, for the bodega has made a speciality of these ever since its foundation. Cooperatives supply the rest of the grapes, and also wine. Red Conde de Castilla is a decent, but unremarkable product of half and half Garnacha and Tempranillo. And in fact the same can be said of the rosé (90 percent Garnacha, 10 percent Tempranillo). Of the three fortified Moscatel wines (which have no DO), the Goya has the most to offer.

Vinos Catalán Bozal 31591 Corella
This firm was established in 1940 and acquired its present name in 1983. It is named after Soledad Bozal, daughter of the founder, and José Luis Catalán her husband. The wines from this bodega are of an average standard. Among the most pleasant are the white Don Julián

Above: Long covered way leading to the church in the wine village of Cascante.

(100 percent Viura) and the red of the same name (formerly 100 percent Garnacha, now with 10 to 15 percent Tempranillo as well). Don Fermín, Marqués de Bajamar and Señorío de Urdaix are other brands.

Bodegas Vicente Malumbres 31591 Corella
A family business dating from 1940 that has had modern equipment at its disposal since 1987. The grapes come exclusively from some 60 ha (148 acres) of its own, where new Tempranillo and Chardonnay vines were planted in 1990. Both the red and the rosé Don Carví and Viña Otinar lack distinction, but the white is very pleasant and stimulating in taste. In it the Viura is the most important grape variety. This bodega does not as yet produce wood-aged wines, but there are plans for casks and a cellar.

Bodegas Cenalsa 31521 Murchante
Since its foundation in the first half of the 1980s, this important concern has grown into one of the biggest and most dynamic producers. The grapes and wines come in from the cooperatives and are processed with up-to-date equipment. Bodegas Cenalsa's speciality is Navarrese wines for drinking young. This is a deliberate choice, taken to make the wines different from the Rioja wines, which are often wood-aged (Bodegas Muerza in Rioja actually belongs to the group). The simplest line is the Campo-Nuevo, with a red that has a supple, pleasing taste with a measure of cherry-like fruit (from 100 percent Garnacha). Rather more colour and depth is offered by the red Agramont (60 percent

Garnacha, 40 percent Tempranillo). The white (100 percent Viura) and the rosé (100 percent Garnacha) are of a very decent quality. The red Verjus (50 percent Tempranillo, 50 percent Garnacha) possesses a smooth, fruity, almost gentle taste and is made by the *macération carbonique* method. Bodegas Braña Vieja and Pleno are subsidiary brands marketed by Bodegas Cenalsa.

Bodegas Príncipe de Viana 31521 Murchante
A Bodegas Cenalsa subsidiary, with in general a somewhat higher quality of wine – particularly the red. Since 1990 the red Príncipe de Viana has been made from 70 percent Tempranillo aand 30 percent Cabernet Sauvignon. Ageing in wood is done here, though usually in fairly limited doses – generally seven or eight months. In 1989 a pure Cabernet Sauvignon was added to the range, and a Chardonnay will also be added.

Bodegas Carricas 31390 Olite
This business began life as Navarra's (and Spain's) first wine cooperative, which decades ago was bought by Cecilio Carricas. Most of its red wines, such as the wood-aged Teobaldo I and the Domaine Mont-Plané, are distinguished by having a fresh core, and a fairly rustic character. The red Viña Mont-Plané, on the other hand, possesses supple fruit. It is made from Garnacha and Tempranillo, by *macération carbonique*. The grapes come from 60 ha (148 acres) of its own land and from growers, and wine is also bought in.

Bodegas Ochoa 31390 Olite
Javier Ochoa is the oenologist under whose direction many experiments are conducted at the Evena research station. He also runs this, his own bodega. Not quite a fifth of the grapes come from Ochoa's own 17 ha (42 acres), the rest being bought in. The wines, sold as Ochoa – or sometimes Viña Chapitel – are notable for their purity. The white (100 percent Viura) and rosé (100 percent Garnacha) are fermented at low temperature and possess both freshness and fruit. The red (60 percent Tempranillo, 40 percent Garnacha) undergo cask-ageing. The *crianza* and the *reserva* both taste smooth and balanced, although the former is fairly simple, while the latter offers more power and depth. In 1990 it launched a lively-tasting, pure Tempranillo and a pure Cabernet Sauvignon, characterized by berry-like fruit.

Bodegas de Sarría 31100 Puente la Reina
The vast 1,500 ha (3,700 acre) estate of Señorío de Sarría was bought by the wealthy contractor Félix Huarte at the beginning of the 1950s. He enlarged the vineyard, which now covers 200 ha (494 acres), and built a cellar complex. Both were taken over in 1981 by the Caja de Ahorros de Navarra. This bank provided a new financial impetus, with the aim of doubling the previous annual production of 400,000 cases. With this in mind stainless-steel tanks were obtained and the number of small casks was increased to 16,000. Chardonnay and Cabernet Sauvignon made their appearance in the vineyard, with 30 ha (74 acres) each. Much credit must go to the oenologist Francisco Moriones, regarded as having one of the best noses in Navarra, for the exceptionally reliable quality of the wines. In principle all the red wines mature in oak casks. The youngest is the Viña Ecoyen *crianza* (50 percent Garnacha, 40 percent Tempranillo, 10 percent Mazuelo and Graciano). This usually tastes dark-toned and reasonably intense. The Señorío de Sarría *reserva* consists of 60 percent Tempranillo, with 20 percent Garnacha, and 10 percent each of Graciano and Mazuelo. It is a fine, aromatic, mouth-filling wine, with shades of wood and fruit. A slightly superior version is produced under the name of Viña del Perdón. Finally there is a red *gran reserva* Señorío de Sarría, which makes a mature, but vital impression. The rosé Viña Ecoyen (80 percent Garnacha, 10 percent Tempranillo, 10 percent Viura) is for drinking young and tastes agreeable, but with less fruit than it might have. The same is true of the white (60 percent Viura, 40 percent Malvasía).

Luis Gurpegui Muga/Bodegas Villafranca de Navarra 31330 Villafranca de Navarra
Since 1970 this has been a subsidiary of Bodegas Gurpegui in San Adrián, Rioja. Mainly simple wines are produced with bought-in grapes and wine. An exception is the *crianza* Monte Ory, a wine composed from Garnacha and Tempranillo grapes with a pleasant, quite full taste in which both fruit and wood can be perceived. Subsidiary brands are San Acisclo, Sestero and Monte Bravo.

Travel Information

Above: The wine estate of Señorío de Sarría.

HOTELS AND RESTAURANTS

Parador Príncipe de Viana, 31390 Olite, tel (48) 740000 Partly housed in a medieval royal castle. Its central location makes the peaceful village of Olite an excellent starting point for trips through the region.

Casa Mauleón, Calle Amaya 4, 31000 Pamplona, tel (48) 228474 The place to have breakfast or lunch after the *encierro* during the San Fermín in July.

Hartza, Calle Juan de Labrit 19, 31000 Pamplona, tel (48) 224568 The Hartza brothers delight their many loyal customers with traditional Basque and Navarrese dishes, based on fresh ingredients, including *merluza* (hake).

Josetxo, Plaza Príncipe de Viana 1, 31002 Pamplona, tel (48) 222097 Stylishly appointed establishment serving elegant versions of regional dishes.

Hostal del Rey Noble "La Pocholas", Paseo Sarasate 6, 31000 Pamplona, tel (48) 222214 Traditional restaurant often visited by Ernest Hemingway.

Sarasate, Calle García Castañon 12, 31002 Pamplona, tel (48) 225102 Inventive, contemporary dishes.

Hotel Tres Reyes, Jardines de la Taconera, 31001 Pamplona, tel (48) 226600 Comfortable, fairly modern hotel on the edge of the old town centre.

Atalaya, 31350 Peralta, tel (48) 750152 New-style Navarrese cuisine here alongside more conventional dishes.

La Conrada, 31100 Puente la Reina, tel (48) 34002 A good address for a country lunch.

Mesón del Peregrino, 31100 Puente la Reina, tel (48) 340075 Small hotel/restaurant with rustic décor, just outside the village.

Hostal Tafalla, 31300 Tafalla, tel (48) 700300 Traditional regional dishes, and a very extensive wine list.

Tubal, 31300 Tafalla, tel (48) 700852 A distinguished restaurant where guests from the nearby Olite Parador often come to eat.

Casa Ignacio, Calle Cortadores 11, 31500 Tudela, tel (48) 821021 Actually more *tapas* bar than restaurant. The *tapas* here are highly original, using every possible vegetable from the region.

PLACES OF INTEREST

Ayeguí In this wine village near Estella stands the Benedictine monastery of Irache which once accommodated a university. Close by is the Bodegas Irache with a small wine museum.

Carcastillo The Monasterio de la Oliva was built by Cistercians in the twelfth century. As in former times it produces table as well as communion wine from a 17 ha (42 acre) site. Bottles are on sale at the monastery. Architecturally, the cloisters and the church are the most interesting parts.

Cascante In this wine village a long arcade leads up the hill to an eighteenth-century church and a small park.

Corella Historic village where many houses have coats of arms; ten or so bodegas are established here.

Estella This town of Roman origin has so many monuments and churches that it has acquired the nicknames "Estella la Bella" and "the Toledo of the North". The oldest church (partly twelfth, partly thirteenth-century) is San Pedro de la Rúa, which has an imposing interior and fine cloisters. The churches of San Miguel, Santo Sepulcro, and the basilica El Santuario de la Virgen del Puy are worth seeing. The latter contains the sword of Carlos III. One of Spain's oldest (secular) buildings is the twelfth-century Palacio de los Duques de Granada et Ega, by the atmospheric Plaza de San Martín.

Fitero The monastery of Santa María la Real was built in the twelfth and thirteenth centuries by the Cistercians. The treasury here is richly endowed.

Funes The remains here of a Roman wine cellar.

Mendigorría According to tradition, the church in this village was built using mortar that was mixed with wine.

Olite This old village is very much dominated by the castle that Carlos III built in 1406 on the foundations of a thirteenth-century stronghold. The Gothic structure was given numerous towers. Part of it functions as a *parador*. In front of the castle is a charming village square and next to it stands the church of Santa María with its richly decorated portal.

Pamplona The San Fermín festival has become world-famous through Ernest Hemingway. Bullfights take place in the second week of July, and there is an *encierro* in which bulls are run through the narrow streets. There is a cathedral to admire (fourteenth and fifteenth-century), and various other churches. The cathedral stands on the edge of the picturesque old centre, as does the Museo de Navarra with its impressive collection of paintings, sculptures, frescos and mosaics.

Puente la Reina This takes its name from an eleventh-century bridge built for the many pilgrims who crossed the Arga. On the north side of Puente la Reina is a bronze statue of a pilgrim. There is a pleasant walk here through the Calle Mayor, which comes out by the bridge.

Tafalla Here there are the ruins of a royal palace, the Convento de la Pu, Concepción (a splendid Flemish altarpiece), the Romanesque Santa María church (a fine retable), and the Convento de San Francisco.

Tudela This town in the fertile Ebro valley has a rather austere-looking cathedral (twelfth to thirteenth-century) with the Bishop's Palace next to it. The *ayuntamiento* is nearby, where a richly decorated coach can be seen.

Ujué This medieval village is built on a hill that dominates the surroundings. Many local couples from the area get married in the Romanesque church of Santa María with its fortified towers. Women picking grapes are carved on the Gothic portal.

WINE ROUTE

Just how far Navarra stretches is shown by the suggested wine route, which is 200 to 300 km (125 to 136 miles) long. It passes through the five wine zones, and through most of the important wine communities. Olite is an excellent starting point.

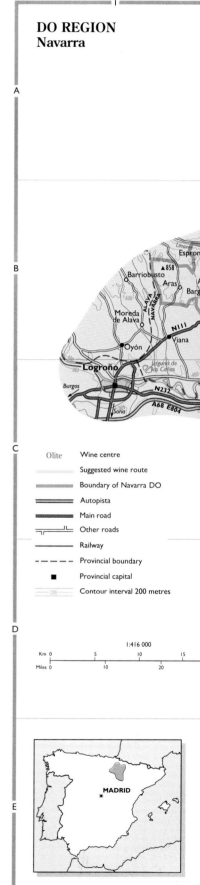

**DO REGION
Navarra**

Olite	Wine centre
	Suggested wine route
	Boundary of Navarra DO
	Autopista
	Main road
	Other roads
	Railway
	Provincial boundary
	Provincial capital
	Contour interval 200 metres

1:416 000

MADRID

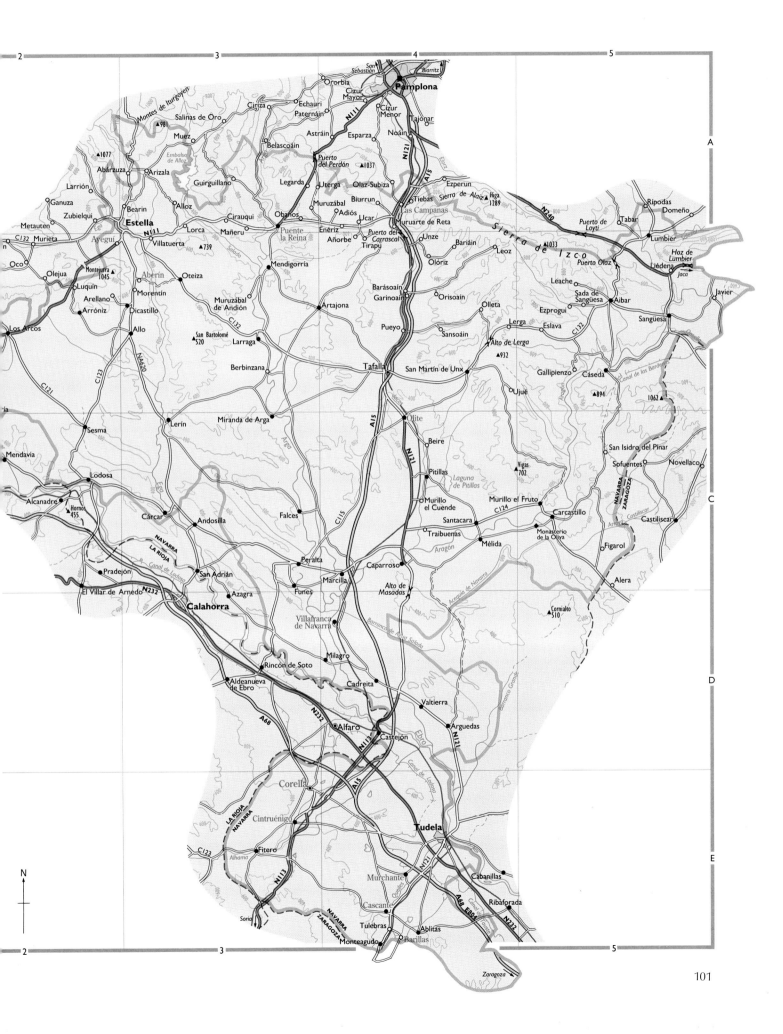

Chacolí de Guetaria (The Basque Country)

Capital: Vitoria
Provinces: Alava, Guipúzcoa, Vizcaya
Area: 7,261 square kilometres
Population: 2,133,002

Above: Spain's north coast offers many dramatic views, but is largely unsuitable for winegrowing, apart from Chacolí.

The north coast of Spain is of little significance in terms of winegrowing. Not only is the terrain distinctly rugged and mountainous, it is also relatively cool and damp: the annual rainfall is 1,500 mm (59 ins). Nevertheless, grapes are cultivated in this coastal strip. With characteristic stubbornness the Basques have for centuries been defying the elements and making their own wine, and in 1990 one of these wines was even given its own *denominación de origen*. This is the white Chacolí de Guetaria, which the Basques themselves call, in *Euokera*, their unique language, the Getariako Txkolina.

The smallest DO

As the name indicates, Chacolí comes from the area around the fishing village of Guetaria, built on a narrow, rocky tongue of land about 25 km (15.5 miles) west of San Sebastián in the province of Guipúzcoa. Besides Guetaria, the DO is made up from part of the area of the seaside resort of Zarauz, and the mountain village of Aia. The vineyards, which consist mainly of small plots, altogether cover an area of not quite 50 ha (124 acres): which makes Chacolí de Guetaria by far the smallest DO in Spain. Its annual production is in the region of 250,000 bottles, almost all of them consumed within the home area.

Grape varieties

Two varieties of grapes are permitted for making Chacolí: white Hondarribi Zuri (85 percent of the vines) and black Hondarribi Beltz (15 percent). No one outside the Basque country has heard of them. They are cultivated by a dozen growers, eight of them in Guetaria itself. By far the biggest of these is Txomín Etxaníz, who owns 12 ha (30 acres). Chacolí is said to be derived from the Arabic *chacalet*, which means weakness or thinness, and certainly the wines are usually light and lean, often with considerable acid and a distinct mousse to them. The best taste juicy, pure and stimulating. They go well with fish and shellfish, and can also be used as an aperitif. Not all the wines, however, are of the same quality: there are Chacolís with so austere and prickly a taste that you almost feel as if you are drinking a glass of pins.

Left: A great deal of fresh fish is landed at Pasajes de San Juan, near San Sebastian, and other harbours on the Atlantic coast; white Chacolí de Guetaria tastes excellent with it. Below: Vines tied up high in the Guetaria area. In this way the plants get maximum ventilation from the wind, thus reducing the risk of moulds caused by too much moisture.

PRODUCERS OF SPECIAL INTEREST

Txomín Etxaníz 20808 Guetaria
With roughly 12 ha (30 acres) this is by far the biggest producer of Chacolí de Guetaria. The cellars are partly equipped with modern stainless-steel fermentation tanks. The wine is composed of 85 percent Hondarribi Zuri and 15 percent Hondarribi Beltz, and is one of the very best from the district. It sparkles well on pouring. The carbon dioxide is certainly discernible in the stimulating, agreeable and fresh taste, in which there is a hint of fruit.

Ameztoy 20800 Zarauz
A family concern that is extending its own modest vineyard area to about 10 ha (24.7 acres). Its characteristic wine is fresh, slightly sparkling and with a touch of fruit.

Travel Information

HOTELS AND RESTAURANTS

Elkano, 20808 Guetaria, tel (43) 831614 Here, with a view of sea and coast, you can eat fresh fish, crustaceans and shellfish in a rustic setting.

Kaia y Asador Kai-Pe, 20808 Guetaria, tel (43) 832414
Simply prepared fish and meat dishes (roasted, fried or grilled) are served downstairs; more elaborate fare upstairs.

Aiten Etxe, Carretera de Guetaria 3, 20800 Zarauz, tel (43) 831825
Traditional Basque cuisine based on fresh fish and *mariscos* (shellfish) cultivated here. The restaurant gives a view of the sea.

Karlos Arguiñano, Mendilauta 13, 20800 Zarauz, tel (43) 130000
Restaurant with a very good reputation where traditional Basque cooking is interpreted in a contemporary manner – Chacolí being served of course. Try the marvellous seafood terrine.

Hotel Zarauz, Avenida de Navarra 26, 20800 Zarauz, tel (43) 830200
A good place to stay, not far from the beach, with a restaurant.

PLACES OF INTEREST

Guetaria A great deal of whaling used to be done from this village (population 2,500) built on a spit of land, which is why the seal of the local *Consejo Regulador* depicts a whale.

The Gothic church of San Salvador, with parts dating from the thirteenth and fourteenth centuries, is one of the most important monuments in the province. It contains a model ship, and underground passages link the church with the fishing harbour. The village council building has murals by the Basque painter Ignacio Zuloaga (*see also* Zumaya right). These depict the voyage made by the Guetaria-born Juan Sebastián Elcano, who set out in 1519 with Magellan on his voyage around the world. After Magellan was murdered in the Philippines, Elcano took over command of the *Vitoria*, the only one of the original five ships to complete the journey. Elcano returned in 1522 and died in 1526. He is immortalized by a statue in Guetaria.

Zarauz At a once-renowned shipyard here was built the *Vitoria*, the ship in which Elcano (see above) sailed around the world. At the end of the nineteenth century it was Zarauz that Queen Isabella II chose for her summer residence, and the town subsequently grew into Spain's most exclusive – and expensive – seaside resort. More recently King Baudouin and Queen Fabiola of Belgium have stayed here. The glory of former days is somewhat diminished, but there is still a splendid sandy beach and some fine villas. The town with its population of 15,000 lies in a natural amphitheatre and possesses one of the most impressive towers in the Basque country. This is the Gothic Luzea tower, overlooking the Calle Mayor. The church of Santa María is also Gothic, but with a baroque altar. The fifteenth-century Palacio de Narros stands close to the beach.

Zumaya Zarauz lies just to the east of Guetaria, and Zumaya is a few miles to the west. This town has a population of just under 8,000 and is of Roman origin. A pleasant walk on a fine summer's day is along the tree-lined *paseo* that leads to the lighthouse. The Basque painter Ignacio Zuloago (1870-1945) lived and worked here, and his villa is now a museum. Apart from works by Zuloago himself the collection includes canvases by El Greco, Goya and others. Next to this building stands the chapel of Santiago Echea, which was used by pilgrims to Santiago de Compostela. The fifteenth-century San Pedro church has fine triptychs.

Castilla y León

Capital: Valladolid
Provinces: Avila, Burgos, León, Palencia, Salamanca, Segovia, Soria, Valladolid, Zamora
Area: 94,147 square kilometres
Population: 2,600,330

There are no fewer than nine provinces in the Castilla y León *autonomía*, making it the biggest in Spain; it covers about one fifth of the country. Avila, Burgos, Segovia, Soria, Valencia and Valladolid belonged to the old countship of Castilla, founded in 951 by Fernán González. León, Salamanca and Zamora were part of the former kingdom of León, which also came into being in the tenth century. Then in 1037 Ferdinand I united Castilla, León and Asturia under the one crown. The name of the present *autonomía* dates from 1983. Before that the area was known as Castilla la Vieja (Old Castile), and still included the provinces of Logroño and Santander.

A chain of strongholds

Ferdinand I was succeeded by his son Sancho II, who was killed in suspicious circumstances, thus making way for his combative brother Alfonso VI. In 1085, after Toledo had been won back from the Moors, this monarch developed a line of forts along the Duero, some of them of Moorish origin. Among the best known are the castles of Berlanga de Duero, Peñafiel (in the middle of the Ribera del Duero wine district), Peñaranda de Duero and San Esteban de Gormaz. Castles had been in Castilla from an early date: *castillo* is the origin of the name.

A wealth of monuments

Castilla y León is thinly populated, but has a number of beautiful towns. Most of them have served for varying lengths of time as royal residences. Among them is Avila with its impressive town walls, with their 88 towers; the cathedral here is the highest above sea level in Europe. Gothic Burgos functioned as Castilla's first capital. Vivar, not far from here, was the birthplace of the legendary eleventh-century warrior Rodrigo Díaz, later known as El Cid. León grew out of a settlement made by the Roman VIIth legion, has been a royal capital, and possesses a splendid cathedral. Segovia, too, has a Roman history, as its towering aqueduct with its two-tier arches shows. Alfonso X (the Wise) had his residence here in the thirteenth century, and the Spanish mint was here between 1586 and 1730. Salamanca was conquered by Hannibal in 220 BC. Its university dates from 1218 and is thus the oldest in the country; Columbus visited it before his departure. Salamanca also has a magnificent Plaza Mayor, and two cathedrals. The royal court spent many periods in Valladolid, the most centrally situated city of Castilla y León. Here Ferdinand and Isabella were married; Charles V reigned – he later abdicated in favour of his son Philip II; and Cervantes wrote the first chapter of *Don Quixote*. The tiny house where Cervantes lived from 1603–1606 is now a museum.

Rolling plateaux

The big towns with their wealth of monuments and interest – and many of the smaller ones – are in striking contrast with the surrounding country, for this is seldom exciting or inspiring. Two-thirds of Castilla y León consists of plateaux at various

Above: The convent of Santa Clara in Tordesillas, Rueda.

heights. A good deal of grain is grown on this rolling terrain, but there are also large areas that are not cultivated, suitable only for grazing flocks of sheep. At best the monotony may be broken by isolated peaks and river valleys. Along the Duero in particular (Castilla y León largely falls within its catchment area) there is much more relief to the landscape, for example between Peñafiel and Pesquera, and near the town of Toro. The climate is generally harsh, with hot summers and cold winters. Only in the north-west, where the Bierzo wine district is situated, does a somewhat moister, more agreeable climate prevail under the influence of the sea.

Nourishing food

The cuisine of Castilla y León is one of nourishing dishes, meant for toilers on the land. Beans and pulses feature in many recipes, and numerous kinds are grown here. A famous dish with chick peas and cabbage is the *olla podrida*, also known as *cocido madrileño*, which includes pieces of pork and beef. Among the specialities there are also roast lamb and sucking pig (locally called *tostón*, *lechón*, *lechoncito* or *cochinillo asado*). In these the meat has to be so tender that you can cut it with the edge of a plate. Some restaurants – José María in Segovia, for example – make a ritual of this and ask their guests to dash the relevant plates to pieces. Veal (*ternera*) is the speciality of Avila, which has its own *denominación de origen*. The hilly regions support game such as rabbit (*conejo*), hare (*liebre*) and partridge (*perdiz*), as well as trout (*trucha*) from the mountain streams.

Wine districts with and without DOs

Winegrowing in Castilla y León is concentrated in a wide circle around Valladolid. To the east of this city is Ribera del Duero,

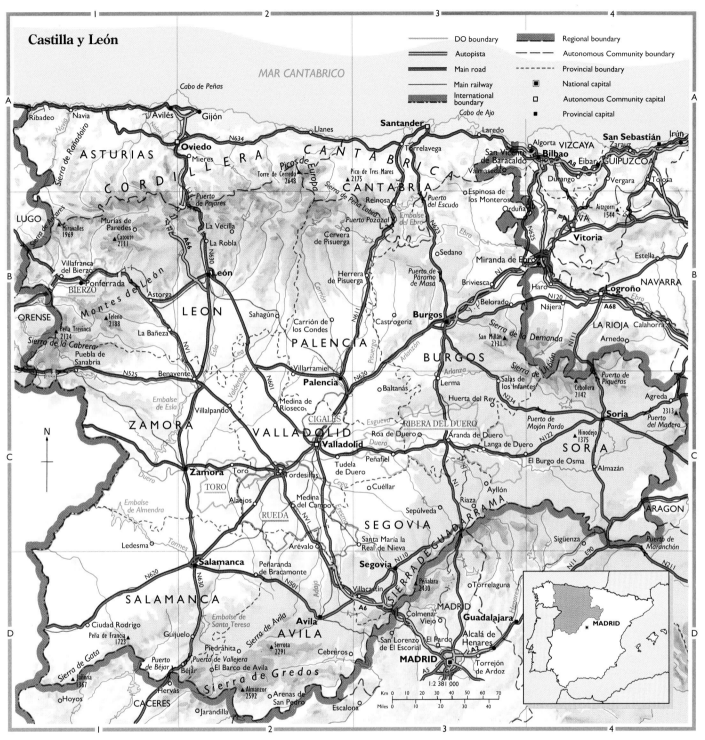

Castilla y León

MAR CANTABRICO

which enjoys a worldwide reputation for its red wines. To the south and south-west are Rueda, which produces excellent white wines, and Toro, known for its fiery reds. To the north of Valladolid is Cigales, which mostly makes dry rosés. The only other DO is Bierzo, up in the north-west. This district bordering on Galicia commands attention with its outstanding red wines made from the Mencía grape. Besides its DO wines, Castilla-León also produces various other kinds. In Cebreros, right in the south of the region and due west of Madrid, it is mainly heady red wines from Garnacha that are made. They are rather like those of Méntrida. The lighter ones are of a more interesting quality, the whites among them. In 1966 a group of go-ahead growers in

Valdebimbre-Los Oteros, just south of León, decided to get together, and invested in modern equipment. Today the red and rosé wines from Bodegas Vinos de León (VILE) are of a most attractive quality, particularly the red, wood-aged Don Suero, which has the local Prieto Picudo as its main grape variety. Another active producer in this area is the Valdebimbre cooperative. Slightly sparkling rosés, the *rosados de aguja* (literally "needle" wines), are a speciality of the district. Areas of rather less interest are Benavente-Campos (rosés and light red wines); Fermoselle (red); La Ribera de Salamanca (rosé and red); La Ribera del Arlanza (rosé and red); La Ribera del Sea (rosé and red); and La Sierra de Salamanca (rosé and red).

105

Ribera del Duero

Halfway between Madrid and Santander lies one of Spain's fastest developing wine regions, Ribera del Duero. It extends over four provinces of which Burgos is by far the most important with about 85 percent of all the vineyard area. Valladolid comes next, with around 10 percent, and Soria and Segovia have the remainder of the vinegrowing land. The Duero flows through the region, its valley bordered in places by flat-topped mountains. The vineyards are found on both the north and the south sides of this valley. In most cases the distance to the river is not more than 1.5 to 3 km (1 to 2 miles). The actual wine zone, however, is much wider, up to 35 kilometres (22 miles) at its broadest. As the crow flies the region is about 110 kilometres (68 miles) long. A tour through Ribera del Duero soon shows that winegrowing is not the only source of income here. You see fields of corn, vegetables and sugar beet interspersed with pastures cropped short by browsing flocks of sheep. The landscape is made up of flat plateaux and hills wooded with pines or deciduous trees. The plots of vines may be very small, or sometimes very large. Some of the most extensive estates are in Valbuena de Duero, Aranda de Duero, Pesquera de Duero and Roa. In many of the sleepy villages here the church tower is adorned with a stork's nest.

Cold nights

The climate in this part of the Duero valley is somewhat more moderate than in the surrounding country, but still not all that congenial. After a dry summer in which the temperature may reach as high as 36°C (97°F) there comes a comparatively wet autumn, followed by a short, cold winter when there can be up to 10°C (18°F) of frost. The risk of frost continues into spring, and often on to the middle of May. Since spring and summer nights can be cold, a sweater can certainly not be regarded as excess baggage. In fact this drop in temperature is very good for the aroma of the grapes – and for that of the eventual wine. Rainfall varies between 450 and 500 mm (17.7 and 19.7 ins) a year. Additional moisture comes from the mists that often spread out from the river.

Most of the vineyards are found at 700 to 800 m (about 2,300 to 2,600 feet) above sea level, on loose, easily worked soils. There is generally a good deal of limestone, and often iron too, which explains the reddish hue of the soil. Vineyards closer to the river are characterized by a considerable clay content. The natural factors of climate and soil make Ribera del Duero perfect for the production of wines of high quality: it is just that it has taken a long time for this to be understood.

Vega Sicilia

The Romans probably cultivated grapes here, but the first concrete evidence for winegrowing dates from the ninth century AD. Monks were responsible for a revival in the Middle Ages: a Cistercian monastery was founded at Valbuena de Duero in the twelfth century, and Benedictines from Cluny in Burgundy are known to have brought vines to Ribera del Duero. From documents it appears that many bodegas were already in existence in the thirteenth century; and at the end of the eighteenth century Charles III became personally involved in viticultural affairs in the region at the request of the winegrowers of Aranda de Duero. None of this alters the fact that there was little to distinguish the region from other Spanish areas. This

Above: At Peñafiel the castle stands proudly on its ridge, like a ship stranded on a rock. The local cooperative, situated at the foot of the hill, has dug out passages in the rock for storing wine.

changed to a modest degree in 1846, for in that year the De Lecanda family established a winery on the south bank of the Duero, opposite Valbuena, taking the name Bodega de Lecanda. Some of its vines came from Bordeaux; thus it was that Cabernet Sauvignon, Merlot and Malbec first appeared alongside the traditional Spanish varieties. In 1890 this wine estate was taken over by the Herrero family, who after a few years decided to change its name to Vega Sicilia. Vega means "fertile plain" and Sicilia is a reference to the little church of Santa Sicilia on the estate, less than a mile from the cellars.

A legendary reputation

For decades Vega Sicilia was the only producer of any significance in the region. During this period the bodega developed into one of the most renowned in Spain. The wines had an almost legendary reputation, not only for their great quality, but also because of their rarity and their high price. Vega Sicilia was a giant among dwarfs, completely overshadowing everything the rest produced. Most of the other winemakers were small producers using archaic methods, generally in cellars that were in fact caves. It was not until the 1950s and 1960s that improvements began to be made. An increasing number of winegrowers came together in cooperatives, where operations were not only on a bigger scale, but were more efficient and up-to-date. Yet most of the wine remained totally uninteresting, mainly being sold in bulk. There was no question of any progress in quality until the 1970s. One man played a key role in this: Alejandro Fernández.

Pesquera

As Alejandro helped his father make wine in Pesquera de Duero he noted that many growers were uprooting their vines to make way for sugar beet. You could drink wine, but sugar beet meant you could eat. Thus at the end of the 1940s the young Alejandro decided to turn his attention to sugar beet. This he did by designing and making machines to harvest the beet, and subsequently sold them throughout the country. A quarter of a century later, Alejandro had saved enough money to set up a bodega of his own. Having seen the success of Vega Sicilia he, too, was convinced of Ribera del Duero's potential. He decided not to imitate Vega Sicilia, however, but to strive for a style of his own, with purely regional grapes. The 1975 was his first full vintage and it immediately made a great impression. Indeed, that year's *reserva*, bottled in 1983, is still a remarkable wine. Until 1982 Alejandro worked "in the Roman manner": the black grapes were not destalked and fermentation often lasted 28 days. From 1982 there was destalking (but not of all the grapes in that first year) and the fermentation period was gradually reduced to the present 8 to 15 days. Since then his wine has had a phenomenal, world-wide success.

Huge investments

The breakthrough came in 1986, when the Pesquera 1982 and 1983 were both highly praised in America. The critic Robert Parker described them in *The Wine Advocate* as two of the best red wines he had tasted that year, compared the 1982 with a great Pomerol such as Pétrus on l'Evangile, and ended his remarks by saying, "Pesquera wines must be tasted to be believed". Because of the initiative of Alejandro Fernández the region itself had by this time achieved the requisite stage of development, so that after provisional recognition in 1979, the definitive *denominación de origen* was granted in 1982. New firms had been established, such as Bodegas Ismael Arroyo in 1979 and Hermanos Pérez Pascuas in 1980, and radical technical changes had been carried through. With Vega Sicilia and Pesquera as shining examples, the great potential of Ribera del Duero quite suddenly became apparent to everyone.

Since 1982 the amount of investment has been tremendous; capital has flooded into this area of the Duero valley from other parts of Spain, and even from abroad – from Sweden for example. One side-effect of this has been the steep rise in the price of land. One Rioja bodega is known not to have gone ahead with a purchase here because it would have proved a much costlier investment than it had anticipated.

Small plots

Within the boundaries of Ribera del Duero there are about 14,000 ha (34,600 acres) of productive vineyards. Out of this total 8,000 to 9,000 ha (19,800 to 22,250 acres) are entitled to the DO, an area that will continue to increase. Small plots are very much a feature of this region, where nearly 90 percent of growers own less than 1 .ha, or roughly 2.5 acres. A logical outcome of this is the large number of cooperatives: there are about a score of them. At the beginning of the 1990s only three of them were bottling wine. However, across the whole of Ribera del Duero the amount of wine being bottled is continuing to increase. During the 1980s there was a rise from not quite half a million bottles annually to between six and seven million. This trend is undoubtedly set to continue, for selling bottled wine is the object in view with all the investment.

Tinta del País

Whereas Vega Sicilia made its name with wines that were often produced from French grapes, Alejandro Fernández opted for one that came almost exclusively from Tinta del País, also called Tinto Fino. This variety is almost, if not completely, identical with Tempranillo. Some growers maintain that there is a difference. Tinta del País, they say, bears slightly larger grapes than Tempranillo. The majority opinion, however, is that they are identical – and the *Consejo Regulador* agrees with this; and it should be remembered that soil and climate give a grape certain specific properties. Compared with the Tempranillo from the best district of that arch-rival, Rioja, namely Rioja Alavesa, Tinta del País appears to be less likely to oxidize, and to have a fuller, stronger structure, more substance, more colour and a somewhat greater acidity. These qualities together result in complex, dark-red wines that are sinewy yet not excessively alcoholic and that can mature over a very long period. Repeatedly I was informed that Ribera del Duero's red wines are probably the longest-living in Spain.

White grapes

Tinta del País accounts for some 60 percent of all plantings, and this share will increase as many new vineyards have been planted exclusively with it. The remaining 40 percent is divided among 10 or so varieties, including whites. The latter are used in small doses to make red wines somewhat lighter and more fragrant. There is in fact no white Ribera del Duero. The most notable of the white grapes is Albillo, which is a synonym for Pardina. As in Toro, this variety used to be planted not only for wine but also to give dessert grapes. The pickers are fond of eating them. According to the rules of the Ribera del Duero DO, French varieties such as Cabernet Sauvignon, Merlot and Malbec may only be planted in districts where they are already being grown.

The fact that Alejandro Fernández has shown what spectacular results can be achieved with almost exclusive use of Tinta del País does not mean that all the other red wines from Ribera del Duero are of similar character and quality. Anyone who goes tasting at the 25 or so bodegas that bottle their products will come across some very different kinds of wine: neutral or striking, supple or dour and unforthcoming, fruity or rustic, moderate or good – with all the variations in between. It is advisable to choose your Ribera del Duero reds with care.

Similarly, the standard of the *rosados*, which are also permitted within the DO, varies greatly. In keeping with local tradition, these dry wines are made largely or solely from Garnacha. However, the best ones have around 50 percent Tinta del País. One firm that produces a relatively large amount of rosé is Bodegas Peñalba López, where this represents about 40 percent of the total. The rosé here is made from 60 percent Garnacha and 40 percent Tinta del País. There is, however, a world of difference between the best red wines and the best of the rosés. Ribera del Duero's vocation is red wine.

PRODUCERS OF SPECIAL INTEREST

Bodegas Peñalba López 09400 Aranda de Duero

The wine firm Torremilanos was established just west of Aranda in 1903. Today Torremilanos serves as the principal brand name for the wines it markets. The bodega is reached via an industrial area. Since being taken over by Pablo Peñalba López in 1974 it has been greatly extended as well as renovated. The same is true for the vineyards, which have grown from a few dozen hectares to their present 200 ha (494 acres). Some of the new planting consists of Cabernet Sauvignon and Merlot. The wine (60 percent red, 40 percent rosé) ferments in stainless-steel tanks. There are some 4,500 casks for ageing the wine, 500 of them made of French oak. Many of the casks have been replaced by new ones in recent years. In terms of quality the wines represent a good average for Ribera del Duero. They do not quite have the depth and concentration to be at the top, but they are very pleasing. The best are the Torremilanos *crianza* (18 months in cask, 6 in bottle; 80 percent Tinta del País, 20 percent Garnacha) and *reserva* (2 years in cask, 1 in bottle; 100 percent Tinta del País). From time to time a *gran reserva* is brought out (2 years in cask, 3 in bottle; 100 percent Tinta del País). The ordinary Torremilanos consists of 60 percent Tinta del País and 40 percent Garnacha. The reasonably lively, slightly fruity *rosado* has the same grapes as its basis. Partly because for foreign customers "Torremilanos" sounds so much like "Torremolinos", the names Peñalba, Vega Lara and Monte Castrilla are employed in some markets.

Viña Buena 09400 Aranda de Duero

A winery founded in 1984 that processes both bought-in grapes and those from its own 40 ha (99 acres). Tinta del País is the sole variety used. Both red and rosé wines are marketed under the Mío Cid name. They are very correct in quality with a generally supple, undemanding taste. The *crianza* is generally considered to be one of the best.

SAT Los Curros 09314 Boada de Roa

A subsidiary of the establishment of the same name in Rueda. Quite firm, good red wines are made, with plenty of colour and some fruit. The rosé is tasty and refreshing.

Bodegas Valduero 09440 Gumiel del Mercado

A dynamic concern that has 100 ha (247 acres) of its own vineyards, and built an entirely new cellar in 1991. The number of casks – 2,500 at present – is to be greatly increased in the coming years. Both the red Viña Valduero for drinking young, and the *crianza* with the same name, are very attractive examples of their kind. The Valduero 1985 *reserva* has distinct merits too. The *gran reserva* El Buen Conde is somewhat rustic.

Bodegas Victor Balbás 09442 La Horra

Since the 1988 vintage this bodega has had a modern vinification area and an underground cellar for its casks. The grapes come from its own 50 ha (124 acres) of vineyard and from other growers. Tinta del País only is used for most of its red wines, though there is a little Cabernet Sauvignon in the *reserva*. The quality of these already good wines has further improved since 1988. This applies both to the fruity, young red Ardal (a proportion of the grapes for this undergo *macération carbonique*) and to the *crianza* Balbás (matured in American and French oak casks), and the refreshing rosé. Since 1984 the firm has been energetically directed by Juan José Balbás, whose family has been making wine in La Horra since 1777.

Bodegas Señorio de Nava 09318 Nava de Roa

Since 1986 the big León-based wine company VILE has invested many millions of pesetas in Bodegas Señorio de Nava, which now has the most up-to-date equipment at its disposal.

In the firm's own 140 ha (346 acre) vineyard Cabernet Sauvignon and Merlot are planted as well as regional grape varieties. The fresh Señorio de Nava *rosado* has plenty of fruit and is among the best produced by Ribera del Duero. It is made from 70 percent Tinta del País and 30 percent Garnacha. The young red wine is a pure Tinta del País with a juicy, supple taste and matures for a year in casks of American oak. It is a quite elegant wine with wood and vanilla as well as mellow fruit. The *reserva* is a wine of much larger dimensions: 1986 was the first vintage. When all the investment in the bodega is completed it will have about 3,000 casks, some of them French. Besides Señorio de Nava, the name Vega Cubillas is used for exactly the same wines.

Bodega Hermanos Pérez Pascuas 09316 Pedrosa de Duero

A rising star in the Ribera del Duero firmament, this family business has been in existence since 1980 and has invested a great deal in the 60 ha (148 acre) vineyard and in a new cellar complex. About 80 percent of the grapes come from the bodega's own land high up in Pedrosa; the rest are bought in. By far the most important variety is the Tinta del País, but some Cabernet Sauvignon, Merlot and Graciano is also used. The young red wine usually has plenty of fruit and quite a full taste. As with the other wines the name Viña Pedrosa is used, but it is also supplied to Spanish restaurants with their own labels (such as Mesón José María in Segovia). The *crianza* is distinguished by a mellow, juicy taste, elegantly firm, and with a suggestion of wood and dark fruit. The *reserva* is still more velvety. The three Pérez brothers plan to increase production by stages to 60,000 cases a year.

Bodega Ribera Duero 47300 Peñafiel

Founded in 1927, this is the region's oldest cooperative. It is located at the foot of the local castle and the cellars, 1,200 m (3,940 ft) long, are cut into the rock. The cooperative has around 230 members, who cultivate some 225 ha (556 acres). Its wines are exceptionally reliable. The young *vino tinto* tastes meaty and nicely fruity, qualities that are also perceptible in the smoother Ribera Duero *crianza*, which in addition has a slight vanilla aroma from its six to seven months in cask. The Peñafiel *reserva* is usually somewhat more substantial in structure, but sometimes actually lighter (it has 12 to 18 months in cask). The *gran reserva* Protos is always a mature, powerful wine with a good dose of wood and vanilla after two years in cask.

Alejandro Fernández 47315 Pesquera de Duero

As you come into Pesquera de Duero from the east, a simple gateway indicates the entrance into this wine estate of world renown. After a modest start in 1972 Alejandro continued to extend his bodega. This now consists of various halls and includes an underground cellar for bottles. In the beginning he covered his expenditure with the money he had earned with his agricultural machines. In the 1980s, however, his wine acquired so great a reputation that it has gone on being sold at very high prices ever since. Alejandro made use of his technological expertise in the bodega, for he built everything himself. He also invented a device that cleaned used casks so well, that they had almost the same effect on the wine as new ones. It was bought by a number of Bordeaux estates. Alejandro's 65 ha (160 acres) are planted almost exclusively with Tinta del País; Garnacha and Albillo account for only some 2 percent. The estate provides about nine-tenths of the grapes required.

Up until 1982 Fernández was still fermenting everything in a strictly traditional way. Grapes were not destalked and fermentation took four weeks. The resulting wines were of very good quality, but fairly rustic, with a lot of tannin but short on fruit. In 1982 Alejandro decided to leave the stalks on just some of the grapes. This was how the *gran reserva* Janus came into being, made with half the grapes destalked, the other half not. This nicely matured, classic wine was joined by the 1982 *crianza*, made solely from destalked grapes. Part of this vintage was later sold as *reserva* and *gran reserva*. With the even better 1983 wines the new-style Pesquera was enthusiastically received. Even the most stringent critics were full of praise. The subsequent vintages, too, had the best possible reviews. A characteristic Tinto Pesquera is a dark wine with an intense, rich taste that has a lot of berry-type fruit in it, a creamy vanilla aroma, energy and life in its character and a finish that lasts for minutes. Even the wine from 1987, a rather thin year, was a delight. This impressive quality is achieved on the one hand by excellently situated vineyards, where the grapes ripen early, and on the other by careful vinification and nurture. Normally the skins are left in contact with the fermenting must for 8 to 15 days, at fairly low temperature. Ageing takes place mainly in used, but thoroughly cleaned casks. Alejandro and his gifted oenologist Teófilo Reyes prefer the rather more neutral American wood to the very distinctive French type, so 90 percent of the casks are American oak, 10 percent French. Usually the *crianzas* mature for 14 months and the *reservas* for two years. However, the time can vary according to the vintage: Alejandro likes things made to measure. A second bodega is now under construction in Roa de Duero, where Alejandro has created a 100 ha (247 acre) vineyard. In his own words his wine estate in Roa is becoming "the most beautiful in

Ribera del Duero", comparable with a Bordeaux château. Nobody doubts his words.

Bodegas Federico Fernández Pérez 47315 Pesquera de Duero
The brother of Alejandro Fernández also makes wine, which has very good quality indeed. It is characterized by a deep red colour and a substantial taste with more wood (and vanilla) than fruit.

Bodegas Ismael Arroyo 09441 Sotillo de la Ribera
In 1979 Ismael Arroyo and his two sons, Ramón and Miguel, decided to start their own bodega. They built a hall with stainless-steel tanks and obtained 500 casks, which were set out in a centuries-old cellar dug out of the rock. The grapes are largely bought in, although the family itself has about 10 ha (nearly 25 acres) of vineyard. The wines are neither too heavy nor too light; and in the *crianza* and *reserva* Mesoneros de Castilla a good balance is achieved between wood and fruit. Another pleasant Ribera del Duero is their Tinto Joven, which does not undergo cask-ageing.

Bodegas Mauro 47320 Tudela de Duero
Since Tudela lies just outside the DO area, the wines cannot be sold as Ribera del Dueros. This did not stop Luciano Suárez from starting a small wine business of his own in this locality, aimed solely at quality. The bodega is housed in a seventeenth-century building and has about 10 ha (25 acres) of vineyard. Bought-in grapes are also processed. After maturing for about three years (partly in new French casks) the red Mauro is sold as *vino de mesa*. It is made on the basis of 85 percent Tinta del País, 10 percent Garnacha and 5 percent Albillo. In its perfume and taste it gives impressions of mellow, ripe fruit, with some spices, a darker note suggestive of coffee, and vanilla. From 500 cases in 1978, production has risen to an annual 4,500.

Vega Sicilia 47359 Valbuena de Duero
For more than a century the Vega Sicilia star shone alone in this part of the Duero valley. This wine estate, established in 1846, was a soloist of world class, performing amid well-meaning amateurs. After 1970 other producers began to make good, and sometimes even very good, wines, but this has not affected Vega Sicilia's unique reputation. This is due above all to owners who have spared neither

money nor effort to maintain, or even improve on, a high standard of quality. From 1965 to 1982 the property was in the hands of Hans Neumann, a Venezuelan of Czech origin, and since 1982 it has been owned by the Spanish entrepreneur David Alvarez Diaz, whose son Pablo runs it. In the 1980s the capacity of the cellars was doubled and stainless-steel tanks, pneumatic presses and new casks were acquired. A château-like grey house stands next to the low, brick cellar complex. The Alvarez Diaz family

Above: A panoramic view over the wide valley and flat-topped hills of Ribera del Duero, where vines are only one of several crops grown.

has spent millions of pesetas in renovating it.

Opposite the bodega, across the road and against a vine-covered slope, there is a cellar containing some of the firm's 6,000 *barricas*. The casks are made and maintained in Vega Sicilia's own cooper's workshop. The estate covers 1,000 ha (2,470 acres), of which 130 ha (320 acres) are planted with vines. Of these 60 to 65 percent are Tinto

del País, followed by other regional as well as French varieties. The Cabernet Sauvignon represents about 20 percent of the total, the Malbec and Merlot some 5 percent each. These French varieties have been there since the year the estate was established, when Eloy Lecanda had them brought in from Bordeaux. For generations they grew in among other types, but gradually they have been replanted in their own groups. Until the late 1960s Vega Sicilia's production remained so modest that the wine was hardly seen outside Spain, and was very scarce inside the country. About 40,000 bottles a year were being produced at that time. Today the total is an annual 250,000 (soon to rise to a maximum 300,000); yet still the demand greatly exceeds the supply, and the very high prices are partly due to this. After picking (by hand) and fermentation, selection by quality takes place. The simplest wine is the Tinto Valbuena 3.o, which matures for an average 18 months in casks (70 percent of them of American oak, 30 percent French) and goes on sale in the third year after its vintage. Next comes the Valbuena 5.o, and finally the Unico. This last wine is the bodega's flagship, which always contains about 20 percent Cabernet Sauvignon and usually spends 10

years maturing, in wooden vats, in large barrels, small casks, and in bottle. All the Vega Sicilia wines have a somewhat reserved personality. They are not characterized by exuberant fruit or great geniality, but rather by a distinguished, firmly based taste with almost always a certain amount of spice, a suggestion of somewhat smoky wood, compact berry-like fruit and a long, complex aftertaste in which a hint of toast is detectable. Their colour is always dark and deep. The Unico has the most depth and the longest lifespan, but both the Valbuena wines are excellent too, with a slightly looser, more open structure, and they are also more rounded, with more fruit. All these wines deserve to be tasted with the utmost attentiveness, for only then do they fully reveal their sometimes subtle nuances.

Above: The cellars of Vega Sicilia, whose wines have a legendary reputation.

Travel Information

HOTELS AND RESTAURANTS

Casa Florencio, Arias de Miranda 14, 09400 Aranda de Duero, tel (47) 500230 Famous for its *asados* (roasts), especially of lamb.
Casa Rafael Corrales, Obispo Velasco 2, 09400 Aranda de Duero, tel (47) 500277 *Asados* of sucking pig and equally young lamb. Try the local cheese.
Mesón de la Villa, Plaza Mayor 3, 09400 Aranda de Duero, tel (47) 501025 Restaurant with a lot of atmosphere. Besides traditional seasonal fare, more inventive dishes can also be ordered.
Asador Mauro, 47300 Peñafiel, tel (83) 880816 Simple eating house where roast young lamb comes perfect from the oven. You will also find surprisingly good wines at attractive prices (Pesquera, Vega Sicilia, etc).
El Chuleta, 09300 Roa, tel (47) 540312 The best place for meat and fish dishes, such as *besugo* (sea bream).
Hostal Sardón, 47240 Sardón de Duero, tel (83) 680307 Roadhouse offering a few simple hotel rooms. Castilian cuisine of good quality, reasonably priced.
Parador, 47100 Tordesilla *see* Rueda
Mesón La Fragua, Paseo de Zorilla 10, 47006 Valladolid, tel (83) 338785 Varnished beams, a tiled floor, low, leather-upholstered

chairs, cowhides here and there. In this masculine atmosphere you can eat sucking pig, roast lamb and other Castilian dishes, as well as fresh fish.
Mesón Panero, Marina Escobar 1, 47001 Valladolid, tel (83) 301673 Cheerful eating place with a busy décor where you can enjoy both regional dishes and more cosmopolitan fare.
Hotel Mozart, Menédez Pelayo 7, 47001 Valladolid, tel (83) 297777 Very comfortable hotel in the old centre. It was totally renovated a few years ago.
Olid Meliá, Plaza de San Miguel 10, 47003 Vallodolid, tel (83) 357200 Modern-looking, comfortable hotel in walking distance of the Plaza Mayor. Fairly noisy.

PLACES OF INTEREST

Aranda de Duero At the entrance to this provincial town (population 28,000) there is a sign with the words *Tierra de vino y cordero* (Land of wine and lamb). Besides these culinary enjoyments the place also offers a few visual ones, such as the churches of Santa María (fifteenth century, Gothic) and San Juan Bautista (small, thirteenth century, Romanesque).
Clunia In the neighbourhood are the remains of a Roman town and theatre, and a splendid view.

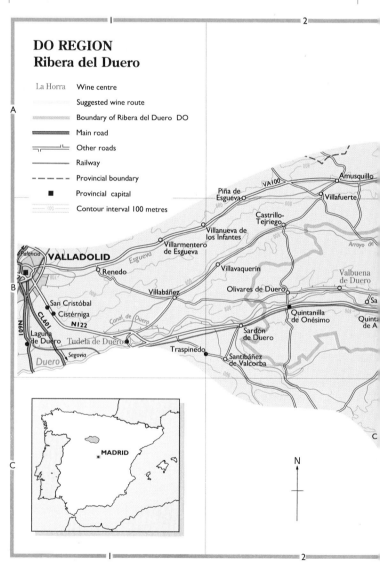

DO REGION
Ribera del Duero

La Horra	Wine centre
	Suggested wine route
	Boundary of Ribera del Duero DO
	Main road
	Other roads
	Railway
	Provincial boundary
■	Provincial capital
	Contour interval 100 metres

Fuentecén Notable crenellated church tower with a statue.

Peñafiel This little town is dominated by its castle, 200 m (656 ft) by 23 m (75 ft), perched on a high ridge looking like a ship on the rocks. The tenth to fourteenth-century structure is well preserved. As well as a number of church buildings, such as the fourteenth-century San Pablo in Mudéjar style, Peñafiel has its Plaza del Coso. This typically Castilian square is wide, covered with sand, and surrounded on all sides by ancient houses. It was in fact laid out for bullfights.

Peñaranda de Duero At its centre, beside the atmospheric Plaza Mayor, is the Miranda palace. This was built in Renaissance style and dates from the sixteenth century. It is open to the public.

Roa de Duero Now that Alejandro Fernández has established his second bodega here, Roa de Duero has become something of an unofficial wine capital for Ribera del Duero. Many of its 2,500 inhabitants

are winegrowers (often members of the local cooperative). The sixteenth-century Santa María church overlooks the Plaza Mayor.

Sardón de Duero The abbey of Santa María de Retuarta can be seen a short distance from the N122. This dates from the twelfth century, but was later rebuilt and extended. It can only be looked at from the outside.

Sotillo de la Ribera A typical small wine village. Try to visit one of the many wine cellars that were hewn out of the San Jorge mountain. The one belonging to the biggest local bodega, Ismael Arroyo, consists of long galleries with an area of 1,200 sq m (1,435 sq ft). Some beautiful landscapes to be seen on the road from Sotillo to La Horra.

Valbuena de Duero There is here the remarkable thirteenth-century abbey built by the Cistercians, and a church and chapel with frescos. The renowned Vega Sicilia wine estate is on the south bank of the

Duero, between the river and the N122. There are security men walking around, not only because of the 900,000 bottles of expensive wine kept on the premises, but because the proprietors also own a security firm.

Valladolid This continually expanding city with almost 340,000 inhabitants has a rich history. The counts, and later kings, of Castilla often resided here, and royal weddings and births took place (Philip II, Henry IV). Vallodolid even became the capital of Spain more than once. The city owes many monuments to this glorious past. Among them are the cathedral (fifteenth to nineteenth century) with a statue of Cervantes in front of it; the San Pablo church with its fine Gothic façade (fifteenth century); and the richly decorated Colegio de San Gregorio (founded in the fifteenth century) which contains Spain's biggest sculpture collection. The house where Cervantes spent the last years of his

life can be visited. Note the rosary along the Paseo de la Católica thoroughfare. Valladolid is also a university town and the seat of a bishop.

WINE ROUTE

The journey mapped out covers mainly the western part of Ribera del Duero, for it is there that the best producers and the most interesting wine-making communities are to be found. Valladolid lies outside the wine zone, but its many monuments make it decidedly worthwhile visiting. The scenery is usually more beautiful north of the river Duero. Two very fine stretches of road are due east of Pesquera de Duero, and between La Horra and Sotillo de Ribera. Southwest of Valladolid you can connect with the Rueda wine route.

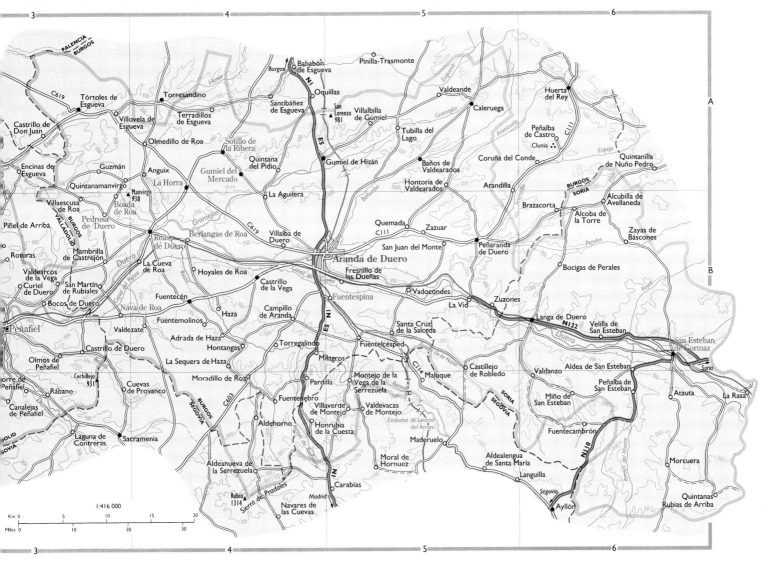

Rueda

In the fifteenth and sixteenth centuries the town of Medina del Campo, 155 km (96 miles) north of Madrid, experienced a time of great prosperity. The kings of Castilla were in residence here, and this was where Isabella the Catholic spent her last years. The presence of the court was a great stimulus to winegrowing, with the result that nearly 500 bodegas flourished in and around the town. At the end of the sixteenth century wines from the Tierra de Medina were being served at the court of Philip III in Valladolid. This monarch even issued a decree to prevent any fraud with his favourite wines. After the court had moved to Madrid the Medina wines remained important. Halfway through the eighteenth century the district had some 29,000 ha (71,660 acres) of vineyards. At the end of that century Charles IV gave his personal permission for wines from Rueda, a village between Medina and Tordesillas, to be shipped to London. Rueda has since become the name for the whole district and the wine produced there, and was officially confirmed with *denominación de origen* status in 1980.

Flat plateaux, low hills

Rueda today is a colourless main road village beside the N6, which links Madrid with Galicia. There are bodegas on both the north and the south side where passing motorists can taste and buy wine, but in the village itself there are few shops where bottles of wine are sold. Unseen by the motorist are the many underground galleries or cellars down in the rock, where the wine used to be made. The one belonging to SAT Los Curros dates from the fourteenth century and is 20 m (65 ft) deep; it is now used only for receptions and banquets.

Rueda is surrounded on all sides by a patchwork quilt of vineyards and other cultivated fields, but the landscape is otherwise rather bleak, consisting of flat plateaux and low hills. Most of the 5,100 ha (12,600 acres) of vineyards are at 500 to 750 m (1,640 to 2,460 ft) above sea level, on sandy and chalky soils, with a good deal of gravel in the best of them. More clay occurs in the valleys of the Zapardiel and other small rivers. About 400 mm (nearly 17 ins) of rain fall annually, most of it in 80 or so days in autumn. The rest of the year is usually dry, with hot summers and hard winters. Frosts occur into the spring.

Discovery of Verdejo

After the district had been stricken by phylloxera it was mainly replanted with Palomino. This grape variety originated in Jerez and resulted in sherry-like wines which were often affected by *flor* yeast. Palomino was often mixed with a proportion of Verdejo, a native variety. Rueda's *vinos generosos* were not very successful: their quality remained inferior to that of sherry, their reputation was largely local, and most of the wine was sold in bulk. In short, Rueda (Spanish for wheel) was standing still.

That the district got moving again is due to Francisco ("Paco") Hurtado de Amézaga and the professor who had taught him at Bordeaux university, Emile Peynaud. Paco's family ran the Rioja bodega Marqués de Riscal and wanted to start making white wine, but the local Viura grape was found to have too little character. Paco and Peynaud therefore went looking in other areas for grapes that they could use – in Penedés, Galicia, La Mancha, and Rueda. It was in Rueda that they discovered Verdejo, a grape that according to Peynaud had great quality potential. The dry wine it made put him in mind of a Sauvignon from the Graves district of Bordeaux.

A new style of wine

After fermenting bought-in must in 1971, the Marqués de Riscal firm decided to build a modern bodega of its own in Rueda. The location chosen was just north of the village of Rueda. It was the first bodega in the area with stainless-steel tanks in which the wine could be fermented at low temperature. To ensure a sufficient supply of Verdejo grapes, Paco paid the growers a considerable premium for them. In addition he decided to lay out a vineyard here. The new style of Rueda wine was received enthusiastically all round the world and now not only is the United States a great customer, but France as well. Indeed, the bodega proudly announced that the French importer had wanted to buy up the whole 1990 vintage. The Marqués de Riscal example has been followed by the other 16 producers here and Verdejo plantings have greatly increased. In the vineyards at least half the vines must be Verdejo before the grower is given permission to plant other varieties, such as Rueda's third white grape, Viura (or Macabeo) for example.

Rueda and Rueda Superior

The naming of the different types of wine was also based on Verdejo. Ordinary Rueda has to have at least 25 percent of this variety. Rueda Superior on the other hand should consist of a minimum 60 percent Verdejo; and if the name Verdejo appears on the label then that minimum goes up to 85 percent. Some of the better producers make pure Verdejo wines. The Martínsancho by Angel Rodríguez Vidal is a delightful example. Good Verdejo wines are characterized by a taste rich in substance with quite a lot of natural glycerine, a touch of aniseed, modest fruit and an unmistakable refinement. They are undoubtedly among the best that Spain has to offer.

Experiments

Although this basic material is already excellent in itself, attempts are being made to add a further dimension to wines from the Verdejo grape, to make them more complex still. Experiments at the Marqués de Riscal bodega have resulted in the Reserva Limousin, a Rueda that is matured in new, or almost new, casks of French oak. At Castilla la Vieja, where the white Marqués de Griñon is made, experiments have been carried out fermenting a pure Verdejo in new casks and then ageing it in them for five months. This same bodega leaves all the white grape skins in contact with the must. During this contact, extra elements of scent and taste are added to the grape juice. Another challenge facing the Rueda bodegas is how to keep their wine fresh and good for as long as possible. The locally based oenological research station has conducted trials with "hyper-oxidation". By clarifying the wine thoroughly and with a large amount of oxygen, it is protected against oxidization. The result of this experiment is very encouraging. Given these developments, Rueda wines may be expected to gain in depth and quality in the years to come.

The rise of Sauvignon

There is a further type of white wine on its way up, one based on Sauvignon. Once again the impulse has come from Bodegas Marqués de Riscal. The Sauvignon grape appears to do well in this area, giving fruity, congenial, well-structured wines with a gentle freshness. The variety's usual slightly vegetal, floral aroma with its tendency towards gooseberries is absent here. The

Above: Characteristic landscape in Rueda. These fields lie directly behind the bodega of Marqués de Riscal.

Rueda Sauvignons have a personality of their own. At Marqués de Riscal they believe in this wine and Sauvignon plantings are therefore to be increased in the bodega's own vineyard. Castilla la Vieja, Sanz, Los Curros, Lagar Noble and other bodegas, too, have begun making Sauvignon. Marqués de Riscal also has at its disposal plots with Chardonnay vines, and there are others planted with Pinot Gris, Riesling, Albariño and Treixadura – the last two varieties from Galicia. The large amount of Verdejo grown, and the increase in the new varieties, does not mean that the area's traditional grapes have disappeared. The Viura, for example, is still grown in abundance and is there as the main grape in all the ordinary Ruedas, and in smaller percentages in most of the Rueda Superiors. Castilla la Vieja has experimented with making a truly commercial wine from the Viura alone, with plenty of residual sugar and *pétillant* with carbon dioxide bubbles. Marqués de Riscal sells some of its pure Viura wine under a second brand name.

Red wines

Palomino has remained on the scene, although on a much more limited scale than previously. The Rueda DO still distinguishes a couple of *vinos generosos* (which also have to contain at least 25 percent Verdejo). Pálido has to develop *flor* and mature for at least four years, the last three in oak casks. Its minimum alcohol content is 14 percent (which probably becomes 15 percent). Pálido usually has a pale gold colour and a fairly dry taste that greatly resembles a very simple sherry. Browner and more mature (from more pronounced oxidization) is the Dorado. There is a faint suggestion here of an *amontillado* from Jerez. Its minimum alcohol content is 15 percent. Again, for this wine four years' ageing is obligatory, the last two in wood. The *rancio* character of various Dorados is achieved by exposing then to the sun in straw-jacketed bottles. So far Rueda has made its name only with its white wines. The *Consejo Regulador*, however, is endeavouring to bring red wines within the DO. Various producers already make red wines, which are sold as *vinos de mesa* or table wines; and the research station is carrying out trials not only with Tempranillo, but also with Cabernet Sauvignon and Merlot. Red wines are certainly nothing new for Rueda, since they were mentioned along with the whites back in the tenth century.

Above: White Verdejo is Rueda's finest variety. Growers have to plant half their vineyards with it before they are allowed to plant different species.
Left: In the square at Medina del Campo, once an important wine village, was held the first known money exchange.

PRODUCERS OF SPECIAL INTEREST

Alvarez y Diez 47500 Nava del Rey
A house that follows traditional methods and makes wines exclusively from grapes from its own 70 ha (173 acres). The least interesting Ruedas from its range are the organic Mantel Nuevo (all kinds of subsidiary elements and vaguely sherry-like) and the wood-aged Mantel Blanco (vanilla, slightly oxidized). The *generosos* are of a better standard for their class – for example, the five-year-old Mantel Pálido and the Dorado with its touch of sweetness.

Angel Lorenzo Cachazo 47220 Pozáldez
The Rueda Superior from this well-equipped bodega is made solely from Verdejo grapes and carries the Martinvillí name. In terms of quality it is among the best from the region, thanks to its slightly floral and fruity touches and a pure, distinguished taste. The ordinary Rueda, the Lorenzo Cachazo brand, is of a decent standard. The firm processes grapes from its own 20 ha (49 acres) of land, and bought-in fruit.

Bodegas de Crianza de Castilla la Vieja 47490 Rueda
This bodega was built in 1976 by Antonio Sanz, of the fourth generation of a wine family. He has at his disposal 26 ha (64 acres) of vineyards and also buys in a lot of grapes. Verdejo grapes from vines 50 to 60 years old are vinified separately for the Marqués de Griñon brand. The wine has depth and distinction. Castilla la Vieja also markets its own Rueda Superior, with a reasonably lively, firm taste. The brand names are Mirador (with a label by José Peñin) and Castilla la Vieja. Also in the collection are a substantial Castilla la Vieja Sauvignon; a fresh but not very refined sparkling Verdejo, Palacio de Bornos (*brut* and *brut nature*); and a number of other kinds, including red and rosé without the DO. Before fermentation begins, the juice from grapes for the Rueda Superior is left with the skins in, with the aim of giving the wines more scent and taste. Trials are going on in the bodega with fermenting in cask.

SAT Los Curros 47490 Rueda
The Gonzalez Vilera family built an entirely new bodega 2 km (just over 1 mile) north of Rueda, replacing an old one that had an underground cellar 20 m (66 ft) deep. About two-thirds of production consists of Rueda Superior. The best of the variants is the Castical, a pure Verdejo with a quite full, meaty taste. The Terra Buena is a correct Rueda, but the other kinds can be disappointing. At the end of 1989 a sparkling wine called Cantosan (100 percent Verdejo) was launched. By the mid-1990s the bodega hopes to have 50 ha (124 acres) of its own vineyards, compared with 6 ha (just under 15 acres) in 1990.

Marqués de Riscal/Vinos Blancos de Castilla 47490 Rueda
The Rioja house of Marqués de Riscal has done pioneering work in Rueda by perceiving the real qualities of Verdejo, and building a brand-new bodega based on them. Then the Rioja people brought Sauvignon to Rueda and are still experimenting with various other white grapes, including Chardonnay. The best wines here are Rueda Superior (80 percent Verdejo), a pleasant-tasting, mouth-filling creation, and the rather more complex Rueda Reserva Limousin. The last thing this Sauvignon wine calls to mind is a Sauvignon. It has some fruit (tending to pears) and a smooth, firm taste. Most of the grapes come from the bodega's own 60 ha (148 acres) of land, plus the same area under contract. Marqués de Riscal was the first firm here to ferment wine at lower temperatures in stainless-steel tanks, and it also makes use of selected yeast cells. There are around 300 casks in the cellar and this number could be increased. Viña Calera is the brand name used for a cheaper pure Verdejo wine.

Vinos Sanz 47490 Rueda
This family firm is right next door to Castilla la Vieja, on the south side of Rueda. Oenologist Juan Carlos Ayala wants eventually to be able to get three-quarters of the grapes he needs from his own land. The area of the latter has therefore been increased from 50 to 80 ha (124 to 198 acres); all of this will be productive by the mid-1990s. The vines here consist of 75 percent Verdejo and 25 percent Sauvignon. Up-to-date equipment is used, including stainless-steel tanks. The Rueda Superior is a successful, quite

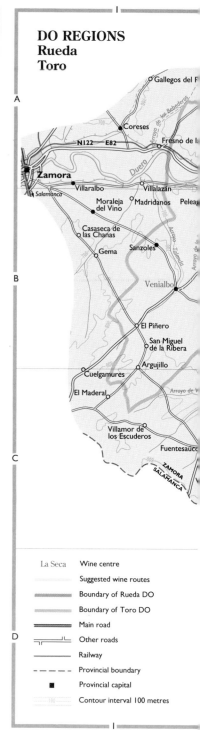

DO REGIONS
Rueda
Toro

La Seca	Wine centre
	Suggested wine routes
	Boundary of Rueda DO
	Boundary of Toro DO
	Main road
	Other roads
	Railway
	Provincial boundary
■	Provincial capital
	Contour interval 100 metres

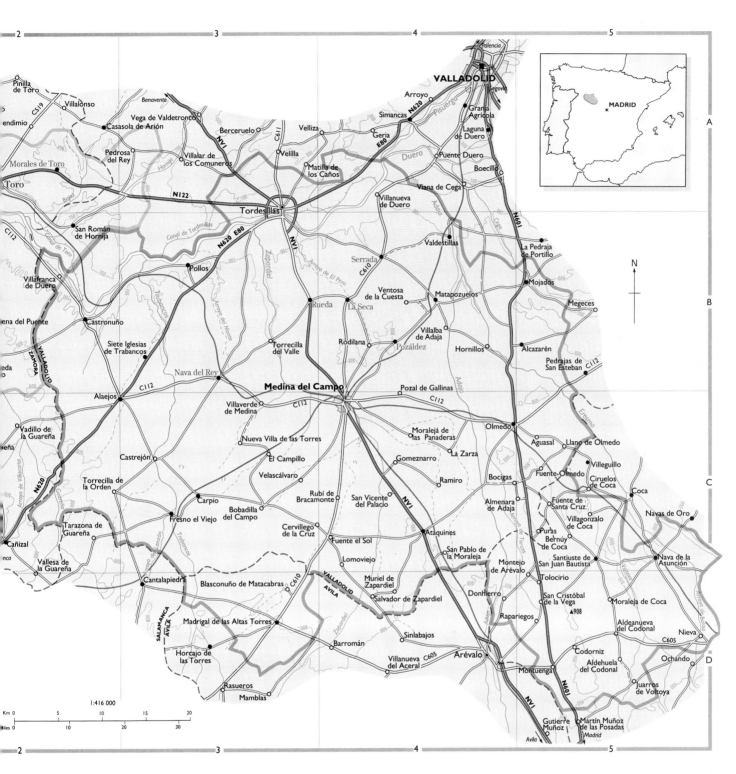

1:416 000

Km 0   5   10   15   20

Miles 0   10   20   30

aromatic wine, somewhat lighter and fresher than others of its kind. This has to do with the fact that Vinos Sanz picks relatively early; often it is the first bodega to do so.

Vinos Vega de la Reina 47490 Rueda

Although this medium-sized bodega mainly produces red and rosé wines without the DO, it also does a decent Rueda Superior with the brand name Vega de la Reina. Often

the slightly aniseed aroma of the Verdejo can be clearly recognized in it, so it is a pure Verdejo.

Agrícola Castellana 47491 La Seca

Marqués de Riscal and this cooperative together control about three-quarters of production in Rueda. The cooperative's members cultivate around 2,000 ha (4,940 acres). Its Cuatro Rayas is a somewhat neutral, yet very

acceptable Rueda Superior (100 percent Verdejo). The concern also produces considerable quantities of Pálido (brand name Campo Grande) and Dorado.

Angel Rodríguez Vidal 47491 La Seca

This bodega has been bottling Martínsancho, its own pure Verdejo wine, since 1981 and has had success with it as far away as America. It is a slightly floral, fruity

wine with depth, a good finish and much charm. The grapes come largely from Angel's own vineyard, high up and covering 15 ha (37 acres).

Bodegas Los Curros 47494 Fuente el Sol

A family firm that aims at quality and has 50 ha (124 acres) of well maintained vineyards (80 percent Verdejo). Its all-Verdejo Castical wine is juicy, fresh and clean.

115

Travel Information

HOTELS AND RESTAURANTS

La Pinilla, 05200 Arévalo, tel (18) 300063 Roast lamb and sucking pig are the specialities here.

El Buen Yantar, 47009 Fuente el Sol, tel (83) 824212 Regional dishes such as *sopa de ajo* (garlic soup) and grilled lamb chops. The lamb from this area is renowned.

Mónaco, 47400 Medina del Campo, tel (83) 801020 Facing the Plaza Mayor, and on the first floor over a gallery. Well-thought-out furnishings and cuisine. The fresh fish comes in from La Coruña practically every day. Try the *croquetas de merluza* (made with hake) to start with.

Parador, 47100 Tordesillas, tel (83) 770051 This two-storey *parador*, set among pine trees, was opened in 1958. It stands a few miles out of town, along the N620. The rooms are comfortable and in the dining room you can enjoy such regional dishes as *conejo* (rabbit) *al vino de Rueda*, *sopa de ajo* and *perdiz de la region escabechada* (marinated cold partridge). This is the best place to stay to visit Rueda, and it could be for Toro, Ribera del Duero and Cigales as well.

El Torreón 47100 Tordesillas, tel (83) 770123 The roasts are excellent here. For dessert try the *tarta de Juana la Loca* or the *dulce de leche*.

PLACES OF INTEREST

Arévalo This old town, just outside the wine district, lies near the confluence of the Arevalillo and Adaja rivers. The two are spanned by a bridge in Mudéjar style. The San Martín church was built in this same style and is easily recognized by its two imposing towers. Another church well worth seeing is La Lugareja, a thirteenth-century, purely Mudéjar structure. Arévalo also has five town mansions, or *palacios*, two of which face the Plaza Mayor, and there are some fine entrances and porches around the Plaza Real. The small castle here dates from the fourteenth century. The belltower has a sixteenth-century interior.

Coca The hill here is crowned by one of Spain's most beautiful citadels, built some five centuries ago in brick, in Gothic Mudéjar style.

Madrigal de las Altas Torres In this town with its thirteenth-century walls is the convent of Madres Agustinas de Nuestra Señora de Gracia, where Isabella the Catholic was born. San Nicolás de Bari is an interesting twelfth-century Mudéjar church.

Medina del Campo Ever since the sixteenth century all the shops here have been closed on Thursdays and open on Sundays, when the market is held. This town, formerly a royal residence, is also where organized currency exchange was first devised. In the fifteenth and sixteenth centuries the markets here (for wool, for example) and the annual fair were among the most important in Europe. Isabella the Catholic spent her last years here, dying in 1504 in a building on the broad Plaza de España. Here, too, is the sixteenth-century collegiate church of San Antolín; on its tower the hours are struck by the figures of a man and a woman. The impressive Mota castle, where Isabella the Catholic held court, is on a hill overlooking the town.

Nava del Rey A wine community with many underground cellars. Most of them belong to the wine firm Alvarez y Diez. The church of Los Santos Juanes displays various styles and has a splendid sacristy.

Olmedo According to an old saying, this walled town has seven monasteries, seven churches, seven squares, seven fountains, seven gates, seven great houses and seven outlying villages. The most beautiful church is that of San Miguel (thirteenth century). It derives its fame from Lope de Vega's play *El Caballero de Olmeda*.

Pozaldéz Two fine churches stand in this village, San Boal and Santa María.

Rueda In the main street here, besides the wine and souvenir shops, stands the baroque church of Santa María, with its façade flanked by two round towers. There is goldsmith's work within. A few hundred yards to the south of this church is a stately looking building that houses the Estación Enológica de Castilla y León. Rueda now celebrates the grape harvest at the end of September, after doing it for the first time in 1990.

La Seca Besides its wine the place has two churches, the baroque Santa Francisco and the Renaissance parish church.

Tordesillas This little town on the Duero was where Spain and Portugal divided lands yet to be discovered between them. High above the river bank is the convent of Santa Clara, with royal connections and built in Mudéjar style. The guided tour enables visitors to enjoy many art treasures, and a richly decorated inner courtyard. Juana the Mad, daughter of Isabella the Catholic, shut herself up in this convent after the death of her husband, Philip the Handsome, in 1506. She was in mourning for 44 years and left state affairs to her father Ferdinand and later Charles I. Not far from the convent is the sixteenth-century church of San Antolín, which now also serves as a museum for sculpture and other art treasures. The Plaza Mayor is a typically Castilian square.

WINE ROUTE

The suggested route covers a large part of the wine region. It takes in not only the most important wine communities (Nava del Rey, Rueda, La Seca), but also the most interesting historic places inside and just outside the boundaries. Westward the route can be extended by a visit to Toro, and Ribera del Duero is not too far to the northeast.

Toro

Pilgrims following the northerly route to Santiago de Compostela used to drink a good deal of the red wines of Toro, a town halfway between Tordesillas and Zamora. They were valued not only for their colour and strength, but also for their healing properties. To assure themselves of a sufficient supply of wine, religious orders in the thirteenth century acquired land around Toro, and sometimes it was donated to them. Thus in 1208 King Alfonso IX of León made a grant of vineyards to the cathedral of Santiago de Compostela. Complimentary references to Toro wine turn up in the fourteenth-century *Libro de Buen Amor* and elsewhere. According to tradition, Columbus not only praised these wines; he placed orders for them. Whether he actually took casks of it with him on his voyage of discovery is, however, uncertain. His ship the *Pinta*, which on 12 October 1492 was the first to sight land, is said to have got her name through Diego de Deza, who was born in Toro. He worked at the court and apparently suggested the name, which means "pint", to Isabella the Catholic.

Effect of phylloxera

In the sixteenth, seventeenth and eighteenth centuries Toro remained an important wine centre. The quantity of wine that was made annually varied from 15,000 to more than 30,000 hl (330,000 to 660,000 gals). But after Toro's vineyards had been laid waste by phylloxera, winegrowing declined sharply, and a revival did not come until the mid-1980s – the Toro *denominación de origen* dates from 1987. At present the region has around 6,100 ha (15,070 acres) of vineyards, of which 3,200 ha produce wine that can be sold as Toro. The annual volume varies around 25,000 hl (550,000 gals). The *Consejo Regulador* expects that this volume – and therefore the vineyard area – will change little for the present.

Wine zones

This wine region is at a height of 620 to 750 m (2,030 to 2,460 feet); and the terrain is mostly fairly flat and rather dull. Vineyards alternate with fields of vegetables or corn, sometimes edged by poplars or other trees. Here and there a flock of sheep grazes. It comes almost as a relief to have a view out over the Duero valley from Toro's collegiate church. The winegrowers distinguish two zones here. The zone around Toro covers about 1,700 ha (4,200 acres) and has a relatively large amount of gravel. The poor soil here yields 2,500 to 3,000 kg per ha (2,230 to 2,675 lb per acre). A few miles further east is the Morales de Toro zone. There the soil consists of fine sand with some clay, and yields around twice as much: 5,000 kg per ha (4,450 lb per acre). According to local experts this considerable economic difference is not really reflected in the wines, differences in quality being small. Both Toro and Morales de Toro, like most of the other wine communities here, come within the province of Zamora; only three of the 15 villages are in Valladolid. One of them, San Román de Hornija, can make either Toro or Rueda wine.

A Tempranillo variant

Toro's many small growers – the average property here is 0.8 ha (not quite 2 acres) – work under severe weather conditions. It usually rains for less than 60 days a year, giving an annual rainfall of 350 to 500 mm (13.8 to 19.7 ins). The summers are dry and hot, up to 40°C (104°F), and the winters hard. Frost can occur

from the last week in October to the first week in May. The Tinta de Toro has been cultivated for centuries now in this climate. It is a close relative of the Tempranillo: "If it isn't a sister then it's a first cousin", said one producer. Wine from Tinta de Toro differs from what the Tempranillo family gives elsewhere in Spain – in Ribera del Duero and Rioja, for example. Red Toro – which has to contain at least 75 percent Tinta de Toro – is a wine with a very great deal of colour, strength and substance: so much so that there has been difficulty getting it accepted as conforming to EC rules.

Earlier harvest

There are references to the potency of Toro in local sayings, such as: *Tomando vino de Toro, más que comer devoro* (Drinking Toro wine is more devouring than eating). Not for nothing has the *Consejo Regulador* limited the alcohol content of red Toro to 12.5 and at most 15 percent. But for the winemakers even that 15 percent is a restriction, for in this area the wines can reach 16 to 17 percent quite naturally. In the *Consejo Regulador* the conviction is that nowadays heady wines are harder to sell than varieties with rather less alcohol. In cooperation with the oenological research station in Rueda, guidelines have been evolved for the production of wines with less alcohol. The most concrete proposal is for earlier picking.

Faithful to tradition, the majority of growers do not begin picking until after 10 October, but according to the *Consejo*, an earlier start gives wines that are not only rather lighter, but also contain more acid. Most of the four private bodegas have followed this advice. However, the two cooperatives, which between them produce 70 percent of the volume, are hesitating. Picking too early

Below: Most of Toro's grapes are grown on flat terrain, where trees such as this Mediterranean pine are rare.

is not necessarily a good thing either, since then the grapes may tend to lose too much of their aroma. According to Manuel Fariña, "The trick is to find exactly the right balance." He himself expects that normally red Toro will have to continue to have 13 to 13.5 percent alcohol.

White and rosé Toros

Tinta de Toro is not the only grape variety here. It represents about two-thirds of plantings and the rest consist of 16 percent Garnacha (which combines excellently with Tinta de Toro) and 18 percent other, mainly white varieties, Malvasía being the most common. There are, too, small percentages of Verdejo, Palomino and Albillo. Just as in Ribera del Duero, this last variety also features as a dessert grape.

A proportion of the white grapes is used, as in other regions, to make the red wines a little lighter and more fragrant. There is, however, white Toro wine; if fermented at low temperature it can sometimes be very good, but it is no match for the wine made by neighbouring Rueda. Relatively speaking, Toro *rosado* is rather more interesting, although it cannot reach the level of the red. The Cabernet Sauvignon variety is conspicuous for being almost completely absent. The six Toro producers believe that their red wine can only succeed nationally and internationally on the basis of maintaining its own personality to the full: Toro is original, and must remain so.

PRODUCERS OF SPECIAL INTEREST

Bodegas Fariña 49800 Toro
Since the creation of the Toro DO in 1987, producers of this wine have had to be established in the wine zone itself. As a result Bodegas Fariña, a family concern founded in 1942, had to move from Casaseca de las Chanas, 9 km (5.5 miles) from Zamora, to Toro. A whole new bodega was built, part of it underground, which has been in operation since 1988. The owner, Manuel Fariña, is very keen to achieve a good balance in his wines between wood and fruit, and he also wants to bring their alcohol down gradually to 13 to 13.5 percent from the present 14 percent.

The wines are made exclusively from Tinta de Toro. The Colegiata is a sinewy, dark wine with some freshness and mellow, ripe fruit. It usually spends two years in tanks and eight months in bottle before it is sold. There is rather more depth to the *crianza* and *reserva* Gran

Colegiata. These full-bodied wines with their suggestion of vanilla and wood taste wonderful with the traditional stews of the region on a cold winter's day. Both wines have 9 to 14 months cask-ageing (in American oak, 20 percent of it new) besides the time in tank and bottle. The Gran Cordelero is a *crianza* that is aged in wood for two months less.

Bodegas Fariña makes its Toro wines with bought-in grapes. The concern's own 30 ha (74 acres) still lie outside the actual zone and provide table wines (*vinos de mesa*).

Bodegas Luis Mateos 49800 Toro
It was in 1942 that Luis Mateos first began to make wine in Toro. Some 30 years later his bodega was converted into a limited company; since 1978 it has been in the hands of the Marcos family, who also deal

Below: The town of Toro is built on a hill high above the river Duero, east of Zamora. It was founded in the 3rd century BC.

in cheese. The grapes come from the company's own 18 ha (45 acres) in Villafranca de Duero, and from contracted growers. The grapes are fermented in concrete tanks. For its *crianza* and *reserva* the bodega has about 450 mainly used casks and large barrels. The best wines are the ones for drinking young, such as the Valdevi (in red and rosé). The wood-aged ones I tasted were all somewhat rustic, and sometimes musty. Relatively speaking the most interesting quality was offered by the *gran reserva* Vega de Toro, a dark-toned, potent wine with a hint of sun-drenched fruit.

José María Fermoselle 49153 Venialbo
To meet the requirements of the Toro DO this dynamic, Zamora-based house was obliged to open a branch within the zone. In 1985 it bought and renovated cellars in Venialbo, a village southwest of the town of Toro. Fermoselle has its own vineyard area of 40 ha (99 acres) and also buys in grapes. Among its most successful wines are the red (80 percent Tinta de Toro, 20 percent Malvasía), rosé and white versions of its Novissimo Señorío, for drinking young, and this is partly due to their pleasant fruitiness. Of the others, El Señorío de Toro Etiqueta Negra deserves attention. This is an almost opaque *crianza* (12 to 18 months in wood) with a meaty, mellow, quite lively taste, with not too much alcohol – usually 13 percent.

Left: Peaceful street scene in Toro. The hill beneath the streets is honeycombed with galleries and cellars where the wine used to be made.

(population 60,000). The *parador* here is a good place to stay.

Zamora prospered and flourished in the Middle Ages, as the many remaining monuments bear witness.

If you walk around the area between the *parador* and the Romanesque cathedral you will pass a number of churches, among them the twelfth-century San Isodoro, with its stork's nest; the twelfth-century La Magdalena; the seventeenth-century Corpus Christi; and the twelfth to fifteenth-century San Ildefonso.

Also in the same part of the town are the thirteenth-century Santa María de la Horta; the twelfth-century Santo Tomé; and the Santiago del Burgo dating from the same period. Not far from the cathedral are the remains of an old castle with a pleasant park in front; this *castillo* offers a panoramic view of the surrounding area. The Plaza Mayor with its trees, terraces and galleries is always a congenial place in the early evening.

WINE ROUTE

The wine route consists of three loops around Toro. The eastern one runs along the right bank of the Duero, through the Morales de Toro and Toro wine zones, and the town itself. The southern loop follows the left bank of the river (there is a viewing point at Castronuño); the western one goes to Zamora. This trip also takes in the wine village of Venialba. A convenient connection can be made with the Rueda wine route via Tordesillas or Nava del Rey.

Travel Information

HOTELS AND RESTAURANTS

Restaurante Alegría, 49800 Toro, tel (88) 690085 Simple eating house where you can order garlic soup, dried cod and goat.
Catayo, 49800 Toro, tel (88) 690060 Restaurant and bar. Regional dishes, including roast lamb.
Juan II, 49800 Toro, tel (88) 690300 Pleasant, comfortable hotel in quiet situation next to the collegiate church. Spectacular view over the Duero valley. Also a decent restaurant.
Parador, 47100 Tordesillas: *see* Rueda
Parador Condes de Alba y Aliste, Plaza Viriato 5, 49001 Zamora, tel (88) 514497 Established in a former fifteenth-century palace. The rooms are situated around an inner courtyard and provided with all amenities. In the restaurant regional dishes are offered.

PLACES OF INTEREST

Toro With its 10,000 inhabitants this is the third largest town in the province of Zamora, after Zamora itself and Benavante. Its origins probably go back to the 3rd century BC. The town was built on a hill beside a sharp bend in the Duero, which has a Roman bridge over it. Inside this hill there is a network of galleries where the wine used to be made. Toro's most beautiful church is the twelfth-century Colegiata de Santa María la Mayor, with a splendidly sculptured Pórtico de la Gloria, which stands on the edge of town. The church has a rose garden beside it, and from here there is a marvellous view across the valley of the Duero. The brick-built San Lorenzo church is a fine example of the Mudéjar style, as is the San Salvador. In the San Sebastián church and museum the works of art include fourteenth-century frescos. Memories of the religious orders that used to make wine in Toro are kept alive by four foundations, among them the fourteenth-century Convento del Sancti Spiritus. You drive into the oldest part of the town below the Torre del Reloj, a clocktower dated 1733 which incorporates a picture in the masonry. By the central square are a number of galleries, with bars, and the eighteenth-century *ayuntamiento*. The painter Delhy Tejero lived and worked in Toro; you can visit her house, which is now a small museum where about 100 of her paintings are displayed.

Toro has one of Spain's oldest Plazas de Toros (bullrings), dating from 1828.
Zamora The distance from Toro to Zamora is only 33 km (20 miles), so you can easily visit this town

Bierzo

In Roman times a town called Bergidum was established in Asturias, in northwest Spain. Later the whole area was to take its name – El Bierzo – from this place. El Bierzo consists of a vast, triangular basin around the valley of the Sil and its tributaries. To the west and north it is screened from Galicia by the mountains of the Cordillera Cantábrica and to the east by the Montes de León. The southern boundary is formed by the Sierra Cabrera and the lower Sil valley. As a result of this situation – not far from the sea yet sheltered – El Bierzo has a gentler, more congenial climate than the other wine districts of Castilla León further south, but it is not so damp as Galicia. Annual rainfall is around 650 mm (25.6 ins) and the average temperature is an agreeable 13°C (55.4°F); which is exactly the same as for the Riojan capital Logroño. Climate alone makes El Bierzo eminently suitable for quality winegrowing.

The pilgrim route

The soil, too, lends itself to winegrowing, at least in El Bierzo Bajo, the relatively low-lying eastern part. Around Cacabelos (Bergidum was sited near here), Camponaraya, the sizeable town of Ponferrada, and Villafranca del Bierzo there are hills, valleys and plateaux that are often clayey and ferruginous (hence their reddish-brown colour), but sometimes there is granite rubble and slate as well. The wine grape does excellently in such soils. It was probably French monks who planted the first vines here 600 years ago: Villafranca is derived from *villa francorum*, "town of the Frenchmen". That the monks chose this area had to do with the pilgrim route to Santiago de Compostela, which crossed El Bierzo. People making this pilgrimage often rested here to gather their strength for the tiring journey over the high mountain passes. One of the places where they lodged was an abbey in Villafranca founded in the twelfth century by Cistercian monks from Cluny, known today as the Colegiata de Santa María.

Below: Vines growing near Villafranca del Bierzo.

The rise of the cooperatives

References to vineyards in El Bierzo occur from the twelfth century onward; and the pilgrims often praised the wine for its good qualities. From the eighteenth century an increasing amount of wine went to Galicia, especially the red, which the region was short of, a situation that continued until well into the twentieth century.

El Bierzo wine was so easy to sell both in its own area and in Galicia that the producers did not bother to improve the quality, or to seek customers elsewhere. Not until the 1960s did this gradually begin to change. Under the pressure of increasing competition from other regions many small wine producers decided to organize themselves into groups – with the result that in 1963 the first cooperative was set up at Camponaraya. Four others were to follow and today the cooperatives control about three-quarters of production. The whole region has about a dozen active producers.

A hint of metal

The region only received its *denominación de origen* in December 1989, a quarter of a century after the establishment of the first cooperative . The wine district comprises 7,500 ha (18,500 acres) of which 5,800 ha (14,300 acres) are entitled to grow DO wines. Many of the vines are old, so that the average yield per acre is low. The most important, and also the most characteristic, grape is the black Mencía. It is probably related to Cabernet Franc, which the medieval monks would have brought with them. Naturally the variety has adapted itself to the soil and climate of El Bierzo, and in so doing has acquired characteristics of its own. Its leaves are rather transparent, and its wine can be recognized by the slight hint of metal or mineral in its taste. Often a modest touch of fruit is also present, together with a little greenness to begin with. In addition, red Mencía wines age in excellent fashion, developing particularly well in bottle.

Big investments

Elsewhere in Spain Mencía is hardly grown at all, and is found mainly in the district of Valdeorras, in Galicia, which borders on El Bierzo. It is with reason therefore that the *Consejo Regulador* has laid down that the red wines must contain at least 70 percent Mencía and the rosés 50 percent. Unlike the region itself the DO bears the name Bierzo, not El Bierzo. It is mainly Garnacha that is used as the second black grape. The best red wines, however, have Mencía only. About a fifth of the plantings in the 22 wine communities here are of white grapes. These may be made into white wines, or mixed with black varieties for rosés. Malvasía is the most cultivated of the white grapes, but in terms of quality the producers speak more favourably of Doña Blanca, a variety of Portuguese origin that gives very fruity wines here. Godello, from Valdeorras, is here too, and so is Palomino, which is slowly disappearing.

Bierzo's *rosados* and white wines are seldom really interesting, a fact that is also acknowledged locally. Here they are firmly convinced that the future of Bierzo lies with red wines, naturally from the Mencía grape. Since the end of the 1980s large investments have been made on the basis of this conviction, both by the cooperatives and by private producers. As a result of this, not only will the quality of Bierzo wines be further raised, but the quantity that is bottled will be increased. In 1990 almost half the vintage was bottled, but everyone expects that the percentage of bottled wine will have gone up considerably by the turn of the century.

Above: The soil around Bierzo is often reddish in colour as there are iron ore deposits in many places. The climate is gentler here than in the more southerly parts of Castilla y León.

PRODUCERS OF SPECIAL INTEREST

Bodega Comarcal Cooperativa Vinos del Bierzo 245450 Cacabelos
This is the largest of the five cooperatives in Bierzo, with some 2,000 members who cultivate 1,000 to 1,500 ha (2,470 to 3,700 acres). Since the 1980s this winery, which dates from 1964, has followed a policy aimed at quality, resulting in a range of attractive wines. The best are the red wines – all 100 percent Mencía – which are matured in wood in the underground cellar, where there are about 500 *barricas* of American oak. The name Vinos Guerra suggests an almost violent wine (*guerra* means war), but it is in fact a very pleasant creation with that characteristic Mencía taste with its metal, dark fruit, some wood and a slight fresh touch to it. It is matured for about three months in cask. More mature, smoother, firmer, and with more wood and vanilla is the somewhat rustic *gran reserva* Guerra, a five-year-old wine given 12 months in cask underground. The cooperative regards the Señorío del Bierzo as its best wine. This is a well-matured, juicy *gran reserva* with a distinct wood aroma, and rustic nature.

Prada a Tope 245450 Cacabelos
In Bierzo the nicest wine firm to visit is Prada a Tope. The way to it is clearly signposted, not just for the motorists but also for the coach drivers who bring people here from all over Spain. The most important attraction in this whole charming complex is a large cafeteria where wine and snacks are served. You can also eat at a proper restaurant here at Prada a Tope. On the other side of the inner courtyard is an inviting shop (with a marvellous smell of ham) selling not only wine, but also spirits, preserves and books.

In another large room the wines are bottled. These come from Prada a Tope's own 15 ha (37 acres) and from cooperatives. One of the wines is the Joven en Rama, for drinking young, which is neither filtered nor clarified. It is a pleasing product with a not too heavy, supple taste and a slight metallic element to it. The wood-aged red wines are usually rather rustic and of average quality. As well as wine the owner, José Luis Rama (who set up the firm in 1984) also makes spirits and excellent preserves, including peppers, chestnuts and cherries (in *aguardiente*).

Cooperative Viñas del Bierzo
24410 Camponaraya
This cooperative – the oldest of the region, founded 1963 – is busy renewing and refitting its equipment. A great deal has been modernized since 1990 and this will be continued in the coming years. One of the aims is to increase the proportion of bottled wine, which was only 10 percent at the start of 1990.

Naraya is a supple, decent wine that spends six months in barrel. The quite generous Gran Bierzo is a good *crianza* of its kind, with 15 months in cask behind it. The cooperative has 1,600 affiliated members with around 800 ha (1,980 acres). Of the bought-in grapes the Mencía accounts for 90 percent.

Palacio de Arganza 24500
Villafranca del Bierzo
Facing a large square and next to Villafranca's *colegio* there stands the Palacio de Arganza (fifteenth century with wings added later) where wine has been made since 1805. Since 1963 the *palacio* and the bodega have been the property of Daniel Vuelta and his family. It is a privilege to enter here, for the interior of the *palacio* is furnished and decorated in an extremely tasteful manner. Its many rooms contain a rich collection of works of art, and are also very comfortable.

The bodega operates solely with bought-in must and wines. Normally there are nearly 20 types in the range, including vintages of 10 to 15 years old. The red wines generally are made from 80 percent Mencía and 20 percent Garnacha grapes. The proportion of Garnacha is higher in wines from the 1970s. The average quality is good to very good. Even the mature wines still possess a wholly vital taste; they also have backbone, wood and vanilla (half of the wine spends time in the 1,000 or so small casks and large barrels), and a sound balance. Of the wines for drinking young, the fresh white is one of the best-tasting in the region.

One point that has been unclear

for years now is the matter of the DO, Palacio de Arganza not being affiliated with the Bierzo *Consejo Regulador*. In principle, therefore, the wines could come from anywhere. Since the end of 1991, however, the most recent white and rosé vintages have carried the Bierzo name, and the same will apply to the reds from the end of 1992. The brand name most used by this producer is Palacio de Arganza, but some of the wines are sold as Señorío de Arganza.

Viñas y Bodegas del Bierzo 24500
Villafranca del Bierzo
The two sisters Flor and Consuelo Alvarez de Toledo took over the business here after the death of their father. Since then it has been built up into one of the very best in Bierzo.

About 80 percent of the grapes come from their own land: between Villafranca and Cacabelos are the almost 35 ha (86 acres) of Viña de los Pinos, a hilly estate with reddish, ferruginous soil. The wine is expertly made in Villafranca's most famous street, the Calle del Agua. The cellars are here, distributed among some extremely large buildings. As well as large barrels, Viñas y Bodegas has around 200 small casks.

The best wines are sold under the Valdeobispo name. Normally the red wine is matured in wood for a maximum six months, so as to leave the fruit and the characteristic Mencía taste intact as far as possible. The bodega then rests the wine in bottle for at least seven months. The result is a delicious wine that can be drunk young, but can also develop further without problems.

With the arrival of a full-time oenologist in 1989 the average

quality of the wines improved still further. There are few other bodegas in Bierzo where the potential of the Mencía is so fully exploited.

Travel Information

HOTELS AND RESTAURANTS
Casa Gato, 24540 Cacabelos, tel (87) 547071 Typical local dishes, but also recipes of their own.
La Moncloa, 24540 Cacabelos, tel (87) 546101 This is the restaurant belonging to the wine and preserves company Prada a Tope. In its rustic ambience you can enjoy roast lamb, *chorizos al vino*, pimientos and other country fare.
Azul Montearenas, N4 km 383, 24400 Ponferrada, tel (87) 417012 Among the specialities are lamb and

chanterelles. Spacious dining room in many shades of light brown.
Ballesteros, Fueros de León 12, 2400 Ponferrada, tel (87) 411160 A good address for fish and meat dishes.
Las Cuadras, Calle Gil y Carrosco 4, 24400 Ponferrada, tel (87) 411299 No menu: you eat *tapas* here.
La Charola, 24500 Villafranca del Bierzo, tel (87) 540175 Decent roadside restaurant on the N6 serving regional cuisine.
Parador, 24500 Villafranca del

Above: Not only is Prada a Tope one of the Bierzo's biggest cooperatives in Cacabelos, but it is also the most visited wine company of the area. Which is why this statue of a grape-picker was placed here in 1983.
Left: A farmer and his wife pass the Santuario de las Angustinas, the most important monument in the wine village of Cacabelos.

Bierzo, tel (87) 540175 After the characterless hotels in busy Ponferrada this *parador* on the way into Villafranca comes as a relief. It is quite a modern building, surrounded by a pleasant garden. *Botillo*, a strange local dish, is sometimes on the menu. It consists of a sort of bag filled with spiced, stewed pork.

PLACES OF INTEREST

Cacabelos The statue (1983) of a man carrying a basket of grapes demonstrates that this is one of the most important wine communities. Not far from this sculpture is an atmospheric little square with trees in the middle and arcading around. Near the bank of the Cúa stands the Santuario de las Angustinas with its classic façade – and stork's nest. Archaeological finds are displayed in the Cacabelos museum, some from the vanished town of Bergidum Corullón. There are also partly overgrown castle ruins with a view. The two village churches, the Romanesque San Miguel and San Esteban, were restored a few years ago.

Pieros Near this village between Villafranca and Cacabelos is a hill topped by ruins; this is the *castro*, the remains of the former fortified town of Bergidum from which El Bierzo derives its name. Parts of the walls and towers remain.

Ponferrada Iron is mined in El Bierzo, and around Ponferrada there are smoking blast furnaces and other industrial plant. Traffic is heavy here and anyone who does not know the way may end up in a maze of one-way streets. The many blocks of flats form a striking contrast with the weathered lines of the Templar castle, completed in the thirteenth century. In the basilica of Nuestra Señora de la Encina (patron saint of El Bierzo) is a sixteenth-century altarpiece. The Torre del Reloj is all that remains of the wall that encircled Ponferrada. Around 8 September every year a festival is held on the large square in front of the seventeenth-century *ayuntamiento* in honour of the patron saint mentioned above.

Villafranca del Bierzo This town, built at the confluence of two rivers, was an important stopping place for pilgrims on their way to Santiago de Compostela. They could safely rest and regain their strength in the twelfth-century abbey, built by French monks from Cluny. Since the sixteenth century this building has been the Colegiata de Santa María; there is a fine altarpiece here. The same

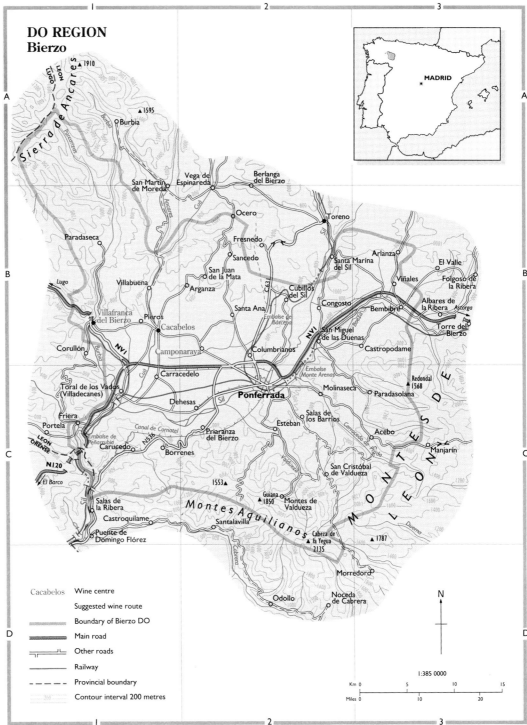

**DO REGION
Bierzo**

MADRID

Cacabelos	Wine centre
	Suggested wine route
	Boundary of Bierzo DO
	Main road
	Other roads
	Railway
	Provincial boundary
	Contour interval 200 metres

1:385 0000

Km 0   5   10   15
Miles 0   10   20

N

Cistercians built the church of Santa María de Cluniaco, which acquired its present form in the sixteenth and eighteenth centuries.

Villafranca also has a Jesuit college, the great Colegio de la Compañía de Jesús, still with its broad seventeenth-century front. On the same three-sided plaza there stands the Palacio de Arganza winery. Villafranca still has three monasteries and one convent. The castle here is surrounded by high walls and cannot be visited. The best-known street in Villafranca is the sloping Calle del Agua (Calle de Ribadeo is its official name), with its many stately houses, some with crests on their frontages.

WINE ROUTE

This takes in the western, more interesting part of the wine zone; and you can if you wish avoid congested Ponferrada. The most southerly road involved is also included in the Valdeorras (Galicia) route. If you follow the latter you come to El Barco de Valdeorras.

Cigales

The Cigales *denominación de origen* has been in existence since March 1991 and stretches north of Valladolid for a distance of about 30 km (19 miles). It is some 15 km (9.5 miles) across and follows the course of the Pisuerga. The landscape is fairly flat, but at an average 700 m (2,300 ft) above sea level. All but one of the 12 communities are in the province of Valladolid; Dueñas belongs to Palencia. Imposing churches and the arms of noble families on houses bear witness to the past prosperity the region has known, but in the twentieth century it is only recently that the wines have come to notice. This was in 1990, when the first bodegas invested in stainless-steel fermentation tanks and the cooling equipment that goes with them. This has meant a big improvement in quality for many of the wines. Cigales produces mostly dry rosés, a kind that benefits greatly from low-temperature, slow fermentation.

Tinta del País

In the better *rosados* from Cigales Tinta del País (the local name for Tempranillo) is always the most important grape. Black Garnacha is generally used with it, and one or more white varieties, among them Albillo and Verdejo. The soils where the grapes are grown vary according to location, but mostly contain clay, supplemented by limestone and gravel. The prevailing climate is continental, only slightly influenced by the sea. Average annual rainfall is just under 410 mm (about 16 ins). In summer the mercury can rise to almost 40° C (104° F) and fall to −12° C (10.4° F) in winter. Winters are usually long and often bring fog as well as frost.

The oenological station at Rueda has contributed greatly to the improvement in quality of the Cigales wines. Every possible test has been carried out with different blends of grapes, different methods of winemaking, and different styles of wine. In the end an aromatic type of rosé was chosen, one that was readily digestible and lighter than the Navarra product. These desirable qualities can only be achieved with a goodly percentage of Tinta del País. This means that in the present area of vineyard – around 2,300 ha (5,685 acres) – this variety is given preference when replanting. Of the existing vines 60 percent are already Tinta del País, but this will obviously increase. About a tenth of the grape harvest goes into red wine, but so far this has been inferior to what neighbouring Ribera del Duero grows. It looks as though rosé will for the present remain the Cigales speciality.

PRODUCERS OF SPECIAL INTEREST

Bodega Cooperativa de Cigales
47270 Cigales
About half of all the winegrowers are associated with this cooperative and between them work some 600 ha (1,480 acres). Modern cellar equipment is part of the reason why this concern, the only cooperative in Cigales, is able to produce an exemplary rosé, the Torondos. This has a fresh fruitiness in taste and fragrance, and is quite simply one of best wines of the region.

Bodegas Frutos Villar 47270 Cigales
A bodega with modern equipment that works on the basis of 70 percent of its grapes from its own 80 ha (198 acres) of vineyard and 30 percent bought in. Its Viña Calderona is refreshing and pure in taste, with sufficient fruit to it. The same owners have three other wine concerns, in Toro, Ribera del Duero and Cigales itself (the last-named for simple table wine).

Travel Information

HOTELS AND RESTAURANTS

For hotels, *see* Ribera del Duero and Rueda.
El Mesón de Cigales, 47270 Cigales, tel (83) 580110
Regional fare: the young lamb and young local rosé taste delightful together.
La Sorbona, 47194 Fuensaldaña, tel (83) 583077 Castilian cuisine.
Bodega la Cuela, 47194 Mucientes, tel (83) 583084 The local winegrowers recommend this restaurant.
Los Tres Arcos, 47194 Mucientes, tel (83) 58223 Regional dishes and wines.

PLACES OF INTEREST

Cabezón de Pisuerga Houses with coats of arms on their façades. The fifteenth-century Santa María church has a high tower and an altarpiece in rococo style. Spanish patriots stopped Napoleonic troops at the large sixteenth-century bridge. There are the remains of a Cistercian monastery at Palazuela 4 km (2.5 miles) from here.
Cigales A majestic hall church that took two hundred years to build, starting in the sixteenth century. There are a number of businesslike bodegas on the slopes around here.
Corcos del Valle Parish church with paintings by Gregorio Martínez.
Dueñas With about 3,200 inhabitants this is the biggest community in the DO. The first meeting took place here between Isabella the Catholic and Ferdinand of Aragón. It has a good deal of atmosphere and many old buildings: the church of Santa María de la Asunción is partly twelfth century. The abbey of San Isidro de Dueñas lies 5 km (3 miles) to the north, where items on sale include its own cheeses.
Fuensaldaña The Castillo de los Vivero (thirteenth to fifteenth century) is wholly restored, and there is a belltower with four round corner turrets. The San Cipriano church is fifteenth century.
Mucientes Wine village with a Gothic church distinguished by a mighty tower.
Trigueros del Valle Here are noblemen's houses, the tenth-century chapel of Santa María del Castillo, a Romanesque church, and the ruins of a fifteenth-century castle.
Valoria la Buena The very large parish church shows the prosperity this village enjoyed in the eighteenth century. The stone here has a golden colour.

WINE ROUTE

A good way of getting to know Cigales is to follow this route from Valladolid: Valladolid – Valoria la Buena – Dueñas – Trigueros del Valle – Corcos del Valle – Cigales – Mucientes – Fuensaldaña – Valladolid.

Galicia

Capital: Santiago de Compostela
Provinces: La Coruña, Lugo, Orense, Pontevedra
Area: 29,434 square kilometres
Population: 2,785,394

If the inhabitants of Galicia, the Galegos, are too long away from their own region they are overtaken by *morriña*, a melancholy homesickness. This comes over them not only abroad, but even when they are elsewhere in Spain, for in many ways Galicia differs greatly from the rest of the country. The *autonomía* of this name is made up of the provinces of La Coruña, Lugo, Orense and Pontevedra. Together they form an out-of-the-way corner in north-western Spain, between the Atlantic and the northern frontier of Portugal. Cape Finisterre is Spain's most westerly point. It used to be thought that the world ended here, but after Columbus had discovered America it pointed the way to adventure, fame and fortune. The sea being so close means that the rainfall is heavy. About 1,300 mm (51.2 ins) a year is measured at the port of Vigo, and inland at Pontevedra it is still 800 to 1,000 mm (31.5 to 39.4 ins). As a result green is the predominant colour in Galicia, the hills and mountains covered with forests.

The rainfall notwithstanding, a genial climate prevails in Galicia: the average annual temperature fluctuates around 14°C (57°F). This not only makes winegrowing possible, but even the cultivation of citrus fruit. The region also produces a good deal of kiwi fruit, as well as commercially grown flowers. Maize and rye are cultivated; *hórreos*, open barns raised on stone supports, were formerly used for drying these grains. Inheritance laws here mean that properties are continually being cut up, so that a lot of cultivable land is taken up by dividing walls. The extent of this fragmentation is shown by the fact that it took Morgadío, a bodega in the Rías Baixas *denominación de origen*, no less than six years to put together a 2 ha (5 acre) plot that had to be acquired from 30 different owners. From the west coast with its *rías*, inlets rather like low fjords, a number of ranges extend far inland. They are not very high, at an average 500 m (1,640 ft), but they mean that Galicia is hilly nearly everywhere.

Below: The rocky coast of Galicia near La Coruña.

Celtic origins

As in two of the other *autonomías* of northern Spain, País Vasco and Cataluña, there is an official second language in Galicia. This comes between Spanish and Portuguese in form; yet Galician culture and tradition are certainly not Portuguese in origin, but Celtic. In this respect the region is reminiscent of Brittany, Scotland and Wales. There are many crucifixes (*calvarios*) along the roads, just as in Brittany, and as in Scotland there is no celebration without the bagpipes; the Galician variant is called the *gaita*, and there is lively, energetic dancing to its music and to the sound of castanet and drum. Architecture is generally quite austere, as can be seen from the *pazos*, large houses built of grey granite for the nobility, often with a coat of arms on the façade as the only decoration. Inland these dwellings sometimes have defensive towers or turrets, a reminder of less peaceful times. Galicia, as part of the kingdom of Asturia, was the bastion from which the Christians began their centuries of struggle with the Moorish invaders. And here, too, was one of Europe's most important places of pilgrimage, Santiago de Compostela. Between the eighth and the sixteenth centuries millions of pilgrims visited this city and its cathedral, where the remains of St James were believed to lie. Every year several thousand people still make the journey on foot, by bicycle or on horseback.

Fish and shellfish

Santiago de Compostela lies about halfway between Spain's two biggest fishing ports, La Coruña and Vigo. It was from La Coruña that the Armada sailed out on its fatal voyage in 1588. In the eighteenth century the city obtained the right to trade with the South American colonies, with the result that ships full of precious cargoes began to land here, to the great benefit of the churches and monasteries of Galicia. Today La Coruña and Vigo supply about a quarter of all Spain's fish and *mariscos* (crustaceans and shellfish). Every day a great number of lorries drive in from the coast to Madrid to provide the capital's wholesalers, shopkeepers and restaurateurs with fresh fish. Often, too, the drivers stop along the way to make deliveries, so that you can enjoy fresh seafood anywhere on the N6 road. Naturally enough a good deal of fish is served in Galicia itself: cod, sardines, tunny, hake, bass, sole, angler fish, eels, octopus and squid; and then there are crayfish, various kinds of prawns, crabs, scallops, oysters, mussels and many other delicacies. Mussels are farmed in the *ría* at Vigo and elsewhere, around floating platforms called *mejilloneras*. Freshwater fish are also caught, especially in the Miño, the river that marks the frontier with Portugal. The wine village of Arbo is famous for its lampreys and occasionally, salmon are caught in the river here.

Enthusiastic trenchermen

The inhabitants of Galicia are energetic, work hard and like to eat well. Anyone who doubts this should order a *cocido gallego* in a restaurant. The population has fed for centuries on this traditional dish. It comprises an awe-inspiring stew with potatoes, cabbage, beans, sausage (*chorizo*), veal, pork (often ears and tail), and chicken. Besides being enthusiastic eaters the Gallegos are also eager drinkers. Wine consumption here is significantly above the Spanish average. A good deal of the region's wine production is therefore drunk locally, and besides this a lot of wine is bought from other areas. The latter consists mainly of red wine, since Galicia produces mostly white. At the end of a lunch or dinner here it is not brandy that appears on the table, but always a white *aguardiente*.

Above: The cathedral of Santiago de Compostela.

A spectacular revolution

The great majority of Galician vineyards are to be found in the provinces of Orense and Pontevedra. Closest to the coast is the Rías Baixas DO, spread over a large area and contiguous with the Ribeiro DO, further to the east. The third DO is Valdeorras, further inland again. This is divided from Ribeiro by some of Galicia's highest peaks. The winding mountain road between the two districts climbs a pass some 1,000 m (3,280 ft) high.

Until halfway through the 1980s most Galician wines hardly merited attention. Since then, however, a spectacular revolution has taken place, with Rías Baixas in the lead. Thanks to considerable investment in modern winemaking equipment, the white wines from these small bodegas have within a short period become so good that today they are among Spain's best. In Ribeiro, too, with its greater concentration of production, both red and white wines have improved in quality. Development has been somewhat slower in Valdeorras, partly because winegrowing there is largely dominated by cooperatives – which by definition are not the most progressive of producers. In this district, however, private initiative restored the Godello grape, a high-quality white variety, to favour. Wines made from it have had such success that Godello plantings have increased greatly in recent years, among cooperative members as well.

Besides its three DOs, Galicia has various other, much less important wine districts. The most interesting of these is Ribera del Sil, between Ribeiro and Valdeorras. Many of the vineyards here climb terraced mountain slopes. In the Sober district the Lapatena group from Valdeorras makes an attractive red wine, called Rectoral Amandi. The isolated district of Valle de Monterrey, up against the Portuguese border, had provisional DO status. This was withdrawn, however, because the producers in this valley were not interested in making quality wine. In Monterrey it is the cooperative that follows the most vigorous policy. Finally there is Valle del Miño-Orense, where mostly white wines are made on a very modest scale from various grape varieties. The nicest example is the Conde de Lagariños, from Bodegas Lagariños in Coles, a village just northeast of Orense and on the north bank of the Miño.

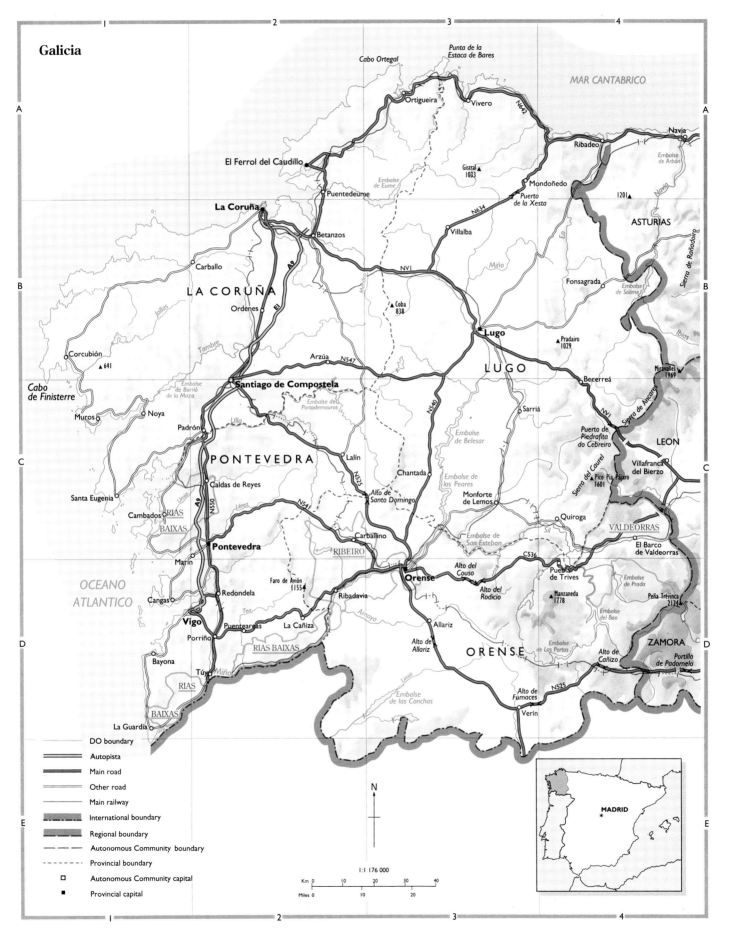

Galicia

DO boundary

Autopista

Main road

Other road

Main railway

International boundary

Regional boundary

Autonomous Community boundary

Provincial boundary

□ Autonomous Community capital

■ Provincial capital

1:1 176 000

N

Km 0   10   20   30   40

Miles 0   10   20

MADRID

Valdeorras

Above: The vineyard of Bodegas Godeval in El Barco de Valdeorras, planted with the Godello variety.

To go from the Bierzo to the Valdeorras wine district is to cross from one *autonomía* to another, from Castilla León to Galicia. Driving up by the Peñarrubia reservoir and through the tunnels the motorist is made aware of this by roadside signs, and by a slight change in the road surface. The vineyards of Valdeorras lie mainly in the valley of the Sil, with El Barco de Valdeorras at their centre. This town of 11,000 inhabitants can be picked out from afar by the tall smoking chimneys of its slate works. El Barco has little of beauty to offer, and the narrow streets in the centre are choked by too much traffic. Yet you do not have to drive far to find a beautiful, peaceful landscape. Quite close to the town there is an idyllic valley with an old Romanesque monastery that has been most tastefully restored and now houses Bodegas Godeval. The frontage, and a charming eleventh-century chapel, do little to suggest from the outside that behind these walls are not only comfortable reception rooms, but an exceedingly modern cellar full of stainless-steel equipment. In the wine country to the west there is much to enjoy, particularly at La Rúa and at the little village of Laroco built on a hill. Often the vines grow right to the sides of the road, climbing high up the slopes from the valley floor.

Black grapes

Of the three Galician *denominaciones de origen* – the others are Ribeiro and Rías Baixas – Valdeorras is furthest from the coast, about 150 km (93 miles) as the crow flies. An impressive mountain chain rises immediately to the west. The winding road across it climbs over passes 700 to 950 m (2,300 to 3,120 ft) high – the Barrio de Trives is one example – and along the tops of impressively deep valleys. The many abandoned terraces bear witness to all the winegrowing there used to be up here; only a few of these upland sites still have vines. They do not, however, produce wine of DO quality. The distance from the coast, and these nearby mountains, make the climate in Valdeorras somewhat drier than the other two Galician wine districts and less moderate, with more extreme temperatures in summer and winter. This local climate favours the growing of black grapes, which are predominant in Valdeorras. Some three-quarters of the vines are black varieties. About half of the total area – 2,500 ha (6,180 acres) – is planted with Alicante, a local pseudonym for Garnacha, which supplies dark firm wines. In second place, with 15 percent of the area, comes Mencía, familiar from Bierzo. This variety is said to have been introduced on the initiative of the La Rúa cooperative. Three other varieties are of lesser importance.

Wines for quick consumption

Most of the Valdeorras red wines, particularly those made from Alicante, are sold in bulk. Wines from Mencía – possibly with a small amount of Garnacha in them – are usually bottled, and are intended for drinking young. The best of them have a good colour, a firm, meaty taste and decent amount of fruit. Some of the makers, the cooperatives at El Barco and La Rúa, for example, age a proportion of their Mencía wine in wood, which sometimes leads to pleasant results – but can also produce wines with too much volatile acid. In this district wines made mainly from the Garnacha grape lack distinction.

Rediscovery of Godello

The white grapes here may be inferior in terms of quantity, but certainly not in quality. In fact it is thanks to its white wines that Valdeorras is beginning to make itself known in Spain and beyond. The future of the area will probably be determined by how skilfully it goes over to producing one particular white wine: the kind made from the Godello grape. As yet this variety represents only 10 percent of the vines. The remainder of the white grapes – a quarter of the Valdeorras total – is made up of Palomino and Doña Blanca. Godello was rediscovered in the 1970s when a committee of wine experts from Valdeorras went looking for the best possible varieties for their area. Mode of planting, vinification and other aspects were all investigated, and Godello, a native variety that had all but disappeared, emerged as the absolute winner. This is why a firm like Godeval, established in 1986, has planted Godello vines exclusively.

Godello is not an excessively productive grape at 12,000 to 15,000 kg per ha (10,700 lb per acre to 13,380 lb per acre), giving 60 to 70 percent wine. It is also susceptible to rot and so cannot thrive if the climate is too wet: Valdeorras is just about the only area in Galicia where it can be successfully grown. The white wine from it is characterized on the one hand by quite a high degree of acid, and on the other by a fruity, aromatic taste with 12 to 13 percent alcohol. If skilfully vinified it is one of Spain's most attractive wines.

A strong comeback

The vigorous comeback made by Godello is demonstrated by figures from the El Barco cooperative. There the weight of Godello grapes processed rose from 2,000 kg (4,410 lb) in 1976 to 50,000 kg (110,000 lb) in 1989 – and it is reckoned that this amount will be trebled by the end of the century. Among the many small growers – 87 percent of them have less than 1 ha (2.5 acres); only 1 percent have more than 5 ha (12.5 acres) – the change to Godello has been greatly stimulated by the high prices for its grapes. At the beginning of the 1990s these were three to four times the average grape price, and double that of Mencía. These high prices are justified by the enthusiasm with which the market has reacted to Godello wines. To date the demand has been so great that around halfway through the year all bottles are sold.

Above: Joaquín Rebolledo specializes in top-quality red and white wines.
Left: Wine was probably first made in Valdeorras by the monks of the isolated Santuario de las Ermitas. A few wine terraces can still be seen on the surrounding hillsides. In former days the white wine was considered to be the best in Valdeorras. Nowadays the bulk of wine produced is red.

PRODUCERS OF SPECIAL INTEREST

Bodega Cooperativa Jesús Nazareno 32300 El Barco de Valdeorras

This cooperative, founded in 1963, has over 500 members who cultivate about 200 ha (495 acres). Production consists of 60 percent red and 40 percent white wine (the latter being above the average for the area). Stainless-steel fermentation tanks and cooling equipment has meant an improvement in quality, notably of the white wines, since the 1990 vintage.

Star of the range is the Viña Abad, a pure Godello. The red Valdouro is very pleasing, with a hint of spice and a distinct vanilla scent. This is achieved by dint of about 12 months in casks of American oak. The supple Menciño (100 percent Mencía), with a similar touch of spice, is meant for drinking young; this also holds good for the decent, pleasant Albar, made mainly from Garnacha grapes.

Bodegas Godeval 32300 El Barco de Valdeorras

Sixteen men decided in 1986 to start a winery, with the aim of producing the best wine possible, and so Bodegas Godeval came into being. Cellars and reception rooms were fitted up in the splendid old monastery of Xagoaza. This stands in a peaceful mountain valley not far from El Barco. In 1986 the building was still a ruin, but it was completely, and very tastefully, restored. The grapes from the firm's own 12 ha (30 acres) – it will be 16 ha (40 acres) by 1995 – are made into wine in a modern tiled cellar with stainless-steel tanks and other state-of-the-art equipment. After thorough research it was decided to plant only Godello vines. This bodega therefore produces only white wine, from this grape variety, with Viña Godeval as the best of the range. This wine is distinguished by a clear, fresh, extraordinarily clean taste with slight elements of fruit, and a sound, firm core of around 13 percent alcohol: a delightful product.

Bodegas Medorras 32356 Petín de Valdeorras

This firm, housed in a sort of chalet, makes Godellón, a good Godello wine. Petín is near La Rúa, on the opposite bank of the Sil.

Bodega Cooperativa Virgen de las Viñas 32350 La Rúa

Although I have tasted disappointing wines from this establishment, it really is beginning to improve. As proof there is the strikingly labelled Pingadelo, a pleasant Mencía wine with a little fruit. The brand name Brisel is used for the white Godello.

Joaquín Rebolledo 32350 La Rúa

Technically well equipped winery with around 20 ha (50 acres) of its own land. The red wine is juicy, meaty, and with fruit; it is 100 percent Mencía and one of the best wines of the area. The white Godello, too, is of top quality. The owner, a lawyer who lives in Orense, is experimenting with Cabernet Sauvignon, Riesling and other varieties.

Above: Haymaking the old-fashioned way in Ribeiro.

DO REGION
Valdeorras

La Rúa Wine centre
Suggested wine route
Boundary of Valdeorras DO
Main road
Other roads
Railway
Provincial boundary
Contour interval 200 metres

1:390 000

N

Travel Information

HOTELS AND RESTAURANTS

Espada, 32300 El Barco de Valdeorras, tel (88) 322683 Modern hotel on the N120, opened in 1990. This is the most comfortable place to stay in the area, with a view over El Barco and the Sil valley. There is an adequate restaurant on the premises.

San Mauro, 32300 El Barco de Valdeorras, tel (88) 320145 Simple restaurant where regional dishes are served. Situated on the Plaza de la Iglesia

Espada, 32350 La Rúa, tel (88) 310075 Belongs to the family that also runs the Espada in El Barco. The rooms are plainly furnished, but clean. Ask for one at the back, because of the heavy traffic. Simple restaurant.

Os Pinos, 32350 La Rúa, tel (88) 311716 Only a middling roadhouse where the TV stays full on during lunch. Avoid the inferior white house wine and order a Godello or red Mencía.

PLACES OF INTEREST

El Barco de Valdeorras
Although this town that took its name from a ferryboat is at the heart of the wine district, it is best avoided. There is little of beauty to see, apart from a few *pazos* or town residences, and the streets are often blocked by traffic. There are also the smoking chimneys of the slate works to contend with. If there is a good time to visit El Barco, then it is the first Sunday in September, during the Fiesta del Cristo folk festival.

El Bollo A hamlet with an ancient castle.

Petín de Valdeorras The monastery of Santa María in its isolated setting is not far from this village.

La Rúa The Romans transported gold through the Sil valley, hence the name Valdeorras, from *val de oro*. La Rúa was one of their settlements, witness the Roman bridge on the road in from the west. Otherwise there is little to see along this rather straggling place. Only the surrounding wine country has visual appeal.

Santuario de las Ermitas The first Valdeorras wine was probably made by the monks of this monastery, beautifully situated and surrounded by terraces. According to an old manuscript, *su principal producción es el vino blanco y tinto de buona calidad* (Its main production is of white and red wine of good quality).

By the beginning of the seventeenth century the monks here had already created a sort of official administration of the surrounding vineyards, and by the end of the eighteenth century the monastery was managing more than 200 vineyards in the region.

WINE ROUTE

Part of the suggested wine route consists of a "pilgrimage" through some beautiful country to the Santuario de las Ermitas, where Valdeorras winemaking was nurtured and flourished centuries ago. This part of the route starts in La Rúa and goes on by way of narrow winding roads (and the village of El Bollo with its castle), eventually bringing you to the N120 again. A pleasant drive from El Barco runs along the south bank of the Sil towards Bierzo and Ponferrada. Going east along the N120 also takes you to Bierzo.

Ribeiro

The vineyards of Rías Baixas and Ribeiro adjoin the common boundary of their respective provinces, Pontevedra and Orense. Less rain falls in Ribeiro than down on the coast, but still a lot in Spanish terms, 800 to 1,000 mm (31.5 to 39.4 ins) a year. In the museum at Ribadavia, historically and artistically the provincial capital, there are figures with straw "coats" of the kind the peasants used to wear to keep off the rain. Winegrowing is concentrated in three green river valleys, those of the Miño, Avía and Arnoya. In among the small vineyard plots, other things are grown – flowers, for example, especially carnations. The vineyards, roughly 3,600 ha (8,900 acres) belong to thousands of small growers. Some 1,200 of them take their grapes to the Cooperativa Vitivinícola del Ribeiro, which is located near Ribadavia. Another group of about 1,000 growers sells its grapes to the futuristic-looking Lapatena winery in Santa Cruz de Arrobaldo, a village halfway between Ribadavia and Orense further east. Then there are another 25 or so smaller firms putting their wines on the market.

An illustrious past

Winegrowing in Ribeiro (from *ribera*, meaning "bank, riverside") has a glorious past. In the sixteenth century, in the time of Philip II, the wines were successfully exported to various European countries, including Italy. A century later England was buying a good deal of it. From documents it appears that in the thirteenth century Ribeiro wine already had a good reputation (*bon vino d'Ourens*), and it is possible that the Romans cultivated vines here: they certainly availed themselves of the hot springs at Orense, and laid the foundations of a many-arched bridge that still stands. In the Ribadavia museum mentioned above there are Roman finds on display. A series of crises, including that of the phylloxera, brought Ribeiro's long period of prosperity to an end early in the twentieth century.

The Palomino grape

When vineyards that had been totally laid waste by phylloxera were replanted, Palomino was used on a big scale; this is the basic grape for sherry (often called *jerez* in Ribeiro). The advantage of this variety is its high yield: around 20,000 kg per ha (17,850 lb per acre). But its disadvantage is that it is a rather neutral sort of wine; it has few faults, but few merits either. The Ribeiro cooperative already mentioned is actively replacing Palomino with higher quality grapes. First among them is Treixadura, a variety also found in northern Portugal, one that gives juicy, lively and quite exciting wines of good quality.

A second type given prominence is Torrontés, from which aromatic, smoothly fresh wines can be made. Yields from these two varieties is from 10,000 to 15,000 kg per ha (8,920 to 13,400 lb per acre), considerably less than Palomino gives. The cooperative makes up for this by paying much more for Treixadura and Torrontés grapes. At the beginning of the 1990s a kilo of Palominos was fetching 70 pesetas, compared with 160 pesetas for the two other kinds. Lapatena is also paying this sort of price. Of the 2,500 ha (6,180 acres) in Ribeiro planted with white grapes, three-quarters had Palomino until a few years ago. The Ribeiro cooperative is endeavouring to get its members to give up Palomino altogether. This conversion of the vineyards is also being encouraged by the research station in Cuñas which has been engaged for years now in selecting the best possible clones of native Spanish grape varieties, including Treixadura and Torrontés.

Technological progress

As in neighbouring Rías Baixas, there is heavy investment in Ribeiro in the latest vinification techniques. Lapatena's cellars provide the most impressive example. This winery, opened in 1990 and belonging to the Caves do Ribeiro company, has at its disposal a great battery of stainless-steel fermentation tanks, modern filters and bottling lines, air-conditioned storage areas, and other facilities that meet the most stringent requirements. At the end of the 1980s the Ribeiro cooperative invested 400 million pesetas in a filter for must (the first in Galicia), stainless-steel fermentation tanks and other equipment. Nor were smaller bodegas left behind: there is, for example, the excellently equipped Sociedad Cooperativa de Viñas 2001. This was founded by four growers in 1989 and is situated in the village of Féa.

To an important extent the quality of white Ribeiro is determined by the technical equipment of the producer in question. There can be no doubt that firms that ferment the must at low temperature in steel tanks make better wines than those that do not. Another important factor is the Palomino content. The lower this is, the better the quality of the wine will usually be. In general a Ribeiro with, say, 60 percent Palomino, supplemented by Treixadura and Torrontés, will have more to offer than one with, for example, 90 percent.

Significantly, one of the most highly praised wines from this district is the white Amadeus produced by the cooperative. This is made very largely from Treixadura (85 percent) and Torrontés, produced in small quantities (a few tens of thousands of bottles), and in good years only (nothing in 1986). The wine has a lively taste, juice and freshness, an elegant structure, and a slightly vegetal aroma. In the experimental bodega in Ribadavia belonging to the *Consejo Regulador* a good wine has been developed on the basis of 60 percent Treixadura, 30 percent Torrontés, and 10 percent Loureira – another regional grape. In addition to still white wines, sparkling wines are beginning to appear; Lapatena's is the first on a commercial basis.

Red wines

Almost a third of the vineyards are planted with black grape varieties. The wines from them are mainly drunk in Galicia itself and hardly ever appear outside the region, let alone beyond Spain's frontiers. This is scarcely a matter for regret, since the bulk of Ribeiro reds are of little interest in terms of quality; white wines are the district's speciality. Nevertheless a few producers are doing their best to raise the standard of their red wines – and with success. Garnacha appears to give wines here that are less heavy, and somewhat fresher, than elsewhere in the country. With this knowledge Lapatena has launched a small number of attractive red wines, including Viñao (exclusively Garnacha), Teluro (90 percent Garnacha), and Rectoral de Amandi (90 percent Mencía. All these wines are distinguished by a deep-red colour and relatively low alcohol, usually 10.5 percent at most); the Garnachas have good fruit and the Mencías a somewhat spicy character. The Ribeiro red wines do therefore have a future, providing they are expertly made from carefully selected grapes.

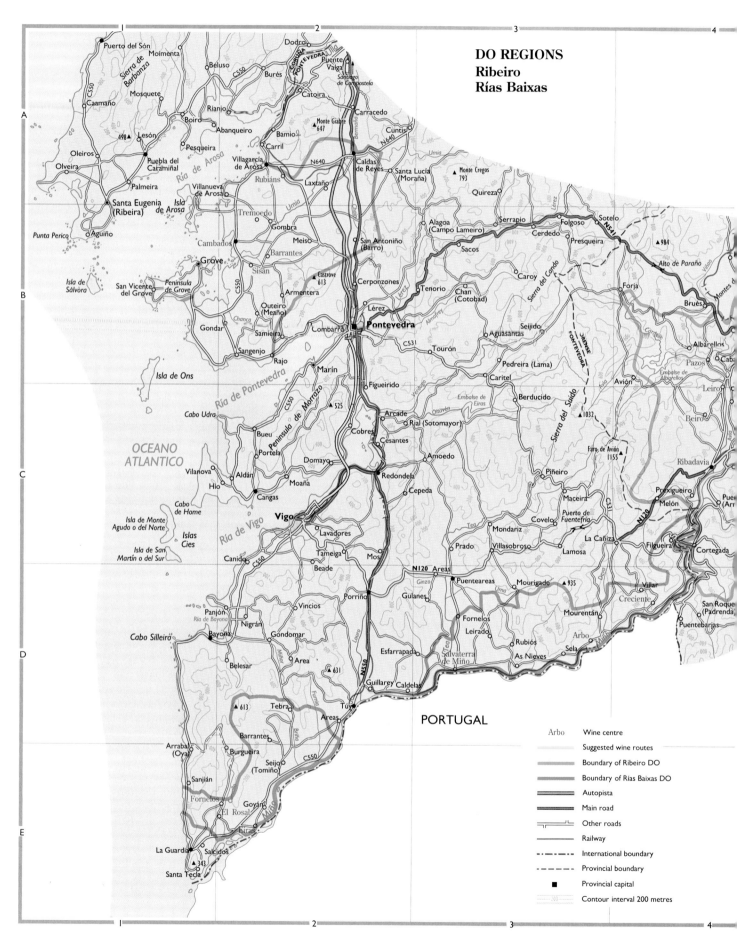

DO REGIONS
Ribeiro
Rías Baixas

Puerto del Són
Moimenta
Sierra de
Barbanza
Beluso
Burés
Dodro
Santiago
de Compostela
Puente
Valga
Catoira
Carracedo
Caamaño
Mosquete
Rianjo
Monte Giabre
647
Cuntis
A
498▲
Lesón
Boiro
Abanqueiro
Bamio
Carril
N640
Oleiros
Pesqueira
Rías de Arosa
Villagarcía
de Arosa
N640
Caldas
de Reyes
Santa Lucía
(Moraña)
Olveira
Puebla del
Caramiñal
Palmeira
Villanueva
de Arosa
Rubiáns
Laxtaño
Monte Cregos
793
Quireza
Santa Eugenia
(Ribeira)
Isla
de Arosa
Tremoedo
Umia
Serrapio
Folgoso
Sotelo
Punta Perico
O Aguiño
Cambados
Gombra
Meiso
San Antoniño
(Barro)
Alagoa
(Campo Lameiro)
Cerdedo
Presqueira
984▲
Alto de Paraño
Barrantes
Sacos
Caroy
B
Grove
San Vicente
del Grove
Península
de Grove
Sisán
Castrove
613
Cerponzones
Tenorio
Chan
(Cotobad)
Seijido
Forja
Brués
Isla de
Sálvora
Chanca
Armentera
Lérez
Aguasantas
Albarellos
Gondar
Outeiro
(Meaño)
Lombarra
Pontevedra
C531
Tourón
Pedreira (Lama)
Avión
Pazos
Embalse de
Albarellos
Leiro
Samieira
Sangenjo
Rajo
Marín
Figueirido
Caritel
Berducido
▲1032
Beiro
Isla de Ons
Ría de Pontevedra
Cabo Udra
▲525
Arcade
Rial (Sotomayor)
Embalse de
Eiras
Faro de Avión
1155
Ribadavia
OCEANO
ATLANTICO
Bueu
Portela
Cobres
Cesantes
Amoedo
Piñeiro
Prexigueiro
Vilanova
Aldán
Domayo
Redondela
Maceira
Melón
C
Hío
Moaña
Cepeda
Covelo
Puerto de
Fuentefría
Cangas
Cabo
de Home
Isla de Monte
Agudo o del Norte
Islas
Cíes
Vigo
Mondariz
La Cañiza
Figueira
Cortegada
Isla de San
Martín o del Sur
Lavadores
Prado
Villasobroso
Lamosa
Canido
C550
Tameiga
Mos
N120
Areas
Mourigade
▲935
Villar
Beade
Porriño
Gulanes
Puenteareas
Creciente
San Roque
(Padrenda)
Panjón
Ría de Bayona
Vincios
Fornelos
Mourentán
Puentebarjas
Nigrán
Bayona
Gondomar
Leirado
Arbo
Cabo Silleiro
Belesar
Area
▲631
Esfarrapada
Salvaterra
de Miño
Rubiós
As Nieves
Sela
D
Guillarey
Caldelas
▲613
Tebra
Túy
PORTUGAL
Arrabal
(Oya)
Barrantes
Areas
Burgueira
Seijo
(Tomiño)
C550
Sanjián
Fornelos
Goyán
El Rosal
Miño
La Guardia
Salcidos
▲343
Santa Tecla

Arbo	Wine centre
	Suggested wine routes
	Boundary of Ribeiro DO
	Boundary of Rías Baixas DO
	Autopista
	Main road
	Other roads
	Railway
	International boundary
	Provincial boundary
■	Provincial capital
	Contour interval 200 metres

PRODUCERS OF SPECIAL INTEREST

Sociedad Cooperativa de Viñas 2001 32940 Féa

In this wine village on the south bank of the Miño four men got together in 1989 to set up a joint venture. They own 7 ha (17 acres) of vineyards, and they also buy in grapes. The best wines from the modern cellars here are the white Viñas 2001 (mainly Palomino) and the Veiga Douro (60 percent Torrontés, 30 percent Treixadura, 10 percent Loureira). The latter wine has a pleasant perfume with both vegetal and floral notes in it, in harmony with the fresh taste.

Cooperativa Vitivinícola del Ribeiro 32417 Ribadavia

This concern dating from the 1950s was originally established in Leiro, but after amalgamating with another cooperative it moved to Valdepeira, a hamlet near Ribadavia. Thanks to large investments in the late 1980s and the beginning of the 1990s, it now has stainless-steel tanks and other up-to-date plant. It is a careful firm, where everything is taken seriously: for example, the filtering and bottling equipment is sterilized nightly.

The grapes come in from 800 members, who work a total 500 ha (1,235 acres), and from 400 other growers. Total production is in the region of 6 million litres (1.3 million gal) a year, all of which is bottled.

In order to reduce drastically the proportion of Palomino used the cooperative, helped by the bank, is encouraging the conversion of the vineyards to the preferred Treixadura and Torrontés grapes.

One of the best of all Ribeiro whites is made from these two varieties, the vital, fresh, slightly vegetal Amadeus. Unfortunately its production remains limited to a few tens of thousands of bottles – and that only in good years. There is, however, an attractive alternative, the Viña Costeira (usually 50 percent Palomino, 40 percent Torrontés, 10 percent Treixadura). This supple, smoothly fresh wine has charm and a slight floral and also vegetal scent. There are two versions of the Pazo brand, one decent and ordinary (almost wholly Palomino) and a somewhat livelier special (mainly Palomino, but with some Torrontés). Also in the range there are sparkling and red wines. A small wine museum has been set up for visitors.

Cosecheros de Vino del Ribeiro 32414 Ribadavia

This firm is situated almost opposite the cooperative, and like Lapatena it belongs to the Caves do Ribeiro company. Lapatena has plenty of space at its disposal, all its equipment is modern, and everything gives the impression of being spotlessly maintained. The accommodation and plant at Cosecheros de Vino del Ribeiro contrast greatly with this. Here only

Above: Green wine terraces along the banks of the Miño.

bought-in grapes are processed. The best wine is the usually pleasant, but unremarkable, Campo Hermoso (40 percent Treixadura, 20 percent Palomino, 20 percent Lado).

Bodega Valdomiño-Avia 2400 Ribadavia

In the austere-looking cellars of this modest, quite recent (1986) winery there are stainless-steel tanks in which the fermentation temperature can be perfectly controlled. The firm's own grapes, from 3 ha (7.5 acres), and bought-in fruit are both used. The star of this bodega is the white Val de Reza, a light, quite fruity wine from seven or so grape varieties (the Torrontés and Treixadura accounting for half). The Valdomiño is 70 percent Palomino, fresh, and has a good taste.

Lapatena 32593 Santa Cruz de Arrobaldo

Near the spot where the Barbantiño flows into the Miño, right in the eastern corner of the Ribeiro district, one of Spain's most striking bodegas was opened in 1990. The building looks like a modern office block, complete with tinted glass and marble floors in the reception areas.

Technologically the cellars are excellent and built for growth. The present capacity of 7 million litres (1.54 million gal) can be increased

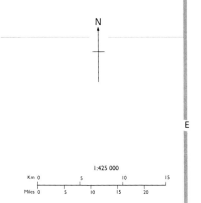

without any problem. The growers are paid considerably more for indigenous varieties such as Treixadura and Torrontés than for Palomino. Lapatena also sells young vines to the growers at reduced prices. The best white wine is the Fin de Siglo (60 percent Palomino, 40 percent Torrontés and Treixadura).

This is juicy, light and clean in taste, and amenably fresh. The Viñao and Abilius are dominated by the Palomino; the latter is the more interesting wine. Some 20 percent of production consists of red wines, among them the Rectoral de Amandi (90 percent Mencía), with a hint of spice and a lot of character; the fruity and fresh, satisfying Teliro (90 percent Garnacha); and the firm but by no means heavy Viñao (100 percent Garnacha). The firm also produces a dry sparkling wine. Lapatena wines can be recognized by their very unusual labels in pastel shades. This model winery belongs to five people from the region, who together also own the Caves do Ribeiro holding company. The Cosecheros de Vino del Ribeiro, mentioned above, also belongs to the latter.

Below: The square of San Clodio gives a view on to the cloisters.

Travel Information

HOTELS AND RESTAURANTS

Martín Fierro, Sáenz Diez 65, 32003 Orense, tel (88) 234820 Locally this restaurant enjoys at least as good a reputation as the much better known Sanmiguel. The fish is good here, though meat dishes are actually the speciality.
Pingallo, San Miguel 6, 32005 Orense, tel (88) 220057 Regional country dishes served here.
San Martín, Curros Enriquez 1, 32003 Orense, tel (88) 235611 The most comfortable place to stay in the district, with air-conditioning and its own garage.
Sanmiguel, San Miguel 12, 32005 Orense, tel (88) 221245 This renowned restaurant deserves a visit simply for its extensive wine list (with many a Galician bottle), but the strongly regional cuisine merits praise. A lot of chestnuts are gathered around Orense, and Sanmiguel uses them in dishes such as *conejo con castañas* (rabbit with chestnuts).
Sila, Avenida de la Habana 61, 32003 Orense, tel (88) 236311 An adequate hotel without much character.
Plaza, Plaza Mayor, 32400 Ribadavia, tel (88) 470576 Restaurant and bar in the heart of the town. Austere décor with a lot of brown. Tasty *entremeses de la casa* (including *jamón serrano*, other kinds of ham, olives and cheese),

and tender *chuleton de ternera* (veal steak). Ribeiro wines are, of course, served.

PLACES OF INTEREST

Castrelo de Miño Village near Ribadavia, with twelfth-century bas-reliefs within the eighteenth-century church of Santa María.
Cuñas A modern oenological research station is established here. In its vineyard it experiments with dozens of grape varieties and their clones.
Féa In this wine village on the south bank of the Miño the single-aisled Romanesque church is worth seeing for its portal.
Orense The capital of the province of this name, which merits a visit. One of the bridges to the west of the centre is the Puente Romano, the foundations of which were laid by the Romans. It was completed by the Spaniards, later destroyed but subsequently restored. In this busy town, with a population of nearly 100,000, it is the centre that has atmosphere. Here there are some delightful squares, such as the Plazuela de Magdalena (there is a crucifix here with the figure of the weeping Mary), and the Plaza del Hierro, which has a fountain from the Osera monastery. The cathedral, with narrow streets all round, is one of Galicia's most beautiful churches.

Its dominant architectural style is Gothic. The Pórtico del Paraíso with its colourful painted figures is particularly fine. The church of San Francisco has Gothic sarcophagi. The Romans settled here because of the hot springs, which still flow. Finds from the Roman and other periods can be seen in the Museo Provincial de Arquelogía, housed in the former Bishop's Palace.
Ribadavia This was the Galician capital when García I had his residence here. The town has around 7,000 inhabitants and a number of monuments, the most striking being the ruins of the castle of the Condes de Ribadavia (now partly an auditorium). The churches of Santiago (also a museum; note the ornate capitals and carved wooden figures) and San Juan are Romanesque. Santa María de Oliveira also has Romanesque elements. The convent church of Santo Domingo is a fine example of Galician Gothic. There is an old Jewish quarter in Ribadavia, with gateways and galleries – as there are around the Plaza Mayor as well. Many archaeological finds are on display in the Museo de Artes y Costumbres Populares, including a very rare dug-out boat. The rural life of long ago is vividly illustrated by reconstructions of rooms with their furniture, old costumes, including straw "raincoats", tools and pottery. At the end of April and the beginning of May the biggest of Galicia's wine fairs, the Feiro do Viño do Ribeiro, is held in Ribadavia, and the grape harvest is celebrated in September. Besides all this, Ribadavia is proud of being the theatrical capital of Galicia.
San Clodio There is a famous Cistercian monastery here with a Romanesque church. The winding road past it leads into a valley with, on the right, a fine *pazo* or country manor.

WINE ROUTE

This consists of three suggested routes around Ribadavia. Two of them run along either bank of the Miño. The one to the east can be combined with a visit to Orense. The third route follows the Avia valley and leads to the San Clodio monastery and the valley beyond; one to the north takes you to the pleasant wine village of Pazos.

Rías Baixas

Spain's intensely green northwest coast is characterized by wide inlets, called *rías*, that reach many miles inland. The northern part of this coastline is called Rías Altas, the southern Rías Bajas. The dividing line comes at Cape Finisterre, Spain's most westerly point. The Galician name for Rías Bajas is Rías Baixas, and this was chosen for the regional DO, one of the country's youngest.

This elevation to DO was the reward for an intensive programme of improvement. Although wines were exported to England, Italy and Germany in the sixteenth and seventeenth centuries, Rías Baixas had gone into a decline by the beginning of the twentieth century. After phylloxera had devastated the vineyards they were largely replanted with hybrids and other inferior grapes. Not until the beginning of the 1980s was there encouragement to replant with better varieties. At the same time many of the wine producers invested in modern equipment. The result was a total metamorphosis. Until 1986 there were fewer than five bodegas producing really good wines, but three years later some 50 brands were offered, all approved by the *Consejo Regulador*.

Investing in Albariño

One of the elements in this success is Albariño, a grape grown here for centuries. It is probably of German origin and is said to have been brought here by Cistercian monks in the twelfth century, when they visited the monastery of Armenteira, which lies between Pontevedra and Cambados. The latter calls itself the "capital of the Albariño", and every first Sunday in August it celebrates with a feast devoted to this grape. The same variety occurs in Northern Portugal, where it is used for Vinho Verde.

There is, however, a world of difference between the Albariño wines of Rías Baixas and the Vinhos Verdes. Most white Vinhos Verdes are low in alcohol, high in acidity, and with a slight sparkle. In Rías Baixas, however, this same grape gives still wines that usually have at least 12 percent alcohol and a more distinctive character. In a typical Rías Baixas both floral and fruity elements are present, with a hint of spice. The tartness is less noticeable than in Vinhos Verdes; in fact most winemakers in these coastal areas favour malolactic fermentation so as to achieve a more amenable kind of acidity. Further inland this is not thought necessary, e.g. in the wines from the Morgadío estate.

Growing Albariño is no simple matter, for Rías Baixas is one of Spain's wettest regions, with an average rainfall of around 1,300 mm (59 ins) a year. Only the summers are relatively dry. Because of the rain, fungus diseases form a great threat to the vines. This is why they are trained up on a kind of pergola. The stems and branches are taken up granite posts about 1.8 m (6 ft) high and along steel wires. Weeds retain moisture and so they have to be cleared regularly – some growers plough their land up to 20 times a year. The *Consejo Regulador* allows a yield of 66 hl per ha (3,588 gal per acre), but in reality 60 hl per ha (3,264 gal per acre) is the most practical quantity for wines of quality. Compared with other white wine areas this is not a high yield. This is one of the reasons why Albariño is Spain's most expensive grape.

Modern technology made its entrance fairly dramatically here. Or, as one grower put it: "In three years our winemaking evolved from doing it all by hand to hi-tech." Pneumatic presses, stainless-steel fermentation tanks and cooling plant became the rule rather than the exception. Various producers use the technique of skin

Above: The northern part of Rías Baixas lies along the wide Ría de Aroso.

contact. Technological devices are also being used in the vineyards. The Fillaboa estate, for example, has a metereological measuring system that indicates exactly when the vines should be treated against mildew.

A new optimism

Going over to Albariño in a big way and investing in technology have given Rías Baixas a new self-respect. The winegrowers are full of optimism so plantings of this variety are steadily increasing. Rías Baixas now has about 1,500 ha (3,700 acres) of vineyards, but this figure will increase significantly by the turn of the century. Almost all the producers I visited had plans for expansion.

Although Rías Baixas is one of Spain's smaller *denominaciónes de origen*, visiting the district demands some time, for the vineyards are spread over a considerable area. Also, the wine district does not form a compact whole, but consists of three zones. Soil composition in Rías Baixas varies according to zone, and even from vineyard to vineyard. But as a rule soils are sandy, slightly acid and not very deep. The most northerly zone is Val do Salnés, which lies between the Ría de Arousa and the Ría de Pontevedra, on a peninsula. Cambados, the "Albariño capital" mentioned earlier, is the centre of wine production here. The second zone is called O Rosal and lies by the mouth of the Miño, the river that forms the border with Portugal. There is a considerable amount of terracing here. Further upstream, where the Tea flows into the Miño, is the third zone, the Condado de Tea. Val do Salnés used to be the zone with the best name, but now an increasing number of the leading producers are in Condado de Tea. Among them are Fillaboa, Marqués de Vizhoja and Morgadío. In all three zones pure Albariño wines are the speciality, but blended whites (simply defined as Rías Baixas) are also produced; these have to contain at least 70 percent Albariño.

Above: The port of Cambados which is considered the capital of Albariño.
Right: Bodegas Marqués de Vizhoja is located in a 18th-century pazo with watch towers. The actual wine cellars lie lower down, at the foot of the hill.

PRODUCERS OF SPECIAL INTEREST

Bodega Morgadío 36420 Albeos
José Antonio López Dominguez and his four friends were dubbed "the madmen of Albeos" when in 1984 they began to buy, and plant, land on the plateaux and slopes around this hamlet near Creciente, in the Miño valley. Locally, people saw no future in creating new vineyards here for the production of quality wines. However, the sceptics were proved wrong for the wines from Morgadío, as the estate was named, turned out to be among the very best produced in Rías Baixas. They were even exported, to the United States and elsewhere.

The vineyard is not quite 30 ha (74 acres) in area, divided into three sites. The manure for them comes from Morgadío's own flock of sheep. After picking, the grapes are vinified in a very modern installation. As soon as the seeds and stalks have been removed from the must, the grape juice and skins start their 14 or so hours contact, at 7 to 8°C (44.5 to 46.5°F). The actual

fermentation then follows, at 17 to 19°C (62.5 to 66°F). Selection is made on the basis of the quality of the grapes and the must. The simplest, but far from unpleasing, white wine is the Carballo do Rei, which contains 45 percent Albariño. The two other kinds are made exclusively from this grape variety. The Torre Fornelos is smoothly fresh in taste, and quite fleshy. In quality, character and depth it is surpassed by the Morgadío. This is a firm, lively wine with slight touches of spice, exotic fruit and flowers. This delightful Rías Baixas has, repeatedly and justifiably, received plaudits and awards in Spain and beyond.

Bodegas Marqués de Vizhoja
36438 Arbo
On the north side of the Miño valley stands an elegant eigheenth-century country mansion with lookout towers. In 1976 Mariano Pelaez Lomana began to plant a vineyard around it. This now covers 12 ha (30 acres) and from it comes the pure, refreshing Torre La Moreira, a wholly Albariño wine with a

slightly fruity and floral scent. The Folla Verde is a simpler Rías Baixas, with 70 percent Albariño. This estate has up-to-date equipment, with cellars built by the house in 1980. The name Marqués de Vizhoja is also used for a successful white wine brand from Mariano Pelaez. However, this has no DO, and in quality comes quite a way behind the wines that do. If you visit this property have a look at the restored chapel.

Benito Vázquez García 36636 Barrantes
A small vineyard of some 3 ha (7.5 acres). Like the property itself, the wine is called Carballal. In a good year this is smoothly fresh, fragrant and lively.

Bodegas Castro Martín 36636 Barrantes
This house processes grapes both from its own 14 ha (35 acres) and from other growers. The brand name here is Casal Caeiro. The quality of this Albariño wine can vary, from refreshing (and slightly sparkling) to dull and almost sweet.

Bodegas Chaves 36636 Barrantes
A dynamic concern that vinifies both grapes from its own 9 ha (22 acres) of vineyard, and fruit bought from elsewhere. It also buys wine ready-made. Castel de Fornos is the top wine here, and 100 percent Albariño. It possesses good structure, a smooth taste with fruit, and a beautiful aftertaste.

Bodegas Salnesur 36639 Cambados
Founded in 1988 and accommodated in a somewhat uncompromising sort of white building, in the hamlet of Castrelo. This firm works with bought-in grapes and technologically it is excellently equipped. Condes de Albarei is the name for its fruity, pure Albariño wine, with a taste that is sometimes more exciting than its scent.

Bodegas de Vilariño-Cambados
36639 Cambados
This winery set up in 1986 processes grapes from 140 growers in the Val do Salnés area. Martín Codax (he was the founder of Vigo) is the chosen brand name. Nowadays this Albariño wine is of better than average quality.

Daniel Alonso González 36760 Eiras
At the end of the 1980s this bodega was thoroughly reconstructed: tradition gave way to modern technology. At the same time Daniel Alonso considerably enlarged his vineyard, from 7 to about 40 ha (from 17 to 100 acres). The O Aforado wine (90 percent Albariño), fermented at low temperature, is reasonably firm in taste, juicy and refreshing, with a little fruit.

Limeres Rodríguez 36770 El Rosal
Makes a very distinctive Albariño, called La Val, with suggestions of fruit, flowers and spice. The property is in the hamlet of San Miguel Tabagón and covers 4 ha (10 acres). Grapes are also bought in. Founded in 1985.

Santiago Ruiz 36770 El Rosal
This firm is more than 100 years old and buys in practically all its grapes. Its white Rías Baixas is sold in a Bordeaux bottle, has around 80 percent Albariño and bears a striking label. The quality of this wine, which has fruit, is good.

Fernández Cervera Hermanos
36770 Fornelos
Wine estate of 26 ha (64 acres) dating from 1982. This belongs to the substantial Rioja house of La

Rioja Alta. The wine is called Lagar de Cervera and is a pure Albariño, reasonably full, supple, smoothly fresh, and with a suggestion of fruit.

Valdamor 36968 Meaño
Striking, stylishly presented Albariño wine with much charm and flawless quality.

Adega Mar de Frades 36619 Rubiáns
The producer of two Albariños, Casabella and Mar de Frades. The latter is the better wine, with a clean and delicious taste that goes perfectly with seafood.

Fillaboa 36450 Salvaterra de Miño
The Fillaboa *granxa* lies where the Tea flows into the Miño. The entrance is beside a Roman bridge. Kiwi fruit is grown here, but the emphasis is on the Albariño grape; 19 ha (47 acres) are planted with it. The wine from these vines is produced in a trim, spacious hall with stainless-steel tanks dating from 1988. Out in the vineyard is an advanced meteorological measuring system that indicates exactly when the vines should be given their anti-mildew treatment. Fillaboa is one of the best of Rías Baixas wines: pale in colour, with a hint of fruit and spice in the taste, and fresh in a smooth way. The first vintages rather lacked depth, a fault that righted itself as the vines grew older. There is a reception hall for visitors where hunting trophies hang on the wall. As well as the wine a fine, mellow distillation of Albariño is also made.

Agro de Bazán 3662 Tremoedo
A firm dating from 1988 that buys in grapes to supplement the harvest from its own vineyard of just under 15 ha (37 acres). It markets two Albariños, both with the brand name Granbazán. The one sold in the brown "flute" is the better as it is made from the first pressing only.

Travel Information

HOTELS AND RESTAURANTS

Parador Conde de Gondomar, 36300 Bayona, tel (86) 355000 This L-shaped, walled *parador*, the best in Galicia, is established in a fine old building. It stands on a small peninsula, surrounded by pine and eucalyptus trees, and offers a view out over the Bayona and Vigo *rías*. As well as seafood the restaurant offers veal as a speciality.
Parador del Albariño, 36630 Cambados, tel (86) 542250 A rather austere-looking *parador*, set up in a former *pazo* (manor house). The restaurant serves a good deal of fresh fish – and, of course, Albariño wines.
O'Pozo, 36880 La Cañiza, tel (86) 651050 Simple hotel, but with bar, restaurant and swimming pool, on the road between La Cañiza and Orense. The rooms at the back are the quietest.
Reveca, 36880 La Cañiza, tel (86) 651426 Strictly regional dishes are served in this soberly furnished restaurant, including a monumental *cocido gallego*, the traditional stew of Galicia. The red house wine goes well with it. Lamb and sucking pig are good here, as well as the *jamón serrano*, a speciality of this village.
Los Abetos, 36209 Nigran, tel (86) 368147 Restaurant on the coast road between Vigo and Bayona. Tasty meat dishes from grill and oven. The fish smoked on the premises deserves a recommendation. Large wine list with many local examples and a goodly selection of Riojas.
Parador Casa del Barón, 36000 Pontevedra, tel (86) 855800 Here you stay in a Galician *pazo* with a beautiful garden and imposing stone steps, and can enjoy fish and shellfish to your heart's content in the restaurant. The *parador* stands in the old centre of the town.
Parador San Telmo, 36700 Túy tel (86) 600309 Fairly small *parador* below the little town and its fortress-like cathedral. A former *pazo*, it offers views of the Miño valley and Portugal. Traditional cuisine, including lampreys.
Amarante, Roupeiro 84, 36300 Vigo, tel (86) 224048 Small restaurant where you can eat well and inexpensively. Many dishes are of Portuguese origin.
Ciudad de Vigo, Concepción Arenal 5, 36201 Vigo, tel (86) 435233 Comfortable, reasonably modern, but otherwise characterless hotel near the harbour. It has a garage.
Estoril, Lepanto 12, 36201 Vigo, tel (86) 436122 Simple, but acceptable (and cheap) hotel near the station.
El Mosquito, Plaza Villavicencio 4, 36202 Vigo, tel (86) 433570 Much liked by the local people. The sole here tastes perfect, as does the *cabrito asado* (roast young goat).
Sibaris, Avenida García Barbón 122, 36201 Vigo, tel (86) 221526 The entrance is tucked away in a small shopping arcade and the restaurant is on the first floor. Elegant-looking, with restful colours. However, the greatest surprise is the food, prepared by the slender Doña Antonia ("Toñi") Vicente. She is one of Spain's (if not Europe's) best cooks and treats her guests to creations of great refinement. Among my memories are a delicious salad with marinated *luabina* (sea bass), heavenly *croquetas de marisco* (shellfish), and *merluza* (hake) with a compote of tomatoes and fragrant with rosemary. Some of the best Albariños are on the wine list.
El Timón Playa, Playa de Corujo, Corujo, 36200 Vigo, tel (86) 490815 One of the best addresses for fresh seafood.

PLACES OF INTEREST

Arbo Near this village there are ever-changing views out over the valley of the Miño. This is also where the Bodegas Marqués de Vizhoja, an excellent wine producer, is situated. Arbo's speciality is lamprey, the freshwater fish also found in the Bordeaux region.
Armenteira The first Albariño vines were possibly brought to the abbey here. This is beautifully situated and dates from the thirteenth century.
Cambados This fishing port is also the "Albariño capital", and on the first Sunday in August holds a festival devoted to it – with decorated carts, musicians, dancers, fireworks, etc. Cambados has a number of fine town houses (*pazos*), the most impressive of which is Fefiñes, on the square of that name.
La Cañiza This village 570 m (1,870 ft) up is famous for its marvellous ham – celebrated in the *Festa do Xamón* held here on August 15.
Combarro Along the *ría* you have a view of the granite *horreos*, the farm buildings where corn cobs are laid out to dry. The place itself has tiled balconies.
Hío The atrium of the Romanesque church of San Andrés has the most beautiful *crucero* in Galicia. Carved from granite, it depicts the Descent from the Cross.
Pontevedra The old centre of this provincial capital deserves a visit, not only for the churches of the Virgen Peregrina (shaped rather like a shell), Santa María la Mayor (sixteenth-century basilica), and San Francisco (partly fourteenth century), but also for the Plaza de la Leña with its special atmosphere, its arcades and weathered crucifix. The Museo Municipal, in two eighteenth-century town mansions, includes in its collection prehistoric finds, an admiral's cabin, an antique kitchen, and paintings by Spanish, Dutch and Italian masters.
Túy From a distance the cathedral in this town built on a hill looks more like a fortress than a church. It has a nave and two aisles, and dates from the twelfth to the eighteenth century, so that various architectural styles are to be seen there. There is a Spanish-Portuguese market every Thursday in this small town, with tradesmen's gear among items on sale. Túy is also famed for its eels.
Vigo This bustling, ever-expanding city (population 260,000) stands on the largest *ría* of the region. It is Spain's most important fishing port, and also has a good deal of industry. From the Castillo del Castro with its surrounding park there is a view across the city and its bay. The atmospheric old town, the Barrio del Berbès quarter, has steep streets. The harbour is close by, and in fine weather you can stroll there past all the yachts. The municipal museum in the southwest of the city has a considerable folklore collection. The zoo, and also the Mirador de la Madroa with its views, are 7 km (4.5 miles) out of Vigo.

WINE ROUTE

The suggested wine route runs through the three zones of Riás Baixas. The section north of Vigo and the circuit south of the city both demand a whole day – certainly if towns and villages are to be looked at, producers visited, and lunch taken en route. If you have just one day available, I recommend the southern route, because of the ever-changing views it affords across the green valley of the Miño.

Above: The sumptuous library of the 16th-century El Escorial monastery, built by Philip II.

The East and Centre

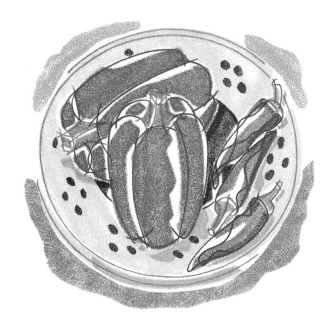

While various wine regions of northern Spain were for decades following a policy directed towards quality and exports, the whole of central Spain was supplying cheap, simple wines mainly in bulk to what was still a protected, uncritical market. Until well into the 1970s there would have been little point in visiting and describing these regions, for their wines were seldom interesting, and only a small proportion of them bottled. In the 1980s, however, a great change of direction took place – towards quality. The giant had awoken at last. The results of this reorientation have been remarkable. Anyone who travels in central Spain today will discover many exciting wines, honestly and expertly made. Cellars have been rebuilt or renovated practically everywhere and investment in modern equipment has been on a large scale.

Widespread revolution

The most spectacular advance has been noted in La Mancha, where the dull, flat wine made from white Airén has evolved into a lively, refreshing, delicious thirst quencher. At the same time the level of many red wines has been raised, which also has been the case in neighbouring Valdepeñas. Naturally, not all the producers in these *denominaciones de origen* have as yet invested in modern equipment, but the laggards cannot really afford to wait much longer, for the time is approaching when not a single market in the Western world will accept the old-style wines. Going over to modern technology is no longer a question of choice, but of survival. This has also been realized by the DOs of Levante, to the east of La Mancha. Thanks to the strength of five large bodegas here, the Valencia area is now well equipped, which is also true of many of the Utiel-Requena producers. In Alicante, Bullas, Jumilla and Yecla only a few producers have so far seen

139

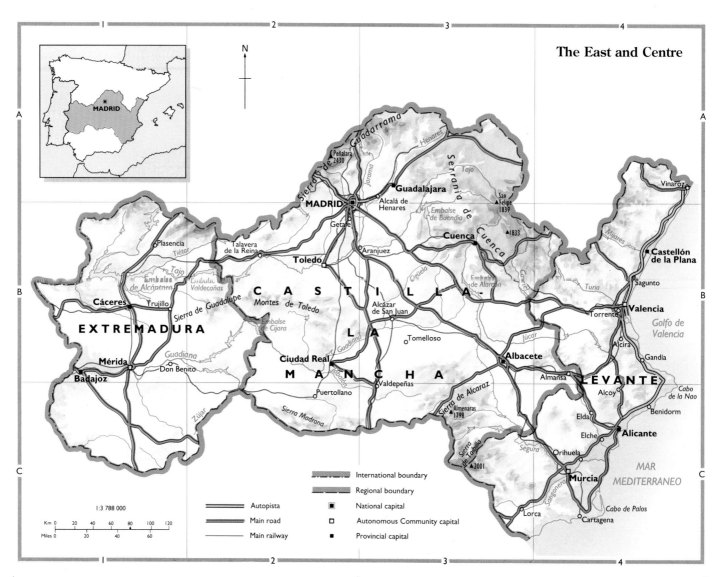

The East and Centre

MADRID

N

Peñalara 2430
Guadalajara
MADRID · Alcalá de Henares
Getafe
Plasencia
Talavera de la Reina
Toledo
Aranjuez
Cuenca
San Felipe 1839
1833
Vinaroz
Castellón de la Plana
Sagunto

Cáceres · Trujillo
Sierra de Guadalupe
Montes de Toledo
Embalse de Valdecañas
C A S T I L L A -
Alcázar de San Juan
Torrente
Valencia
Golfo de Valencia

EXTREMADURA
Embalse de Cijara
L A
Alcira
Gandía

Mérida
Don Benito
Ciudad Real
Tomelloso
Albacete
Almansa
L E V A N T E
Alcoy
Cabo de la Nao

Badajoz
M A N C H A
Valdepeñas
Sierra de Alcaraz
Almenaras 1798
Elda
Benidorm

Puertollano
Elche
Alicante

Sierra Madrona
2001
Orihuela
Segura
MAR MEDITERRÁNEO

Murcia
Cabo de Palos

Lorca
Cartagena

1:3 788 000

Km 0 20 40 60 80 100 120
Miles 0 20 40 60

International boundary	
Regional boundary	
Autopista	■ National capital
Main road	□ Autonomous Community capital
Main railway	■ Provincial capital

Above: The magnificent, richly decorated cloisters of the monastery of San Juan de los Reyes in Toledo.

the light, but others will undoubtedly follow. North of La Mancha are the DOs of Méntrida and Vinos de Madrid.

The wine districts around the capital are fully committed to development, but Méntrida is so far the only DO of central Spain that shows little or no movement: the proverbial exception to the rule. That it is possible to produce wines of high quality there is demonstrated most eminently by the Marqués de Griñon: just south of Méntrida this gifted grower makes splendid, much-praised wines from mainly French grape varieties. Wine is also grown to the west of La Mancha, albeit on a modest scale. The leading area here is Tierra de Barros, towards the Portuguese border, near Badajoz. In the lead in terms of quality is Inviosa (Industrias Vinícolas del Oeste) in Almendralejo. Its red, wood-aged wines have Tempranillo as the principal grape and have already won a good deal of international recognition. They are called Lar de Barros.

Rich heritage

The centre of Spain not only furnishes the traveller with some surprises in the sphere of wine; it is also where an important part of the country's heritage is to be found. To walk around Toledo with its many art treasures and monuments is to go back in time; Christian, Islamic and Jewish civilizations all flourished in this city. Under the Moors, it became a great centre of learning.

Above: The Roman aqueduct which spans the city of Segovia.

Arts and crafts

Another characteristic of central Spain is its arts and crafts in all their various manifestations. Pottery of a high degree of craftsmanship is made in the province of Valencia, and in such towns as Talavera de la Reina and Toledo; the latter is of course famed for its jewellery and its steel – swords in particular – a legacy of its Moorish heritage. Lacemaking is carried on in various towns and villages, examples being Almagro in La Mancha and Monóvar in Alicante. Many of these crafts have been practised for centuries and make the visitor to this part of Spain realize just how strong the historical connections are.

Enormous tolerance was shown towards Christians and Jews alike. The fourteenth-century El Tránsito Synagogue, richly decorated with both Mudéjan and Hebraic work, shows how this tradition continued, while Toledo became famous for its School of Translators, who spread to the West a knowledge of Arab medicine, culture and philosophy. Toledo was also the home of El Greco, and the sumptuously appointed cathedral holds several of his paintings.

In Elche, near Alicante, you might think yourself in Arabia, for thousands of palm trees grow here. Then not far to the north you enter a once powerful feudal state that was protected by medieval castles; they are still there, among them Chinchilla de Monte Aragón, Sax and Villena. Strongholds from the period when Christians and Moors were fighting each other are also to be seen on and around the high plain of La Mancha; others there date from the time before Castilla and Aragón were united.

The Man from La Mancha

But here in the heart of Spain you are reminded most often of a character from a book: Don Quixote. His name and likeness adorn the fronts of buildings, signboards, wine labels and all kinds of tourist wares. Don Quixote, the "Man from La Mancha", was the creation of Miguel de Cervantes. He was born in 1547 in Alcalá de Henares, then a university town, just to the east of Madrid. The writer himself led an adventurous life, being wounded when soldiering in Italy and spending five years as a slave in Turkey. After publishing a number of other works, he wrote the first volume of *Don Quixote* in 1605, a brilliant satire in which he held his society and the established order up to ridicule, in a subtle and often humorous way. The nobility of the time would lay claim to wealth while in reality suffering hunger – and were as thin as Don Quixote. In the book this elderly knight errant wants to make the world a better place in his idealistic way, accompanied by his faithful, simple, yet shrewd squire Sancho Pancha. Together they have numerous adventures, including the famous fight with the windmills. In 1615 Cervantes wrote the second and final volume of *Don Quixote*. A year later he died, on 23 April 1616 – the same day as Shakespeare. How widely influential Cervantes has been is clear not only from the fact that his book is still read, but also from the many editions of it that have appeared. The Cervantes museum in El Toboso, La Mancha, has 400 editions; that at Castillo de Perelada, in Ampurdán-Costa Brava, has 1,000 in 30 different languages.

Below: Landscape at Camporrobles, Utiel-Requena.

141

Castilla-La Mancha

Capital: Toledo
Provinces: Albacete, Cuidad Real, Cuenca, Guadalajava, Toledo
Area: 29,226 square kilometres
Population: 1,665,029

The former Castilla la Nueva (New Castile) is now an *autonomía* made up of five provinces: Albacete, Cuenca, Ciudad Real, Guadalajara and Toledo. In the south and east it borders on the Madrid *autonomía*. The most characteristic element in the Castilla-La Mancha landscape is the *meseta* in the south, a vast upland plain between the Tajo valley and the Sierra Morena. In the eighteenth century a British major, William Dalrymple, rode on horseback from Gibraltar to Galicia, and wrote that this plateau reminded him of a calm sea. Referred to by the Moors as the *manxa*, "dry land", this plateau is at an average height of 700 m (2,300 ft) above sea level. Scorching, parching heat prevails in summer and a biting cold wind blows through the long winter. The two seasons account for a temperature range from 44° down to −22°C (111 to 7.5°F). Rain falls infrequently, and given these inhospitable conditions the presence of many busy towns and villages here is really somewhat surprising. The houses are

Below: A view over the vineyards near Almansa.

usually grouped close together, as if seeking protection from the elements. On the other hand they often have notable central squares; the Plaza Mayor in many places is quite splendid. Two of the finest are at Almagro and San Carlos del Valle, but there are also good ones at Daimiel, La Solana, Tembleque and elsewhere.

Hunting area

La Mancha's tableland is not the only kind of terrain in this *autonomía*. Almost the whole of its western part is comprised of the Montes de Toledo, a much-eroded, lonely mountain range that is linked by a wide hilly area with the Sierra Madrona further south. There is also a range in the east, the Serranía de Cuenca, which is richly endowed with natural beauty. In the southeast there is the Sierra de Alcaraz, where a number of rivers rise, such as the Mundo with its high waterfall, and the Guadiana. The latter system irrigates the southern part of the plateau, sometimes flowing underground. All kinds of game can be hunted in the mountain areas, so that in the season large groups of sportsmen – some from outside Spain – make their way to Castilla-La Mancha

Windmills

The white windmills made famous by the story of Don Quixote have come to symbolize the high plateau, but they are to be found in only a few places, such as at Alcázar de San Juan, Campo de Criptana (the most charming town in La Mancha according to British professor Walter Starkie), Consuegra, Mota del Cuervo and Valdepeñas. They mostly stand in groups; the oldest of them date from the sixteenth century and Dutch technology was used in building them. The windmills are a reminder of the time when La Mancha mainly produced grain. Today, however, the *meseta* supplies vast quantities of wine, as well as grain and olives, and the cylindrical silhouettes of fermentation tanks are now much more typical of La Mancha.

Emphasis on white wine

For hundreds of years Castilla-La Mancha was a kind of no man's land between the Christians and the Moors, and so for a long time winegrowing was of little importance. But in the thirteeth century, when the Moors had been driven from the plateau (and the town of Valdepeñas had been established in the south), the number of vines planted increased greatly. The military monastic order of Calatrava contributed a good deal to this. Later some of the wines were even served at the Spanish court. Nevertheless in 1764 a Frenchman called Fleuriot was to write that no amount of money would induce him to drink the wine of La Mancha unwatered, for it tasted of sulphur, was inky dark in colour, and so strong that one glass would make you drunk. A century later, the Reverend Joseph Townsend reported that he had tasted excellent wines in Manzanares which combined the fragrance of the best burgundies with the strength of port. Since the beginning of the twentieth century, however, plantings have been mainly of white Airén. This variety provides both the basic wine for the

Above: Windmills are a familiar sight on the high plain of La Mancha.

brandy industry in Jerez and white table wines – the latter sold pure or blended with red. In terms of quality, pure Airén wines only became interesting in the 1980s, after modern vinification equipment had been introduced. The second grape on the *meseta* is Tempranillo, known locally as Cencibel. Of the two *denominaciones de origen* on the plateau, La Mancha and Valdepeñas, the former has around 75 percent Airén, the latter about 85 percent. With its 170,000 ha (420,000 acres) La Mancha is not only the biggest wine region in Castilla-La Mancha, but also in Spain and even in Europe, and has some 420 active bodegas.

Other wine districts

The two other DOs are on the edge of the tableland, and here different grape varieties are predominant. To the north-west of medieval Toledo the Méntrida district produces heady red wines from Garnacha; and in the extreme south-east Almansa, a town with a castle, has given its name to a DO making firm red wines from Monastrell, Garnacha Tintorera and Cencibel grapes. Only a small proportion of some 80,000 families in Castilla-La Mancha who make their living from wine reside in non-DO districts, of

which there are only two. The larger of these is Manchuela, situated between La Mancha and Almansa, and Utiel-Requena in the Levante. Black Bobal is the most cultivated grape here. The bulk of the wines disappear anonymously into tanks for blending; one of the few bottle lines is at the cooperative at Iniesta, in the province of Cuenca. The Mondéjar-Sacedón wine district is in Guadalajara province and stretches eastwards from the Vinos de Madrid DO. The Malvar grape is the usual basis here for white wines, with the Cencibel for red. For practical reasons the Vinos de Madrid DO is included in the Castilla-La Mancha region. In this DO, dating from 1990, the most prevalent grapes are white Malvar, black Tinto Fino (Tempranillo) and Garnacha.

Regional cooking

It is alleged that King Philip II made Madrid his capital in 1561 because it offered a much more suitable place for hunting parties to meet than Valladolid further to the north. There was a good deal of hunting in Castilla-La Mancha then, as there is now.

Above: Vineyard in Valdepeñas.

Naturally enough game, especially small varieties, features prominently in the regional cuisine. This is demonstrated by the *gazpachos*, *manchegos*, or *galianos*, which are served everywhere. These have nothing to do with the cold *gazpacho* of Andalucía, but are traditional hunter's and shepherd's dishes made with various kinds of small game (and often chicken, too), wine, herbs, frequently tomatoes, onion and peppers, and *torta*, a type of flat bread baked on a hot stone. Quite often a piece of the bread is used as a spoon. Another classic dish is *pisto manchego*, a savoury combination of cooked vegetables: Spain's answer to ratatouille. Small game, other meat and vegetables are all cooked together in *tojunto*: it is said that this easy dish was invented by the women of Almagro, who thus had more time for their lacemaking. The stews called *cocidos* are often served here, as is garlic soup. Meals in La Mancha often start with a piece of Manchego cheese, which can vary in taste from mild and fresh to piquant and dry. This is Spain's best-known and most-produced cheese, made from sheep's milk. Finally there is marzipan, which is a speciality of Toledo; probably this delicacy of Arab origin has been made here since the thirteenth century.

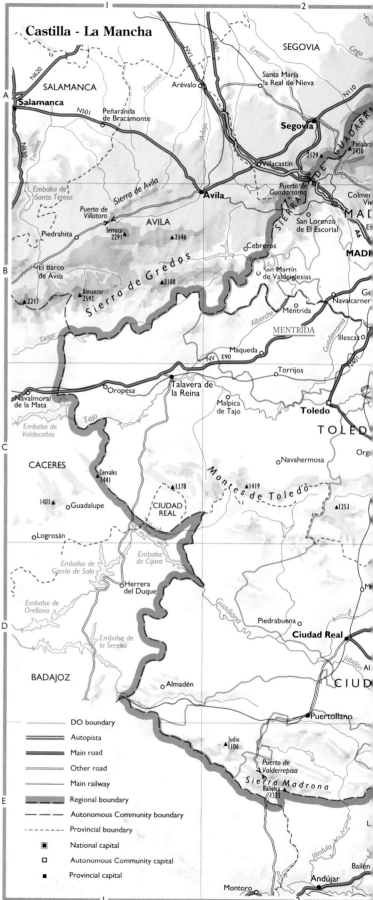

Castilla - La Mancha

DO boundary
Autopista
Main road
Other road
Main railway
Regional boundary
Autonomous Community boundary
Provincial boundary
■ National capital
□ Autonomous Community capital
■ Provincial capital

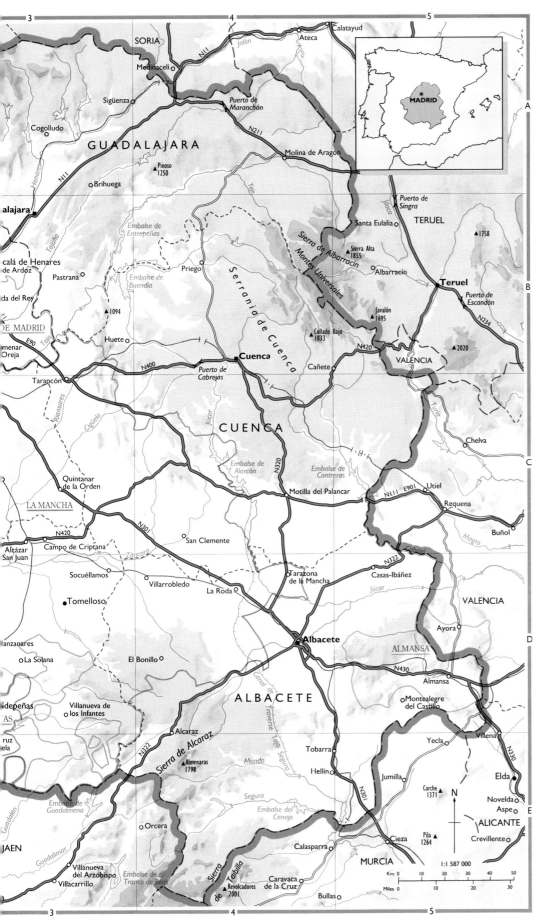

SORIA

Calatayud
Ateca

Medinaceli

N II

Sigüenza

Puerto de
Maranchón

Cogolludo

N 211

GUADALAJARA

Molina de Aragón

Pinoso
1250

Brihuega

alajara

N II

Henares

Tajo

Puerto de
Singra

TERUEL

Jiloca

Santa Eulalia

1758

calá de Henares
de Ardoz

Embalse de
Entrepeñas

Priego

Sierra Alta
1855

Sierra de Albarracín

Pastrana

Embalse de
Buendía

Serranía de Cuenca

Montes Universales

Albarracín

Teruel

da del Rey

1094

Javalón
1695

Puerto de
Escandón

E MADRID

Tajo

Huete

Collado Bajo
1833

N 420

2020

N 234

menar
Oreja

Cuenca

Cañete

VALENCIA

Tarancón

N 400

Puerto de
Cabrejas

Ransares

Ciguela

CUENCA

Júcar

Chelva

Turia

Embalse de
Alarcón

N 320

Embalse de
Contreras

C

Quintanar
de la Orden

Motilla del Palancar

N III E 901

Utiel

LA MANCHA

Requena

N 420

N 301

San Clemente

Buñol

Alcázar
San Juan

Zancara

Magro

Socuéllamos

Villarrobledo

Tarazona
de la Mancha

Gabriel

anzanares

Tomelloso

La Roda

N 322

Casas-Ibáñez

Júcar

VALENCIA

La Solana

Albacete

Ayora

D

ALMANSA

N 430

depeñas

Villanueva de
los Infantes

El Bonillo

ALBACETE

Almansa

AS

Alcaraz

Montealegre
del Castillo

ruz
ela

N 322

Sierra de Alcaraz

Travense Tajo

Canal de

Tobarra

Yecla

Villena

N 330

Almenaras
1798

Mundo

Segura

Hellín

Carche
1371

Elda

N 301

Jumilla

Novelda

Aspe

Embalse de
Guadalmena

Segura

Embalse del
Cenajo

N

ALICANTE

Guadalen

Orcera

Pila
1264

Crevillente

JAEN

Guadalimar

Calasparra

Cieza

MURCIA

1:1 587 000

Villanueva
del Arzobispo

Embalse de el
Tranco de Beas

Sierra de Taibilla

Revolcadores
2001

Caravaca
de la Cruz

Km 0   10   20   30   40   50

Villacarrillo

Bullas

Miles 0   10   20   30

MADRID

A

B

*Above: In spring the hillsides are
carpeted with wild flowers.*

Vinos de Madrid

The harvest festival which took place on 7 October 1990 on the Plaza de Colón had a very special meaning for the wine-growers of Vinos de Madrid: they were also celebrating the fact that their region had just received its DO as a result of a six-year-old campaign. The bonds of the Tierra de Madrid with the capital naturally date from much further back. From ancient documents it appears that in the fifteenth and sixteenth centuries the inhabitants of Madrid already drank much wine from the neighbouring villages, which are identified by name. Thus the wine from San Martín de Valdeiglesias was called *vino de reyes* because it was drunk by the royal court, as was that of Valdemoro. Even Spanish literature mentions the wines produced in the region of Madrid; Casanova himself greatly admired them. But after a period of strong growth during the seventeenth century many vineyards disappeared as a result of growing urbanization. Note that the DO only covers some 13,000 ha (32,100 acres) which is not even half of the vineyards in the region.

Area of the DO

The present DO consists of 55 communes, all situated in the south of the province – on the map it forms a semi-circle around the capital and its suburbs. The distance between the most eastern and western wineproducing villages is a good 100 km (62 miles). In the south the region goes just beyond Aranjuez which is not far from the high plateaux of La Mancha. The region enjoys a continental climate: in the summer the temperature easily rises to 38°C (100.4°F), while in the winter it will sometimes go as low as −5°C (23°F). There can be frost as early as mid-October and as late as mid-May, although the climate is slightly more pleasant than that of La Mancha. The average rainfall is also slightly higher, at 450 mm (17.7 ins) rather than 400 (15.7).

Sub-zones

The *Consejo Regulador* of Vinos de Madrid distinguishes three sub-zones: Arganda (east), Navalcarnero (centre) and San Martín de Valdeiglesias (west). Arganda is by far the most important of these districts as it covers half the vineyards of the region. The soil is rich in clay and lime. The amounts of lime can be considerable, giving the soil a rather whitish appearance. Arganda produces quite a bit more white than red and rosé together. It is the only sub-zone which produces a substantial amount of white wine, totalling over 95 percent of all white Vinos de Madrid. The regulations allow two white grape varieties, Malvar and Airén. Malvar is the most commonly grown and traditional of the two. It is only cultivated around Madrid where it is also eaten as a dessert grape, though the grapes are small, with a tough skin. The wine is supple and fruity with a hint of nuts and some acidity. The Arganda winegrowers are also experimenting with other white grape varieties such as Macabeo and Parellada. This district dominates the others not only with its white wines but also – in terms of quality – with its reds. In Arganda red wines are made either from Tinto Fino or Tempranillo, while in the other two sub-zones they are made exclusively from Garnacha. There are very few pure Tinto Fino wines, at least bottled. They can be of outstanding quality with a rich colour, a lot of tannin, strong taste of fruit and a good level of acidity. The most commonly produced wines are made from the must of black and white grapes so that there are more *claretes* than *tintos*. Ambitious bodegas in Arganda are now experimenting with Cabernet Sauvignon and Syrah. The results achieved by Jesús Díaz e Hijos in Colmenar de Oreja are extremely promising.

Navalcarnero

While Arganda covers 27 villages, the district of Navalcarnero which lies slightly to the west only covers 19. The vineyards of this district represent around 15 percent of the region's total. The composition of the soil is very different here; it contains very little lime and its colour is reddish brown; it also holds moisture very well. The landscape is gently rolling, in contrast with some parts of Arganda which are very hilly. This district produces almost entirely red and rosé wines, and being based mainly on Garnacha they tend to be rather strong. Only those wines which are fermented under controlled temperature deserve to be bottled. The early harvesting of the grapes also improves the quality of the wine. The minimum alcohol percentage of the *tintos* and *rosados* produced in Navalcarnero is – like those from the third and last zone of San Martín de Valdeiglesias – half a percent higher than those produced in Arganda, i.e. 12 percent instead of 11.5 percent.

San Martín de Valdeiglesias

The most westerly vineyards of the sub-zone of San Martín de Valdeiglesias are situated in the foothills of the Sierra de Gredos. The landscape is slightly hilly as in Navalcarnero, but the soil here is different again, consisting of a thin, rather infertile top layer of brown earth with a granitic sub-soil. The vines, which are mainly of the Garnacha variety, produce red and rosé wines which are vigorous and contain very little acid. The bulk of it is used anonymously in the bottling plants around Madrid. White wine is also made here, but only around 3 percent. The grape variety used for making this white wine is Albillo. This early-ripening variety is typically Castilian; its wines are quite aromatic with a high alcohol content. It is rarely bottled. Covering nine villages and around 35 percent of the vineyards, San Martín comes second as far as quantity is concerned. The importance of cooperatives is even greater here than in the other districts: the percentage of wine produced by the cooperatives is over 90 percent here, against approximately 85 percent in Navalcarnero and almost 75 percent in Arganda. It is obvious from these figures that the future of the Vinos de Madrid will be determined by these establishments.

Tanks and *tinajas*

Meanwhile it is very promising that several cooperatives have now started to use stainless-steel fermentation tanks and the cooling plant which goes with it, as well as the traditional concrete tanks lined with synthetic resin. Some of the privately owned bodegas have also invested in modern plant. In fact it is quite common to find three "generations" of fermentation tanks in the cellars of the same wineproducers: the traditional *tinajas* (giant clay amphoras, very common in La Mancha), concrete tanks, and stainless-steel containers, which are all still in use. Both cooperatives and individual producers are increasing their investment in bottling plants. Over 20 of the 30 bodegas are now able to bottle their own wine. But the amounts are still small: less than 10 percent of all Vinos de Madrid reaches the consumer in bottled form with a numbered *Consejo* label. The sub-zone which has been involved longest in bottling is Arganda; most bottles are sold in Spain and only a few on the still-limited foreign markets.

PRODUCERS OF SPECIAL INTEREST

Bodegas Castejón 28500 Arganda del Rey
This firm with 50 ha (124 acres) of its own land specializes in supple red wines, often made with 50 percent white grapes. The youngest red, the Viña Rey, is often the best.

Bodega Francisco Figueroa 28380 Colmenar de Oreja
Estate with some 35 ha (86 acres) of vineyards. The red Figueroa is made from 50 percent Tempranillo and 50 percent Garnacha and is meant for drinking young. At the yearly wine competition of Vinos de Madrid it has several times been named best in its category.

Jesús Díaz e Hijos 28380 Colmenar de Oreja
This bodega is the best known wine producer of Vinos de Madrid. The company owns some 60 ha (148

acres). Two thirds of these are planted with Malvar and the rest with Tinto Fino. The high proportion of Malvar is one of the reasons why the red wine (in reality a *clarete*) consists of 60 percent Malvar and 40 percent Tinto Fino. It is a supple, firm product with a very pleasant taste. Under the guidance of the oenologist Juan José Díaz the bodega is also experimenting with red wines produced from Cabernet Sauvignon (80 percent plus 20 percent Malvar), Syrah (with 30 percent white must) and pure Tinto Fino. These experiments have led to excellent results; there is no doubt that several new red wines will be added to the existing range. Both the white wine (100 percent Malvar) and the rosé (100 percent Tinto Fino, only the first juice) are very reliable with stimulating freshness and a good amount of fruit. Most of their wines are sold under the brand name of Jesús Díaz e Hijos, but for some

markets such as the United States they use the label Colmenar.

Cooperativa Nuestra Señora de la Concepción 28600 Navalcarnero
This cooperative, founded in 1957, has some 200 members and handles around 10 percent of the production in Vinos de Madrid. The most pleasant wine is the red Valdecepa, firm but not too heavy and quite lively, made from Garnacha.

Bodegas Orusco 28511 Valdilecha
The red Viña Main produced by this family business is a *crianza* matured in wood with a smooth, pleasant taste and firm body. It is made from 85 percent Tempranillo and 15 percent Malvar. This bodega owns in all some 130 casks while part of the wine is left to ferment in stainless-steel tanks. The Orusco family own over 12 ha (30 acres) of vineyards and often buy over two

Above: The palace and statues of the Jardín del Príncipe give Aranjuez a Versailles-like air.

million kilos (1,968 tons) of grapes. They are one of the few producers who export on a regular basis.

Laguna 28360 Villaconejos
Energetic producer with an estate of 80 ha (198 acres) and some modern equipment. The white Valdeguera (100 percent Malvar) is clear in taste and is one of the best such wines from this area. The rosé too, is of a good standard, and the red is pleasing.

Algaco 28590 Villarejo de Salvanés
Both the pure fruity white Jeromín (100 percent Malvar) and the dry rosé (70 percent Tempranillo, 30 percent Garnacha) have class. A quarter of the grapes come from the estate's own 50 ha (124 acres).

Above: Local bars are large buyers of Vinos de Madrid.

Travel information

HOTELS AND RESTAURANTS

Casa Pablo, Almíbar 42, 28300 Aranjuez, tel (1) 8911451 Carefully prepared regional dishes (pheasant) as well as less specifically Castilian cuisine served in a traditional setting.

Cafe de la Iberia, 28370 Chinchón, tel (1) 8940998 Probably the best place to eat in the area and also beautifully situated in the magnificent Plaza Mayor.

Mesón Cuevas del Vino, 28370 Chinchón, tel (1) 8940206 This restaurant, which will greatly appeal to wine lovers, consists of several rooms in a converted olive oil mill. Regional dishes such as *chorizo asado*.

Parador, 28370 Chinchón, tel (1) 8940836 Seventeenth-century Augustinian monastery converted into a hotel and restaurant.

La Cantina, 28380 Colmenar de Oreja, tel (1) 8944426 Regional, and more sophisticated and creative dishes. Good wine list. Situated outside Chinchón.

Felipe IV, 28600 Navalcarnero, tel (1) 8110913 Ideal place to stop for a delicious lunch on the suggested wine route: fish and roast lamb. The restaurant is situated slightly to the east of the town.

Mesón Les Arcos, 28680 San Martín de Valdeiglesias, tel (1) 8610434. You can eat out on the terrace when the weather is right. Delicious goat dishes. The local wine is used in the preparation of peach *al vino tinto*.

Carlos V, 45001, Toledo *see* Méntrida

Parador Conde de Orgaz, 4500 Toledo *see* Méntrida

La Ochava, 28511 Valdilecha, tel (1) 8738180 Typical Castilian cuisine in a genuine wine village.

PLACES OF INTEREST

Aranjuez This green oasis on the edge of the Spanish plateau is situated on the confluence of the Jarama and the Tajo. In the sixteenth century Philip II began the construction of a royal palace here which was later completed by Charles III. It was conceived in the style of Versailles, complete with a magnificent throne room. The Jardín del Príncipe which stretches between the Palace and the Tajo contained many different kinds of trees, statues and even a small temple. There are also statues and fountains in the Jardín de la Isla, an island garden on the Tajo. In the Jardín del Príncipe you may admire the Casa del Labrador, built around 1800 in the style of the Petit Trianon at Versailles and sumptuously furnished and decorated. Joaquín Rodrigo composed his *Concierto de Aranjuez* in homage to this beautiful town.

Arganda del Rey The parish church of San Juan Bautista dates back to the sixteenth century and has an altarpiece which comes from a convent in Calatayud.

Cadalso de los Vidrios Small town built at an altitude of 800 m (2,630 ft) with a sixteenth-century castle, the Palacio de Villena, surrounded by beautiful gardens.

The Calle Real is lined with some attractive town houses; at the end of the street are the ruins of two Moorish towers.

Chinchón The Plaza Mayor in this delightfully picturesque village is one of the most beautiful in Spain, and is often used in film sets, as well as for bullfighting. It has an irregular shape and is surrounded by many arcades and balconies. You can also visit the ruins of two castles, the Castillo de Casasola (fourteenth century) and the Castillo de los Condes de Chinchón (fifteenth century). In the sixteenth-century church of the Asunción hangs a painting by Goya representing the Ascension. Chinchón is known in Spain for its anis or aniseed liqueur. It is also interesting to know that quinine was named after Chinchón: in the seventeenth century it was used in Peru to cure the first Countess of Chinchón. The Countess brought the tree bark back to

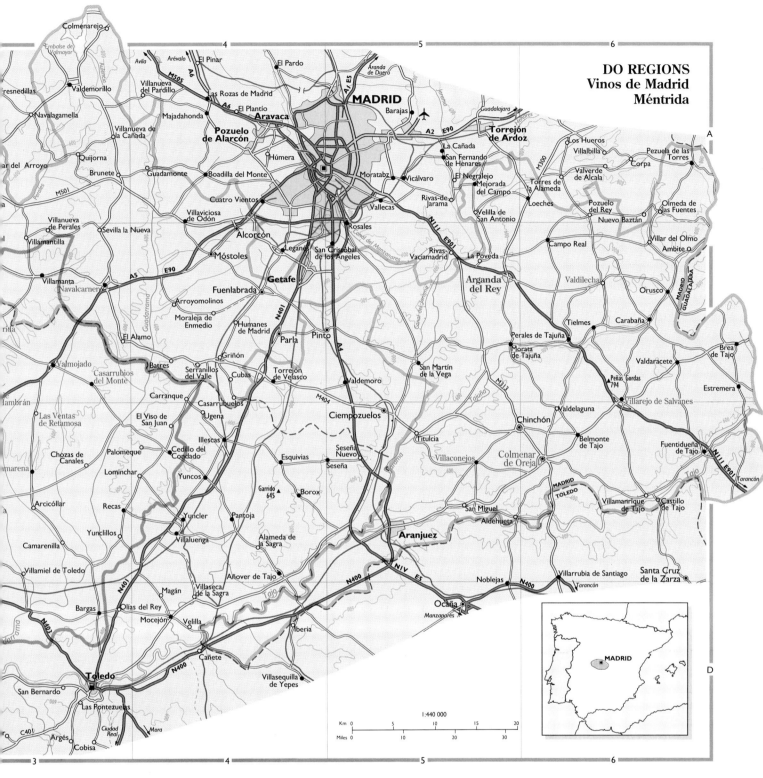

DO REGIONS
Vinos de Madrid
Méntrida

Europe where it became known as *chinchona*.

Colmenar de Oreja This town, which probably dates back to Roman times, has a beautiful Plaza Mayor with arcades. The eighteenth-century *ayuntamiento* which overlooks the Plaza houses many paintings by the local painter Ulpiano Checa (1860-1916) including his impressive work *The last days of Pompeii*. The Arco de Zacatin, a tunnel built in 1794, runs under the Plaza Mayor. The parish church dates from the sixteenth century.

Navalcarnero Provincial capital founded in 1499. Large Plaza Mayor with arcades and small cobblestones. The church of the Asunción built in various architectural styles can be recognized by its baroque spire.

San Martín de Valdeiglesias Market town with a fourteenth-century castle which is being restored. The sixteenth-century church is one of seven after which the town was named: Valdeiglesias comes from *Val de las siete iglesias*.

Villa del Prado Of Roman origin. The parish church which dates from the fifteenth century has a massive entrance door covered with metal spikes.

Villarejo de Salvanés The village is dominated by an enormous tower which is all that remains of a castle.

WINE ROUTE

The proposed route covers almost the whole wine region and would make an ideal day trip – especially if you stop to visit a few places of interest and some wine producers, including a delicious lunch somewhere. The trip can be made from Madrid or Toledo and will take you quite close to Méntrida, in the west of the region.

Méntrida

With over 30,000 ha (74,000 acres) Méntrida is one of Spain's largest wine regions, yet few people have heard of it. The fact that it is crossed by two busy main roads, the N5 (Madrid-Caceres) and the N401 (Madrid-Toledo) has probably not helped, but there is another reason: approximately three-quarters of the entire production is sold in bulk, and what is bottled is rarely found outside Madrid, Toledo and the Méntrida region itself. The bars in Madrid have been large consumers of Méntrida wine for centuries, and in the past a little honey would sometimes be added to improve the taste of this rough wine.

Terrain

The Méntrida wine region covers 53 communes in the north of the province of Toledo and two in the southwest of the province of Madrid. Not far from its southern border flows the Tajo. Méntrida's landscape consists mainly of low hills, the quiet wine-growing villages nestling on the slopes or in the valleys. The soil is mostly reddish brown and chalky, but in the north of the region it is more sandy. Many vineyards consist of smaller or larger plots, surrounded by fallow land or other kind of cultivation. There are very few trees, so the grey silhouette of the Sierra de Gredos can almost always be seen: the mountain ridge, with peaks of over 2,000 m (6,500 ft), which lies to the northwest of the region. The Alberche, which flows through the region before joining the Tagus, has its source in these mountains. A few dozen kilometres to the east flows the Guadarrama, which is also a tributary of the Tajo.

Mainly Garnacha

This wine region, which is at an altitude of approximately 550 m (1,800 ft) has a continental climate with hot, dry summers (up to 35°C/95°F) and cold frosty winters. Frost is possible well into spring and can cause serious damage to the vines. Garnacha is by far the most cultivated variety: it is grown in around 85 to 90 percent of vineyards. The other varieties are Tempranillo (Cencibel, Tinto Fino) and Tinto Madrid. The former is becoming increasingly popular with winegrowers while the rather disappointing second variety is slowly disappearing from the scene. Most of the vinestocks are old, their average age being well over 30 years. This means that little wine is produced per hectare, usually about 15 to 20 hl (130 gals per acre).

Colour and strength

Traditionally, winegrowers here have always been paid a price per hectolitre per degree of alcohol. They therefore leave Garnacha grapes on the vine for as long as possible in order to obtain the highest sugar content possible. The result is heavy, heady red and rosé wine. The law stipulates that it must contain at least 13 percent alcohol; this can even go up to 18 percent. The strongest wines are hardly suitable for consumption if unblended, and are thus used to give lighter wines from other regions more colour and backbone. Méntrida also produces *doble pastas* by allowing the must to ferment with a double quantity of skins. This type of wine is used exclusively for blending. The very small amount of Méntrida wine which is bottled is not distinguished as far as quality is concerned. Most of it is robust, concentrated and rather fatty; you could almost chew it. The reds in particular, which are very dark, are at their best in winter, and the locals also

Above: One of Spain's most beautiful castles is in Guadamur.

use this wine for cooking partridge. But whether the rest of the world will take to this kind of wine is another question.

A new approach

What Méntrida really needs is a producer who understands and exploits this wine's natural potential for quality, as has happened in other regions (Rueda, Ribera del Duero, etc.). A producer with the right kind of approach could get the entire region moving again. Méntrida has not kept up with the times and is producing wine which no longer suits modern taste: in other words the region currently has little prospect of commercial success. There have even been attempts from certain quarters to take away its DO unless substantial improvements are made. There is no doubt that it is possible to produce quite excellent wines in this part of Spain – this is clearly shown by the wines produced just outside the Méntrida region. Indeed, one of Spain's best red wines is produced on the south bank of the Tajo by Carlos Falcó, Marqués de Griñon.

Marqués de Griñon

After studying agriculture at Louvain (Belgium) and Davis (California), Carlos Falcó decided in 1973 to plant vines, including French grapevines, on the large family estate near Malpica de Tajo. Then in the 1980s Falcó started producing a red wine made exclusively of Cabernet Sauvignon, on the advice of Professor Emile Peynaud of Bordeaux. The first vintage, which came out in 1986, was a great success. Since then Falcó's wine, which can now also contain 10 percent of the Merlot grape, has acquired a great reputation both in Spain and abroad. It has an intense, meaty taste with undertones of wood and a fruity aroma of berries. Its official category is simply *Vino de mesa de Toledo* but its quality is far higher than that of the Méntrida DO wines. Méntrida's only hope lies in the interest shown by Cosecheros Abastecedoros: this group, which operates in Valdepeñas as Bodegas Los Llanos, is now considering the possibility of starting an outlet in Méntrida too.

PRODUCERS OF SPECIAL INTEREST

Marqués de Griñon 45692 Malpica de Tajo

In 1973 Carlos Falcó, Marqués de Griñon, decided to plant vines on the 1,400 ha (3,450 acres) family estate of Casa de Vacas. This idea first came to him when he was studying agricultural sciences at Davis University, California, and met the head of the wine department. Most of the vinestocks were brought illegally from France and smuggled into Spain by an apple grower. At first the Marqués knew little about grapes, but in the early 1980s he met Alexis Lichine who put him in touch with Professor Emile Peynaud. The latter travelled to Malpica where he tasted the wine made from Cabernet Sauvignon and Tempranillo, and also the pure versions. Peynaud was very enthusiastic about the wine made exclusively from Cabernet, so Falcó decided to concentrate on that. After the very successful launch of the 1982 vintage (at the Dorchester Hotel in London), the Marqués de Griñon continued to produce excellent vintages. The wine, which can contain up to 10 percent of Merlot, matures for 14 to 26 months in French casks. It usually has plenty of colour, a meaty, intense taste and a complex aroma of wood, vanilla and berries. The grapes come from a vineyard which is growing gradually. Besides the 13 ha (32 acres) of Cabernet Sauvignon and 1 ha (2.5 acres) of Merlot some 5 ha (12 acres) of Syrah were added, as well as several plots of Cabernet Franc. The very dry climate of the region has necessitated drip irrigation for the Cabernets. Falcó was given permission to do so by the Minister himself, "because we do not irrigate for quantity but for quality". At the beginning of 1990 the Marqués added to his house (dating from 1793) a magnificent underground cellar and a dining-room for 60 people.

Meanwhile he is also producing excellent wines in other regions such as Rueda, where he works with Antonio Sanz. From Aragón, there is Tastavins, a white wine made from Garnacha Blanca; from the Duero valley comes red Durius, which is made from the local Tempranillo variants; and from Almansa comes the Tagus, a blend of Monastrell and Garnacha – and there are already plans to add further to this range.

Cooperativa Nuestra Señora de la Natividad 45930 Méntrida

Above: The wine property of Marqués de Grinon lies at Malpica de Tajo.

The 250 members of this cooperative, which lies slightly out of town, cultivate some 700 ha (1,750 acres). The cooperative, re-established in 1963, has been bottling approximately one-fifth of production since the late 1980s. It consists of 75 percent red and 25 percent rosé. One of their best wines is the soft, warming (15 percent) red Vega Berciana. The cooperative receives financial support from the Caja Rural de Toledo.

Bodegas Garva 45930 Méntrida
This family business, over a hundred years old, owns around 30 ha (75 acres) of vines and buys grapes in as well. They use only the Garnacha variety. Of the various wines produced by the bodega the three-year-old Cuevas de Castillejo is one of the most successful.

Cooperativa Cristo de la Salud 45920 La Torre de Esteban Hambrán
Their rosé Señorío de la Torre, made exclusively from Garnacha, has its good points. This cooperative dating from 1975 has 190 members who together cultivate some 1,300 ha (3,250 acres).

Bodegas Valdeoro 45940 Valmojado
This is undoubtedly one of the most energetic among the DOs. The owners of this limited company work with bought-in must. Besides the more conventional fermentation tanks they have also invested in some stainless-steel tanks. Production is equally divided between red and rosé. Red *reservas* such as Ambicioso, Castillo de Maqueda and Tio Felipe mature for six to twelve months in oak vats. Their rosé Castillo de Maqueda is among the better wines of the region.

Travel Information

HOTELS AND RESTAURANTS

Mesón Gregorio II, 45180 Camarena, tel (25) 8174372 This restaurant, situated in an ancient convent, serves regional dishes.
Hotel Beatriz, Avenida de Madrid 1, 45600 Talavera de la Reina, tel (25) 807600 Modern, centrally located with comfortable rooms. Its restaurant Anticuario is among the best in the province, with an excellent wine list.
Hostal del Cardenal, Recarredo 24, 45004 Toledo, tel (25) 224900. This hotel/restaurant is actually a former cardinal's palace on the edge of the old town. The stewed partridge is delicious.
Carlos V, Plaza Horno Magdalena 1, 45001 Toledo, tel (25) 222100 Friendly, reasonably priced hotel in a quiet location between the cathedral and the Alcázar.
Parador Conde de Orgaz, Paseo de los Cigarrales, 4500 Toledo, tel (25) 221850 Wonderfully situated on the bank of the Tajo with an unforgettable view over the town.
El Mesón, 45500 Torrijos, tel (25) 760400 Homely hotel and restaurant serving regional dishes.

PLACES OF INTEREST

Casarrubios del Monte Fourteenth-century castle with an elegant tower with cupola.
Cebolla Village situated between the wine region and the Tajo. You will find here the ruins of the Castillo de Villalba (eleventh and twelfth centuries).
Erustes Part of the fifteenth-century parish church is built in the Mudéjar style.
Escalona Walled town with an important citadel which has also been used as a palace. Also note the convent of the Inmaculada Concepción (sixteenth century).
Fuensalida The present castle was restored in the sixteenth century; the parish church shows Mudéjar and Gothic influences.
Guadamur Near this village (southwest of Toledo) stands one of the most beautiful castles in Spain, certainly worth a visit.
Hinojosa de San Vicente The ruin of the Castillo of San Vicente (twelfth century).
Hormigos Sixteenth-century parish church with three naves.
Illescas The hospital of Santuario de la Virgen contains paintings by El Greco. Town gate in Mudéjar style.

Malpica de Tajo Well-preserved citadel of the fourteenth century on the Tajo. It is the home of the nephew of Carlos Falcó, Marqués de Griñon. 6 km (4 miles) south of Malpica lies the estate of the Casa de Vacas where the Marqués has his vineyards and cellars.
Maqueda Fifteenth-century castle built on the site of an Arab citadel. Walls and towers show Mudéjar influences. The living quarters within are more recent.
Méntrida The heart of this small wine town is the Plaza de España. You can admire tile pictures with two fountains, one for water and one for wine. The plaza is surrounded by eighteenth and nineteenth-century buildings.
La Puebla de Montalbán This village boasts a castle with a beautiful fifteenth to sixteenth-century ceiling. The Renaissance influence is felt in the Torre de San Miguel.
Talavera de la Reina Famous for its pottery, which can be seen in the museum of Ruiz de Luna, this town also boasts interesting churches and the chapel of Nuestra Señora del Prado.
Toledo Arabs, Jews and Christians have here created an amazing wealth of interesting architecture; the old centre of Toledo is one large museum. The town is extremely picturesque with a maze of narrow, winding streets and little squares. The French Gothic cathedral, which dates mainly from the fifteenth century, contains many art treasures. There are also two synagogues, many churches, the Flemish-Gothic Monasterio de San Juan de los Reyes and the imposing Alcázar, which was built on the highest point of the town. In or around 1577 El Greco arrived in Toledo. The Museo del Greco is dedicated to him and his work, and you can visit his house. From the road which goes round Toledo following the south bank of the Tajo there is a most wonderful view over the old town.

WINE ROUTE

The route has been marked through the central part of Méntrida where the most important wine communes are situated. The route which branches off in a southerly direction takes you to Malpica de Tajo and the estate of the Marqués de Griñon.

La Mancha

The vastness of La Mancha is overpowering. When you travel through this enormous wine region situated on a high plateau you will often drive along roads which are lined for miles and miles with vineyards stretching as far as the eye can see. The monotony of this landscape dominated by vineyards is only interrupted by the brightness of the white-washed barns, small groups of trees dotted here and there, cornfields and, perched on hills from time to time, windmills such as those Don Quixote used to fight. Now and again the slopes are speckled with the silvery green of olive trees. The ancient villages are almost always flanked by what appear from afar to be watchtowers but which in reality are metal wine tanks. Indeed this region produces unimaginable quantities of wine. The region is also known for its Manchego cheese; after people, sheep are La Mancha's most important inhabitants.

"Winter and hell"

The high plateau is situated between the Tajo to the north and the foothills of the Sierra Morena to the south. It was the Moors who named this region *Manxa*, dry land. It rains very little here, with a yearly rainfall of 400 mm (15.7 ins). The summers are extremely hot. It has been known for the temperature to rise to 44°C (111°F) and above. The winters on the other hand can be bitingly cold, with frosts of −22°C (−7.6°F). This explains the expression used to describe La Mancha's climate: "nine months of winter and three months of hell". The soil of this gently rolling, rarely truly hilly region, is loamy and quite chalky. Sometimes the lime comes in the form of a stony substratum.

Europe's largest wine region

The wine region, which acquired its present shape in 1976, covers parts of four provinces: Albacete, Ciudad Real, Cuenca and Toledo. The vineyards cover some 170,000 ha (420,000 acres) which makes La Mancha Europe's largest wine region, even larger than the whole vineyard area of some of the smaller wineproducing countries. Wine is therefore produced here on a large scale. There are cooperatives whose members cultivate 10 to 15,000 hectares (25 to 37,000 acres) of vineyards and quite a few bodegas which produce between 15 and 20 million litres (3.3 and 4.4 million gals) of wine a year.

The largest proportion of vineyards are situated in the province of Ciudad Real (45 percent), followed by Toledo (25 percent), Cuenca (20 percent) and finally Albacete (10 percent). Even this last figure represents some 16 to 17,000 ha (40 to 42,000 acres) which is still more than the surface area of about 20 other Spanish DOs.

Brandy

The ocean of wine which La Mancha produces annually only goes in part to the consumer. Very large amounts are distilled and sent to Jerez to make brandy. La Mancha also produces industrial alcohol made from wine; Tomelloso has the largest distilling plant in the region. As a result of the dry climate, the large number of old vinestocks and the fact that there are relatively few vines per hectare, the yield in La Mancha is only 21 to 25 hl per ha (185 to 220 gals per acre). Irrigation would increase this figure considerably but the winegrowers are not interested. Increased production would lead to great problems, including a new wine lake within the EEC.

Airén

The fact that part of the harvest can be used to make brandy is due to the fact that La Mancha produces an enormous amount of white wine. Over three-quarters (around 77 percent) of the vines are of the white Airén grape variety. The remainder are mainly black grape varieties such as Cencibel (identical to the Tempranillo, with 17 percent) and Garnacha (6 percent). These figures have been rounded off to account for the fact that there are also very small amounts of white Macabeo, Pardilla and Verdoncho as well as blue Moravia and the increasingly popular Cabernet Sauvignon. With some 130,000 ha (321,000 acres) of Airén in La Mancha alone the latter is not only the most common grape variety in Spain but probably also in the world. Its grapes have a thick skin and the vines grow low and close to the ground in order to preserve the little moisture there is. In regions with a higher rainfall this would undoubtedly lead to rotting and various other problems, but in the very dry climate of La Mancha this could never happen. The exception was in 1989 when a large part of the harvest was lost because of mildew. As a rule the cooperative of Nuestro Padre Jesús del Perdón of Manzanares produces 14 to 15 million litres (3.1 to 3.3 million gals) of wine, but in 1989 production went down to 8 million litres (1.8 million gals).

Above: The famous windmills that Cervantes' Don Quixote tilted at.

Spectacular growth

People were already making wine in La Mancha as early as the Reconquest. This is clear from a document dating back to 1150 in which King Alfonso VII gives large parts of the region to the Order of the Templars while also referring to wine. The black grape varieties were probably brought to the region by French monks (*see also* chapter on Valdepeñas) which explains why La Mancha has been producing mainly red and light red wines, the so-called *claretes*, for centuries. These were the wines whose praises were sung by the Spanish authors of the sixteenth and seventeenth century. The references in Spanish literature to the wines of Ciudad Real, Manzanares and Membrilla are extremely complimentary, while Gabriel Téllez judges the wines of Ocaña "the best in Spain". Airén was already cultivated at the time – it was then known under the name of Lairén – but it was sometimes accused of producing wines lacking in strength. It was only in the twentieth century, after the phylloxera outbreak in 1900 and the ensuing crisis, that Airén was planted on a large scale. The acreage planted with Airén suddenly increased again in a spectacular fashion after the Civil War, and La Mancha started producing enormous quantities of cheap white wine. Madrid was a great consumer of these white wines. The wine writer José Peñin writes in a history of the region that it was quite common in the 1950s to see building workers in the capital with a bottle of white La Mancha and a straw so as to be able to drink straight from the bottle.

Giant amphoras

The white wine produced at the time had not much to recommend it. The grapes were usually picked too late in the season and then fermented at a temperature which was too high to be able to preserve the wine's fruit and freshness. Moreover the alcohol content was usually around 13 to 14 percent, which made the wine very soporific. *Tinajas*, giant amphoras made of clay, were usually used for the fermentation and storage of the wines. They are still very common in La Mancha and the surrounding regions as well as in Montilla-Moriles. These 3-m (10-ft) high containers which can hold between 3,000 and 7,000 litres (660 and 1,540 gal) are made from a special kind of clay, usually from around Villarrobledo. Rows of new *tinajas* can often be seen along the ringroad which by-passes the town. There are also concrete versions, but these are cylindrical in shape. In spite of the *tinajas'* long tradition many winegrowers have switched to stainless-steel fermentation tanks. This trend became firmly established in the 1980s when the storage capacity in stainless-steel tanks rose by tens of millions of litres. Producers also invested in modern cooling plants on a large scale. They were led to do so because the old-style Airén wine was becoming increasingly less acceptable to the consumer. The demand was for light, fresh wines with plenty of fruit. In La Mancha this could only be achieved by using modern equipment. Rodriguez & Berger were one of the early pioneers in the field. The grapes are picked earlier in the season in order to make the white wines less heavy than they used to be. Grape picking often starts at the end of August now instead of at the end of September. The more progressive bodegas now work with selected yeast cells, and are also blocking the malolactic fermentation in many white wines in order to achieve maximum freshness.

New thrust

All these developments have given La Mancha a new lease of life. The era of mindless mass production is now a thing of the past. The new-style white La Mancha wines are even beginning to win prizes in competitions as well as being extremely popular with the consumers. It often happens that they sell out before the new vintage arrives on the market, so that producers are left without reserves for several months. Further reflecting the growing self-confidence of La Mancha is the increasing production of sparkling wines. They too are made from Airén grapes, either on their own or blended with Macabeo. The technological developments in the science of winemaking have also resulted in better rosés such as Zagarrón, made from a must of black grapes and white which is an attractive, lightly fruity, fresh wine produced by the cooperative of Nuestra Señora de Manjavaces of Mota del Cuervo, a village with windmills.

Better quality red wines

Red wines have also improved enormously in quality. The wines destined for immediate consumption have gained in fruit and liveliness, and taste much nicer than those boring, heavy wines of the past. The better quality wines are made exclusively and mostly from Cencibel, sometimes by the method of *macération*

carbonique. More wines are now also matured in wood. Bodegas Fermín Ayuso of Villarrobledo was not only the first to produce red wine in this village but also the first in the whole of La Mancha to build an underground storage cellar which now contains some 7,000 *barricas.* This example was soon followed by other producers, such as the largest in the region, the Vinícola de Castilla in Manzanares which owns 2,500 casks.

Cabernet Sauvignon

While the Cencibel variety has been greatly improved during the past decades, La Mancha growers are also very interested in new varieties and more especially in Cabernet Sauvignon. Some producers have been experimenting with the latter for quite some time. Thus Bodegas Cueva del Granaro had already planted Cabernet Sauvignon as early as the beginning of the 1970s. But Fermín Ayuso, on the other hand, only experimented with it in 1990. Growers working with Cabernet Sauvignon do not always achieve the expected high quality, but the results are sufficiently encouraging to make it almost certain that this variety, merely tolerated up to now, will soon be allowed to join the DO.

Above: The desolation of La Mancha is occasionally relieved by a solitary farm, or castle.

Increasing bottling

La Mancha has always produced a lot of bulk wine. Even as recently as the late 1980s less than 30 percent of the production was sold in bottles. But in view of the great success of the new-style white wines and of the much improved rosés, the marketing prospects of bottled wine seem very promising. The number of producers with bottling capabilities is therefore increasingly steadily. Almost a quarter of the 415 producers have now the facilities to bottle their own wine and this figure will undoubtedly increase. Many privately-owned bodegas have invested in bottling plants, but the number of cooperatives who bottle their own wine is also increasing.

PRODUCERS OF SPECIAL INTEREST

Rodriguez & Berger 13720 Cinco Casas

Rodriguez & Berger was founded in 1919 near the station of Cinco Casas. It still belongs to the same families. Over 80 percent of their production consists of white wine which is made from bought-in grapes (first pressing only). Selected yeast cells are added when the must has cooled down. Afterwards fermentation takes place at a low temperature. Rodriguez & Berger are among the first producers to have used this process of winemaking. No malolactic fermentation takes place after the alcoholic fermentation has been completed. The Viña Santa Elena is the best among the white wines bottled by the bodega. They also produce a lot of white wine in bulk. Their customers (among whom are various English wine merchants) can buy their wine "made to measure". This is made possible by the fact that Rodriguez & Berger work with a large number of relatively small tanks. The red wine – which is also sold under their own label of Viña Santa Elena – is bought in a ready form and is slightly less lively than the white.

Bodegas Cueva del Granaro
16417 Los Hinojosos

The landscape east of Quintanar de la Orden is quite a lot hillier than in other regions of La Mancha. This is where you will find the estate of Cueva del Granaro which is of about 1,000 ha (2,500 acres). Some 500 ha (1,250 acres) are planted with vineyards, partly with young vines. It is expected that they will all be producing in the mid-1990s. The energetic, forward-looking owners have also planted new grape varieties such as Chardonnay (30 ha/74 acres), Merlot (40 ha/99 acres) and Cabernet Sauvignon (which they had already started planting in the 1970s, 120 ha/300 acres). They are also experimenting with Syrah, Ruby Cabernet (a cross between Carignan and Cabernet Sauvignon) and others. Only the old Airén vines have been preserved (134 ha/330 acres), and there is also some Cencibel (140 ha/345 acres). The company has invested in modern winemaking equipment and hopes that soon it will be able to bottle half its production. The wines are sold under the label of Cueva del Granaro. The wines are usually still young when they come onto the market. Both the red Cencibel and the Cabernet Sauvignon range from

Above: The Manjavacas cooperative is one of those that have invested heavily in modern equipment.

decent to good as far as quality is concerned. There is also a red *crianza* made from Cencibel, a firm, tannic wine which has been allowed to ripen in tank and bottle.

Cooperativa Nuestro Padre Jesús del Perdón 13200 Manzanares

The average quality of La Mancha wine would be significantly higher if all 100 or so cooperatives of La Mancha were as well equipped as this one. The white grapes produced on 8,250 ha (20,385 acres), 99 percent of which are Airén, are processed in their up-to-date installations. Half the production is free-run juice from the pressure of the weight of the fruit itself, and this is treated separately from the must obtained through pressing. The free-run juice is first cooled and cleaned. This company was the first in La Mancha to build specially tiled tanks for this purpose. Fermentation then takes place, at approximately 16°C (61°F). The first wine to be bottled is the white Lazarillo which is destined for immediate consumption, a fairly firm wine with fruit and freshness. It is often sold out after eight to nine months. They also make a delicious, tasty, fruity red which is sold under the same label. It too is bottled young. The most important range produced by this company is Yuntero. In character these wines are between the new and the old-style wines. The white is allowed to mature for about 18 months in tank and bottle. Its taste is clean and pleasant: an ordinary good wine. The regular red is also in that category. The Selección Limitada is left to mature for 30 months in the tank and 20 months in the bottle. It is the pride and joy of the 840 members of the cooperative: meaty

and well-rounded with a taste of soft fruit and a hint of brown in the colour. Only 20,000 bottles are produced. The company has bought 50 casks in order to study the effects of maturing in wood. Another brand which has not been mentioned is Casa la Teja.

Vinícola de Castilla 13200 Manzanares

This company which was founded in 1977 by the Rumasa Group is extremely efficient. The buildings are streamlined and modern; there is nothing romantic about the place. In 1982 it was taken over by a wealthy family who then expanded it. The cellars are very clean and equipped with the latest equipment, such as carpet presses for white wine and rotating stainless-steel tanks for red and rosé wines. Vinícola de Castilla have clearly shown that their methods of winemaking are ideal for producing good wine even with production figures of around 14 million litres (30 million gals) per year. The white and red wines of their Señorío de Guadianeja range (sometimes abbreviated to S & G) are among the best in La Mancha. The white has an extraordinarily clean taste with a remarkable freshness, lightness and charm. The red is characterized by a taste of noble wood with a firm, stimulating, slightly fruity taste. The wine is allowed to mature for 14 to 18 months in new casks made of American oak. Their Cabernet Sauvignon, sold under the same label, is also matured in wood (around 30,000 bottles). They also produce a cheaper range under the label of Castillo de Alhambra whose whites and reds are both very pleasant. The red (100 percent Cencibel) which is made by the

macération carbonique method is very supple, attractive with a hint of fruit; a small red. Their Finca Vieja and Gran Verdad ranges are slightly less interesting. The sparkling wines, marketed under the Cantares label, still lack the class and distinction of their still wines. Vinícola buys grapes from vineyard owners with whom it has long-standing agreements. The company is very successful both at home and abroad and is La Mancha's largest exporter.

Cooperativa Nuestra Señora de Manjavacas 16630 Mota del Cuervo

The village of Mota del Cuervo can be recognized miles away by the white windmills which overlook it from the hill above. The local cooperative which was founded in 1948 has specialized in new-style white wine and rosé. Old-style wines are still produced but these are usually sold in bulk. The white Zagarrón is fresh and light. The *rosado* of the same name has a definitely fruity taste. It is produced from the must of Airén and Cencibel, the black grapes being left in contact with the juice for 24 hours. The 2,200 members own some 8,000 ha (20,000 acres).

Bodegas Julián Santos Aguado 45800 Quintanar de la Orden

This family-owned bodega was founded way back in 1900. But it was mainly during the 1960s and 1970s that the company started to expand on a large scale when they bought 1,200 ha (30,000 acres) of vineyards. These now produce almost one-third of their requirement. This figure will soon increase as a result of the extra 500 ha (1,250 acres) the estate is about to acquire. This bodega has been bottling its wines since 1984. These have been of average quality up to now. The best of them is usually the *crianza* Don Fadrique which is allowed to mature in the cask for 12 months. The wine is velvety, with a firm body, and has a definite aroma of wood and vanilla.

Fermín Ayuso 502600 Villarrobledo

The very industrial-looking complex housing this bodega which was founded in 1947 is situated on the outskirts of the town. The Ayuso family have always had a progressive outlook towards the business. They were the first in Villarrobledo to produce red wine, the first in La Mancha to build an underground storage cellar for their casks and the first in the region to install a bottling plant. Almost the entire production of 15 million litres (3.3 million gals) is bottled; 40 to 50 percent of the production is red. The house markets its wines under several labels with and without DO such as Mirlo, Viña Q, Armiño, Don Nino, Ayuso, Castillo de Utrera and Estola. The latter is by far the strongest label, having greatly contributed to the bodega's serious reputation both at home and abroad. The cool-fermented white is pleasant with a good deal of freshness and fruit. The red is produced in two versions: the *reserva* (12 to 18 months in the cask) and the *gran reserva* (36 to 42 months in the cask). Fermín Ayuso has some 7,000 casks for this wine. They last around ten years and are made mostly of American oak. The *reserva* is usually a dark red, velvety, rather meaty wine with a taste of wood and delicate hint of fruit. The *gran reserva* has dark aroma and a riper taste, but is still lively. Both red Estola wines are made exclusively from Cencibel.

Bodegas Torres Filoso
Villarrobledo 02600
This family business, modest in La Mancha terms (it produces one million litres/220,000 gals), combines the modern techniques of winemaking with the classic *élevage* in wooden casks for red wines. This interesting approach produces a series of interesting wines. The Arboles de Castillejo (100 percent Cencibel) is among the better *reservas* of La Mancha, as is the Juan José (100 percent Cencibel), which is of limited availability. The Torres Filoso, velvety with a good aftertaste, is matured for a slightly shorter period and is usually made from 60 percent Cencibel, 30 percent Garnacha and 10 percent Airén. The white of the same name is a stimulating, new-style Airén wine of good quality. The house was founded in 1921.

Travel Information

Above: The formidable castle at Belmonte. This 15th-century stronghold is well-preserved both inside and out.

HOTELS AND RESTAURANTS

Ercilla Don Quijote, 13600 Alcázar de San Juan, tel (26) 543800 Rather homely hotel providing adequate comfort, while the Sancho restaurant is probably the best around. Serves both regional and Basque dishes.
Parador, 13270 Almagro, tel (26) 860100 This magnificent *parador* to the southwest of the town is housed in a former Franciscan convent. The restaurant specializes in regional cuisine.
Granada, 13200 Manzanares, tel (26) 610400 Rather modern building, slightly outside town (on the south side). The rooms are good, but the "grand buffet" formula offered by the restaurant lacks a certain culinary finesse.
Venta de Quichote, 13650 Puerto Lápice, tel (26) 576110 This large but atmospheric restaurant is strongly geared to tourism. In spite of this their typically Castilian dishes are delicious.
Hotel Castillo, 02600 Villarrobledo, tel (67) 143311 Modern, nice, homely but dull.
Ideal, 02600 Villarrobledo, tel (67) 140009 Situated close to the central square (and near a parking garage). Serves lamb, partridge and other regional dishes, as well as Manchego cheese. Has a bar too.

PLACES OF INTEREST

Alcázar de San Juan The archaeological museum of Fray Juan Cobo houses a collection of Roman mosaics while the Torre de Don Juan de Austria has become a heraldic museum. Some parts of the church of Santa María la Mayor date back to the thirteenth century. Slightly to the south of the town – where the *Consejo Regulador* also has their headquarters – are several windmills.
Almagro Town of Roman origin. In the sixteenth century a university was founded here whose main building has beautiful carvings. The Plaza Mayor is one of the most beautiful and remarkable in the whole of Castillà-La Mancha. It is oblong in shape and is lined on two sides by stone columns supporting wooden façades pierced with many windows. At number 11 you will be able to visit the rectangular-shaped Corral de Comedias, Spain's oldest theatre, still in use (it also houses a museum). Equally worth a visit is the Convento de Calatrava.
Belmonte The village is overlooked by an imposing fifteenth-century citadel, flanked by two round towers, built on a hill. It is well preserved and has beautifully decorated ceilings. The Gothic parish church also dates

back to the fifteenth century (interesting chapels and paintings). Many dwellings in Belmonte are adorned with coats of arms.
Campo de Criptana It is said that Don Quixote fought his famous battle near the white windmills of this extraordinarily charming village. It is also the home of Spain's first cooperative which was founded in 1901 and which still exists today.
Ciudad Real This town of almost 52,000 inhabitants was founded in 1255, straddling the boundary between the Moorish and Christian civilizations. The Moorish influence is clearly visible in the Puerta de Toledo. This gate was part of the fourteenth-century walls which surrounded the city. The Gothic cathedral of María del Prado (fifteenth century) is one of the rare ones with one nave only. Even older is the church of San Pedro where you will be able to admire the beautiful tomb of the precentor Coca. The palace of the Diputación Provincial houses a collection of paintings by La Mancha artists.
Consuegra The ruins of a twelfth-century castle and several windmills dominate the village. There are many potters in Consuegra, but the village is even more famous for its saffron. This incredibly expensive

spice is picked each autumn when the purple crocus is in bloom.

Daimiel Beautiful arcades along the Plaza Mayor as well as two ancient churches, that of Santa María (fourteenth century) and that of San Pedro (sixteenth century). To the north-west is Parque Nacional de las Tablas de Daimiel where you will be able to see many waterbirds.

Horcajo de Santiago In the church there are paintings by an unknown fourteenth-century artist known as the "Master of Horcajo".

Manzanares Busy, small town with pretty Plaza Mayor. Its parish church, Nuestra Señora de Altagracia, dates back in part to the fourteenth century. There is also a thirteenth-century castle, that of Pilas Bornas.

Mota del Cuervo Overlooked by hill with windmills, one of them very ancient. Parts of the thirteenth-century parish church are in the Mudéjar style.

Puerto Lápice This is where Don Quixote is said to have been knighted. More windmills, Roman ruins and a very popular restaurant serving regional cuisine.

Ruidera Village built along the Lagunas de Ruidera, a series of small lakes stretching over 60 km (37 miles). In summer this is a very popular holiday resort.

El Toboso The local Cervantes Museum takes great pride in its collection of 400 editions of *Don Quixote*, translated into 30 languages.

Villarrobledo Small town rather lacking in personality. In the Plaza Mayor stand the late sixteenth century *ayuntamiento* and the church of San Blas which has a beautiful main altar. The ring road to the southwest of the town is often lined with rows of newly-made *tinajas*; the clay of Villarrobledo is used to make these enormous amphoras.

WINE ROUTE

The suggested route covers mainly the central and most interesting part of La Mancha. The route will take you not only through the important wine-producing towns and villages but also through places of more general interest to the tourist. Thus you will see many of La Mancha's famous windmills. You can easily continue the trip from Almagro, Manzanares and La Solana by following the Valdepeñas route.

Above: White-walled country dwelling on La Mancha's winegrowing plain.

Above: Almagro's fine town square, lined with stone columns, is one of the most notable in all Castilla-La Mancha.

Valdepeñas

The wine region of Valdepeñas is totally encircled by that of La Mancha except along its southern border, and in fact for a long time it belonged to La Mancha. It only became independent in 1968 although the region and its wines have been known under their own name for much longer. It is said that the town was founded by the mother of Ferdinand III, Doña Beringuela from Navarra, who also gave it its name. She called it Valdepeñas after the surrounding countryside: the name is derived from *val de peñas*, valley of rocks. The town was placed under the authority of the monastic order of Calatrava. The Cistercians used as their headquarters the castle of Calatrava, near Calzada de Calatrava, and it was probably the monks who first brought the black grapes to the region.

Influence of the court

Winegrowing developed both in quantity and quality under the Order of Calatrava, who ruled the region until 1582. In the reign of Philip II and his successors the court at Madrid was a great consumer of Valdepeñas wine, a taste which was shared by the inhabitants of the capital. This is what led Charles III to levy a duty on it during the second half of the eighteenth century; the income was used to finance the building of monuments in Madrid.

When Spain fought the War of Independence against the French in 1808 Valdepeñas put up a brave resistance, suffering severe losses; but Manzanares (La Mancha), 30 km (19 miles) to the north, surrendered without a fight. The inhabitants of Manzanares are still known disparagingly as "the French" by the people of Valdepeñas.

The nineteenth-century English traveller Richard Ford visited Valdepeñas and has nothing but praise for its wine. He also mentions a Dutchman called Muller who made wine so expensive that the furious inhabitants raided his cellars and nearly killed him. *Clarete*, a light red wine made from black and white grapes, has been a speciality of Valdepeñas for centuries. However, they have also long produced true red wines: thus in 1840 the French author Théophile Gautier mentions a wine whose colour was as rich as blackberry syrup.

After the railroad from Valdepeñas to Madrid was opened in 1861, sales to the capital increased spectacularly; Luis Palacios, the largest wine producer in Valdepeñas, sent a train with 25 trucks loaded with wine to Madrid every day. The wine region of Valdepeñas was in fact extremely prosperous from this period up to the Spanish Civil War. This is clearly reflected in the fact that at least 62 newspapers were published in the town of Valdepeñas between 1885 and 1936. Moreover, the town had electricity installed in 1906, the telephone very soon after and in 1925 their drinking water system. Phylloxera invaded the vineyards here as elsewhere in 1911, but because of their large reserves this region suffered less than others. The capital still drinks a lot of Valdepeñas; Luis Megía alone sells 1,600 cases a day.

Present DO

The present *denominación de origen* comprises 10 communes covering altogether 34,600 ha (85,500 acres) of vineyards. A large part of these, 60 percent, are situated within Valdepeñas itself. The vines are usually planted on flat terrain at an altitude of 700 to 750 m (2,300 to 2,500 ft). It is only in the south of the region that the vineyards take on a more rolling aspect. The colour of the soil

ranges from sandy to rusty brown; the subsoil often contains loam and sometimes clayish sand. The climate of Valdepeñas is rather similar to that of La Mancha, which is of a continental type: during summer the temperature can rise to over 40°C (104°F), while in very severe winters it goes down to −10°C (14°F). The rainfall is on average around 400 mm (16 ins), but there have been years when the rainfall has been much higher, such as in 1979, when the Jabalón – which crosses the region from east to west – overflowed and flooded many cellars in Valdepeñas.

Increased planting of Cencibel

Only two grape varieties may be used in the production of Valdepeñas wine, white Airén and black Cencibel (which is another name for Tempranillo). The Airén variety is the most prevalent of the two with 85 percent of the planting. This predominance of Airén will however gradually diminish, since the new planting programme only allows the use of Cencibel. The percentage of Cencibel has risen considerably (by about half) during the 1980s as a result, and the trend is continuing. This is of vital importance for Valdepeñas because the region produces mainly red wines. In order to be able to satisfy the demand for red wine, some 3,000 tonnes (2,950 tons) of Cencibel had to be "imported" from elsewhere during the period 1989-1990. This decision was taken by the *Consejo Regulador* with a majority of votes, but still caused quite a stir. While most producers have to fight for Cencibel, some of them have plenty. The wine producers

Above: An old tinaja *is a landmark in this vineyard.*

Casa de la Viña, for instance, own vineyards covering almost 1,000 ha (2,500 acres) planted with this variety, thereby dominating one-fifth of the total production. And over two-thirds of the 270 ha (670 acres) which the Domaine Pozo Blanco will have in production in the mid-1990s will be planted with Cencibel.

The *Consejo Regulador* is considering the possibility of allowing other grape varieties, such as Cabernet Sauvignon. Bodegas Los Llanos has planted 20 ha (50 acres) with this variety, the Casa de la Viña 10 ha (25 acres) and Bodegas Espinosa has already brought a pure (but not brilliant) Cabernet to market. Félix Solís has also been experimenting with Cabernet Sauvignon as well as with white Macabeo. The Casa de la Viña have also planted some Pinot Noir and Merlot, while the Domaine Pozo Blanco has some Garnacha and Aragon.

White wines

Until early 1990 55 percent of all wine produced in Valdepeñas was white. Many producers have invested in modern equipment in order to make this wine as refreshing and fruity as possible. Stainless steel fermentation tanks are now being used as well as the older concrete vats and the traditional *tinajas*. Bodegas Luis Megía have been real pioneers in the cool fermentation of white wine. The Marqués de Gastaña produced by this firm is in fact among the better white wines of this kind. It has been subjected to

malolactic fermentation, but Félix Solís does not use this process for its Viña Albali. Quite often Airén grapes are picked earlier than usual in order to produce more acid in the wine. In spite of all this even the most successful whites remain merely average, middle-of-the-range wines. This can be explained by the fact that the Airén grape variety is not of truly noble character. For this reason it is good that Valdepeñas is concentrating increasingly on black grapes and red wine. Rosé wines are not particularly important in Valdepeñas and make up only three percent of the total production. This is to be expected since *clarete*, which is closely related to rosé, is still produced in large quantities.

Clarete

As in the past *clarete* is made from black as well as white grapes. It is illegal to mix together the wines so produced, but the regulations do allow the juices of both kinds of grapes to be blended, and this takes place before fermentation. The mixture must contain at least 20 percent Cencibel. A typical *clarete* from Valdepeñas is a supple, gently refreshing, light red wine which is easy to drink and does not cost much. It is eminently suitable as an ordinary table wine or for drinking in bars and pubs. Ordinary red Valdepeñas, which contains a very high percentage of Cencibel, has rather more colour, strength and personality. The bulk of the production is bottled when young and is destined for immediate consumption. The various Valdepeñas wines can in fact differ quite a lot, ranging from rather dull to very fruity and lively. Surprisingly, even the better wines are still in the lower price range.

Both the *Consejo Regulador* and the large producers find this too narrow a base to build up the reputation and identity of Valdepeñas wines, certainly compared with the much larger wine region of La Mancha. This is why during the 1980s winegrowers concentrated increasingly on wines matured in wood, rather than on wines for immediate consumption. Naturally this was only possible with large-scale investment in casks. Luis Megía still uses second-hand sherry casks, while also experimenting with small French *barriques*. At Félix Solís they had to make room for an extra 1,000 casks on top of the thousands they already had. The La Invencible cooperative (which bottles almost 20 percent of all Valdepeñas), the Casa de la Viña, Visan and Bodegas Aranda own several hundred casks. But it is the Bodegas Los Llanos which owns by far the largest number of barrels. Some 12,000 casks are stored in the imposing underground cellars of this establishment, thereby providing the most important facilities in Castilla-La Mancha for storage in wood.

The arrival of *crianzas*, *reservas* and even *gran reservas* has added a new dimension to the range of Valdepeñas wines. Here too, as in other wine regions in Spain, it appears that the wine made from the Cencibel grape has a good resistance to oxidization, which makes it possible for the wine to mature in casks for a longer period. The problem (or art) for the bodegas is to find the right balance between the quantities of second-hand and new casks used by them (there is also a financial aspect here) as well the correct duration of the period of maturation. Indeed, in the case of excessively long maturation the taste of wood will dominate at the expense of the fruit. Thus the *gran reserva* Pata Negra produced by Los Llanos has a lot more class – and fruit – than the Señorío also produced by them because the former matures for a shorter time in wood. Compared to other wood-matured wines those of Valdepeñas are very reasonably priced. This gives the region a serious advantage on the market, both abroad and in Spain.

Above: The square Plaza de Toros of Las Virtudes is one of the oldest in the country.

PRODUCERS OF SPECIAL INTEREST

Domaine Pozo Blanco 13345 Cózar

When this vineyard was taken over by three Frenchmen and one Spaniard in 1968 it covered 40 ha (100 acres) planted with Airén and interspersed with olive trees. They pulled up almost all the existing vines and replaced them with Cencibel. They then started on a large-scale planting programme. The owners hope that by the mid-1990s they will have almost 270 ha (670 acres) in production, of which 180 (450) will be Cencibel (100 ha/250 acres with older vines, 80/200 with young plants). The other varieties are Airén (11 ha/27 acres), Garnacha and Aragon. The last two are tolerated by the *Consejo Regulador*. Winemaking is approached in a very scientific way under the guidance of an oenologist from Bordeaux. The bodega only produces wine for immediate consumption. The best is Finca Corlita, a pure Cencibel with an aroma of berries, a meaty, clean taste and slightly tannic. It is always made from grapes from a particular spot, with relatively old stocks. The ordinary Valdepeñas is also successful. It is a supple, firm wine with a very pleasant aftertaste which contains 70 percent Cencibel, 10 percent Airén and 20 percent Garnacha plus some Aragón. The estate markets its wine under different brand names among which are El Pozo, Pozo Blanco, Bodega Castillo la Serna and Bodega Corlita. Production could still increase considerably because the whole estate now covers 660 ha (1,630 acres).

Visan 13730 Santa Cruz de Mudela

Limpieza, limpieza, limpieza (Cleanliness, cleanliness, cleanliness) reads a board near the cellars of this domaine – thereby underlining the importance of hygiene in the making of good wine. These cellars are situated near an old, somewhat run-down but very picturesque quarter of the town. The bodega makes decent wine produced mainly from grapes from their own vineyards (165 ha/410 acres) which provide 60 percent of the grapes. Top of the range are two *reservas* both made exclusively from Cencibel: Castillo de Calatrava which matures only in the bottle while Villa del Duque is left to mature in the casks (the house has 250 to 300 *barricas*). The former is relatively fresh and elegant, while the latter is slightly more complex. All Visan wines are made exclusively from Cencibel. Bodegas Castillo de Mudela, Viñedos y Bodegas San Miguel and Bodegas Morenito all belong to the same group.

Casa de la Viña 13240 La Solana

Undoubtedly the most important estate in Valdepeñas, boasting the largest planting of the Cencibel grape, with 950 ha (2,350 acres) out of 1,000 ha (2,470 acres) cultivated by the estate. Up to 1986 most of these grapes were sent to other producers. But in 1987 the group Bodegas y Bebidas took over the estate, since when the harvest has been processed on the spot. The group invested in a large number of stainless-steel fermentation tanks as well as the necessary cooling systems. The cellars too were enlarged in order to provide sufficient space for casks, a bottling plant and storage of bottles. The quality of their wines ranges from good to very good, especially from 1986 onwards (although the 1985 *reserva* Casa de la Viña was already delicious). The older wines which are still on the market at the moment have a rich and pleasing taste; but what we are really waiting for are the *crianzas* and *reservas* produced under the new management. The bodega markets its wines under three names: Señorío de Val (red and white wines for drinking young), Vega de Moriz (red, rosé and white wines for drinking young plus a red *reserva*) and Casa de la Viña (special selections of *crianza* and *reserva*). The rather isolated estate is definitely worth a visit because Bodegas y Bebidas, in spite of their heavy investment in modern plant, have left the actual appearance of

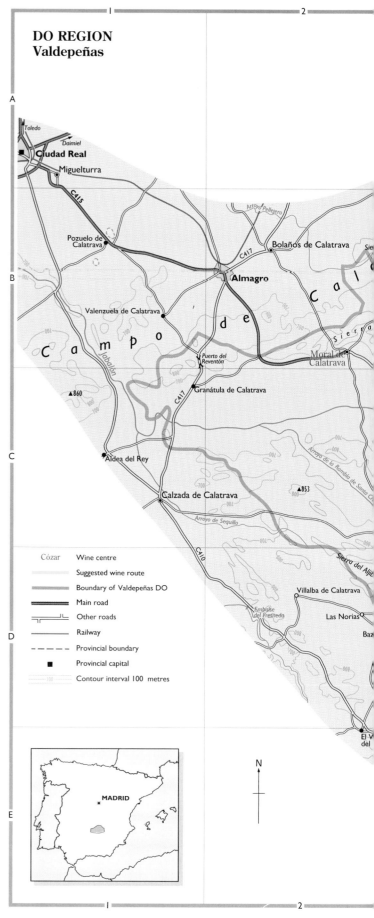

DO REGION
Valdepeñas

Cózar	Wine centre
	Suggested wine route
	Boundary of Valdepeñas DO
	Main road
	Other roads
	Railway
	Provincial boundary
■	Provincial capital
	Contour interval 100 metres

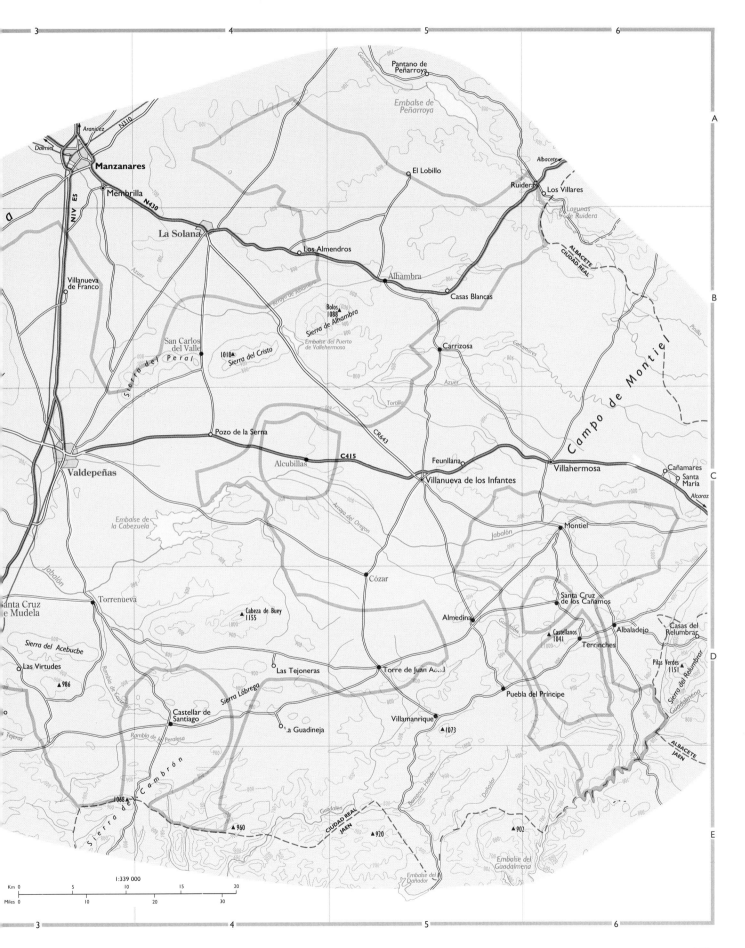

Km
1:339 000

Km 0   5   10   15   20
Miles 0   10   20   30

the ancient bodega untouched, so that both the small and large inner courtyards still retain the atmosphere of times gone by. The estate of almost 2,900 ha (7,170 · acres) also provides grazing lands for 2,000 sheep, as well as shooting for the family and friends of Bodegas y Bebidas in the hilly parts of the domaine in season.

Cooperativa La Invencible 13300 Valdepeñas

The 220 or so members of this cooperative cultivate about 9,000 ha (22,240 acres) of vineyard. The production represents about one-fifth of the entire region's output. In this cooperative the wine is still partly fermented in *tinajas*: a most impressive sight. The wine may be stored either in concrete and metal tanks or in 300 casks which the cooperative also owns. The wines are of average quality, supple and straightforward without much character. The red Viña Lastra is made up of 50 percent Cencibel and 50 percent Airén, while the red Valdeazor is made exclusively of Cencibel, the skins of which are only allowed to ferment for 24 hours with it.

Bodegas Félix Solís 13300 Valdepeñas

This large family business founded in 1945 is situated to the west of Valdepeñas and is distinguished by its large number of tanks. This bodega has a total storage capacity of over 40 million litres (10.6 million gals). They buy in grapes, must and wine while their own vineyards of 1,300 ha (3,200 acres) yield about 20 percent of the grapes. The plant is modern. The standard quality red and white Valdepeñas are sold under the brand names of Los Molinos and Soldepeñas. Los Molinos is usually the more robust of the two. The quality improves further in the Viña Albali range; the *reservas* are stored in casks in a special cellar elsewhere in the town. White Viña Albali is a fresh, clear-tasting, rather light product: a pleasant spring and summer wine. It is made with grapes which have been picked relatively early in the season. The red *reserva* (7 to 10 months in barrels) is a full-bodied wine with plenty of American oak, a dark aroma and velvety taste. They sometimes also make a *gran reserva*. Their more general range of wines are marketed under a variety of brand names such as Bonus, Rucio, Cerro de los Pastores, Viña Grand Chaparral and Diego de Almagro. A subsidiary company of Félix Solís produces *vino de mesa*

exclusively; it is called Bodegas Cruzares.

Bodegas Los Llanos 13300 Valdepeñas

The old buildings of this establishment which was founded in 1875 are situated in Valdepeñas itself and now house only a museum. The wine is made in a large complex on the outskirts of the town, not far from Félix Solís. Since 1973 it has been owned by the Cosecheros 'Abastecedoros group. This limited company has invested substantially in Los Llanos, which now concentrates on producing quality wines.

The pride and joy of the bodega is an imposing underground cellar which contains around 12,000 barrels. This firm was also one of the first in the region to use casks on a large scale. 10 to 15 percent of the grapes come from their own vineyards which cover 250 ha (620 acres); this proportion will increase. 20 ha (50 acres) are planted with Cabernet Sauvignon. The house has specialized in *reservas* and *gran reservas* matured in wood. The *reserva* Señorío de los Llanos is a supple, well-rounded wine, slightly rustic and characterized by overtones of wood. The velvety *gran reserva* is a ripe, well-balanced wine with a taste of cherries, having more distinction and firmness than the *reserva*. Even fruitier is the *gran reserva* Pata Negra which matures for a shorter time in the barrel. They also produce white and rosé wines which are marketed under the name Señorío de los Llanos, but they are not so good as the red. In addition the company produces two ranges of more ordinary wines

under the brand names Don Opas and Toreo, while Armonioso is the name of a young white wine. Los Llanos use mainly stainless-steel fermentation tanks and other up-to-date plant for their vinification.

Bodegas Luis Megía 13300 Valdepeñas

The buildings of this bodega are spread throughout the town. Luis Megía have always concentrated on the home market (namely Madrid) but have recently started to export. Not owning any vineyards themselves they buy in grapes for 90 percent of their production, the remaining 10 being bought as wine. The house was the first producer in Valdepeñas to experiment with cool fermentation, in 1970. The white and rosé wines produced for immediate consumption are made in this way. The white Marqués de Gastañaga is a lively, fresh, beautiful wine of such quality that the *Consejo Regulador* has used it as a benchmark for tastings. The red wines of the same name are at their best one year after the harvest. The most prestigious red wines are the Duque de Estrada *reserva* and *gran reserva*, two succulent, meaty wines with a gentle freshness; the *gran reserva* is the more rounded of the two. Two-year-old wines are marketed under the name of Tenorio and three-year-old wines under that of Luis Megía. The semi-sweet and white is sold under the name of Isolero. Since 1989 the bodega has been owned by Collins, a Spanish company with a few French shareholders. Luis Megía was founded in 1946.

Travel Information

HOTELS AND RESTAURANTS

Parador, 13270 Almagro. *See* La Mancha.
Parador, 13200 Manzanares. *See* La Mancha.
La Aguzadera, N4 in a northerly direction, 13300 Valdepeñas, tel (26) 323208 This restaurant specializes in regional dishes, some of them very traditional.
El Baviera, Calle 6 de Junio 30, 13300 Valdepeñas, tel (26) 324050 Restaurant above a bar (where you can eat good *tapas*) serving delicious lamb and rabbit dishes.
Hotel Gala, Arpa 3, 13300 Valdepeñas, tel (26) 323857 Central but peaceful location, simple hotel. Also has a restaurant.
Meliá El Hidalgo, N4 in a northerly direction, 13300 Valdepeñas, tel (26) 323254 Motel complex with slightly rustic-looking but comfortable (and expensive) rooms. The restaurant has a good reputation for its regional food, but lacks atmosphere.
Melody, Calle 6 de Junio 26, 13300 Valdepeñas, tel (26) 320021 Old-

fashioned eating-house. Regional food.
Molino El Gobernador, N4 in a northerly direction, 13300 Valdepeñas, tel (26) 320757 Old converted mill. Serves country dishes.
El Tigre, El Peral (hamlet on the road to La Solana), 13300 Valdepeñas, tel (26) 325000 Good restaurant. Cuisine with occasional French overtones: the owner has a French wife.

PLACES OF INTEREST

Alhambra This village (its name simply means 'fortified place') has the remains of a Moorish castle.
Calzada de Calatrava To the southwest of this village, along the CR504, lie the ruins of the castle of Calatrava and the convent of the same name. It is from here that the monastic order of the Cistercians ruled over Valdepeñas for several centuries.
San Carlos del Valle The

eighteenth-century Plaza Mayor was designed by Charles III's architects. Near it stands a baroque church with round towers.

Santa Cruz de Mudela Village founded by the crusaders with a very old Plaza de Toros and a sixteenth-century parish church. Running parallel to the road to Torrenueva (but before you get to the station) is a wide road with low houses; at the end of it you will find the Visan wine producers.

La Solana Spacious, pretty, church square surrounded by arcades. Even the fifteenth-century church has arcades, high on its facade. The estate of the Casa de la Viña is situated between La Solana and Villanueva de los Infantes, a few kilometres beyond a small reservoir.

Valdepeñas Along the various roads leading to this small town of 25,000 inhabitants stand bodegas with a whole network of underground cellars beneath them. The northern approach along the N4 is a wide road lined by *tinajas* (Avenida de Tinajas). North of this is a building where the tourist can go for information, wine and cheese. On the south side stands an imposing white mill which houses a museum where the work of the local painter Gregorio Prieto may be admired.

More paintings and sculptures as well as curiosities are exhibited at the town's museum. The centre of Valdepeñas is the Plaza de España which is dominated by the partly Gothic church of the Ascunción. In the square itself there is a fountain depicting winemaking. The buildings of the old Los Llanos bodega now house the wine museum.

North of the town is a monument built on a hill dating from the time of Franco (who was not very popular with the local people), while to the south there is a white mill built on top of the San Cristobal hill.

Villanueva de los Infantes Village with many historical buildings and a square in the Renaissance style. The parish church in this square is late Gothic. There are also three convents in this village as well as the tomb of the poet and satirist Francisco Gómez Quevedo (1580-1645).

Las Virtudes Here is one of the oldest square Plazas de Toro in the country (1641).

El Viso del Marqués The castle of the Marqués de Santa Cruz which has beautiful painted ceilings also houses the archives of the Spanish navy.

WINE ROUTE

Because the roads of Valdepeñas do not follow the borders of the wine region exactly, there are some places and villages on the route (such as La Solana and Villanueva de los Infantes) which are part of the La Mancha wine region. El Viso del Marqués is in fact in neither of the two wine regions. However the proposed circuit will give an excellent impression of the Valdepeñas wine region, its countryside and interesting villages.

Above: Castle ruins at Calatrava. Monks from the monastery there were probably the first to plant black grapes in this district.

Almansa

The tall rock 1,200 m (3,400 ft) high which dominates the town of Almansa and the surrounding countryside has played a decisive role in the history of this region. During the Moorish occupation the Arabs built a citadel on the steep rockface where several battles and engagements were fought. Jaime I drove off the Moors in 1233, but in 1265 the king was forced to dislodge them from their stronghold again. During the centuries that followed the castle had several owners, including the Order of Templars. The castle was rebuilt in the fifteenth century after being damaged during a siege. In 1707, during the War of Spanish Succession, the Battle of Almansa ended in a victory for the Bourbon dynasty, thereby giving the Spanish throne to Philip V. Present-day Almansa is a small, peaceful provincial town with some 20,000 inhabitants and a small amount of industry. The castle, which lost all military connections a long time ago, was declared a public monument in 1921 by royal decree.

Wines in bulk

Winegrowing around Almansa probably dates back to the sixteenth century and has developed steadily ever since. This wine region, at an altitude of 700 m (2,300 ft), is the most easterly of Castilla-La Mancha and is closer to the wine zones of the Levante than to those of Valdepeñas and La Mancha. Moreover, it also borders on Jumilla and Yecla, two Levantine regions. This is why the winegrowers of Almansa have always had close contacts with the merchants on the coast, such as those from Tarragona. Consequently the bulk of the wine produced in Almansa was not made for drinking in its natural state but for blending with other wines. This is still the case today. In recent years only one firm, Bodegas Piqueras, has bottled wine on a consistent basis. There are two other bodegas which also sell bottled wine but these date back respectively to the late 1980s and to more than a decade ago. The winegrowers are just not interested, so that the production is almost exclusively of wine in bulk. They have no problem in selling all their grapes and there is no mention of any surplus.

Terrain

The DO, which dates back to 1975, consists of nine communes covering some 7,600 ha (18,800 acres) of vineyards. The soil is very rich in lime with some clay here and there. The climate of Almansa is slightly less extreme than that of La Mancha but the summers are still very hot and the temperature can easily rise to 40°C (104°F). The rainfall is only 400 mm (15.75 ins) per annum. Most of the vineyards are situated on flat terrain, although vines are sometimes seen growing on the surrounding mountain slopes. The most commonly cultivated variety is Monastrell, which is much more characteristic of the Levantine regions (such as Jumilla and Yecla) than of Castilla-La Mancha. About half the vines are of that variety. Traditionally Monastrell has always been blended with Almansa's second most common variety, Garnacha Tintorera, which represents around 35 percent of the vines planted. It is this variety which gives most Almansa wines

Below: Almansa vineyards are generally on fairly flat terrain.

their particular character and which makes them so attractive to the merchants on the coast.

Garnacha Tintorera

Garnacha Tintorera produces wines with a dark, opaque colour, and is one of the few black grape varieties with coloured flesh. It makes wines with a strong flavour, a lot of tannin and high alcohol content and little acid. On their own they are undrinkable but they are ideally suited for strengthening lighter wines – even after having been mixed with Monastrell. It is important not to leave the grapes of this particular Garnacha variety too long on the vine because otherwise they tend to fall from the stems. That is why the harvest usually takes place towards the end of September and beginning of October. In order to secure the future of the Almansa DO, the *Consejo Regulador* has decreed that more wine should be bottled. This explains why the planting of Cencibel or Tempranillo is now taking place. Chairman Mario Bonete (of Bodegas Piqueras) has given the lead to other winegrowers by using mainly Cencibel for his own red wines. Moreover the *Consejo* is also trying to persuade the growers to produce wines with a lower alcohol content, such as 12 to 12.5 percent rather than the usual 14 to 15 percent.

The efforts to improve the overall quality of the wine has not been in vain, with the quantity of Cencibel already around 15 percent and probably still rising. The *Consejo* recommends that bottled wine should contain a majority of Cencibel plus a certain amount of Monastrell and Garnacha Tintorera. According to Mario Bonete there should be no more than 10 percent Garnacha at the most. His own wines usually consist of 65 percent Cencibel, 25 percent Monastrell and 10 percent Garnacha Tintorera. Considering the great success of the Bodegas Piqueras wines it is amazing that the other producers have not followed suit. But the situation can still change – if only to ensure the survival of the Almansa DO.

PRODUCERS OF SPECIAL INTEREST

Bodegas Piqueras Almansa 02640 Bodegas Piqueras are the only wine producers to have given the Almansa DO a character of its own as a result of the impressive quality of their bottled wine. Their buildings are situated in a rather anonymous-looking street, not far from the centre.

This company, which dates back to 1915, has no land of its own but has entered into an agreement with several growers, who together cultivate almost 40 ha (100 acres). Bodegas Piqueras stipulate when the harvest must start, which is earlier than usual in order to avoid wines with an excessively high alcohol content. To produce their wine Mario Bonete and his well-schooled son Juan Pablo buy in 65 percent of Cencibel, 25 percent of Monastrell and 10 percent of Garnacha Tintorera. From 1991 the fermentation of these grapes is taking place partly in stainless-steel tanks.

The bodega has specialised in wines matured in wood. They have invested in 1,500 casks which they bought in Catalonia. Instead of the usual 225 litres (50 gals) these casks hold 300 litres (66 gals) which the Bonetes prefer. The wood is American oak. The largest cask is in fact not used for storing wine but as a tasting room.

Castillo de Almansa is the name under which the *crianza* is marketed. The wine is supple, not too heavy, with an almost velvety taste, a hint of freshness, some wood, ripe fruit (especially berries) and a good balance. The *reserva* of the same name is firmer in structure, with a stronger taste and hints of spices and chocolate as well as berries. Both the *reserva* and the *crianza* are usually allowed to mature for some 18 months in cask. For the *reserva* Marius this period has been reduced to 14 to 15 months – which seems very good for the wine. It is more succulent and lively than the Castillo de Almansa, with sufficient wood and vanilla and a hint of a toasted flavour.

Above: Almansa's imposing castle, and the Palacio de los Condes de Cirat.

is the Palacio de los Condes de Cirat – also known as Casa Grande – with a superb baroque façade. A few kilometres to the west of Almansa is the Embalse de Almansa, which is the oldest reservoir in Spain and dates back to 1348.

Alpera Slightly to the north of this wineproducing village are prehistoric caves with coloured rock paintings. One of these caves is known as the *Cueva de la Vieja*.

Chinchilla de Monte Aragón Old, very picturesque village built at the foot of a rock which contains many cave dwellings and on top of which stands a castle. The splendid elegance of the buildings clearly reflect the town's importance in the past; it had even been the capital of the province. The *ayuntamiento* was completed at the end of the sixteenth century.

Travel information

HOTELS AND RESTAURANTS

Parador de la Mancha, N 301, 02006 Albacete, tel (67) 229450 Rather boring appearance but peaceful location – and on the right side of the equally uninteresting Albacete to visit Almansa. Also has a restaurant.

Mesón de Pincelín, Calle Las Norias 10, 02640 Almansa, tel (67) 340007 Typical regional cuisine including *gazpacho manchego* and fresh fish dishes. The wines of Bodegas Piqueras may be sampled here.

Los Rosales, 02640 Almansa, tel (67) 340750 Travellers' hotel-restaurant with bar. Presently situated on the by-pass, but might move to a new location on the motorway.

PLACES OF INTEREST

Albacete Large but not particularly picturesque country town of around 100,000 inhabitants. It is known for its knife and scissor industry as well as for its artichokes and saffron. The Museo Arqueológico Provincial houses a large collection of prehistoric and Roman antiquities.

Almansa The fifteenth-century castle, built on top of the Mugrón, lies to the east of the town, only a few streets away from the centre. Next to the castle stands the parish church of Santa María de la Ascunción which has a magnificent Renaissance portal. Near the church

WINE ROUTE

The Almansa countryside is not particularly beautiful, nor are there many places of interest to visit; and of course there is a near-absence of bottling bodegas. But it is possible though to find a pleasant route to visit the region.

Starting in Almansa you take the C3212 in a southwesterly direction towards Montealegre del Castillo (ruins of a castle) and then turn right towards the wineproducing village of Bonete. In Bonete you go in a westerly direction towards Pétrola and then through Horna to Estación de Chinchilla. A few kilometres to the west rises the rock on which Chinchilla de Monte Aragón has been built and which is certainly worth a visit.

From Chinchilla follow the N430 in the direction of Almansa and then left towards Higueruela where almost all the vineyards are planted with Garnacha Tintorera. Then on to Alpera via Casillas, north of which are some prehistoric caves. Finally from Alpera back to Almansa. You can continue towards Jumilla and Yecla which are to the south of Almansa.

Levante

Capital: Valencia
Provinces: Alicante, Castellón, Murcia (*autonomía*), Valencia
Area: 34,622 square kilometres
Population: 4,786,287

Levante, which stretches along the east coast of Spain, consists of two *autonomías*, those of Murcia and Valencia. The former corresponds with the province of the same name; the latter is made up of Alicante, Castellón, and Valencia. As in Cataluña, many different peoples have established themselves in this region, among them the Phoenicians, Greeks (who founded Valencia), Romans, Visigoths and Moors. It was the legendary El Cid who temporarily won back Valencia from the Moors, and ruled there for five years, until his death in 1099. Both Murcia and Valencia have been kingdoms, springing from earlier Islamic domains. The Moorish influence persisted for some time in Murcia, which is why the regional dialect contains so many Arabic words. Valencia was part of the kingdom of Aragón and Cataluña for a long time, with the result that the people here speak their own version of Catalan. Something else the Valencians have in common with the Catalans is an intense local patriotism. History shows that time and time again they rose against the rulers in Madrid, such as the monarchs Charles V and Philip V.

Blue-domed churches

In both Murcia and Valencia there are some fine historic monuments built in the baroque style. These include the cathedral in the city of Murcia, which began as a Gothic structure, but after being badly damaged was rebuilt to the baroque designs

Above: The church of Santa Maria Magdalena in Novelda, a pretty little village just to the south of Monovar.

of a Valencian architect. A characteristic of Valencian baroque is the use of intensely blue, glazed tiles to cover domes on churches. These can be seen all through the region, and on the cathedral at Murcia. There are often colourful tiled pictures as well. The art of making ceramics and tiles was first introduced by the Moors; the splendid results can be seen in many parts of Spain, where they are still produced by traditional methods. Murcian baroque produced a famous sculptor, Francisco Salzillo (1707–83), and his polychrome wooden carvings stand in numerous churches, chapels and monasteries. Murcia, the city of his birth, has a museum devoted to him.

Fertile plains

The coast of Levante consists in fact of two huge bays, around Valencia and Alicante respectively. On either side of these large industrialized ports are many miles of sandy beaches invaded every year by hundreds of thousands of tourists. In places these beaches are interrupted by rock formations; the most easterly of these is Cape Nao, which marks the boundary between the Costa del Azahar to the north and the Costa Blanca to the south, which of course includes Benidorm. Between the sea and the mountain-

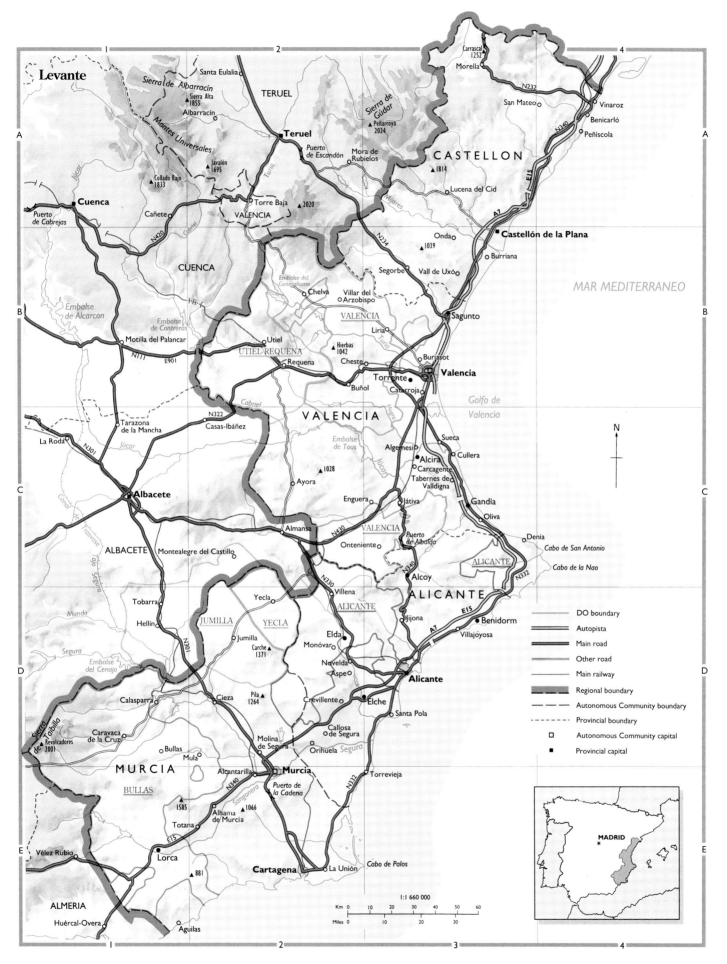

Levante

Sierra de Albarracín
Santa Eulalia
▲Sierra Alta 1855
Albarracín
Montes Universales
Collado Bajo 1833
▲Javalón 1695

TERUEL
Teruel
Puerto de Escandón
Mora de Rubielos

Sierra de Gúdar
▲Peñarroya 2024

Carrascal 1252
Morella
N232
San Mateo
Vinaroz
Benicarló
Peñíscola

CASTELLON
▲1814
Lucena del Cid

Cuenca
Puerto de Cabrejas
Cañete
Torre Baja
▲2020
VALENCIA

CUENCA
N420

Onda
Ondo ▲1039
Castellón de la Plana
Burriana

Embalse de Alcarcon
Embalse de Contreras
Motilla del Palancar
N111
E901
UTIEL-REQUENA
Utiel
Requena

Segorbe
Vall de Uxó
Chelva
Villar del Arzobispo
VALENCIA
Liria
▲Hierbas 1042
Cheste

Sagunto

MAR MEDITERRANEO

Burjasot
Valencia
Torrente
Catarroja
Buñol

Golfo de Valencia

La Roda
N301
Tarazona de la Mancha
N322
Casas-Ibáñez

VALENCIA
▲1028
Ayora

Sueca
Algemesí
Alcira
Carcagente
Cullera
Tabernes de Valldigna

Albacete

ALBACETE
Montealegre del Castillo

Almansa
N430
Onteniente
VALENCIA
Puerto de Albaida

Enguera
Játiva
Gandía
Oliva

Denia
Cabo de San Antonio
Cabo de la Nao
ALICANTE

Tobarra
Hellín
JUMILLA
YECLA
Yecla

N330
Villena
ALICANTE
Alcoy
ALICANTE

Jijona
Benidorm
Villajoyosa
E15
A7

Jumilla
Carche ▲1371
Monóvar
Elda
Novelda
Aspe

Calasparra
Caravaca de la Cruz
Sierra de Taibilla
▲Revolcadores 2001

Bullas
Mula
Pila ▲1264
Cieza

MURCIA
BULLAS
▲1585
Totana
Alhama de Murcia ▲1066

Crevillente
Callosa de Segura
Orihuela

Alicante
Elche
Santa Pola

Alcantarilla
□ **Murcia**
Puerto de la Cadena

Torrevieja

DO boundary
Autopista
Main road
Other road
Main railway
Regional boundary
Autonomous Community boundary
Provincial boundary
□ Autonomous Community capital
■ Provincial capital

Vélez Rubio
Lorca
▲881
Cartagena
La Unión
Cabo de Palos

ALMERIA
Huércal-Overa
Aguilas

1:1 660 000
Km 0 10 20 30 40 50 60
Miles 0 10 20 30

MADRID

167

ous interior are the *huertas*: steppe-like plains, originally dry, but transformed by irrigation into fruitful areas of cultivation (it was the Moors who first introduced the techniques of irrigation to the arid wastes of Spain). They grow amazing quantities of vegetables and fruit (including many citrus fruits), as well as almonds and sugarcane. Winegrowing mainly takes place on the margins of the *huertas* and further inland.

The wine districts

Altogether Levante has six important wine districts. The most northerly is Valencia, which chiefly produces light, fresh wines for drinking young, with the emphasis on white wines from the Merseguera grape. But in fact many more wines are shipped out of the port of Valencia than are grown in its own *denominación de origen*. The big firms established there handle millions of gallons of bulk wine from all over the country. Immediately to the west of the Valencia DO lies that of Utiel-Requena, where delicious rosés are made from the black Bobal, while the production of interesting red and white wines is increasing steadily. Black Monastrell holds sway in the Alicante, Yecla and Jumilla DOs. The red wines made from it vary greatly according to the producer, ranging in character from supple, fresh and fruity to rustic, wood-aged and heavy – with all possible grades in between.

In Bullas, the most southerly wine district, Monastrell is again predominant, but here two-thirds of the crop goes into rosé. In terms of both quantity and quality the level drops sharply in the other three Levante districts, and the chance that these will ever acquire DOs is minimal. The little district of Beniarrés lies north of the Alicante DO and drinks practically the whole of its own

Below: View looking towards Jumilla.

Above: Mountainous terrain near the town of Jumilla.

production of principally red wines – and some Moscatel. Campo de Cartagena circles the port of Cartagena and makes white and red wines of no significance whatever. San Mateo, finally, is an inconsiderable district in the north of the province of Castellón; here both the potent white and the red wines show all kinds of defects.

The origin of paella

Ever since Moorish times Valencia has grown rice as well as fruit and vegetables, and so this is an important ingredient in many regional dishes. Paella is the best known of these. All kinds of variants of it are served in Valencian restaurants, with large prawns, for example. In Chiva there is even an annual competition to see who can make the best paella. The Valencian cuisine also has delightful recipes for eel and duck (both from the Albufera storage lake), and every possible sort of fresh seafood. Murcia offers many kinds of salad and dishes such as *pastel murciano*, a tasty meat tart; fish baked in coarse sea salt, or *dorada a la sal*; and *olla gitana*, a kind of stew of gipsy origin.

Bullas

The Bullas wine region lies in the west of the province of Murcia, between Jumilla and the Mediterranean. It acquired its name from the unremarkable small provincial town of Bullas, which with six other communities makes up this provisional *denominación de origen*. By far the biggest of these places, in area and population, is the historic town of Lorca. The region is predominantly agricultural – about a third of the working population is in this sector.

In the Bullas region the produce grown includes almonds, apples, apricots, cereals, olives and peaches. Much of the fruit is processed in local canning factories. There is also a small furniture industry here. Vines are planted on about 7,500 ha (18,530 acres), with Monastrell the most important variety – it accounts for 95 percent of the total. This is very hilly country, with considerable areas of plateau in among the heights, and extends over three zones. The most westerly lies at 400 to 500 m (about 1,300 to 1,650 ft) above sea level, and has the lowest annual rainfall at 300 to 350 mm (11.8 to 13.8 ins); grape picking starts earliest here. The second zone is further inland, at a height of 500 to 600 m (about 1,650 to nearly 2,000 ft) and slightly wetter, and picking begins 9 or 10 days later. In the third zone, directly to the south of the towns of Bullas and Cehegín, the height above sea level rises to 600 to 800 m (from nearly 2,000 to over 2,600 ft).

Annual rainfall here is 450 to 500 mm (17.7 to 19.7 ins) and the grape harvest usually starts three to four weeks later than in the first zone. The *Consejo Regulador* (called the *Centro Gestor* until 1991) has in fact been gradually bringing forward the start of picking over the whole region, with the aim of producing wines of lower alcoholic strength. The soil is chalky to a greater or lesser degree over practically the whole of the region. It is hoped to increase plantings of Tempranillo and even Cabernet Sauvignon grapes.

Four producers

Wine production in Bullas consists very largely of rosés (65 percent) and reds (35 percent). There is also some white wine made, but the volume is insignificant. At the end of the 1980s and the beginning of the 1990s the four active producers – two in the Bullas area, two in Cehegín – invested heavily in modern cellar equipment, with an improvement in the average wine quality as a result. This does not alter the fact that even the best Bullas wines do not as yet have the kind of appeal that attracts national and international attention. As a rule they lack fruit and finesse, and the wood-aged varieties are somewhat rustic. Yet the potential for really good wines is here, particularly if the wines are made on the basis of grapes from the highest, and relatively wettest, of the zones.

Below: The imposing castle at Caravaca de la Cruz, in the northwest of the region. The town is noted for its religious festivals.

PRODUCERS OF SPECIAL INTEREST

Bodegas Carrascalejo 30180 Bullas

140 ha (346 acres) of vineyard supplies 60 percent of the grapes required. Rosé and red wines are made, both exclusively from Monastrell grapes. The rosés are quite firm and reasonably fruity. At a higher level are the powerful red wines, including the Carrascalejo, for drinking young, and the *reserva*, which is aged for a year in cask.

Cooperativa Agro-Vinícola Nuestra Señora del Rosario 30180 Bullas

About half of the total volume of wine from the region is produced by this cooperative. Its 1,200 members own nearly 5,000 ha (12,360 acres). The concern is equipped to include *macération carbonique* in its winemaking methods. If the grapes for this are delivered within half an hour of picking, and intact, the growers are paid a 15 percent premium. Most of the supple, firm and readily drinkable Don Hidalgo is made by this process. The Señorio de Bullas *crianza*, which spends eight months in used casks, is more rustic in character.

Travel Information

HOTELS AND RESTAURANTS

Avenida, 30180 Bullas, tel (68) 652345 Regional cooking, with plenty of hotpots in season.

Flipper, 30180 Bullas, tel (68) 652987 Despite its curious name one of the better restaurants, favoured by wine growers.

Restaurante El Sol, 30403 Cehegín, tel (68) 740064 Situated in the attractive quarter that draws tourists. Strictly regional cooking.

Alameda, Musso Valante 8, 30800 Lorca, tel (68) 467500 The only decent hotel in the region, in the centre of Lorca. It has air-conditioning.

Los Naranjos, Jerónomo Santa Fé 43, 30800 Lorca, tel (68) 465942 Eating house with quite a lot of atmosphere and good food, particularly regional specialities. Has a faithful local clientele.

PLACES OF INTEREST

Bullas This is the heart of the wine region of the same name. Just under 11,000 people live here. The only building of any significance is the Romanesque church.

Caravaca de la Cruz Belonged once to the Bullas DO, but is no longer part of it. This town 15 km (9 miles) west of Cehegín is known for its religious festivals and has an imitation of the Escorial, with a relic of the True Cross.

Cehegín Also called the Capital of Cave Art because of the important prehistoric paintings to be found in nearby caves. This town with its strongly agricultural interests possesses the remains of a Moorish castle; the fifteenth-century Ermita de la Concepción, with colourful roofs in Mudéjar style; the church of Santo Cristo; the Santa María Magdalena, built a little later, with its baroque façade with a wooden statue, some fine paintings and other religious art; the Duque de Ahumada ethnographical museum, which includes a collection of coaches; the Museo Arqueológica, with prehistoric finds; and the eighteenth-century baroque monastery of San Esteban. Besides these there are noblemen's houses to be seen. Reddish-coloured marble

Above: The collegiate church of San Patricio, Lorca

from nearby quarries is used in many of the buildings.

Lorca This town stretches out over quite a large area, and reaches back far into history. The remains of the Moorish Castillo de Lorca (restored in the nineteenth century) tower over the old quarter of the town, which climbs up a slope. The town has suffered from natural disasters and from the violence of war, yet it has a number of fine buildings. Among them are the baroque town hall with its two wings; the richly decorated Casa de los Guevara with its splendid façade and inner courtyard; and the sixteenth-century collegiate church of San Patricio – the only one in Spain to be named after the Irish saint. The impressive tower shows work in a number of architectural styles. There was an important colony of painters here in Lorca in the seventeenth century.

WINE ROUTE

With Lorca as the starting point the following route will show you a good deal of the wine region: Lorca – Zarzadilla de Totana – then by way of a winding mountain road to Bullas – Cehegín – Caravaca de la Cruz – Lorca.

Left: Picturesque view over the rooftops of Cehegín.

Yecla

The town of Yecla lies about halfway between Albacete and Alicante, where two country roads cross. As a result the streets are thronged with a continuous stream of traffic. In the seventeenth century Yecla had the byname *Bodega Mayor*, the "Great Bodega", as wine was then its main concern. Today, however, Yecla is best known for its furniture industry. A number of these factories stand along the roads into the town and a great furniture fair is held here every March.

Even more people come to Yecla between December 5 and 8, when the fiesta is celebrated. People go about in nineteenth-century costumes and many of them carry an *arcabuz* or blunderbuss – the old firearm of the flintlock type. During these fiesta days even the noise of the traffic is drowned out.

Winegrowing area

Although winegrowing used to be of greater importance for the Yecla economy than it is today, there are still around 29,000 ha (72,000 acres) planted with vines here. About 20,000 ha (nearly 50,000 acres) produce wine entitled to the Yecla *denominación de origen*. The vineyards lie in a rough rectangle around the town of Yecla, all of them within the municipal boundaries. This is in fact Spain's only DO with its total area confined to a single community. The growers distinguish two zones about equal in area. The northern zone is called Campo Arriba and rises to 750m (2,460 ft) above sea level. The soil here is stony, with relatively little clay. The southern zone, Campo Abaja, is at a height of 630 to 650m (2,070 to 2,130 ft), and is fairly flat, with quite a lot of clay. When there are heavy falls of rain – as at the end of summer – drainage becomes a problem here. The northern area yields less wine to the hectare, but both quality and alcohol content are higher than in the southern zone. Over the whole Yecla area wine grapes take up to 40 to 45 percent of agricultural land. A lot of apples and olives are grown and the local cooperative produces a considerable amount of olive oil as well as wine.

Varieties grown

In contrast to the compactly built town, the winegrowing land around Yecla has a broad, open aspect. Its slopes are gentle, and mainly to the north, but beyond mountains rise on almost every side. The climate is generally dry, with an annual rainfall of only 300mm (11.8 ins). It is very similar to that of neighbouring Jumilla, but with slightly more rain and less extreme summer and winter temperatures. The mean annual temperature is 15.8°C (60.4°F). Of white grape varieties, Yecla grows just slightly more than Jumilla. Officially only Merseguera and Verdil are permitted, but at present Airén is also accepted. Thus Bodegas Castaño makes a white wine from 70 percent Airén and 30 percent Merseguera. White wine, however, is very much a sideline: in Yecla the accent is definitely on red.

The red wines largely have the Monastrell grape as their basis and this variety represents 80 percent of all the vines grown. In many cases it is the only grape used, but it may also be mixed with Garnacha. The proportion of Garnacha can vary from 10 to 30 percent. Garnacha is always vinified by the traditional method,

Below: Yecla is surrounded on nearly all sides by mountains.

Above: Young and old grape-picking during the harvest in Yecla's highest zone, Campo Arriba.

PRODUCERS OF SPECIAL INTEREST

Bodegas Castaño 30510 Yecla
A dynamic family concern with modern equipment, near the Plaza de Toros. In order to have the greatest possible control over grape quality an estate of 280 ha (695 acres) has been created. This grows about half of the grapes required; the rest are bought in. Some 10 to 15 percent of the volume of wine is produced by *macération carbonique*, giving firm wines with fruit that carry the Castaño label. For the wines made by the ordinary method the name Viña Las Gruesas is used. The red is a good, pleasant wine made from Monastrell grapes plus 10 to 15 percent Garnacha. The name Pozuelo is borne by a *crianza* that is given wood and bottle ageing. The resulting wine has refinement, a restrained touch of vanilla and good quality. The grapes used are 70 percent

Monastrell and 30 percent Garnacha.

Cooperativa La Purísima 30510 Yecla
The 1,300 or so members of this large cooperative cultivate about 7,000 ha (17,300 acres). Here 85 percent of the vines are Monastrells. In recent years the concern has invested a good deal of money in modern equipment, to the benefit of the average quality of the wine. The bottled red wines are usually made exclusively from Monastrell grapes. The Estio and the Iglesia Vieja wines are generally supple and uncomplicated. There is a step up in quality with Alfeizar, a wine with fruit and some meatiness, vinified by *macération carbonique*. Wines with the Calp label are somewhat rustic in style.

Dominio de las Torres 30510 Yecla
This wine estate to the south of

but for certain wines some producers use *macération carbonique* for Monastrell – and the results clearly show that this grape variety is eminently suitable for this method. Bodegas Castaño was the first to employ this winemaking technique; other producers, including the cooperative, soon followed suit.

For generations the great merit of the red wines of Yecla was their high alcohol content. Wines with 14 to 16 percent were quite usual, both ordinary reds and *vinos de doble pasta* (made with a double quantity of skins). The latter were not meant for drinking on their own, but for strengthening weaker products. A number of producers have now started to make lighter wines in a more contemporary style, but many growers are still paid according to the potential alcoholic strength of their grapes. This has led Ramón Castaño, for example, to decide to acquire as much vineyard area as possible – since only then would he be able to obtain grapes with the sugar content he wanted. Therefore alongside the traditional, heady kind of Yecla there is also a more elegant version with just 12 to 13 percent alcohol. The proportion of this type of wine is growing steadily and lends itself perfectly to sale in bottle in Spain and abroad. Even so this does not alter the fact that most Yecla wine is still shipped out in bulk and is intended for anonymous blending with other kinds. For example, the cooperative La Purísima, whose members cultivate 7,000 ha (17,300 acres), bottles only one-fifth of its total vintage. However, La Purísima and some of the other bodegas expect to increase their percentage of bottled wines considerably by the year 2000.

The character of the bottled Yecla wines varies considerably according to producer and type. There is no question of any homogeneity. For drinking young – preferably within a year – the *macération carbonique* wines can be very agreeable, with a supple taste, fruit and some rounding, based on 12 to 12.5 percent alcohol. Wines made in the traditional way differ markedly and may be lively and harmonious, or dull and ill-balanced. Yecla also produces wood-aged wines on a modest scale, both *crianzas* and *reservas*. These vary in character from refined and elegant to rustic and robust. The white wines only achieve any kind of standard when they are vinified by modern methods, and the same applies to the Yecla rosés.

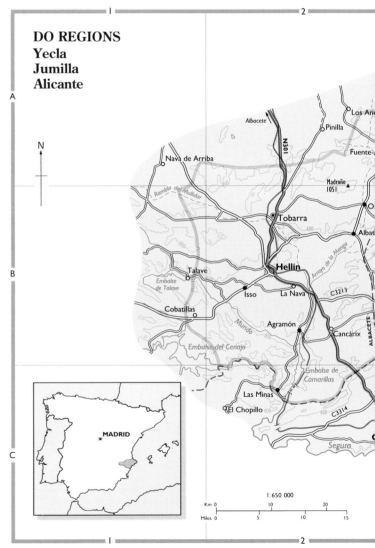

**DO REGIONS
Yecla
Jumilla
Alicante**

Travel Information

Yecla was bought by Frenchmen from Bordeaux at the end of the 1980s. Thanks to a good deal of new planting it now covers around 100 ha (nearly 250 acres). Monastrell is by far the most important grape here. In addition, experimentation with Cabernet Sauvignon and other varieties is being carried out on a modest scale. Manager Michel Jaubert starts harvesting when the grapes have a potential 12.5 to 13 percent alcohol. In addition he leaves the grape skins in the must for quite a long time. The result is a dark-red, well-balanced robust wine with vitality and tannin. The labels used are Dominio de las Torres, Moro, Torrepaloma, Castel Real and Châteauvalon.

HOTELS AND RESTAURANTS

Hostal Avenida, San Pascual 5, 30510 Yecla, tel (68) 790189 (hotel), (68) 79513 (restaurant). This is the better of Yecla's two hotels. The rooms are clean, albeit somewhat sparsely appointed. The hotel is noisy. Behind the basement bar is the Aurora restaurant with an interior that suggests a tent in a greenhouse. Its kitchen offers carefully prepared country dishes such as *gazpacho yeclano-manchego* and kid chops. In addition there is an adequate selection of regional wines. Hotel and restaurant are in the centre of town, just inside a pedestrian zone.
Arabí, 30510 Yecla, tel (68) 790525. Local dishes, including leg of lamb.
La Parra, 30510 Yecla, tel (68) 792908. Many meat dishes, including roasts.
Club de Tenis, 30510 Yecla, tel (68) 792502. This local tennis club is just outside Yecla, in the Maneta direction. The restaurant occupies a modern building and is open to non-members. Fish dishes and regional cooking. A large-screen television is usually on during lunch.

PLACES OF INTEREST

Yecla This rather grey town is built at the foot of a hill surmounted by a basilica and ruined castle. In the centre are the churches of La Asunción (sixteenth century) and San Francisco (with a group by the eighteenth century sculptor Francisco Salzillo). In the *ayuntamiento* (seventeenth century) are works by the local painter Andrés Ginés de Aguirre, who lived in the eighteenth century. Archaeological finds are exhibited in the Casa de la Cultura. The best way to become acquainted with Yecla is to take a short walk through the traffic-free zone.

WINE ROUTE

The best way to see this wine district with just the one community is to take the roads that go through the vineyards and circle round the area. In the south this would link up with the Jumilla wine route. In the southwest you are close to the Alicante route; in the north there is the attraction of the wine town of Almansa with its castle.

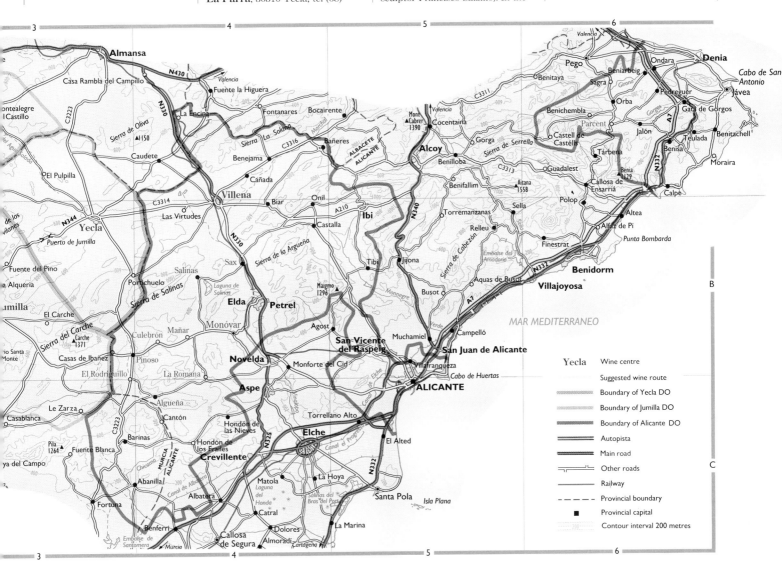

Jumilla

From Yecla you reach the similarly sized town of Jumilla by way of the Puerto de Jumilla, a pass 800 m (2,625 ft) high. The distance between the two towns is about 25 km (15.5 miles). The wine districts bearing these two names border on each other and so they have very much the same climate, except that temperatures in Jumilla are a little more extreme, going from 41°C (106°F) in summer to − 5° to − 7°C (23° to 19°F) in winter. Average rainfall is just under 300 mm (11.8 ins) a year. Summers are generally exceedingly dry. October is the wettest month, and there is usually some rain in spring. The vine is the most important plant growing in the often chalky soil – and has been for centuries. The Romans practised winegrowing here; and the cathedral archives from Murcia show that in the seventeenth century, Jumilla paid its tithes in wine. Apart from wine, Jumilla today produces only olives and almonds.

A splendid landscape

Jumilla's vineyards stretch over rolling plateaux that are surrounded by imposing mountain chains. These generally rise abruptly and most run parallel to each other, from southeast to northwest. A tour around the vineyards here provides magnificent views. The region looks its best in autumn, when the vine-leaves shade from dusty green to reddish brown, colours that harmonize beautifully with the brown-green of the nearby heights and the grey-blues of the mountains further off. The stillness is disturbed only by the chugging drone of the tractors towing the grape harvest back to the bodegas.

Most of the wine firms are based in and around Jumilla, a town with a population of 21,000, built around a twelfth-century castle. Close to this stronghold is the oldest part of the town, with its low, white-stuccoed houses. Other sections have fifteenth-century and Renaissance buildings, and there are many modern blocks of flats. Since 1972 Jumilla has had a well-attended wine festival during the second half of August. During this *fiesta de la vendimia* practically any kind of wine can be sampled in the *Consejo Regulador*'s pavilion, and thirst can be slaked at an 1801 fountain in the Jardín de la Glorieta – which flows with wine for a week. Ceremonies include trampling the grapes, and religious offering and sampling of the new must. The high point of the festivities is the *cabalgata del vino*, a wine parade held on the last Saturday of the event with about 50 decorated floats.

Monastrell

About a dozen of Jumilla's bodegas market bottled wines. The volume represents about a third of the total; most Jumilla is still sold in bulk. As in other Spanish regions, however, there is a tendency to bottle more and more of the wine locally. Jumilla wine has been greatly influenced, for better or worse, by the San Isidro cooperative, founded in 1934. This has nearly 2,000 members, who work 20,000 ha (49,500 acres) out of Jumilla's total 47,000 ha (116,140 acres) of vineyards. Now the cooperative has an increasing amount of modern equipment at its disposal, and there has been an investment in some 2,500 oak casks. Of the millions of pounds of grapes the cooperative handles annually, something in the region of 90 percent is Monastrell. Taken over the whole of Jumilla, this black grape variety represents about 85 percent of the vines. The cooperative's oenologist was right when he remarked, "Monastrell is our mistress".

Restructuring the vineyards

Monastrell is a sturdy variety that can cope with the often harsh Jumilla climate and can also stand up well to phylloxera. In fact in many vineyards there seemed to be no need to protect the vines against this parasite by grafting on to American rootstock. Nevertheless, all new plantings do now involve this procedure. The reason is not only one of immunity from any possible phylloxera outbreak, but one of yield. On average Jumilla only achieves 17 hl per ha (150 gal per acre) and 12 hl per ha (105 gal per acre) on cooperative members' vineyards. With grafted vines these results can be drastically improved to bring them to a more acceptable level. It is hoped that with financial help from the EC, between 6,000 and 7,000 ha will have been reorganized in this way by the year 2000. Research into the best Monastrell clones is being carried on at the Jumilla oenological station which recommends picking Monastrell earlier than usual – as soon as the grapes are fully ripe, and not at the customary time in mid-September.

Bringing the harvesting forward results in less heavy wine, of better quality. In 1990, for example, the station started picking the grapes on August 24; the rest of the area did not follow suit until September 10. The station also gives important advice on vinification. For red wines meant for drinking young it recommends *macération carbonique*; for wines that are to be made in the traditional way a longer period of macerating the grapes is advised, namely six to seven days rather than two to four. The red wine should then ferment at a temperature of 25° to 28°C (77° to 82°F) maximum. And if the wine is aged in wood, then five to six months is usually enough. Longer in wood may bring oxidization

Above: Jumilla's peaceful wine country is marked by striking mountain ranges that often rise abruptly. A tour through the area provides many beautiful views.

Above: The monastery of Santa Ana del Monte in its lofty setting lies not far to the south of Jumilla. It contains many examples of religious art.

problems. The research institute applies techniques of this sort in its own establishment and can demonstrate the excellent results to be obtained, and thus Jumilla's potential as a quality wine area. The station also carries out experiments with grapes new to the district, such as Cabernet Sauvignon. Apparently this variety will thrive here, provided it is given drip irrigation; however, this is not as yet allowed in Jumilla. The necessary advice and recommendations are also given for white and rosé wines; the best *rosado* I was given to taste in Jumilla was at the oenological station.

Divergent qualities

The great majority of Jumilla red wines are made exclusively from Monastrell since the other black varieties there – Garnacha and Cencibel or Tempranillo – are scarce. In itself this is no bad thing for, as the oenological station and some of the bodegas show, wines of distinction can certainly be made from Monastrell. Unfortunately, by no means all producers exploit this potential – not even bodegas that bottle on a big scale. The result is Jumillas that are dull and characterless, or heady, rustic and quite often oxidized. Together with the bulk wines – by definition cheap – these uninteresting products have done Jumilla's image no good. The region has a particularly poor reputation in Spain itself. This led Vitivino, one of the best producers, not to put its very superior Monastrell on the home market labelled with the district name:

instead, a brand name that did not clearly indicate the origin was chosen. Besides Vitivino, the San Isidro cooperative and Bodegas Viña Umbría also follow a policy of quality.

Divergent wines

That very different wines can come from the Monastrell grape is not only demonstrated by the run of ordinary Jumillas. From this same grape various producers make naturally sweet wines. A delightful example is the Lacrima Christi from the cooperative, a dark-brown, wood-aged wine with a coffee-and-cocoa aroma. Monastrell also lends itself to the making of attractive dry rosés that, given low-temperature fermentation, can be lively and fruity. For the true devotee some firms market wood-aged rosés. Thus it was that at Asencia Carcelén I came to be given a glass of nine-year-old *rosado* that had spent two years in the vat – with complete oxidization as a result.

Finally, a proportion of Monastrell grapes is still processed into *doble pasta* wines meant for blending. These are made by being fermented with double the usual quantity of skins, which gives them a great deal of both colour and tannin.

PRODUCERS OF SPECIAL INTEREST

Asencio Carcelén 30520 Jumilla
This firm, founded in 1876, has 1,200 ha (2,965 acres) of its own vineyards, which provide about 70 percent of the grapes it needs, the rest being bought in. Although in their information material high percentages of Cabernet Sauvignon, Cencibel etc. are sometimes quoted for the red wines, in practice they are made from 98 to 99 percent Monastrell. These wines are rustic in character, particularly the wood-aged kinds such as the Bullanguero, Acorde and Con Sello. When the grapes contain extra sugar, a luxuriously sweet red wine called Sol y Luna is made. This firm is especially worth visiting for its charming wine museum, housed in a building immediately behind the bodega itself.

Bodegas Cooperativas San Isidro 30520 Jumilla
This cooperative, originally called El Progreso, was first set up in the centre of Jumilla, but in the 1960s it moved to the edge of the town. There are nearly 2,000 members associated with it, who work some 20,000 ha (49,400 acres). Of the vines, 90 percent are Monastrell. As far as its bottled wines are concerned, the emphasis is strongly on quality. Two wines fermented at low temperature, the white Sabatacha (100 percent Airén) and rosé of that name (100 percent Monastrell) are attractive, pure, and have a good amount of fruit. They are at their best within a year of their vintage. The red San Isidro is made by the *macération carbonique* method; quite lively in taste and juicy, it is best in the spring after its vintage. It is a pure Monastrell wine, which also holds for the Casa Alta. This is fermented at around 25°C (77°F) and for 12 days the skins are left in contact with the must. The wine usually has a firm, supple taste. A more traditional style is represented both by the wood-aged Sabatacha *crianza* (two years in cask, and sometimes 15 percent alcohol), and by the naturally sweet Lacrima Christi, with its coffee and cocoa-like aroma, which has two to three years in cask, and as a rule has 15 percent alcohol.

J. García Carrión 30520 Jumilla
A large firm that exports a great deal and is prominent in Spain itself, not only with its wines in the bottle, but especially with Tetrapak. The knowledge is there to make, or

Above: Old building in the centre of Jumilla, near the Santiago church.

select, really good wines; but even the best wines in the range, those with the brand name Castillo San Simón, scarcely reach a middling level. Improvement in quality is, however, being considered – by using *macération carbonique*, for example.

Bodegas Viña Umbría 30520 Jumilla
This relatively young firm (founded 1983) has 1,000 ha (2,470 acres) of vineyard and also buys in grapes. Its equipment is modern, with stainless-steel tanks, and it has some 600 casks in an underground cellar. The wines, for drinking young, are sold under the Umbría Novel brand name. The red is aromatic – impressions of plums and prunes – and the rosé is one of Jumilla's best. Both are pure Monastrell wines.

Bodegas Vitivino 30520 Jumilla
The modest-sized range of wines from Bodegas Vitivino offers the highest average quality in Jumilla. This wine estate covers some 225 ha (555 acres) and with its cellars lies about 10 km (6 miles) from Jumilla. Most of the vines are around 30 years old, but many new ones have been planted since 1987. It was in that year that the estate was taken over by Jacques Germain, a wine dealer and grower from Bordeaux. For the day-to-day running of the establishment he engaged a Bordeaux-trained oenologist who set aside the traditional Jumilla mode of winemaking and introduced Bordeaux techniques. One of these was a long period of macerating and fermentation – 13 to 20 days. Vitivino produces a small amount of cask-aged red wine, from very old vines that yield only 9 hl per ha (80 gal per acre). The ordinary red wine

is not matured in cask, but is aged for a year in tanks. This Jumilla (100 percent Monastrell) is characterized by its deep-red colour and meaty taste, with some fruit, a lively freshness and a good aftertaste. The wine is sold as Altos de Pio, Dominio de Alba and Taja (exclusive to Mähler-Besse). Also produced is a pleasing, smoothly fresh, fragrant white wine made from Airén grapes.

Jumilla Unión Vinícola 30520 Jumilla
This firm came into being through the amalgamation of several bodegas, including Pedro Gil. It has its own vineyard of 400 ha (990 acres) and also buys in grapes. The most successful wine is the light, fruity, red Cerrillares, made purely from Monastrell grapes and vinified by *macération carbonique*.

Travel Information

HOTELS AND RESTAURANTS

Jumilla has no decent hotel. Possible places to stay are hotels in Yecla, Almansa and Hellín.
Hellín, Antigua Carretera N301, 02400 Hellín, tel (67) 300142 Simple hotel in a somewhat dull town about 40 km (25 miles) from Jumilla.
Bar Central, 30320 Balsa-Pintada (near Fuente Alamo), tel (68) 597835 Situated by the village square. A Basque cook works here.
Fuente del Pino, 30528 Fuente del Pino, tel (68) 780354 Good restaurant by the church square. Local dishes are the speciality.
Campo Nuevo, 30520 Jumillo, tel (68) 782698 Just outside Jumilla on the C3213. Grilled lamb is the speciality.
Casa Sebastián, Avenida de Levante, 30520 Jumilla, tel (68) 780194 Simple and inexpensive place to eat. Regional cuisine.
Mesón San Agustín, Avenida la Asunción 64, 30520 Jumilla, tel (68) 781314 Regional dishes are served, often with fresh fish such as grilled swordfish.

PLACES OF INTEREST

Jumilla From a good way off you can see the well-preserved castle, on a hill above the town, which dates from the twelfth century and is of Moorish origin. A fortified keep was added in the fifteenth century. Jumilla's oldest monument is El Casón, a fifth-century funerary chapel at the end of the Avenida de la Libertad. In the oldest part of the town, below the castle, there are even cave dwellings that are still inhabited.
Nearby is the Santiago church, built between the fifteenth and nineteenth centuries. The oldest part is late Gothic, but there is a Renaissance altar (1583). According to tradition the upper part of the tower is in a different architectural style from the lower because of a

prohibition issued from Murcia by the cardinal. He stopped the building for fear that Jumilla's tower would overtop that of the cathedral in Murcia.
Close to the former church is the sixteenth-century Antiguo Concejo y Longa which is being completely restored: the intention is to house the law court here. Also in the centre is the municipal museum, with archaeological finds, religious art and Roman mosaics on display. The nineteenth-century *ayuntamiento* is housed in a former prison. Of the same century is the striking Vico theatre (opened 1883).
A walk around Jumilla will also reveal admirable fifteenth- and sixteenth-century houses. Wine lovers can visit two wine museums. The municipal one occupies a restored former railway station (at the end of Paseo Lorenzo Guardiola). In addition the wine firm of Asencio Carcelén has its own small museum. Visitors should ask at the bodega if they want to look round it.
Embalse de Talave To the west and southwest of Hellín there are a number of reservoirs where you can cool off on hot summer days.
Monasterio Santa Ana del Monte This Franciscan monastery stands on high ground 6 km (nearly 4 miles) south of Jumilla. The church here dates from 1580 and has some fine sculptures, including *Christ at the Column* by Francisco Salzillo.

WINE ROUTE

To the west of the town of Jumilla the route goes through a good deal of beautiful landscape; to the east it connects with the Yecla and Alicante wine routes. A narrow road runs up the southern slope of the Carche mountain, past a salt mine. From this road (not marked on the map) you have tremendous views over the surrounding countryside.

Alicante

The Alicante archaeological museum displays both Greek and Roman artefacts, silent witnesses to the city's long history. The city was famed for its light: the Greeks called it *Akra Leuka*, or "white citadel", the Romans called it *Lucentum*, "city of light", and in the eighth century the Arabs made it *Al Lucant*. Nowadays Alicante is best known as a seaside resort. Every year tourists in their thousands come to the sheltered bay here, just as they do to the long beaches of Benidorm 45 km (28 miles) further north. A favourite walk for the many visitors to Alicante is along the Explanada de España, a broad, palm-shaded boulevard by the harbour with mosaic paving. On foot, by car or lift you can reach the sixteenth-century Castillo de Santa Bárbara, an impressive fortification built on a rock 200 m (656 feet) high, and dominating the city. That Alicante is also associated with wine comes as a surprise to most foreigners, for only a minute amount of the wine exported is bottled: usually less than 1 percent. Spain itself takes three-quarters of production – but of this, too, only 20 to 25 percent is sold in bottle.

The vineyards

Visitors who keep to the beaches or town are not very likely to see the vineyards. These lie further inland, past the fertile *huerta*, where almonds and other crops are cultivated. The most important wine communities of the *denominación de origen* are Pinoso and Villena, both some 55 km (34 miles) from Alicante. On the other hand, dessert grapes are grown closer to the coast; the area is a big producer of these. At its creation in 1975 the DO consisted only of a zone around and to the west of Alicante. About 10 years later a second zone was added. This lies roughly 75 km (47 miles) from Alicante and north of Benidorm, and is called La Marina. There the vineyards are found on the headland that separates the Gulf of Alicante from the Gulf of Valencia; they produce about a sixth of all Alicante, with the emphasis on sweet white wines made from Moscatel. In the original zone black Monastrell predominates. Of the 17,000 ha (42,000 acres) that the Alicante DO covers, 13,000 ha (32,125 acres) are planted with this vine.

Differences in climate and soil

Whereas the coastal strip has an average annual temperature of 18°C (64.4°F), further inland this drops to 13°C (55.4° F). This has to do with the difference in elevation of the vineyards. Pinoso is about 570 m (1,870 ft) above sea level, Villena more than 500 m (1,640 feet). The interior can have frosts between December and February. The climate is indeed cooler than on the coast, but less extreme than, for instance, in Jumilla and Yecla, the two bordering wine districts still further inland – where again Monastrell is the most important grape. According to the Alicante growers, their red wines are therefore different from those from Yecla and Jumilla. This effect is further heightened by soil differences. The soils here, mainly clay, sand and limestone, tend to be deeper and more fertile than in the neighbouring areas. This applies particularly to the lower-lying parts of the DO, the sometimes broad valleys of the hinterland. According to the director of the Mañan cooperative, all this results in "red wines

Below: Vines in the neighbourhood of Villena, where Bodegas Eval, a leading producer, is established.

with more colour, more aroma and more quality".

In the Alicante *denominación de origen*, 90 percent of the grapes are processed by cooperatives. They make not only red and rosé wines from the Monastrell grape, but considerable amounts of *tintos doble pasta* as well. These are not meant for direct consumption but for blending with other wines. The ordinary red wines from the bodegas that do their own bottling show great differences in character and quality. A number of the firms make traditional, fairly rustic wines that at best could be regarded as decent. But there are some with up-to-date equipment where the wines attain a higher level of quality.

A model bodega

The best-known example is Bodegas Eval in Villena. This independent firm has some 260 ha (640 acres) of its own land and also buys in a lot of grapes. As far as possible the owner, Augustin de la Torre, tries to buy Tempranillo, since this grape combined with Monastrell makes better red wines than those from Monastrell alone. The firm is also experimenting with other varieties, including Cabernet Sauvignon. It has been found that one third Monastrell, one third Tempranillo and one third Cabernet Sauvignon give even better wine than the Monastrell-Tempranillo combination. A wine so made can stand cask-ageing, as one 1985 example has shown, so that the possibility is there to give it that kind of extra dimension. Wines made exclusively or mainly from Monastrell are less suitable for ageing in cask because of the tendency of this grape to oxidize. Trials are also being conducted, in the Bodegas Eval cellar with all its stainless-steel tanks, with *macération carbonique*, experiments that include Cabernet Sauvignon. The firm has been bottling wines since the end of the 1980s and this might well be the means by which the Alicante DO becomes more widely known. Two other houses with managements that aim at quality are Gutiérrez de la Vega in Parcent (on the promontory between the two gulfs) and Salvador Poveda in Monóvar.

An Alicante speciality

That it is possible to make attractive, fresh, fruity rosés from Monastrell has been shown by the Jumilla oenological station among others. One of the conditions, however, is that the grapes should be fermented at low temperature, which by no means all of the Alicante cooperatives are able to do. The quality of certain of the *rosados* is therefore not the best possible – which does not alter the fact that none-too-critical holiday visitors readily drink huge quantities of them. Salvador Poveda's Viña Vermeta is probably the best-selling rosé from the Alicante DO. Besides some powerful, luxuriously sweet Moscatels the district also produces dry white wines, usually made from Merseguera by itself, or in combination with the Airén grape. The same problem arises here as with the rosés.

Fondillón

A wine speciality unique to Alicante is Fondillón. When I was tasting fermenting red wines with the *Consejo Regulador*'s oenologist, he announced when he came to the sweetest of them: "In 15 years it will make a beautiful Fondillón". This wine is made from Monastrell grapes with a very high sugar content and is aged for 6 to 10 years in barrels, then for a considerable time in bottle. Its alcohol content is from 16 percent to 18 percent and its mature taste, strongly influenced by wood, can be either dry or sweet. In the area itself, Fondillón is recommended as a digestif, instead of brandy or liqueur.

PRODUCERS OF SPECIAL INTEREST

Salvador Poveda 03640 Monóvar
This family firm founded in 1919 has 20 ha (49 acres) of its own land. This yields about half the grapes needed for producing *denominación de origen* wines. Contracts have been drawn up for the other half with the Mañan cooperative and other suppliers. Pure Monastrell wines are the speciality of this house, such as the supple Viña Vermeta with its slightly spicy undertones; the somewhat rustic Viña Vermeta Reserva with its ripe fruit; and the excellent, slightly sweet Fondillón. This last wine has about 18 years in cask. Salvador Poveda's 200 or so casks have a capacity of 1,500 litres (330 gal). Tourists can visit this bodega, where bottles of wine are sold to private individuals.

Gutíerrez de la Vega 03792 Parcent
The village of Parcent lies in the Moscatel zone of the Alicante *denominación de origen*, on the promontory north of Benidorm. Gutíerrez de la Vega, named after its owner, markets strikingly designed bottles, with labels dedicated to various writers. Dry, slightly sweet and very sweet Moscatels are of good quality here. They are sold with the Casta Diva label. Try the rosé Viña Alejandria, which is full of character. This is composed of various grapes, with some Cabernet Sauvignon among them.

Bodegas Eval 03400 Villena
Since 1985 Augustin de la Torre, who lives in Madrid, has been the owner of Bodegas Eval, the biggest private wine concern in the Alicante *denominación de origen*. It lies about 10 km (5.5 miles) from Villena on the road to Yecla and is surrounded by vineyards. The house's own 260 ha (640 acres) supply about one-third of the grapes required, the rest being bought in. In the spacious vinification hall most of the fermentation tanks are of stainless steel and the bodega's other equipment is modern too. It was decided after experiments to age progressively more of the wines in cask. In addition, trials were carried out with *macération carbonique*, with Cabernet Sauvignon as well as Monastrell. The ordinary red Lopez de la Torre is a decent, although not exciting wine, but the quality rises with the version that is made from 70 percent Monastrell and 30 percent

Above: Near the Bodegas Eval premises is the Santuario Virgen de las Virtudes.

Tempranillo. The latter also has significantly more fruit. A still more exciting variant is made to the formula of one third Monastrell, one third Tempranillo and one third Cabernet. This has greater depth to it than the two previous kinds, and moreover a pleasant bouquet of wood and vanilla. It spends six months in casks of new oak and six in used barrels. This last type is made only in good years. There is also a cask-aged Monastrell, but this lacks real class. Visitors are very welcome at Bodegas Eval. During the season the firm even makes arrangements with hotels to send parties of tourists.

Above: The castle of Santa Bárbara, above Alicante.

Travel Information

HOTELS AND RESTAURANTS

Curricán, Canalejas 1, 03001 Alicante, tel (96) 5140818 Fairly refined Mediterranean cuisine.
Delfín, Explanada de España 12, 03001 Alicante, tel (96) 5214911 The most famous place to eat here. In the elegant interior the emphasis is on dishes with fresh seafood, as incorporated in the attractive Menú Alicantino.
La Goleta, Explanada de España 8, 03002 Alicante, tel (96) 5214392 Well known for its paellas.
Meliá Alicante, Playa de El Postiguet, 03001 Alicante, tel (96) 5205000 A large, luxurious modern hotel.
Palas, Cervantes 5, 03002 Alicante, tel (96) 5209211 Pleasant, atmospheric hotel in an old building.
Palas, Plaza Ayuntamiento 6, 03002 Alicante, tel (96) 5206511 Three-star comfort in the heart of the city.
Racö del Plaä, Calle Dr Nieto 42, 032001 Alicante, tel (96) 5219373 Regional and Mediterranean dishes

(some with rice) and good *tapas*.
Ramón, Carretera Estación, 03640 Monóvar, tel (96) 5473319 Chalet-like restaurant with garden on the road to Elda. Good *arroz con conejo* (hare with rice), regional *gazpacho* and other traditional dishes.
Xiri, Parque de la Alameda, 03640 Monóvar, tel (96) 5472910 Interesting creations based on fresh ingredients. The restaurant stands in a rectangle of park with pine trees.
Doñana, Calle Marqués de Villores 11, 03400 Villena, tel (96) 5808252 Nicely prepared regional dishes.
Vary-Messy, Calle Isabel La Católica 17, 03400 Villena tel (96) 5801047 Homely, strongly regional dishes with a few more international ones.

PLACES OF INTEREST

Alicante This capital of the province of the same name has a population of over 250,000. It is dominated by the Santa Bárbara castle, not far from the sea and standing proudly on a rock more than 200 m (656 ft) high. The oldest parts are said to have been built by the Carthaginian general Hamilcar Barca in the third century BC. This *castillo* can be reached by lift as well as by car or on foot. The castle museum has satirical figures that are "rescued" from the flames during the spring festival (which shows similarities to Valencia's *Las Fallas*). On the north side of the city there is another fortification, the smaller Castilla de San Fernando (early nineteenth century). Alicante's *ayuntamiento* has an imposing façade with baroque doorways, and the inside deserves a visit. The most important church is the cathedral of San Nicolás de Bari dating from the seventeenth century. The archaeological museum has a stimulating collection of artifacts from times long past. A famous promenade, the Explanada de España, runs beside the harbour, with terraces, palms and colourful mosaic paving. In the Museo de Arte the collection includes works by Braque, Miró and Picasso.
Biar Worth visiting for its medieval castle and the Calle Jesús, a beautiful street.
Elche This sizeable town has Spain's biggest palm plantation. In the Huerta del Cura, the part open to the public, other Mediterranean trees, shrubs and flowers are also grown.
Ibi Many of Spain's toys are made here. Various factories can be visited and these sell their products at attractive prices.
Monóvar One of the most attractive monuments here is the Ermita de Santa Bárbara, a white-stuccoed monastery chapel with a blue dome, in the north of Monóvar. The Torre del Reloj is a sixteenth-century belfry that rises over the town. One house here has a museum dedicated to the writer Azorín (José Martínez Ruiz). There is, too, the pleasant Museo de Artes y Oficios with exhibits including an old kitchen, a furniture maker's workshop and items connected with wine. Crafts and trades are esteemed here: there is, for example, a school for lacemaking.
Pinoso A wine community not far from the border with the Jumilla district. It is also known for its red and pink marble.
Salinas This village, on the wine route, is in one of the most beautiful of the wine valleys. The church tower is surmounted with a cupola.
Sax Dominated by a steep cliff with a well preserved castle on top.
Villena A decent-sized town with a rich past. It stretches around the foot of a hill with a castle of Moorish origin on top. In the Museo Arquelógico, housed in the town hall, there is the "Villena treasure": artifacts of gold from the Bronze Age. The sixteenth-century church of Santiago is Gothic.

WINE ROUTE

The suggested wine route itself covers a considerable distance, but it can be further extended with visits to the "toy town" of Ibi and Elche with its palms. West of Villena the route stops at Bodegas Eval, but can of course be continued towards Yecla. The circuit west of Monóvar, around mountains of some 900 to 1,000 m (2,950 to 3,280 ft) comprises the more or less official *ruto del vino* created by that community.

Valencia

The present city of Valencia originated with the Greek settlement of Thuris (later changed to Roman Valentia) which under Moorish rule became the capital of a prosperous kingdom. In the course of the centuries Valencia has repeatedly suffered the violence of war, the last time being during the Spanish Civil War, when many churches here were pillaged. Nevertheless the old centre with its narrow, winding streets still has many fine buildings and monuments, among them the cathedral, the late Gothic Lonja de la Seda (Silk Exchange), and a large covered market. Outside the old centre there are modern districts with blocks of flats and heavy traffic. The old bed of the river Turia winds across the city, though the river itself was diverted through the suburbs after floods in 1957.

Some 750,000 people live in Valencia, making it Spain's third largest city. Not only are there many industries here – cars, computers and jeans are among the products – but Valencia is also an important centre for orange-growing. Millions of citrus trees grow in the *huerta*, the flat, fertile land immediately west of the city. Before the Civil War rice was the most important crop, hence the many rice dishes in Valencian cuisine, such as paella, and there are still many ricefields to the south of the city in the Albufera district. Valencia derives part of its prosperity from its port, El Grao, the biggest in the country. Some of the old sheds there are decorated with pictures of oranges and bunches of grapes. For generations now vast amounts of wine have been shipped out from El Grao – at present as much as a quarter of all the non-fortified and still wine that Spain produces goes out through this port.

A long history

When Hans Christian Andersen visited Valencia in the 1860s he wrote of "grapes as big as plums, the wine fiery and potent". Valencian winegrowing then had already been in existence for a long time; the Greeks and Romans both practised winegrowing here, and even in the Moorish period wine was being produced. When Valencia later became a Christian kingdom, the first attempt was made to set up a system of wine classification. A more precise classification was made in 1626 when a document was drawn up by the Monzón parliament that distinguished three categories of Valencian wine to which different excise tariffs applied.

At the end of the eighteenth century the area around Valencia was dotted with distilleries, but a century later wine had again become predominant. The destructive effect of phylloxera meant that French wine producers were searching elsewhere for strong-coloured, powerful wines for blending. A trade treaty was signed between France and Spain, and so the volume of wine exports from Valencia rose sharply and dramatically. In 1883 more than 1 million hl (22 million gal) were sent out through El Grao; some 20 years earlier it had been only 30,000 hl (660,000 gal).

Not only did wine exports achieve an impressive volume, but there was a sharp increase in the total vineyard area. The great reverse came at the beginning of the twentieth century, when Valencia too was afflicted with phylloxera. Tens of thousands of acres of vines were uprooted, mainly in the fertile *huerta* area. They were replaced by orange and almond trees, and by other crops. Valencian winegrowing became concentrated further inland – which is still the situation today.

Before the advent of phylloxera though, Valencia's flourishing wine trade attracted not only Spanish but foreign entrepreneurs too – just as had happened in Bordeaux and Champagne – and firms sprang up with names like Steiner and Teschendorff. Many of these houses have since amalgamated, or simply disappeared. It is a striking fact that of the five great wine businesses that remain, three are wholly Swiss: C. Augusto Egli, Schenk, and Cherubino Valsangiacomo. The two other houses, Vicente Gandía Pla and Vinival, have Spanish owners.

The port area

Originally all these firms were situated in the area around the port. Vicente Gandía Pla, however, has left (to an ultra-modern bodega just outside Chiva) and at least two of the other firms are considering moving. There used to be plenty of space around the docks, but residential development there has made it increasingly difficult to reach the commercial and industrial sites with trucks and tankers. However, there is no need for tourists to lament the departure of wine firms from the area, for they are simply not geared to visitors, and none of the bodegas would win prizes for the beauty of their setting.

The big producers

The five big firms are run on their bulk sales. Four of them bottle only 15 to 20 percent of their wines. Only at Vicente Gandía Pla is the proportion higher. In the early 1970s this was the first firm to sell wine in bottles; it now bottles more than a million cases a year. Various bodegas in the region have prestigious estates of their own, but by far the greater part of the wine they process does not come from their vineyards.

recent years they have given much thought both to selling bottled wines, and to bringing out lines that will enhance the prestige of the Valencia DO.

Three districts

The present DO covers about 19,000 ha (47,000 acres) and is subdivided into three districts. By far the biggest of these (with 60 percent of the vineyards) is Valentino. This lies west of the city of Valencia and is at the centre of the province of that name, with Chiva as its own midpoint. Various grapes are grown, on limestone, including white Merseguera, Malvasía and Pedro Ximénez, and blue Bobal and Garnacha. Valentino itself is again divided into four subdistricts, at heights varying from 175 to 550 m (575 to 1,805 ft) above sea level.

Northwest of Valentino is Alto Turia, a hilly district with 10 percent of the vineyards. The best white Valencia wines come from here, made mainly from Merseguera. Alto Turia has sand as well as limestone. Because of its height – an average 625 m (2,050 ft) – it is somewhat cooler here than in the other districts. The most important town in this scenically beautiful district is Chelva. Alto Turia and Valentino border on each other, but Clariano, with 30 percent of the vineyards, lies by itself in the south of the province, to the west of Gandía. The undulating terrain goes from 100 to 400 m (330 to 1,310 ft) and limestone is the main component. Some of the vineyards are laid out in terraces. Here, too, there is a subdistrict, with rather more clay. Clariano has a good reputation for its red wines made from the Monastrell grape, but Bobal and Garnacha are also grown here as well as white varieties. Districts and subdistricts are seldom stated on labels, even when the wines are not blended. At present the information is of more interest to visitors than to consumers.

White wines

White wines represent the greater part of production in the Valencia *denominación de origen*. The better kinds always have a good percentage of Merseguera, or are made exclusively from this grape, which represents 40 percent of all vines here. Provided they are fermented at low temperature these wines have a clear, juicy and refreshing taste, with some discreet fruit. They are meant for drinking within one year. Castillo de Liria from Vicente Gandía Pla is a good example of a pure Merseguera wine. At Augusto Egli Merseguera is mixed with Planta Nova and Macabeo, which results in a splendid, gently fresh wine that also offers agreeable nuances. It is labelled Rey Don Jaime. Schenk combines Merseguera with Moscatel in the light white wine Cavas Murviedro, and the Moscatel aroma is clearly perceptible here. There are also pure Moscatels, the best of them sumptuously sweet, often with 14 percent alcohol. They make delicious dessert wines.

Rosés

Bobal is the grape chiefly used for rosé wines, the same variety that predominates in the vineyards of neighbouring Utiel-Requena. These Bobal *rosados* usually have a colour that comes midway between soft pink and orange, and a dry, fresh, but never acid taste, with some fruit and a quite slender structure. They are ideal thirst quenchers on summer days. Among my favourites are the Castillo de Lira from Vicente Gandía Pla, Cavas Murviedro from Schenk, and Perla Valenciana from Augusto Egli. This last house also makes a truly complete *rosado* under the Rey Don Jaime name; this wine is given an extra dimension by the addition of Garnach and Tempranillo.

Above: The port of Valencia.

The firms buy in grapes, must, or wine from dozens of cooperatives. In the Valencia area these cooperatives are often not efficiently or effectively equipped, and so selling grapes rather than wine they have bottled is a more attractive option: modernizing the cooperatives is seen by the wine merchants as one of the most urgent problems. From the basic material available to them the five big firms create a great diversity of wines. Often this is done to their customers' specifications: buyers from all the chain stores of Europe can, as it were, order to measure – and always at a reasonable price. Sangria and must are also exported. One firm, for example, supplies must to Britain (where a soft drink is made from it) and to Japan (for wine). These five big firms are not short of brand names: at Schenk alone the various buyers have 40 or 50 to choose from.

Valencia DO

By no means all the wines sold have a *denominación de origen*, and of those that do only a fraction comes from the Valencia wine district. Valencia wines represent only about 15 percent of the total volume from Vinival (Valencia's largest bodega), and similar percentages apply to the other bodegas. Thus of all the wines shipped from the Valencia area, most originate from elsewhere. In the wines with the Valencia DO, quality and character vary greatly. The whites can range from meagre, semi-sweet little efforts to lively, pure and smoothly fresh creations of an attractive standard, and great differences also occur in the reds and rosés. None of this does Valencia's image and identity any good. However, the big firms are fully aware of this problem and in

Above: The cathedral at Valencia, which has been built in a variety of styles, from Romanesque and Gothic to Renaissance and baroque.

Red wines

In many Valencian red wines Bobal is again the most used grape, generally supplemented by Garnacha and Tempranillo, and/or Monastrell. Then come wines made from Monastrell alone (Schenk); Garnacha Tintorera (Cherubino Valsangiacomo); Tempranillo (Vinival); Tempranillo and Garnacha (Augusto Egli); and various other combinations. Together these provide a good diversity of wines. Most of them are intended for drinking within two years of vintage, but there are also some wood-aged *crianzas*. In the Schenk cellars, for example, there are several hundred second-hand casks from Bordeaux. Cherubino Valsangiacomo has some 1,700 barrels; a *reserva* is matured in some of these, the Marqués de Caro from the Clariano subdistrict Valle de Albaida. Combining Bobal with other varieties seems to result in some pleasing wines. The ones made for drinking young mostly have a supple, lightly fruity taste with a lively freshness. The cask-aged wines are usually more powerful; besides impressions of ripe fruit they often offer deeper, darker notes and, of course, a wood and vanilla aroma. That good red, rosé and white wines can be produced within the Valencia DO is certain. We can only wish that the consumer saw more of them.

PRODUCERS OF SPECIAL INTEREST

Vicente Gandía Pla 46018 Chiva
This dynamic family business was the first of Valencia's big bodegas to move out of the port area. In Chiva, about 30 km (19 miles) west of Valencia, an ultramodern establishment was built, including a large bottle plant. In the early 1970s Vicente Gandía Pla was the first important firm to bottle Valencian wine. Now it sells more than a million cases a year. The new bodega has a capacity of 30 million litres (6.6 million gal). The rosé and white wines are produced at Chiva, basically from bought-in must. Red wines come ready-made from the cooperatives. Wines for drinking young are the speciality of this house, which is strongly export-orientated.

Among the best products are the refreshing white Castillo de Liria (100 percent Merseguera), the fruity rosé Castillo de Liria (100 percent Bobal) and the juicy, supple, smoothly fruity red wine with the same name (Bobal, usually with Monastrell, but sometimes Garnacha and Tempranillo). The same wines are sold with the Marqués del Turia label. The golden Moscatel, rich in fruit, is also worth noting. In 1985 Vicente Gandía Pla celebrated its 100th anniversary. With the opening of its hi-tech plant in Chiva the firm has started out on its second century full of confidence.

C. Augusto Egli 4600 Valencia
After setting up a wine business in Zurich in 1894 the Swiss C. Augusto Egli opened a branch in Valencia in 1903. It still flourishes on its site in the dockside area and is directed by the Swiss parent company. The firm has many stainless-steel storage tanks and other modern equipment. In great contrast to the clinical-looking Valencian cellars is the rural Casa lo Alto, the firm's own wine estate in Utiel-Requena (q.v.). The house makes a number of good wines, including the clear-tasting white Perla Valenciana (from Merseguera); the white, gently fresh, Rey Don Jaime, with some nuances (Merseguera, Planta Nova, Macabeo); the *rosados* Perla Valenciana (Bobal and the fine, fruity Rey Don Jaime (Bobal, Garnacha, Tempranillo); and the smooth, pleasing red Perla Valenciana (Tempranillo, Garnacha). The red Rey Don Jaime has rather more taste and strength to it, but this is a Utiel-Requena wine.

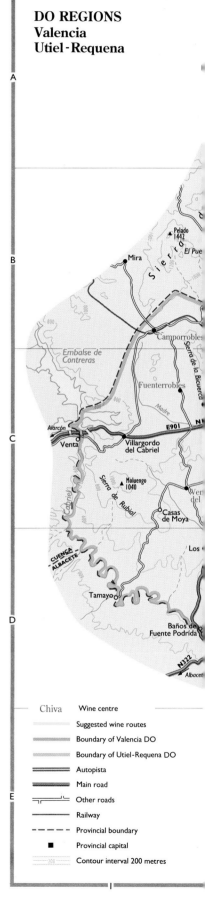

DO REGIONS
Valencia
Utiel-Requena

Chiva — Wine centre

— Suggested wine routes

— Boundary of Valencia DO

— Boundary of Utiel-Requena DO

— Autopista

— Main road

— Other roads

— Railway

— Provincial boundary

■ Provincial capital

— Contour interval 200 metres

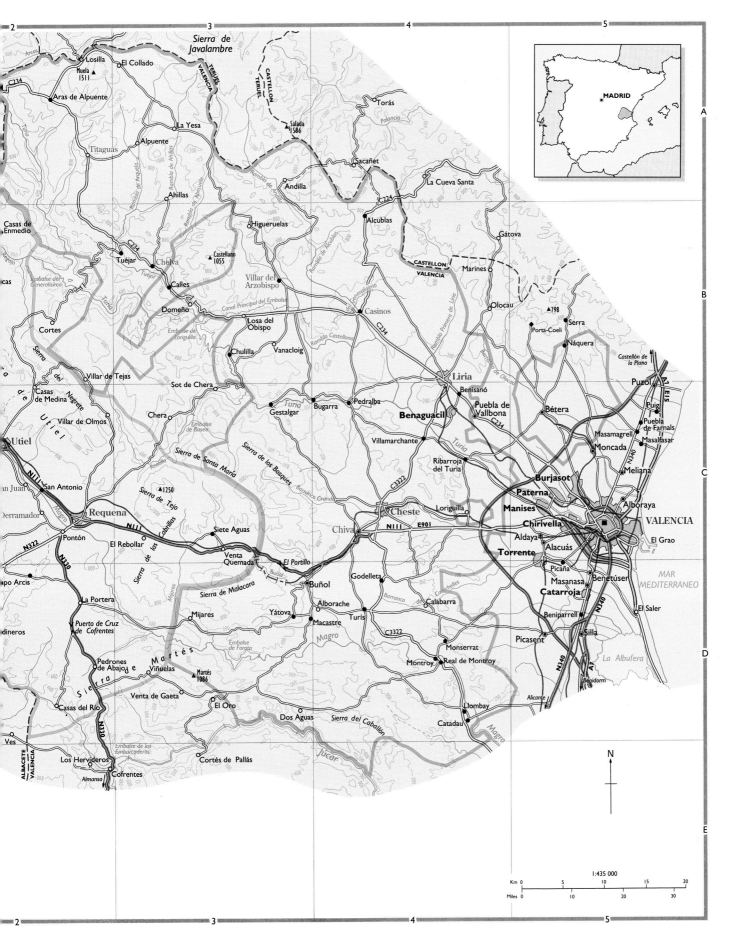

MADRID

Sierra de Javalambre

Losilla
El Collado
Muela 1511
Aras de Alpuente
C234
La Yesa
Alpuente
Titaguas
Ahillas
Casas de Enmedio
Tuéjar
Chelva
Calles
Castellano 1055
Domeño
Cortes
Villar del Arzobispo
Losa del Obispo
Chulilla
Vanacloig
Villar de Tejas
Sot de Chera
Chera
Casas de Medina
Villar de Olmos
Utiel
San Antonio
Requena
Pontón
El Rebollar
Derramador
Siete Aguas
Venta Quemada
El Portillo
Buñol
La Portera
Mijares
Yátova
Macastre
Turís
Alborache
Godelleta
Puerto de Cruz de Cofrentes
Pedrones de Abajo
Viñuelas
Martés 1086
Venta de Gaeta
El Oro
Dos Aguas
Casas del Río
Los Hervideros
Cofrentes
Ves
Cortés de Pallás
Almansa
Júcar

Torás
Salada 1586
Sacañet
Andilla
La Cueva Santa
Higueruelas
Alcublas
Gátova
CASTELLON VALENCIA
Marines
Olocau
Casinos
Serra
Porta-Coeli
Náquera
Castellón de la Plana
Liria
Benisanó
Puebla de Vallbona
Bétera
Pedralba
Benaguacil
Bugarra
Gestalgar
Villamarchante
Ribarroja del Turia
Masamagrell
Masalfasar
Moncada
Meliana
Puzol
Puig
Puebla de Farnals
Burjasot
Paterna
Manises
Alboraya
Loriguilla
Cheste
Chiva
Chirivella
VALENCIA
Aldaya
Alacuás
El Grao
Torrente
Picaña
Masanasa
Benetúser
Catarroja
Calabarra
Beniparrell
El Saler
Silla
Picasent
Monserrat
Montroy
Real de Montroy
La Albufera
Alicante
Llombay
Catadau
Magro

MAR MEDITERRANEO

N

Km 0   5   10   15   20
1:435 000
Miles 0   10   20   30

Cherubino Valsangiacomo 4600 Valencia

This firm, which has remained Swiss, was founded at Monóvar, Alicante, in 1830 and subsequently moved to the harbour area in Valencia. It is the smallest of the big five, but nevertheless handles around 100 million litres (22 million gal) a year. It produces widely differing wines and related lines, including vermouth. The wood-aged Vall de Sant Jaume is correct in its quality (60 percent Garnacha, 20 percent Bobal, 20 percent Tempranillo). The standard rises with wines bearing the Marqués de Caro name. The agreeable white is made from Merseguera, the rosé from Bobal (from Utiel-Requena), and the red mainly from Garnacha Tintorera. Cherubino Valsangiacomo is contending with serious problems of space in its location near the harbour, which is hampering the modernization of its equipment. The firm, however, is considering leaving Valencia and building outside the city.

Bodegas Schenk 46023 Valencia

This large Swiss company has had a branch in the port of Valencia since 1927. Like the other big bodegas, it specializes in bulk wines, but increasing attention is being paid to bottled wines. It brings the best of them out with the Cavas Murviedro name, which used to indicate a brand, but now a separate firm. Most of the Cavas Murviedro wines carry the Valencia DO, but the range also includes some good wines from Utiel-Requena, where Schenk has its own cellar. White Cavas Murviedro is made from Merseguera and Moscatel; the fruit scent of the latter grape is clearly present. A German-style wine was created on the basis of the Merseguera, Moscatel and Malvasía. The quite firm rosé is a pure Bobal wine. Some diversity comes with the red wine for drinking young – in its rather lively taste. It is made from Bobal with Garnacha, Monastrell and a little Tempranillo. There is also a cask-aged *crianza* version, which tastes rather sturdier and darker; Bobal and Monastrell are the grapes used here. A small amount of wood-aged wine is also made from the Monastrell grape only – the Tinto Monastrell. Schenk's casks are bought second-hand in Bordeaux and then remain in use for three or four years. The Estrella is a relatively light (11.5 percent), naturally sweet Moscatel wine; the Real Copero tastes heavier, more syrupy and more traditional. A

Above: The old Lonja de Seda (Silk Exchange) in Valencia.

delicious, meaty red wine from Utiel Requena is pure Tempranillo.

Bodegas Vinival 46120 Alboraya

Valencia's largest bodega by far is Vinival, in which the majority of shares is held by the Bodegas y Bebidas group. It sells nearly 100 million litres (22 million gal) a year, dispatched by ship, truck and train. The business was founded in 1969 by a number of separate private concerns, which subsequently amalgamated in 1975. A large building went up in the port area for the storage and handling of wine. The thick, semicircular towers of brown brick have various nicknames. About 15 percent of the volume is bottled by Vinival. The greatest merit of most of these wines is their low price; they certainly are no recommendation for the Valencia DO. The most interesting of the wines are the red and rosé Viña Calderon. These, however, come from Utiel-Requena, where Vinival has its own wine estate, the 100 ha (247 acre) Dominio del Arenal. The supple, smooth red is made from Bobal, Garnacha and Tempranillo grapes; the *rosado* from Bobal and Garnacha.

Travel Information

HOTELS AND RESTAURANTS

Levante, 46181 Benisanó, tel (6) 2780721 Famous for its paellas. Many regional wines served.
Hotel Sidi Saler, 46012 El Saler, tel (6) 1610411 Quietly situated, very comfortable seafront hotel 8 km (5 miles) from Valencia.
Parador Luis Vives, 46012 El Saler, tel (6) 1611186 Modern *parador* in the middle of an 18-hole golf course; 7 km (4.5 miles) south of El Saler.
Bergamonte, 46137 Puebla de Farnals, tel (6) 1461612 Situated on the seafront in a typical Valencian *barraca*. The food is very good value for money, and offers a good mix of regional and international dishes. The village lies 18 km (11 miles) north of Valencia.
Taberna Alcazar, Mosen Fermades 9, 46002 Valencia, tel (6) 3529575 In the south of the old centre, a place where you eat outside in summer. Specializes in fresh fish dishes. The *tapas* are also good.
Astoria Palace, Plaza Rodrigo Botet 5, 46002 Valencia, tel (6) 3526737 Civilized comfort near the cathedral. Avoid the first floor as there is a disco below.
Don Ramón, Calle Salva (not far from Calle Poeta Querol), Valencia A very good *tapas* bar.
La Hacienda, Navarro Reverter 12, 46004 Valencia, tel (6) 3731859 Valencia's most famous restaurant, where you eat well and are elegantly served. *Langosta a la mostaza* is one of the specialities.
Ma Cuina, Gran Vía Germanías 49, 46006 Valencia, tel (6) 3417799 Typical Valencian and other traditional Spanish dishes.
Larrad, Navarro Reverter 16, 46004 Valencia, tel (6) 3742002 Order the *paella de langosta* (lobster paella).

PLACES OF INTEREST

Alpuente A village high up in Alto Turia with an old castle.
Benisanó The centre here is still partly walled. On the side towards Liria there is a well-preserved feudal castle. The town also has a medicinal spring.
Calles An aqueduct and a village with atmosphere.
Chiva The parish church here has a blue cupola, characteristic of the region, with frescos inside by José Vergara. The ruins of a Moorish castle with a chapel can be seen here. In the first half of August a three-day food festival is held. Dozens of teams compete for prizes (for the best paella, for instance) and 3,000 to 4,000 people join in the feasting. The ultra-modern Vicente Gandía Pla bodega is between Chiva and Cheste.

Domeño Village in Alto Turia built originally by the Moors. In the houses in the old part of the village, the front room used to be for a cow or donkey. Near Domeño are the ruins of a Christian-built fort.
Liria Three rival orchestras are active in this "town of music". The church here is worth seeing.
Tuéjar Deep in the Alto Turia. Here you savour the atmosphere of old Spain. The village has a famous spring.
Valencia The old heart of this city is a cultural treasure house with many impressive buildings, a good number of churches among them. The biggest is the cathedral, displaying a number of architectural styles: late Romanesque, Gothic, Renaissance and baroque. The last of these is particularly in evidence in the exuberant interior. On Sunday evenings a market is held at the foot of the striking octagonal tower. Behind the cathedral there is a large square with terraces and a fountain. Through a maze of little streets (where you can easily get lost without a map) you come to the Lonja de Seda (Silk Exchange), a sublime late Gothic building. Opposite is one of Spain's biggest covered markets. The National Ceramic Museum is housed in the splendid Palacio del Marqués de Dos Aguas. Spanish and specifically Valencian paintings are displayed in the Museo Provincial de Bellas Artes. This stands just outside the old centre, across the original course of the Turia. Next to it are the Jardines del Real, the former royal gardens and now Valencia's biggest park. Northwest of the centre is the extensive Jardin Botanico, one of the best botanical gardens in Europe. In mid-March Valencia celebrates its famous festival of *Las Fallas* in which gigantic papier mâché figures are paraded through the streets and then burned.
Villar del Arzobispo Typical wine village in Alto Turia, with many springs.

WINE ROUTE

Most of the suggested wine route runs over narrow, winding roads in mountainous Alto Turia. The peace and natural beauty come as a relief after crowded Valencia and the intensively cultivated *huerta*. In addition, Alto Turia has many ancient villages, often of Moorish origin. Here you experience the atmosphere of old Spain.

Utiel-Requena

As you drive from Valencia along the N111 the road climbs steeply not far past Buñol. Here the fruitful flat land gives way to a rugged, mountainous landscape with pine trees. This is the border between the Valencia and Utiel- Requena *denominaciónes de origen*. If you follow the N111 in an easterly direction you see vineyards on both sides, on the slopes and in the valleys. At first they are isolated plots, but in the neighbourhood of Requena the landscape opens up. Vines are grown on most sites, so that the vineyards are almost continuous: unlike Valencia, with its oranges and other crops, in Utiel-Requena there is almost a monoculture.

Formerly the area subsisted mainly on cereal crops and silk culture, but from the sixteenth century winegrowing became steadily more important; and by the eighteenth century the vineyard area had already risen to more than 20,000 ha (49,400 acres). After the phylloxera infestation at the beginning of the twentieth century, the wine region took on its present form,

except that at first there were two separate districts, Utiel and Requena. Their amalgamation resulted in a region that at present covers 39,000 ha (96,400 acres) of vineyards. The region is contained between two mountain ranges and the valleys of the Turia and Cabriel at an average height above sea level of 800 m (2,625 ft), forming the most easterly part of the province of Valencia. The climate, however, is slightly less Mediterranean than that of Valencia, with fairly cold winters and relatively fresh, short summers. The soil consists mainly of porous limestone and varies in colour from pale to almost orange-brown.

The predominant variety

The towns of Requena and Utiel lie 15 km (9.5 miles) apart, linked by the N111. This busy road runs parallel with the Magro, which forms the axis of the region, and cuts through a great plateau absolutely full of vines. About half of all the vineyards come within the boundaries of Requena, while the wine-growing area in Utiel represents only a quarter of the total. The rest is distributed

Below: The most frequently planted grape species in Utiel-Requena is blue Bobal, used to make excellent rosés.

over seven communities, of which Camporrobles at 907 m (2,976 ft) is the highest.

Of the vines planted, Bobal represents about 85 percent. This is a variety that has been here since the ninth century AD and does best high up, with summers that are not too hot – two conditions that Utiel-Requena fulfils admirably. This grape lends itself perfectly to making fresh rosés, with fruit; it is the boast of the growers in this area that they produce Spain's best *rosados*. The percentage of Bobal has in fact been even greater in the past, but it has been deliberately reduced by the planting of other varieties. Pure Bobal wines in fact age badly. This is no problem for rosé wines, but it is for red *crianzas*. This is why additional varieties were brought in, notably Garnacha and Tempranillo. The oenological station and the viticultural school at Requena have also carried out successful experiments with Cabernet Sauvignon and Syrah. Trials with foreign grape varieties were likewise conducted on the beautifully situated Casa lo Alto wine estate belonging to the Valencia firm of C. Augusto Egli. Thus alongside Bobal, Tempranillo and Garnacha vines there are small plots with other black varieties, Cabernet Sauvignon, Cabernet Franc, Graciano and Syrah.

In Utiel-Requena a modest amount of white wine is also produced. In the best kinds Macabeo is always there – in combination with, for example, Planta Nova. The white Casa lo Alto is in fact made exclusively from this grape. On the estate of that name Chardonnay, Sauvignon Blanc and Verdejo are also grown.

Close links with Valencia

That Utiel-Requena has the potential to be a quality wine district is shown, for example, by rosé and red wines from C. Augusto Egli (both through the Casa la Alto estate and the red Rey Don Jaime); Cherubino Valsangiacomo (Marqués de Caro rosé); Schenk (Tempranillo from Cavas Murviedro); and Vinival (rosé and red Viña Calderon). It is no coincidence that these are without exception Valencian firms, for their hold on Utiel-Requena is considerable. There are various reasons for this. In the first place Utiel-Requena is in the same province and borders on the Valencia DO. Also, the wines of Utiel-Requena and Valencia complement each other perfectly; one district produces mainly rosés and reds, the other whites. Lastly, the Utiel-Requena cooperatives (which make 95 percent of all the district's wine) produce huge quantities of red wine that lends itself to mixing with other kinds or for shipping in bulk – two activities that form the backbone of the Valencian wine trade. Just how important the bulk wine production is can be seen from the fact that only about 15 percent of the wine from this DO is sold in bottle – again largely through the Valencia firms.

What is notable, too, is that it was not until the early 1980s that wines from Utiel-Requena were exported in bottle for the very first time. In view of the strong interests the big Valencian bodegas have in Utiel-Requena they are seeking an amalgamation of the two *denominaciónes de origen*, with subzones and, possibly, communities under the newly combined name. So far Utiel-Requena's *Consejo Regulador* does not think much of this proposition, for fear of losing its identity. Significantly, the *Consejo* has imposing premises of its own in Utiel, in a former round wine cellar (Bodega Redonda). It is particularly well furnished and besides offices and tasting rooms, it houses the Museo del Vino de la Comunidad Valencia.

Above: Entrance to the wine estate of Dominio del Arenal in San Juan, which belongs to Vinival in Valencia.

PRODUCERS OF SPECIAL INTEREST

Cooperativa Agricola Virgen del Loreto 46313 Las Cuevas de Utiel
The fermentation and storage tanks of the cooperatives stand tall in every village of the Utiel-Requena district. The collective enterprise at Las Cuevas de Utiel makes and bottles a pleasant red wine, supple and with an undertone of fruit, called Alto Cuevas.

Torre Oria 46390 Derramador
This wine estate deserves a visit not only for its beautiful *fin de siècle* house with its tiled façade, minaret-style tower and underground cellars, but also for its wines. The still varieties have the name Villa Iñigo (the same as the house). A lively taste, with fruit, characterizes the red variant, which is made from 60 percent Tempranillo and 40 percent Bobal. It is matured for a year (not in wood) before being sold. The *rosado*, from Bobal grapes only, tastes smoothly fresh and has a little fruit; the white (60 percent Planta Nova, 40 percent Macabeo) has something of a nutmeg aroma. Torre Oria produces about 200,000 bottles of still wine a year, with double this amount of sparkling wine. The latter is called Cava Torre Oria and comes in six varieties. The *brut nature* is the best: generous sparkle, elegant taste, attractive scent. But the ordinary *brut* and the *brut rosé* are good of their kind. Since 1982 Torre Oria has belonged to six families in the area. The *finca* here used to cover 10,000 ha (24,700 acres), but today the firm no longer has any vineyards of its own.

Bodegas Coviñas 46340 Requena
This firm was founded in 1965, at first with the aim of buying must from a group of cooperatives. Not long afterwards it began to make and bottle wine. Today Coviñas produces about half a million bottles a year; about a fifth of this wine will have aged in wooden casks. Among the best wines in the range are the rosé Viña Enterizo (100 percent Bobal; juicy, supple, with fruit), and the Enterizo *reserva*, wood-aged (Tempranillo and Garnacha; a lot of wood, firm, traditional in style).

Sociedad Cooperativa Vinícola Requenense 46340 Requena
In September 1976 a bottling line was set up here. Two of the most attractive products are pure, quickly bottled Tempranillo wines: the rosé Palacio del Cid and the red Tempranillo.

Dominio del Arenal 46390 San Juan
Wine estate belonging to Vinival of Valencia. It covers about 100 ha (247 acres), which yields some of the grapes for the rosé and red Viña Calderon. The estate is partly walled and you enter through a charming gateway with a little clocktower. The cellars and their equipment are efficient. Both the rosé and the red Viña Calderon are of a decent quality. Besides the native grapes grown here trials are conducted with the Cabernets and Merlot.

Casa lo Alto 46310 Venta del Moro
Casa lo Alto, probably dating from 1794, stands on a hill forming the midpoint of a 200 ha (494 acre) estate, of which about 135 ha (334 acres) are planted with vines. Bobal,

Tempranillo and Garnacha predominate, but Macabeo and Malvasía are also planted here, as well as a number of experimental varieties. Among the latter are the black Cabernet Sauvignon, Cabernet Franc, Graciano and Syrah. Trials are also carried on with white Chardonnay, Sauvignon Blanc and Verdejo. The standard of the wines made here is high. The red Casa lo Alto is composed of half Tempranillo and half Garnacha, and after fermentation it matures for a short time in oak casks. It is characterized by an aroma of ripe fruit, an element of noble wood, a firm structure and more breadth to it than many other Utiel-Requena wines. The white is made exclusively from Macabeo and possesses a pleasing freshness, combined with fruit. The estate is the property of the Valencian firm of C. Augusto Egli (see Valencia), which also uses this property for business receptions.

Cherubino Valsangiacomo (see also Valencia) 4600 Valencia
The best rosé from the range here is the Marqués de Caro, a pure Bobal wine from Siete Aguas in Utiel-Requena.

Bodegas Schenk 46023 Valencia
Has a successful pure Tempranillo from Utiel-Requena. The ordinary version of this has six to seven months in cask; but for some customers the wine is bottled sooner – and thus has less wood.

Above: Casa lo Alto, about two centuries old, which produces high-class wines.

María, which you enter through a weathered Gothic portal. Some rooms in the Museo Municipal are devoted to the wine history of the area; exhibits include old wine presses. The Museo de la Fiesta de Vendimia, which is housed in the Torre de la Fortalez, the remains of a Moorish castle, has photographs of dozens of vintage celebrations. And at the end of the great *avenida* that runs through the centre of the town is a unique, 18 m (59 ft) statue devoted to the grape harvest: the Monumento Universal a la Vendimia. The first such festival in Spain was held at Requena in 1948.
San Juan Near this hamlet between Requena and Utiel is the wine estate of Dominio del Arenal, which belongs to Bodegas Vinival in Valencia.
Utiel The *Consejo Regulador* of Utiel-Requena is housed in and beside the remarkable Bodega Redonda. This round structure dates from 1891 and for many years functioned as a wine cellar. It is now mostly a museum; all of Valencia's wine districts are represented here. Near the Bodega Redonda and opposite the station are the large Utiel cooperative and Schenk's local cellar. During the grape harvest the streets here are full of tractors waiting to deliver grapes. The 12,000 townspeople of Utiel are proud of having Valencia's oldest *plaza de toros*.

Travel Information

HOTELS AND RESTAURANTS

Fuente Chica, 46315 Caudete de las Fuentes, tel (6) 2171973 Regional dishes served here in a village some 10 km (6 miles) west of Utiel. Among the specialities of the district are sausages such as the *longaniza* (pale in colour) and *morcilla* (dark).
Mesón del Vino 46340 Requena, tel (6) 230000 Comfortable restaurant where regional dishes and wines are served. The *cordero asado* (roast lamb) is excellent.
San José, 46340 Requena, tel (6) 2300087 The best place for regional dishes, as recommended by local wine growers.
El Vegano, 46300 Utiel, tel (6) 217008 This hotel, which was opened at the end of the 1980s, stands in the centre of the town. Rooms are trim and spruce, albeit a little austere. Across the road is the busy restaurant of the same name, with quite a lot of fish dishes on the menu as well as simple meat ones. The TV is often on, especially during football matches.
Venta de l'Home, 46360 Venta Quemada, tel (6) 1184515 On the N111, near the boundary between the Valencia and Utiel-Requena *denominaciónes de origen*. This 200-year-old inn is furnished with odds and ends of old furniture and has a regionally based cuisine.

PLACES OF INTEREST

Casas de Medina Just north of this village in the Sierra de Utiel stands the fine Ermita de Nuestra Señora del Remedio. From this chapel – dedicated to Utiel's patron saint – there are views out over the mountain landscape.
Derramador Near this hamlet between Requena and Utiel a remarkable house was built at the centre of a wine estate in 1897. The façade has colourful tiled pictures, and next to it stands a minaret-like tower designed by a pupil of Antoni Gaudí. A large cellar complex extends under the house. Nowadays still and sparkling wines from the firm of Torre Oria are produced there. The owners, six families from the area, bought the dilapidated building in 1982 and have since restored it with great taste. Wines can be tasted and bought in a reception room there.
Embalse de Contreras Reservoir with a viewpoint on the N111, on the western boundary of the district.
Embalse de los Embarcaderos Anyone wanting to drive from Requena to Almansa will arrive – after negotiating the Puerto de Cruz de Cofrentes, a pass 710 m (2,330 ft) high – in a magnificent valley where three rivers flow into a reservoir, the Embalse de los Embarcaderos. In this valley and its extension are picturesque villages such as Jarafuel and Teresa de Cofrentes. Unfortunately, however, this idyllic scene is marred by a large nuclear power station close to Cofrentes.
Requena With about 18,000 inhabitants, this is the biggest town in the area. On a hill on the east side is the atmospheric La Villa, an old part of the town with narrow streets and the church of Santa

WINE ROUTE

The northern part of the suggested route runs partly through a mountain area with quiet, winding roads. The southern section goes through vineyards, wine villages and beside the famous Casa lo Alto estate of C. Augusto Egli (Valencia). To reach this estate, take the N322 out of Requena in a southwesterly direction to Los Isidros. Then turn right just past this village in the direction of Los Cojos. Just before the latter place, bear right in the direction of Caudete de las Fuentes. Casa lo Alto is on a hill to the right of the road. There are some old cellars opposite the house.

Above: Demonstrating the architectural wealth of Sevilla is the Plaza de España.

The South

A blazing sun, whitewashed houses, flamenco music, beaches, *tapas*, palm trees, Moorish monuments, bullfights, gipsies, processions and *copitas* of cool sherry are some of the images associated with southern Spain. For this sun-suffused region is not only rich in natural beauty, but also in its traditions, its culture, and its gastronomic pleasures. It consists of a single *autonomía*, Andalucía, which is made up of eight provinces. The most westerly, next to the Portuguese border, is Huelva, the most easterly Almería; in between are Cádiz, Córdoba, Granada, Jaén, Málaga and Sevilla. In the south Andalucía is bounded by the Atlantic and the Mediterranean coasts, in the north by the Sierra Morena. Between the city of Granada and the coast rises the Sierra Nevada, the highest mountain system of the Spanish mainland. Altogether some two-thirds of Andalucía is mountainous; the dominant feature of the remainder is the Guadalquivir river basin.

Olive trees and vineyards

Where the mountains give way to extended plateaux and rolling hills, the soil is fertile and is often covered with countless olive trees, their silver-green foliage stretching to the horizon. Between Córdoba and Málaga the olive groves alternate with thousands of acres of vines, forming a complex patchwork of waving green. Some of Andalucía's other crops are citrus fruits, almonds, sugar cane, rice, vegetables, grain and cotton. The fact that this dry region is so abundantly cultivated is partly due to the industry and ingenuity of the Moors, who ruled here for some seven centuries. With their advanced water engineering, they managed as if by magic to turn these arid plains into fruitful fields.

Majestic monuments

In other aspects, too, the Moors left their imprint on the region. During their rule Al-Andalus, their 'land in the west', grew into

Above: Interior of the Mezquita, the famous mosque at Córdoba, built between the eighth and tenth centuries.

one of the most prosperous and culturally rich areas of Europe, with an important university in Córdoba. In the Moorish period much majestic architecture was created, and fortunately many of these splendid monuments have been preserved. Thus Sevilla has a dozen minarets, including the beautiful La Giralda; Córdoba has its masterpiece of a mosque; and the Alhambra in Granada is one of the world's most famous buildings. The textile industry was developed under the Moors, as were the ceramic arts. They also introduced hitherto unknown fruits to Spain, among them apricots, oranges and peaches; and the same is true for rice and cotton. The exciting sounds of guitars, clicking castanets, stamping feet and rhythmic hand clapping of flamenco music are another Moorish legacy – which, thanks above all to the gipsies, remains today.

Religious processions

With the fading of Moorish civilization Andalucía entered into centuries of economic problems, which continued into the twentieth century. Vast numbers of people left the region; from Málaga, for example, thousands of families emigrated to South America. As a result of government measures in recent decades, however, the tide has now turned. Andalucía's new self-confidence has been expressed in the organization of a world fair for 1991 in Sevilla, the city that between 1503 and 1718 had the monopoly of trade with the American colonies. By tradition the Andalusians are very devout, as is clear from the many religious events. These reach their culmination in Holy Week, when there are processions in many towns and villages; that at Málaga is one of the most famous. But Andalucía is also the land of *alegría*, of

joy, for there is nearly always a celebratory feast after the solemnities. People here are also wont to enjoy life outside of these high points: sessions at table are intensive and long-lasting.

Tapas and other specialities

Before the meal itself begins the diners first tuck into *tapas*, small starters washed down with several glasses of sherry or montilla. Devising and preparing *tapas* has been raised to an art in Andalucía. Some of these little snacks are quite straightforward, such as that marvellous *jamón de Jabugo*, one of the world's finest hams, others subtle and refined. The word *tapa*, "cover, lid", comes from the slice of bread, cheese or ham that was laid on a

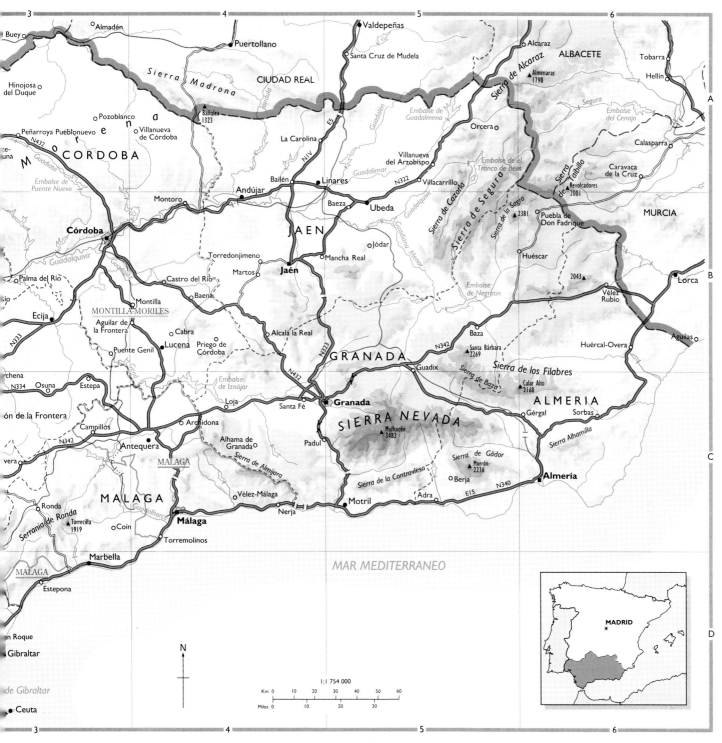

wineglass to protect the contents from flies and dust. A typical selection of *tapas* might include marinated olives, marinated mussels, *fritos* (deep-fried scallops, mussels, clams etc in batter), tiny skewers of grilled ham, mushrooms or chicken livers, garlic shrimps, salt-cod fritters, and tiny canapés of all kinds – tuna, sardines, anchovies, chicken etc.

During the meal fresh fish and shellfish are often served, in all possible variations and prepared in all kinds of ways. Gazpacho, a substantial soup served cold, is a typical Andalusian speciality; and olives are included in such dishes as *pato a la sevillana* (duck). Also traditional are recipes with meat from bulls, and *calderata de cordero*, a lamb casserole. The Moorish influence is most clearly

seen in desserts, although the El Caballo Rojo in Córdoba is one restaurant that has revived old Hispano-Moorish main courses. Many sweet dishes based on almonds are, like *mazapán* (marzipan), of Moorish origin.

As you will see, most wines are fortified, or so strong that they need no added alcohol: i.e. those from Jerez, Montilla, Condado de Huelva and Málaga. Practically all the other districts sell their whole vintage in bulk, or just bottle some wine for the local market: these areas are Aljarafe (fortified white wine), Bailén (light red), Costa-Albondón (fortified white), Laujar (red, rosé), Lopera (strong white), Los Palacios (mistela and white), Torreperogil (light red), and Villaviciosa de Córdoba (white).

191

Jerez

"Sekeris is a strong town of average size surrounded by walls. The country around it is beautiful to behold and contains vineyards, olive trees and fig trees." So wrote the Moorish geographer Ibn Adbd al-Mun'im nearly a thousand years ago. In fact, not a great deal has changed in the course of the centuries, except the name. Jerez de la Frontera is still an important centre, a place now with just under 200,000 inhabitants, surrounded by a pleasant landscape in which vineyards are predominant. The terrain is one of gently sloping hills with dead-straight ranks of green vines, miles long and growing in chalky earth. This almost dazzlingly white soil is called *albariza* and is indeed chalky; it is to this that sherry owes part of its character. In Moorish times the vineyards lay more to the other side of Jerez, to the east, just as they did at the beginning of the present era. Since then the winegrowing acres have gradually shifted to the *albariza* area which extends mainly between the three sherry towns, Jerez de la Frontera, El Puerto de Santa María and Sanlúcar de Barrameda. The zone has the form of an untidy triangle, is the nucleus of the *denominación de origen*, and is called Jerez Superior.

Increasing plantings on chalk

In about 1960 not more than 50 percent of the vineyards were in Jerez Superior. In 1980 this had gone up to 80 percent – and the proportion is still increasing, albeit slowly. Spain's oldest *Consejo Regulador*, that of Jerez-Xérès-Sherry and Manzanilla de Sanlúcar de Barrameda, is today doing a great deal to promote winegrowing on the good chalky soils. The offer of lucrative premiums for uprooting poorer quality ·vineyards has tempted many small growers – there are 4,500 to 5,000 – to take this step. At the same time a contraction of the total vineyard area is the order of the the day. The sherry region has readjusted to a stable world demand, estimated at the equivalent of 155 million bottles per annum. Besides this rooting up of vineyards the *Consejo* has received petitions from many small growers outside Jerez Superior to leave the DO so that their grapes are no longer eligible for sherry making. This results not only in reduced production, but also in an improvement in quality. The small producers, most of them members of one or other of the cooperatives, usually do not have the means to maintain their plots properly, to make improvements, or to provide efficient transport of the harvested grapes to ensure that they arrive at the presses in optimum condition.

Reducing stocks

Thus the total vineyard area has been reduced to 12,950 ha (32,000 acres): half what it was in 1980 and 5,000 ha (12,355 acres) less than in 1991. The stock of sherry in the bodegas will also have to be reduced to an eventual 700,000 casks of 500 litres (132 gal). To achieve this shrinkage an average vintage should nowadays be no greater than 165,000 casks – slightly less than the current demand for sherry. It is also realized that it is vitally important to boost the sherry image. This is in fact happening in all kinds of

Below: The best grapes come from the chalky albarizas. *Many bodegas, like Sandeman's, have cellars and pressing facilities built in the middle of the vineyard.*

ways – increasing bottling in the region itself is one of them. About 80 percent of all sherry now goes into its bottles locally. To this end all large houses such as Harvey's and Gonzalez Byass have closed down their bottle lines in the UK. Local bottling in fact is also a precondition for the *denominación de origen calificada* that this region, emulating Rioja, hopes to achieve.

The problems that the sherry region is now contending with are the direct result of 1974 estimates, based on more than 20 years of growth in export figures. The Netherlands in particular showed itself to be a sherry-drinking country. The United Kingdom, which in absolute figures had long been in first place, did not look in danger of losing its lead at that point; it has now, after consumption, halved from 70 to 35 million bottles per annum, mainly, the sherry producers claim, because of UK tax discrimination. To be able to meet demand during the boom period of the 1970s, the vineyard area was doubled within the decade to 23,000 ha (56,850 acres). Bodegas were renovated and extended, and *soleras* assiduously enlarged – which did not do the quality of the wine much good. The sherry region began to live in some style, with no heed for the consequences. As in the nineteenth century, when a similar situation arose, the results were unfavourable.

Rumasa

Throughout the 1960s and 1970s a special role was played by Rumasa, the enterprise headed by José María Ruiz-Mateos. In good times and bad this Jerez producer acted as a kind of catalyst. Rumasa in the end became a financial empire, by Spanish standards, of 18 banks and 400 other businesses in possession of about one third of both investment and production in Jerez. The end of the story came on 24 February 1983. Premier Felipe Gonzalez's government, not quite three months old, announced the expropriation of Rumasa, so that at a stroke the state became the biggest sherry producer. It was about a year before the government had a clear picture of all the Rumasa operations and could proceed to a phased re-privatization, with sherry houses (grouped in six units) among the firms on offer. The Rumasa affair came to a virtual conclusion only in 1989 with the sale of Williams & Humbert.

Palomino Fino

A notably equable climate prevails in this part of Spain. From May to the end of September the weather is dry and warm most of the time. In August the thermometer can rise to 40° C (104° F), but the moderating influence of the sea means that the average summer temperature is a very acceptable 30.8° C (87.4° F). In an annual average of 70 days with rain, some 635 mm (25 in) falls. The region therefore has more rain than, for example, Haro in Rioja, which has 500 mm (19.7 ins). Some of the moisture is retained by the *albariza*. This soil is able to absorb large quantities of water and thus build up a reserve that the vines can draw on during the hot summer months. The white Palomino Fino grape does extremely well in these conditions. This is the sherry grape par excellence, although the *Consejo* allows three other varieties: Palomino de Jerez, Moscatel and Pedro Ximénez. Long ago it was mainly Palomino de Jerez that grew in the chalky soil but this grape, also known as Palomino Basto, has largely been replaced by Palomino Fino. The latter originated in the Sanlúcar area and not only provides a higher yield, but is also considerably less susceptible to diseases. There is also more refinement to its wine, and about 95 percent of the total area is now planted with it.

Above: One of the enormous bodegas belonging to Gonzalez Byass, producer of the excellent fino *Tío Pepe.*

Other grape varieties

After Palomino Fino, Moscatel is the most important grape, at least in terms of quantity. This variety represents three percent of plantings and is mainly to be found in the sandy areas around Chipiona, just south of Sanlúcar. The Pedro Ximénez grape has had to yield a lot of territory since the 1950s. Only 0.3 percent of the winegrowing land is planted with it: some 40 ha (99 acres) in Jerez, 13 ha (32 acres) in the Lebrija area, and 2 ha (5 acres) in Sanlúcar. Like Palomino, Pedro Ximénez is eminently suited to the *albarizas*. It is principally used for making sweet wines, but trials at various houses, including Gonzalez Byass, have shown it to be also suitable for dry sherries. Moreover, the excellent results with Pedro Ximénez in Montilla-Moriles speak for themselves. That this variety has never achieved a breakthrough as a sherry grape has to do with the fact that looking after it in the Jerez vineyards is more labour intensive than Palomino, it is more susceptible to disease, and its wines are less refined and less stable.

Flor

The first phase in the making of sherry is practically identical with that for ordinary white wine. The real differences only come after fermentation is completed and the new wine is put in oak casks. The wine is then fortified with wine alcohol, and terms like *flor* and *solera* come into the story. *Flor* – or *flor del vino* – is a layer of yeast cells that forms spontaneously on the surface of the wine. It starts with yellowish-white flecks that look rather like flowers, hence the "flower of the wine" name. These continue to grow and after a few weeks the whole surface of the wine is hidden by a thick layer that resembles lightly whipped cream. This cuts the wine off from the air, while the yeast cells are nourished by oxygen. Thus the wine is protected from oxidation – one of the most important functions of *flor*. New cells are made the whole time, and the dead ones sink to the bottom of the *bota* (oak cask). The most active periods come in late spring (April and May) and in autumn (October and November). At these times the *flor* is thick and nicely white in colour. During the summer and winter months the more extreme temperatures mean practically no formation of new cells and so the layer becomes thinner. The influence of the sea means that temperatures are more moderate in Sanlúcar de Barrameda and El Puerto de Santa María than in Jerez de la Frontera, and there is greater humidity. This is good for the development of *flor* and so the layer is thicker and more active in these coastal areas than in Jerez; and the stronger and healthier the layer, the greater its influence on the wine. A good thick layer vouchsafes pale-yellow, bone-dry, delicate wines with some spiciness and a gently bitter hint afterwards. The last words in *flor* wines are therefore to be found more particularly in Sanlúcar de Barrameda and El Puerto de Santa María. This is already recognized in the case of the former district, for the sherry produced there has its own DO: Manzanilla. Until recently, *flor* was represented as the great mystery of the sherry region, but today it is a controlled phenomenon. It is allowed to develop in the casks, and so for this reason the casks are not completely filled.

The *criaderas* and *solera* system

Long ago sherries were aged in the same way as vintage wines in most other regions. However, to obtain a measure of uniformity of quality and style, the makers went over to the *criaderas* and *solera* system. As simple as it is ingenious, this is a method of enabling *criadera* (literally, nursery) wines gradually to acquire the character of mature *solera* ones. The system consists of a number of layers of casks all containing the same style of wine. In practice the *botas* or casks with the oldest wine are nearest the floor and form the *solera* (probably derived from *suelo*, "ground"). Above this bottom layer are the *criadera* layers with casks holding a blend of wine that gets younger the higher up the stack you go. There can be nearly 40 layers of *criaderas*, particularly in the *manzanilla*-producing town of Sanlúcar (*see also* Barbadillo below). A specific amount of wine, the *saca*, is drawn off regularly from the *solera*. This wine that is removed is replaced by the same amount from the next *criadera* above, which in turn is replenished from the one above, and so on until the top or last *criadera* is reached. This is then topped up with wine from any number of given years, from another *solera*, or even, but very unlikely, from the most recent vintage. In this way the *solera* gives a wine that is a complex blend – on the one hand maintaining the characteristics of the sherry in question, and on the other removing any variations in quality between different vintages. This system has been of great importance in the marketing of the wine, since it enables a consistent standard of quality to be supplied. Another advantage of the solera system is the uniformity of the maturing process, which again benefits the quality.

Manzanilla

There are many aspects to sherry, but it can be divided into three main groups: *fino*, *oloroso* and *palo cortado*. These basic types can be further subdivided according to the average age, character and quality of the wine. The *fino* group consists of wines with *flor*, and of these *manzanilla* is the lightest. This wine can only be grown in Sanlúcar de Barrameda with its particular microclimate. Locally

Above: A demonstration barrel showing flor *growing.*

this delicate, sometimes almost salty sherry – which, as we have seen, has its own DO – is often drunk as a table wine and comes in half-bottles of dark glass. On the front at Sanlúcar there are a number of eating houses where in hot weather you sit in the shade, while a soft sea breeze brings a little coolness. With a few *copitas* of *manzanilla* you can enjoy prawns and other delights fresh from the sea. In the Sanlúcar bodegas *manzanilla* has developed over the years from *manzanilla fina* to *manzanilla pasada*, eventually to become *manzanilla amontillada*. This last type, however, is seldom seen. The name *manzanilla* probably derives from the time when the growers used to bring their wine into Cádiz, where it would be drawn off from the cask as required. The last drops always seemed to have a lot of *flor*. It was just at this point that there would be a great demand for the wine, for people found that it had the same beneficial effect on their stomachs as camomile tea. And so Sanlúcar sherry eventually became known by the Spanish word for camomile.

Fino

The pale yellow *fino* exceeds *manzanilla* many times over in volume, and comes from Jerez de la Frontera and Puerto de Santa María as well as from Sanlúcar de Barrameda itself. The Jerez *finos* are generally rather more rounded and substantial in taste than the often ultra-fine *finos* from Osborne, Luis Caballero, and other bodegas in El Puerto de Santa María. In other words the *finos* from the latter district form a stage between the delicate *manzanillas* and the rich, more classic *finos* from Jerez. At present *fino* and *manzanilla* represent around 15 percent of the total volume of sherry produced, but their share is continuing to rise sharply. More and more bodegas are turning to them, for these sherries are the only ones in the range that can take on the competition from white wines made in the modern way in other regions. It is not for nothing that many *finos* are already being exported at 15.5 percent alcohol. At the same time more and more houses are making sure that the wines are as fresh as possible when shipped. The house of Barbadillo (among others) also produces an unfortified white table wine from the Palomino grape. It is called Castillo de San Diego and has a somewhat neutral, but pleasant taste. The same firm is also experimenting with a sparkling wine.

Amontillado

If *finos* and *manzanillas* are allowed to mature further in the *solera*, they develop into *amontillados*. The *flor* then becomes less and less active, and the alcohol content is raised to 17.15 percent. In addition the sherry is moved to the youngest *criadera* of a *solera* with *amontillado* only. Oxidation becomes very much part of the maturing process there, and the wine changes in colour from golden yellow to amber, and becomes more concentrated with greater acidity. The alcohol content must not exceed the prescribed legal maximum of 20.9 percent. A true *amontillado* has a dry, robust taste and a nutty, quite penetrating scent.

Oloroso

The two other main groups, *oloroso* and *palo cortado*, are subject to little or no growth of *flor*, are in contact with the air and consequently oxidized in character. *Oloroso* is the more important by far. Its name indicates that this is an aromatic type – it is Spanish for "sweet-smelling", "fragrant". It is less obviously expressive than an *amontillado*, but in dry, mature form there are often amazing nuances to it, and it is luxurious in character and velvety in taste. It was casks of *oloroso* that Francis Drake carried off to England in 1587, after setting fire to the Spanish fleet at Cádiz. It is thanks to these 2,900 casks that the English first learned to drink sherry – something the whole kingdom has gone on doing. In 1598 sherry – once again it was probably *oloroso* – was immortalized by Shakespeare in *Henry IV Part 2*, where Falstaff exclaims: "If I had a thousand sons the first principle I would teach them should be, – to forswear thin potations, and to addict themselves to sack."

Palo cortado

Like a characteristic *oloroso*, *palo cortado* has an alcoholic content that varies from 18 to 20.9 percent. Yet the wines are not alike, for *palo cortado* is in fact a maverick in the world of sherry. It comes between an *amontillado* and an *oloroso*, and is actually a rare freak of nature. It is a wine that is not suitable to proceed as a *fino*, and has little growth of *flor* or none at all. Nevertheless, its aroma has a good deal of the *amontillado* about it, while taste and colour put you in mind of an *oloroso*. Depending on its age this rare kind of sherry is subdivided into *palo cortado*, *dos cortados*, *tres cortados* and *cuatro cortados*. There are few bodegas that have a *palo cortado* in their regular range. Among the best known of these wines are the Dos Cortados from Williams & Humbert and the Capuchino from Agustín Blazquez.

Conditions for ageing

Not all the types of sherry mentioned above have to be matured in

Below: The inner courtyard of Antonio Barbadillo.

a *solera*. In principle this is only necessary for *finos* and *manzanillas*. The growth of *flor* essential for these wines needs a system of continuing refreshment, which the *solera* provides. To obtain *amontillado, oloroso, palo cortado* sherries the producer can in theory do without the latter system. In practice, however, the *solera* is equally used for these wines. For all types of sherry there is a stipulated minimum ageing period of three years, in casks of American oak; and this can only be carried out in Jerez de la Frontera, El Puerto de Santa María, and Sanlúcar de Barrameda.

Sweet blending wines

Of the above-mentioned bone-dry wines, only a modest amount is bottled in the pure form. Most of the sherry that comes on to the market is a blend of various wines. Usually these comprise a dry wine with one or two sweet and/or dark wines. The latter category consists of sweet wines (*vinos dulces*) and colouring wines (*vinos de color*). The sweet wines are made from Pedro Ximénez or Moscatel grapes, the former giving the better quality. These are laid out to dry in the sun for 10 to 15 days, which greatly increases their relative sugar content. The fruit is then pressed. Because of the amount of sugar in it, the must undergoes a slow and only partial fermentation, or alcohol may be added immediately. The procedure is the same for Moscatel. Both wines are dark, intensely sweet and sometimes almost treacly thick. Pedro Ximénez is notable for a slightly sharp, apple-syrupy kind of taste, Moscatel for a touch of nutmeg. The *vinos dulces* are intended primarily for sweetening sherries, but Pedro Ximénez has been traditionally and is increasingly being bottled and marketed under its own name, and makes an excellent dessert wine. Like Málaga it is a perfect accompaniment to chocolate

desserts. The region itself does not produce enough Pedro Ximénez wine to meet the great demand. Therefore some is bought in from Montilla-Moriles, where Pedro Ximénez is the most-planted variety. These "imported" wines have to be inspected by the *Consejo Regulador* before they can be used, mainly for sweetening.

Pale Cream was launched in the 1970s (*see* Croft below) and is a golden-yellow sweet sherry requiring a gold-coloured sweetening wine. At present this is made from Pedro Ximénez grapes that have not been dried in the sun, but pressed immediately after picking. Alcohol is then added to the must to prevent fermentation. The wine is aged in a *solera* made up of old *fino* casks (since these do not colour the wine). These casks are hermetically sealed to prevent oxidation as far as possible. Another name for this wine is *dulce blanco*.

Colouring wines are intended in the first instance to give colour to a blend. A good *vino de color*, however, will also improve the quality of the sherry in question. A boiled-down must is prepared – a process that was copied from the Moors, who used the thick, dark-brown syrup as a sweetener. This boiled-down must is then mixed with unfermented grape juice or young wine to make the *vino de color*.

Limitless possibilities

With their bone-dry and sweet wines the bodegas can create an almost unlimited number of blends. For every taste there is a sherry that can be put together. Many importers still order their sherries to measure. In addition the shippers themselves have blended their own sherries, some of which are brands that have gone around the world. Some of the best-known blends are Bristol Cream from Harveys, and Dry Sack from Williams & Humbert. Every bodega has its own formulas for the various blends, but a cream nearly always consists of an *oloroso* sweetened with a Pedro Ximénez. The Amoroso type has a similar composition, but tastes less sweet (Character from Sandeman, for example). Other blended sherries are Vino de Pasto (sweetened *amontillado*); Old East India (sweet *oloroso*); Brown Sherry (*oloroso*, blended with Pedro Ximénez and – or – Moscatel, and quite often colouring wine as well). Then there are simple varieties such as Medium, Medium Dry, and so on, also blended from various dry and sweet wines. The market for these semi-sweet types in particular is declining; the future of sherry may be largely dominated by the dry wines, mainly *fino* and *manzanilla*. For all the other kinds, long life seems likely to be their lot only if they are of high quality. Finally it should be noted that quite a few sherry houses are also big brandy producers. The wines used for this hardly ever come from the sherry region, but usually from La Mancha.

Left: Inspection of the mature amontillado *at Valdespino.*

PRODUCERS OF SPECIAL INTEREST

Agustín Blazquez 11400 Jerez de la Frontera

This firm, established in 1795, caused quite a furore in the 1980s with its Carta Blanca. This *fino* has settled at the top by consistent high scoring at tastings. It has also become a much-served drink in the Jerez *tapas* bars, rightly so, for Carta Blanca is a good, concentrated sherry with a great deal of finesse. It is clean-tasting and smooth, with that characteristic slight bitterness in the aftertaste. All the Blazquez sherries are in fact produced in Puerto de Santa María, as their style shows.

The *amontillados* Carta Plata and Carta Oro, the *oloroso* Carta Roja, and the *palo cortado* Capuchino are all characterized by their high degree of refinement. Blazquez is one of the few firms in the sherry region that includes old wines in its regular range. You will, for example, find a 40-year-old *amontillado* on the list, and a *palo cortado* of the same age. Since 1973 Agustín Blazquez has been a subsidiary of Domecq, but operates completely independently: a few years ago it bought the parent company's bodegas in Puerto and spent a great deal of money renovating them.

Bobadilla 11400 Jerez de la Frontera

After several tumultuous years in which one take-over after another fell through, Osborne finally became the owner in 1990, after first buying the splendid El Caballo vineyard from the family. Osborne stated quite openly that it was only interested in the vineyards (particularly those in the *fino* production area) and in the brandy. The Bobadilla sherries do not correspond with the Osborne concept of this wine, and so their days seem numbered. This is a great pity for it means not only the disappearance of that classic Jerez *fino*, the Victoria, but also of a splendidly rounded, rich cream like La Merced. Osborne, one of Spain's biggest brandy producers, is of course trying to profit from Bobadilla's reputation for its brandy, and its share of the market. For this sherry house, founded in 1837, has built up a name as a great brandy maker in the last 30 years. Its Brandy 103 was for a long time one of the best-known brands in Spain. A large proportion of the Bobadilla wines are still fermented in wooden casks, which endows

Above: Antonio Barbadillo of Sanlúcar.

them with a distinctly classic character.

Bodegas Internacionales-Diez Merito 11400 Jerez de la Frontera

This bodega was once the showpiece of José María Ruiz-Mateos, the man behind Rumasa. The firm's cellar complex was put up in 1977 to provide space for the wines from the many small sherry houses that fell prey to Rumasa: Bertola, Pemartin, Diestro, Varela and Marqués de Misa, to name just a few. The wines were moved en masse to the vast bodega, at that time the world's biggest, just outside Jerez. The small, historic and picturesque bodegas in the city were left empty, and some of them are now on the point of collapse. The *soleras* were combined and, depending on the market, one of the old trade names would simply be recycled. Bodegas Internacionales did in fact launch a brand of its own as well. This was the Duke of Wellington, still on the market. It was later joined by the Currito. This is a *fino* selected for its colour and finesse from the Duke of Wellington *solera*, which then goes to the Currito *solera* with its three extra levels. Despite an average age of seven years this exceptionally pale wine remains fresh, dry and altogether refined. The origin of Diez Merito goes much further back, to 1875. That was when the Frenchman Salvador Diez, together with his two brothers, set up the sherry firm of Diez Hermanos. Their best-known wines were the Fino Imperial, which at that time was an excellent *amontillado*, but has not maintained its quality; and the *oloroso* Victoria Regina. In 1976 Diez Hermanos took over the firm of

Marqués de Merito and was subsequently known as Diez Merito. After the restructuring of the nationalized Rumasa companies, Diez Merito acquired the Don Zoilo range, hitherto marketed by Zoilo Ruiz-mateos. In 1985 Marcos Equizabal bought Bodegas Internacionales and Diez Merito from the Spanish state. This businessman, who had acquired a few firms in the Rioja as well (including Paternina and Bodegas Franco-Españolas), continued the rationalization the state had begun, fusing the two houses into one large sherry producer.

Croft 11400 Jerez de la Frontera

This might be characterized as a young firm with an old name, for although the connections with wine go back to the seventeenth century, Croft Jerez has only been in existence since 1970. Getting a sherry house established today had been thought impossible, yet this company brought it about in just a few years. In doing this it was able to draw on the Gilbey family's old *soleras*, which were stored in the Gonzalez Byass bodegas. These now form the basis of the sherries that Croft markets. Old *olorosos* such as the Doña Gracia and Doña Beatriz, and *amontillados* such as Don Gaspar and MZ, are stored in one of the biggest *sacristías* in Jerez. Croft's belated decision to enter the sherry trade has had its advantages. It has, for example, profited greatly from the mistakes other producers have made. Centralization has been the guiding principle. The site is readily accessible and spacious in layout. This fledgeling producer came out straight away with a revolutionary wine called Croft Original, a Pale Cream, which was an immediate success. Romanticism is kept to a minimum in the Croft bodegas, and this applies to production as well. Continuous presses and computer-controlled vinification have little of the old winemaker's craft about them. The firm has done well with its taut, austere mode of management, and Croft is one of the most successful sherry houses, despite the fact that its wines are of less than top quality.

Garvey 11400 Jerez de la Frontera

The 1980s were a turbulent time for Garvey, for this sherry firm, known above all for its San Patricio *fino*, had problems with swift changes at the top. Regular changes of ownership do not promote stability, either of management or of product, and the reputation of the San

Patricio has suffered as a result. Once this classic Jerez *fino*, still a good, refined wine, belonged among the top sherries. After the Rumasa take-over, however, its *solera* was spoiled and the quality of the wine speedily declined – all this in a firm that had been in at the birth of this type of sherry. From 1823 onwards Garvey, originally based in Sanlúcar, was regularly exporting *pajizos* ("pale wines") to Britain. There could have been no question of any large-scale production at that stage, for it was not until the end of the 1840s that the terms *criadera* and *solera* appear for the first time. Some of the bodegas – the Guadalete complex, named after the river – are in the centre of Jerez. The most striking of them is the San Patricio, which for more than a century was the biggest bodega in the sherry region. With its casks ranged in the San Patricio *solera*, this building is still worth seeing. More romantic is the Sacristía de las Banderas, which has old wines inscribed to some fairly well-known persons. The future for Garvey is not yet clear. At present it is being restructured, which might be a preliminary to a new sale. And what is more, vineyard land in the Jerez Superior zone was sold to Osborne at the beginning of 1991. Nevertheless this bodega is busy trying to improve its somewhat tarnished image by bringing out some lovely old sherries, such as the Amontillado Tío Guillermo and the Oloroso Ochavico.

Gonzalez Byass 11400 Jerez de la Frontera

As far as the familiarity of its name is concerned this firm, founded in 1835, has to yield pride of place to its own top wine: the *fino* Tío Pepe, the world's biggest-selling sherry brand. To some extent this excellent product is still made by the classic cask fermentation method and is aged in the Gran Bodega Tío Pepe – the only three-storey bodega in the region. The rising cost of building land, and lack of space, led Gonzalez Byass to decide to put up this massive concrete structure. The great complex here borders on the Alcázar and has a number of other, more attractive bodegas, among them La Concha, La Unión and La Constancia – not to mention the splendid garden and the picturesque Los Ciegos alleyway. In recent years Gonzalez Byass has been rather more concerned with its old wines. Most of these Rare Old Soleras are between 25 and 30 years old, and together they make a fine collection. Los Aposteles is an old, slightly

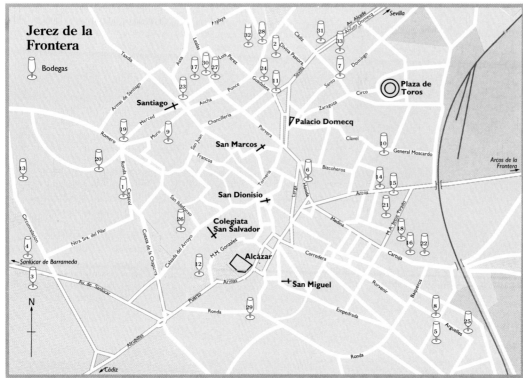

Jerez de la Frontera

Bodegas

Santiago
San Marcos
San Dionisio
Colegiata San Salvador
Alcázar
San Miguel
Palacio Domecq
Plaza de Toros

Sevilla
Arcos de la Frontera
Sanlúcar de Barrameda
Cádiz

N

1 Antonio Nuñez
2 A.R. Valdespino
3 B. M. Lagos
4 Bobadilla
5 Bodegas Rayon
6 Cayetano del Pino y Cia
7 Croft
8 Diez-Merito, S.A.
9 Emilio Lustau
10 Emilio M. Hidalgo
11 Garvey
12 Gonzalez Byass
13 Herederos Marqués del Real Tesoro
14 J. H. E. S. A.
15 John Harvey & Sons
16 John Harvey & Sons
17 José Bustamante
18 José de Soto
19 José Esteve
20 José M. Guerrero Ortega
21 La Riva
22 Luis G. Gordon
23 Luis Paez
24 Manuel de Argueso
25 M. Gil Galán
26 Pedro Domecq
27 Sánchez Romate Hnos
28 Sandeman
29 Tomás Abad
30 Viñas
31 Williams & Humbert
32 Wisdom & Warter
33 Consejo Regulador Jerez-Xérés-Sherry-Casa del Vino

sweet *oloroso*, the first cask of which was laid up around the middle of the nineteenth century. The Pedro Ximénez Noé is a complex, slightly tart creation with a taste of apple syrup and raisins. In addition there is the stylish Amontillado del Duque and the opulent, slightly sweet *oloroso* Matusalem. Besides these specialities, Gonzalez Byass also markets a large number of sherries. They are never disappointing, which is characteristic of this solid firm, which sells nearly 30 million bottles a year.

John Harvey & Sons 11400 Jerez de la Frontera
Until 1970 this was purely a firm of shippers, but in 20 years it has succeeded in building up a vast consortium in Jerez. For many years John Harvey & Sons sold wines under its own name without ever owning a vineyard or a bodega. Reliability with regard to the consumer was one of the reasons that compelled the firm to establish itself in the sherry region. Another was the ending of the contract with Ruiz-Mateos. In 1970 it bought the British house of Mackenzie & Co with its 45 ha (111 acres), thereby gaining a foothold in Jerez for the first time since 1796. From that moment developments followed in swift succession.
A large production concern was set up in Gibalbin, with continuous presses. These were revolutionary

for the sherry area; Croft adopted the process later. In the course of the following years just under 1,400 ha (3,460 acres) of land was bought and of this more than 1,000 acres (2,470 acres) has now been planted. In 1979 Harveys purchased the Marqués de Misa and Merito bodega complexes, then six years later the firms of Fernando H. de Terry and Palomino & Vergara (Jerez) were acquired: the former for its brandy, and the latter in particular for its *fino* Tío Mateo, well known in Spain. Both of these businesses have been fully integrated. Thus it is that, once again, several sherry houses have disappeared from the scene. The name Palomino & Vergara remains purely as a decoration on the Tío Mateo labels, and de Terry is no more than that for the brandy.
Most of the sherries from these various bodegas have been integrated into the Harvey *solera* systems. The company needs vast quantities of wine to be able to meet the demand for Bristol Cream alone. Tío Mateo will slowly change in style, for Palomino & Vergara's production methods were rather different from the way that Harveys makes its *finos*. Moreover, the latter wants to move towards a lighter type. The Tío Mateo launched on the Japanese market already has this new, young character. If it pleases the customers, the rest of the world will have to accept it.

Emilio Lustau 11400 Jerez de la Frontera
The exceptionally dynamic firm of Emilio Lustau has made a particular name for itself over the last 10 years with a number of specialist sherries. First of all it came out with the so-called *almacenistas*: sherries that Lustau bought in from small private producers (who were often doing it as a hobby), bottled in very small quantities, and then suitably marketed. This approach has done the sherry image no harm at all. It is by no means strange that Lustau should have done things this way, for the firm itself has an *almacenista* background. José Berdejo y Veyan, a lawyer, set the firm up in 1896 as a hobby. Decades later his son-in-law Emilio Lustau put the sherries on the market. Lustau therefore has a special feeling for these amateurs not shared by other companies. Besides this, with only a few dozen acres of vineyard, the firm's freedom of manoeuvre was limited. Until recently Lustau bought mainly from cooperatives, with all the risks this entails. This meant the firm had insufficient control over quality; and not all cooperatives have the best of equipment. To survive Lustau had to be there in the market with all manner of not very usual items. This did not do a great deal for the firm financially, but it spread abroad the Lustau name for quality. Some change has come about recently, for in the autumn of 1990 Luis Caballero, of Puerto de

Santa María, bought Lustau. This has given the latter more elbow room, for the Montegillilo vineyard of 120 ha (297 acres) is now at its disposal and so it can be involved in the production of sherry from start to finish. Other Lustau activities in years past have included launching the East India Solera and the Landed Age sherries. The latter are – literally – shipped to England to spend a further few months ageing in cellars by the Thames. Only then are they bottled.

Pedro Domecq 11400 Jerez de la Frontera
At certain times in the history of sherry it has been Pedro Domecq that has instigated new developments. Domecq was the first firm to bottle all its sherries within the production area. And in the last decade it has taken up the struggle against oxidation in *fino* wines. Domecq believes absolutely in the great future that lies ahead for *fino* sherries that are fresh and refined, and has spared neither cost nor trouble in its effort to control the whole production and bottling process to the maximum. Oxidation has to be combated at all levels for the greater glory of its refreshing, elegant and bone-dry La Ina. To avoid oxidation, Domecq began to fit a screwcap to its bottles. At first the other bodegas were shocked; since 1991, however, Osborne has been using screwcaps for all its sherries. Domecq is the oldest of all

the big sherry houses, having been set up by the Irishman Patrick Murphy in 1730. Dating from the same year is its fine El Molino bodega, named after the olive oil mill that must once have stood on this site. Besides several old *soleras* this bodega houses the *sacristía* with casks inscribed to William Pitt, Nelson and the Duke of Wellington, those heroes of the wars with Napoleon. On the other side of the road, on a hill on the outskirts of Jerez, stands the La Mezquita bodega. With its imposing forest of columns, this rather resembles the Mezquita, the great mosque, in Córdoba. Housed here are the casks of La Ina, which takes its name from Aina!, the Moorish battle cry. Next to the Mezquita are the production bodegas with a capacity of 135,000 hl (2.97 million gal). That Domecq's heart is not just in pawn to the *fino* is clear from the three superior sherries that it has been selling for several years now: the old, slightly sweet *palo cortado* Sibarita; the Pedro Ximénez Venerable, tart and tasting of raisins and apple syrup; and the complex Amontillado 51 1a.

Sandeman 11400 Jerez de la Frontera

The history of this firm is somewhat like that of Harveys. For a long time Sandeman, too, was purely a shipper, giving its own name to the wines. However, the bankruptcy of Pemartin, one of its most important producers, compelled this British house to become involved in sherry production. As the largest creditor, Sandeman took over Pemartin's bodegas and old stocks of sherry. Some 25 years later a big collection of *olorosos* was added. These still form the basis of the excellent range of *olorosos* the house has in stock. Sandeman remained in the hands of its family until 1980. In order to escape the persistent attempts by Rumasa to take it over, it fled to the arms of Seagram, the Canadian multinational. The sherry firm was subsequently taken in hand and totally modernized. In Britain, David Sandeman has made successful efforts to raise the image of sherry. For example, he has taken bottle-aged sherries to auction to demonstrate that these were indeed exceptional wines. In addition he has promoted the rarer sherries in the Sandeman range. Among the best are the Royal Esmeralda, a sweet *amontillado* about 25 years old; the 28-year-old Royal Ambrosante, a *palo cortado* and also sweet; the sweet *oloroso* Royal

Top: Rolling barrels outside John Harvey and Sons' bodega in Jerez de la Frontera.
Centre: The Marqués de Bonanza of Gonzalez Byass is the great-grandson of one of the founders.
Bottom: The family firm of Valdespino is run by Miguel Valdespino. Its Inocente Bodega is one of the oldest in Jerez de la Frontera.

Corregidor, also 28 years old; and finally the concentrated and particularly complex Imperial Corregidor, more than 40 years old. For the present the Don Fino, Sandeman's best *fino*, is not likely to be so successful; it is perhaps too classic to enchant many people, yet does not have quite the finesse to rank among the top sherries. A younger and fresher type would not come amiss here. In 1990 Sandeman celebrated its second century. The firm has entered very confidently into its third century with the renovation and extension of its bodega complex in Jerez.

A.R. Valdespino 11400 Jerez de la Frontera

The old romanticism of the classic Jerez family business can still be savoured at this establishment where the head of the firm, Miguel Valdespino, stubbornly insists that love for a centuries-old craft should be the keynote in the making of wine, although the firm is equipped with all the modern device. For example, Valdespino mainly sticks to fermentation in wooden casks for its Fino de Inocente. The quality of this Fino, a model of refinement and style, symbolizes the craftsmanship of the bodega. The Tío Diego, an excellent *amontillado*, is at this same level of quality; and in fact the two wines come from the same vineyard. The firm's most beautiful bodega is only a stone's throw from the office. This is the Inocente bodega, part of a former monastery. Little has changed here since the eighteenth century; today the casks are still ranged under a low roof in what is one of the oldest bodegas in Jerez.

Williams & Humbert 11400 Jerez de la Frontera

The last ten years have not been lucky for Williams & Humbert. It formed part of Rumasa from 1972, then after the latter had been taken over by the Spanish government the firm remained too long under the state umbrella. This was all due to the difficulties surrounding Dry Sack. There was in fact a lawsuit to establish that this brand name belonged not to Rumasa but to Williams & Humbert. Subsequently there were many prospective buyers for this well-known sherry house, but it was Barbadillo that got in first. However, it proved to be rather too big a proposition for the Sanlúcar firm and so at the beginning of 1991 it sold off 60 percent of the holding to two Dutch firms: 40 percent to Bols, which had been on the warpath in Jerez for some years; 20 percent to Ahold. During all these developments sales of Dry Sack, a supple and elegant blend of *oloroso*, *amontillado* and Pedro Ximénez, had declined considerably. Williams & Humbert, however, went indefatigably on. The house did in fact hold a number of aces: the Dos Cortados, for example, a beautiful *palo cortado* with a subtle bouquet and an elegant, clean taste; and the Pando, a fino with body. Then there is Walnut Brown, a classic Brown Sherry; A Winter's Tale, a nice medium *amontillado*; and its slightly sweeter *oloroso* counterpart, As You Like It. Britain has always been an important market for Williams & Humbert.

Wisdom & Warter 11400 Jerez de la Frontera

Wisdom & Warter (founded in 1854) have not been independent for very long. In 1930 the company was bought by Gonzalez Byass. After Warter's death in 1914, they went through rather unsettled times, as it had relied rather heavily on this whimsical character. Wisdom did

Above: Grape-picking at Osborne's.

not live in Jerez but in London, where he led a rather quiet and unobtrusive life, always remaining slightly in the background. This led to the saying in Jerez: Wisdom sells the sherry and Warter makes it. Wisdom & Warter owe their survival to Gonzalez Byass' helping hand. In spite of being taken over, this small sherry producer (which must have produced some 3.6 million bottles in the past few decades) has succeeded in steering a relatively independent course. Although the grapes (part of which come from their own model vineyard Bodogonera) are processed at the large production bodega of the mother company, the

fermentation (mainly in stainless steel tanks) and maturing take place in Wisdom & Warter's bodegas in the old centre of the town of Jerez. The company (which has a wide range of classic sherries) is especially known for its fine choice of *amontillados*. The best of them are Tizon, and Very Rare Solera, a powerful sherry with enormous concentration. The typical Jerez *fino* Olivar (ripe, bone dry and displaying the characteristic impressions of almond) is also of a high standard.

Luis Caballero 11500 El Puerto de Santa María

The family firm of Luis Caballero, founded in 1830, resembles Valdespino in being one of those typical Spanish sherry houses. Although it is far from small, its great strength lies in the home market, and export forms only 30 percent of total turnover. The Ponche de Caballero, a mixture of brandy and orange juice, is very popular in Spain; but the Fino Pavon, from Puerto itself, is also a success. Recently this *fino* has been produced by a system developed by Caballero. When the sherry is about five years old and ready for bottling it is blended with a *fino* from the *sobre tablas* (wine of the most recent vintage), and then spends several weeks in bottle. By this means Caballero "rejuvenates" the *fino* and increases its *flor* aroma. The impression is given of a fresh *fino* –

which is another means of combating oxidation. The long history of the house is marked by two important feats. The first of these was the purchase in 1933 of the sherry producer José de la Cuesta, which also brought the renowned house of John William Burdon into Caballero's possession. Although both these firms were totally absorbed into the parent company, the two brand names continued in use for the foreign market. Burdon in particular falls more easily on the ears of English speakers than Caballero. The second feat was of much more recent date, namely the take-over of Lustau, which showed Caballero's fine nose for quality. The whole of production has been focused on *fino*, for according to Caballero this is the ultimate sherry; the rest, *amontillados* and *olorosos*, are only a side show.

Osborne 11500 El Puerto de Santa María

This is perhaps the most successful firm of late. This house, still controlled by the Osborne family, had by the early 1990s grown into Spain's biggest producer of wines and spirits. Thomas Osborne arrived in Cádiz around 1800. There he got to know James Duff, who had been in the sherry trade since 1768 and had set up Duff Gordon in 1832 with William Gordon. In 1832 Osborne became a partner in Duff's business and four years later took charge of the firm. It was not until 1890 that the Osborne name appeared on casks and bottles, but this did not mean giving up Duff Gordon. A division was made, with the Osborne name used for the home market, Duff Gordon for exports – mainly to Britain. Osborne has been out raiding in recent years and in the contest for various bodegas, Williams & Humbert among them. In the end Bobadilla was acquired, Osborne being particularly enchanted by its stocks of brandy and the vineyards in the Balbaina district, a *fino* area par excellence. Osborne in fact is supported by two important pillars, namely *fino* and brandy. Like the other big producers – Domecq, Gonzalez Byass and, to a lesser extent, Caballero – Osborne believes fully in the pale yellow *fino* that is seen to full advantage in Puerto in particular. Everything therefore must yield pride of place to the Fino Quinta. Vineyards are being bought up one after the other in the *fino*

Left: Pressing house of Williams and Humbert in the albariza *vineyards.*

districts; bodegas are being adapted to create the most favourable microclimates for *finos*; and Osborne is going over to screwcaps to restrict oxidation as far as possible.

In the meantime Osborne has also been active in the international market with – besides Quinta (the Duff Gordon *fino* Feria) – the young *amontillado* Coquinero; the sublime *oloroso* Bailen; and the rich Pedro Ximénez 1827. The splendid Osborne bodegas are worth a visit, La Palma in particular.

Antonio Barbadillo 11540 Sanlúcar de Barrameda

This is by far the biggest producer in Sanlúcar; about 70 percent of all the bodega space in the area belongs to this firm. Its headquarters is housed in the beautiful El Palacio de la Cilla, the former bishop's palace. The firm was founded in 1821 but did not count for much until 1966, when it got hold of the big Harvey wine orders. Since then the house has not looked back and every year supplies an average 6 million litres (1.32 million gal) of sherry. Written up in large letters on one of its bodegas are the proud words *Proveedores* (Suppliers) *de Harveys of Bristol*. The Harveys connection has done Barbadillo no harm. The firm did in fact become a little reckless and bought Williams & Humbert, then had to divest itself of 60 percent of it later. In earlier years Barbadillo had already acquired Pedro Romero and 50 percent of Los Infantes Orleans-Borbón, both of them in Sanlúcar. The whole of Barbadillo's wine production is centralized in the big Gibalbin complex, which was set up together with Harveys. After fermenting, the wines are transported to Sanlúcar, where they are further matured in the bodegas in accordance with a complicated system. Thus the most recent *manzanilla* (the Fina Eva) passes through 19 *criaderas*; the oldest, a *manzanilla pasada* (Solear), has by the end of the process been through nearly 40 levels, by which time it is some 16 to 17 years old. The house carries a strikingly large range. There are at least six brands for each of the lightest styles. In addition the firm has four current dry *olorosos* and *amontillados*. The same numbers apply for the sweet versions. Not liking the modern trend towards a more limited range, Barbadillo has clung to the traditional big selection of sherries.

Right: One of the most recently established bodegas is that of the Marqués del Real Tesoro.

José Medina y Cía 11540 Sanlúcar de Barrameda

This house, dating from 1821, did not sit still during the 1980s. Within a short space of time it bought up a fistful of firms: Hijos de A. Pérez Megía, known for its elegant Manzanilla Alegría, R.M. Lagos, Juan Vicente Vergara, and Luis Paez. Ahold, the Dutch food concern, has had a majority interest in this last-named house since February 1980. Although these various firms operate independently as far as possible, and are therefore responsible for the nurture of the wines, vinification is centralized at Medina in Sanlúcar. Fermentation takes place partly in stainless steel, partly in the classic *tinajas*. From the production bodega the wines are distributed among the other firms. Luiz Paez receives its due share and subsequently sells the sherries under the Rey de Oro and Conqueror names.

Herederos de Argüeso 11540 Sanlúcar de Barrameda

This *manzanilla* specialist works in the traditional way by fermenting its wines – from 70 ha (173 acres) in the Jerez Superior zone – in old casks steeped in wine. The only modern tanks here are used for cold stabilization of the wines shortly before bottling. Both the ordinary *manzanilla* Viruta and the *manzanilla* Pasada San León are of exemplary quality, and are right at the top in their categories.

Above: Sampling in the Emilio Lustau bodega.

Hijos de Rainera Pérez Marín 11540 Sanlúcar de Barrameda

In the nineteenth century there was a steadily increasing demand for the *manzanilla* from this house, which dates from 1825. Those placing orders used to be asked whether they had enough *guita*, or money. The repeated use of this expression gave the bodega the idea of giving its best *manzanilla* the brand name La Guita. This still exists and the wine in question is a characteristically excellent *manzanilla*. It is aged in a *solera* with eight levels. The firm owns no less than 205 ha (507 acres) in the Jerez Superior zone.

Los Infantes Orleans de Borbón 11540 Sanlúcar de Barrameda

Barbadillo run Los Infantes Orleans, 50 percent of which is owned by the largest producer in Sanlúcar and the remaining 50 percent by the Spanish royal family. Most wines are left to mature in the bodegas of Barbadillo. Los Infantes only have Las Caballerizas at their disposal, namely the old horse stables of the castle, built in the Burgundian style in the centre of Sanlúcar. This is also where a part of the refined *manzanilla pasada*, Tizona, is stored. The castle was sold to the town in 1970 and having been thoroughly renovated it is now the town hall. Some wines are still vinified in the traditional manner, such as those of the Torre-Breva complex, south of Sanlúcar, which covers some 150 ha (370 acres). Here, after the grapes have been pressed, the wines are fermented in *tinajas*.

In early spring, after the first classification, the wines are moved to the bodegas of Sanlúcar, where they are in part integrated with the reserve of Barbadillo. This is why a number of wines of the two houses are surprisingly similar to each other. Top of the list in the range are, besides the Tizona (also sold under the name Torre-Breva), the *manzanilla fina*, the La Ballena *manzanilla olorosa*, the splendid Ataulfo *amontillado* and the well-balanced Fenicio *oloroso*.

Travel Information

HOTELS AND RESTAURANTS

Jerez de la Frontera At the beginning of the 1980s Hotel Jerez de la Frontera was the only hotel of any consequence in the city. Today, Jerez has a number of good hotels, and others are always being built. The swift development of this area is there to be read in the way in which this aspect of tourism is being tackled.

Hotel Avenida, Avenida Alvaro Domecq 10, 11405 Jerez de la Frontera, tel (56) 347411 Situated opposite the Royal Sherry Park, in a converted block of flats. The hotel has a three-star standard of comfort and is furnished in a severely functional style. The quality of the cooking leaves something to be desired.

Bodega La Andana, Parque de la Serrana, 11400 Jerez de la Frontera, tel (56) 307385 Typical *tapas* bar in one of the modern suburbs of Jerez. The fish specialities are particularly good. Other bars where good to very good *tapas* are served are: Mesón La Tasca, Plaza del Caballo; El Buen Comer, Plaza de Toros; La Venencia, Calle Larga; and Maypa, Cruz Vieja.

El Bosque, Avenida Alvaro Domecq, 11405 Jerez de la Frontera, tel (56) 333333 The most prestigious of the Jerez restaurants, nicely situated and with architecture that is more English than Spanish. The cuisine is international, but includes Andalucian specialities.

Las Botas, Santo Domingo s/n, 11400 Jerez de la Frontera, tel (56) 338977 Takes its name from the many casks of sherry stored here. Specialities of this atmospheric *tapas* restaurant, besides its *serrano* ham, include *tortilla de camarones* (tortilla with shrimps).

Camino del Rocio, Avenida Nuestra Señora de la Paz, 11400 Jerez de la Frontera A *tapas* bar for the late evening. When the clock strikes 12 the lights go out and a candle is lit before the image of the Virgin Mary, after which the idea is that everyone joins in singing a devotional song. The *tapas* are good, as is the *berza gitana*, a casserole with meat and ham.

Hotel Capele, Corredera 58, 11400 Jerez de la Frontera, tel (56) 346400 Simple but good three-star hotel, renovated and extended at the end of the 1980s. It is in the centre of Jerez and within walking distance of various tourist attractions, such as the San Miguel church, the covered market and certain bodegas (Gonzalez Byass and Diez Merito, for example).

Hotel Jerez, Avenida Alvaro Domecq 35, 11405 Jerez de la Frontera, tel (56) 300600 A five-star hotel of the Ciga chain, on the outskirts of Jerez. Still the city's most important hotel and the meeting-place of the sherry trade. The Jerez provides every comfort and there is a fine garden and swimming pool. The restaurant serves both regional and national specialities. There is also a terrace restaurant (barbecue).

Bar Juanito, Pescaderia Vieja 8–10, 11400 Jerez de la Frontera, tel (56) 334838 Small bar in the old part of Jerez. Excels in the original Jerez *tapas*. This place should not be missed if you want a good idea of *tapas* and all that goes with it.

La Orca Gorda, Santo Domingo 11, 11400 Jerez de la Frontera, tel (56) 335152 Spanish national dishes presented in a French manner. This is one of the better Jerez restaurants, but not the place for typical Andalusian fare.

La Mesa Redonda, Manuel de la Quintana 3, 11403 Jerez de la Frontera, tel (56) 340069 Tucked away in an arcade below a block of flats, this restaurant serves good quality food. A number of regional dishes are on the menu, but also many of the chef's own creations, in which fish figure largely.

Hotel Royal Sherry Park, Avenida Alvaro Domecq 11, 11405 Jerez de la Frontera, tel (56) 303011 Modern four-star hotel with a functional atmosphere. Spacious, fully equipped rooms, swimming pool, restaurant and much-patronized bar. In walking distance of the city centre, and not far from the Williams & Humbert and Garvey bodegas.

Tendido 6, Circo 10, 11405 Jerez de la Frontera, tel (56) 344835 The most famous dish at this restaurant, opposite Entrance 6 of the bullring, is the *cola de toro*, or bull's tail. The *angulas* (elvers fried in olive oil with Spanish pepper and garlic) are also delightful. In the restaurant's *tapas* bar, one of the nicest in Jerez, there is a large assortment of excellent snacks on the menu.

El Puerto de Santa María Much the same can be said of this town as of Jerez, although developments here got under way rather later. For a long time the town had only one hotel of a decent standard; today it has four.

Casa Flores, Ribera del Río, 11500 El Puerto de Santa María, tel (56) 863512 Excellent *tapas* bar, known especially for its splendid *serrano* hams.

La Goleta, Carretena de Fuentebravia, 11500 El Puerto de Santa María, tel (56) 854232 Good fish restaurant, where even the lobster has remained affordable; the presentation tends to be French in style. Not far from the road from Puerto to Rota.

Hotel & Yacht Club, Puerto Sherry, 11500 El Puerto de Santa María, tel (56) 874004/873000 The Puerto Sherry complex just outside the town consists of a yacht harbour; Pueblo Sherry, the Andalusian village; and the Hotel & Yacht Club. This four-star hotel has all the comforts. The complex also has six restaurants, bars, three swimming pools, saunas, Turkish baths, tennis and squash courts. The Vista Hermosa golf course is close by.

Hotel Meliá El Caballo Blanco, Avenida de Madrid 1, 11500 El Puerto de Santa María, tel (56) 863745 The town's oldest hotel of a decent standard. It is in the four-star category and stands a few hundred metres (yards) from the road from Puerto de Santa María to Cádiz, and 548 m (600 yds) from the beach. There is of course a swimming pool and the hotel is surrounded by a beautiful garden and dozens of pine trees.

Mesón del Asador, Rufina Vergara/Plaza Herreria, 11500 El Puerto de Santa María, tel (56) 864022 Meat, especially grilled, is the order of the day here – which is exceptional for Puerto. Try the marvellous potato salad.

Mesón del Pescador, Calle Jesús de los Milagros 11, 11500 El Puerto de Santa María, tel (56) 871897 As the name indicates, this restaurant with its glamorous décor specializes in fish. The building itself is no less chic.

Hotel Monasterio San Miguel, Calle Larga 27, 11500 El Puerto de Santa María, tel (56) 864440 This four-star hotel in the centre of Puerto was opened in 1990 and occupies a nicely restored eighteenth-century monastery. The roof terrace offers a splendid view out over the Bay of Cádiz. The swimming pool is in the walled garden. The restaurant and *tapas* bar are reasonable.

Los Portales, Ribera del Río/ Ribera del Marisco, 11500 El Puerto de Santa María, tel (56) 862116 Good restaurant and a *tapas* bar of at least the same level. Being right on the harbour, there are many fish specialities.

Hotel Santa María, Avenida de la Bajamar, 11500 El Puerto de Santa María, tel (56) 873211 Reasonable, three-star hotel, opposite Puerto's fishing harbour and within walking distance of the centre of town. The swimming pool and sun terrace is on the hotel roof. A pleasant *tapas* bar.

Sanlúcar de Barrameda The hotels here do not amount to much, and if you are visiting it is better to drive out from Puerto de Santa María or Jerez. However, there are plenty of restaurants and *tapas* bars here, often of a surprisingly good quality.

Casa Bigote, Bajo de Guía, 11540 Sanlúcar de Barrameda, tel (56) 362696/363242 One of the most famous restaurants in Andalucía. The two brothers, Fernando and Paco, have made a concept of it; they are former fishermen who have brought ashore the kind of cooking practised aboard fishing vessels. It is a straightforward cuisine, with fish and all the rest the sea has to offer in the main role. Especially popular are dishes with such fried fish as *acedias*, *salmonetes* and *puntillitas* (tiny squid). No refrigerator here: everything is fresh.

Café-Bar El Tunel, Plaza del Cabildo 25, 11540 Sanlúcar de Barrameda, tel (56) 362513 A good eating-place in the centre of the town, specializing in shellfish and grilled fish.

Restaurante El Veranillo, Barrios 6, 11540 Sanlúcar de Barrameda, tel (56) 362719 Traditional cuisine, with much use of wine – i.e. sherry – but in a more contemporary style. To be recommended.

PLACES OF INTEREST

Arcos de la Frontera One of the best-preserved examples of a medieval town with a Moorish tradition. Numbers of narrow streets and steps climb steeply, and small entranceways form practically the only openings in and among the tall, massive buildings. This picturesque place – the best known of the white-walled *pueblos blancos* – stands high up on a narrow ridge and is washed on three sides by the Guadalete. From a much-visited balcony of the well-preserved castle of the Dukes of Arcos there is a truly magnificent view out over the surrounding countryside. The largest church, Santa María de la

Asunción, is a repository of architectural styles. Romanesque, Gothic, Renaissance and Mudéjar influences are all to be seen in this monument: not surprising, since building began in the seventh century and went on into the eighteenth.

Cádiz The provincial capital Cádiz is one of the oldest cities of southern Spain. By about 1,000 BC the Phoenicians had established themselves on the narrow spit of land here on the Andalusian coast. Cádiz was another of those places whose great prosperity came when trade with the New World got under way. That period of prosperity largely determined the character of the city. The old, romantic part of Cádiz, with such districts as El Populo and Santa María, took its shape then in a maze of alleyways and passages. The cathedral towers over this old section of the city, with only the Campo del Sur to separate it from the Atlantic Ocean. Black columns divide its nave from the aisles on either side. Among those buried in the crypt is the composer Manuel de Falla. The Santa Cruz, also called El Sagrario, is smaller, but no less beautiful than the cathedral. It dates from the thirteenth century, but was rebuilt in Renaissance style after its destruction in 1596. Its most precious treasure is a silver monstrance 3 m (nearly 10 ft) tall. Other fine churches are the Capilla de Santa Catalina, with paintings by Bartolomé Murillo; the Santa Cueva, with work by Francisco de Goya; the seventeenth-century monastery church of Santo Domingo, known for its high altar with spiralled columns; and the Oratorio San Felipe Neri, the seat of the Cádiz parliament during the Napoleonic wars.

Chiclana de la Frontera A proportion of the wines produced from the vineyards around Chiclana are sent to Jerez or the other two sherry towns, where they are usually used in the cheaper blends. Chiclana used to be better known for its white pasto-wines which have now become rather rare. The little town, which has over 40,000 inhabitants, is also famous for its mostly hand-made dolls and the sulphur baths of Balneario de Fuente Amarga which are taken in Spain as a cure against rheumatism. The town of white-washed buildings is dominated by the dark Iglesia Major, which looks very much like a fortress. The church of the Augustinian nuns and the Hermitage of Santa Anna are also very interesting and deserve a visit.

Above: Training in the famous riding school of Jerez de la Frontera.

Chipiona Recently, Chipiona has become especially known for its horticultural production, including large numbers of flowers such as chrysanthemums, carnations and pinks. Tomatoes and melons are also grown. But the sweetest moscatel sherries are still made from the grapes grown on the sandy soil (the *arenas*) around Chipiona. Because of its wonderful climate and beautiful sandy beaches the town has always been a popular seaside resort, but only among the Spanish, because it has not yet been discovered by international tourism.

Chipiona was probably named after Scipio Africanus. The ruins of the towers, built in honour of this Roman commander (235–185 BC), and those of a Roman settlement, can still be seen nearby.

Jerez de la Frontera Cádiz may be the provincial capital, but that is what Jerez feels itself to be – and certainly has the air of one. The fine town mansions, the picturesque old part of the city with its many historic monuments and its imposing bodegas give Jerez a certain distinction. Jerez had an important role in the distant past, for it was an important border fortress in the wars between the Catholic monarchs of Castilla and León and the Moors; hence the title "de la Frontera". Its strategic siting is still there to be read in its strong walls and the Moorish Alcázar, a stone's throw from the Gonzalez Byass bodegas. The citadel was built in the eleventh century on the foundations of a Roman fort, which explains its rather plain, rectilinear form. Its octagonal tower dates from the fifteenth century. Within the Alcázar are the thirteenth-century Capilla de Santa María and a twelfth-century mosque. During repair work in the Torre del Homenaje at the beginning of the twentieth century, the remains of Moorish baths were discovered. The restoration of this piece of the Moorish heritage was begun in the second half of the 1980s and is continuing. Close to the Alcázar stands the Colegiata San Salvador, the cathdedral. This dates from the first half of the eighteenth century and replaced an earlier Gothic structure, traces of which, such as pointed arches, are still visible. A free-standing belfry, with a lower section that belonged to a vanished Mudéjar castle, rises beside the cathedral façade, which is in the decorative Plateresque style of the Spanish Renaissance. Not far from the Plaza El Arenal, the great square in the heart of Jerez, stands the church of San Miguel, with a splendid blue-tiled Mudéjar spire that can be seen from afar. This fifteenth-century Gothic church emulated the cathedral at Sevilla with its Giralda tower. The interior of San Miguel has recently been restored. This church is noted for its imposing high altar. The fine Madonna on one of the side altars should also be seen. (If it is too dark, the priest will gladly put the lights on for a few pesetas.) A busy shopping street with various tapas bars (La Venencia among them) leads into the Plaza El Aremal. At the other end of this street, near the Puerta de Sevilla, is the Palacio Domecq, the former residence of the

Marquises of Domecq. The arms of this family, two white gloves, are to be seen everywhere. This building is used for receptions and is only very occasionally open to the public. One of the great rooms is kept permanently ready for a visit by King Juan Carlos. The *ayuntamiento* or city hall lies outside the old town walls; Jerez has quite a number of buildings that fulfilled this function in the past – such as La Atalaya, once the property of the Vergara family and now a clock museum. The oldest part of Jerez, with its ancient street layout and narrow alleyways, might be compared with an open air museum. It is true that many of the old buildings are undergoing restoration, but a great deal that is beautiful remains for the visitor to discover. There is, for example, the Casa de Cabildo Viego. This former *ayuntamiento*, which now houses the city library, dates from the end of the sixteenth century; the coat of arms of Philip II adorns its Plateresque front. There are two fine churches in this area: the fifteenth-century San Dionisio has a tower like a minaret, while the late Gothic San Marcos is worth seeing for its main altar covered with Moorish tiles, and its side chapels built in Mudéjar style are of great art historical interest. The Santiago church in the lively gipsy quarter of Jerez is rather reminiscent of St Mark's. Two of its chapels have Mudéjar roofs and one is in rococo style. In the centre of the city there is the archaeological museum to visit, with finds that emphasise the ancient history of wine in the region. The Spanish Riding School, the Escuela Andaluza de Arte Ecuestre, is an important and interesting tourist attraction; the dancing horses give a show every Thursday at 12 o'clock. La Cartuga is a Carthusian monastery, dated 1463, that lies some 4 km (2.5 miles) southeast of the city. It is a splendid group of buildings with some stirring history. During the Carlist wars around the mid-nineteenth century the monastery was closed; earlier, in the Napoleonic conflict, it was used as a military barracks and stables. Since those days the monastery has returned to its rightful Carthusian owners. What is particularly noticeable is the multiplicity of architectural styles. The Gothic monastery church of Nuestra Señora de la Defensión has a Plateresque portal; a good many of the art treasures of this church have been stolen over the years, and a number of images have disappeared from the high altar. The *claustrillo* is a courtyard

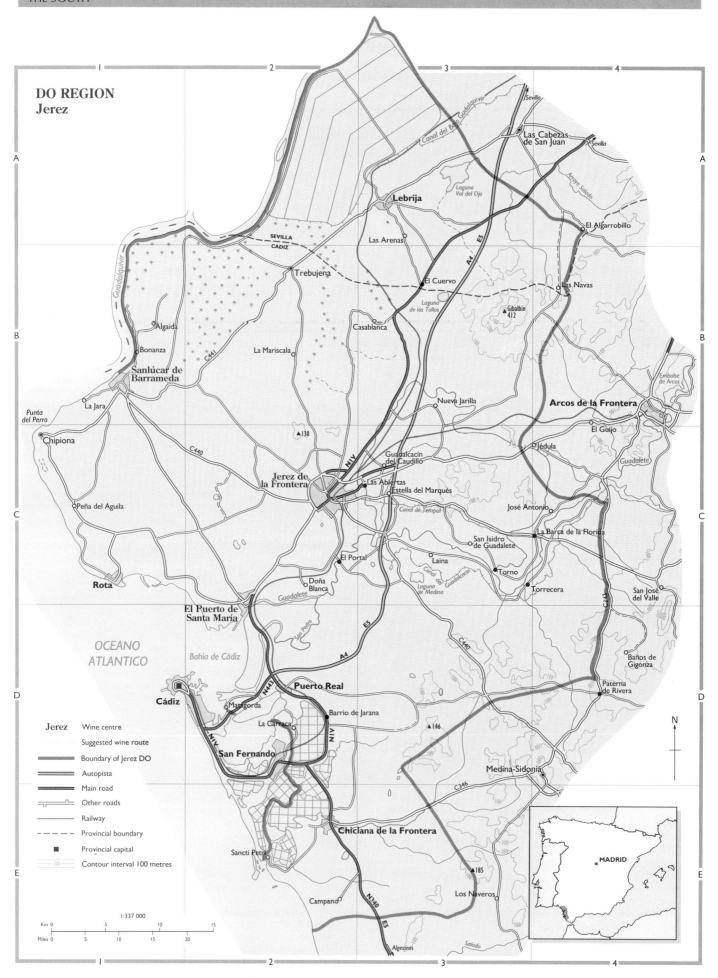

DO REGION
Jerez

SEVILLA
CADIZ

Las Cabezas
de San Juan

Sevilla

Lebrija

El Algarrobillo

Laguna
Val del Ojo

Las Arenas

Sevilla

Guadalquivir

Trebujena

El Cuervo

Las Navas

Gibalbín
412

Algaida

Casablanca

Laguna
de los Tollos

Bonanza

La Mariscala

C441

Embalse
de Arcos

Sanlúcar de
Barrameda

Nueva Jarilla

Arcos de la Frontera

La Jara

El Guijo

Punta
del Perro

Jédula

Chipiona

C440

▲130

Guadalete

Guadalcacín
del Caudillo

Jerez de
la Frontera

Las Abiertas
Estella del Marqués

José Antonio

Peña del Aguila

NIV

Canal de Tempul

La Barca de la Florida

San Isidro
de Guadalete

El Portal

Laina

Torno

San José
del Valle

Rota

Doña
Blanca

Canal

Guadalcacín

Torrecera

Guadalete

Laguna
de Medina

El Puerto de
Santa María

San Pedro

Baños de
Gigonza

OCEANO
ATLANTICO

Bahía de Cádiz

A4

E5

C440

C443

Paterna
de Rivera

Puerto Real

NIV3

Matagorda

Barrio de Jarana

▲146

Cádiz

La Carraca

NIV

San Fernando

Medina-Sidonia

Jerez   Wine centre

Suggested wine route

Boundary of Jerez DO

Autopista

Main road

Other roads

Railway

Provincial boundary

Provincial capital

Contour interval 100 metres

Chiclana de la Frontera

Sancti Petri

C346

▲185

MADRID

N

Los Naveros

Km 0   5   10   15

Miles 0   5   10   15   20

Campano

N340

E5

Algeciras

Salado

1:337 000

surrounded by Gothic cloisters, which the monks' cells open on to, and where in earlier times they used to be buried. This sherry city also has a goodly stock of noblemen's houses; the collection around the Benavente square is especially impressive.

El Puerto de Santa María Down through the centuries Puerto has been able to hold its own reasonably well against Jerez. It has had one important advantage, namely the presence of a harbour, and this has been of inestimable value to the sherry trade. The sixteenth and seventeenth centuries were a golden age for Puerto de Santa María because of the expanding trade with the New World. The Casa del Cabildo dates from this time. So does the Iglesia Mayor, or Nuestra Señora de los Milagros, the church that Alfonso Rodriguez built and in so doing created one of the town's most precious monuments. The south portal, the Puerta del Sol, is particularly beautiful. This is a good place to see how an originally Gothic piece of architecture developed into Plateresque. To the right of the high altar is the chapel with the figure of Nuestra Señora de los Milagros, patron saint of Puerto. Richly decorated town mansions also went up during the years of prosperity, such as the Casa de Bizarrón on the Plaza del Castillo. Smaller merchants, too, benefited from the prosperity and had their houses built in a style that was to become characteristic of Puerto de Santa María. There are still plenty of these often impressive villas in the town, especially around the harbour, and they are furnished with a kind of turret. From these *atalayas* (the Moorish word for lookout) the occupants can watch the ships sail in and out. Also worth seeing are the Plaza de Toros, with Spain's biggest arena, and the Castillo San Marcos, the property of the sherry family Caballero. In 1990 restoration work on an old bodega, built against the castle wall, was finished off and the fine result is now in use for receptions. According to tradition Columbus and his crew prayed in the castle chapel on the eve of one of their voyages to the New World.

Lebrija This is the only town in the sherry production region which does not lie in the province of Cadiz. The outline of the town standing out against the horizon is easily recognized with the ruins of the medieval castle at the top of a hill. The most important church is Santa Maria, which was built in the 16th century, parts of an old mosque being used as building material. The style is a mixture of Gothic and Renaissance. The Mudéjar tower dates from the 18th century.

Sancti Petri The island of Sancti Petri lies off the Spanish coast opposite the town of Chiclana. The Phoenicians built a famous temple to Hercules here, and it was also here that the Spanish composer Manuel de Falla wrote his *Atlantico*.

Sanlúcar de Barrameda The growing reputation of *manzanilla* is ensuring that Sanlúcar is confidently coming out of its shell. For long this seaport let Jerez show the way. Yet Sanlúcar was once an important place, and prominent in the sherry trade before Jerez acquired all the power for itself. The pomp and splendour of times past have lost much of their lustre now, but the place still has its charm; thus this former fief of the Dukes of Medina Sidonia holds a wealth of monuments. In addition to the seat of this ducal family there is a palace, built in Burgundian style, that belonged to the Spanish royal house of Bourbon. This was bought by the town in the first half of the 1980s and, after thoroughgoing restoration, now serves as the town hall. Like every town in southern Spain, Sanlúcar has an abundance of churches. The most beautiful of them is the fourteenth-century Santa María, with fine portals. The townscape here is dominated by the ponderous Castillo de Santiago, built on the foundations of a Roman fort. This castle, which has been undergoing careful refurbishing, is surrounded by the Barbadillo bodegas, and the firm has named its white table wine after the castle. In the centre of Sanlúcar is the Plaza de Cabildo, a square with atmosphere, orange trees, fine houses, a fountain and a café. This is where people meet one another after Sunday mass. The Sanlúcar seafront, too, is a good place to linger, not least for the restaurants serving fresh fish, shellfish, and cool *manzanilla*. In 1498 Columbus departed from the nearby harbour on his second voyage to the New World; and later Francisco Pizarro sailed out to search for treasure in Peru.

WINE ROUTE

Naturally enough the wine route through the sherry region takes in its three most important places, Jerez de la Frontera, Puerto de Santa María and Sanlúcar de Barrameda. The road between Jerez and Sanlúcar leads across the chalky *albariza* terrain of the wine slopes. From Sanlúcar to Puerto de Santa

Above: Cork trees growing on the Sierra Blanquilla, east of Cadiz.

María it runs along the coast for part of the way, and round the American base at Rota. From Puerto you can make the trip to Cádiz. Northeast of Jerez there is the attractive Arcos de la Frontera, which merits a visit and is therefore included in the route.

Condado de Huelva

Although Condado de Huelva borders on the sherry area, it can only be reached by way of Sevilla, after making a great detour north of the Guadalquivir delta with its Coto de Doñana National Park. Obviously the climate here is practically identical with that of the sherry country: in other words hot, dry summers and mild, fairly damp winters. Nor does the average rainfall differ much at 650 mm (25.6 ins) a year. The annual average temperature is 17.5° C (63.5° F). The vine is the most important plant grown in the mainly chalky soil (there are only a few vineyards here on alluvial soil), and this has been the case for many centuries.

As in the sherry region it was the Phoenicians who introduced winegrowing, and later the Romans profited from it to the full. Huelva thus has a long tradition in wine. Some seven centuries ago its wines were already being shipped to northern European countries. In *The Pardoner's Tale* Chaucer refers to the very strong white wines of Lepe, a town between Ayamonte and Huelva. Geoffrey Chaucer (c. 1340–1400) was the son of a vintner and so knew what he was talking about. In other words, Huelva wines already had an image, which they maintained for several centuries. It is clear, too, that the first wines drunk in the New World would have come from Huelva. At all events Columbus had a number of casks of wine with him when he sailed from the local port of Palos de la Frontera in 1492 on the voyage that was to take him to "India". The first document indicating that a brisk wine trade was developing with America dates from 1502. Great days were dawning for Huelva.

Reduced production

But in the second half of the seventeenth century a decline set in, and this decline continued into the twentieth century. For decades half of Huelva's production went to Jerez bodegas, to disappear anonymously into the *soleras* there. The rest of the wines were not widely distributed, as the producers in Condado de Huelva were poorly equipped to do this. In addition, the 1980s saw a reduction in the demand for the classic fortified wines the region was exclusively producing at that time. Many producers therefore went over to other branches of agriculture – such as growing strawberries. By the end of the 1980s some 130 million kg (about 11,800 tons) of these were being picked. The vineyard area dropped from 18,622 ha (46,016 acres) in the mid-1970s to 15,631 ha (38,625 acres) in 1981, and then down to the present 12,000 ha (29,650 acres). To tackle these problems a number of bodegas resolved to adapt themselves to the new fashion for light, fruity white table wines. These have now come to account for about a third of the total annual production of 165,000 hl (3,630,000 gal).

Cooperation

In 1979 Condado de Huelva was the first Andalusian district to be given permission to produce white table wine within its *denominación de origen*. A number of producers promptly banded together to set up Sovicosa, a company with modern equipment installed. Since then only white table wine has been made there, including the successful Viña Odiel. Not long afterwards the biggest of the cooperatives, Vinícola del Condado, bought modern equipment and began to produce unfortified wines alongside its fortified kinds. Grapes for the unfortified table varieties are usually picked a few weeks earlier than usual, in order to give the wines their requisite freshness.

The gently sloping Condado de Huelva vineyards, at 50 to 200 m (165 to 655 ft) above sea level, are mainly concentrated in the neighbourhood of Bollullos par del Condado. This charming little town between Sevilla and Huelva is at the heart of the winegrowing area, with dozens of bodegas and distilleries almost side by side. Zalema is the most common grape variety in the district, accounting for 75 percent of plantings. Just under 20 years ago it was still at 90 percent. The local *Consejo Regulador*, however, has promoted planting of Palomino. This is because Zalema is not altogether adequate for the classic wines, whereas Palomino offers much more refinement. The Zalema percentage has therefore gradually dropped. At present, however, numbers of producers are hesitating: their traditional grape variety is, in contrast to the neutral Palomino, very suitable for the lucrative making of white table wines. The enthusiasm for rooting out Zalema is therefore diminishing steadily. The expectation is that the proportion of Palomino, despite the *Consejo*'s efforts, will not increase much now. Other grape varieties permitted in this DO are Moscatel and Garrido Fino, but these are of only minor importance.

The classic wines

From early days there has been a great deal of contact with the sherry area. This can be seen in the production and the maturing of the fortified wines here, which show many similarities to what happens in the sherry towns. Thus the classic Condado de Huelva wines – the area was given its DO in 1963 – are comparable to some of the sherry types. The Condado Pálido and Condado Viejo, like the *vinos generosos*, are fortified wines. The former is rather like the *fino* sherries, but lacks their finesse. The Pálido, which is also subject to *flor* (see page 194), has rather more substance to its taste and colour. This is largely because the development of the *flor* is less intensive. Its alcoholic strength varies from 15 to 17 percent.

In the past Pálido wines matured in the *solera* were always called *finos*, but sherry producers objected strongly and use of the name was prohibited. However, one of the Huelva producers went to court to contest this ban. He won his case and since 1985 use of the term *fino* for Pálido wines has been allowed (except in the UK). The Condado Viejo is the equivalent of the Jerez *oloroso*, a wine where oxidation has featured in its maturing. Here, too, the Huelva wine is usually the lesser of the two kinds. Compared with the *oloroso* the Viejo lacks both intensity and complexity. Its alcoholic strength varies from 15 to 23 percent. The Viejo comes in versions ranging from dry to sweet (*seco*, *semiseco*, *semidulce* and *dulce*). All fortified wines from Condado must have had two years' cask ageing – one year less than the sherries – in one of the communities within the DO.

The cooperatives

With 85 percent of the total, the Condado de Huelva cooperatives have by far the biggest share of wine production. Until recently the 19 cooperatives (of which only five can be regarded as really important) sold practically all their wines in bulk to private producers in their own region, or to bodegas in Jerez. Of late, however, some of these concerns have set their wine production on a new path. They have opted for quality, a quality moreover that applies particularly to white table wines. The best example is Vinícola del Condado, in Bollullos par del Condado, which at present is good for 30,000 hl (660,000 gal) of white table wine a year, compared with 140,000 hl (3,080,000 gal) of the classic Condados.

PRODUCERS OF SPECIAL INTEREST

Bodegas Andrade 21710 Bollullos par del Condado
The house of Andrade, nearly 50 years old, has mainly concentrated on producing white table wines in recent years. At present half of the grape harvest is vinified in stainless-steel tanks; the resulting Castillo de Andrade is a fresh, fruity wine of reasonable quality, made solely from Zalema grapes, which has to be drunk young. The Doceañero, a 12-year-old amber-coloured Viejo, is the best of the classic Condado wines here. The firm's *oloroso* is 100 percent Palomino. Not all the production comes from Andrade's own vineyards, which cover about 120 ha (nearly 300 acres); both grapes and wine are also bought in from small producers in the region.

Bodegas A. Villaran 21710 Bollullos par del Condado
At present this bodega only produces classic Condado wines. It has the whole range of Pálido, including Pedro Ximénez (which does not come within the DO). For the million litres (220,000 gal) of wine it makes every year, Villaran has recourse to its own 50 ha (124 acres), and also buys grapes and young wines from other local producers. In recent years the firm has invested in stainless-steel tanks for temperature-controlled fermentation. Nevertheless a proportion of the wines still ferment in concrete vats. Among the best wines in the range are the Solera 1934, a Condado Viejo made from Zalema grapes; and the Pedro Ximénez Villaran, a wine with the aroma of dried fruit and a well-structured, somewhat tart taste.

Manuel Sauci Salas 21710 Bollullos par del Condado
This firm, founded in 1925, is one of Huelva's few quality houses working with traditional methods. It is small, owning just 7 ha (17 acres) of vineyard, and wholly dedicated to the classic local wines. Only one third of production is bottled, the rest being sold in bulk. The bottled wines are of outstanding quality. The eight-year-old Pálido Espina Pura (100 percent Palomino), for example, has a generous dose of *flor*, a structured taste, and is of a satisfactory refinement. The Riodiel, 15 years old and also made from Palomino grapes, is a good wine with a nutty fragrance to it. The good measure of acid shows the age of this Viejo.

Top: Detail of the church tower of El Rocío, a village on the outskirts of the Doñana National Park. Once a year tens of thousands of pilgrims come to worship Nuestra Señora del Rocío. The wetlands of Doñana is Spain's largest National Park. It is the home of many rare birds and animals, including two of Europe's most endangered species, the imperial eagle and the lynx.
Bottom: Wine estate near Almonte. The custom of planting palm trees in front of the house dates from the time of the Moors; it symbolizes hospitality.

Sovicosa 21710 Bollullos par del Condado
A number of producers set up the high-tech Sovicosa bodega in 1984 purely and simply to make a white table wine. This was the Viña Odiel, a fruity, juicy wine made wholly from Zalema grapes. It must be drunk young. Later the Viña Saltes, a semi-sweet version, was added but this has not achieved the level of the dry wine.

Vinícola del Condado 21710 Bollullos par del Condado
Following Sovicosa's example Vinícola del Condado, with its 1,800 members the biggest cooperative in the region, changed course completely in 1986. The most advanced winemaking equipment was bought: modern presses, stainless-steel tanks for computer-controlled fermenting, and facilities for cold stabilization. This cooperative, accounting for 4,500 ha (11,120 acres), was yet another producer that saw a future in white table wines. The classic wines were not to be forgotten and they still represent 80 percent of annual production. Nevertheless Sovicosa had set the tone for the coming years, plotting a course for winegrowing in Condado de Huelva. As in Rueda, producers will devote more and more attention to white table wines. The classic fortified wines will have to give ground, but without disappearing altogether. Vinícola del Condado has at present five white table wines in its range, all made wholly from the Zalema. The best is the refreshing Viña del Mar 92. This cooperative also makes a reasonable red wine called Barón Rojo. Its classic Condado wines, too, are generally of good quality; in particular the characteristic Fino Mioro, made from 90 percent Palomino and 10 percent Garrido, is very worthwhile.

Cooperativa San Isidro Labrador Almonte, postcode 21730
With around 800 affiliated producers, who together account for 1,600 ha (3,955 acres), San Isidro Labrador is one of the region's bigger cooperatives. It is one of the youngest bodegas, founded in 1972, but its equipment is far from modern and it still makes use of *tinajas*. However, its Los Tejares table wine, made from 100 percent Zalema grapes, is of reasonable quality. The cooperative also makes a dry and a sweet Condado Viejo and a red wine also called Los Tejares. This *tinto*, made from Zalema grapes and *doble pasta* from Jumilla, has no DO.

Travel Information

HOTELS AND RESTAURANTS

El Reñiero, Cruz de Montañina 6, 21710 Bollullos par del Condado, tel (55) 410875 The place to go for regional fare in this small town, 48 km (30 miles) from Huelva and typical of this rural area. The town is the seat of the Consejo Regulador del Vino del Condado. Among the specialities of the restaurant are hams from the area (*Jabugo*) and fish dishes such as *rape a la marinera* (angler fish).

Las Candelas, Carretera de Punta Umbria, 21000 Huelva, tel (55) 318301 The consistently high quality of the food it serves makes this one of Huelva's best restaurants. It uses produce that is fresh on the day, and fish and meat dishes are cooked over charcoal. Service is professional and good.

La Cazuela, Garcí Fernández 5, 21000 Huelva, tel (55) 258096 A restaurant that, like so many here, specialises in fish dishes.

Doñana, Martin Alonso Pinzón 13, 21000 Huelva, tel (55) 242773 Restaurant with a pleasant atmosphere. Specialities are the casseroles and dishes with pork from the Iberico pig, which also provides joints of ham. Try the *rape al vino blanco*, angler fish with a sauce based on white wine.

Los Gordos, Carmen 14, 21000 Huelva, tel (55) 246266 This restaurant applies itself to cooking fish dishes, which taste splendid, and the shellfish is particularly good; but it also serves excellent hams.

Luz Huelva, Alameda Sundheim 26, 21003 Huelva, tel (55) 250011 One of the region's better four-star hotels. It has a fine garden, a swimming pool and tennis courts.

La Muralla, San Salvador 17, 21003 Huelva, tel (55) 255077 Regional dishes are prepared and presented in an elegant way; the starting point is what fresh produce the market has to offer. An extensive wine list, which includes the regional varieties.

Tartessos, Alonso Pinzón 13, 21003 Huelva, tel (55) 245611 Very much a tourist hotel, with three stars and a reasonable restaurant.

Parador Cristóbal Colón, 21130 Mazagón, tel (55) 376000 This *parador* is close to an extensive sandy beach, and not far from the Coto de Doñana National Park.

La Parrala, Plaza de las Monjas 22, 21800 Moguer, tel (55) 370422 Simple restaurant with typical regional dishes on the menu.

Hostería de la Rábida, La Rábida, 21810 Palos de la Frontera, tel (55) 350312 A small three-star hotel with five rooms, situated beside the the de la Rábida monastery. The restaurant specializes in fish and has a large stock of Condado wines.

PLACES OF INTEREST

Bollullos par del Condado This is Condado de Huelva's wine town, where most of the producers are established and the *Consejo Regulador* is based; the latter has set up a *casa del vino* here, a pavilion where wine can be tasted and bought. A wine festival takes place in mid-September, during a big agricultural and trade fair. The *ayuntamiento* and the Santiago church both date from the eighteenth century.

Coto de Doñana The Coto de Doñana National Park covers 750 sq km (290 sq miles) in the southern part of the Guadalquivir delta. The area, an important resting place for migratory birds, is notable for the contrasts in its landscape. Dunes, beaches, pinewoods and marshes alternate, and the great range of vegetation provides for an equally varied fauna. The Parque Nacional de Doñana is the domain of many kinds of birds of prey, of herons and pelicans. Deer, wild boar, marten and lynx also have their habitats here; and there are even dromedaries. You can only visit Coto de Doñana in the company of a member of the staff. For information the address is: Diputación Provincial del Ministerio de Información y Turismo, Calle Paraquay 1, Sevilla.

Huelva The town in fact lies

Above: The statue of Columbus, south of the town of Huelva

outside the production area, but is nevertheless worth a visit. Huelva was built on a neck of land between the Tinto and Odiel rivers. The Phoenicians first founded the town and named it Onuba. Many centuries later the Moors called it Ghelbah. From 1468 Huelva belonged to the Dukes of Medina Sidonia. Preparations for Columbus's first voyage must have been made in the neighbourhood. Just southeast of Huelva is Palos de la Frontera, from where the discoverer set sail with his three ships, the Santa María, Pinta and Niña. Since 1929 a 36 m (118 ft) high statue of Columbus commemorating that voyage has stood at Punta del Sebo, at the confluence of the Río Tinto and the Río Odiel. The monument is the work of the American Gertrude Vanderbilt Whitney.

Although the warfare of past centuries, and the earthquake of 1755, have destroyed many buildings and monuments in Huelva, there are still things to see. In the north of the town there is a Moorish aqueduct that has remained in excellent condition. There is also the San Pedro, a sixteenth-century church that was rebuilt after the earthquake. It stands on the site of a mosque, remains of which can be seen, including a splendid screen. Also worth seeing are the churches of La Concepción and San Francisco. Exhibits in the Museo Provincial de Bellas Artes include archaeological finds from prehistoric chambered tombs in the area.

Left: View of the wine country of Moguer. The parish church has a 16th-century Mudéjar tower.

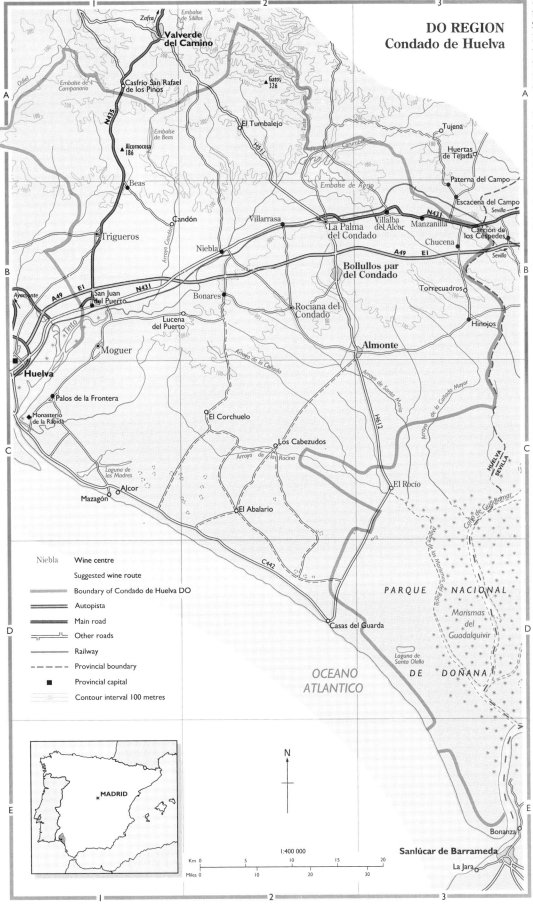

DO REGION
Condado de Huelva

Moguer On a hill near this small town there stands the 14th-century Santa Clara monastery, built in Mudéjar style. The church here, where Columbus offered a prayer of thanksgiving after his safe return from the New World, holds many treasures. There are, for example, a 17th-century altarpiece, alabaster tombs, a diptych of the Sienese school, and choirstalls in Granadine Moorish style; these last are unique in Spain. Also in Moguer is the sixteenth-century Nuestra Señora de la Granada with its fine Mudéjar tower, which rather resembles the Giralda in Sevilla.

Monasterio de la Rábida If you drive from Huelva to Palos de la Frontera you pass this famous Franciscan house after about 10 km (6 miles). It was built on its hill in the fifteenth century. The earlier (fourteenth-century) church has the remains of fifteenth-century frescos. Columbus gained support for his voyages of discovery at this monastery. In 1484 the prior, Juan Pérez de Marchena, offered shelter to Columbus and his son Diego, and acted as mediator in the negotiations with the Catholic kings.

La Palma del Condado Wine town where the regional baroque style is beautifully represented in the parish church of San Juan Bautista. This is flanked by a tall steeple, and in front there is a square with palms and a fountain.

Palos de la Frontera This village is an early Spanish settlement. It was from the harbour here, now silted up, that on 3 August 1492 Columbus began his voyage to "India", and to which he returned on 15 March 1493. Palos has many prehistoric monuments, including a chambered tomb over which the Romans later built a fort. Later still the Moors made a lookout tower of it. The church of San Jorge rose on the foundations of an early Christian basilica, and there is a fine west portal in Mudéjar style.

El Rocío With its small houses and unsurfaced roads Rocío has much of a Wild West ghost town about it. But once a year, at Whitsuntide, it is thronged with tens of thousands of pilgrims who come here to pray to Nuestra Señora del Rocío.

WINE ROUTE

The suggested route not only goes through the various important wine communities, but also close by the Coto de Doñana, through Huelva, past the statue of Columbus just southeast of Huelva, and past the Monasterio de la Rábida.

Málaga

Málaga has a glorious past as a wine region. It takes its name from the city that was founded by Phoenicians about 3,000 years ago. They called it Malaca, probably from the word *malac*, which meant "salt" – fish was salted here. It seems likely that the Greeks were practising wine growing around Málaga – which they called Mainake – by about 600 BC, and also introduced methods of pruning. The Romans made wine here too, as demonstrated by the Roman wine cellar that was found near Cártama, to the west of Málaga. During the Moorish period wine remained part of the way of life. The Moors called it *xarab almalaqui*, which meant "Málaga syrup", and it is possible that this name was chosen to obscure the alcoholic character of wine. It became apparent in 1214 that Málaga wine enjoyed a great and almost universal reputation, after a commission in Paris spent two months analysing the world's best wines. As a result, Cypriot wine was given the honorary title of "Pope of Wines", and that of "Cardinal of Wines" was awarded to the Málagan product.

Wine fraternity

Later, the winegrowers of Málaga began to protect the quality standards of their wine. To this end they established a fraternity in 1487, the Hermandad de los Viñeros de Málaga, a body that also carried out charitable work. In 1552 the town authorities took measures against wine fraud, particularly in the taverns. The following century saw a very great increase in exports: in some years 15,000 casks out of the 20,000 produced went overseas, but the real golden age was yet to dawn. It came between 1787 and 1829, when wine became the backbone of the local economy. At the end of the eighteenth century Málaga wine was more famous than that of Jerez. In 1791 the Spanish ambassador in Moscow presented the Empress Catherine II with some cases of Málaga. These pleased her so much that she gave permission for Málaga to be imported free of duty, on condition that it was wine approved by the Hermandad.

In 1851 the region was afflicted with mildew, and then in 1876 an even greater disaster struck – phylloxera. Málaga had the doubtful honour of being the first Spanish wine district to be affected, and the effect on the vineyards and the economy was calamitous. With just under 113,000 ha (279,000 acres) of vineyards, Málaga was then Spain's second wine region – but within a few years all the vines had been destroyed, and many winegrowers emigrated to South America. Recovery came slowly and only to a modest degree. The Spanish Civil War, during which the city of Málaga was largely destroyed, represented another low point. In addition, sweet fortified wines went out of fashion. As a result of all this Málaga largely sank into oblivion, to the extent that just under 900 ha (2,225 acres) of vineyards is all that is cultivated today, and the area is among the smallest of Spain's *denominaciones de origen*.

Below: Antequera, originally a Roman town, is dominated by the remains of a Moorish castle.

Four zones

The vineyards that Málaga still has are spread over four zones. By far the most important is the Zona Norte. This is separated from the city of Málaga and the coast by a broad range of mountains and consists of a rolling plateau, the monotony of which is relieved by a few low hills. Geologically there is limestone with fine sand and thin layers of clay. Height above sea level varies from 380 to 480 m (1,245 to 1,575 ft). Rainfall is about 530 mm (20.9 ins) a year, and the annual average temperature is, at 15.3°C (59.5°F), the second coolest of the four zones. Half the plantings consist of Pedro Ximénez, half of *vidueño*; the latter is a collective name for non-traditional, fairly neutral grape varieties such as Airén, or Lairén, and Doradillo. Most of the zone's vineyards are around the white-walled village of Mollina, where some of the large bodegas have their own winepresses.

Moscatel grapes

The next zone is the Zona Montes, in the mountains directly to the north of Málaga. The slopes here used to be covered with vines, but today there are only a few sites left, near Colmenar. The climate in the mountains is cool, with an annual average temperature of 13.2°C (55.8°F), and relatively damp – about 810 mm (31.9 ins) of rain a year. It is warmer and drier further east, in the Zona Axarquía, where the land rises from sea level up to the mountains. The annual average temperature varies between 18.6 and 19.5°C (65.5 and 67.1°F), depending on location, and annual rainfall between 415 and 543 mm (16.3 and 21.4 ins). By no means all the grapes are used for wine, however, and many reach the shops in the form of raisins.

The fourth and last zone is the Oeste which, as the name indicates, is in the west of the region, some 100 km (62 miles) from the city of Málaga. The annual average temperature is around 18.5°C (65.3°F), with an average rainfall of nearly 650 mm (25.6 ins). Here, as in the Zona Axarquía, Moscatel grapes are grown, mainly for eating and only to a limited extent for wine. The classic Málaga wines are always made with a preponderance of Pedro Ximénez (in various forms, including concentrated), but the region cannot supply enough of this variety by itself. For one thing, plantings in the Zona Norte are insufficient, and importing Pedro Ximénez from neighbouring Montilla-Moriles is permitted to a legally prescribed maximum of 10 percent of volume.

Great variation

The law lays down that all Málaga wines must be matured in the city of that name, so that is where all the storage cellars and bottle lines are situated. The 100 or so bodegas that Málaga once had were in the centre of the city, near the harbour. The few that remain are scattered over industrial estates. Generally they look businesslike and efficient; there is scant investment in atmosphere. Although there are few bottle lines now, it is still possible to taste a considerable number of different wines. Some houses carry a large range of Málagas: Scholtz Hermanos, for example, has nearly 20 and López Hermanos still more. What is fascinating is that every firm has its own recipe for combining the different wines, for most Málagas are composed of various, very precisely measured, elements.

Sun-dried grapes

The traditional Málaga is made on a basis of sweet white wine from the Pedro Ximénez grape (often called Pedro Ximén locally). The sweetness is generally obtained by interrupting fermentation

Above: Terracing in the Zona Axarquía, east of Málaga. Here Moscatel grapes are mostly grown.

through adding alcohol. Sometimes, however, the grapes have so much sugar that not all of it ferments out. This is particularly the case with *vino tierno*, which is made from grapes that have been dried in the sun for 7 to 20 days. After two days the sugar content of the fruit rises by 15 percent, and after nine days by nearly 60 percent. Making *vino tierno* is a labour-intensive activity and sometimes the grapes have to be covered to protect them from the rain. The yield is low: usually the grapes give not more than 16 litres of must per 60 kg – roughly equivalent to 60 gal per cwt, or 60 gal per ton (53 gal per US ton). What results from fermentation is an extremely sweet wine. Most *vino tierno* comes from Pedro Ximénez, but a version from Moscatel is also produced.

Boiled-down must

Another element that occurs in classic Málagas is *arrope*. This is must that has been boiled down to 30 percent of its volume. It may be added to the basic wine either before or after fermentation. The next step up from *arrope* is *vino de color*, also called *pantomina*, for which the must is boiled longer. The winemakers also have *vino maestro* at their disposal, which can be compared to *mistela*. This consists of grape juice fortified with seven to eight percent alcohol. Finally there is *vino borracho*, a blend of half wine, half alcohol. Some bodegas use this last type rather than pure alcohol for fortifying wine, because it disturbs the balance of the wine less. Wines from the neutral *vidueño* grapes also have a part to play – although most producers prefer not to talk about this. Certainly the quality houses speak disdainfully of firms that make *arrope* as cheaply as possible, for example by adding figs and peaches.

Complex composition

The winemakers set about their work of composition on the basis of this sweet white wine and a series of remarkable ingredients. Some houses use a lot of *arrope*, because its somewhat burnt, caramelly taste is what many faithful drinkers of Málaga expect.

On the other hand many firms, notably Larios, limit the amount of *arrope* so as to achieve a more elegant, less syrupy wine. In the classic Málaga wine, besides the basic sweet wine, there can be *arrope*, the concentrated must; *vino tierno*, wine rich in sugar from sun-dried grapes; *vino maestro*, grape juice fortified with alcohol; and an amount of extra alcohol, or *vino borracho*, a mixture of half alcohol, half wine. The art of the winemaker lies in creating a harmonious whole from all these elements – a most complicated task. It is not without reason that a computer programme has been developed to do this at Larios. The basic wine naturally has much influence on the eventual result. The top quality is called *lágrima*; formerly obtained by treading the grapes. Today *lágrima* is wine from the first pressing only, whether or not enriched by *arrope* or other ingredients.

The classic Málaga is, of course, sweet and has a taste rich with nuances of dried fruit (such as raisins), caramel, cocoa and coffee, often with a suggestion of nuts, and sometimes a hint of spice (nutmeg for example), and banana. A fragrance of wood is also present to some degree: two years' cask ageing is obligatory for Málaga. Like sherry, the top qualities come from *soleras* and have an even longer average life. Traditional Málaga is a delight with chocolate desserts, and also with fruit, nuts, and blue-veined cheese instead of port. Málaga can be so rich, however, that a glass of it by itself makes a perfect finish to a meal.

Moscatels

As well as the sweet Málaga made mainly from Pedro Ximénez grapes, all the bodegas have a Moscatel in their range. Usually this is made from Moscatel grapes only, but sometimes with a little *vidueño* too. The grapey, fruity scent of the Moscatel is always strongly present in these wines. Málaga of the classic kind benefits a lot from its compulsory two years in wood – it enables the different elements to blend for one thing – but the Moscatel does not. The charm of this wine is its fruit, a quality that is lost in cask ageing. This is why firms are arguing for a reduction of the present obligatory ageing period for Moscatel to six months. And to demonstrate this point there are houses that have anticipated such a change, improving the quality of the wine. Moscatel grapes can also be used in the classic kind of Malaga, albeit as the lesser proportion. Spain's best-selling Málaga is the Málaga Virgen by López Hermanos, which consists of 75 percent Pedro Ximénez and 25 percent Moscatel.

Dry Málaga

The third main type of Málaga is the dry version. This usually has the highest alcohol content, as it is made from fully fermented wine: a characteristic dry has 17 to 18.5 percent whereas the sweeter kinds generally vary in strength from 15.5 to 17 percent. The best dry Málagas are given a long period of ageing in cask, and in character they closely resemble an *oloroso* from Jerez or Montilla-Moriles. They usually have a nutty, mature aroma, while the alcohol present adds a generous touch to the pronouncedly dry taste. They make an unusual and intriguing aperitif. There are various other categories between the dry and the classic sweet Málagas, but these are of less interest. All in all, Málaga in its various forms is a unique wine, one that can give particular pleasure at carefully chosen moments. It is furthermore a wine whose medicinal properties have been renowned for centuries. An excuse for drinking Málaga is always to hand. This attribute, and the fame of the drink, led Dostoyevsky to write, in *The Village of Stepanchikogo*, "He is asking for a bottle of Málaga wine to make him well again. Nothing less than a Málaga?"

Above. The inner courtyard of the Larios bodega

PRODUCERS OF SPECIAL INTEREST

Larios 29000 Málaga
This is Spain's largest gin maker, with a very modern factory on an industrial estate, towards the airport. It produces not only gin and other distilled drinks but also a considerable amount of Málaga. The grapes for this – 1.5 to 1.7 million kg (3.3 to 3.75 million lb) annually – are bought in the Zona Norte. In addition, some Moscatel is obtained from Axarquia. Blending is done with the greatest care. For the Málaga Larios, a traditional kind, more *tierno* is used than *arrope*, so that the wine does not take on too much of a burnt caramel element in its taste. The wine has a dark colour, a sun-steeped scent that includes cocoa and raisins, and a sweet, nuanced taste that lingers without being syrupy. The dry Málaga Benefique is an amber-coloured wine, quite mature and elegant, with considerable wood. Once a year 5,000 to 10,000 litres (1,100 to 2,200 gal) are drawn from a *solera*. The sweet Málaga Moscatel is juicy and balanced in taste. It is decidedly sweet and the Moscatel fragrance is strong.

López Hermanos 29000 Málaga
This family firm is more than a century old. It is difficult to find, tucked away in an industrial district on the edge of the university area. In the past this bodega exported wine to Russia, and as a result of this trade received two large pinewood vats from that country, which are still in use. In 1990 the owners bought 500 ha (1,236 acres) of vineyards in the Mollina area. Since then most of the Pedro Ximénez grapes used have come mainly from this, their own estate. The López Hermanos share of the Spanish market is about 75 percent. Its Málaga Virgen is classic in character, a dark, sweet, pure product, elegant in style. It is blended from 75 percent Pedro Ximénez and 25 percent Moscatel (in addition, 8 percent *arrope* is included in this). The fruity Moscatel Cartojal, which was launched at the end of the 1980s is also sweet and elegant in taste. The dry style is represented by the Trajinero. This wine, too, has a quite elegant structure, despite its 18 percent alcohol. To these specialities should be added the Málaga Virgen Solera, a splendidly opulent and distinguished wine, about 35 years old.

Scholtz Hermanos 29000 Málaga
As you come from the airport or from Torremolinos, this is the first wine estate that you see, for it lies right beside the Málaga to Cádiz road. It was established in 1807 by Christian Scholtz, a German, and remained German until 1945, when it became the property of the Spaniard García Gómez. After his death it passed in 1990 to his son-in-law Pedro Gil-Delgado, of the Distilerías y Crianzas group. Since 1945 the day-to-day running of the firm has been in the hands of succeeding generations of the Dutch Ankersmit family.

Scholtz Hermanos has no vineyards of its own, and generally buys its must (Pedro Ximénez) from the local cooperative in Mollina. It is then transported by tanker to Málaga. The firm has a total storage capacity of 2 million litres (440,000 gal) in wooden vats and casks. Most of the Málaga produced is the Dulce Negra, which is made

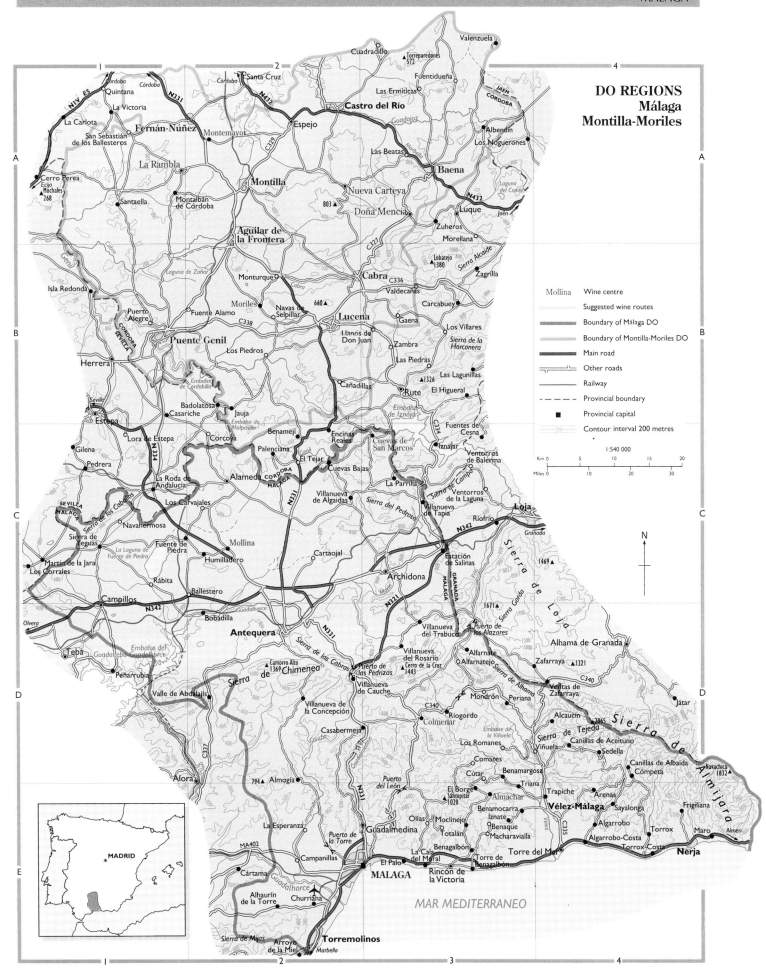

DO REGIONS
Málaga
Montilla-Moriles

Mollina	Wine centre
	Suggested wine routes
	Boundary of Málaga DO
	Boundary of Montilla-Moriles DO
	Main road
	Other roads
	Railway
	Provincial boundary
■	Provincial capital
	Contour interval 200 metres

1:540 000

Km 0   5   10   15   20
Miles 0   10   20   30

N

MAR MEDITERRANEO

MADRID

from half-fermented grape must, 15 percent *arrope* and 3 percent *vino de color*. The speciality of the house, however, is the Solera 1885, a wine with a strength of 18 percent that consists of three *lágrimas*, some 10-year-old dry wine, and a little concentrated Moscatel. In the complex bouquet of this brown-coloured wine there are suggestions of sweet dried fruit, such as raisins, coffee, cocoa and caramel; and the taste is firm and with comparable nuances. Other wines worth recommending from the range of 17 are the very sweet, orange-brown Golden Moscatel; the intense Lágrima 10 Años with its modest richness; and the Seco Añejo 10 Años, a very dry, mature wine that makes a beautiful aperitif. The most precious possession of Scholtz Hermanos consists of casks of very old *lágrima*, the 1885 and 1787. Both wines are still completely vital, and so concentrated that a few drops on a cloth give off fragrance for a week.

Travel Information

Above: Sunset in Archidona, a town along the wine route.

HOTELS AND RESTAURANTS

Parador, 29200 Antequera, tel (52) 840261 Modern, low-built *parador* in quiet situation, surrounded by a garden. The restaurant serves mainly Andalucian dishes.
Antonio Martín, Paseo Marítimo 4, 29016 Málaga, tel (52) 222113 This modern-looking restaurant is on the front, close to the old city centre and the Plaza de Toros. In fine weather you can eat out on the terrace. Fish dishes, such as *fritura malagueña*, and other regional specialities are prepared with care.
Casa Pedro, Quitapenas 121, Playa de El Palo, 29017 Málaga, tel (52) 290013 One of the biggest restaurants on the coast, situated on the sea front and specializing in fish – grilled sardines, for example.
Hotel Guadalmar, Carretera de Cádiz, 29080 Málaga, tel (52) 231703 Large, comfortable hotel on the sea front, to the southwest of the city. Has a dining room in rustic style, and a lot of holidaymakers.
Los Naranjos, Paseo Sancha 35, 29016 Málaga, tel (52) 224316 Fairly small hotel on the east side of the Gibralfaro hill, less than a mile from the sea front.
Parador de Gibralfaro, 29016 Málaga, tel (52) 221903 Situated on the Gibralfaro hill, beside the castle of that name. Offers a splendid view and a restaurant serving regional specialities.
Parador del Golf, Apartado 324,

29080 Málaga, tel (52) 381255 Modern *parador* with its own golf course and a restaurant. Too close to the flightpath into the nearby airport for perfect peace.
La Taberna del Pintor, Maestranza 6, 29016 Málaga, tel (52) 215315 Known for its good meat dishes. Has a rustic ambience.
Las Vegas, Paseo Sancha 22, 29016 Málaga, tel (52) 217712 This hotel has recently been extended and renovated.
Hotel Molino de Saydo, 29532 Mollina, tel (52) 740475 The rather spartan rooms are built around a small inner courtyard. The hotel is in a quiet setting, between the autopista and the village of Mollina. There are sometimes big celebrations and parties here at weekends.

PLACES OF INTEREST

Antequera A town of Roman origin that later became a stronghold of the Moorish kingdom of Granada. The angular remains of a Moorish castle high up on a hill are a reminder of that time. After its reconquest by the Christians, no fewer than 24 churches were built in Antequera. One of the most beautiful is the Carmen church, with its huge retable and ceiling in Mudéjar style. The minster church of Santa María la Mayor dates from the sixteenth century and is a

national monument. The municipal museum, in a former palace, displays many finds from prehistoric and Roman times, among them a famous first century sculpture, the "Bronze Youth of Antequera". Around the town there are a number of prehistoric burial chambers. Some of these dolmens – called *cuevas* here – are about 4,500 years old. Directly to the north of Antequera stretches the rolling plateau where most of the grapes for Málaga wine are harvested; and to the south of the town there is the El Torcal national park with its weathered, whimsically shaped rock formations.
Archidona The wine route takes in this town because of its medieval walls, castle ruins, and notable plaza.
Colmenar One of the few wine villages in Málaga's Zona Montes. The Ermita de la Candelaria here is said to have been built by people from the Canary Islands. Just to the east of Colmenar and its white-walled houses is Ríogordo, where a passion play is performed during Holy Week.
Málaga Most tourists who arrive here at the new airport, opened in 1991, see Málaga with its half a million inhabitants only from the air, for they go straight on to the Costa del Sol and stay there. Yet this large city on its bay is certainly worth a visit. The old centre and the

harbour are dominated by an oblong-shaped hill with terraced gardens on its southern side. On the lower slopes there is the Alcazaba, a Moorish castle complex, and on the northern side are the remains of a Roman amphitheatre. In the castle itself there is an archaeological museum, with a splendid collection of Moorish ceramics among its exhibits. In line with the Alcazaba, at a height of 130 m (427 ft), stands the Castillo de Gibralfaro, a fourteenth-century stronghold with a former mosque and beautiful gardens. Near the hill and not far from the harbour stands the *ayuntamiento*, a yellow building in Spanish Renaissance style. It is not far to walk from here to the imposing cathedral, which was begun in the sixteenth century, but never completed. A good place to take a rest and eat some *tapas* or a light lunch is the Café El Jardin, on a corner near the cathedral. Also near the cathedral is the Museo de Bellas Artes, with works from the sixteenth and seventeenth centuries, as well as sketches and paintings by Pablo Picasso. He was in fact born in Málaga, in 1881, a few hundred yards from this museum in a house on the corner of the Plaza de la Merced. A foundation has arranged a small display in this house, and a short film is also shown here. Holy Week is celebrated with great intensity in Málaga, with processions and other events, beginning on Palm Sunday. The Museo de Semana Santa (away from the old centre, in the Plaza San Pedro on the west bank of the Guadalmedina) exhibits many pictures of these processions.
Mollina The most important wine village of the Málaga DO consists of a number of white houses built up a low hill. Some bodegas in the city of Málaga have their own facilities for pressing grapes here.

WINE ROUTE

Since the Zona Norte grows by far the largest amount of Málaga grapes, that is where the wine route from the city, and from hotels on its outskirts, is concentrated. Just before Antequera, after the drive through the Montes de Málaga, you have a splendid view out over the northern plateau. The first vineyards do not come into view until you are near Mollina. Beyond that village they soon give way to almost uninterrupted stretches of olive plantations. The journey can be continued into Montilla-Moriles by way of the N331.

Montilla-Moriles

Once a year a group of Roman soldiers parade through the streets of Montilla, beating drums and sounding trumpets. This takes place during Holy Week, so that there are churches as well as bars on the route taken by these men in ancient garb. The tradition harks back to the Roman period, which greatly stimulated local winegrowing. Roman pottery decorated with grape harvest motifs has been found, and statues of Bacchus and remains of primitive wine presses have been dug up. The orator Seneca the Elder and his son, the philosopher Seneca the Younger, both lived in Córdoba, then called Baetica, and the latter spoke with pride of his own vineyards. During the centuries of Moorish rule winegrowing was prohibited in large areas of Spain, but hardly at all around Córdoba – which is why Arabic-Andalusian poems in praise of wine have been found in this region. In the nineteenth century, thanks to the opening of a canal between Córdoba and Sevilla, the local wines became known far beyond their own region – even as far as Britain. In 1945 the region acquired its own *denominación de origen*, using the name Montilla-Moriles after its two most important places in terms of quality.

A green, rolling landscape

The present wine region starts about 30 km (19 miles) south of Córdoba and covers the southern part of the province of that name, as far as the border with Málaga. The peaceful landscape is made up chiefly of low hills and small plateaux, covered with the green of grapevines, olive and almond trees. It is like a rolling green sea in which the villages resemble eddies of white foam, for they are nearly always built on hilltops. In fact, Montilla-Moriles was once a sea. Not only have shells been found here, but even the skeleton of a whale. The area is now 300 to 600 m (985 to 1,970 ft) above sea level and a continental climate prevails. Summers are long, hot and dry: quite often the temperature reaches 40 to 45°C (104 to 113°F), usually dropping sharply at night. Winters are short and not really cold. In many of the small plots almond and olive trees grow close to the vines, not only for economic reasons but also because of the climate: their shade protects both the grapes and the pickers from the fierce sun. The first grapes are harvested here as early as the middle of August.

Below: In the green rolling landscape of Montilla-Moriles the rock La Lengue [the tongue] forms a remarkable landmark. It stands on the road between Montilla and Cabra, not far from the bodegas of Montebello.

Some two-thirds of the soil in Montilla-Moriles is made up of reddish sand with some clay and limestone; this is called *ruedos* here, and from it come the simpler wines. The *zonas de superior calidad*, usually called *alberos*, are of a different composition. They look whitish, contain a great deal of limestone and resemble the *albarizas*, the best soils of Jerez. They occur directly east of Montilla, in the slightly cooler Sierra de Montilla, a group of hills that rise some 100 m (330 ft) above the surrounding terrain. They are also found around Moriles, in the zone called Moriles Alto. The limestone. soil not only gives the grapes their special qualities, but in summer forms a hard crust. This reflects the sunlight and restricts the evaporation of the moisture present in the soil – which with an annual rainfall of 650 mm (25.6 ins) is no luxury. These superior zones yield less wine to the hectare, namely 60 rather than 80 hl (roughly 535 gal per acre instead of 710 gal per acre). The growers here are paid an extra three to six percent for their grapes.

Pedro Ximénez

The vines grown on the not quite 15,000 ha (37,000 acres) of the Montilla-Moriles DO are almost exclusively Pedro Ximénez. Its share amounts to 90 percent. It is less than 100 percent because traditionally some other white varieties were planted in most of the vineyards to produce a slightly less alcoholic wine. Pedro Ximénez appears very well able to stand up to the heat of Montilles-Moriles, unlike Palomino, for example, the characteristic sherry variety. Experiments with the latter grape have been unsuccessful. Properties are small here: the average amount of land held is 2 ha (5 acres) per grower. More than half of all the grapes are therefore taken to cooperatives. These put little wine on the market on their own account, most of them selling must or

Above: Tinajas at Alvear. These are still used in many bodegas for fermenting and storing wine.

wine to bodegas with facilities for storing and ageing. The bulk of these houses are in the town of Montilla, where nearly three-quarters of all the dealing in wine takes place. Moriles on the other hand has no commercially operating bodegas of any significance.

The warm local climate and the naturally high sugar content of Pedro Ximénez result in wines that achieve 15 percent alcohol without any problems. If the variety is used as a basis for aperitif wines there is often no need for it to be fortified. This is in contrast to comparable wines from Jerez, which are always given extra alcohol. The lightest and finest aperitif wines from Montilla-Moriles are the *finos*. Today these wines are mostly fermented in stainless-steel tanks, but many *tinajas* are also in use. Most of these huge earthenware vessels can hold 3,000 to 7,000 litres (660 to 1540 gal) – and sometimes even 10,000 litres (2,200 gal). These vast jars are also found in La Mancha, Valdepeñas and other areas – but rarely in sherry country. Nowadays in the big bodegas *tinajas* are used chiefly for malolactic fermentation and for initial storage.

Flor

Just as in Jerez, the *fino* wines develop a growth of *flor*: a thick , sometimes double, layer of grey yeast cells appears on the surface of the stored wine. This protects it from oxidation and at the same time gives it a distinct scent. The most important phase in the maturing process for the development of *flor* – in a wholly natural way – comes while the wine is in cask: which is why the casks are never completely filled. For unfortified wines ageing should last for at least one year. The casks used are mostly 500 litre (110 gal) *botas*; the maximum capacity permitted is 1,000 litres (220 gal). In the sherry region a moister, less harsh climate prevails and *flor* develops more readily than in Montilla-Moriles. To give nature a helping hand the bodega floors in the latter area are regularly sprinkled with water to increase the humidity.

It is principally the better zones that supply *finos*. Those from the Sierra de Montilla are rather lighter and more elegant than those from the Moriles Alto district. In theory it should be possible to nurture and bottle these types separately, but this seldom happens. An experiment was once carried out at the Pérez Barquero bodega in which three casks were left to age separately: one with pure Sierra de Montilla, one with pure Moriles Alto, and one with a blend of the two. The last of the three *finos* was clearly the best. The wines from the region can in fact be sold as Montilla-Moriles, Montilla, or as Moriles. In the two latter cases the wines similarly come from the whole region, not just from the places named.

Similarity to sherry

Although the Montilla-Moriles *finos* are not made from the Palomino grape variety and are different, too, in that they are not usually fortified, nevertheless they show a striking likeness to their Jerez equivalents. Even very experienced tasters, including some from Jerez itself, have been unable for example to distinguish a Gran Barquero from Pérez Barquero from famous sherries, and have rated it at least as highly.

You can find out just how delicious a young *fino* from Montilla-Moriles can taste, in the bars of the region, where the wine sometimes comes straight from the cask – even with flecks of *flor*. The C.B. from Alvear is a successful young *fino*, with several million bottles sold every year in Spain. The truly great *finos*, however, undergo a long period of cask ageing. As in Jerez, the bodegas here apply the *solera* system. Usually they have four layers, or *criaderas*, of casks for each type of wine. The wine is drawn only from the bottom layer, or *solera*. Topping up takes place via the uppermost layer; in this way a continuous process of blending is achieved, resulting in a consistent quality of wine. The great *finos* sometimes pass through two *soleras*. Thus at an average age of eight years the Gran Barquero is drawn off from the first *solera* and used as the youngest wine for the next one. The art of making a great *fino* lies in getting the right balance between the longest possible ageing and the maximum possible freshness. A mature *fino* is more intense in taste than a young one; the fragrance of the wine lingers much longer in an emptied glass.

Amontillado and *oloroso*

About three-quarters of all Montilla-Moriles wine consists of *fino*. Another basic type is *amontillado*: a fortified, venerable *fino*. At Pérez Barquero the best kind is twice the age of the Gran Barquero, an average 16 years in other words. An *amontillado* usually has a brown colour and a nutty scent with a lot of wood. At the end of the eighteenth century, and especially in the nineteenth, this type of wine was taken to the sherry region, where it was later to be produced from Palomino grapes. Whereas *fino*, and therefore *amontillado* as well, is made from juice from the first, light pressing, *oloroso* is prepared from the second pressing. The juice is less fine, and has more solids in it and more colour. There is no growth of *flor* with *oloroso* and the casks are therefore completely filled. Then again, this wine is always fortified, and in Montillo-Moriles it is used in particular for blending. A type that comes between an *amontillado* and an *oloroso* is the *palo cortado*. This is fairly rare and comes in both dry and slightly sweet forms. I have pleasant recollections of the dry *palo cortado* from the house of Cobos.

A very special place among the Montilla-Moriles wines is held by the *dulce*, an intensely sweet, almost syrupy wine made from grapes that have been allowed to dry in the sun. By the end of this process they have lost about half their moisture. The modern pneumatic presses do not work with these grapes; only the old-fashioned hydraulic kind exerts enough pressure to get all the juice out of the flesh of the fruit. A considerable amount of both the must (in concentrated form or otherwise) and the wine goes to Málaga and to the sherry region for blending.

A down-market image

In 1925 the Italian oenologist Sannino rated Montilla-Moriles wine among the six best in the world. Today the great *finos* – and in fact the *amontillados* and *dulces* as well – remain wines that are full of character. The problem is that their existence is hardly known of outside Spain. One reason is that they are difficult to distinguish from the comparable sherries, which come from a richer region, and one that in terms of publicity completely overshadows Montilla-Moriles; the other is that the area has to contend with a down-market image. Since an estimated half of its wines do not need to be fortified (which puts them in a different category when it comes to the duty payable), and the required period in cask for unfortified wines is one year, not the three stipulated for the fortified kinds, the region has largely become a supplier of cheap alternatives to sherry. Thus many good basic wines disappear anonymously into some not very inspiring blends. This even applies to many *finos*. Take any medium Montilla – say one for a large supermarket chain – and you may find it composed of, for example, *fino*, *oloroso* and concentrated must. Very many people, importers too, therefore come to look on Montilla-Moriles wines as inferior kinds of sherry. It is going to take a great deal of effort on the part of the serious producers to get themselves out of this situation. In the meantime many firms have gone under because of the downward spiral of prices, which has led to a high degree of concentration in the sector. Thus at present there are just three groups controlling production and export: Alvear, Compañía Vinícola del Sur, and Navisa. This could be a good thing, for it is only by combining forces in this way that the producers can improve the somewhat down-at-heel image of Montilla-Moriles.

Light table wines

In order to survive in the short term most bodegas here have other alcoholic drinks in their range. Alvear, for instance, is one of Spain's biggest vermouth producers. A relatively recent phenomenon, successful on the home market, are the unfortified table wines. These are light – with 10 to 11 percent alcohol – and are made from early picked grapes. Most of them are generous in scent and have a gently fresh, fairly neutral taste. Nearly all of them are made solely or mainly from Pedro Ximénez grapes, which explains their slightly sweet aroma. This variety is not present, however, in the Viña Carreron from Cobos, a wine that is among the very best from the region, thanks to its dry, refreshing and slightly fruity taste. The owners of Cobos – the Navisa group – are also experimenting with black grapes, Cabernet Sauvignon and Tempranillo. The first harvest of these came in 1986 and may mark the starting point for the official return of red Montilla-Moriles, a wine made in plenty before phylloxera.

PRODUCERS OF SPECIAL INTEREST

Alvear 14550 Montilla

The history of Alvear goes back to 1729, when Diego de Alvear of Córdoba moved to Montilla and set up a bodega there with his son. The firm's oldest buildings stand in the centre of the town, but for several decades now most of the casks have been housed in an extensive complex further out, facing a small park. Alvear, which still belongs to the same family, has some 40 ha (99 acres) of vineyard, which yields about five percent of the grapes required. The rest of the requirement is bought in, as grapes, must and wine. The firm has a large *lagar*, Las Puentes, in the Sierra and presses grapes there after destalking them. Fermentation takes place there in both stainless-steel tanks and *tinajas*. For ageing the wines are taken to Alvear's nearly 20,000 casks in Montilla.

The most important brand is the Fino C.B., fragrant, elegant, fresh and with fruit. This wine with its 15 percent alcohol is also sold by big customers under their own labels – such as Sainsbury's in Britain. The C.B. is about two and a half years old. More mature, at six to seven years, is the Fino Festival, which is an excellent wine in its category. Some of the other specialities are the old *amontillado* Carlos VII; the still more mature, very intense *amontillado* Solera Fundación, and two rich, sweet, almost syrupy *dulces*, the 1927 and the 1930. Alongside these wines of character Alvear, like the other big producers, also makes a series of simpler Montillas. These are often made to the requirements of large purchasers. Conde de la Cortina is a subsidiary of Alvear. Its casks stand in bodegas belonging to, and are filled with wines from, the Alvear concern. There are, too, buildings on the Alvear estate devoted to the Cruz Conde brand. Almost half of the total Alvear production is exported.

Cobos 14550 Alvear

The wines of Cobos are pressed and fermented in the Bodegas Montebello *lagar*. Here they also undergo part of the maturing process before being taken to Montilla for further ageing, either in the bodegas jointly owned by Cobos and Valesco Chacón, or in those of Bodegas Montulia. This confusing

Right: Some of the 20,000 barrels in which Alvear matures its wines.

situation arises because Cobos, like the other firms mentioned, is in the Navisa group (which is also a grocery wholesaler). After the take-overs this group increasingly concentrated its various activities. As a result, the differences between the wines produced by the various houses have been steadily reduced. Thus the Cobos Fino, of its kind an attractive, clean-tasting wine, differs very little from the Montebello Gran Fino or from Velasco Chacón's Las Incas. Another *fino* from the Cobos range, with wood very much present, is the Pompeyo (about five years old).

The good Cobos Amontillado carries a label with the original design from 1906, the firm's foundation year; the Precursor is a powerful, dark-toned *oloroso*; and the Tres Pasas is a *dulce* of high quality. The collection also includes a successful, dry *palo cortado*. The Viña Carreron, made from Baladí and Lairén grapes, is one of the very best table wines from the region: refreshing, slightly fruity, and really dry. Exactly the same wine is sold by Velasco Chacón as Viña Rama. It was the Cobos family, by the way, who built Las Camachas, Montilla's best restaurant (*see* Travel Information, page 219).

Compañía Vinícola del Sur 14550 Montilla

This firm belongs to the holding company of the same name, as do Gracia Hermanos, Pérez Barquero and Tomás García. Its buildings are set around a large, bricked inner courtyard, and the name Bodegas Monte Cristo is painted on the outside – for this is the most important brand. All the wine is exported and is in general fairly commercial in character. It is of a very decent quality, but you would look in vain for a truly superior *fino* under this name.

Gracia Hermanos 14550 Montilla

A firm dating from 1959 that was taken over at the end of the 1980s by the holding company Compañía del Sur. Its premises are large, severe-looking halls beside the railway line. The grapes come from the firm's own 125 ha (310 acres), and from more than 100 growers, who account for 85 percent of production.

The best of the wines is the María del Valle *fino*, a refined creation of graceful charm, with a sound balance between wood and fruit, which is aged for about 10 years. The standard qualities are largely marketed by customer firms under their own labels. About 15

percent of the total volume consists of Viña Verde, a supple, smooth and light table wine.

Montebello 14550 Montilla

Part of the Navisa group. The firm has a total of 150 ha (370 acres) and processes the grapes using modern equipment in an octagonal *lagar*, where there are also facilities for ageing. The top wine is the Montebello Gran Fino, which resembles the best *finos* from the other houses in the group, Cobos for example. The ordinary *fino*, the old *oloroso* and the *dulce* also merit attention.

Montulia 14550 Montilla

The ageing and bottling facilities for the Navisa group are being increasingly concentrated here, and there are also presses for both ordinary and sun-dried grapes. In addition there are *tinajas* in plenty for fermenting and storage. There is ample space, for the complex covers 30,000 sq m (about 323,000 sq ft).

This firm has belonged to the Navisa group since July 1990 and the latter's head office is here. Wines are also to be produced under the Montulia name. The Navisa group has a total of around 10,000 casks at its disposal, most of them at Montulia.

Pérez Barquero 14550 Montilla
This firm, which stands beside the road into Montilla from the south, is the flagship of the Compañía Vinícola del Sur and it produces the best wines. A fifth of the grapes come from its own 100 ha (247 acres), the remaining requirement being bought in as grapes and wine. The grapes are pressed at its own *lagar* in the Sierra de Montilla. After fermentation the wine is brought to Montilla for ageing in the 10,000 casks here. This lasts an average eight years for the Gran Barquero Fino, with the oldest wine from one *solera* used as the youngest in the next. This particular *fino* belongs among the very best and offers everything that can be expected of wines of this kind: refinement, purity, a noble taste and perfect balance. Even experienced tasters have been unable to distinguish it from the best *finos* from Jerez.

Travel Information

HOTELS AND RESTAURANTS

La Casona, 14920 Aguilar de la Frontera, tel (57) 660439 For roast meat dishes.
Mesón del Vizconde, 14940 Cabra, tel (57) 521702 Here you can eat fish and *mariscos* – with a half bottle of *fino* to accompany them.
Bandolero, Medina y Corella 6 y 10, 14003 Córdoba, tel (57) 476491 A good tapas bar.
El Blasón, José Zorilla 1, 14000 Córdoba, tel (57) 480625 After drinking an aperitif on the patio you go on to enjoy elegant, inventive cooking.
El Caballo Rojo, Cardenal Herrero 28, 14003 Córdoba, tel (57) 475375 This is the most famous restaurant in the city, if not the province. The owner has interpreted numerous old recipes – such as *cordero a la miel* – in a contemporary way. The establishment, which also has a bar, lies directly behind the Mezquita.
Casa de Montilla, Ximénez de Quesada 17, 14000 Córdoba, tel (57) 410104 Excellent for *tapas* and a few glasses of *fino*.
El Churrasco, Romero 16, 14003 Córdoba, tel (57) 290819 This atmospheric restaurant is in the old Jewish quarter. The speciality is meat dishes. Ask if you can see the wine cellar.
Sol los Gallos, Avenida Medina Azahara 7, 14005 Córdoba, tel (57) 235500 A modern, comfortable hotel, just west of the old centre.
Maimónides, Torrijos 4, 14003

Somewhat younger – four to five years – but also very sound is the Los Amigos *fino*. Other stars of the collection are the Gran Barquero Amontillado (16 years old), the Gran Barquero Oloroso, and the Gran Barquero Pedro Ximénez.

Tomás García 14550 Montilla
The Carbonell group (big in olive oil and other lines) used to own this bodega, but sold it to Bodegas Bobadilla of Jerez at the end of the 1980s. The latter house in turn made over all the casks, wine, brand names and so on to the holding company Compañía Vinícola del Sur at the end of 1990. Only the buildings, in Aguílar de la Frontera, were not taken over. Montillas for Carbonell are now among the Tomás García products, and are commercial in character. The best *fino* offered under the firm's own name is the Verbenera.

Córdoba, tel (57) 471500 Situated by the Mezquita. A decent standard of comfort. A patio and (absolutely necessary here) a garage.
Parador de la Arruzafa, Avenida de la Arruzafa, 14012 Córdoba, tel (57) 275900 A few miles north of the city, in the El Brillante direction. This *parador* is a large, modern building of several storeys. Many rooms (and balconies) offer a fine view. Restaurant on the premises.
Castillo de Montemayor, 14530 Montemayor, tel (57) 384253 Hotel opened in 1990 beside the Córdoba-Málaga trunk road. Nice if somewhat spartan rooms. Always ask for one at the back, because of the traffic. Often a lot of noise at weekends from a hall at the back used for parties. A good restaurant with friendly service.
Los Arcos, Plaza de la Risa 1, 14550 Montilla, tel (57) 650036 Bar in the heart of the town. Serves tasty *tapas*, such as *salpicón de mariscos*, and a fresh *fino* of the house.
Las Camachas, 14550 Montilla, tel (57) 650004 You reach the pleasant dining room through an always crowded bar. The cooking here is sound, substantial and without frills with, for example, fresh *gambas*, grilled hake (*merluza*), and *chuletas de cordero*. Half bottles of *finos*.
Don Quichote, 14550 Montilla, tel (57) 651271 Pleasant and affordable restaurant with regional cuisine. Also a *tapas* bar.

PLACES OF INTEREST

Aguilar de la Frontera On a hill with a ruined castle. The Plaza de San José here is notable for its octagonal shape.
Cabra Picturesque village with its church built on a hill, which forms a viewing point. There is an auditorium beside the river (Fuente del Río). The Ermita Virgen de la Sierra nearby is a place of pilgrimage for gipsies.
Córdoba Although this city was probably founded by the Phoenicians and also has a Roman past, it only really began to flourish during the first three centuries of Moorish rule, from AD 711. That was when Córdoba grew into one of the most important cities of Europe, becoming a centre of culture, science and scholarship. The most tremendous monument from this period is the Mezquita, a masterpiece with more than 800 columns, and arches in red and white marble. In the sixteenth century a cathedral was built within this mosque.
Around the Mezquita is the Judéria, or Jewish quarter, made up of narrow streets – some thronged with tourists, others peaceful. Through open doors here you glimpse cool patios, often full of flowers. Within, or near, this quarter there are a number of museums, including the Museo Arquelógico Provincial, with prehistoric, Roman and Moorish artefacts; the Museo Municipal Taurino, devoted to bullfighting; the Museo Provincial de Bellas Artes, with works of art from the region; and next to the last-named institution the Museo de Julio Romero de Torres, dedicated to the well-known Andalucian artist. The fourteenth-century Alcázar, with fine mosaics, is close to the Judéria; you can climb the tower. Córdoba has a host of beautiful churches and houses, as well as monasteries and other imposing buildings. Directly opposite the Mezquita there is a Roman bridge over the Guadalquivir, and on the south side stands the Torre de la Calahorra, a compact fourteenth-century watchtower. Since 1980 Córdoba has had botanical gardens, stretching for 700 m (766 yd) along the riverside.
Espejo Great fifteenth-century castle of the Dukes of Osuna.
Fernán Nuñez The eighteenth-century palace of the local dukes.
Lucena Famous for the craftsmanship of its bronzes, but not especially attractive as a town.
Montemayor You can enjoy a panoramic view out over the

landscape with its vineyards from the 14th-century castle above this village. An old church tower rises behind this stronghold and there is also a small chapel.
Montilla This town, with about 22,000 inhabitants, is built on and around a rectangular hill. It was the birthplace of Gonzalo Fernandez y Aguílar, known as El Gran Capitán. In the service of Ferdinand and Isabella, the Catholic Monarchs, he fought with success against the Moors and the Italians. He built a great castle in Montilla, but after a disagreement with the crown, it was ordered to be demolished. The Montilla townsfolk refused to do this and so it was carried out by the people of Aguílar de la Frontera; since then there has been some strain in the relations between the two communities. Montilla today is a somewhat untidy assemblage of old and new buildings. Outside the town are a number of very large bodegas. The large Santiago church is built on a hill behind this square. Off to its left is the small atmospheric Escuchuela quarter. Elsewhere in the town there is the Santa Clara convent, which has a church with a richly decorated interior. Next to the *ayuntamiento* in the main street is the former hospital where Cervantes wrote his novella *Dialogo de Perros*. A small museum is dedicated to "the Inca", Garcilaso de la Vega, (1539–1616) a historian who published works on Peru.
Monturque Set on a steep hill. A Roman burial place here.
Moriles Neat but somewhat dull village with many low-built, white-walled houses.

WINE ROUTE

The journey goes through the heart of the Montilla-Moriles region, with the town of Montilla as its starting and finishing point. To the right of a hill alongside the Montilla to Cabra road there stands a striking pointed rock called La Lengua ("the Tongue"). According to tradition this is part of a meteorite. It is also said that the rock grows a few inches every year. Not far past this rock, on the left-hand side, are buildings with the wine presses of Montebello, Alvear and Pérez Barquero. Between Montilla and Montemayor there is a small museum set up by a nougat manufacturer.

NB The terms *fino, amontillado* and *oloroso* are not currently permitted to be used for Montilla wines in the UK, where they are reserved exclusively for sherry from Jerez.

Above: Sunset in Lanzarote.

The Islands

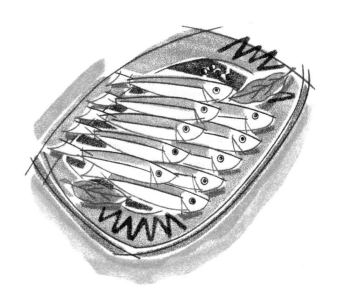

The millions of tourists who throng the Spanish islands every year usually have no idea that wine is made there. This is in fact a good thing, for the volume of island wines produced is so small that shipments are tiny. The Balearics, which together form a province, are the closest of the islands to mainland Spain. The largest of the group are Mallorca (with the capital, Palma de Mallorca), Menorca, Ibiza and Formentera. All have been inhabited since the Bronze Age, as is clear from the dozens of *talayots* – burial chambers made of large stones – that have been found, mainly on Menorca, but also on Mallorca.

The Balearic Islands are characterized by a splendid climate and luxuriant vegetation. In the mountainous parts you find thickly wooded slopes and ravines; and on the plateaux and the lower hillsides almonds, olives, figs and other fruits are grown. The olive trees are sometimes centuries old and formed into weird shapes by the wind. Grapes are grown almost exclusively on Mallorca, and it was here that Spain's first *denominación de origen* away from the mainland, namely Binissalem, was created. The only other Balearic wine district of any significance is Felanitx, also on the main island.

Traditional dishes

It is said that Mallorca looks towards Spain, Menorca to France, and Ibiza to Africa, for the islands have had links in the past with various Mediterranean peoples. Also, Menorca was British for practically the whole of the eighteenth century. These different influences can be traced in the islands' cuisine. Thus turkey with stuffing, that very British dish, is still eaten on Menorca, and *maccarons con grevi* is macaroni with gravy, no less. On Mallorca there are a number of traditional recipes with pork: *sobrasada*, for example, is a soft, spreadable sausage seasoned with peppers. *Sobrasada* is sometimes used in the local *empanadas*, a dough

round like a pizza which may also be filled with lamb or pork, onion and herbs. Pork dripping is used in making *ensaimada*, a sweet-tasting flat loaf that varies in size from a small disc to a wagonwheel. Mallorcan soups are in fact mostly stews, with vegetables, peppers and often some pork. *Tumbet* is also a stew, made with meat or fish, aubergines and potatoes. And of course, they eat a good deal of fish and shellfish. The best cheese from the Balearics is the *Mahón*, made on Menorca from sheep's milk.

The shortest distance from the Balearics to the Spanish coast is about 100 km (62 miles). The same applies to the Canary Islands – except that the coast in question is the African, not the Spanish coast. Spain is nearly ten times as far away. The group consists of seven large and six smaller islands, divided into two provinces, Las Palmas and Santa Cruz de Tenerife. The biggest island is the triangular Tenerife, with an area of roughly 2,000 sq km (770 sq miles), which is about half the size of Mallorca. The "Fortunate Islands" has been another name for the group, which was known to the Greeks before the beginning of the present era. The Arabs, Genoese, Portuguese and French all had trading posts there, but the first expedition to conquer the islands came in 1402. It took nearly another century before all the islands were under Spanish rule. The native population, the Guanches, still living in the Stone Age, were finally defeated in 1496 by Alonso Fernández de Lugo, who thereupon became the first governor.

Volcanic origin

The Canary Islands are of volcanic origin, and so most have the characteristic cone silhouette. Eruptions – the most recent was on La Palma in 1971 – have refashioned and coloured the landscape in many places. On Tenerife there are *cañadas*, lava channels; some plateaux bring landscapes of the moon to mind; and beaches

Above: Vines grown on volcanic ash at Lanzarote. They are planted in saucer-like indentations surrounded by walls to protect them from the heat.

may be black, brown or white. A dry climate prevails throughout the year in the islands, with temperatures between 18 and 30°C (48 and 86°F), but the trade winds ensure that the north sides of the islands are relatively moist. This combined with irrigation systems has produced abundant growth. On Gran Canaria and Tenerife there are extensive banana plantations, and in addition fruits such as mangoes, melons, oranges and papaws are cultivated, as are tobacco, coffee, tomatoes, nuts, grain and potatoes. The Canary Islands cuisine is very much dominated by fresh fish, and tropical fruit is often on the menu. A traditional stew is *puchero canario*, which may include meat, pumpkin, sweet potato, maize and other ingredients. The south of the islands is much less green, being swept by a searing wind from the Sahara.

There is winegrowing on five of the islands: Gomera, Hierro, Lanzarote, La Palma and Tenerife, the latter being the most important. Harvests from the group consist of roughly half red and half white wines: very little rosé is produced here. Only a small proportion of the total volume, about a fifth, is bottled. In terms of quality Tacoronte-Acentejo on Tenerife is the most interesting wine district, and this is described separately. The following producers from the other districts are worthy of note: Bodega Montijo in La Orotava-Los Realejos (Tenerife); Bodegas Teneguia, a cooperative, in Fuencaliente (La Palma); Bodegas Mozaga in La Geria (Lanzarote); the Frontera cooperative (Hierro); and the Agrupación Noruega (La Gomera). Wine districts not yet mentioned are Icod de los Vinos, Sur de Tenerife, Valle de Güimar (all on Tenerife); El Mazo (La Palma); and Santa Brígida (Gran Canaria).

Binissalem
(Balearic Islands)

Capital: Palma de Mallorca
Province: the Balearics are an *autonomía*
Area: 5,014 square kilometres
Population: 754,777

Mallorca, the biggest of the Balearic Islands, has been inhabited from the second millenium BC onward. Since those prehistoric inhabitants, the island has been occupied by Phoenicians, Greeks, Carthaginians and Romans. Viniculture was certainly practised by the Romans, and Pliny the Elder made mention of Mallorcan wine. Late in the eighth century the Balearic Islands were conquered by the Moors, who were to remain there for five centuries. They created an irrigation system, developed agriculture and gave many towns and villages their present names. One of these is Binissalem, centre of the wine district.

On the last day of 1229 the Moors were defeated by James (or Jaime) I of Aragón, and under his rule the Balearics, the French province of Roussillon, and Montpellier were united into a short-lived kingdom. Mallorcan wines were served at the court of Aragón, and in 1257 James I gave personal permission for more vines to be planted on Mallorca. As elsewhere in Spain at that time it was the monasteries that dominated winegrowing. Wine exports became so important for the island economy that a new harbour, Alcudia, was specially built for this trade on a bay on the north coast. The reputation of Mallorca's wines continued to grow, with regular references to those from Binissalem. The legend on a map dating from 1784 states that Binissalem is famous for its *vino de superior calidad*. In this same period priests from Mallorca went to California, where they founded missions that were to grow into cities such as San Diego and San Francisco. They built these missions in Mallorcan style, and it is likely that they took vines there with them.

In the nineteenth century the most famous Mallorcan wine was the sweet Malvasía from Bañalbufar, on the steep west coast, and it enjoyed at least as great a reputation as Madeira. It was drunk by George Sand and Frédéric Chopin, who spent the winter of 1838–9 on the island. Malvasía was aged for three to four years in 500 litre (110 gal) casks that had been treated with rum. Since those days all the vines have disappeared from those terraces around Bañalbufar and Mallorca's Malvasía is only a memory. Around 1880 the island's wine production increased sharply as a result of the phylloxera then ravaging France. The total vineyard area on Mallorca rose from 20,000 to 35,000 ha (49,400 to 86,500 acres). From Porto Colóm, on the east coast, and other harbours the wine ships sailed straight to Marseille and Sète. This period of prosperity did not, however, last long for in 1891 the vines on Mallorca fell victim to the phylloxera. Figures from the Porto Colóm customs speak volumes: in 1887 the authorities received around 50,000 pesetas from levies on wine; in 1897 less than 3,000. Mallorcan winegrowing has never got over this reverse. The present vineyard area – 2,500 ha (6,180 acres) – differs hardly from that at the beginning of 1900.

About 400 ha (988 acres) belongs to Binissalem, Spain's first *denominación de origen* beyond the mainland, created in

February 1991. The district consists of five communities: Binissalem, Consell, Sancellas, Santa Eugenia and Santa María del Camí. They all lie northeast of Palma de Mallorca on El Pla, the central plateau. All the vineyards are east of the C713, the road linking Palma with Alcudia. A mountain chain along its northwestern side shelters this plateau from cold, wet winds. The mountain tops rise to around 1,400 m (4,590 ft), which is sufficient to limit the average annual rainfall to the east of them to less than 500 mm (19.7 ins). The vines grow in soils with a good deal of limestone, some clay, and in places a lot of stones. The vineyards do not form a continuous whole, but are interspersed with orchards – almonds, figs, apricots, olives – and fields of vegetables. It is wonderfully peaceful here, even at the height of the season, for tourists seldom visit this part of Mallorca.

The grapes grown in the Binissalem DO are mainly native varieties. Around half the plantings consist of black Manto Negro; the red wine from this is elegant, but also firm and aromatic enough to undergo ageing in cask. Another Mallorcan grape is Callet; and Monastrell and Tempranillo are also grown here. The most common white variety is Moll (or Prensal Blanc), which gives a fresh wine with both fruit and a touch of spice. Parellada and Macabeo, too, are planted. Binissalem's most important producer, Bodegas José L. Ferrer, quite deliberately uses only the varieties just mentioned, so as to make wines with a distinct personality of their own. The smaller producer, Herederos de Hermanos Ribas, has a different philosophy, increasingly working with imported grape varieties, among them Cabernet Sauvignon, Merlot, Rubí Cabernet, Syrah, Chardonnay, Chenin Blanc and Riesling. But Binissalem wines have to be made with a considerable proportion of native grapes: a minimum 50 percent of Manto Negro for red wines, and 70 percent Moll for white.

Felanitx

To the east of Binissalem there is another wine district, called Felanitx. It comprises the town of that name and 13 other communities. It has no DO and is going through a difficult period. This is shown by the fact that the biggest producer, the Felanitx cooperative, has missed a couple of vintages. But there are some bright spots. Miguel Oliver in Petra is producing a delightful, gently fresh Muscat with a lot of fruit in scent and taste, and the Celler Son Calo white and the Mont Ferrutx red *reserva* are also worth discovering. Another good producer is Jaume Mesquida in Porreras. The specialities here are Cabernet Sauvignon, Pinot Noir (also as a rosé), Gewürztraminer and Chardonnay. The last-named also goes into Jaume Mesquida's sparkling wine, the first from Mallorca. Finally, a recent (1985), modern firm called Florianopolis is active in Andraitx, west of Palma. This was founded with Swedish capital and will soon have some 80 ha (198 acres) of vineyards planted with French grape varieties.

PRODUCERS OF SPECIAL INTEREST

Bodegas José L Ferrer 07350 Binissalem

After a stay in France, José Luis Ferrer decided to become a winegrower, thus continuing the parental tradition. His idea was to establish a wine cooperative in Binissalem, which he did in 1931, but lack of cooperation among the members led to its becoming a private concern in that same year. Ferrer's descendants, José Luis Roses and his brother Sebastián, are the present owners of Franja Roja, the parent company to which Bodegas José L. Ferrer belongs. The grapes come from some 150 ha (370 acres), of which about 70 ha (173 acres) are run directly by the firm. The temperatures of red, white and rosé wines are carefully regulated during fermentation. Their average quality is very good. The Blanc de Blanc is made exclusively from Moll grapes and has a refreshing, clear taste with a hint of spices. The delicious Viña Veritas is somewhat more complete and also gentler; its basis is 80 percent Moll and 20 percent Parellada. When it comes to red wine this bodega believes in wood ageing – there are around 600 casks of American oak in the underground cellar. The wines matured in them are all made from about 80 percent Manto Negro and 20 percent Callet grapes. They are usually characterized by a firm elegance, a lively, racy and full-flavoured taste, a smooth, unobtrusive structure, a deep aroma and elements of wood – which grow stronger the longer the wine is in cask. The range includes *crianza*, *reserva* and *gran reserva*. About 70 percent of production consists of red wine. It is due to the high quality standards of this producer that the Binissalem DO was created. The bodega is prominently situated near the road into the town from the south.

Herederos de Hermanos Ribas 07330 Consell

Although the origins of this bodega go back to the beginning of the eighteenth century, it has been functioning in its present form only since 1986. The wines come from the firm's own estate of about 50 ha (124 acres) and are in part processed with modern equipment. In addition to native grapes, imported varieties are also used – Chardonnay, Chenin Blanc, Riesling, Merlot, Pinot Noir, Rubi Cabernet, Syrah and Cabernet Sauvignon. A wine made solely from Cabernet Sauvignon is in fact

Above: Statue of grape-pickers in the church square at Binissalem.

produced. So far the wines have been of a decent quality. The standard will probably rise as the vines mature, and as a result of the technical experiments that have been conducted here for several years. The bodega's brand name is Herederos de Ribas.

Above: In the reception room of the Bodegas José L. Ferrer, an old picture on the wall praises the wine of Binissalem. It is mainly thanks to the high quality of this producer's wines that the Binissalem DO was granted. Mallorca boasts numerous monasteries, like the one depicted here. Most winemaking was controlled by monasteries in the early days.

Travel Information

HOTELS AND RESTAURANTS

Celler Ca'n Amer, Pau 39, 07300 Inca, tel (71) 501261 Established in an old wine cellar – hence the casks – and specializing in authentic Mallorcan dishes. A good selection of the island wines.

Koldo Roya, Paseo Marítimo 3, 07014 Palma de Mallorca, tel (71) 457021 This restaurant is named after its owner and chef, a brilliant Basque cook who surprises his guests with his refined creations.

Palladium, Paseo Mallorca 40, 07012 Palma de Mallorca, tel (71) 712841 Around the Bay of Palma there are scores of hotels that are very much geared to sea-front tourism. This, however, is a pleasant place to stay in the town itself, close to the old centre. The rooms offer a decent standard of comfort and the service is very friendly.

Sol Jaime III, Paseo Mallorca 14b, 07012 Palma de Mallorca, tel (71) 725943 Centrally situated, reasonably comfortable hotel, with a good shopping street around the corner.

Taberna O'Arco, Calle Concepción 34, 07012 Palma de Mallorca, tel (71) 721042 In expensive Palma this is a very affordable small restaurant where the owner does the cooking. There is a cheap dish of the day, and tasty fish and meat courses. It is close to the hotels mentioned above.

Xoriguer, Fábrica 60, 07013 Palma de Mallorca, tel (71) 288332 Classic cuisine based on ingredients fresh from the market. Reasonably priced wines.

Celler Sa Sinia, 07670 Porto Colóm, tel (71) 824323 For very fresh fish.

PLACES OF INTEREST

Binissalem In this little wine town the grape harvest is celebrated every year in the Festa de's Vermar, held on the last Sunday in September. It takes place on the church square, where there are statues of a man and woman with bunches of grapes. The stone used for these sculptures, the church itself and many other buildings in the town is a local kind, cream coloured with orange flecks. About 4,700 people live in Binissalem, including a number of Germans: there is even a German school.

Deyá Small village high above the sea, near Sóller, made famous by the English writer Robert Graves, who lived here for many years. The local bar is still frequented by writers and artists. Wonderful views from here of the mountains inland, terraced with ancient olive trees.

Felanitx Small, agricultural town with some 15,000 inhabitants. It has a large thirteenth-century church that was restored in the seventeenth century. Also here are buildings of monumental dimensions, and craftsmen producing ceramic objets d'art. The monastery of San Salvador is in the neighbourhood, 500 m (1640 ft) up on top of a steep, rocky slope. The view from there is magnificent.

Inca The Thursday market attracts a great many people to this town, where a very big trade fair is organized every November. Inca is the most important town in central Mallorca, with a fair amount of industry (textiles, leather, shoes). *Concos*, rather neutral-tasting biscuits, are also made locally. The church of Santa María la Mayor has a Gothic tower, and there are baroque cloisters at the Franciscan monastery.

Palma de Mallorca More than half of all the inhabitants of the Balearics live in this town, and every year many tourists come here. Palma enjoys great prosperity, evidence for which includes the many jeweller's shops and the high

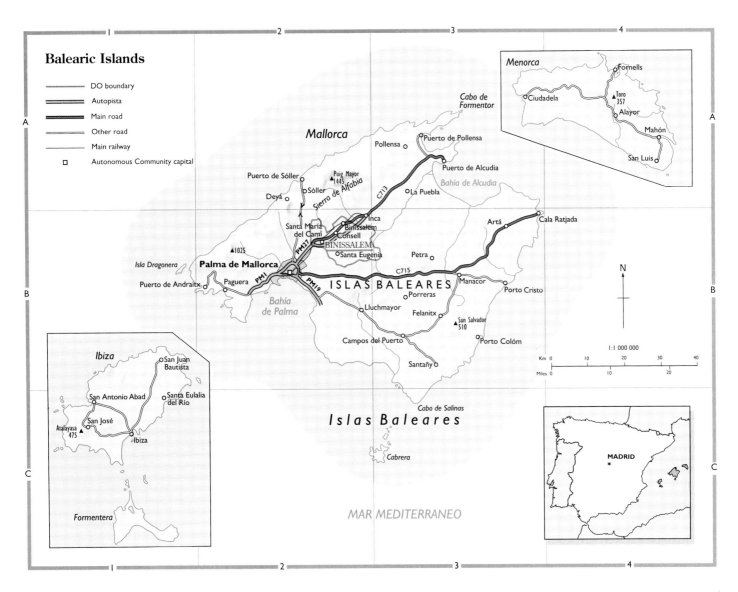

Balearic Islands

Legend:
- DO boundary
- Autopista
- Main road
- Other road
- Main railway
- □ Autonomous Community capital

Mallorca

Menorca — Fornells, Ciudadela, Toro 357, Alayor, Mahón, San Luis

Cabo de Formentor

Puerto de Pollensa
Pollensa
Puerto de Alcudia
Bahía de Alcudia
Puerto de Sóller
Puig Mayor 1445
Sóller
Deyá
Sierra de Alfabia
C713
La Puebla
La Puebla
Inca
Santa María del Camí
Consell
BINISSALEM
Artá
Cala Ratjada
Isla Dragonera
▲1025
Palma de Mallorca
Santa Eugenia
Petra
Paguera
PM27
PM1
PM19
ISLAS BALEARES
C715
Manacor
Puerto de Andraitx
Porto Cristo
Bahía de Palma
Porreras
Lluchmayor
Felanitx
San Salvador 510
Campos del Puerto
Porto Colóm
Santañy
N

Ibiza
San Juan Bautista
San Antonio Abad
Santa Eulalia del Río
San José
Atalayasa 475
Ibiza

Formentera

Cabo de Salinas

Islas Baleares

Cabrera

1:1 000 000
Km 0 10 20 30 40
Miles 0 10 20

MADRID

MAR MEDITERRANEO

---

prices in the restaurants. The harbour is dominated by the cathedral, La Seo, built on a hill and lit up at night. It was worked on for more than three centuries, and had to be partly rebuilt after an earthquake in 1851. This explains the various architectural styles seen in the structure. It is a vast monument and contains no fewer than 18 chapels. Palma's old centre lies behind the cathedral, with many narrow, atmospheric streets and beautiful buildings. Certainly worth a brief visit are the Moorish baths, dating probably from the tenth century. They are set beside a garden and the biggest room has a dome and a dozen supporting pillars. The seventeenth-century Consulado del Mar houses a maritime museum. Art of the province can be seen in La Lonja, which is fifteenth century and by the harbour, to the west of the cathedral. Just to the west of Palma there is the Pueblo Español, an open

air museum with replicas of famous buildings from all over Spain. In a large park to the south of it stands the Castillo Bellver, which contains an archaeological museum. This thirteenth-century structure is Spain's only round castle. A good address in central Palma for buying local wine is Malvasía, Santo Domingo 11.

Petra Here in 1713 was born Fray Junípero Serra, the great Franciscan father, founder of Los Angeles, Monterrey, San Diego, San Francisco and San José. He was educated in the local monastery and gave these towns the names of its various chapels. There are statues of this priest on the square in Petra and in the Hall of Fame in Washington, DC. The house where he was born can be visited and has a wine cellar. It was donated to the City of San Francisco some years ago, and contains a small museum.

Porreras Church where there is a Gothic Templar's cross.

Santa Eugenia Pleasant wine village overlooked by an old flour mill.

Santa María del Camí The town hall is in baroque style, and the parish church has some baroque elements. There is a museum of costume in the Convento de los Mínimos.

WINE ROUTE

Because of the small area covered by the Binissalem wine district the route is extended to take in the most interesting of the Felanitx communities. Visits can be made on the way both to wine producers and monasteries, such as that of San Salvador near Felanitx. You can also make a detour to get to the Castillo de Alaró, which is set high up on a mountain northwest of the wine villages of Santa María del Camí and Consell, and offers a splendid panoramic view of the surrounding country.

Tacoronte-Acentejo (Canary Islands)

Capital: Las Palmas de Gran Canaria/Santa Cruz de Tenerife
Provinces: Las Palmas de Gran Canaria, Santa Cruz de Tenerife
Area: 7,273 square kilometres
Population: 1,614,882

There was a time when Canary Island wines were famous: 30,000 casks a year used to be exported, and the wine was even served at European courts. In Shakespeare's *Henry IV*, Falstaff is called "Sir John Canaries" because of his great consumption of the wine and other authors, Sir Walter Scott among them, also make mention of Canaries wine.

What was referred to in all cases was the rich, sweet Malvasía – a wine so strong that a rare 1760 was still vigorous in taste in 1981. It was chiefly produced on the islands of La Palma and Lanzarote. Malvasía is still made today, in both its sweet and semi-dry forms, but interest in this kind of wine has declined so sharply that the modest amount still made is mainly consumed in the islands themselves. Significantly enough, Malvasía has not been granted a *denominación de origen*.

The only wine district that is at DO level is Tacoronte-Acentejo. This is on Tenerife, the biggest of the *Islas Afortunadas*, the Fortunate Isles. Tenerife is triangular in shape. Its name is derived from an old expression meaning "snow-covered mountain", for the island is dominated by a huge volcano that is indeed covered with snow from November to April. This is Teide, at 3,718 m (12,198 ft) the highest Spanish mountain. A ridge of mountains extends from Teide; to the south of this the climate and plant life are almost desert-like, while to the wetter north the vegetation is luxuriant. Here there are not only banana plantations, but trees and other plants that grow nowhere else in the

Below: Vines growing at La Victoria de Acentejo, one of the seven wine communities of Tacoronte-Acentejo.

world – such as the Canaries pine, the Canaries palm and the dragon tree, which can often be more than 1,000 years old. The last-named has a parasol shape and can easily be 6m (20 ft) across. In 1496 Tenerife was the last island of the group to fall to Alonso Fernández de Lugo, after his defeat of the native Guanches.

The wine district

Tacoronte-Acentejo takes the first part of its name from Tacoronte, 25 km (15.5 miles) west of Santa Cruz de Tenerife, the island's capital. Altogether the wine district comprises six communities plus part of La Laguna (the second-largest town on Tenerife). The region is narrow in shape, follows the coast, and is 23 km (15 miles) long. About half of all the winegrowers live in Tacoronte. Then, in order of importance, come El Sauzal, La Victoria de Acentejo, Tegueste, La Matanza de Acentejo, Santa Ursula, and La Laguna. The vines are usually planted in reddish-brown soil and grow quite high. Some of the vineyards are flat, others slope, and a third category is terraced. The height above sea level varies from 100 to 800 m (330 to 2,625 ft), and some 2,500 ha (6,180 acres) is cultivated. This represents 40 percent of Tenerife's vineyard area, and 20 percent of the total for the whole island group.

Mention is made at various points in the history of Tacoronte-Acentejo of measures to safeguard quality – in 1563, for example, it was laid down that no wine could be imported from outside the island. Yet it is only recently that the area has begun to make its mark in terms of quality. It was not until the end of the 1980s that a number of individual producers and cooperatives made much-needed investments in modern cellar equipment. An experimental bodega was set up for the whole DO, where the work includes testing new grape varieties – the Cabernet Sauvignon, for instance, or the Rubí Cabernet (a cross between the Carignan and the Cabernet Sauvignon). The very active *Consejo Regulador* hopes gradually to raise annual production from around 5,300 to 7,000 hl (116,600 to 154,000 gal), and also to increase the proportion of bottled wine. For the Canary Islands as a whole 15 percent of the wine is bottled, but in Tacoronte-Acentejo the percentage bottled is already near to 50 percent.

The accent here is on the production of red wines; the Listán Negro grape represents 80 percent of plantings, and Negramoll – also black – accounts for 12 percent. The most prevalent of the remaining kinds is Listán Blanco, or Palomino. Listán Negro is regarded as a black version of the same grape. The climate here would in fact allow two grape harvests a year, but for the sake of quality growers stick to just one. The Canary Islands are the only Spanish region never to have been afflicted by phylloxera. Thanks to improved vinification techniques, Tacoronte-Acentejo red wines are in general much fresher and fruitier than they used to be, while their alcoholic strength is usually limited now to 12.5 to 13.5 percent. Most of them have to be drunk young. Various white wines have also gained in quality, developing into refreshing, pleasant accompaniments to salads and fish courses. The two foremost producers are a cooperative, SAT Viticultores del Norte de Tenerife, in Tacoronte, and the Bodegas Monje in El Sauzal, but there are other producers who are also making a name for themselves. The improved quality of the wines has made the people of Tacoronte-Acentejo more confident. The *Consejo Regulador* moved into new premises in 1991 and the region is now well represented at wine fairs in Barcelona and Madrid, where professionals and wine-lovers are proudly shown the new-style island wines. There is no doubt that their next step will be the export of their wines.

Above: The Consejo Regulador *of Tacoronte-Acentejo took over these new headquarters in 1991.*

PRODUCERS OF SPECIAL INTEREST

Bodegas Flores 38370 La Matanza de Acentejo
Small family firm that processes the grapes from its 4 ha (10 acres) of vineyards, spread over three villages. Its best wine is the red Viña Flores. This is somewhat rustic in character, has a good structure and possesses a modest amount of fruit (with some floral hints), and is made from three grape varieties – of which Listán Negro is the most important.

Bodegas Monje 38360 El Sauzal
Miguel González Monje is one of Tenerife's foremost independent winemakers. He owns nearly 12 ha (30 acres) of vineyard, from which he produces some good wines. The dry white Drago Blanco is an engaging pure Listán Blanco wine that tastes good with fish dishes. It is surpassed in quality by the red wines, the Monje in particular, which is marketed as a *vino nuevo*. This wine is supple in taste, with fruit (redcurrants); it is slightly meaty and a little earthy. It should be served fresh.

Cooperativa SAT Viticultores del Norte de Tenerife 38350
Tacoronte
Dynamic cooperative with modern installations and about 80 members. The brand name is Viña Norte, but in addition the labels often give the name of the grower who supplied the grapes for the particular wine. In this way different red wines are produced from the same grape harvest. In general these are intended for drinking young. In addition to having a substantial core of alcohol they are often characterized by a supple, meaty taste and a touch of candied fruit. White Viña Norte is usually very decent.

Bodegas La Isleta 38260 Tejina
This modest bodega beside the church square at Tejina has been producing wine since 1969. The white La Isleta is simple and sometimes has too high an acid content but the red, made from 70 percent Negramoll grapes, has a pleasant taste, possesses character, and charms with its fruit. The firm uses the grapes from just under 5 ha (12.5 acres) of vineyard.

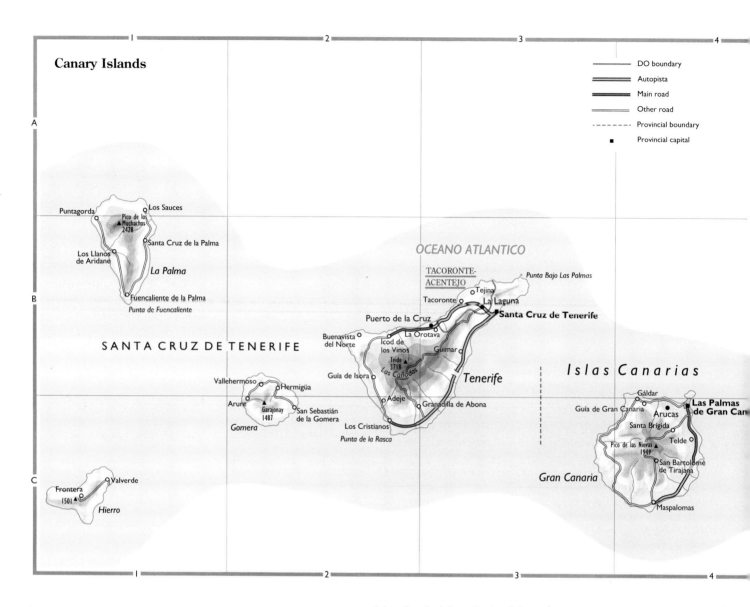

Canary Islands

DO boundary
Autopista
Main road
Other road
Provincial boundary
■ Provincial capital

Puntagorda
Los Sauces
Pico de los ▲ Muchachos 2428
Santa Cruz de la Palma
Los Llanos de Aridane
La Palma
Fuencaliente de la Palma
Punta de Fuencaliente

OCEANO ATLANTICO

TACORONTE-ACENTEJO
Punta Bajo Las Palmas
Tejina
Tacoronte
La Laguna
Puerto de la Cruz
Santa Cruz de Tenerife
Buenavista del Norte
La Orotava
Icod de los Vinos
Güimar
Teide 3718
Las Cañadas
Guía de Isora
Tenerife

SANTA CRUZ DE TENERIFE

Islas Canarias

Vallehermoso
Hermigüa
Arure
Garajonay 1487
San Sebastián de la Gomera
Gomera
Adeje
Granadilla de Abona
Los Cristianos
Punta de la Rasca

Gáldar
Guía de Gran Canaria
Las Palmas de Gran Can
Arucas
Santa Brígida
Pico de las Nievas ▲ 1949
Telde
San Bartolomé de Tirajana
Gran Canaria
Maspalomas

Valverde
Frontera 1501▲
Hierro

Travel Information

HOTELS AND RESTAURANTS

Parador, 38300 Las Cañadas del Teide, tel (22) 232503 Chalet-like *parador* with a fine view, and restaurant. It has Spain's highest swimming pool.

Casa Ramallo, 38200 La Laguna, tel (22) 263202 Very reliable eating place, with a splendid fish soup among its offerings.

Café del Príncipe, Plaza Príncipe de Asturia, 380000 Santa Cruz de Tenerife, tel (22) 278810 A locally very popular, atmospheric establishment with a garden, terrace, and Canaries cuisine.

La Caseta de Madera, Regla, 38000 Santa Cruz de Tenerife, tel (22) 210023 Fresh fish is always on the menu here. The service is friendly in this renowned restaurant.

Colón Rambla, Viera y Clavijo 49, 38004 Santa Cruz de Tenerife, tel (22) 272550 There are many tourist hotels overlooking the beaches of Tenerife, but this one is in the capital. Here you can rent an apartment at a reasonable rate complete with kitchen. No air-conditioning.

Mencey, Avenida Dr José Naveiras 38, 38001 Santa Cruz de Tenerife, tel (22) 276700 Large, luxurious hotel with nearly 300 rooms, in a residential quarter and on the edge of the old centre of the town. Has a restaurant.

La Riviera, Rambla General Franco 155, 38001 Santa Cruz de Tenerife, tel (22) 275812 There is creative cooking in this restaurant

based on fresh ingredients – fish and meat, including young lamb. A good wine list.

El Calvario, Calle Calvario 65, 38350 Tacoronte, tel (22) 563734 Specialities are cod and roast chicken.

El Campo, Carretera General del Norte 350, 38350 Tacoronte, tel (22) 561761 This is one of the meat restaurants typical of Tacoronte and its neighbourhood. The meat here is grilled, and the ambience is rustic.

Club Parque Mesa del Mar, 38350 Tacoronte, tel (22) 561300 Modern, nicely situated hotel complex with gardens, shops, and a discothèque.

Mesón El Drago, 38280 Tegueste, tel (22) 543001 This restaurant is accommodated in a listed building, a Canaries nobleman's house. Besides the traditional fare (fish, shellfish, lamb) there is also more inventive cooking. At weekends the local *puchero canaria* stew is served here.

PLACES OF INTEREST

Las Cañadas del Teide No visitor to Tenerife can miss this national park area. It consists of a vast crater with a circumference of 45 km (28 miles), largely surrounded by steep walls. The landscape within the crater is almost unearthly, with freakish rock formations, solidified streams of lava and a basalt floor. From the park you can take a cable car to the top of the Teide, the highest mountain on Spanish soil.

Icod de los Vinos Built on a hillside Icod looks out over the coast. Its monuments include some noblemen's houses, the Castillo de San Miguel, and the sixteenth-century parish church of San Marcos, with many fine carvings. An enormous dragon tree grows in Icod, nearly 17 m (56 ft) high.

La Laguna Part of this town comes within the Tacoronte-Acentejo wine district. La Laguna (it took its name

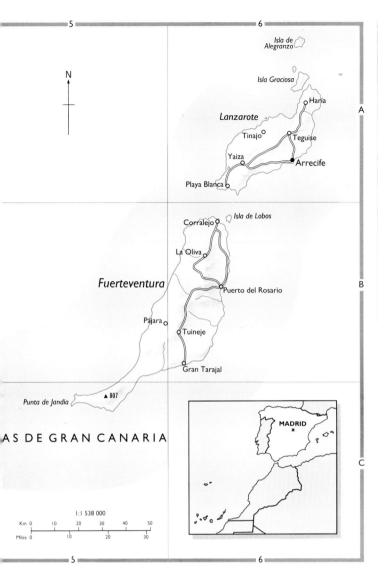

Above: Wine festival at Romeria de Tegueste, Tenerife.

from a lagoon that subsequently dried up) was the first town to be established on the island, in 1496 by Alonso Fernández de Lugo. Building began around the Concepción church, which is distinguished by a seven-storey bell tower. The cathedral, with an eighteenth-century Flemish altarpiece, acquired its present form at the beginning of the twentieth century – building having started in 1515. It contains the tomb of De Lugo, who died in 1525. The imposing crucifix he brought to the island now stands on a silver altar in the Santuario del Cristo, a chapel beside the Franciscan monastery. It is carried through the streets in a great procession in mid-September. La Laguna also has the first, and only, university in the Canaries. In the centre of the town there are many colonial dwellings with the arms of noble families on their façades. Here, too, is the Plaza de Adelante, with all its atmosphere,

and around it the sixteenth-century *ayuntamiento*, the Santa Catalina religious house, and the partly baroque Palacio de Nava. Elsewhere in the centre there stands the bishop's palace, which has a beautiful inner courtyard and a seventeenth-century façade. La Laguna is famed for its ceramics and during the Feast of Corpus Christi large, very artistic designs made with small coloured stones are put together in the streets.

La Matanza de Acentejo In 1494 Alonso Fernández de Lugo suffered a bloody defeat near this wine village at the hands of the Guanches. It was to be their last victory.

La Orotava Picturesque place on a mountain slope, with many typically colonial houses, that have projecting balconies. The Concepción church was built in Rococo style.

Santa Cruz de Tenerife The capital of Tenerife with nearly

200,000 inhabitants has an important harbour and a fair amount of industry, including an oil refinery. Not a great deal is left of the old town. One of the most beautiful churches is the Concepción, dating from the 16th century, but rebuilt after a fire in the 17th. It contains the Cruz de la Conquista, commemorating the final defeat of the native Guanches, as well as a couple of flags captured from Nelson. The British admiral had attempted in vain to take Santa Cruz, and lost his right arm in the battle. The cannon that fired the fatal shot is called El Tigre and stands in the military museum at the Castillo de Paso Alto. Behind the Iglesia de la Concepción there is the Museo Municipal de Bellas Artes, which mainly has works by Canaries artists. The archaeological museum shows how the Guanches lived.

El Sauzal In the district of La Baranda there is the Casa Museo del Vino, a wine museum contained in a characteristically low-built Canaries farmhouse. Just west of the village, on the Finca de San José, stands a large old wine press.

Tacoronte In this town with its population of 17,000 the biggest wine event of the Canary Islands is organized, usually at the end of May, and lasts a week. Most of the activities are concentrated in and around the Alhóndiga, a plain, austere-looking building of the seventeenth century. It formerly served as a grain store for the town, but is now a craft museum. The seventeenth-century church of Santa Catalina is one of the most beautiful

on the island and merits a visit for its altarpieces, sculptures and silverwork. The church of the former Augustinian monastery contains the impressive Cristo de Dolores, a 17th-century wooden crucifix. The altar is of Mexican silver and the roof is in Mudéjar style. A walk through Tacoronte (the Paseo José Izquerdo is the most attractive street) shows that arts and crafts are practised here, including various kinds of wood carving and pottery. Nougat is made here. A number of dragon trees grow in the town.

La Victoria de Acentejo After his reverse at La Matanza, De Lugo had his revenge in 1496 when he decisively defeated the Guanches here. Today La Victoria is best known for its pottery, and there is also winegrowing here.

WINE ROUTE

The best way to explore Tacoronte-Acentejo is to take the narrow, winding road to Tegueste from La Laguna. The route then continues by way of Tejina and Valle Guerra to Tacoronte. It goes on through El Sauzal, La Matanza de Acentejo, La Victoria de Acentejo, and Santa Ursula. You can then return eastwards on the *autopista* to La Laguna (and Santa Cruz de Tenerife), but it is also possible of course to take a trip westwards to Icod de los Vinos or, via La Orotava, to Las Cañadas del Teide national park.

Glossary

Almacenista Private stockholder who ages fine sherries.
Albariza Intensely white soil, up to 80 percent pure chalk, found in the Jerez region. It has high water-retaining properties, and is responsible for the particular character of sherry.
Amontillado A type of sherry and Montilla-Moriles, obtained by maturing well-aged *fino* in oak, which gives a nutty flavour.
Amoroso A sweet dessert sherry.
Año Year
Arrope Wine reduced by boiling it down to one-fifth of its original volume. It is used for colouring and sweetening blends.
Autonomía Autonomous community. Spain is now divided into 17 *autonomías*.
Ayuntamiento Town hall.
Barrica Cask, usually 225 litres (50 gal), used for maturing wine.
Barrique bordelaise Oak cask used for maturing Bordeaux wines. Some DOs have adopted their use.
Blanco White wine.
Bodega Literally, a wine cellar. Used in this book in its extended sense of a place where wine is made as well as matured.
Botas Wineskins
Brut Extra-dry, used only of sparkling wine.
Brut nature Former term for dry sparkling wine.
Castillo Castle
Cava Cava is both a DO, and the sparkling wine produced by the traditional champagne method which carries this DO.
Clarete Light red wine. The term is now obsolete, but may be found on older bottles.
Consejo Regulador Literally, Regulating Council. Each of the denominated wine regions of Spain has its own Council, responsible for quality control and awarding the *denominación de origen*.
Cooperativa Cooperative
Copita Traditional glass used for sherry.
Cosechero Winegrower, usually on a small scale, who vinifies his own wine.
Crianza Wine that has had at least six months' ageing in cask. In Rioja, where the term is most commonly used, the wine must have spent at least twelve months in oak casks.
Denominación de origen Qualification applied to wine of an approved type and standard, from a defined district.
Doble pasta Wine produced with double the amount of grapeskins and a single portion of must, giving good colour and body.
Dulce Sweet. Wine with a sugar content of more than 50 grams per litre.
Embotellado por Bottled by.
Fino Pale, delicate dry wine aged under *flor*.
Flor Naturally occurring yeast cells which form a crumbly greyish-white layer on the surface of certain types of fortified wines. The cells feed on oxygen, so the wine itself does not become oxidized. This phenomenon occurs in the Jerez area, as well as Montilla-Moriles and Condado de Huelva, and is responsible for the development of *fino* wines.
Gran reserva Wine of good quality that has been aged. Red wines must be aged for at least 2 years in oak cask, followed by 3 years in bottle.
Huerta Irrigated land.
Lagar Old-fashioned wine press in the form of a stone trough, used for treading grapes.
Lágrima Literally, a tear. Wine made from the first pressing of the grapes.
Macération carbonique Method of fermentation whereby whole bunches of grapes are put into a vat filled with carbon dioxide. Fermentation begins inside the skins of the intact grapes. The juice of the grapes at the bottom, crushed by the weight, also begins fermenting in the normal way.
Malolactic fermentation Secondary, non-alcoholic fermentation that takes place after the main fermentation. It converts the malic acid in the wine into lactic acid (and carbon dioxide). Reduces the total acidity of the wine, and makes it more stable. Essential for all red wines, but with white wines may be desirable to retain a higher degree of acidity.
Manzanilla A *fino* sherry aged in the town of Sanlúcar de Barrameda.
Mistela Mixture of must and wine alcohol.
Modernista Literally, modern. The Spanish equivalent of art nouveau.
Mudéjar Moorish architectural style which developed under Christian rule.
Must Fresh grape juice and skins which has not begun fermentation.
Oloroso A dark, full-bodied type of sherry.
Oxidation Chemical reaction of wine to oxygen in the atmosphere. An indispensable process in the ageing of wines. If it occurs involuntarily it can damage the aroma, taste and colour.
Pajizos Yellow tone found in young wine.
Palo cortado A type of sherry that comes between *amontillado* and *oloroso*. Has an alcoholic strength of 18–20 percent. Only a few bodegas produce palo cortado.
Parador State tourist hotel of a good standard, often housed in a building of historic interest.
Pasada A well-aged Manzanilla.
Phylloxera Plant louse which attacks vine roots. It appeared at the end of the last century and destroyed many vineyards on the Spanish mainland as well as in the rest of Europe.
Rancio An old white wine, maderized and sometimes fortified.
Reserva Red wine of good quality, aged for at least 3 years in cask and bottle.
Río River
Rosado Rosé
Sacristía Sacristy
Santuario Sanctuary
Seco Dry
Sierra Mountain range.
Sin crianza A wine that has not been aged in cask.
Solera A system of fractional blending used to age sherry, Málaga and Montilla.
Tannin Naturally occuring substance in wine that has a preservative effect.
Tapas Snacks
Tinaja Traditional-style earthenware jar used for fermenting and maturing wine.
Tinta Red
Toneloro Cooper
Vendimia Vintage
Verde Young wine, white or red, which is slightly sparkling.
Vino Wine
Vino borracho A blend of wine and alcohol, used to fortify Málaga.
Vino de color Wine used to give colour to a blend. Made from must boiled down to a thick, dark-brown syrup.
Vino de Mesa Table wine.
Vino de la Tierra A wine from a specific region in Spain – equivalent of the French *Vin de Pays*.
Vino dulce Sweet wine.
Vino tierno Málaga wine made from sun-dried grapes.

Bibliography

Abdon Arjona Algaba et al., *Los vinos Valencianos y su comercialización*, Valencia 1988

David Baird, *Excursions in Southern Spain*, Fuengirola 1991

David Baird, *Inside Andalusia*, Fuengirola 1988

Desmond Begg, *Traveller's Wine Guide: Spain*, London 1989

F. Bosch i Torrent et al., *Denominación d'origen Penedès*, Barcelona 1989

Cristina Cebrián Sagarriga, *El vino Albariño*, Vitoria 1988

Jaume Ciurana, *Los vinos Catalanes*, Barcelona 1980

Club de Gourmets, *Guía BMW Gourmetour 1990/1991*, Madrid

Club de Gourmets, *Guía de vinos Gourmets 1990/1991*, Madrid

Harry Debelius, *Spain*, London 1988

Fernando Delgado Cebrián, *Los pueblos de Madrid*, Madrid 1981

Hubrecht Duijker, *The Good Wines of Rioja*, London 1987

Cayetano Enríquez de Salamanca, *De viaje por Andalucía*, Málaga 1988

Escalas, *Guide of Majorca*, Palma de Mallorca 1985

Dana Facaros & Michael Pauls, *Spain*, London 1989

Antón Gil, *Vinos y licores*, Murcia 1988

Miguel Golobardes Vila, *Perelada*, Figueras 1965

Everest, *Jumilla*, Madrid 1989

Dennis Gunton, *Spain*, London 1990

F. Gurri Serra et al., *La guía de Catalunya*, Barcelona 1989

Ellen Hoffman et al., *Bantam Travel Guide: Spain*, New York 1990

Hans Hoogendoorn, *ANWB Reisgids: Spanje*, The Hague 1989

Icex, *The Challenge of Spain*, Madrid 1989

Julian Jeffs, *Sherry*, London 1982

Rob Kerstens, *De wijnen van Spanje en Portugal*, Haarlem 1985

Tony Lord, *The New Wines of Spain*, London 1988

Ana Martínez et al., *León rutas turisticas ineditas*, León 1985

Garry Marvin, *Coping with Spain*, Oxford 1990

Franz N. Mehling, *Spanje*, Amsterdam 1987

Janet Mendrel Searl, *Cooking in Spain*, Fuengirola 1989

Charles Metcalfe & Kathryn McWhirter, *The Wines of Spain and Portugal*, London 1988

Wim Mey, *Sherry*, Baarn, Netherlands 1987.

Michelin, *España Portugal 1990/1991*, Madrid

Michelin, *Spain*, London 1987

David Mitchell, *Travellers in Spain*, Fuengirola 1990

Jordí Olavarrieta, *Cava*, Barcelona 1981

Andreu Parra & Miquel Sen, *Viajes por los vinos de España*, Barcelona 1989

Luis Pastrana, *El Bierzo*, León 1981

José Peñín, *Vinos y bodegas de España 1990*, Madrid

Plaza y Janes, *Guía del viajero España 1990/1991*, Barcelona

Jan Read, *The Mitchell Beazley Pocket Guide to Spanish Wines*, London 1988

Jan Read, *The Wines of Spain*, London 1982

Jan Read, Maite Manjón & Hugh Johnson, *The Wine and Food of Spain*, London 1987

Javier Rivera Blanco, *Guía del Bierzo*, León 1978

Ian Robertson, *Blue Guide: Spain*, London 1989

Jancis Robinson, *Vines, Grapes and Wines*, London 1986

Jorge Sauleda, *The Wines of Navarra*, Pamplona 1989

Marimar Torres, *The Spanish Table*, New York 1986

Miguel A. Torres, *Los Vinos de España*, Madrid 1984

Miguel A. Torres, *Mil años de viticultura en Cataluña*, Barcelona 1990

Miguel A. Torres, *The Distinctive Wines of Catalonia*, Barcelona 1986

Félix Valencia Díaz, *Monografía sobre los vinos de Málaga*, Málaga 1990

Adolfo Vasserot Fuentes, *Málaga Wine*, Málaga 1978

Frans Verbunt, *De wijnen van Spanje*, Utrecht 1988

Frans Verbunt, *Vinos de Castilla-La Mancha*, 1978

Ben van Wakeren & Marloleine Rijke, *Noord-Spanje*, Haarlem 1989

Mark Williams, *The Story of Spain*, Fuengirola 1990

PERIODICALS

Alles über Wein (Germany)

Bouquet (Spain)

Club de Gourmets (Spain)

Decanter (United Kingdom)

Goede Smaak (Netherlands)

Gourmetour (Spain)

Lookout (Spain)

Marco Real (Spain)

La Prensa de la Rioja (Spain)

Sobremesa (Spain)

Vinum (Switzerland)

Wine (United Kingdom)

The Wine Advocate (United States)

The Wine Spectator (United States)

Wine & Spirit (United Kingdom)

Index and Gazetteer

The index includes references to grape varieties, vineyards, estates and producers, cooperatives, towns and wine villages, and locations of general interest to the visitor. Map and grid references are given with the page number of the main reference in the text, for all important points on the maps.

PICTURE CREDITS

Abbreviations: Alan Williams – AW; Hubrecht Duijker – HD; Michael Busselle – MB; Archivo Icongrafico SA – AI; Mick Rock/Cephas Picture Library – MR/C; Cephas Picture Library – C; Francesco Venturi/KEA Publishing Services – FV/KEA; Susan Griggs Agency – SG.

Key: left – L; right – R; top – T; bottom – B

P. 2–3 AW; 6 Miguel Torres SA; 7, 8 AW; 10 Robert Frerck/ SG; 11 Vatican Museum/Scala; 13, 18, 19, 20–1 AW; 22 Zefa; 23 AW; 24 Roy Stedall/C; 26T/B, 27, 28 AW; 30 HD; 31 AI; 33 AW; 34 Miguel Torres SA; 35L/R MR/C; 36, 37, 40, 41, 42T/B, 43, 44 AW; 45L/R HD; 46, 48, 49, 50 MR/C; 51, 52, 53L/R AW; 54 AI; 55 MR/C; 56 HD; 57, 59T FV/KEA; 59B Robert Frerck/ SG; 60T Zefa; 60B MR/C; 61, 62 AGE Photostock; 63 AI; 64, 65, 66, 69, 70L/R, 72 HD; 73L/R AI; 74, 75, 77, 78, 79, 80, 81, 82, 83, 84L/R, 85, 86–7, 87T/B, 88, 89, 90, 91, 94, 95, 96 AW; 98, 99, 100, HD; 102, 103L MB; 103R HD; 106, 109 AW; 110, 113 HD; 114L AW; 114R MR/C; 116 MB; 117, 118 MR/C; 119, 120,

121, 122L AW; 122R HD; 125 AGE Photostock; 126 Spectrum Colour Library; 128 HD; 129L AI; 129R HD; 130 Nik Wheeler/ SG; 133 Robert Frerck/SG; 134 HD; 135 Robert Frerck/SG; 136L MB; 136R HD; 138–9 Michael Holford; 140 MB; 141T HD; 141B, 142, 143, 144, 145 AW; 147 FV/KEA; 148 HD; 150 MB; 151 HD; 152–3 AW; 154 FV/KEA; 155 HD; 156 AW; 157T HD; 157B, 158–9,160 AW; 162 HD; 163, 164 AW; 165 HD; 166, 168T/B AW; 169 Mike Feeney; 170T AGE Photostock; 170B Mike Feeney; 171 AW; 172 HD; 174–5, 175 AW; 176 HD; 177 AW; 178 HD; 179 Eugen/Zefa; 180–1 Rob Cousins/SG; 182 AGE Fotostock; 184 Victor Englebert/SG; 185, 186 AW; 187 HD; 188–9 Spectrum Colour Library; 190 Adam Woolfitt/SG; 192, 193 AW; 194 HD; 195, 196, 197 AW; 199T John Harvey and Sons; 199C/B AW; 200T Osborne Y Cia SA; 200B Williams + Humbert Ltd.; 201T Emilio Lustau SA; 201B AW; 203 HD; 205 AW; 207T/B AW; 208T/B, 210 AW; 211 Roy Stedall/C; 212 HD; 214, 215, 216, 218 AW; 220–1 Spectrum Colour Library; 222 Angus Reid/C; 224T/B, 226, 227 HD; 229 D.Burrows/C.